TEACHER MANUAL

STREET LAW

A COURSE IN PRACTICAL LAW

TENTH EDITION

networks™
There's More Online!

Cathy Ruffing
Senior Director, Teacher Professional
Development Programs & Curriculum
Street Law, Inc.

Lee P. Arbetman, M.Ed., J.D.
Executive Director
Street Law, Inc.

The work of Lena Morreale Scott was essential to
the development of this teacher manual.

Mc
Graw
Hill

Cover Credits:

Pixtal/AGE Fotostock, artisteer/Getty Images, zennie/Getty Images, Photographs in the Carol M. Highsmith Archive, Library of Congress, Prints and Photographs Division., iStock/Getty Images Plus

mheducation.com/prek-12

Send all inquiries to:
McGraw-Hill Education
8787 Orion Place
Columbus, OH 43240

ISBN: 978-0-07-681503-6
MHID: 0-07-681503-X

Printed in the United States of America.

4 5 6 7 LHN 25 24 23 22 21

The tenth edition of *Street Law: A Course in Practical Law* builds upon the success and popularity of earlier editions. Incorporating their best features, this edition provides new information, practical advice, and inquiry-based, competency-building activities designed to provide students with the ability to analyze, evaluate, and resolve legal disputes. More broadly, *Street Law* is a powerful civic education vehicle that helps build critical thinking and problem-solving skills as young people prepare for thoughtful, democratic engagement.

The student text and this Teacher Manual reflect the changes in law and legal procedure that have taken place at the national level since the publication of the ninth edition. In response to increased interest and demand, a chapter on environmental law has been added to the tenth edition. A deliberation feature that presents students with multiple perspectives on contemporary issues has also been added to each unit. Students will use deliberation techniques to engage in civil discourse on controversial topics, while learning the advocacy skills needed to communicate effectively with peers and elected officials. We have added text and problems dealing with the most current law-related public issues, including intellectual property, marriage equality, immigration, terrorism, and technology. The chapter-based feature "Taking Action: Law and Democracy" challenges students to consider steps they can take to help address some of the nation's most difficult issues. Students are asked to plan inquiries, gather evidence, draw logical conclusions, and articulate reasonable action steps that can be taken to solve problems and strengthen communities.

Another chapter-based feature, "Investigating the Law Where You Live," asks students to find and explain local and state variations in the law. Many aspects of law are not federal and vary significantly from place to place. This feature asks students to explore local laws, procedures, and resources where they live. More than one hundred such investigations are included throughout the student text.

Street Law's approach to civic learning (also called democracy education) is to provide practical information and problem-solving opportunities that develop in students the knowledge and skills necessary for meaningful democratic engagement. While the program has been developed and tested extensively with high school students (as opposed to law students), there is no mistaking the considerable intellectual rigor required to learn about the law—even at this introductory level. The curriculum includes case studies, deliberations, mock trials, role-plays, small-group exercises, and visual analysis activities. For optimal results, the *Street Law* program strongly encourages the use of community resource people such as lawyers, judges, law students, police officers, consumer advocates, and others to help teachers implement lessons in the classroom. *Street Law* also promotes community experiences such as court tours, observations of legislatures, and police ride-alongs. This approach allows students to be active participants in their own education, and models the civic engagement that is a critical outcome of all high-quality social studies programs.

ADVICE TO READERS

Law varies from state to state and is constantly changing. Therefore, someone confronted with a legal problem should not use this text as a substitute for legal advice from an attorney.

TABLE OF CONTENTS

Preface...iii
About Street Law, Inc. viii
Professional Development Opportunities ix
Street Law Supplements ix
Introduction to the Street Law Curriculum T1
    Content and Organization of the Student Edition..............................T1
    Special Features in the Student Edition T2
    Organization of the Teacher Manual T3
Acquiring or Presenting New Content T4
    Brainstorming T4
    Categorizing T4
    Each One—Teach One T5
    Gallery Walk or Carousel T5
    Jigsaw T6
    Mind Walk..T7
    Small Group Work/Cooperative Learning in Small Groups..............T7
    Think-Pair-Share..T9
    Accessing Community Resources T9
    Field Trips T10
    Analyzing Supreme and Appellate Court Cases..............................T11
    Case Studies...T11
    Unmarked Opinions T12
    Classifying Arguments T12
    Applying Precedent T12
    Moot Court T13
    Fishbowl Tag...T13
    Quick Activities to Introduce or Wrap Up Discussions T13
    Discussing and Exploring Controversial Issues...............................T14
    Deliberations T15
    P-R-E-S T16
    Simplified Civil Conversations T16
    Take a Stand, Fair/Unfair, and Continuum......................................T16
    Analyzing and Interpreting Media and Websites T17
    Evaluating Websites...T18
    WebQuest..T18
    Evaluating Media Coverage of Legal Issues T19
    Simulations and Role-Plays T20
    Mock Legislative Hearing...T21
    Mock Mediation T23
    Mock Negotiation...T24
    Mock Trial T25
    Moot Court T27
    Mini-Moot Courts T29
    Pro Se Court T30
    Role Plays T31

TABLE OF CONTENTS

Related Publications from Street Law, Inc. T33
Civic Learning in America T34

UNIT 1 Introduction to Law and the Legal System

CHAPTER **1** **What Is Law?** 2

CHAPTER **2** **Lawmaking** 12

CHAPTER **3** **Advocacy** 17

CHAPTER **4** **Settling Disputes** 25

CHAPTER **5** **The Court System** 30

CHAPTER **6** **Lawyers** 39

UNIT 2 Criminal Law and Juvenile Justice

CHAPTER **7** **Crime in America** 46

CHAPTER **8** **Introduction to Criminal Law** 60

CHAPTER **9** **Crimes Against the Person** 65

CHAPTER **10** **Crimes Against Property** 72

CHAPTER **11** **Defenses** 81

CHAPTER **12** **Criminal Justice Process: The Investigative Phase** 85

CHAPTER **13** **Criminal Justice Process: Proceedings Before Trial** 103

CHAPTER **14** **Criminal Justice Process: The Trial** 110

CHAPTER **15** **Criminal Justice Process: Sentencing and Corrections** 123

CHAPTER **16** **Juvenile Justice** 133

TABLE OF CONTENTS

UNIT 3 Torts

CHAPTER **17** Torts: A Civil Wrong 145

CHAPTER **18** Intentional Torts 157

CHAPTER **19** Negligence 166

CHAPTER **20** Strict Liability 178

CHAPTER **21** Torts and Public Policy 184

UNIT 4 Consumer Law

CHAPTER **22** Contracts 191

CHAPTER **23** Warranties 196

CHAPTER **24** Credit and Other Financial Services 200

CHAPTER **25** Deceptive Sales Practices 210

CHAPTER **26** Becoming a Smart Consumer 217

CHAPTER **27** Major Purchases 226

UNIT 5 Family Law

CHAPTER **28** Law and the American Family 244

CHAPTER **29** Marriage 247

CHAPTER **30** Parents and Children 259

CHAPTER **31** Foster Care and Adoption 271

CHAPTER **32** Separation, Divorce, and Custody 279

CHAPTER **33** Government Support for Families
and Individuals 287

TABLE OF CONTENTS

UNIT 6 Individual Rights and Liberties

CHAPTER **34** Introduction to Constitutional Law 301

CHAPTER **35** Freedom of Speech 305

CHAPTER **36** Freedom of the Press 323

CHAPTER **37** Expression in Special Places 331

CHAPTER **38** Freedom of Religion 340

CHAPTER **39** Due Process 350

CHAPTER **40** The Right to Privacy 355

CHAPTER **41** Discrimination 366

UNIT 7 Contemporary Issues in Law

CHAPTER **42** Immigration Law 394

CHAPTER **43** Intellectual Property 408

CHAPTER **44** Law and Terrorism 414

CHAPTER **45** Rights and Responsibilities in the Workplace 424

CHAPTER **46** Environmental Law 437

About Street Law, Inc.

The *Street Law* materials are a product of Street Law, Inc., a global, nonpartisan, nonprofit organization with more than 45 years of experience developing classroom and community programs that educate young people about law and government. Street Law programs and materials help advance justice by empowering people with the legal and civic knowledge, skills, and confidence to bring about positive change for themselves and others.

Street Law lessons use interactive, student-centered methods to teach substantive information about law and government, while building important civic skills, including problem solving, critical thinking, cooperative learning, communication, advocacy, and conflict-resolution skills.

Many Street Law programs partner volunteers from the legal community with educators to deliver lessons. These volunteers include police officers, judges, law students from more than 100 law schools worldwide, and legal staff from more than 50 major corporations and law firms. These "community resource people" bring the law to life through real-world examples and experiences and give students the opportunity to consider possible careers in law, law enforcement, and government.

Street Law staff and consultants are global leaders in civic education with unmatched experience in curricula creation, program design, classroom teaching, customized technical support, and professional development for educators. Their expertise is available to school districts, law schools, corporations, law firms, juvenile justice system settings, community- based organizations, and others wishing to educate young people about law and government.

In addition to *Street Law: A Course in Practical Law*, the organization's publications include:
- *United States Government: Our Democracy* (2018, McGraw-Hill Education)
- *Street Law: Understanding Law & Legal Issues* (2011, McGraw-Hill Education)
- *Street Law's Classroom Guide to Mock Trials and Moot Courts* (2005, McGraw-Hill Education)

For more information, please contact:

Street Law, Inc.
1010 Wayne Avenue, Suite 870
Silver Spring, MD 20910
USA
Tel.: 301-589-1130
Fax: 301-589-1131
website: www.streetlaw.org
email: learnmore@streetlaw.org

Professional Development Opportunities for Street Law Teachers

Street Law offers professional development for law, government, history, and civics teachers. Street Law's professional development programs blend legal and civic content with interactive teaching strategies. We train teachers to use simulations to engage students in the content, and provide teachers with up-to-date, comprehensive information about important legal, constitutional, and public policy issues.

Street Law's most well-known professional development program is the Supreme Court Summer Institute for Teachers, offered in partnership with the Supreme Court Historical Society. This program helps teachers strengthen and expand their instruction about the Supreme Court of the United States, constitutional concepts, and current cases and improve their use of student-centered instructional strategies. Many teachers of the Street Law curriculum have participated in this Institute and found it helpful.

Street Law, Inc. also designs and delivers customized professional development events to meet the needs of particular programs or schools. For more information, visit www.streetlaw.org.

Street Law Supplements

The Street Law instructional program consists of the *Street Law: A Course in Practical Law*, Student Edition, plus the following integrated supplements:

- **Teacher Manual**—This manual includes chapter overviews, special projects, and additional resources for each unit. Each chapter includes detailed materials such as learning outcomes, additional background information, discussion topics, student activities, answers to each numbered problem in the Student Edition; and answers to caption questions for each photo and graphic in the Student Edition.

- **Online Student Edition**—*Street Law's* new tenth edition is part of McGraw-Hill Education's **Networks**, a social studies learning system. The Online Student Edition offers all of the same core content as the printed Student Edition. Go to connected.mcgraw-hill.com. Then enter a username and password. Create a new account using the redemption code you were issued. Click on your program to launch the home page of the Online Student Edition.

- **Online Lesson Plans**—*Street Law's* new tenth edition is part of McGraw-Hill Education's **Networks,** a social studies learning system. Go to connected.mcgraw-hill.com. Then enter a username and password. Create a new account using the redemption code. Click on your program to launch the home page of your Online Lesson Plans. In addition to offering all of the same materials that are provided in the print Teacher Manual, the Online Lesson Plans include:

  - Presentation Slides that include a text or graphic stimuli followed by discussion questions to spark student interest. These Presentation Slides can be found under the Resources tab of the Online Lesson Plans.

- **Online Assessment Center**—Unit and chapter question and activity banks are available in the Online Assessment Center. You can use the existing test questions, edit them to meet classroom needs, or create your own questions and tests from scratch. After you've logged in to the Online Lesson Plans, follow these steps to utilize the Online Assessment Center: (1) Click on the Assess tab for test preparation activities and rubrics, and to access the Test Generator; (2) Click the Online Assessment Center launch image to open the Online Assessment Center test generator; and (3) Click New Test and add questions from your Question Bank or write new questions.

Street Law began in 1972 as a one-semester experimental course in two District of Columbia public high schools. Taught by law students from Georgetown University Law Center, Street Law expanded to become a credit-bearing elective in all District of Columbia public high schools. Today, law students from more than 70 law schools participate in Street Law programs in the United States. More than 50 law schools overseas also send law students into school and community settings to teach empowering practical law lessons, based generally on the original Georgetown Law Center model.

The curriculum, *Street Law: A Course in Practical Law,* was first published as a separate textbook for the District of Columbia in 1974. It was a product of several revisions of earlier materials based on the written evaluations of high school students, social studies teachers, and law students.

After field testing and revision, the local edition was adapted and republished as a national textbook in 1975. This text was designed to give students a basic knowledge of law that could be of practical use to them in everyday life. Subsequent editions were published in 1980, 1986, 1990, 1995, 1999, 2005, 2010, and 2016. Used by students and teachers all over the country, *Street Law* has now been expanded and updated in this new tenth edition (copyright 2021).

Incorporating the best features of the earlier editions, the tenth edition provides new and updated legal information, as well as competency-building activities designed to provide students with the ability to analyze, evaluate, and, in some situations, resolve legal disputes. Over time, this practical law focus has broadened into a powerful vehicle for promoting civic learning. Student involvement is emphasized through the use of problems, case studies, deliberations, role-plays, cooperative learning activities, simulations, research using the Internet, and a variety of other activities. The updated curriculum is designed to appeal to a wide variety of student learning styles.

Street Law is published with this accompanying Teacher Manual. As part of McGraw-Hill Education's **Networks,** a social studies learning system, the new tenth edition is also available as an Online Student Edition and Online Lesson Plans that include worksheets, presentation slides, and assessment.

The goals of the *Street Law* program focus on developing in students the knowledge and skills necessary to participate meaningfully in our constitutional democracy. The *Street Law* program:

1. provides a practical understanding of law and the legal system that will be of use to students in their everyday lives.
2. improves understanding of the fundamental principles and values underlying the U.S. Constitution, laws, and legal system.
3. promotes awareness of current issues and controversies relating to law and the legal system.
4. encourages effective and informed civic participation in our democracy.
5. brings about a greater sense of justice, tolerance, and fairness.
6. develops a willingness and an ability to resolve disputes through informal and, when necessary, formal mechanisms.
7. improves basic skills, including critical thinking and reasoning, communication, observation, and problem solving.
8. improves understanding of the roles that law, lawyers, law enforcement officers, and the legal system play in our democracy.
9. provides exposure to the many vocational opportunities that exist within the legal system.

CONTENT AND ORGANIZATION OF THE STUDENT EDITION

The *Street Law* Student Edition is organized into seven units with 46 chapters.

Each unit begins with a brief overview of the chapters in that unit. Following the introduction, the chapters are divided into major sections or content areas. Each of these sections represents a topic for classroom study. Practical legal information and competency-building activities are provided in each chapter. In addition, the Student Edition includes activities designed to promote active student learning, higher-level thinking, classroom involvement, and civic engagement.

SPECIAL FEATURES IN THE STUDENT EDITION

The *Street Law* Student Edition is quite different from most texts designed for use in high school classrooms. Other texts tend to present review questions at the end of each section and chapter, questions which too often fail to challenge students' abilities to think critically but simply ask students to repeat what they have just read. Throughout the *Street Law* Student Edition, readers will find cases, problems, and other features which are intended to function as part of the text and present opportunities for students to think critically, express judgment, and demonstrate comprehension.

The Student Edition includes a number of special features designed to promote student learning and enhance understanding of the textbook material. The following features are found throughout the Student Edition.

Photographs Each chapter contains a number of carefully selected photographs. These photos illustrate various facets of the law in action. In addition, the photos can serve as focal points for classroom discussion and can be used to develop student inquiry and visual analysis skills. To assist the teacher, teaching captions and questions accompany the photographs.

Case Studies Brief case studies are presented throughout the Student Edition. These cases illustrate legal issues and processes in the context of real-life situations. They also promote the development of reasoning, as well as analytical and critical thinking skills. Finally, case studies vividly illustrate the ways in which social, economic, moral, and political issues affect and are affected by the law. A guide for teaching the case study method is included in the front of this Teacher Manual.

Figures A number of tables, diagrams, graphs, and documents are included throughout the Student Edition to amplify the material presented in the text. Some figures provide students with the opportunity to read and draw inferences from quantitative data. Documents and forms give students the opportunity to analyze, and obtain a working knowledge of everyday legal documents.

Investigating The Law Where You Live Written for students throughout the country, the Student Edition reflects the laws and legal procedures that exist in most states. However, there is necessarily a gap between what can be offered in any textbook and the variations in law that exist on the state and local level. The Law Where You Live feature bridges this gap by drawing attention to many common local variations in practical law.

Additional state-specific information may be available online through state bar associations and from statewide civic education organizations.

Unit-Based Feature The tenth edition includes a Deliberation feature in each unit. This feature presents students with the opportunity to explore multiple perspectives through civil discourse.

Chapter-Based Features Taking Action: Law and Democracy features puts students in the position of policy makers, judges, and civic activists to identify and solve important problems. For Your Information (FYI) features provide additional reference material, not necessarily of a legal nature, to supplement the main text. Steps to Take features provide general legal information that students and their families can use when they encounter certain legal problems. However, it is important to remind students that the law varies from state to state and changes over time; *Street Law* cannot substitute for the legal advice provided by an attorney.

Legal Documents The Appendix of the Student Edition contains the full text (with annotations) of the U.S. Constitution and all constitutional amendments, the Universal Declaration of Human Rights (original text and the plain language version), and a summary of major federal civil rights laws.

Vocabulary Words, Glossary, and Index Vocabulary words and legal terminology have been set bold and highlighted in the body of each Student Edition chapter. Such treatment focuses student attention on unfamiliar words and phrases and helps build a legal vocabulary. Terms and definitions are printed in the margins at point of use the first time they are used. They are also listed and defined in the Glossary, located in the Appendix at the back of the Student Edition. A detailed Index, also included in the Appendix, can be helpful with research questions.

ORGANIZATION OF THE TEACHER MANUAL

Street Law teachers do not need formal legal training, but some background knowledge and information is useful to help answer the many questions raised by students. This Teacher Manual was created to assist teachers with the *Street Law* curriculum and is organized to closely follow the Student Edition. After a brief unit overview, which includes a summary of the chapters in the unit, recommendations for special projects, and references for additional resources, each chapter of the Teacher Manual corresponds to the Student Edition. For the major sections of each chapter there are learning outcomes, additional background information, suggested discussion topics, answers to the questions in the captions for the photos and graphics, additional activities and resources, and answers to the numbered problems in the Student Edition. Please note that since many of the problems in the Student Edition ask for opinions, the answers in the Teacher Manual do not necessarily reflect "right" answers. Instead they suggest common legal thinking and how courts have addressed similar questions. Endnotes provide citations to cases—generally those decided by the U.S. Supreme Court—mentioned in the Teacher Manual and the Student Edition.

Every teaching strategy listed here is designed to help students acquire new information and skills in ways that are student-centered and engaging.

****

BRAINSTORMING

Purpose Brainstorming encourages students to use their imaginations and to be creative. It helps elicit numerous solutions to any given problem. Once a brainstormed list is created, responses can be reorganized, combined or modified to create solutions that more directly address the problem.

Procedures

1. Provide a whiteboard, flip-chart pad or paper to record and post ideas for all to see.
2. State the problem or question to be addressed.
3. State the rules for brainstorming:

   - At this point, we are not evaluating ideas or judging how useful they are.

   - Think creatively. No idea is too crazy.

   - Generate as many ideas as you can. The more ideas the better.

   - Build upon the ideas of others (combine, modify, etc.).

4. Ask for ideas and record them as fast as they come. Do not edit what they say or how they say it.
5. Discourage derisive laughter, comments, or ridicule of any ideas.
6. Continue as long as the ideas keep coming, then at the conclusion, discuss and evaluate the ideas generated.

****

CATEGORIZING

Purpose This is a good strategy to help students learn or review the differences between several concepts. It requires students to apply their knowledge to specific cases or examples and it allows them to move around the room, making it a more physical or kinesthetic learning activity.

Procedures

1. Choose a broad topic or concept that has several important parts. For example, if you are teaching about the First Amendment, a broad concept might be "freedom of religion" and subtopics might be "the free exercise clause" and "the establishment clause." If you are teaching about the broad concept of intellectual property, the underlying categories could be "trademarks", "patents" and "copyrights". Make signs naming the categories and post them on the walls in different corners of the room.
2. Create various note cards or strips of paper that include characteristics or examples of each category. You may use words, hypothetical situations, pictures, or other visual media to illustrate the concepts. For example, you might include photos of students praying at football games, summaries of key Supreme Court cases about religion, etc. In the intellectual property example above, students might get pictures of logos and products and need to decide which ones are depictions of trademarked products, patented products, and copyrighted products. You should have at least one card for each student.
3. Once class begins, explain the purpose of the activity and the directions for students. Confirm they understand their tasks.
4. Distribute the note cards or strips of paper described above. Each student may get one or several.
5. Ask students to decide which category their example fits in. If this is the first time the students are encountering this material, you will want to provide them with a textbook or handout that defines each category. Students may work on their own or in groups to decide.
6. Once students have figured out which category their cards relate to, they should walk to the sign that best fits their example and attach their card or paper or product to the wall beneath that sign and then return to their seats.
7. Once all the examples are affixed to the wall, lead a discussion of each category—asking students to contribute the reasons why a particular example was placed in that category. If the students decide

that something has been misplaced, they should move it.

8. Conclude the activity with a whole-class discussion and debrief about the broad concepts, categories, and examples.

****

EACH ONE—TEACH ONE

Purpose   With this teaching strategy, students first learn about one fact, definition, or a small amount of information. Then, they share what they have learned with classmates who studied different information. This method is good for building student interest when introducing a unit or summarizing the points learned when ending a unit.

Procedures

1. Prepare fact cards or strips. Put a fact or definition on an index card or a strip of paper, one per student. With larger groups, you may replicate facts among more than one student.
2. Distribute one card to each student.
3. Each student should spend a few minutes reading the information on the card. You may want to ask them to put the information into their own words or think of an example that illustrates the concept or fact. Circulate and check that students understand the information they have received.
4. Tell the students to circulate around the room and teach their fact to <u>one person at a time</u>. For each interaction, students will share their own fact and learn one fact from the person they are speaking to. It may be helpful for students to take notes about what they learn.
5. Conclude the activity by asking students to share something they learned from another student.

****

GALLERY WALK or CAROUSEL

Purpose   This activity gives students the opportunity to share their work in a "carousel" fashion with other students. It requires students to create a piece of work, such as a poster, that illustrates their research or ideas

about a particular topic or unit. In addition to showing their ideas, students talk to others who circulate around the gallery or carousel. In this way, students can teach and learn from each other. This activity has the added benefit of requiring that students get up and move while they learn.

Procedures

1. Arrange the room so students can spread out along the perimeter.
2. Ask students to find a partner.
3. Ask each set of partners to stand together. The pairs should spread out along the perimeter of the room, forming a large circle or square.
4. Instruct students to tape, hang or display their work product on the wall behind them. If students created their work online and it must be shown that way, arrange for computers to be available to display the work.
5. Ask one student from each pair to come to the middle of the room. Explain that these students will have the first chance to check out the work of the other students. They will be the "moving learners". (Other students will get a chance to be moving learners shortly.) Ask the other student to stand by their displayed work products. They will be the "standing student teachers".

    Explain that in a moment, the "moving learners" will spread out across the room to speak to the "standing student teachers" who are standing along the wall near their work. At your cue, ask the "moving learners" to choose a "standing student teacher" to talk to. The "standing student teachers" should share their work, explain how it relates to the topic of learning, and answer any questions from the "moving learners". Tell students they will have two or three minutes to share for each rotation. Confirm students understand the instructions.
6. Begin the first round. After about two minutes, give your cue. That should signal the "moving learners" to rotate and meet with a different student teacher. After two or three rounds, ask students to switch roles and switch places. Now, the "standing student teachers" get to be "moving learners" and vice versa. Again, the "moving learners" should move

upon your cue. Follow the same pattern until this second set of "moving learners" have had a chance to circulate around the room to see at least two or three sets of student work.

7. Call the students together and back to their seats for a brief discussion. Ask students:

   - What were you able to learn from explaining your work to other students?

   - What were you able to learn from seeing and discussing other students' work?

8. If possible, keep the student work hanging around the room for the rest of the class period or even into the next class period.

****

JIGSAW

Purpose   In this method students teach each other. Peer teaching is one of the most effective ways to learn content and practice many important skills, such as explaining difficult information, asking questions, listening, and communicating. This approach is designed to allow students to work together to learn a large amount of information in a short time (oftentimes in place of a long lecture or presentation.) It can be used to teach and learn about multiple related concepts such as several Supreme Court cases, several key ideas relating to a particular legal concept, multiple primary or secondary source documents, etc.

Procedures

1. Select 3-4 concepts or cases that you want the students to grasp. For example, if you wanted the students to learn about negligence, you might select: duty and breach of duty, causation, and damages. Or, if you wanted students to learn about important student expression cases, you might include the *Hazelwood*, *Tinker*, and *Bethel* cases.

2. Prepare a "compilation" worksheet or capture sheet that has space for each of the cases or concepts. You should also prepare a separate handout or reading on each of the topics you want students to learn. These should be brief: no more than one page. The handout should also include three or four questions you want students to answer about the concept or case. (Alternatively, you could list these questions on the compilation sheet.)

3. Put students into groups. If you select three topics, you need three students in each group, if you select four topics, you need four students per group, etc. Assign a letter to each group. These are the students' "home" groups. Direct students to write their home group letter at the top of their worksheet.

4. Then assign one student in each home group to become an "expert" on each concept.* In this example, one will become an expert on the *Hazelwood* case, another student becomes an expert on *Tinker*, etc. Confirm students know which topics they are assigned.

5. Now ask students to move so they are sitting with other students who will become experts on the same topic. These new groups are called "expert groups." Students assigned to the first concept (*Hazelwood*) should sit in one area of the room, and the second (*Tinker*) in another area, etc. (Depending on how many students are in your class, you may want to further divide the expert groups so the expert groups include no more than three to five students.

6. Give each expert group a reading about their topic. Ask students to read it and discuss it with others in their expert group. They should then decide which portions of the material the students in the other groups need to learn about. They should create a list of talking points to teach other students.

7. After the allotted "expert" time, ask students to return to their home (letter) groups. Each student will be asked to spend 5-7 minutes teaching about their case or concept. Other students should listen, take notes, and ask questions.

8. After students teach their home groups, every student should have studied one case or concept in depth and learned about several others. Conclude the activity with a whole-class discussion about how the concepts relate to each other, or to emphasize especially important points.

(*) Note: This strategy suggests each student is responsible for one concept or case. If you have an uneven number of students, or if you have some students that would struggle with serving as a solo expert to teach others, you may wish to create "home groups" that are larger than the number of concepts. In that case, you could double up on experts for some concepts.

****

MIND WALK

Purpose This activity demonstrates the many ways in which law touches our lives. It will illustrate how regulations affect students' lives and the importance of knowing about them. Students will recognize the influence of laws on daily life and realize that laws are made not only to control social behavior but also to regulate and protect citizens. It can be adapted easily to focus on a specific area of law or government such as an exploration of family law with a story about being born, growing up, getting married (or not), having children (or not), etc.

Procedures

1. Tell students that you are going to narrate a "story" and that they should stop your narration when they think you have mentioned something that pertains to the law.
2. Begin to narrate your daily activities. For example: "This morning I woke up at 6:00 am. I took a shower, got dressed, ate a breakfast of cereal and coffee, and then I got in my car and drove to school. I picked up my mail in the office, etc."
3. The students should have stopped you at a number of places to mention points such as the following:

   - Time is regulated by law. The official clock in Washington, D.C., is set in accordance with Greenwich Mean Time.

   - Water for showering is inspected by city officials and must meet standards regulated by law.

   - Clothing must have the contents listed on a label.

   - Cereal boxes are required by law to list the ingredients on the box. Milk must be pasteurized and meet standards regulated by the law.

   - Cars must have safety and pollution control devices that are regulated by law.

   - Drivers must be licensed and must obey traffic laws.

   - Streets are built and maintained under standards regulated by law.

4. As an alternative, you may ask the students to challenge you—ask them to name something that is not regulated by a law, and you will try to explain how it is. Examples:

   - Breathing- is regulated by air quality laws and pollution control standards.

   - Talking to a friend- may be regulated by free speech laws, noise ordinances, hate speech laws, etc.

5. Conclude the activity with a discussion. You might ask:

   - What surprised you?

   - What did you learn?

   - What do you want to know more about?

   - Who makes laws?

   - Who makes regulations? How are they different than laws?

   - Who chooses the people who make laws and regulations?

   - Which level of government is responsible for the laws and regulations we discussed? (Local, state, federal?)

   - If you wanted a new law or regulation—or if you wanted to amend or remove one—what steps could you take? Who could you contact?

Then segue into the specific area of law or policy that is the focus of the lesson today.

****

SMALL GROUP WORK / COOPERATIVE LEARNING IN SMALL GROUPS

Purpose A primary characteristic of high-quality, law-related education classes is an emphasis on student participation. One of the best ways to maximize participation is by using cooperative small-group instruction. Students working in a small-group setting can practice critical civic skills including: cooperating, leading, communicating, resolving differences, learning from peers, and developing appreciation for diverse viewpoints.

Procedures

Cooperative small-group instruction requires advance planning of the activity and the group assignments.

Take these steps before class begins:

1. Select an activity. Choose a problem that requires students to work together to complete it.

2. Think carefully about what students need to know and to be able to do to be successful with the activity. Be sure they have that prior knowledge before you begin small group work.

3. Decide in advance how large you want the groups to be. Generally, group size should be limited to three to five students.

4. Decide if you want to prearrange groups, if you want students to choose their groups, or if you want to put them together randomly (like by counting off) when the activity begins.

5. Think about how you want the groups to function. Each member of group should have at least one role to promote active learning. (For smaller groups, students may have multiple roles.) Sample roles could include:

   - **facilitator**—keeps discussion moving, makes sure all group members are contributing, but does not dominate or direct the decisions of the group

   - **recorder**—takes notes on ideas and decisions

   - **reporter**—communicates the group's decisions and reasons when the whole-class discussion begins

   - **time keeper**—notes the time given for the group assignments and helps the group meet the time limit

6. Write a handout that includes necessary background information and directions for the group activity. Directions should be clear and limited in number. You may also want to include a list of roles and job descriptions for members of the group. (See above.)

Take these steps once class begins.

7. Introduce the general topic and framework of the activity.

8. Form the groups and ask students to move to their groups and sit in a small circle. If the task requires students to use desks or tables, be sure all students are facing each other and can see and hear each other easily. This will facilitate engagement, cooperation and communication.

9. Assign roles or allow students to choose them. Review the responsibilities for each role. (See job descriptions above.)

10. Distribute the handout that explains the task the group should complete. Provide a time limit and write it on the board. Confirm students understand the task before the groups begin to work.

11. Circulate and facilitate. Move among the groups to ensure that they are on track. Monitor the time and adjust the limit if students need more time. If some groups finish before others, challenge them with an extension activity.

12. Once the group work has been completed, you will usually want the groups to report back. Where appropriate, record the results of the group work (e.g., on a grid on the board or on large sheets of paper). Be sure to ask for reasons for each group's decisions. Time permitting, some groups may wish to question others about their reasoning. Ask a few volunteers to describe how the process worked in their group.

13. You may want to give each student the opportunity to reflect on the activity and his or her role. An exit card or journal entry could include some or all of the following questions:

    - Do you think everyone in the group could contribute ideas?

    - Did everyone listen to other students' ideas and consider them fairly?

    - Do you think everyone was willing to compromise and to cooperate?

    - Did your group experience any conflict when people had different ideas? If so, what was the conflict about? Was your group able to resolve that conflict? If so, how?

    - What could you do differently or better next time you work in a small group?

****

THINK-PAIR-SHARE

Purpose In this strategy, students take time to think alone and then discuss their ideas with a partner. After that, each pair shares their ideas with other students. This method is an excellent way to increase student participation in a discussion, to ensure that all students have an opportunity to consider a question and formulate a response, and to draw out students that might be too shy to speak in front of the group. It can also be used to develop critical thinking, persuasion and debate skills.

Procedures

1. Pose a discussion question or a hypothetical situation to the students.
2. Ask students if they have any clarifying questions about the facts or what the question is asking.
3. Give students a short amount of time to think about possible answers or solutions on their own.
4. Divide the students into pairs to discuss their ideas with their partner. They should try to come to an agreement or consensus on the answer or solution.
5. Then, begin a large, whole-class discussion by inviting each pair to share their answer and reasoning with others.

ACCESSING COMMUNITY RESOURCES

In every community many resources are available to enrich law-related education classes. Use of community resources (also known as Legal Resource People or Outside Resource People) can take two forms: resource persons can be brought into the classroom, or the class can take a field trip into the community. Community-based education is essential to make law-related education realistic and to give students a firsthand look at the legal system.

Purpose One of the best practices in law-related education is the use of community resource people in the classroom. They can provide students with a wide array of information, materials, and experience not available in any textbook. The use of community resources can also expose students to vocational opportunities involving the law, and broaden students' viewpoints and perspectives.

Procedures

Most teachers likely have an idea about whom to invite as a "guest speaker" for their students. Typically, those "guest speakers" lecture, take part in a panel, or participate in a question and answer session with students. The research on best practices in law-related education suggests a different approach—one in which community resource people co-teach interactive student-centered lessons with you. They serve as coaches or advisers for mock trials, role plays involving traffic stops, mock legislative hearings, etc. In this approach, the resource person does less "speaking" and more co-teaching lessons you have designed.

Before class, follow these steps:

1. Select a resource person based on the unit of study and the goals of the class. Among the most common are lawyers, law students, and police officers. Other possibilities include probation or parole officers, paralegals, jury consultants, federal law enforcement officers, real estate agents, consumer advocates, social workers, housing inspectors, elected officials, judges, journalists, and representatives of various government agencies or public interest organizations.
2. Prepare the resource person and the class. The resource person should be given some background information on the students and their prior knowledge of the topic of discussion. The resource person should be told the objectives of the class. If you have a copy of the lesson plan, send it to the resource person and discuss how you will co-teach the lesson. If you do not have a specific lesson plan, create one with the resource person. Encourage him or her to avoid lecturing.
3. A few days prior to the class, confirm the visit. If necessary, explain your school's procedures for visitors. For example, is there a designated visitor's parking area? Does he or she need to bring an ID? Will you or one of your students meet him or her in the front office?, etc.
4. Tell students how the resource person fits into the goals of their class. They should do some background study on the topic of the visit and should prepare a list of questions, preferably in writing, prior to the visit.

When class begins, follow these steps:

5. Introduce the resource person and remind students the purpose of his or her visit to their classroom.

6. Assume responsibility for class management, rather than depending on the resource person to do so. If the activity involves small-group work, you might consider putting students into groups.

7. Introduce and conduct the student activity you have planned. The resource person will advise, coach, observe, make suggestions, etc.

8. As the student activity concludes, involve the resource person in the closing discussion. Focus on how the activity compares to "the real world", local laws and procedures, etc. Be sure to leave enough time for students to ask questions that may not have been addressed in the activity such as:

   • What education and training is required for your job?

   • What inspired you to do this work?

   • What is a "typical" work day for you?

   • What are the best/worst parts of your job?

After the class:

9. Discuss the visit through questions such as these:

   • What did you learn from the resource person?

   • What else would you like to have learned?

   • How did the resource person's remarks relate to other information you have learned on the same topic?

10. Write a thank you note or email to the resource person. At a minimum, it should come from you. It would be even better if students write or sign it. If possible and appropriate, copy the resource person's supervisor.

****

FIELD TRIPS

Purpose   Field trips are exciting to students and an excellent way to engage students in law-related education. They give students a look at the "real world" of the legal system and government in action, and they make it possible for students to apply what they have learned to what they see in their own community.

Procedures

Careful advance planning is the key to a successful field trip. Each school or school system has its own rules about how far in advance teachers must request field trips, which forms must be completed, which transportation may be used, how many chaperones are required, what time students can leave the building and when they must return, etc. Be sure to build in enough lead time to understand and comply with those requirements. The following general steps will help you plan and maximize the success of your field trip.

1. **Decide where to go.** Among the common locations visited by law or government classes are court buildings, correctional facilities, police departments, crime labs, and government agencies. You might also consider your state capitol or local government building. If you live near a federal court, contact the federal court's educational outreach program at www.uscourts.gov.

2. **Plan the visit.** Students should be prepared for the visit, and every effort should be made to involve the personnel of the agency or facility visited. For example, if students are going to court, contact the clerk of the court to find out the best time of day and most interesting proceeding to attend. Consider asking a judge or attorney to speak to the students as a way of better explaining the visit. Prepare an observation sheet for students to record what they see and learn on the visit.

3. **Conduct the visit.** As with any class, students should be prepared to ask questions, to watch for specific things, and to record their reactions on an observation sheet.

4. **Debrief and discuss the visit when you return to school.** You might ask students:

   • What did you see?

   • How did you feel about what you saw?

   • What did you learn from the visit?

   • How did what you learned relate to what we are studying or your prior knowledge?

   • What else would you now like to know?

****

ANALYZING SUPREME AND APPELLATE COURT CASES

Purpose Analyzing cases that have been decided by (or are under consideration by) the United States Supreme Court is a quintessential teaching strategy in law-related education. Analyzing cases gives students the opportunity to understand how the law affects real people. The process requires students to consider and understand challenging legal problems, to reach decisions and to understand the impact of the outcomes of a case.

There are a variety of effective methods to teach about court decisions, including case studies, classifying arguments, unmarked opinions, applying precedent, and moot courts. They are listed below in order from the most basic to the most complicated method. Most teachers use a variety of these methods to teach important content and skills. NOTE: Street Law, Inc. has an extensive library of free and ready-to-use cases on its website at: www.streetlaw.org

CASE STUDIES

Procedures

Before class begins, follow these steps:

1. Select the case materials: (You may want to use one of the many cases on Street Law's website. They are free and ready-to-use at www.streetlaw.org) If you choose to use a different case, consider the following when you select which case to teach:

   - Is the content of the case relevant to your course, to a specific school outcome or worth knowing?

   - Is it interesting to students?

   - Are community resource people available to assist with the lesson?

   - Is there an underlying value conflict that is important for students to examine?

2. Prepare the student materials and decide if you want students to work alone or in groups.

Once class begins, follow these steps:

3. Distribute the case materials to students and review the facts. Clarify any facts that are not clear to students. Ask students:

   - What happened in this case?
   - Who are the parties?
   - What facts are important?
   - Is any significant information missing?

4. Help students frame the issue. Students should pinpoint and discuss the issues or problems presented by the case. The legal issue is the question of law on which resolution of the case turns. An issue should be posed in the form of a question. While most cases revolve around a legal issue, students should also consider issues of public policy, values in conflict, and practical reality. For example, a case study involving drug testing in schools might involve the following issues:

   (Legal issue) Can public schools require mandatory drug tests for students who participate in extracurricular activities?

   (Public policy issue) Should schools require drug tests for students who participate in extracurricular activities? Why or why not? Do such tests reduce drug use? Do such tests protect the safety of students in those schools?

   (Values in conflict) Which value is more important, student safety, student health, or student privacy? Why?

   (Practical) Do such tests reduce drug use? Do such tests protect the safety of students in those schools? Who would pay for the testing? Who would administer the test? What would be the consequences for students who fail the drug test?

5. Discuss the arguments. In this step, students develop and discuss the arguments that can be made for and against each of the issues. Students should consider questions such as the following:

   - What are the arguments in favor of and against each point of view?

   - Which arguments are most persuasive? Least persuasive? Why?

   - What might be the consequences of each course of action? To the parties? To society?

   - Are there any alternatives?

NOTE: In discussing the various arguments, it is important to foster a climate of acceptance and openness. Students must know that all opinions are welcome and that their ideas will receive a fair hearing and analysis no matter how controversial the issue. In other words, students should be encouraged to listen to, consider, and evaluate points of view.

6. Reach a decision. Ask students to reach their own conclusions before you tell them what the Court decided (if it did). Possible questions to ask:

   - How would you decide the case? Why?

   - (Once you have conveyed the Court's actual decision) Do you agree or disagree with the Court's decision?

   - What reasons did the Court give for its decision?

   - What consequences do you anticipate with the decision?

****

UNMARKED OPINIONS

Procedures

1. Give students the facts, issues, and arguments for a case. Then give them two an unmarked judicial opinions. One should be marked "Opinion A" and the other "Opinion B." One should include excerpts or a paraphrase from the Court's decision and the other excerpts or a paraphrase from the dissenting opinion. Participants are not told which of the Court opinions is the actual decision (majority) or dissenting.

2. Ask students to select the opinion with which they agree with and explain why.

3. Later, give students the actual marked opinions and ask them to compare their reasoning and result against the Court's decisions.

****

CLASSIFYING ARGUMENTS

Procedures

1. Provide students with the facts and issues in a case, then provide them with a list of arguments. The list of arguments should include some arguments for

each side. If you choose to use one of Street Law's hundreds of case summaries available free on our website, download the word document, delete the headings for the arguments, and cut and paste the bulleted arguments in random order. If you use a case not on our website, depending on the skills and experience of your students, you may want to use actual quotes from the decision or from the written briefs or oral arguments. As an alternative, you may want to paraphrase the arguments.

2. Ask students to read and evaluate each argument and decide whether it is an argument for the petitioner or the respondent.

3. After students have classified the arguments, ask them to choose one argument for each side that they think is most persuasive. Ask students to explain why they found them compelling.

4. Conclude the activity with a discussion about the decision. Ask students to reach their own conclusions before you tell them what the Court decided (if it did). Possible questions to ask:

   - How would you decide the case? Why?

   - (Once you have conveyed the Court's actual decision) Do you agree or disagree with the Court's decision?

   - What reasons or arguments did the Court give for its decision?

   - What consequences do you anticipate with the decision?

****

APPLYING PRECEDENT

Procedures

1. Using this approach, give students the facts, issues, and arguments of a case.

2. Then provide students with the decisions in similar past cases that might serve as precedent, or as a guide for decision making in the present case.

3. Ask students to take on the role of a judge to determine whether the cases that may serve as precedent apply to the case. For each precedent listed, answer the following questions:

- How is the precedent similar (analogous) to the current case?
- How is the precedent different (distinguished) from the current case?
- In your opinion, how does this precedent apply to the current case?

4. After analyzing the possible precedents, have students determine how the case should be decided and ask them to explain their reasons.

****

MOOT COURT

See "moot courts" in the Simulations and Role Plays section.

****

FISHBOWL TAG

Purpose   Fishbowl tag engages students in carefully-constructed discussions and requires effective listening skills. It works well in many types of classrooms, including classes that include students with a wide range of skills and experiences, because it draws on personal knowledge and opinions.

Procedures

1. Write down several open-ended questions. Place these questions in a fishbowl or other container.
2. Arrange five to eight chairs or desks to form a small circle. Arrange a second set of five to eight chairs or desks to form an outer circle. Arrange the rest of the desks or chairs around the circles.
3. Assign students to sit in each chair or desk and explain that all students will have at least one chance to sit in each section through the course of the activity.
4. Explain how the discussion will work:

- One student from the "inner circle" will choose a question from the fishbowl. Then, all of the students in the inner circle will discuss that question. Once they have contributed to the discussion at least once, they may choose to stay in the circle and continue discussing the question, or, they can tag someone in the "outer circle" to take their place.

- Students in the outer circle may raise their hand if they want to contribute to the discussion, but they may only speak if and when someone in the inner circle calls on them and switches seats.
- Students who are in neither circle are assigned the role of "active observer" and should be prepared to discuss what they heard when the whole-class discussion begins.

5. Confirm that students understand their roles and then begin the first discussion. When you feel the question has been fully discussed, begin a whole-class discussion by asking the "active observers" these questions:

- What did you hear that was important?
- What did you want to say that was not discussed?
- Which arguments discussed were most persuasive? Why?
- What questions do you still have about the discussion?

6. After one discussion topic or question has been fully explored and the larger class discussion about that topic has concluded, ask students to switch places. Five to eight students who were "active observers" should move to the inner circle. People who were in the inner circle move out one level, etc. Ask an inner circle student to choose the next question and continue the pattern until all questions have been explored and all students have had an opportunity to join the inner and outer circles.

****

QUICK ACTIVITIES TO INTRODUCE OR WRAP UP DISCUSSIONS

Purpose   There are hundreds of excellent activities to help introduce students to a new concept or to wrap up a lesson or unit of study. Sometimes, teachers want a simple and fast strategy. A few stand out in law-related education classes as particularly effective for promoting critical thinking skills. They are opinion polls and rank-order exercises.

Conduct an opinion poll. Typically, a poll allows for a range of opinion (e.g., strongly agree, agree, undecided, disagree, and strongly disagree). An opinion poll can serve as a springboard for classroom discussion; give you feedback on the students' values, attitudes, and beliefs; and help assess changes in student attitudes following instruction.

1. Decide how you want to conduct the poll. Do you want to use a simple show of hands? Do you want to use a free online polling tool such as "Survey Monkey" or "Poll Everywhere"?

2. Decide how many questions you want to include in the poll (typically, a few questions are more effective than many), and compose the questions.

3. Conduct the poll, first asking students to express their own opinions. This can be as simple as having students write down their answers on a scrap of paper.

4. You should then develop a class composite. This can be done by a simple show of hands.

5. Ask students to explain their opinions and to listen to opposing points of view.

6. You may wish to follow the opinion poll with a case study on the subject of the discussion. For example, suppose a number of students respond to an opinion poll on criminal law by strongly agreeing with the statement "Criminal offenders should be rehabilitated and not punished." This poll could be followed by a case study about a violent offender with a long record.

Use a rank-order exercise. Another approach to analyzing and discussing student beliefs is a rank-order activity. The rank-order activity involves making choices between competing alternatives. For example, students might rank certain offenses from most serious to least serious. By putting items in rank-order, students have to prioritize and evaluate various options.

****

DISCUSSING AND EXPLORING CONTROVERSIAL ISSUES

Teaching about controversial issues helps students consider polar positions and alternative solutions to controversial issues and important public policy problems. Teachers are sometimes reluctant to introduce controversy, fearing that students will be unable to discuss emotionally charged subjects or ambiguous

issues rationally. Nevertheless, teaching about controversial issues helps raise student interest in the lesson and engages students in learning and practicing meaningful skills through reasoned debate. It also teaches decision making, social participation, careful listening, defending a position, and conflict management skills. The following suggestions can help make controversy constructive and educational:

✓ Encourage students to examine and present conflicting views even if they do not agree with these views. Be sure all sides of an issue are equally explored. Raise any opposing views students may have missed.

✓ Help students identify specific points of agreement and disagreement, places where compromise might be possible, and places where compromise is unlikely to occur.

✓ Keep the students focused on ideas or positions, rather than people.

✓ Emphasize that the outcome or the decision that your students reach is not as important as their ability to support a decision and express it in a civil manner.

✓ Conclude or debrief the activities or discussions, summarizing all of the arguments presented and exploring consequences of any alternatives suggested.

✓ Before using a teaching strategy in which class discussion and sharing of opinions are critical components, you may wish to establish some ground rules. For example:

- Everyone will get a chance to talk. Only one person will talk at a time.

- Wait your turn. Do not interrupt.

- Do not argue with people. Challenge specific reasons or ideas.

- You may change your view or opinion. Be prepared to give your reason for changing.

- Listen to reasons and ideas presented by your classmates. You will be called on to tell which one of your classmates' ideas you found most persuasive.

****

DELIBERATIONS (ALSO KNOWN AS STRUCTURED ACADEMIC CONTROVERSY)

Similar to civil conversations, deliberations are civil discussions among students about public policy.

Purpose For a democracy to flourish, citizens must be able and willing to express their ideas, to exchange their ideas with peers and their elected leaders, and to reach conclusions about important and sometimes controversial public policy questions. Deliberations help students develop these important skills.

The purpose of this method is to explore controversial topics effectively ensuring a "best case fair hearing" for the issue, followed by informed decision making and consensus building among students. It also demands engaged participation from every student in the room. By following a highly-scaffolded process, students will be able to advocate both for and against an issue/policy, determine the most relevant and convincing arguments, and search for consensus in small groups.

This is often an ideal method to introduce controversial issue discussions in a highly structured and non-threatening way, laying the foundation for large group and whole class discussions.

Note: This method works best in cases where there are two clear opposing viewpoints.

This teaching method was developed by the Johnson brothers at the University of Minnesota and adapted through a partnership between Street Law, Inc., the Constitutional Rights Foundation Chicago, and the Constitutional Rights Foundation in their project *Deliberating in a Democracy*. Street Law's deliberation method was further refined and new deliberations were created through the 2018-2019 pilot of the New Perspectives program.

Procedures

For free deliberation materials, handouts, and lesson plans, and an instructional video, visit https://store.street-law.org/deliberations/. Information about the New Perspectives program can be found at https://www.street-law.org/programs/new-perspectives-deliberation-training.

1. While planning, watch the instructional video available at https://store.streetlaw.org/deliberation-resource-bundle-and-video/.
2. If you choose to use one of Street Law's deliberations, simply go to https://store.streetlaw. org/deliberations/ and download all of the needed materials. If you want to do a deliberation of a different topic, choose a text or texts that provide balanced background and more than one viewpoint about a controversial public policy. Then, prepare a specific deliberation question. The question should be binary, meaning it should require a "yes" or "no" answer. For example, if the topic is juvenile justice, the question might be: "Should our state punish violent juvenile offenders as adults?" After you write background on the issues, be sure to include an equal number of arguments for and against the question. Try to keep the reading short, no more than five pages double spaced. If possible, number the lines of the text to help students refer to specific points more easily during the deliberation. For examples, go to https://store.streetlaw.org/deliberations/.
3. **Introduction**—Review the meaning of deliberation, the reasons for deliberating, and the norms for deliberation. You may choose to do this step the day before the full deliberation.
4. **Careful Reading**—Instruct students to read the text together. They should identify confusing terms and note interesting facts or ideas. You may prefer students do the reading as a class or they could do it in groups of four.
5. **Clarification**—Check for understanding of the terms and content, and that students understand the deliberation question.
6. **Prepare and Present Positions**—Put students into groups of four and then divide each group into pairs, Team A and Team B.

   - Team A prepares for their presentation, finding at least two reasons to say YES to the question. They should take notes about their ideas.

   - Team B does the same, but finds at least two reasons to say NO to the question.

   - Then each team shares their most compelling reasons for or against the proposal with the other team.

7. **Reverse Positions**—Instruct the students representing the "A" viewpoints to select the best reason they heard from the other pair (B) and to state it. They should then add at least one additional compelling reason from the reading to

support the "B" position. Then flip the discussion so the students who initially represented the "B" viewpoints follow the same pattern. Tell students to record their notes.

8. **Free Discussion**—Allow students to drop their assigned roles and deliberate the question in their small groups. Tell each student to reach a personal decision based on evidence and logic.

9. **Search for Common Ground**—Ask students to search for a consensus on the question. (This may not be possible, but they should try to find consensus on some part (perhaps even that they all agree it is a problem that needs to be addressed)). They might simply find that both "A" and "B" agree on the cause or significance of the problem.

10. **Whole-Class Discussion**—Lead the class in discussion to gain deeper insight into the question, democracy, and deliberation. Debrief by instructing students to:

   - Raise your hand if you changed your position on the issue. (There will probably be very few or no hands.)

   - Raise your hand if you considered a new opinion that you had not considered before today. (There will probably be a few more hands.)

   - Raise your hand if you felt listened to during the deliberation. (Almost all hands should be raised.)

     Follow up by asking students, how they might translate this activity to conversations outside the classroom.

11. **Student Reflection**—Ask students to reflect about the content and skills they learned through the activity. A suggested self-reflection format is available with the deliberation materials at the Street Law website.

****

P-R-E-S (POINT OF VIEW–REASONS–EXAMPLES–SUMMARIZE)

Purpose This method provides students with a tool to develop their arguments and opinions. It helps them clarify their thoughts and articulate and present their opinions clearly and concisely. The P.R.E.S. method provides a useful format for conducting controversial issue discussions and public policy lessons.

Procedures

1. Post or provide a handout with the four steps in the P.R.E.S. method.
   (P) State your point of view
   (R) Give one reason for your point of view
   (E) Give an example to clarify your reason
   (S) Summarize your point of view

2. Clarify the steps and answer any questions. Give an example of each step. An example of the formula is:
   (P) I am opposed to people smoking inside.
   (R) Smoking is unhealthy for the smoker as well as the non-smokers in the room.
   (E) Research has showed that second-hand smoke causes cancer.
   (S) I am opposed to people smoking inside because of the negative health impact on non-smokers.

3. Introduce the discussion topic that is the focus of the lesson. Circulate and guide students in applying the P.R.E.S. method.

****

SIMPLIFIED CIVIL CONVERSATIONS

Purpose Among the most important civic skills students can learn are the skills relating to exchanging ideas about public policy in a thoughtful and civil manner. This teaching strategy helps students practice those skills. Civil conversations are carefully constructed discussions among students about public policy issues. Students are usually given a text to read (which could be written or some form of electronic media) and then grouped with a few other students to analyze and discuss the text. For more information about this strategy, please visit the website of the Constitutional Rights Foundation at https://www.crf-usa.org/t2tcollab/ where you will find step-by-step instructions, lesson plans, and student discussion guides on the topics of current events, government, economics, U.S. history, and world history.

TAKE A STAND, FAIR/UNFAIR, AND CONTINUUM

Purpose The take a stand, fair/unfair, and continuum methods have similar purposes and procedures. They are especially useful to help frame a discussion on controversial issues because they invite students to share their opinions about an issue. They expose students to the diversity of viewpoints on the topic and they provide students an opportunity to express positions on controversial issues and to practice communication skills. They are good starting activities to assess student knowledge before a lesson. They can also be useful to assess student understanding after a lesson. Because the method involves physical movement of students, it often motivates students to speak out who are normally quiet in class.

Procedures for a continuum/take-a-stand activity

1. As you plan, watch the instructional video available free at https://store.streetlaw.org/take-a-stand-bundle/.

2. Before the class begins, select a controversial issue that has two or more legitimate, opposing viewpoints for which there is no correct answer. Then, compose a question or statement that gets to the heart of the issue. For instance, if the subject of class is the Equal Protection Clause or *Brown* v. *Board of Education*, you may want to pose the question, "Does treating people equally mean treating them the same?" In a lesson about employment law, you might post a hypothetical situation such as "Alex got a tattoo over the weekend. When he returned to work, his supervisor said she did not like the tattoo and fired him. Is this fair?"

3. If the question requires a "yes" or "no" answer, post signs at opposite ends of the classroom with each of these responses. If a statement is posed to students, place signs at opposite ends of the classroom with the words "agree" and "disagree" on them. You could also use signs for "fair" and "unfair", or signs that express a range of views such as "strongly agree, agree, disagree, and strongly disagree."

4. When class begins, describe the activity in a general way. Post and discuss rules for the activity. You may ask students to help you create rules.

5. Begin the activity by writing or projecting the question or statement where all can see it. Give students a minute to think about their answer and compelling reasons for their position.

6. Ask the students to stand up and move to the sign that most clearly describes their position,

or a spot in between the signs if their opinion falls somewhere in between. (In the example above, someone might be standing in the middle, towards the "Fair" end, if they believe that it was fair as long as a no-tattoo policy had been outlined in Alex's company handbook.)

7. Invite a few students to state their position and to explain their reasons. Invite students from different areas along the continuum to respond.

8. Ask if there are students who have changed their minds and would like to move. Ask them to share their reasons for moving.

9. Ask students to state the most compelling reason they heard from people who hold opposing views.

10. You may wish to extend the activity changing the wording to reflect a nuance of the question or hypothetical situation. Another alternative is to introduce factual material that may sway students' positions on the issues, asking students to reposition themselves along the continuum after each fact is unveiled. You might ask students to consider the consequences of their decision such as "If we allow employers to fire everyone with a tattoo, what could happen as a result?" "If we treat everyone exactly the same, what could be the intentional or unintentional results?" You might also conclude by asking students to identify what the law says rather than their opinions.

11. Debrief the activity by asking students what, if anything, compelled them to change postilions.

There are some public policy questions or issues for which people have to decide yes or no and the middle ground is not an option. For example, if people are voting on a ballot measure, there is no "maybe or sometimes" on the ballot. To give students practice at reaching decisions on these types of questions, you may want to drop the continuum and simply offer the options or "yes" or "no".

****

ANALYZING AND INTERPRETING MEDIA AND WEBSITES

ANALYZING POLITICAL CARTOONS and PHOTOGRAPHS

Purpose   Photographs or political cartoons can be used to generate interest in a topic, to recall earlier experiences, to reinforce learning, to enrich and encourage reading, to develop observation and critical-thinking skills, and to clarify values.

For strategies and a student worksheet, visit the National Archives website at https://www.archives.gov/education/lessons/worksheets/cartoon.html.

****

EVALUATING WEBSITES

Purpose   As with any source, websites vary when it comes to presenting high-quality information about a particular topic. Since websites are frequently used for research, students should learn how to evaluate the sites they encounter. This activity provides a framework for evaluating websites as sources of information.

Procedures

1. Before the class begins, choose several websites you want students to evaluate. You may want to write their addresses on the board or hyperlink them in an email you send to the students or other accessible document. You should also create a handout or web-based document they can access that has a graph on it. One axis would include each of the websites to evaluate. The other would have the evaluation criteria listed below. Students will use this sheet to record their notes and scores.

2. In addition, either print the document below or establish a way for students to access them online.

   • "Evaluating Web Pages: Questions to Consider." From the Cornell University Library (http://guides.library.cornell.edu/evaluating_Web_pages)

3. When class begins, ask students to review the analysis guides and to note the definitions of the following terms:

   • Authority

   • Accuracy

   • Objectivity

   • Currency

   • Coverage

4. Assign students to groups of three, giving each student in each group a letter. Each letter corresponds to a category or categories, as follows:

A = authority and accuracy
O = objectivity
C = currency and coverage

5. Tell students to work independently, and visit each of the designated websites you assign. Students should evaluate each site based on the assigned category or categories. Students should select a score of 0-3 to each site in their assigned category or categories (with 1 being the lowest and 3 being the highest, or best score). Use the following guidelines in the scoring process:

   0 = does not meet the criteria
   1 = meets some of the criteria
   2 = meets most of the criteria relevant to this particular site
   3 = meets or exceeds the relevant criteria for this particular site

6. Have students share their findings with the other members of their group and explain why they gave each site the score that they did. Then ask students to add up the total of points each site received (from all group members) and write the total score in the last column of the chart.

7. Conclude the activity with a whole-class discussion. Questions to consider:

   • Was the website with the highest score the "best" site? What made it a good site?

   • Would you use the websites? Why or why not?

   • Is there any value in using the website that received the lowest score? Why or why not?

   • How will the process of evaluating these websites assist you in understanding the case or subject we are studying?

   • How will you use this website evaluation guide in the future?

****

WEBQUEST

Purpose   A WebQuest is an inquiry-oriented exercise using websites. Students explore online resources to obtain answers to questions, conduct research, or learn more about particular positions. A WebQuest has students synthesize, analyze, solve problems, or apply knowledge to real-world situations. For example, the WebQuest in *Texas v. Johnson* could help prepare for a legislative hearing about flag burning by researching the positions of different interest groups on the issue. Many WebQuests use group-based work, with a division of tasks among students. It is usually best to build the activity around preselected resources so that students can spend time engaging with information, not searching for it.

Procedures

Before class begins:
1. Decide on the problem or issue students will address through the WebQuest. Locate helpful resources online that will help students address this problem or issue. When appropriate, look for a variety of sources with a variety of perspectives.
2. Create a list of websites for students to use. Indicate whether these websites are required or optional, and if you want them to find additional resources.

   (optional) If you have a classroom website or space on a learning management system like BlackBoard, Google Classroom, Edmodo, etc., you might consider posting this worksheet including hyperlinks to the sites so students can find them quickly. If students will be working in groups to gather information, you might consider creating the worksheet as a Google Doc or similar document so students can collaborate and share their work more easily.
3. Devise a task for students to complete that incorporates information from the various sites. The task should involve higher-order thinking and not simply summarizing the content contained on websites. Some examples of tasks include creating a multimedia presentation, participating in a discussion, debate, or deliberation, participating in a simulation, presenting possible solutions to a problem in a multimedia format, or publishing solutions on a website.
4. Develop a rubric or another written set of expectations to give to students so they know how they will be assessed.

When class begins:
5. Introduce students to the general goal of the activity.
6. Frame the problem, issue or task for students. Explain how and why the websites will be the source of information and drive the activity.

7. Distribute assignment sheets and assessment rubrics or tools.
8. If you want students to work in groups, spend time reviewing the roles and how each student is expected to contribute.
9. After students have completed their tasks, debrief the activity by discussing what they learned, as well as possible extensions and applications of the information.

EVALUATING MEDIA COVERAGE OF LEGAL ISSUES

Purpose   Given the importance of information in a democracy, one of the most vital civic skills is to effectively evaluate media coverage of events and issues. Good media coverage is balanced, substantive, coherent, and accurate. It avoids sensationalizing complex issues. Media evaluation assignments are particularly interesting when a local or national case is prominent and receiving heavy media coverage. Court decisions—including rulings by the U.S. Supreme Court—also offer opportunities for students to examine and assess coverage. Such assignments can focus on one medium, for example, newspaper coverage, or they may ask students to team up to compare several media sources. The assignments can vary, too. In one assignment, students could measure coverage in terms of minutes or column inches. In another assignment, students might distinguish between facts and opinions. In a more challenging assignment, students might infer ideological slants and other nuances.

Procedures

1. Ask students where they typically go when they want to know more about the news and why they choose that news source. Discuss the strengths, weaknesses, and reliability of those sources.
2. Assign small groups of students to cover a news story about an important case or law. Each group should learn about the story from a different news medium (print newspaper, print magazine, network television news, public television news, cable television news, commercial radio news, public radio news, online news sources, blogs, etc.). They should not be assigned to analyze editorial or opinion pieces unless you intend to teach students about the distinction between those and straight news.

3. Ask students to work with their group to answer some (or all) of the following questions about the coverage:

- How much space did your news source devote to the story? (Number of minutes for a television or radio news, total number of words or columns for print media, number of pages for online sources, etc.)

- How much prominence did your news source give to the story? (On which page did it appear in print? Was it above the fold in the newspaper? Was it a leading story for television or radio news? Was it designated as a "top story" on the website's home page?)

- Did photos, graphics, sidebars, or other images accompany the news story? If so, what did they depict?

- Try to find out who owns the news source you researched. Is the station owned by a private company or group, a powerful individual, or by the public? Do you think that might influence the way this story was reported?

- Generally, do you think the story was reported in a way that would either flatter or embarrass the individuals or groups involved? What was the tone of the reporter when he or she interviewed people for the story?

- Do advertisements appear on the same page as the story? Are there links to other websites? If so, are the ads or links to any groups that might have a special interest in the legal news story?

- Do you think the news was reported without bias? If so, how do you know?

- Consider the sources quoted or referred to in the article. Did the reporter identify them? Do the sources have expertise in the field?

- Do you think the information was reported in a way that gives you a deep and broad understanding of the topic? Or was the story too brief or superficial to explain much?

4. After students have analyzed news stories within their groups, ask students in different groups to compare what they found. (This could be done through an informal jigsaw activity or by having

groups report to the class.) Then ask students to discuss some or all of the following questions:

- Which news source provided the most coherent story?

- Which provided the most balanced (least biased) story?

- Which had the most accurate story?

- Which had the deepest and broadest coverage?

- Which news source will you go to for information about the law or legal issues in the future? Why?

- Why do you think the First Amendment right to a free press is so important in a democracy?

****

SIMULATIONS AND ROLE-PLAYS

MOCK INVESTIGATION

Purpose This activity helps students understand an investigation by putting them in the roles of investigators, witnesses, and someone who is accused of wrongdoing. It can be used to teach many concepts such as criminal investigations or a workplace investigation into an alleged violation of a company employment policy like sexual harassment.

Procedures

(optional) Invite one or more members of your community to assist you with this activity. For a criminal investigation, you could invite a police officer. For an employment investigation, you might invite an attorney who specializes in employment law. (See the section Accessing Community Resources.)

1. Before the lesson begins, write a fact pattern that illustrates what a person is accused of doing. It should refer to multiple witnesses (five or six) and explain who is investigating the charge or allegation. For example, in an employment law dispute, witnesses might be co-workers, supervisors, the accused person, or witnesses to the alleged activity. This fact pattern should be very brief, no more than ¾ of a page. Based on the fact pattern, determine how many student volunteers you will need to conduct the role-play. You may also want to include a description of the policy or law that

is under consideration if it is complicated. Make copies of the fact pattern for all students. Invite students to play the roles of the witnesses.

2. When the lesson begins, review the company policy (ex: sexual harassment policy) or the law that the accused person is being investigated for violating.

3. Explain the fact pattern—it works well to have an accuser address the students in character.

4. Review techniques for interviewing witnesses.

   • Relax, put the witness at ease.

   • Ask open-ended questions, especially at the beginning of the interview.

   • Avoid loaded or leading questions.

   • Once the facts surface, build new questions off of the facts shared by the witness.

   • Make sure you take notes during the interview.

5. Divide the students into groups of two or three, and ask them to sit at tables around the room. (There should be the same number of tables as there are witnesses. Try to arrange the tables far apart so students will not hear conversations from other groups.) Then, ask one witness to sit at each table.

6. Give students five minutes with each witness. Every five minutes, blow a whistle or ring a bell and have the witnesses move to the next group of students. Each student should lead the questioning for at least one witness. Students should take notes during their interviews.

7. Facilitators and witnesses can help prod groups towards certain questions and help them shape their investigation if they are having trouble.

8. After the witnesses have been interviewed by each group of students, ask students to work in their groups to discuss the information uncovered, to decide whether the policy was violated, and what course of action they recommend. Give students several options. (Ex: fire the person, provide a warning, transfer the person, do nothing)

9. In a whole-class discussion, invite students from different groups to share their conclusions with the entire class. Ask students:

   • What facts made you come to this decision?

   • Did your group get information from a witness that contradicted or called into question the "facts" of the case?

   • Did you encounter any witnesses that contradicted each other?

   • Did any witnesses seem biased? How do you know?

   • What was the best tactic to get to the truth?

   • Did you wish you had more information? If so, what else would you want to know before you had to decide?

10. Debrief the lesson by asking students: What did you learn about investigations today?

(optional) If a resource person joined you for this activity, ask him or her to discuss how the students' investigation and process would be similar to or different than the way their department would have handled a similar situation. Encourage students to ask questions.

****

MOCK LEGISLATIVE HEARING

Purpose Simulating a legislative hearing provides students with an opportunity to gain an understanding of the purposes and procedures of such hearings, as well as the roles and responsibilities of committee members. Students also gain experience in identifying and clarifying the ideas, interests, and values associated with the subject being discussed in the legislative hearing.

Procedures

Before class begins, follow these steps:

1. Identify a lesson that calls for a legislative hearing, create one of your own, or visit https://store. streetlaw.org/ and search for "legislative hearing" for full lesson plans. Choose a topic that is a current public policy debate that will interest students. It could be on any issue that might come before a town council, state legislature or the United States Congress.

2. Think about how to involve as many students as possible in the role play. Options include:

   • **Legislators:** Five legislators is a practical number for a committee but this number may vary to meet class requirements. Designate one legislator as committee chairperson.

- **Witnesses:** These students will testify in favor of or in opposition to the bill under consideration. They typically represent interest groups or others who have an opinion and/or a stake in the bill. They should represent a diverse range of views with a variety of reasons to oppose or support the bill. The number and nature of the witnesses will depend upon the topic being discussed and how much time you can allow for the hearing.

- **Recorder:** Select a student to keep a record of proceedings and of recommendations.

- *(optional)* **Journalist(s):** This person or group will observe and report on the preparation and actual hearing. You may want to challenge the journalist to be impartial or you might choose to have different journalists represent sources that are typically considered liberal or conservative to see how the stories may be different.

3. If there are many students in your class, you might consider assigning two students to represent each interest group so they can prepare their testimony and co-present. Better still, you might consider running two legislative hearings (on different topics) to maximize participation. Provide background information about the topic in the form of a fact sheet or data set(s). You may also allow students to conduct their own research.

4. Prepare a handout of the student instructions. Include background information on the topic, if necessary, a description of the roles you have chosen and steps for the preparation and hearing. Leave space for students to take notes. You may either provide the students with a bill to discuss, provide a list of possible legislative options, or have the legislators create their own legislation based on the hearing.

5. *(optional)* Contact the local legislature, local interest groups, or local chapters of national organizations that have a concern about the topic of the lesson for information on the topic. Invite appropriate staff to attend class. (For additional suggestions about best practices for using resource people, see that section of this document.)

6. Arrange your classroom to look like a committee hearing room. You will need a table for the

legislators at the front of the room, a desk for the recorder, and a desk that faces the lawmakers and/or podium for the witnesses. Other desks or chairs should be set up to face the front of the room.

If your classroom will not accommodate this set up, you might use a theater, media center, or other space in your school. It would be even more exciting if you could arrange to use a hearing or committee room of your local legislative body or school board.

7. *(optional)* Find a gavel for the committee chairperson and nameplates or table tents to identify each of the lawmakers and witnesses.

Once class begins, follow these steps:

8. Describe the activity in general terms. Assign students to their roles.

9. Explain to students the purpose of the legislative hearing and the procedures to be followed. Distribute the handouts you prepared, if any. Confirm students understand their tasks and how much time will be allotted for each step.

10. Allow time for students to prepare for the legislative hearing in accordance with their assigned roles. Once the research is complete, each student should prepare for the hearing by writing a witness testimony, preparing questions for witnesses, etc.

Once the hearing begins, follow these steps:

11. The committee chairperson calls the legislative hearing to order, states the purpose of the hearing, and announces the order and time limits for witness testimony and questions from committee members. The following time limits are suggested:

    - Two to five minutes for a witness statement.

    - Five to ten minutes for questions from the chairperson and other committee members.

12. Each witness is called to present a statement for a set amount of time, followed by questions from lawmakers on the committee. The chairperson is the first to question the witness followed by each of the other members of the committee.

13. After the witnesses have been heard, the legislators on the committee review the testimony,

discuss the problem, and make recommendations on what their next step(s) will be.

14. Conclude the activity with a whole-class discussion and debrief. Here are some questions to consider:

- What did you learn about the current issue we considered?

- Which facts and arguments were most persuasive and what made them compelling?

- Which facts and arguments were least persuasive and what made them so?

- Did you agree with the perspective of the role you were assigned?

- What was most difficult about your role?

- What did you learn about lawmaking from this activity?

- Dropping your role, how do you think this issue should be addressed?

- Assume for a moment that this issue passed out of committee, what would happen next in the process before it could become law? Who would be involved in that process?

- Do you think our (real local, state, or national) legislature should address this issue?

- If so, who could we contact to express our views? How should we contact them?

(optional) If a community resource person has helped to lead this activity, allow him or her to comment on the students' work and to reflect on how it compares to "real life" hearings and the legislative process.

****

MOCK MEDIATION

Purpose Mock mediations give students the opportunity to learn the stages of a conflict resolution that involves the help of a mediator. Students learn the skills of articulating point of view, advocacy, compromise, and finding areas of agreement (if possible). Typical mediations may include a business contract or a conflict between two people or groups that both parties want to resolve.

Procedures

(Optional) Invite members of your community, such as lawyers or professionals involved in conflict resolution to help facilitate this activity. If you include them, decide in advance whether they will play the role of mediators or coach students as they take on those roles. Note: The directions below presume students will play the roles of moderators.

1. Before class begins, write a short description of a conflict involving two people or two groups. It should be short — no more than ½ of a page. Leave space for students to take notes to prepare for their mediations and to record agreements they reach in the mediation session. If students are new to mediation, you should also create a handout of the steps to a mediation.

2. Begin the activity by introducing mediation and describing the situation or dispute to be resolved in general terms. Review a fact pattern with students.

3. Review different dispute resolution strategies and discuss the pros and cons of mediation. (found in Chapter 4)

- Informal Talk
- Negotiation
- Mediation
- Arbitration
- Court Action

4. Review mediation steps.

- Introduction
- Telling the Story
- Identifying Positions and Interests
- Identifying Alternative Solutions
- Revising and Discussing Solutions
- Reaching an Agreement

5. Divide the class into three groups—one for each side of the dispute and one group of mediators. With larger classes, you will need to further divide the class so the number of groups is a multiple of three. These "prep groups" should not have more than six students. Tell each group which party of the dispute they represent.

6. Ask the groups that represent parties in the dispute to discuss their side's objectives and the arguments to support their point of view. They should also discuss their ideal result, fallback result, and unacceptable result for each point of the disagreement. They should also consider which points are most important to their side. The mediator group(s) should review mediation techniques and brainstorm options that might allow the two sides to reach "common ground" or an agreement. Allow at least 15 minutes for this stage.

7. Rearrange students to create new groups—two students representing each side and one or two mediators.

8. Review the process for the mediation. The process might be: introductions, opening remarks from each side, individual sessions with the mediator, then a joint session with all parties. As students are working, circulate to keep the groups on track, answer questions, and offer suggestions. Allow 20–30 minutes for the mediation.

9. **Stop the mediation.** Ask each group to explain the result of their mediation and compare group results.

10. Ask students:

    - What was the most challenging part of this exercise? The easiest?

    - What did you learn about mediation?

    - Was your side pleased with the result?

    - What qualities should a good mediator have?

    - What types of disputes are best suited for mediation?

11. *(optional)* If a resource person has joined you to co-teach this lesson, ask him or her to tell students about real-life mediations, how they are structured, and the role that legal professionals play in mediations. He or she should also describe his or her own experiences with mediations and take questions.

****

MOCK NEGOTIATION

Purpose   Like mock mediations, mock negotiations give students the opportunity to learn the stages of a negotiation and to practice negotiation skills, such as advocacy, compromise, and finding areas of agreement (if possible). Typical negotiations may include a business contract or a conflict between two people or groups that both parties want to resolve.

Procedures

(Optional) Invite members of your community, such as lawyers or professionals involved in conflict resolution, to help facilitate this activity.

1. Before class begins, write a description of a conflict involving two people or two groups. It should be short—no more than ½ of a page. If students are new to negotiation, you should also create a handout of the steps to a negotiation.

2. Introduce the activity by describing the situation/contract to be negotiated and by reviewing fact pattern with all students.

3. Review negotiation strategies through role-playing or demonstration.

4. Divide students into two or more groups to prepare for each side of the negotiation. With large classes, you will need to split into at least four groups (2–3 for each side). These "prep" groups should not have more than six students. Assign each group to represent one side of the negotiation, and have at least one facilitator with each group.

5. Ask the prep groups to discuss their side's objectives and review strategies for reaching agreement on deal points. Each group should discuss the ideal result, fallback result, and unacceptable result for each deal point. Allow at least 15 minutes for this stage.

6. Create negotiating groups of four—two students representing each side—by seating them together at a table or set of chairs.

7. Tell groups to begin negotiating. Have facilitators circulate to keep the groups on track, answer questions, and offer suggestions. Allow 20–30 minutes for negotiations. Ask students to record the decisions reached on each deal point.

8. Stop the negotiations and shift to a whole-class discussion. Ask students:

    - What agreement did your group reach, if any? (As each group reports, ask them to compare their agreements with those of other groups.)

- What was the most challenging part of this exercise? The easiest?

- What did you learn about negotiations?

9. **(Optional)** If a resource person is assisting with this activity, ask him or her to compare the process the students used to the process in his or her work environment.

****

MOCK TRIAL

Purpose   A mock trial is a simulation or enactment of a judicial proceeding. Mock trials provide students with knowledge of the judicial system, legal process, and courtroom procedures. Mock trials help to: develop students' questioning skills, critical thinking, and oratory skills; demonstrate the roles of various actors in the legal system; and provide the class with exposure to legal resource people, such as judges, attorneys, and law school students. Mock trials may be based on historical events, cases of contemporary interest, or hypothetical situations and fact patterns. The format of a mock trial can be either formal or informal. The format chosen depends on the objectives of the activity, the time available, and the students' skills and prior experiences. To access a collection of free civil and criminal mock trials go to https://store.streetlaw.org/, and click on the mock trials tab. You may also be interested in a publication *Street Law's Classroom Guide to Mock Trials and Moot Courts*, which is available from Street Law, Inc. at https://store.streetlaw.org/classroom-guide-to-mock-trials-and-moot-courts/.

Simplified Rules of Evidence

In United States courtrooms, elaborate rules regulate the admission of evidence. These rules ensure that both parties receive a fair hearing and exclude evidence that is irrelevant, untrustworthy, or unduly prejudicial. For purposes of a classroom mock trial, the rules of evidence may be greatly simplified. The following rules are those most commonly applied to a classroom mock trial.

Form of Questions:

- **Leading questions** are permitted during the cross-examination but not during direct examination of a witness. A leading question is one that suggests the answer desired by the person asking the question. For example, "Mr. Hayes, isn't it true that you were drinking on the night of July 23rd?"

- **Direct questions** are generally phrased to evoke a narrative answer. For example, "Mr. Bryant, can you please tell us what happened to you on the night of July 23rd?"

- **Questions that call for witness opinions:** As a general rule, witnesses may not voice their opinions. They should confine their testimony to matters of personal knowledge (i.e., what they did, saw, heard, smelled, etc.). Certain witnesses who have special knowledge or experience in a certain field, however, may be qualified as "expert witnesses." An expert witness may express an opinion about his or her area of special expertise. For example, an attorney might ask: "Doctor, what medical condition caused the patient to die?" If the doctor was a veterinarian, the question would not be allowed. If the doctor were a medical examiner or forensic pathologist, it likely would be allowed.

- **Questions that call for hearsay:** Hearsay is information the witness gathered from other people and did not personally witness. For example, suppose a witness says, "I heard that John Bryant has a criminal record." This is hearsay if offered to prove that John Bryant has a criminal record. Such statements as "I was told...," "I heard ...," "I was informed...," are other typical examples of hearsay statements. As a general rule, hearsay is not permitted as evidence in a trial. Students should learn, however, that there are exceptions to the rule against hearsay and that it is sometimes permitted in an actual trial. The most common exceptions are statements the witness heard the defendant or a deceased person say regardless of content. For instance, it is an exception to hearsay if a witness testifies that the defendant told them, "I heard my wife was cheating on me."

- **Questions that are irrelevant:** Only relevant testimony may be presented. Irrelevant testimony is that which has nothing to do with the issues in the case. For example, if a lawyer asked, "Mr. Hayes, are you having an extramarital affair?" That question would not be pertinent to a DUI case, however it would be permissible in a divorce case.

Introduction of Physical Evidence:

If there is any physical evidence (e.g., documents, photographs, etc.) that either side wishes to have introduced at trial, this may be done by:

- Asking the judge for permission to have an item marked for identification (e.g., "Your Honor, I ask that this letter be marked for identification as Defendant's Exhibit A.")

- Showing the item to the attorneys on the other side to give them an opportunity to make any objections.

- Asking the witness on the stand to identify the item (e.g., "Mr. Kay, this has been marked Defendant's Exhibit A. Could you please tell us what it is?")

- Moving the item into evidence (e.g., "Your Honor, I offer this letter for admission into evidence.")

Impeachment:

If a witness's testimony contradicts the facts as offered in the witness statement or other witness statements, attorneys on the opposing side can impeach the witness on cross-examination. "Impeach" means that the opposing side can point out the contradiction and thereby call into question the truthfulness of the witness.

To impeach a witness, the opposing side should:

- Show the witness statement to the person on the stand.

- Ask, "Is this your sworn statement?"

- Ask the witness to read the portion of the statement that contradicts his or her testimony.

- Point out the contradiction to the court.

In classroom situations, student attorneys may object if the other side introduces evidence that cannot reasonably be deduced from the fact pattern given.

Procedures

1. Prior to the mock trial, students should be familiar with the simplified rules of evidence (objections).

2. Distribute the mock trial materials to the class. All students except jury members should read the entire set of materials including facts of the case, witness statements, and any other material.

3. Assign or have students volunteer for the various roles in the mock trial. Depending on the type of trial, students should be selected to play the roles of attorneys, witnesses, bailiff, and court reporter. You can form a jury using students from your class, students from outside the class, or adult volunteers to serve "jury duty." Generally teachers play the role of the judge in order to ensure proper courtroom procedure.

4. Divide the class into training groups and allow several classes to prepare:

- Plaintiff team (a prosecution team in a criminal trial)—ask students to prepare opening statements, prepare direct and cross-examination questions, prepare witnesses for their testimony on the stand, and closing arguments. Be sure to share the rules of evidence with students as they prepare for the trial.

- Defense team—ask students to prepare opening statements, prepare direct and cross-examination questions, prep witnesses for examination and cross-examination, and prepare closing arguments. Be sure to share the rules of evidence with students as they prepare for the trial.

5. Before the mock trial begins, set up the classroom to simulate a courtroom and decide where the jury will deliberate (preferably in secret).

6. **Conduct the trial.** A civil trial with two witnesses on each side involves the following steps. (If you are conducting a criminal trial, replace the term "plaintiff" with "prosecution.")

- Plaintiff' team opening statement

- Defense team opening statement

- Direct examination of plaintiff witness #1

- Cross-examination of plaintiff witness #1

- Optional: Re-direct of plaintiff witness #1

- Direct examination of plaintiff witness #2
- Cross-examination of plaintiff witness #2
- Optional: Re-direct of plaintiff witness #2 (continue until all plaintiff's witnesses have been questioned)
- Direct examination of defense witness #1
- Cross-examination of defense witness #1
- Optional: Re-direct of defense witness #1
- Direct examination of defense witness #2
- Cross-examination of defense witness #2
- Optional: Re-direct of defense witness #2 (continue until all defense witnesses have been questioned)
- Plaintiff team closing argument
- Defense team closing argument

7. Once closing statements have concluded, explain the deliberation guidelines to the jury and ask the jury to leave the room to deliberate. Consider asking one jury member to serve as foreperson. Once the jury has come to a verdict, ask the jury to return to the room. Either the judge or jury foreperson can read the judgment or verdict.

8. Conclude the trial by asking the jury to explain how they came to their verdict. Administer any assessments or reflection activities at this point.

****

MOOT COURT

Purpose   A moot court is a role play of an appeals court or Supreme Court hearing. The court, composed of a panel of justices, is asked to rule on a lower court's decision. No witnesses are called. Nor are the basic facts in a case disputed. Arguments are prepared and presented on a legal question. Moot courts are an effective strategy for focusing student attention on the underlying principles and concepts of justice.

Procedures

The following procedures are a slight adaptation of appellate procedures. The changes make the moot court an appropriate activity for high school students.

To prepare students for a moot court, follow these procedures:

1. Select a case that raises a constitutional issue. Street Law has a library of free and ready-to-use cases on its website at: www.streetlaw.org If you choose to use a different case, consider the following when you select which case to teach:

   - Is the content of the case relevant to your course, to a specific school outcome (e.g., civic literacy or citizenship), or worth knowing?
   - Is it interesting and accessible to students?
   - Is it a topic of current interest in your community?
   - Are community resource people available to assist with the lesson?
   - Is there an underlying value conflict that is important for students to examine?

2. Read, review, and clarify the facts of the case. Have pairs of students ask each other the following questions:

   - Review these terms with the students:

     - *Petitioner/Appellant:* The person/organization/company who appeals the lower court decision to a higher court.

     - *Respondent/Appellee:* The person/organization/company who argues that the lower court decisions were correct.

   - What happened in this case?
   - Who are the people/organizations/companies involved?
   - How did the lower court rule on this case?
   - Who is the petitioner? Who is the respondent?

3. Ask the class to identify the issue(s) involved in the case. An issue should be posed in the form of a question. Ask the students to phrase the issue as a question by thinking about these questions:

   - Example: Did the Virginia Military Institute (the actor) violate the Fourteenth Amendment's right to equal protection (part of the Bill of Rights) of women (affected by the action) by not allowing them to attend VMI (cause of the controversy)?

- Who was/were the actor(s)?

- What is the specific part of the Constitution involved?

- Who was affected by the action(s)?

- What caused the controversy?

4. Select an odd number of students (7 or 9) to be the justices of the court.

5. Divide the remaining students into two teams. One team will represent the person or group appealing the lower court decision (the petitioner or appellant). The other team will represent the party that won in the lower court (the respondent or appellee).

6. To increase student participation, several students can be selected to play the role of journalists.

7. Each team of litigants should meet to prepare arguments for its side of the case. The team should select one or two students to present the arguments to the court. When discussing the arguments, students should consider:

- What does each side (party) want?

- What are the arguments in favor of and against each side?

- Which arguments are the most persuasive? Why?

- What are the legal precedents and how do they influence this case? (A precedent is a previously decided case recognized as the authority for future cases on that issue. Using precedents allows for the development of more sophisticated arguments.)

- What might be the consequences of each possible decision? To each side? To society?

8. Students should consider all of the facts that have been established in the lower courts. Teams may not argue the accuracy of the facts.

9. Arguments do not need to be rooted in legal technicalities. Any argument that is persuasive from a philosophical, theoretical, conceptual or practical standpoint can be made. Teams should rely on

principles found or implied in the United States Constitution.

10. The justices should meet to discuss the issue involved and any case precedents. They should prepare at least five questions for each side that they need answered in order to reach a decision. The justices should select one student to serve as Chief Justice. The Chief Justice will preside over the hearing. He or she will call for each side to present its case as well as hold each side to time limits.

To conduct the moot court, follow these procedures:

11. Seat the justices at the front of the room. The attorneys for each side should sit on opposite sides of the room facing the justices. The other team members should sit behind their respective attorneys.

12. The chief justice should ask each side to present its arguments in the following order. The justices may ask questions at any time.

Each side should have three to five minutes for its initial argument and two minutes for rebuttal. (This time may need to be lengthened if the justices ask a lot of questions. You may need to adjust the time for students, particularly if they are new to moot courts.)

During and/or after each presentation, the justices should question the attorney in an effort to clarify the arguments. Attorneys may ask for time to consult with other members of their team before answering questions. (This time is included in the total time allowed for the presentation.)

13. After all arguments have been presented, the justices should organize into a circle to deliberate a decision. The rest of the class can sit around the outside of the circle and listen, but they cannot talk or interrupt the deliberations of the court.

14. In the circle, the justices should discuss all of the arguments and vote on a decision. Each justice should give reasons for his or her decision.

15. The Chief Justice should then tally the votes and announce the decision of the court and the most compelling arguments for that decision. A decision is reached by a majority of votes. A dissenting opinion may be given.

16. Conclude with a class discussion of the decision and the proceedings. If you are using an actual

case, share the court's decision with the students after the student court has reached a decision. In the event the students' decision and the Court's decision are different, it is helpful for the students to understand the reasoning in the dissenting opinions as well as the majority. The students are not wrong, but the majority of the real Court was influenced by different compelling arguments. Ask students to evaluate the reasoning the Court used in the majority and dissenting opinions and compare these to their reasoning. Continue to debrief the activity by discussing the significance of the decision for both sides and for society.

****

MINI-MOOT COURTS

Like moot courts, mini-moot courts are simulations of an appeals court or Supreme Court hearing. Mini-moot courts generally take less class time to prepare and conduct, each student in the class is more fully engaged than in full moot courts, and different decisions may be reached and considered by each mini-court.

Procedures

The following procedures are a slight adaptation of appellate procedures. The changes make the mini-moot court an appropriate educational activity for high school students. While planning, watch the instructional video available at https://store.streetlaw.org/mini-moot-courts-resource-bundle-and-video/. There you will also find classroom instructions and all student handouts.

Use the following steps to prepare students for mini-moot courts:

Follow steps #1 through #3 of the moot court procedure.

4. Assign roles by distributing grouping cards for mini-moot Court. The #1s will become the justices/judges, the #2s the petitioners, and the #3s the respondents. Each group gathers in a separate part of the room, ideally with an instructor or resource person, to develop both their argument and their rebuttal (for lawyers) or their questions (for justices/judges). Use the Justice, Petitioner, and Respondent Signs to label the area of the room where each group will meet. If groups are larger than five students, it is suggested that the groups be subdivided.

5. Prepare for roles. For full instructions visit: https://store.streetlaw.org/mini-moot-courts-resource-bundle-and-video/. The petitioners (#2s) and respondents (#3s) should meet to collaborate on arguments for their side of the case. When discussing the arguments, students should consider:

   - What does each side (party) want?

   - What are the arguments in favor of and against each side?

   - Which arguments are the most persuasive? Why?

   - What are the legal precedents and how do they influence this case? (A precedent is a previously decided case recognized as the authority for future cases on that issue. Using precedents allows for the development of more sophisticated arguments.)

   - What might be the consequences of each possible decision? To each side? To society?

6. Arguments do not need to be rooted in legal technicalities. Any argument that is persuasive from a philosophical, theoretical, conceptual or practical standpoint can be made. Teams should rely on principles found or implied in the United States Constitution.

7. The justices should meet to discuss the issue involved and any case precedents. They should collaborate to prepare at least five questions for each party that they need answered in order to reach a decision. Justices must focus on the facts that have been established in the summary and may not argue the accuracy of the facts or ask questions for which the attorneys do not have access to answers.

8. After an adequate period of preparation (suggested: 30 minutes), instruct students to move to their mini-moot triads using the letters on their Grouping Cards. Each triad has a student from group 1 (justice/judge), a student from group 2 (petitioner), and a student from group 3 (respondent). Then

the 'As' from each group will form one triad, the 'Bs' another, and so on until all triads are formed. You may also wish to pair students up and have two students from each group form a group of six. Tables and chairs should be moved again so each triad or group of six is sitting together.

9. Give instructions for the activity and check for understanding. The student justice/judge runs the mini-moot court. They should ask each side to present their case.

10. The justice/judge may ask questions at any time in an effort to clarify the arguments. Time continues to run as the justice/judge interrupts to ask questions. You (the instructor) will be the official timekeeper of the proceedings.

11. After all arguments have been presented, the justice/judge should consider the arguments and reach a decision. They should write their decision and a brief explanation of the reason they reached that decision including specific arguments and precedents.

12. Handing down decisions: Students return to their original seats and the instructor asks each justice/judge to hand down their decisions and the reasons behind them. If you are using a case that has already been decided by the Supreme Court or appellate court, share the Court's decision with the students after the student mini-courts have shared their decisions.

13. Debrief the mini-moot courts.

- Ask the students to evaluate the reasoning the mini-moot courts used in their decisions and compare these to the reasoning used in the actual case.

- Discuss what various decisions might mean for the petitioner, respondent, and society.

- Ask about the process. Did it seem fair? Did each side have an adequate opportunity to present its arguments?

PRO SE COURT

Purpose The pro se court (also known as a Do-It-Yourself Court or Hearing) strategy provides students with a simplified look at judicial decision-making. It allows all students in the class to role-play a case with a small num-

ber of students and simple rules of evidence. The court is a triad, consisting of: a judge, who will hear arguments from the two sides and make the final decision; a plaintiff, who is the person bringing the action before the judge; and the defendant, who is accused of wrongdoing. Many teachers use the pro se court strategy to introduce students to the adversary system and to give students a basic experience before they conduct a more formal moot court or mock trial.

Procedures

(optional) Invite an attorney or judge to act as a community resource person. Call the local bar association, particularly the young lawyers' association, for volunteers.

1. Divide the class into three equal groups (judges, plaintiffs, and defendants).

2. Give students in each group time to prepare for the hearing.

- Judges should be instructed in "court procedure" and given time to prepare questions for the plaintiffs and defendants.

- The plaintiffs should be given time to prepare their opening statements and arguments.

- The defendants should be given time to prepare their opening statements and closing arguments.

3. Move students into new groups of three. Each group should have one judge, one lawyer for the plaintiff, and one lawyer for the defense. Inform judges that when they have a plaintiff and a defendant, they may begin "court."

4. Conduct the pro se court, using the following procedures:

- Opening statements by the parties (first by the plaintiff and then by the defendant). An appropriate time limit should be imposed on these statements.

- Plaintiff is questioned by judge.

- Defendant is questioned by judge.

- Closing arguments by the parties (first by the plaintiff and then by the defendant).

- Judge makes a decision and explains his or her reasons.

5. Once the judges deliver their decisions, call the class together to debrief the activity as a large group. Ask students:

- What was the most challenging part of this exercise? The easiest? Which part did you like best?

- Was your side pleased with the result?

- What were the strongest arguments on your side? What were the other team's strongest arguments?

- For judges: Was it difficult to make a decision? What factors did you consider? What did you find most persuasive?

6. *(Optional)* Ask the resource person to discuss the decision-making process and decisions given. How would the resource person's decisions and rationale compare to the decisions given by the student judges

****

ROLE PLAYS

Purpose   Role-playing is an activity in which students assume the role of another person and act it out. Students are usually given an open-ended situation in which they must make a decision, resolve a conflict, or act out the conclusion to an unfinished story.

Role-playing is designed to promote student empathy and understanding of others. It also gives students a chance to be imaginative and creative. In acting out the role of another person, it is easier for students to see others' points of view, including how other people think and feel. Building on these insights, students can develop a wider range of ideas about how to solve problems. Role-playing can give students the opportunity to learn behavior appropriate for various situations. Role-playing is also useful for developing critical-thinking, decision-making, and assertiveness skills.

Procedures

Before class begins, follow these steps:
1. Select one or more role-play situations that fits with your unit of study. Many situations lend themselves to the use of a role play, including individual dilemmas (e.g., dealing with a pushy salesperson, observing a crime, or testifying in court) and conflict resolution situations (e.g., a tenant negotiating with a landlord over the terms of a lease or a police officer confronting a suspected shoplifter). Finally, role plays are useful for developing student skills as an interviewer, negotiator, assertive consumer, investigator, or lawmaker, etc.

2. When you devise the scenarios, keep each "cast" relatively small so everyone has an important part to play. Ideally, you would choose enough situations so that each student had a role in at least one scenario. Initial role plays should be simple and then become more complex. Give students several opportunities to role-play, including a chance to do a role-reversal (switch roles and re-enact the same scenario).

3. Make the situations and problems realistic and avoid reinforcing stereotypes. While role plays can help students understand multiple perspectives, do not design an activity that would require a study to portray a historical person such as Hitler, Pol Pot, or the founder of the KKK. Nor should you design a role play that requires students to portray a hypothetical person who is bigoted. If those perspectives are essential to a lesson, choose a different activity such as a primary document analysis or careful reading of a text.

4. Preassign roles or to select volunteers when class begins.

5. If you are planning a role play that is complex, prepare written materials that will help students succeed without providing too much information or scripting the role play.

When class begins, follow these steps:

6. **Introduce the activity and its general purposes.** Tell students about the situation and the various roles they will play.

7. **Select students for the role plays.** Students can either be assigned roles or you can ask for volunteers. If you have opted to have some students act as observers, explain what they should be watching for and what they should be prepare to discuss.

8. **Prepare students** by giving them the handout you created before class or by explaining the scenario and roles carefully. If the lesson plan

involves multiple role plays, let each group practice or get ready simultaneously. Remind the students they can be creative and have fun, but they should avoid stereotypes.

9. **Conduct the role play(s)** at the front of the class. You should not interrupt except to get things moving in case students get bogged down. After conducting the role play, it is sometimes useful to have students reverse roles or to conduct the same role play again. If time permits and it would move the lesson forward, you could let students conduct the role play a second times with reversed roles.

10. **Conclude each role play with a short discussion and debrief.** The discussion should prompt students to think about what happened, what procedures or actions were followed, what alternatives the people in the scenario might have considered, etc.

If necessary, take time to explain how the situation might be handled differently in "real life." Discussion questions could include:

- Was the problem solved? Why or why not? How was it solved?

- Is this situation similar to anything that you have experienced?

- Was the role play realistic? How was it similar to or different from real life?

- What, if anything, could have been done differently? What other outcomes were possible?

- What did you learn from the experience?

- If you had the opportunity to do the role play again, what would you do differently? The same?

- If you ever find yourself in a situation similar to the one in the role play, what would you do differently?

Information about ordering all of Street Law's publications can be found at https://store.streetlaw.org/publications/.

- *Street Law's Classroom Guide to Mock Trials and Moot Courts* (2005) provides instructions for organizing and conducting mock trial and moot court exercises. This guide prepares teachers to conduct nine mock trials and six moot courts.

- *The Response* educational package includes a DVD of the 30-minute film and access to materials developed by Street Law, Inc. *The Response* gives students a unique opportunity to see the inner workings of the Combatant Status Review Tribunals held at the U.S. Naval Base at Guantánamo Bay, Cuba from 2004 to 2007. The open-ended film asks viewers to determine how to balance the rights of detainees with national security interests. The film works as a dynamic constitutional law primer to explore the courts, civics, civil liberties, habeas corpus, and much more. The materials move students from a general understanding of the Combatant Status Review Tribunals to a specific discussion of the issues, ideas, and societal values at stake.

- *Street Law for Police & Teens* provides law enforcement officers with lesson plans for use in school and community settings. The lesson plans are designed to be co-taught by a classroom teacher (or community educator) and a law enforcement officer. The four-unit, 20-lesson plan curriculum is full of interactive strategies that promote problem-solving and critical thinking skills. Group discussions and hands-on activities help participants explore the roles and responsibilities of both police officers and members of the community. The result is an open, two-way dialogue that builds (1) understanding of the officers' role in the community, (2) ability of students and/or community members to voice their concerns, (3) empathy for the role of the police officers, (4) awareness of the needs of the public, and (5) mutual trust between police and students and/or community members.

- *Legal Life Skills Lessons* are a great option for youth-serving organizations wishing to integrate education about the law into their program offerings. The lessons are designed to boost participant knowledge and build key life skills like conflict resolution, decision-making, communication, analytical thinking, and advocacy. The lesson library is an ideal fit for organizations serving youth in the juvenile justice system, youth in the child welfare system, crossover youth who are impacted by multiple systems, re-entry youth and adults, LGBTQ+ youth, homeless youth and adults, youth in alternative education settings, girls and women, and survivors of intimate partner violence

- *Street Law: Understanding Law and Legal Issues* (Community College Textbook © 2012 McGraw-Hill Education; ISBN: 978-0-07-662405-8) is an informative law-based, civic learning text for use in community college courses. The text promotes civic involvement by providing practical information about areas of the law that affect the daily lives of all U.S. residents and activities that develop analytic and advocacy skills. The text introduces students to fundamental civil, criminal, and constitutional law principles and provides a platform for guided discussion of important public policy issues concerning crime, discrimination, health care, and immigration.

- *United States Government: Our Democracy* (© 2018 McGraw-Hill Education), co-authored by Street Law, Inc., Dr. Richard Remy, and Dr. Donald Ritchie, helps educators teach students about government and how to "do democracy." This text is innovative in many ways, especially in its focus on interactive activities that help students build critical civic skills, such as constructing arguments, discussing public issues, listening to others, looking for compromise, evaluating claims, assessing source credibility, and making informed decisions.

Street Law is an active member of two national consortia that promote high quality civic education. The civics renewal network (www.civicsrenewalnetwork.org) consists of more than 20 nonpartisan nonprofit organizations that share access to free programs and teaching materials through a common website. The civXnow coalition (www.civXnow.org) is a broad based group of civics providers that advocate for expanded, improved civics programming for American schools.

Street Law, Inc. is also a long time member of the National Council for the Social Studies (NCSS), the national membership organization for social studies teachers. Street Law staff often present on the agenda of the NCSS annual meeting. Street Law encourages teachers to participate in NCSS and in their state and local social studies councils. For more information, visit www.socialstudies.org.

For research information on civic and political participation, Street Law recommends the work of CIRCLE, the Center for Information and Research on Civic Learning and Engagement. Their information is easily accessed at www.civicyouth.org.

UNIT 1

Introduction to Law and the Legal System

CHAPTER 1
What Is Law?
Chapter 1 provides the definition of law and discusses the kinds of laws that exist. The chapter also examines how law is related to values, human rights, and responsibilities within the framework of the U.S. Constitution.

CHAPTER 2
Lawmaking
Chapter 2 illustrates how laws are made by U.S. legislatures and regulatory agencies and by appellate courts that establish precedents.

CHAPTER 3
Advocacy
Chapter 3 explores the roles of citizens in influencing the formation of laws. It also discusses advocacy and will teach students how to develop and implement plans for taking action to solve problems in their community, state, and country.

CHAPTER 4
Settling Disputes
Chapter 4 focuses on settling disputes outside of court through negotiation, mediation, and arbitration. Students will learn how to make decisions when they encounter conflict.

CHAPTER 5
The Court System
Chapter 5 introduces international courts and the parallel systems of federal and state courts in the United States. Students will learn about trial courts, appeals courts, military courts, and tribal courts, as well as the power of the Supreme Court within the U.S. system of justice.

CHAPTER 6
Lawyers
Chapter 6 helps students determine when a lawyer is needed and how to find and work with lawyers. The chapter also discusses the career path to becoming a lawyer.

This Unit will provide students with a foundation and basis of reference for all that follow.

Within the context of American government, students will take a new perspective on laws and explore the difficulties that citizens, legislators, attorneys, and judges who work to preserve and strengthen our system of justice.

UNIT 1
Introduction to Law and the Legal System

networks™

Unit 1 provides students with a foundation and frame of reference for their study of law. Within the context of American government, students will gain a new perspective on laws and explore the crucial roles and duties of citizens, legislators, attorneys, and judges who work to preserve and strengthen our system of justice.

CHAPTERS IN BRIEF

CHAPTER 1
What Is Law?
Chapter 1 provides the definition of *law* and discusses the kinds of laws that exist. The chapter also examines how law is related to values, human rights, and responsibilities within the framework of the U.S. Constitution.

CHAPTER 2
Lawmaking
Chapter 2 illustrates how laws are made by U.S. legislatures and regulatory agencies and by appellate courts that establish precedents.

CHAPTER 3
Advocacy
Chapter 3 explores the roles of citizens in influencing the formation of laws. It also discusses advocacy and will teach students how to develop and implement plans for taking action to solve problems in their community, state, and country.

CHAPTER 4
Settling Disputes
Chapter 4 focuses on settling disputes outside of court through negotiation, mediation, and arbitration. Students will learn how to make smart decisions when they encounter conflict.

CHAPTER 5
The Court System
Chapter 5 introduces international courts and the parallel systems of federal and state courts in the United States. Students will learn about trial courts, appeals courts, military courts, and tribal courts, as well as the power of the Supreme Court within the U.S. system of justice.

CHAPTER 6
Lawyers
Chapter 6 helps students determine when a lawyer is needed and how to find and work with lawyers. The chapter also discusses the career path to becoming a lawyer.

SERVICE LEARNING AND SPECIAL PROJECTS

1. **Court Visitation:** As students are studying Chapters 5 and 6, they might visit a court, ideally observing both trial and appellate proceedings. Have students observe differences in procedures, the voir dire process, roles of jurors and attorneys, consequences of illegal behavior, etc. Students might be assigned to play the roles of journalists covering a trial. After visiting the court, students can assess whether the adversarial judicial process results in justice.

2. **Student Advocacy:** Using the guidelines provided in Chapter 3, students might select a controversial bill being introduced to the student government, city or town council, or state legislature. After they have formulated their opinion on the proposed law, have students determine when hearings are scheduled and seek permission to speak during the hearings. Students should plan and rehearse testimony and develop additional aspects of their advocacy plan.

3. **Service Learning:** While community service is educational and meaningful on many levels, service learning takes it to "the next level" by connecting service with classroom learning and reflection. The following activities are suggested to help students enhance what they learn in Unit 1 by serving their communities.

   - Students can teach younger students about why we have laws.
   - Students can write a play about how the three branches of government are involved in lawmaking and perform it for younger students.
   - Students can work on a voter registration drive or drive elderly people or others who need a ride to the polls on Election Day.
   - Students can participate in (or help create) a school-based mediation program or organize a conflict resolution program for their classmates.
   - Students can develop and then distribute a pamphlet or poster that lists the programs that provide free legal services to low-income people in their community.

UNIT RESOURCES

Using Legal Resource Persons

One of the "best practices" in law-related education is to invite outside resource people to co-teach lessons in your classroom. These guests should not be asked or expected to lecture on a topic, but to engage students in interactive activities that showcase student work with the guidance of an expert. It is ideal to ask a particular resource person to work with the same group of students repeatedly. This significantly amplifies students' retention of the content and has also been shown to increase the likelihood that those students will pursue careers in the legal field.

1. Judges might be invited to address topics from Unit 1 such as the merits of adjudication versus mediation; the relationship between human rights and the U.S. system of justice; the roles of judges, attorneys, prosecutors, and jurors; and legal ethics.

2. Jurors might be willing to describe their experiences in court. Topics of discussion could include: how they came to the conclusions they did in rendering a judgment, whether they view the court system differently than they did before the experience, and how they feel about the responsibility of citizens to serve on juries.

3. Attorneys could share insights about topics including professional ethics, when the advice of counsel is necessary, how to evaluate a prospective attorney, why they chose a career in law, and the satisfying and dissatisfying aspects of their work.

Law and legal philosophy are viewed through the lenses of history, morality, and culture, resulting in many definitions of *law*. For the purposes of the *Street Law* text, *law* is defined as the rules made and enforced by government that regulate the conduct of people within a society.

INTRODUCTION (PP. 2–3)

Learning Outcomes

After completing this section, students should be able to:
1. define the term *law*;
2. explain several reasons for having laws;
3. explain why the rule of law is important in a democratic society; and
4. list a number of laws that affect daily life in our society.

DISCUSSION—WHY STUDY LAW?

Ask students: How do laws differ from rules? Do parents make the "law" at home? Who makes the law at school?

ACTIVITY—WHY LAW?

Step A: The Ring Game This introductory game will help students develop a definition for *law*, an appreciation for the necessity and purpose of rules, and some basic ideas about fairness. The game can be easily adapted to meet the needs of your classroom and is recommended for the first day of the course.[1]

1. Announce that the class will begin its study of *Street Law* by playing a game.

2. Give several rings (or paper clips, or pencils, etc.) to the first student in each row. Once each row has an equal supply of objects, tell students to begin playing.

3. Students will be confused by the lack of direction and may become frustrated, perplexed, or even angry. Jot down some of their comments. After a minute or so, "explain" the game, telling students to pass the rings to the back of the row and then back to the front, one at a time. The first team to finish wins.

4. Get the game started, using the rules you just explained. Then quickly stop students. Tell them they forgot to pass the objects over their left shoulders only. Students will immediately complain of not having been told about this rule. Do not respond to their complaints, but note some if possible.

5. Now change the rule to "passing over their right shoulders only," and disqualify a row for violating it.

6. Allow the objects to come back to the front and then start again, this time stopping the game because one of the rows has more (or fewer) boys (or girls). Explain that because of this "rule," that row will have to pass two extra rings back and forth in order to win.

7. Restart the game and allow it to conclude.

8. When the "winners" are announced, most of the remaining students will probably express frustration and anger about the way you conducted the game.

Step B: Discussion Students' frustrations with the Ring Game can become the basis for the following discussion:

1. What made you frustrated or angry about the way the game was played?

2. Why was it unfair? If you wrote down relevant comments during the game playing, you may want to share them with students.

In discussing responses, emphasize three key elements:

a. A game cannot be enjoyed without a clear and consistent set of rules announced to all participants in advance. Vague or unclear rules can ruin a game.

b. The rules cannot be changed in the middle of the game without resulting in confusion, hurt feelings, or frustration.

c. Rules must be applied equally and consistently to all; certain groups of individuals cannot be discriminated against arbitrarily.

Step C: Discussion Use the following questions as you ask students to relate the rules of the Ring Game to a society's laws:

1. What was needed for the game to run effectively from the start? *Answers may include references to fairness, lack of discrimination, knowledge and understanding of the rules.*

2. What is needed to make laws effective? *Answers should be similar to those in question 1.*

3. Why would a course about law start off with a game like the one we just played?

Finally, ask students to develop a definition for law based on the class experience with the game. *Law is the set of clear and consistently enforced rules a group or community uses to regulate the conduct of the people within it.*

Ask students why they might want to study law. Have students brainstorm law-related topics they would like to study. Individually or in small groups, have students compare these topics to those listed in the Student Edition Table of Contents.

PROBLEM 1.1 (p.3)

This activity has several purposes:

a. to illustrate the pervasiveness of law in our daily lives;

b. to show that law is both civil and criminal;

c. to illustrate the positive nature of law in our lives, i.e., most laws are protective rather than punitive.

Students may complete this activity, which might be viewed as a kind of "mind walk," either individually or in small groups. Students should brainstorm a list of daily activities and identify those that are affected by law. The chart in **1.1 TM Figure** below can be used to approach the question in more depth and in a more structured way.

FIGURE

1.1 TM Figure

Activity	Affected by law?	Federal, state, or local law	Reasons for the law?	Should the law be changed? Why?
1.				
2.				
3.				

LAW AND VALUES (PP. 3–6)

Learning Outcomes

After completing this section, students should be able to:

1. give examples of how laws reflect economic, moral, political, and social values; and
2. analyze a case in order to explore the relationship between law and morality.

DISCUSSION—PURPOSES OF LAWS

Complete the following exercise with students before reading pages 3–6. Then compare students' answers with the views presented in this section of the text.

1. Have students brainstorm purposes of laws. Ask students: Why do societies create laws, and what do they hope their laws will accomplish?

2. Consider the goals students identify and speculate about situations in which these goals may conflict with each other.

3. Identify societal problems that laws cannot solve.

4. Suggest that a society's values will be reflected in its laws. For example, how might laws in a society that values order and safety compare to laws in a society that values individual freedom and creativity?

CAPTION ANSWER (P. 3) Economic values are often placed in conflict by environmental protection laws.

THE **CASE** OF...

The Shipwrecked Sailors

PROBLEM 1.2 (p.4)

For information on the various ways to use cases mentioned in *Street Law*, refer to the front of this Teacher Manual for a discussion of Teaching with Case Studies.

This case presents a moral dilemma: Should Dudley and Stephens be punished for what they did?

Issues that can be discussed in answering such questions include:

- the historical, moral, and religious roots of prohibitions against killing;
- the relationship of law to society;
- the effect of the agreement;
- the impropriety of cannibalism under any circumstances;
- the verdict actually rendered in this case;
- the issue of whether or not law should be flexible in how it is enforced or more uniformly applied to all who break it.

This problem is based on the actual 1884 case of *Regina* v. *Dudley and Stephens*.[2] An English court found both men guilty of murder and sentenced them to death. The court said, "We are often forced to set up standards we cannot reach ourselves, and to lay down rules which we could not ourselves satisfy. But a man has no right to declare temptation as an excuse nor allow compassion for the criminal to change or weaken the legal definition of the crime." Ask students: What did the court mean by this? Soon after the verdict, Queen Victoria commuted the sentence to six months imprisonment. Why do you think she might have done this?

The questions following the case emphasize reasoning skills; there are no correct answers.

a. Students may argue that Dudley and Stephens should be tried for murder since they willfully took the life of another human being. Those who disagree may argue that given the circumstances, the actions of the two men did not constitute murder. Rather, they should be charged with a less serious offense such as manslaughter, or not charged at all.

b. Dudley and Stephens could argue that mitigating circumstances must be considered, and that even though they did kill another human being, the situation was such that they should not be punished further. Their attorney could argue that going 25 days without food changed the defendants' perceptions of right and wrong (i.e., a possible insanity defense). They might also argue that Brooks had made a contract that should be honored. They could also argue that the killing was necessary for survival. Although necessity is never a good defense in a homicide case, it is sometimes recognized in other cases of criminal law. The state could argue that human life is sacred and that a person who takes another's life must be tried for breaking the law in order to deter others. To do otherwise is to condone what happened. The prosecutor could also note that Brooks had withdrawn his consent before the killing or that consent to an illegal activity is never valid.

c. Ask students how the different rationales for punishment (retribution, deterrence, rehabilitation, and accountability) would be served by convicting Dudley and Stephens. It could be argued that punishing them would not really serve as a deterrent because the situation was unique, and that there is not a strong argument for rehabilitation since it is unlikely that Dudley and Stephens would ever commit such a crime again. The strongest rationale for punishment is retribution and accountability for what many consider a heinous act even under the given circumstances.

d. Answers will vary. Seek reasons for the different positions taken on the issue of punishment. After discussing the point, the students may be interested to learn the actual verdict and sentence, noted on the previous page.

e. Traditional ideas of morality prohibit taking the life of another person under almost any circumstance. However, there are also moral precepts in support of what the sailors did (taking action to protect and preserve their own lives). There are legal arguments on both sides of this case. However, these arguments tend to be technical (Were Dudley and Stephens insane? What law applied on the raft?) rather than broadly moral conceptions of right and wrong. The relationship between law and morality can be seen in laws prohibiting murder. Intentionally killing another person may be legally permissible based on moral principles such as self-defense and justified war.

f. Students should try to articulate acts that may be legal but immoral, or moral but illegal. For example, a person who observes a crime but does not report it may be acting legally but immorally. People who are engaged in civil disobedience may be acting illegally even though their actions may be considered morally justified.

CAPTION ANSWER (P. 5) Allowing women in traditionally male-only positions reflects society's changing ideas about gender equality.

PROBLEM 1.3 (p.6)

Students' answers will vary for both questions but should include a rationale. If students need prompting, remind them of the previous section of the chapter in which they considered the moral, economic, political, and social values reflected in laws. Are there any problems in any of those areas that could be solved by law? Are there any laws pertaining to those values that should not exist?

ACTIVITY—TRACING THE EVOLUTION OF LAW AND JUSTICE

If your students are interested in the evolution of law and justice in our society, you may consider using the friezes that adorn the courtroom of the U.S. Supreme Court to introduce students to influential lawgivers from history. Explain to students that sculptor Adolph A. Weinman designed the friezes on the north and south walls of the courtroom so when the justices looked up, they would be reminded of the "great lawgivers of history" who contributed to the U.S. system of laws.

Have students visit the Supreme Court website to read about the 18 lawgivers on the friezes at https://www.supremecourt.gov/about/northandsouth-walls.pdf. Ask students to determine who made the most important contribution to our current judicial system. Students should be able to support their decision with evidence. You may restrict students to only the information on the website or invite them to research lawmakers further. You may also ask students to rank the importance of the allegorical figures (fame, authority, light of wisdom, history, liberty and peace, right of man, equity, and philosophy) in order of their importance to the pursuit of justice.

HUMAN RIGHTS (PP. 6–7)

Learning Outcomes

After completing this section, students should be able to:
1. define the terms *human rights*, *covenant*, and *reservations*;
2. identify at least five rights included in the Universal Declaration of Human Rights, the International Covenant on Civil and Political Rights, and the International Covenant on Economic, Social, and Cultural Rights;
3. describe the extent to which the U.S. government recognizes and enforces international human rights agreements and treaties; and
4. analyze and critique situations which may or may not reflect human rights violations in the United States.

PROBLEM 1.4 (p.7)

This problem is best answered in small groups. Have each student create an individual list and then compare and contrast it with the lists of other group members. Each group should then compile a master list of ten human rights and reasons for those rights. Bringing the whole class together, a spokesperson from each group should present that group's master list. To generate a class list, have students go through questions **a.–d.** as a class. Question **e.** will illustrate to students that most of the rights they came up with are also in the Universal Declaration of Human Rights (UDHR) and are accepted by most people. Question **f.** provides an opportunity to introduce students to the U.S. Constitution, found on pages 578–597 of the Student Edition.

ACTIVITY—COMPARING HISTORICAL DOCUMENTS

In these four activities, students systematically compare amendments to the U.S. Constitution with the Universal Declaration of Human Rights (UDHR). Both documents are located in the back of the Student Edition.

1. You can expect that students may not have heard of the UDHR. Give them additional background to help them understand the philosophical basis and historical context of both documents. You may want to discuss the role that political economies play in shaping public opinion. For example, people living in countries with a socialist orientation and people living in countries with a history of capitalism are likely to have different viewpoints about human rights. People in socialist countries tend to emphasize economic rights associated with subsistence (the rights to adequate food, clothing, shelter; universal medical care; employment), while people in capitalist countries tend to emphasize political rights associated with freedom (the rights to free speech, assembly, and the press). Ask students to identify the core values inherent in each of these ideologies. After this background discussion, ask students to compare and contrast rights guaranteed by the two documents. Have students list the rights guaranteed by the UDHR that are not guaranteed by the Constitution (e.g., Article 24,

the right to rest and leisure; Article 25, the right to an adequate living standard). Ask students to compare the general position of the United States on the death penalty with the stance of other countries. After they compare the documents, ask students to discuss why they think the Constitution failed to provide many of the rights guaranteed by the UDHR and to provide evidence to support their conclusions.

During this activity, you should explain to students that the rights guaranteed under the U.S. Constitution go beyond those explicitly stated in the text and include constitutional rights recognized by U.S. Supreme Court precedent. For example, the right to privacy does not appear anywhere in the Constitution but has been recognized as a part of the right to liberty guaranteed by the Fourth Amendment and other amendments.

Since the right to life is stated as an absolute in the UDHR, you might also refer students to the Cornell University Law School website at www.law.cornell.edu/states/listing.html for state death penalty information. To illustrate a particular difference between the documents, ask students to examine the human right to life.

2. Divide the class into two groups to prepare for an informal debate to decide which document is superior. Students should first identify specific criteria for superiority and then devise arguments to support their document's superiority. Many issues can be raised in support of each side. One issue is the enforceability of each document. Some people believe it is impractical to enforce the guarantees and rights enumerated in the UDHR (the right to adequate shelter, food and clothing; the right to own property; the right to adequate rest and leisure). Furthermore, there is no enforcement mechanism for the UDHR. Constitutional amendments are enforceable by the U.S. government. Another issue to consider is whether the rights in each document are guaranteed absolutely or with reservations.

Some people believe that the UDHR guarantees some rights (Article 3, liberty; Article 13, freedom of movement) without reservation, but for society to function these rights may have to be abridged. Amendments to the Constitution fail to qualify some of their clauses, providing for an absolute right to free speech, when this right is limited in a number of ways by common law, statute, and ordinance. A third issue to consider is the extent of the rights in each. Amendments to the Constitution fail to provide for essentials of human existence, such as food, shelter, and health care. A fourth issue to consider is how flexible and modern each document is. Constitutional amendments might also be criticized for failing to take into consideration legitimate concerns that have come to the attention of lawmakers in the modern era with the development of a broader-based social conscience (e.g., the need to protect the interests of the poor).

3. After the debate, ask students to assess the value of the Universal Declaration of Human Rights. Why bother producing a document fraught with unenforceable provisions and lacking an effective enforcement mechanism? Ask students to speculate about the possible influence of the Holocaust on those who framed this document just a few years after World War II ended. How did this disaster illustrate the need to articulate the rights that all human beings should possess— irrespective of culture, country, religion, or political or economic system? Why did humans at that time deem it essential to state these rights, even when no government had yet found an effective way of guaranteeing them? Discuss how this document expressed the felt need to set goals and expectations for future human conduct. You might offer the notion of a "continuum of human progress"—the idea that humanity inexorably grows more enlightened and advanced as the years pass. Expect student reaction to this assertion to be vocal and contentious.

4. Ask students to assume that the year is 1948. Each should produce an editorial, letter to the editor, or speech arguing for or against U.S. Senate ratification of the Universal Declaration of Human Rights.

ACTIVITY—DEBATING THE APPLICATION OF HUMAN RIGHTS IN THE UNITED STATES

After students read about the Universal Declaration of Human Rights, pose the following questions for debate:

- Should the U.S. Constitution, laws, and court decisions be the only standards Americans look to, or should globally accepted human rights also be considered and/or enforced by U.S. courts?
- Who is responsible for protecting and guaranteeing basic human rights? Who bears the cost? For example, who would pay for the translation of all texts into the languages of a diverse student body? Who would pay for adequate housing and food for all? Who should pay for the

medical care of people who cannot afford it? Is cost a legitimate factor in decisions about the protection of human rights?
- Consider that the quality of schools varies dramatically from one community to another. Often the better-equipped schools are located in wealthier suburban communities that can raise more money in property taxes than urban and rural schools. Is this a human rights violation? If so, what can/should be done about it?
- Should the government guarantee a job for everyone? Is this desirable or even possible?

RULE OF LAW (P. 8)

Learning Outcomes

After completing this section, students should be able to:

1. Define the *term rule of law*.
2. Explain why the rule of law is important in a democratic society; and
3. Explain how each of the following factors relates to the rule of law: constraints on government, absence of corruption, open government fundamental rights, order and security, regulatory enforcement and civil justice

DISCUSSION – HOW IMPORTANT IS THE RULE OF LAW TO DEMOCRACY?

Ask students what life in the United States without each of the following factors might be: constraints on government, absence of corruption, open government, fundamental rights, order and security, regulatory enforcement, and civil justice. Discuss whether democracy can thrive without any or all of these factors. Ask which factors work to ensure fair elections? Which factors allow people to communicate with and influence their elected officials? Which factors affect how much trust citizens have in their government and why is this important in a democracy? Conclude by asking students to rank the factors in order of their importance to democracy.

ACTIVITY – RAISING THE UNITED STATES' RULE OF LAW INDEX SCORE

Instruct students to explore the United States' current Rule of Law Index Score at https://worldjustice-project.org/our-work/research-and-data/wjp-rule-law-index-2019. Have them select "View Full

Profile" to see the detailed report. Divide the class into 7 groups. Assign one of the following factors to each group: constraints on government, absence of corruption, open government, fundamental rights, order and security, regulatory enforcement and civil justice. After looking at the breakdown of their assigned factor's score, have students brainstorm what reforms might raise the United States' score for that factor. Have each group compose a plan to increase the United States' score on that factor and present their recommendations to the class. In a whole class discussion, seek consensus on 5 recommendations that would increase the overall rule of law score and strengthen democracy in the United States.

PROBLEM 1.5 (p.10)

a. The rule of law index scores can be found at https://worldjusticeproject.org/our-work/research-and-data/wjp-rule-law-index-2019. As of October 2019, the 3 highest index scores belonged to: Denmark (1), Norway (2), and Finland (3) which all achieved higher scores than the United States.

b. The rule of law index scores can be found at https://worldjusticeproject.org/our-work/research-and-data/wjp-rule-law-index-2019. As of October 2019, the 3 lowest index scores belonged to: the Democratic Republic of the Congo (124), Cambodia (125), and Venezuela (126) which all received lower scores than the United States.

c. To strengthen its rule of law index score, the United States could address the areas that received the lowest scores for instance discrimination and corruption in criminal and civil justice systems. You may choose to complete "Activity – Raising the United States Rule of Law Index Score" as a class.

BALANCING RIGHTS WITH RESPONSIBILITIES (PP. 9–10)

Learning Outcomes

After completing this section, students should be able to:
1. describe the relationship between rights and responsibilities; and
2. identify reasons critics object to the emphasis the United States puts on individual rights.

THE **CASE** OF...

The Apathetic Bystanders

PROBLEM 1.6 (p.10)

a. There are many possible reasons the bystanders did not intervene. It is possible that some of them simply did not care. Others may have been selfish or were afraid to get involved. Some may have been jaded by the ubiquitous crime in the city. Perhaps societal factors such as the violent images that people are exposed to in the media have led Americans to become callous about such things. Perhaps the bystanders did not call the police due to a mistrust of, or animosity toward, the police.

Although many valid opinions can be offered to explain the situation, social scientists tend to explain such behavior in terms of the "bystander effect." That is, the more bystanders there are in a situation, the less likely any individual bystander will help. In such a situation there is a diffusion of responsibility as people assure themselves that one of the other bystanders will act.

In one experiment done at New York University, for example, students were told that they would be asked to discuss personal issues in telephone conference groups of two, three, or six people. During each conference an experimenter, pretending to be one of the students in the conference call, faked an epileptic seizure. In the groups of two, in which the students thought they were the only people to hear the seizure, the students promptly sought aid for the victim 81 percent of the time. However, in the groups of six, in which each student thought that four other students also had heard the seizure, students acted only 31 percent of the time.

Though many people could hear Kitty Genovese's screams, each bystander may simply have assumed that someone else would call the police.

b. In general, failure to assist a person in need is not a crime or a tort unless the relationship between the bystander and the victim gives rise to a legal duty to act. For example, parents have a legal duty to help their children, and spouses have a legal duty to help one another because of their relationship. An affirmative duty to act may also arise because one party has assumed responsibility, either by contract or otherwise. For example, a day-care center would have a legal duty to call an ambulance if a child under its care was seriously injured. However, a day-care worker walking home from work would have no duty to help a child who was seriously injured on the side of the road. A lifeguard would have a legal duty to assist a drowning swimmer in the area he or she was guarding. However, a nearby swimmer who was a certified lifeguard could generally not be held criminally responsible for failing to help.

A duty to help also exists where one person has caused the situation. For example, a negligent driver who hits another car, injuring the other driver, has a legal duty to call an ambulance for that other driver, whereas a passerby does not.

c. The problem is an excellent illustration of how it is possible to be morally wrong while still acting within the confines of the law. Regardless of students' individual backgrounds or values, many will accept that it is immoral to simply allow someone to die when it would take very little effort or risk to save the person. However, this point could be reasonably argued. Students should consider morality a strong motivating factor in the creation of laws in a pluralistic society in which people have differing values.

d. Some states have considered "Duty to Rescue" laws, which would require citizens to help others in need of assistance. Students should discuss the pros and cons of such proposals. They should consider how much aid the law might require witnesses to give (e.g., up to the point where there is a risk of further harm in attempting to help). Would the type of victim (a child, for example) make a difference? Should the law impose civil or criminal liability on a bystander who fails to help?

The main pros are that such laws promote citizen responsibility and morality, aid police by ensuring that police will be notified of crimes in progress, and may help save lives. Possible cons are that such laws are difficult to enforce and to prosecute since there are many legitimate reasons for failing to act. In addition, such laws are inconsistent with the right of citizens to be left alone while minding their own business and not actively doing anything wrong.

e. Students' answers will vary. Responses should include a header such as, "All bystanders are responsible for..." and may include responses such as "coming to the aid of others who are in distress."

KINDS OF LAWS (PP. 10–11)

Learning Outcomes

After completing this section, students should be able to:

1. distinguish between the two major groups of laws: criminal and civil;
2. define the terms *criminal law, felony, misdemeanor, civil law, civil action, defendant, plaintiff, prosecutor, beyond a reasonable doubt,* and *preponderance of the evidence;* and
3. describe the difference between misdemeanors and felonies.

PROBLEM 1.7 (p.11)

a. Possible answers include: taking the car, ignoring the handicapped parking sign, leaving trash on the park bench, and possessing illegal drugs.

b.–c. The following types of laws are involved in this story:

- unauthorized use of a motor vehicle— criminal
- parking violation—criminal
- licensing (street vendor)—criminal
- warranty law (tablet)—civil
- littering—criminal
- tort of negligence—civil
- breaking and entering—criminal; trespassing—civil or criminal
- larceny—criminal; conversion of property—civil
- search and seizure—criminal
- possession of illegal substances— criminal
- leaving the scene of an accident— criminal
- arrest—criminal

OUR CONSTITUTIONAL FRAMEWORK (PP. 12–15)

Learning Outcomes

After completing this section, students should be able to:

1. define the terms *limited government, separation of powers, statute, checks and balances, veto, judicial review, unconstitutional, federalism,* and *Bill of Rights;*
2. identify how powers of the executive, legislative, and judicial branches are separated by the Constitution;
3. give examples of how each of the three branches of government check and balance the other two;

4. describe how judicial review can be used to interpret the Constitution and protect individual rights;

5. explain how the principle of limited government is reflected in the Bill of Rights and in our system of federalism; and

6. describe how and why constitutions may be amended.

DISCUSSION—GOVERNMENT AND THE CONSTITUTION

Use the following discussion questions to reinforce basic principles about the Constitution.

1. Why do you think the Framers of the Constitution felt citizens needed protection from government? *Students' answers will likely suggest that the Framers wanted to avoid creating the kind of tyrannical government they had suffered under when they were controlled by the British government.*

2. How does the Constitution protect American citizens from the government? *Students should answer that the Bill of Rights contains a list of rights people have that limit what the government can do. Ask students to give an example of how the Constitution protects citizens from the government. Students may say for example, that the First Amendment begins with the phrase: "Congress shall make no law respecting..." establishing a religion or prohibiting free exercise of religion, restricting the rights to free speech, press, petition, assembly, etc.*

3. Suppose there was just one branch of government rather than three.

   a. Would there be any advantages to such an arrangement? *Some students may suggest that the government would be more efficient.*

   b. What kinds of problems would develop? *Students may suggest that an unchecked branch might increase or abuse its power, threatening individual rights and the Constitution's goals.*

4. Suppose there was no system of checks and balances among the three branches of government. What kinds of problems would citizens face? *Answers may include that citizens might find their rights against the intrusion of government power limited.*

5. Should constitutions be easier to amend than they are now? Explain. *Students' answers will vary. A constitution that is too easy to amend threatens a government's stability. A constitution that is too difficult to amend can become outdated.*

CAPTION ANSWER (P. 12) The Constitution sets forth the basic framework of government. It lists the powers of the government, as well as the limits of these powers.

ACTIVITY—DETERMINING THE CONSTITUTIONALITY OF LAWS

Use the following activity to acquaint students with the U.S. Constitution and the issue of constitutionality. Students should use the U.S. Constitution and the Bill of Rights to decide if the following laws would be constitutional or unconstitutional and name the amendment in question.

- One cannot vote without a college degree. (*unconstitutional—Fifteenth Amendment*)
- Newspapers are prohibited from publishing negative statements about a town's mayor. (*unconstitutional—First Amendment*)
- Handguns are denied to those who are convicted felons. (*constitutional—Second Amendment*)
- Someone is arrested and convicted without the benefit of legal counsel or a trial. (*unconstitutional—Fifth and Sixth Amendments*)
- Someone who is arrested for a crime may refuse to take the witness stand at his or her trial. (*constitutional—Fifth Amendment*)

CAPTION ANSWER (P. 14) The federal government intervenes to protect the constitutional rights that are infringed by government action. Most provisions of constitutional amendments limit the power of the local, state, and federal government.

PROBLEM 1.8 (p.15)

a. A federal court strikes down a state law that violates the Constitution (checks and balances, federalism, and judicial review).

b. When the legislative branch puts requirements on the day-to-day operations of the judiciary, it raises a genuine question about the separation of powers. An argument for allowing this law is that Congress funds the Court and might be able to condition the Court's funding on its televising public sessions (separation of powers, checks and balances).

c. The state court prevents the legislature from subjecting the prisoners to unconstitutional deprivation of rights (checks and balances). However, the court does not have the power to spend the money directly and funding must come from the legislative branch (separation of powers).

d. The existence of federal and state laws both regulating marijuana and the prosecution in federal court are evidence of federalism. The federal government seizure of the drug is also an exercise of national supremacy. The task of enforcement falling to the DEA and lawmaking falling to the legislative branches is an example of separation of powers (federalism and separation of powers).

e. The Supreme Court is exercising its power of judicial review and checks and balances by declaring flag burning laws unconstitutional. Congress then uses its power to propose amendments to the Constitution to check (if the amendment is ratified) the ruling of the Court (judicial review, separation of powers, and checks and balances).

f. This scenario, based on *U.S. v. Nixon* (1974), demonstrates checks and balances when the Supreme Court limits the president's executive privilege and supports the subpoena of evidence from the courts thus checking the president's power. In the Supreme Court case, *U.S. v. Nixon*, Nixon's attorneys argued that allowing the court to enforce the subpoena would be a violation of separation of powers, but the Supreme Court did not find in his favor. Judicial review is seen in this case when the Supreme Court rules that the invocation of executive privilege exceeded the power the Constitution granted to the president.

NOTES

(1) The "Ring Game" is an adaptation of a lesson written by Linda Riekes and Sally Ackerly that originally appeared in the *Law in Action* series (West, 1975).

(2) L.R. 14 Q.B.D. 273 (1884). Both the Case of the Shipwrecked Sailors (Chapter 1) and the Case of the Unclear Law (Chapter 2) are based on ideas originally presented in Harvard law professor Lon Fuller's famous book, *The Problems of Jurisprudence* (1949).

netw⊘rks

LEGISLATURES (PP. 16–21)

Laws come from many sources. The U.S. Constitution sets forth certain laws that people must obey. It also gives state and federal legislatures the power to make laws. City and county governments are involved in making laws at the local level. Administrative agencies make laws to protect workers, businesses, the environment, and many other groups. In addition, the courts make laws when they decide appeals.

Learning Outcomes

After completing this section, students should be able to:
1. describe the role of the legislative branch of government;
2. distinguish among the types of laws typically made at local, state, and federal levels of government;
3. define the terms *ordinance, supremacy clause, statute, bill,* and *legislative intent;*
4. identify and explain the supremacy clause of the Constitution;
5. identify two rules that judges follow when determining legislative intent;
6. interpret a law using the concept of legislative intent; and
7. draft an ordinance by applying the suggested guidelines for drafting laws.

CAPTION ANSWER (P. 17) Although there was not unanimity of national opinion, there was a national consensus emerging that opposed racial segregation. Some states stubbornly and even violently resisted this change and continued to deny African Americans civil rights guaranteed by the federal Constitution.

ACTIVITY—TAKING A FIELD TRIP

Plan a field trip for students to visit a local city or county council, school board, or other lawmaking body. Students should examine some laws enacted by these bodies and learn the procedure for passing the laws. If possible, prior to the legislative session, make an appointment with an elected legislator or someone from his or her staff to discuss what students are likely to observe and what bills will be under consideration during the upcoming session. Have students read this section of the student text and write questions to ask a legislator or staff member if they have an opportunity to interview them.

ACTIVITY—DEBATE OR LEGISLATIVE HEARING

Have students debate the following proposal for a state law: "All persons riding skateboards, scooters, in-line skates, and shoes with embedded wheels are required to wear a helmet." Encourage students to prepare by considering the power of the state legislature to exercise control over the safety of its citizens and the importance of considering the needs of all constituents in formulating laws.

Alternatively, students might prepare testimony for a legislative hearing on this issue from the perspectives of different groups of citizens. Roles could include young people, parents, owners of sporting goods stores, emergency room physicians, and local legislators.

At the conclusion of the debate or hearing, ask students to evaluate the effectiveness of the testimony or debate and to suggest how the arguments could have been made more convincing. Discuss how the arguments and responses in this role-play are similar to and different from "the real thing."

LEGAL RESOURCE PERSONS

To clarify the roles of the legislative, executive, and judicial branches of government, invite a representative from each local branch to discuss laws of interest to students. For example, a member of the city council could discuss how the laws were conceived and passed, a police officer could discuss how the laws are enforced, and a judge could discuss how the courts resolve any disputes that arise in interpreting the laws.

PROBLEM 2.1 (p.18)

a. The parking regulation is a local ordinance.

b. Required school attendance is a state law.

c. Both state and federal laws prohibit bank robbery.

d. The vendor's licensing requirement is a local ordinance.

e. Employment discrimination is prohibited by federal law (*Title VII* of the *Civil Rights Act* of 1964), some state laws, and some local ordinances.

f. Airline searches involve federal statutes and federal constitutional law.

Additional examples include a federal law against treason, a state law that prohibits murder, and a local ordinance that sets a curfew for teenagers.

Investigating the Law Where You Live

(p. 18) Many Internet sites provide the public access to state laws or statutes. The Cornell University Law School site is one of the easier ones to use. Encourage students to visit https://www.law.cornell.edu/states/listing. This website should prove useful throughout your course, as students compare what they learn from the *Street Law* text about laws on a national level to laws in their own states.

THE **CASE** OF...

The Unclear Law

PROBLEM 2.2 (p.19)

This case illustrates how laws, once written, may be susceptible to different interpretations.

Step 1: Before directing students to analyze parts **a.–h.** of this problem, be sure that they read and understand the law and background

Then organize the class into small groups. Ask each group to decide whether or not the vehicle described in **a.–h.** should be allowed in the park. Instruct students to try to persuade the members of their group to agree with their point of view. Each group should reach a consensus on their answers and be prepared to provide reasons for their decisions.

Step 2: After each group has analyzed the cases, group members should rewrite the law to make it clearer.

Step 3: Groups may appoint one spokesperson for the entire exercise or have a different spokesperson provide the answer and accompanying rationale for each case study and read their revised law.

Groups will need about 10 to 15 minutes to arrive at decisions for the cases and another 5 minutes to rewrite the law. Write the ending time on the board. Draw a grid on the board to record responses. The grid should list the case letters along one axis and the group numbers along the other. Below the grid, write "Law Revisions," where you will record the changes each group makes in the law.

Emphasize that reasoning is the most important part of this activity, not arriving at the correct answer. Once groups announce and explain their answers, debrief the activity. Record group responses for each case on the grid, and ask for the rationale of the decision makers where appropriate.

In the debriefing, ask students:

1. How should emergency situations be provided for in the law? Who should determine what constitutes an emergency?

2. What is an appropriate penalty for violating this law? Should the penalty be explained in this law?

3. Who should enforce the law? Is there any remedy available to citizens if those who are supposed to enforce the law break it themselves?

4. How can this law be redrafted to avoid the inconsistencies that now plague it?

5. Should laws be written in such a way that they can be adapted to meet changing situations? Can they be both detailed and flexible?

6. Why do you think the Framers of the Constitution separated the power to interpret laws from the power to make laws?

7. This activity asks us to consider the intent of the legislators who wrote the law. Should laws always be interpreted in a manner consistent with legislative intent?

Point out how the decisions of the student groups reflected reasons based on:

- their understanding of the "letter of the law";
- what they thought the lawmakers actually intended;
- their own sense of values; and
- their perception of what the law's impact on society would be.

TAKING ACTION: LAW AND DEMOCRACY

Drafting a Law Simulation

PROBLEM 2.3 (p.20)

This simulation may begin with students answering questions **a.–c.** individually, in pairs, or in groups of three to five students.

a. Answers will vary according to each student's (or group's) view of what should be done, or not done, about smoking in public places. Prompt students to explain their details and the reasons they included those details in their new ordinance.

b. You may want to refer students to page 20 in the Student Edition, which gives suggestions for drafting a bill.

c. Answers will vary according to the details of the ordinance students are suggesting. Remind students to explain their predictions about which group(s) would support and which might oppose their ordinances.

Each group should present its results to the class. You may consider inviting fellow students to comment on their classmates' proposed laws and to suggest improvements in and solutions to any problems with the proposals.

ACTIVITY—LEGISLATIVE ANALYSIS

Obtain a draft of a bill from your local, state, or federal legislature to analyze.

1. What information is readily apparent on first reading the bill?

2. What groups of people would you expect to support this bill? Oppose it?

3. Is the bill amending, enacting, or repealing parts of the federal, state, or local law?

4. What is required or prohibited by this bill?

5. How clear is the language in this bill?

6. What is the enforcement mechanism for the legislation? What responsibilities, if any, are given to administrative agencies?

7. Is the legislative intent of this bill clear? (Have students interpret this bill, using the same rules that judges use, found on page 20 of the Student Edition.)

8. Does this legislation require the government to spend money? If so, where will the money come from?

If students determine that the legislative intent of the bill is unclear, challenge them to redraft vague sections and send it to their representative(s) for consideration.

AGENCIES (PP. 21–23)

Learning Outcomes

After completing this section, students should be able to:

1. describe how agencies are involved in the lawmaking process;
2. name several federal administrative agencies and describe their work;
3. define the terms *regulation* and *public hearing*;
4. give examples that illustrate how regulations have the force of law; and
5. explain why administrative agencies may be viewed as "hidden lawmakers."

CAPTION ANSWER (P. 21) The Department of Homeland Security is needed to prevent, protect against, and respond to acts of terrorism on U.S. soil.

CAPTION ANSWER (P. 22) Legislative bodies authorize administrative agencies to develop rules and regulations to make laws more specific. Such rules and regulations influence almost all aspects of our daily life, including working conditions, the environment, and local zoning issues. Regulations issued by administrative agencies become law without being voted upon, but agencies usually hold public hearings to give individuals and businesses a chance to express their views.

PROBLEM 2.4 (p.23)

a. Students' answers will vary. Ask each student to present a brief report on what he or she discovered in researching the agency. Then ask:

- Which agencies seem essential? Why? Who might disagree with you? Why?
- Are there any agencies that do not seem necessary? Explain. Who might disagree with you? Why?

b. Students' answers will vary. Have each student briefly report on the agency and action they researched. Students could make oral presentations, write a report, or create a display. After students have shared their reports, ask:

- Was the action taken by the agency essential? Why? Who might disagree with you?
- How might a member of the public impact the work of this agency? Is there evidence that the public has or is currently impacting the work?

ACTIVITY—BUSINESS REGULATION INTERVIEW

Ask students to interview local business people to obtain specific examples of regulations imposed on various businesses and the names of agencies—local, state, or federal—that enforce these regulations.

Students might also ask:

- Which regulations seem reasonable? Which do not? Why?
- Which agencies oversee your business? How consistently, effectively, and ethically do they enforce regulations?
- Should there be any new regulations? If so, which ones? Why?
- What would you say about the regulations if you had the opportunity to testify in an agency hearing?
- Have you joined any organizations that seek to influence regulatory agencies and lawmakers?

After students have completed their research and reported their findings, follow up with a discussion of reasons why members of the business community often seek regulatory reform and reasons why workers and consumers may resist such reforms.

COURTS (P. 23)

Note: This section merely introduces courts in terms of their lawmaking power. Chapter 5 provides a more comprehensive introduction to the U.S. court system.

Learning Outcomes

After completing this section, students should be able to:
1. define the terms *trial*, *appeal*, *appellate court*, and *precedent*; and
2. explain how the decisions of appellate courts can have the force of laws.

ACTIVITY—ASSESSING LANDMARK DECISIONS

Ask students to think about decisions made by the Supreme Court that have become law. You may want to remind them of some important cases that they have studied in their United States history classes. Once they have identified a few cases, ask students to assess the impact of these rulings. For example, *Plessy* v. *Ferguson*[1] established that "separate but equal" facilities for African Americans did not violate the U.S. Constitution. This ruling essentially made segregation legal, establishing patterns of segregation that persist today in some areas. Ask students how the precedents established in *Dred Scott*[2] and *Brown* v. *Board of Education of Topeka*[3] functioned as de facto laws and how they affected individuals and the nation. Visit https://www.landmarkcases.org/ for additional information about these and other Supreme Court landmark cases.

INTERNATIONAL LAWMAKING (PP. 23–25)

Learning Outcomes

After completing this section, students should be able to:

1. define the terms *treaty* and *extradition*;
2. list examples of the types of activities typically regulated by treaties;
3. describe who in the United States must sign and ratify a treaty before it becomes law; and
4. explain the role of the international courts of the United Nations.

CAPTION ANSWER (P. 24)   Members of the EU have the opportunity to be involved in the European Parliament, and therefore may influence lawmaking in the region.

PROBLEM 2.5 (p.25)

a. Students' answers will vary. One of the key questions for people in the United States to consider is under what circumstances it should commit its troops to protect the lives of people in other countries. Some people feel that we should not risk American lives for others under any circumstance. Other people believe we have a duty to protect human rights and to save lives anywhere in the world. Students should consider hypothetical questions such as how many troops and weapons might be needed, how long the troops might need to stay, whether the troops should be involved in keeping the peace after the war ends, and whether U.S. troops would fight under military leadership from other countries or whether our troops would only fight under U.S. direction. Students may recognize that this scenario is similar to the current situation in the Darfur region of western Sudan, or the situation in Syria, where many people died before the United Nations, the United States, or any other country intervened.

b. Answers will vary. Students should consider how other countries will treat the United States if we do not support them, and whether the United States would support other nonmilitary actions the international community could take to pressure the leaders of that African nation. What does it mean to be a member of the United Nations (UN)? Must all countries abide by the decisions of two-thirds of the countries? Or can member countries disregard UN decisions? What is likely to happen if countries do not abide by UN decisions?

c. Answers will vary. Students should explain the benefits and risks of "going it alone," particularly the strength of their commitment to do what they think is right, how the international community might react to the United States in the long term and short term, and the chances of military success as one nation versus many nations using force collectively. This situation is similar to the situation in 2003 before the beginning of the Iraqi war, when the United States, Britain, and a few other countries invaded Iraq without the support of the governments in the majority of countries. Ask students what they think is the result of such an action.

NOTES

(1) *Plessy* v. *Ferguson*, 163 U.S. 537 (1896).

(2) *Dred Scott, Plaintiff in Error,* v. *John F. A. Sandford*, 60 U.S. 393 (1856).

(3) *Brown* v. *Bd. of Educ. of Topeka*, 347 U.S. 483 (1954).

Encouraging and teaching about positive involvement in public affairs is one of the most important goals of *Street Law*. Citizen involvement can influence the lawmaking process in several ways. In a democracy, usually through their elected representatives, the people are responsible for making laws. Voting is one way citizens can voice their concerns in support of or in opposition to the government. Citizens can also work to change laws and policies that are not helping to solve problems in their communities, cities, or states. They can do this through such advocacy activities as lobbying and forming special-interest groups.

THE ART OF ADVOCACY (PP. 26–27)

Learning Outcomes

After completing this section, students should be able to:
1. describe the role of citizens in making laws;
2. define the term *advocacy*; and
3. given specific public policy issues, identify groups of people who advocate for or against those policy proposals.

TAKING ACTION: LAW AND DEMOCRACY

Changing the Law: Research and Role-Play

PROBLEM 3.1 (p.27)

Organize the class into five groups. Have groups analyze one of the proposed laws listed by answering questions **a.** through **d.** If you wish to extend the activity, students might research which lobbyists or advocacy groups are concerned with their assigned issues.

Ask students to take on the roles of legislators, citizens and lobbyists. After the lobbyists try to persuade the legislators, ask both groups to evaluate the effectiveness of student lobbyists. To extend question **c.** ask students to create mock-ups of the social media posts that reflect their views on the proposed law they researched.

LOBBYING (PP. 28–30)

Learning Outcomes

After completing this section, students should be able to:
1. define the terms *lobbying* and *grassroots lobbyist*;
2. describe the various methods that lobbyists use as they attempt to influence legislation;
3. write or e-mail an effective letter to a public official; and
4. evaluate the impact of lobbying and campaign contributions on lawmaking.

BACKGROUND—WHAT IS LOBBYING?

Federal law defines *lobbying* as any oral or written communication (including an electronic communication) to an official in the executive or legislative branch that is made on behalf of a client with regard to:

- the formulation, modification, or adoption of federal legislation (including legislative proposals);
- the formulation, modification, or adoption of a federal rule, regulation, executive order, or any other program, policy, or position of the United States government;
- the administration or execution of a federal program or policy (including the negotiation, award, or administration of a federal contract, grant, loan, permit, or license); or
- the nomination or confirmation of a person for a position subject to confirmation by the Senate.[1]

In 2016, the Center for Public Integrity compared the number of lobbyists registered in each of the 50 states to the number of state legislators and found that there was an average of six lobbyists for every state lawmaker. For more or updated information, visit https://publicintegrity.org/state-politics/amid-federal-gridlock-lobbying-rises-in-the-states/.

Despite the unseemly reputation of some lobbyists, lobbying is an important component of democracy. Most lobbyists contend that their efforts focus on the information they provide to lawmakers and their staffs—not on making back-room deals. In addition to grassroots lobbying, constituents make their wishes known to their representatives through boycotts, petitions, strikes, protests, demonstrations, and acts of civil disobedience. (The First Amendment implications of these forms of political expression are dealt with in Unit 6 of the Student Edition.)

BACKGROUND—LOBBYING REFORM

Discuss the following criticisms and reforms with students. Be sure to invite their input about how lobbying influences democracy.

- Many people criticize the lobbying system for giving moneyed interests too much power in Congress and in state and local legislatures. The high cost of political campaigns may make campaign contributions from these wealthy donors seem essential to candidates.
- Some people criticize former government officials who go through the so-called revolving door and then lobby the people with whom they had previously worked. According to the national nonprofit organization Public Citizen,

as of 2019 nearly two-thirds (59%) of the former legislators who return to the private sector became lobbyists. Critics of this practice say "Ordinary citizens cannot afford to buy this sort of access. Regular people do not have former officials and Capitol Hill aides representing their health care interest before Congress and the Administration. Groups like the Health Insurance Association of America do."
- In September 2007, after much debate, Congress passed and the president signed the *Honest Leadership and Open Government Act of 2007*. According to Public Citizen, the main reforms provided in this legislation are:

- lobbyists will be required to post on the Internet their fundraising events and contributions to lawmakers;
- senators will have to wait two years to become registered lobbyists;
- lobbyists must report their lobbying activities every three months on the Internet;
- lobbyists may no longer give any gifts (of any amount) to lawmakers and their staffs; and
- organizations that employ lobbyists must significantly cut back on the number and type of trips they pay for legislators and their staff to take, and those "junkets" must be preapproved and reported publicly.

PROBLEM 3.2 (p.29)

a. The purpose of this question is to encourage students to consider how organizations use different persuasive techniques to further their interests. The issues students select may be social or political, local or national, or may be related to themselves as students or as teenagers. By visiting the website of advocacy groups, students will see that organizations use various techniques of persuasion, including using facts to appeal to logic, arguing against an opposing viewpoint, or playing on people's emotions, fears, or desires. Students should also consider how to discern the truthfulness of the information provided. For example, does the website rely on scientific studies? Does the organization use statistics? Are references to reliable sources provided on the website?

b. Suggest that students review *Steps to Take* "Writing a Public Official" on page 28 in the Student Edition before drafting their letters. A model letter or email to senators is shown in **3.1 TM Figure.** Remind students that there are additional methods of influencing public officials, including phone calls, e-mail, petitions, and demonstrations.

c. Students' responses will vary. You may choose to debate this question at this point or at the end of the chapter. To help students learn more about campaign finance reform, suggest that they research the *McCain-Feingold Act,* which enacted several sweeping changes and has been challenged in the U.S. Supreme Court several times. Additional information about two of these cases (known as *McConnell* v. *Federal Election Commission* and *Citizens United* v. *Federal Elections Commission*) is available at http://www.oyez.org/.

LEGAL RESOURCE PERSONS

A number of legal resource people might be helpful with this topic. Lobbyists might discuss the process and reasons for registration, as well as the strategies they use in their work.

In addition, the Center for Responsive Politics provides extensive information in their Lobbyists Database, available online at http://www.opensecrets.org/lobby/. The site provides information on individual lobbyists, clients, and lobbying firms in any given economic sector.

STEPS TO TAKE

Guidelines for Advocates (p. 30)

Review the "Guidelines for Advocates" and "Three Golden Rules for Advocacy" found on page 30 of the Student Edition. It is important to emphasize to students that few advocates pass from step one to step eight directly. For example, after people become experts on an issue, they often need to go back to revise or refine their goals.

Then ask students to select an issue they care about and follow the guidelines for changing a rule or public policy to improve their school or community.

After students select an issue or problem to focus on, invite two or more community advocates or other experts to discuss the issue and answer students' questions. Ideally, these resource people will represent opposing points of view. Have students prepare questions for this discussion in advance. Students should also ask about strategies that might be most effective to accomplish their goal.

Step 1: Identify the issue. Most effective advocacy projects begin with a careful analysis of the underlying cause of the problem. And then, action projects address those underlying causes.

Step 2: Set a goal. Remind students that setting a specific goal supports the first golden rule of advocacy: clarity. A goal that students might create is that curbside recycling should be provided by local government by a

---

FIGURE

3.1 TM Figure

Date

The Honorable (Senator's Name)
Senate Office Building
Washington, D.C. 20510

Dear Senator _____,

   I am writing regarding the proposed Strip-Mining Bill, S._____. As one of your constituents, I urge you to vote for it when it comes before the full Senate later this month.

   My friends, family, and I love the outdoors and make considerable use of parks and other open spaces. This bill allows the private sector to develop much needed energy at a profit while preserving the environment by restoring lands that have been strip-mined. Many other members of our community also support this bill, and I would like to share your position with them.

   Please let me know your position on the bill. I look forward to hearing from you.

                                         Respectfully,

                                         _____
                                         Name
                                         Address

specific date. Step 2 asks students to state how the community would be improved if their policy were implemented. They might visualize the impact of this public policy as less litter; less consumption of resources; reduced waste; and increased civic pride.

Step 3: Become an expert on the issue. After conducting research, students should identify facts and arguments that all sides would use to support their points of view. Students should interview community leaders, neighbors, friends, and business leaders for a well-rounded perspective.

For example, students should identify sources of reliable information on recycling. Resources for student research include local, state, and national recycling and environmental advocacy groups and government agencies, as well as journalists who have covered the issue.

Step 4: Recruit allies. Identify Roadblocks. Explain to students that the more people they have supporting their cause, the more likely they are to be successful. This follows the second golden rule of advocacy: quantity. Have students brainstorm a list of stakeholders, or potential allies and opponents concerned with their issue.

For example, people in the community who are likely to share their recycling concerns may include local recycling coalitions, environmentally friendly businesses, waste management companies, other students, and parents. Remind students that they should also consider the viewpoints of people who may try to block their efforts. Opponents may include industry leaders, businesses, and taxpayer unions. Students should identify what these individuals and organizations have to gain or lose if recycling is mandated in the community.

Step 5: Identify your strategies. This work should be done in several stages. Students should first brainstorm potential action strategies and then compare their lists to the one that appears on page 30 of the Student Edition. They should then systematically weigh the merits of each strategy in relation to their specific goal.

For example, students may decide that conducting a survey on community support for recycling will provide the numbers they need to be successful in their cause. Or they may decide that a petition to mandate recycling would have maximum impact during an election year. Others may decide to write emails to legislators or county officials. They may also attend community meetings held on the issue. To complete this step, students should also evaluate their strategies based on their resources, available time, and the potential effort the strategy may require.

Step 6: Plan for success. Once the group has worked through Steps 1–5, they should put their plan on paper. Students should use **3.2 TM Figure** as a model for identifying specific steps to be taken.

Step 7: Work with the media. Explain to the students that it is important to get their message out repeatedly to as many people as possible (golden rule number three: frequency).

Have students examine Step 7 on page 30 of the Student Edition. Considering the audience they are trying to persuade, students should select one or two media strategies to implement. Facts, statistics, and personal anecdotes derived from the research they conducted in Step 3 can be used to persuade the public. For example, students might write letters to the editor of a local newspaper or share their podcast with local radio or cable television stations. Many of the media advocacy strategies can be completed in the classroom, such as starting a blog. Others, such as holding a press conference, may need to take place after school.

Step 8: Create a resource pool. Students should discuss their own talents and how they would be useful in the effort to improve their community.

FIGURE

3.2 TM Figure

Activities/ Action	Person Responsible	Deadline(s)	Resources/Help Needed	Publicity Plan
1.				
2.				
3.				
4.				
5.				
6.				

Perhaps there is an exceptional writer in the group who could draft press releases and letters to the editor. Another student might be a talented artist who can create flyers, brochures, or posters. Someone else may be well organized and can help keep the team on track, while another student may be an excellent public speaker who should testify at a public hearing, and another could be good at recruiting other students to join in the advocacy project.

Students should identify additional resources, including local organizations and individuals who might donate materials or collaborate with students in arousing public sentiment for their issue.

Step 9: Follow Up and Reflection. After students implement their advocacy plan, have them evaluate its success. Students should be reminded that few advocacy efforts are an instant success. Some advocacy efforts can take many years, such as the campaign to eliminate smoking from restaurants. Students should state what they might do differently to advocate more effectively if they had a second chance to pursue this project.

ACTIVITY—HOW INTEREST GROUPS INFLUENCE SUPREME COURT CASES

Street Law, Inc., has created a lesson plan about the influence of interest groups on the selection of cases heard by the U.S. Supreme Court. To download a free copy, visit https://store.streetlaw.org/interest-groups/.

VOTING (PP. 31–35)

Learning Outcomes

After completing this section, students should be able to:

1. define the terms *initiative*, *referendum*, and *recall* and explain their purpose;
2. describe the basic qualifications needed to vote;
3. identify at least three places where a person can get a voter registration form;
4. identify constitutional amendments and laws that made it possible for African Americans, women, Native Americans, and others to vote;
5. develop hypotheses to explain low voter turnout; and
6. evaluate the importance of voting and voter turnout in maintaining our system of representative democracy.

DELIBERATIONS AND OTHER ACTIVITIES—RECALLS, INITIATIVES, AND REFERENDA

Have students examine copies of ballots from current or recent elections to identify any initiative, referendum, or recall items. Contact your local registrar for assistance. Ask students to debate the items informally and then find out how voters decided these issues. For ballot issues relating to initiatives and referenda, ask students to speculate about why these efforts were dealt with through direct voter participation. For recall efforts, ask students to find out what prompted the recall movement. Do students believe, as some critics of recalls do, that recalls are based on single-issue politics and not on serious offenses?

Discuss the concept of "tyranny of the majority." Laws passed through the initiative or referendum process may fail to protect the rights of minorities. Because the majority outnumbers minorities, majority interests tend to win out in direct votes, while comparatively few representatives consistently vote against minority interests in legislatures.

DELIBERATION

Should voting be compulsory in the United States? (pp. 34–35)

An overview of the deliberation method is discussed in the front of this Teacher's Manual. For free deliberation materials, student handouts, and an instructional video visit https://store.streetlaw.org/deliberations/.

If this is your first deliberation, consider devoting significant time to establishing norms for deliberations and civil discourse. Introduce the process of deliberations, including careful reading, clarification, preparing and presenting initial positions, reversing positions, free small group discussion, search for common ground, and whole-class discussion.

Begin class by introducing the deliberation topic: compulsory voting. Ask students if voting is important to our democracy? Ask what happens when people choose not to vote? Invite students to give their ideas for how voter turnout could be increased. Explain to students that this deliberation will help students explore one possible policy to address low voter turnout and that students will strive to reach consensus on some aspect of the issue but are not required to agree on an outcome.

Take students through the deliberation steps as outlined in the front of this Teacher Manual.

Debrief by instructing students to:

- Raise your hands if you changed your position on the issue.
- Raise your hand if you considered a new opinion that you had not considered before today.
- Raise our hand if you felt listened to during the deliberation.
- Follow up by asking students, how they might translate this activity to conversations outside the classroom.

Consider having students perform a self-assessment on the process and their contribution to it.

For the most recent voter turnout statistics and analysis, visit the Pew Research Center at https://www.pewresearch.org/topics/voter-participation/. For current information on compulsory voting around the world, consult the International Institute for Democracy and Electoral Assistance (IDEA) at https://www.idea.int/data-tools/data/voter-turnout/compulsory-voting.

LEGAL RESOURCE PERSONS

Invite a representative of the League of Women Voters, a local political party activist, or someone from your local voter registration office to explain the process involved in registering to vote, voting in your community, and absentee voting.

BACKGROUND—SOME STATES REQUIRE VOTERS TO SHOW IDENTIFICATION

As of April 1, 2019, 17 states require voters to show a photo ID. These laws are surrounded by partisan controversy. Many Republican lawmakers argue that the laws are needed to prevent voter fraud and that photo ID is necessary for many parts of modern life. Many Democrats argue that voter impersonation is a miniscule problem, and the laws make it much harder for people without a photo ID—often poor, minority, and elderly people who often vote for Democrats to exercise their right to vote.

As mentioned in the Student Edition on page 33, the Supreme Court ruled in *Crawford* v. *Marion County* that requiring voter ID cards did not violate the Constitution.[2] Since that 2008 decision, subsequent challenges to different voter ID laws have had mixed successes and failures.

DISCUSSION—WHO CAN VOTE IN PRESIDENTIAL ELECTIONS?

Voting-rights reforms have eliminated literacy tests and poll taxes and liberalized other voting barriers, including residency requirements and voter registration procedures. *The National Voter Registration Act of 1993* (also known as the Motor Voter Act) made it easier for individuals to register to vote by incorporating voter registration into other transactions citizens must complete to comply with regulations at other public agencies. For example, voter registration can be accomplished while applying for a driver's license, public assistance benefits, food stamps, Medicaid, WIC, or disability services. Almost three in ten people who have registered to vote since January 1, 1995, did so when they obtained or renewed their drivers' licenses.

Some advocates have proposed that government take these steps to increase registration and voting:

- Provide citizens easier access to absentee ballots.
- Declare a national holiday for all general elections.
- Hold elections on weekends.
- Permit citizens to vote by postal mail or e-mail.

Another interesting issue is whether all U.S. citizens should have the right to vote. Citizens in the District of Columbia (D.C.), Puerto Rico, and the Trust Territories can vote in presidential elections but cannot elect senators or representatives. Should they be allowed to do so, or should their jurisdictions first be required to become states? Ask students the reasons for or against voting representatives for these entities.

BACKGROUND AND DISCUSSION— YOUTH VOTING

Youth voting—or failure to vote—has been studied by a number of researchers. The Center for Information & Research on Civic Learning and Engagement (CIRCLE) is a good source of information on youth engagement and voting. Its website provides a wide array of resources on the topic. (www.civicyouth.org). According to CIRCLE, the following are important factors in encouraging young people to vote: (1) contact with an organization or candidate, (2) ease of registration, (3) information about when and where to vote, (4) high-quality civic education, and (5) family members who are engaged and vote.

Direct students to the Census Bureau website site at http://www.census.gov/ to conduct research to identify the reasons other groups did not vote. Students should use the search term "reasons for not voting." If they want to compare the reasons people in other age groups did not vote in the same election, direct them to use the additional search words "Youth Vote Participation." They can also enter the election year they are most interested in. On the same site, students will also see a breakdown of why people in various demographic groups did not vote, including a breakdown by gender, race, educational attainment, state, marital status, and duration of residence.

After reviewing the data, students should conduct their own polls of friends and family members who were eligible to vote in a presidential election, but did not, to determine whether their answers mirror the survey results.

Finally, ask students to propose solutions and get out the vote campaigns that could maximize positive factors and minimize negative factors for young voters. Ask students: Will you vote when you are eligible? Why or why not? What will you need to know in order to vote? How can you learn that?

Beginning in 1990, several groups began efforts to increase voting among young people. Youth Vote.org is dedicated to involving young people in the political process in many ways, including voting. Rock the Vote campaign (http://www.rockthevote.com/) often features recording artists and other entertainers participating in public service announcements encouraging young people to vote.

Have students visit the websites for these projects. Then ask them if they find the website and programs motivating. Ask them to evaluate the effectiveness of the programs. Conclude the research activity by asking students to describe advertising techniques that would and would not succeed with their generation.

CAPTION ANSWER (P. 32) Some people believe that voting is the most important political right because it allows citizens to influence their government and its lawmaking activities.

Investigating the Law Where You Live

(p. 33) The League of Women Voters Education Fund has a website (www.vote411. org) with information about registering to vote, residency requirements, and voting places and times. Students may have to do more digging to find answers at http://www. rockthevote.com/, http://congress.org/, or the site run by the Federal Election Commission at http://www.fec.gov/. As students are conducting research about election procedures where they live, suggest they also find out if their state requires voters to present a photo ID.

PROBLEM 3.3 (p.33)

a. Students can make their lists of reasons individually or in groups.

b. Students' answers will vary. Some possible reasons for and against each of the proposals are noted below.

- Registering and voting on the same day would enable voters to "kill two birds with one stone." However, it might cause long delays at some polling places, as poll workers would have to verify voter eligibility. Thus, registering on the same day would probably require more time of the voters.

- Even though lowering the voting age to 16 might result in more people voting, this proposal does not address the problem of those who already can vote but do not. Some would argue that 16-year-olds are not politically aware enough to vote in an informed fashion. Others argue that it would enable students to practice citizenship while in school instead of being limited to discussion and hypothetical choices.

- Students might believe keeping polls open for a week would allow more people to vote because it provides more flexibility to schedule a time to vote. Those opposed to the idea may argue that it would be difficult to stop candidates from continuing to campaign during that period of time and to limit undue influence by the media and other voters on those who vote late in the process. Also, many schools, libraries, and public buildings close on election days so those facilities may be used as polling places. Keeping the polls open for a week may force those places to close for a longer period time or may force election officials to find new sites.

- Automatically registering every one to vote who obtains a driver's license would increase the number of eligible voters, but since most states allow driving beginning at the age of 16, the age requirements of voters may prevent this proposal from moving forward. Those without licenses would still have to register in a separate procedure.

- Allowing citizens to vote up to a month early could increase voter participation and include voters who may otherwise not be able to vote. However, voting precincts would need additional resources to handle the early voting, which could cost taxpayers.

ACTIVITY—INCREASING VOTER PARTICIPATION

After completing Problem 3.3, organize the class into groups of three or four and have students brainstorm a list of ways to increase voter participation.

Give students time to brainstorm. Then ask each group to pick out its three best ideas. List them on the board. How practical is each idea? Could the ideas be implemented? What would be required for each idea to be implemented? Will elected officials support proposals to increase voter participation?

Students may suggest options involving punishment for failure to vote. You should emphasize, however, that in a democracy many people believe that the freedom to speak also implies the freedom not to speak. Thus, the freedom to vote may include the freedom not to vote as well.

DISCUSSION—VOTING RIGHTS IN THE CONSTITUTION AND UNIVERSAL DECLARATION OF HUMAN RIGHTS

Have student explore additional issues related to voting:

1. What does the Universal Declaration of Human Rights (UDHR), Article 21 say about voting rights? Consider the case of South Africa. Ask students if they have seen photos of seemingly endless lines of black South African citizens waiting to vote in the first election in which they were permitted to participate. Ask students to speculate about why voter turnout was so high there, why it is comparatively low in the United States, and why the low participation rate for African Americans is ironic, especially considering efforts to achieve the franchise for African Americans.

2. Go to the Department of Justice website at http://www.justice.gov/crt/about/vot/. Examine the documents there and explain what practices they prohibit.

3. Examine the Twenty-fourth Amendment to the U.S. Constitution. What does it prohibit?

CAMPAIGN FINANCE REFORM (PP. 36–37)

Learning Outcomes

After completing this section, students should be able to:

1. name at least two reasons why some people want to reform the campaign finance system;
2. describe the connection between campaign contributions and free speech protections guaranteed by the First Amendment;
3. explain how recent campaign finance laws have changed the campaign finance system;
4. describe the role of the Federal Election Commission; and
5. summarize the Supreme Court decision in the cases of *Buckley* v. *Valeo* and *Citizens United* v. *FEC*.

BACKGROUND, CASE STUDIES, AND MOOT COURT ACTIVITIES—CAMPAIGN FINANCE

If students want to learn more about the Supreme Court cases of *Buckley* v. *Valeo* or *Citizens United* v. *FEC*[3], they should check out the website www.oyez.com.

In addition, Street Law has prepared multiple lesson plans to help students understand recent Supreme Court decisions relating to campaign finance. The lessons are free and available under the "resources" tab of the organization's website: www.streetlaw.org. There you will find resources about teaching methods such as case studies and moot courts as well as background information and case summaries.

PROBLEM 3.4 (p.37)

There is no single right answer to these problems. Reasonable people disagree about the nature of both the problems and the solutions.

a. The three statements present the three main schools of thought: full federal funding, no limits, and full disclosure. Some of the proposals that have been made are combinations of these ideas. In dealing with this problem, it might also be helpful to look at state and local campaign finance reform models. There is additional information available on this topic at the website site of the League of Women Voters, http://lwv.org/.

b. Students' answers will vary. Ask students to explain their views on each of these statements based on what they have learned and believe about judicial independence, democracy, and elections.

NOTES

(1) 2 U.S.C. Section 1602 (1995).

(2) *Crawford* v. *Marion County*, 553 U.S. 181 (2008).

(3) *Citizens United* v. *Federal Election Commission*, 558 U.S. 310 (2010).

networks™

INTRODUCTION (P. 38)

BACKGROUND—CONFLICT IN DAILY LIFE

Conflict is a natural part of everyday life. Disputes can arise at the personal level among friends or between a husband and wife battling over child custody. Disputes can also occur between consumers and stores, between companies, and even between governments. It is important to know how to resolve disputes because conflict is common in many areas of life. Many conflicts are settled out of court through mediation, negotiation, and arbitration.

Hardly a day goes by when we are not conscious of conflict and its effect on our lives. Conflict is a possibility in every encounter we have, whether it be with family members, friends, coworkers, or strangers. Sometimes it takes only a few seconds for a casual encounter to escalate to an exchange of angry words, or even to physical contact or a threat of litigation. The reality of conflict in daily life underscores the importance of studying conflict and conflict management.

Society's dissatisfaction with lawsuits as a process established to settle disputes has led to new ways of approaching conflict. Community mediation programs have cropped up around the country to help people explore new forms of dispute resolution. The success of these programs and their effect on participants has contributed to their growth.

The study of conflict can be both positive and educational. With the proper tools, people can benefit from learning how to handle conflict. Mediation and conflict-management programs are changing the way people think about conflict.

This edition of *Street Law* purposefully introduces students to alternative methods for settling disputes before it covers adversarial and court-based approaches. The assumption is that litigation often can and should be avoided and that people should understand and consider alternative methods before resorting to litigation.

Several significant concepts underlie this assumption:

1. Conflicts and disputes are a normal part of human relationships.

2. Skills that can be applied to resolving conflict should be part of curricula in many courses, including law.

3. If people view them as potential opportunities rather than as crises, conflicts can produce positive outcomes for all involved.

Students who are interested in learning about conflict resolution around the world may be interested in the work of a nonprofit group called Search for Common Ground. The group strives to help people from various cultures and histories resolve conflicts without violence and with cooperative solutions. To learn more about this group and their work internationally, have students visit www.sfcg.org.

METHODS FOR SOLVING DISPUTES
(PP. 38–43)

Learning Outcomes

After completing this section, students should be able to:

1. list, describe, and distinguish among the three most common methods for settling disputes out of court;
2. define the terms *negotiation, settlement, arbitration, mediation,* and *ombudsperson;*
3. analyze disputes in order to determine which method the parties should use to resolve a conflict; and
4. identify different steps to take to resolve a dispute through negotiation and through mediation.

DISCUSSION—RESOLVING DISPUTES

Review Figure 4.1, Methods of Dispute Resolution, on page 39 of the Student Edition to help students understand the variety of ways to deal with disputes. In addition, two methods not noted in the Student Edition are fact-finding and administrative procedures. Fact-finding uses a third party to recommend a settlement after an investigation. Administrative procedures are similar to adjudication (decision making in the judicial process) but are less formal.

CAPTION ANSWER (P. 39) Negotiation involves only the parties involved in the conflict, while mediation involves a third party to help the disputants resolve their conflict. During arbitration, the disputing parties look to one or more outside parties to listen to their arguments and make a decision for them.

BACKGROUND—ADJUDICATION AND MEDIATION

A comparison of adjudication and mediation can help students gain a greater understanding of when each method should be used. Mediators often work for an agency affiliated with the courts or for a private agency. There are also independent mediators who are hired by the two parties and paid an hourly or set fee for the mediation. Mediators' primary methods of solving disputes involve first allowing each side to work through their emotions so the disputed issues can be identified, and then helping to generate options in order to shape an agreement between the opposing parties. It is important to note that a mediator does not decide the case but instead helps the parties come to their own agreement.

ADJUDICATION AND MEDIATION: A COMPARISON

1. **Who defines the dispute and identifies the issues?**
   Adjudication: In criminal or civil conflict, the state (or judge) defines the specific issue to be resolved.

   Mediation: As part of the process, the disputing parties define the conflict. Both sides discuss what they feel are relevant issues.

2. **What due process is provided?**
   Adjudication: In a criminal matter, the accused has a right to the assistance of an attorney and to a speedy trial held in public and judged by an impartial third party. The trial must comply with the Fourth, Fifth, Sixth, Eighth, and Fourteenth Amendments. In a civil case, both parties also have the right to due process, including a jury trial (Seventh Amendment), but in civil cases, a person who cannot afford an attorney may not be given one by the state.

   Mediation: The parties may represent themselves at the mediation meeting; sometimes they may have an attorney present, or the parties may ask their attorneys to review an agreement before it becomes final. Statements made during the mediation process are considered confidential. Mediation should be conducted impartially. There are no rules of evidence limiting what may be discussed.

3. **What is the orientation of the settlement?**
   Adjudication: Trials focus on past actions and the intent is to determine fault, liability, or guilt. Occasionally court orders regulate the future behavior of parties.

   Mediation: The focus is on the future. The past is discussed only to allow both sides to air their frustrations and to anticipate future behavior. The facts are whatever both parties accept as truth. The settlement helps to define future behavior.

4. **Who decides?**
   Adjudication: A judge or jury decides what to accept as fact and then renders a decision.

   Mediation: Mediators help resolve disputes, but the parties involved must decide for themselves what will be included in the settlement.

5. **Whose interests are served?**

Adjudication: By prosecuting a criminal, the state punishes the wrongdoer, protects society, establishes norms, sets precedents, and deters others from similar actions. In a civil case, the parties get a hearing in court, and one side will receive a favorable decision. The winner's interest is served much more than the loser's, although the winner has to wait for the judgment, and a significant portion of the money recovered must be paid to the lawyer.

Mediation: When mediation works, the disputing parties clarify and improve their relationship, satisfy their individual interests, set ground rules for future interactions, and maintain privacy. Their interest in being able to communicate better in the future is served. However, some people are unable to mediate their disputes.

6. **Who enforces the agreements?**

Adjudication: The state enforces the judgment of the courts.

Mediation: The parties involved take action to see that the settlement is honored. It sometimes is incorporated into a court decree, such as a divorce decree, and then enforced by the court.

Another way to determine which form of dispute resolution should be used is to ask:

- Should one of the parties be punished for his or her actions?
- Is one of the parties dangerous to society?
- Is it important to announce that the disputed behavior is inappropriate?
- Is it necessary to set a precedent about the behavior?

If the answer is "yes" to any of the questions above, adjudication is appropriate.

- Is there a past relationship between parties, and will they have to maintain a relationship in the future?
- Is mending and maintaining the relationship important?
- Is solving the dispute without being adversaries important to the parties?

If the answer is "yes," to any of the questions above, mediation is appropriate.

CAPTION ANSWER (P. 40) It is important to separate the demands from what each party really wants so that the terms of the negotiation are clear. If the terms are unclear, the agreement may be easily broken.

DISCUSSION—HOW CONFLICT AFFECTS US

Students invariably have extensive experience with conflicts and disputes, and their experiences can be explored in class to motivate discussion.

1. Ask students to jot down issues that have resulted in disputes with siblings, friends, bosses, co-workers, or parents. For example, disputes might involve who has access to the TV remote control or a video game, what happened to the shirt loaned to a friend, what time curfew should be, or who should be able to use the car.

2. Have students volunteer to discuss what they wrote. Explain that in law the different "sides" in a dispute may be called "parties" or "disputants." Ask them to identify:
   - disputes that could be solved by the disputants themselves, and
   - disputes that had to be solved with the help of a third party (e.g., a parent, guidance counselor, mutual friend, etc.).

3. Ask students to volunteer to describe emotions they have felt during conflicts with others. Discuss how emotions complicate the process of resolving disputes. Why is it crucial to be able to clearly identify one's feelings while struggling with conflict?

4. Ask students to identify examples of disputes or conflicts that, however painful or difficult at the time, ultimately helped them learn or grow. Families and friends find, for example, that in facing a conflict they become closer to one another and gain mutual understanding.

5. Ask students to brainstorm examples of instances when going to court could actually make a problem worse or be otherwise disadvantageous.

Discuss the concepts of "win-lose" and "win-win" in relation to settling disputes. In litigation (a lawsuit), one side wins and the other loses, with consequences that may ultimately be disadvantageous for both sides. By using alternative methods, both sides can enter into a conflict-resolution process with a win-win goal, where the solution can accommodate the interests of both sides. Litigation may be adversarial. It often escalates the problem and generally promotes hostility between the parties. The methods of negotiation, mediation, and arbitration offer both parties the potential of a win-win outcome, so hostility may be diminished.

(p. 42) If students want to learn about noncourt conflict-resolution programs in your community, suggest that they contact a local attorney who could explain the options available and what types of disputes those community programs handle.

Another option is to direct students to the Association for Conflict Resolution at www.acrnet.org. The site includes a helpful "Frequently Asked Questions" page as well as a search function to find a mediator or arbitrator in a specific geographic area.

To find out if their campus has a conflict mediation program, students can ask at the Student Services office. If a program is available, they should learn how to become involved as a mediator or under what circumstances they can and should refer a conflict to this group for assistance in resolving it.

PROBLEM 4.1 (p.42)

Have students solve Problem 4.1 after completing the discussion about conflict described above and after instruction about the differences between negotiation, arbitration, mediation, and litigation.

In discussing each situation, remind students that there may not be one best answer. Variables that students should consider include the availability of arbitrators and mediators, the presence of complicating issues, such as whether the couple wanting a divorce has a custody dispute, and time and money factors.

a. This situation might best be handled by an informal discussion between the sisters. If this fails, they may opt for a more formal negotiation or mediation by someone who knows and cares for both of them, such as a parent.

b. This situation might best be handled with help from an outside agency or small claims court. Before going to an outside agency, the consumer should first speak directly to the store's owner or to the salesperson's supervisor. If this is unsuccessful, locate a consumer protection agency, such as the state attorney general's office, that can help negotiate or mediate the dispute. If this assistance is not available, you may choose to go to small claims court.

c. The landlord and tenant should try to solve this problem through informal discussion or negotia-

tion. If this is unsuccessful, the next logical approach would be to request that a housing inspector investigate. If this does not resolve the dispute, they might consider asking a housing mediator to help them, if one is available in their community. The landlord or tenant could also go to court or to a landlord/tenant commission.

d. Disputes between workers and employers are often resolved through negotiations between the two sides. In some labor disputes, where workers are in union, the union and management will agree beforehand to submit disagreements to binding arbitration. Mediation and litigation are also sometimes used to help solve such disputes.

e. You might settle your dispute with the IRS through informal discussion. The IRS has established dispute resolution procedures. If these do not prove satisfactory, you may wish to hire an attorney. However, unless you qualify for legal aid, the attorney's fees might be more than the $2000 in question. In that case, the most practical approach may be to simply pay the disputed amount.

TAKING ACTION:
LAW AND DEMOCRACY

Problems at the Mall

PROBLEM 4.2 (p.43)

Before students answer questions a.–e., organize the class into two groups. One group should imagine they are store owners. The other group should imagine they are the teens in the scenario. Each group should answer the questions from their unique perspectives.

a. Answers will vary. The teenagers are likely to be concerned about their own freedom and dignity. They do not wish to be presumed guilty when they have done nothing wrong. They may feel discriminated against since this requirement applies only to people between the ages of 16 and 18. They might also feel that their free speech rights are violated because they cannot even criticize the new policy. The students answering as teens may state the issue as, "The store policy that limits shopping by persons aged 16 to 18 to one pair at a time is discriminatory and must be eliminated."

The store owners' concerns are likely increased costs due to vandalism and shoplifting, which they attribute to youths aged 16 to 18. They may also be concerned that if they raise prices to cover the increased costs, all customers may choose to shop elsewhere. Their issue is that: "Youths aged 16 to 18 are responsible for the economic losses to our businesses through shoplifting and vandalism, and the policy limiting their access to the stores is necessary."

b. Answers will vary. The teens' starting position is that the stores' policies must be thrown out and teens be treated exactly as other customers are treated. The teens really want to be free to shop.

The store owners' starting position is that teens must be restricted, and the policies must stay to reduce the costs of shoplifting.

c. The teens' best conceivable outcomes are that the policies will be lifted and they will be welcomed in the stores.

The store owners' best conceivable outcomes are that vandalism and shoplifting will be eliminated, related expenses will be minimized, other customers will feel safe, and teens can shop freely in the stores.

d. Teens may think the store owners' starting position is to keep the policies in place. They may think that the store owners' underlying interests are to keep teens out of their stores.

The store owners may think the teens' starting position is to let them run free throughout their stores. Store owners may think the teens' underlying interests are unlimited freedom without responsibility.

e. Answers will vary. Workable solutions might begin with distinguishing between vandalism and shoplifting and getting information about why the store owners believe teens are primarily responsible for the shoplifting. A new policy could be established that all shoppers must leave backpacks, large purses, and bags at the counter when they shop. Students could conduct an educational campaign on the impact of shoplifting on local stores and consumers. There may be other actions the store owners can take against shoplifting that would be more effective and apply to all customers.

After students complete Problem 4.2, review with them the FYI feature "Steps In A Typical Mediation Session" on page 41 in the Student Edition. Then organize students into groups containing at least one teenager, one store owner, and one mediator (the mall manager). Lead students through the mediation session and have each group announce the resulting solution to the rest of the class.

networks™

The U.S. judiciary consists of parallel systems of federal, tribal, and state courts. Each of the 50 states has its own system of courts whose powers are derived from its state constitution and laws. The federal court system consists of the Supreme Court and lower federal courts established by Congress. Federal courts derive their powers from the U.S. Constitution and federal laws.

RECOMMENDED INTERNET RESOURCES

The "Teaching Methods" section in the front of this Teacher Manual contains an annotated list of websites recommended by Street Law for teaching about the U.S. Supreme Court. These sites offer lesson plans as well as general information about the history, decisions, and activities of the Court.

TRIAL COURTS (PP. 44–49)

Learning Outcomes

After completing this section, students should be able to:
1. define the terms *trial court, parties, plaintiff, prosecutor, defendant, adversarial system, inquisitional system, plea bargain, stare decisis, voir dire, removal for cause,* and *peremptory challenge;*
2. state one argument in favor of and one argument against the adversarial system; and
3. describe the roles of judges, juries, defense attorneys, prosecutors, and plaintiffs in a trial.

BACKGROUND AND DISCUSSION—THE ADVERSARIAL SYSTEM

Understanding the adversarial system of justice in the United States will be important throughout this Street Law course. This is a concept to which you may wish to return in later chapters. For example, in Chapter 6 students will consider the ethics of attorneys who represent "guilty" clients. However, by helping students recall the adversarial system here, you can enable them to understand that the system requires that lawyers zealously represent their clients and not take on the roles of judges or juries.

Ask students to review the arguments supporting and criticizing the adversarial system discussed in the Student Edition. With which viewpoints do students agree? With which ones do they disagree?

CAPTION ANSWER (P. 45)   Judges working in an inquisitional system are active in questioning witnesses and in gathering and presenting evidence.

> **PROBLEM** 5.1 (p.46)

a. There is no single right answer to this question. The Student Edition lists several considerations for and against the adversarial system. Additionally, students should think about the fact that the adversarial system rests on the presumption that opposing lawyers are evenly matched. Since the outcome of the trial depends greatly on the skill and time commitment of individual lawyers, and since lawyers' fees often depend on these two factors, the party with greater financial resources often has an advantage.

On the other hand, the U.S. system is designed to provide skilled representation to all litigants, an objective third party (the judge) to resolve disputes, a well-developed set of procedural rules designed to achieve fairness, and an opportunity to appeal many decisions.

b. The criminal justice system, with its substantial burden of proof, operates in a manner consistent with the quotation. Guilty persons, technically, do not go free, because a person is not "legally" guilty unless and until proven so. The quotation probably refers to defendants who are filtered out of the criminal justice system at some point (e.g., when police stop but do not arrest the person, an indictment is not returned, probable cause is not proven, or the defendant is not convicted because the prosecution did not prove its case). Clearly, some "morally guilty" persons do go free.

c. The question whether the students would defend someone who they know committed a crime may generate strong opinions. Many attorneys choose not to work in criminal law because they do not wish to represent potentially guilty people. Attorneys who do represent criminal defendants believe that they are fulfilling an essential role to keep the adversarial system fair.

Attorneys understand that they operate in an adversarial system where each side presents its position in the best light possible. It is the job of criminal defense attorneys to present evidence that helps to exonerate their clients or at least raise reasonable doubt as to their guilt. Then either a jury or judge decide the case. The involvement of defense attorneys helps ensure that police and prosecutors act legally and fairly. Knowing that a client committed the crime in question is not relevant to a defense attorney's job. The defense attorney looks to see if procedures were properly followed and rights protected (arrest, search and seizure, right against self-incrimination, etc.), and makes sure the defendant's position is represented.

ACTIVITY—ANALYZING A TRIAL

Walk students through the step-by-step process of a trial. Use the *FYI* feature "Steps in a Trial" on page 47 of the Student Edition to explain what happens during a trial. You may also wish to do one or more of the following:

1. Show a recording of a trial (available at <u>courttv.com</u>). Stop the tape after each part of the process and point out the appropriate step number in the text. If the video does not show the complete trial, ask students which step(s) in the process is not represented.

2. Arrange to observe proceedings in your local, state, or federal courts. Try to see both a trial and an appellate hearing. If possible, arrange for a briefing on the case beforehand. If students are able to observe a variety of types of trials, ask them how the proceedings differ from each other. What evidence of the adversarial system did they observe?

BACKGROUND—JURIES

Juries are becoming more involved in the adversarial process. In some courtrooms, judges sometimes allow jurors to take notes and even to query witnesses through written questions submitted to the bench. This is part of a new movement called "jury liberation." You may wish to discuss the pros and cons of jury liberation with the class. Some arguments for liberation include the fact that it produces more reliable and accurate verdicts, it keeps jurors involved and attentive, and it helps lawyers clarify their presentations. Others contest this procedural change, noting that juries will no longer remain neutral throughout the proceeding but may become advocates for one side of the dispute. Although the jury liberation movement is still in its infancy, it is becoming more common in some courts.

Another controversy involves jury nullification, which occurs when a jury disregards the facts or a judge's instruction because it believes it must do so to dispense justice.

People have looked at ways to make juries more diverse so that defendants may be more likely to truly have a "jury of their peers." In the past, states have typically drawn the list of potential jurors from lists of registered voters. However, this group tends to be less diverse than the general public. Some states are now drawing jurors from lists of people who apply for state identification cards, such as driver's licenses. While this group is more diverse than registered voters, contact information is often out of date, particularly for people with lower incomes because they tend to move more often. For example, in one Wisconsin county, the number of jury summonses determined to be undeliverable was 17 percent overall, but nearly 50 percent for minorities. In that same county, minorities made up 9 percent of the general population, 3 percent of jurors, and 37 percent of the jail population.[1]

Another controversial issue is whether or not attorneys should be able to do extensive background research on individual jurors. Wealthy clients sometimes pay for investigations of jurors so that their attorneys can "pitch" their cases to the specific background, attitudes, and values of the jurors. Jury consultants are sometimes hired to write jury questionnaire, compose jury selection questions, and advise attorneys on which jurors to strike from the jury. Ask students to list the pros and cons of this practice. More information regarding jury selection can be found in Chapter 13, "Criminal Justice Process: Proceedings Before Trial."

When lawyers use peremptory challenges, they excuse potential jurors based on intuition or probability. The U.S. Supreme Court has ruled that judges and lawyers cannot use peremptory challenges to remove potential jurors based on race[2] or gender[3]. Still, reasons for peremptory challenges are difficult to prove. For example, some think that a white defendant will benefit from an all-white jury. Prosecutors may want more women on the jury in rape cases. Ask students if they think these assumptions are true and if peremptory challenges contribute to justice. In conjunction with this section, ask students whether or not the jury system itself is fair. Are any changes needed to ensure that defendants are tried by a jury of their peers? If so, what would they be?

CAPTION ANSWER (P. 48) Attorneys for both the defense and the prosecution may request the removal of any juror who appears to be incapable of rendering a fair and impartial verdict. In addition, peremptory challenges allow attorneys to remove jurors who they feel will not be sympathetic to their case without stating a cause, provided it is not based on the race or gender of the juror.

LEGAL RESOURCE PERSONS

1. Invite a judge to your class to discuss qualifications required of jurors. Ask how voir dire works and the judge's role in the proceeding. Discuss merits of the jury system.

2. Invite a panel of citizens, perhaps parents, who have acted as jurors to discuss their experiences.

3. Invite attorneys with trial experience to explain how the jury system works in your area. Questions he or she may address include:
   - the voir dire process and their role in it,
   - how jurors are selected,
   - how many jurors are required for civil and criminal trials, and

- whether a unanimous verdict is required for a civil and/or for a criminal trial.

ACTIVITY—STUDENTS AS JURORS

Many schools are located in areas where law schools conduct mock trials for law students. These sometimes are part of mock trial competitions, law school clinics, or trial practice courses. Bar associations also often have trial practice programs. These programs or courses often need people to play the role of jurors. These experiences can be arranged by calling the local law school or bar association.

PROBLEM 5.2 (p.49)

a. Some people think that police officers, firefighters, physicians, and members of the armed forces should be excused from jury duty because the nature of their work can involve emergencies that require their immediate attention. Lawyers are seldom excluded by local court rule, but as a practical matter they are often struck in the voir dire process.

Convicted felons are excluded because their conviction deprives them of certain civil rights, including jury duty. The duration of this deprivation varies from state to state, and some states permit eventual restoration of civil rights. Persons who are unable to speak or understand English or who are incapable of serving by reason of mental disability are excused. Some people think no citizens should be excluded, because the responsibilities of citizenship, including jury duty, should apply to all people. With our rights as citizens come responsibilities. It is argued that if we want a system in which cases are decided by our peers, we ourselves must be willing to serve.

b. A defense attorney might ask some of the following questions: Do you know any of the parties in this case? Do you have any underlying prejudice against the defendant in this case? Have you been exposed to any pretrial publicity and/or formulated any opinion about the defendant's guilt or innocence? Would you feel pressured to change your vote if everyone else on the jury voted for conviction but you were not convinced of the defendant's guilt beyond a reasonable doubt? Do you believe in capital punishment? Could you render a guilty verdict if it might result in the death penalty?

c. An attorney might use peremptory challenge if he or she believed that a potential juror would not be impartial, even though the attorney may not be able to prove to the judge that the juror is unfit to serve on the jury. For example, for a defendant on trial for a rape, the defense attorney may use peremptory challenges to strike a juror who is visibly uncomfortable when the topic of rape is discussed.

APPEALS COURTS (PP. 49–50)

Learning Outcomes

After completing this section, students should be able to:
1. define the terms *appeals court, error of law, precedent, dissenting opinion*, and *concurring opinion*;
2. describe conditions under which a case can be appealed to higher courts; and
3. distinguish among and explain the functions of majority, concurring, and dissenting opinions.

BACKGROUND—HOW APPEALS WORK

A common misconception about courts is that anyone can appeal a case if he or she does not like the outcome. In reality, the opportunities for successful appeal are limited. The appealing party must point out an error or errors of law in the trial. In addition, the error of law must be so serious that, had it not been made, the appealing party could otherwise have prevailed. Less serious errors of law, that do not determine the outcome, are frequently considered "harmless error."

To help students gain more than a mechanical understanding of the "error of fact" versus "error of law" rule for appeals, review "The Case of Taking the Car by Mistake" on page 50 of the Student Edition. Then, further illustrate the concepts with two examples of baseball disputes. In the first dispute, the batter hits a slow ground ball to the shortstop, who throws to first base just in time to beat the runner. The umpire declares the runner was out. The team at bat objects to the call but cannot protest the umpire's call. The alleged error is one of fact (whether or not the ball beat the runner to first base), not one involving a rule or law. In the second dispute, the batter hits the ball down the left-field line and the ball lands on the white foul line. The umpire says the ball is foul because it hit the foul line. Here, the decision could be appealed. The issue concerns a rule (whether a ball hitting the foul line is, under the rules, fair or foul), not a fact (all agree that the ball hit the line).

Appealing alleged errors of law, but not those of fact, makes sense. From the sports analogies above, the protestors in the second situation can frame an issue (a question of law) that some third party (here, the commissioner of baseball; in the legal system, an appellate court) can decide: does a batted ball's landing on the foul line constitute a fair or foul ball? In the first situation, only the umpire (or trial judge) is in a position to decide the facts of the play (or case).

THE **CASE** OF...

Taking a Car by Mistake (p. 50)

Ask students if appeals courts should take into consideration only errors of law—as in "The Case of Taking a Car by Mistake"—or if they should also consider broader issues of justice and fairness.

Ask students to think back to the beginning of Unit 1 and to consider again the purpose of law. Is the law merely punitive, or does the role of justice or fairness play a part? Ask students to articulate the purpose of the appeals process from the perspective of fairness or justice. Remind them that mitigating factors could include the insanity plea or a situation in which a judge vacates (annuls) a decision of a jury he or she feels is unfair.

STATE AND FEDERAL COURT SYSTEMS (PP. 50–54)

Learning Outcomes

After completing this section, students should be able to:
1. define the term *probate*;
2. list various types of courts and explain the types of cases they deal with; and
3. classify cases according to jurisdiction of specific courts.

BACKGROUND—STRUCTURE OF THE COURT SYSTEMS

Direct students to Figures 5.1 and 5.2 in the Student Edition. Discuss the two graphics to help students understand the two separate court systems (state and federal) and the organization of circuit courts in the United States. Students should know the names and locations of the trial and appellate courts in their state. Most cases are heard in state courts, as opposed to the federal court system. Over the last decade many state courts have become overcrowded. Some feel this is because "state courts are increasingly becoming social service providers."[4] "The justice system—which was created as a last stop for resolving disputes that could not be settled elsewhere—is being asked to resolve complex societal problems (such as domestic relations problems) it was not designed to handle."[5] Several organizations are working to come up with solutions to this overcrowding. The National Center for State Courts and the American Bar Association are two such groups. They are studying ways in which technological advances, arbitration, mediation, etc., can improve state court efficiency and accessibility.

With respect to Figure 5.2, there are eleven regions covered by federal courts of appeal. In addition, there is a D.C. Circuit Court of Appeals and a Federal Circuit Court of Appeals, both located in Washington, D.C. The D.C. Circuit, similar to the other circuit courts, handles appeals from the federal district court. The Federal Circuit handles cases involving actions against the U.S. government, public contracts, and patents. It also hears appeals from the Court of International Trade, the Patent and Trademark Office, and other federal administrative agencies.

CAPTION ANSWER (P. 51)   Both state and federal court systems have an appeals process that can lead up to the Supreme Court of the United States. However, state courts are courts of general jurisdiction (they can hear cases dealing with state or federal law), while federal courts are courts of limited jurisdiction (they are limited to deciding certain types of cases).

Investigating the Law Where You Live

(p. 51) The website for the National Center for State Courts will help students learn about courts in their community, the types of cases those courts handle, how appeals are handled in their state, and basic information about the highest court in their state. Have students visit www.ncsc.org, and choose the called "Information & Resources" and then "Browse By State." As students investigate, suggest they look for a diagram of their state's court system. If they cannot find one, suggest they create their own diagram and share it with the class.

Investigating the Law Where You Live

(p. 52) Have students use the map on page 53 of the Student Edition to determine which circuit they are in. They can use the same map to figure out which federal court handles appeals from federal trial courts in their community.

PROBLEM 5.3 (p. 53)

a. A case in which one state sues another state can be tried in a federal district court and then appealed to a U.S. Circuit Court of Appeals. Such a case can also be tried before the U.S. Supreme Court, which may have original jurisdiction in this instance.[6]

b. Divorce cases are heard in state court (municipal or county court) and may be appealed to the state's court of appeals or directly to the state supreme court (in those states without an intermediate court of appeals).

c. An assault charge would be tried in either a state or local criminal court and could then be appealed to the state court of appeals.

d. Since both drivers are from the same state, the case will be tried in local or state court. It can be appealed to the state's court of appeals or, in smaller states, to the state's supreme court.

CAPTION ANSWER (P. 53)   Students' answers will vary.

BACKGROUND—INDEPENDENT COURTS AND THE ELECTION OF JUDGES

Like much of the U.S. system of government, the system of judicial independence was inherited from Great Britain. In the 1600s the king or queen could assign judges to the bench and then remove them summarily if they did not represent the sovereign's interests. In 1689, the English Bill of Rights was established, which provided judges a measure of constitutional protection, including the promise that they would not be removed if they showed "good behavior." The U.S. Constitution provides in Article III that "Judges, both of the supreme and inferior Courts, shall hold their Offices during good Behaviour." This term has been interpreted to protect judges from being removed at the political whims of executive or legislative officeholders.

Many critics say that the process of electing judges undermines the important principle of judicial independence. Such elections, they say, require campaigning and fundraising—potentially placing judicial candidates under debts and obligations to individuals, political parties, politicians, corporations, and interest groups. These critics say that when seeking financial support, the election process makes judges prey to the pressure for favors, conditions, and deals that all elected officials face. To ensure future elections, judges may feel compelled to issue rulings favorable to parties who they know support them. Even the impression of such favoritism tarnishes the principle of judicial independence.

Not everyone shares these concerns. Opinion polls show that a large proportion of the American public has confidence in the courts as they now exist. However, members of minority groups and other disadvantaged Americans tend to have less confidence in the courts. As for the legal profession's opinion on the issue, the American Bar Association stated in a report that while some of the concerns regarding judicial elections are merited, "the current state of judicial independence is relatively sound." In 2015, the U.S. Supreme Court heard a case involving the same issues as those presented in this problem. In the case of *Williams-Yulee* v. *Florida Bar*, (U.S. Supreme Court, No. 13-1499) the Court considered this question: Is it a violation of the First Amendment for a state to ban candidates for elected judicial office from soliciting donations themselves? The Supreme Court ruled that Florida's rule banning solicitation of donations by judicial candidates did not violate the First Amendment. Because the public must have faith that the judiciary is fair and acts with integrity in order to trust the system, the government had a compelling interest in restricting the candidates' speech. The Court said the rule specifically targeted the speech that could give the appearance of corruption, and that the rule still left open other ways for the candidates to speak. Therefore, it was constitutional.

Independent Courts (p. 54)

a. It is not uncommon for those running for the office of state judge to ask individuals and corporations for campaign contributions. However, if Mr. Sanchez makes a contribution and Marsha Monroe wins, it would not be proper for Judge Monroe to hear any cases involving Sanchez, members of his family, or his corporation. This is because the judge's ruling might reflect more favorably the point of view of the party who supported her election.

b. In our system of checks and balances, the Congress controls the "purse strings" of the government, including the budget of federal courts so the Congress could reduce the overall budget. However, Congress cannot reduce the salaries of justices or federal judges. Article III of the U.S. Constitution states: "The judges, both of the supreme and inferior courts... shall, at stated times, receive for their services, a compensation, which shall not be diminished during their continuance in office." Therefore it would be unconstitutional for their salaries to be reduced.

c. A distant cousin, unless the judge happens to have a close relationship with this particular relative, is not likely to influence the ruling in this case. However, if the party who loses to the corporation learns of this connection, it may constitute an appearance of favoritism. Some would argue that the judge should recuse (excuse) himself from this case to avoid this appearance of injustice.

d. Unless these sentences are illegal under the sentencing laws of the state, or it can be proven that the judge gave these sentences only because of the upcoming election, it is doubtful that the judge's decisions will be overturned on appeal. However, this example points out the potential problems with electing judges, because some may do what they think the voters want and not what they believe the law requires.

TRIBAL COURTS (P. 55)

Learning Outcomes

After completing this section, students should be able to:
1. define the terms *inherent powers* and *delegated powers* in the context of tribal courts and give examples of each; and
2. explain which court(s) have jurisdiction over criminal and civil matters that take place on reservations.

BACKGROUND—JURISDICTIONS

Tribal courts have jurisdiction over tribal members and other Native Americans and Alaska Natives.[7] Tribal courts may have jurisdiction over non–Native Americans in some circumstances,[8] but it should not be assumed. Tribal courts never have criminal jurisdiction over non–Native Americans.[9] State jurisdiction over Native Americans and Alaska Natives varies from reserva-

tion to reservation. State courts always have jurisdiction over Native Americans who are off the
reservations. Except for the few exclusively federal
jurisdictional reservations, state courts also have
jurisdiction over non–Native Americans who are on
the reservations.

CAPTION ANSWER (P. 55) Several hundred Native
American tribal groups operate as semi-autonomous nations within
the United States. These "domestic dependent nations," as the U.S.
government refers to them, retain certain legal authority over their
respective reservations.

ACTIVITY—RESEARCHING

Ask students to find out whether there are any
tribal courts in their state. If so, ask students to
explain what types of cases the tribal courts have
jurisdiction over. For help finding which types of
courts exist in your state (including tribal courts)
direct students to www.ncsc.org/Information-and-
Resources/Browse-by-State/State-Court-Websites.
aspx.

MILITARY COURTS (PP. 55–56)

Learning Outcomes

After completing this section, students should be
able to:

1. name the set of laws that are unique to the
   military;
2. describe the purposes of military courts and
   tribunals; and
3. identify which branch of government has the
   authority to write the Uniform Code of
   Military Justice.

BACKGROUND

Military courts in the United States derive their
power from Article I, Section 8 of the Constitution and
from the Congress, which wrote its special set of laws
known as the Uniform Code of Military Justice (UCMJ).
All service members take an oath to uphold the UCMJ.

Students may be surprised to learn that actions that
may be legal in civilian life could be crimes under the
UCMJ. Ask students to speculate about why there
might be differences in military and civilian laws. (For
example, service members must live and work where
they are told. They must be respectful, obey orders, and
risk their lives when ordered to do so.)

You may want to point out to students the following differences:

- While service members are protected by the
  Constitution's First Amendment, according to
  the UCMJ, their freedom of speech may be
  more limited. Commissioned officers can be
  court-martialed if they "use contemptuous
  words against the President, the Vice
  President, Congress, the Secretary of
  Defense," and several other specifically titled
  people (UCMJ Article 88). Ask students why
  there might be more restrictions on free
  speech for service members.
- Service members are also protected the
  Fourth Amendment to the Constitution; however, the military has more latitude in
  searches and seizures. For example, the military can conduct inspections of living spaces,
  entry and exit to working area (or base), and
  there are more situations when a warrant is
  not necessary to conduct a search.

If your school is near a military base and your students are interested in military law, you may consider inviting a Navy JAG lawyer to speak with your
students.

ACTIVITY—DELIBERATING MILITARY
TRIBUNALS AT GUANTANAMO BAY

The Response is a short film (about 25 minutes)
that depicts a hearing of an alleged enemy combatant
held at Guantanamo Bay. The script is based on
actual transcripts of secret hearings held there and is
considered a fair and accurate depiction of the workings of the military court there. The film and lessons
written by Street Law prompt students to determine
how to balance the rights of detainees with national
security interests. To order a copy, go to: https://store.
streetlaw.org/the-response-dvd-and-lesson-plans/

THE SUPREME COURT OF THE UNITED
STATES (PP. 56–59)

Learning Outcomes

After completing this section, students should
be able to:

1. describe the benefits of having the courts
   follow precedent and adhere to stare decisis;
2. describe the process for appealing cases to
   the Supreme Court;
3. define the terms *due process, petition for
   certiorari,* and *stare decisis;* and
4. explain the types of cases which are likely to
   be granted certiorari by the Supreme Court.

PROBLEM 5.4 (p. 56)

a. The precedent set by the Supreme Court in the *Gideon* case was that any indigent defendant (someone who cannot afford an attorney) charged with a felony (a crime punishable by imprisonment of more than one year) must be provided with a lawyer at the state's expense.[10] All courts must follow Supreme Court decisions.

b. If the case was decided by the state Supreme Court, the precedent would have to be followed by the lower courts in that particular state.

c. The precedent in the *Gideon* case did not answer the question as to whether a defendant charged with a misdemeanor must be provided a free attorney. In 1972, however, the Supreme Court ruled that an attorney must be provided in all cases before a prison term can be imposed.[11] The *Gideon* opinion does not apply to criminal cases where no prison term is possible or to civil cases, and the Supreme Court has never guaranteed the right to an attorney to persons sued in a civil case.

Additional online activities and resources related to the *Gideon* case and other Supreme Court landmark cases are available through a joint project of Street Law, Inc., and the Supreme Court Historical Society at https://www.landmarkcases.org/.

CAPTION ANSWER (P. 57) Except for a small number of "original jurisdiction" cases which is must hear, the Supreme Court sets its own agenda, usually deciding to hear a case when there is a difference in rulings among lower courts on the issue presented. The Court also grants petitions for certiorari to cases concerning national issues where a ruling appears necessary or appropriate.

BACKGROUND AND RESOURCES— THE SUPREME COURT

Street Law, Inc and several other organizations offer excellent resources for teachers, students, and the general public to learn about and to follow the actions of the Supreme Court. These are among the best:

- www.scotusblog.com has daily features, articles about cases the Court is considering taking, live blogs by journalists who are present when the Court announces decisions, statistics about the Court, plain English versions of Court opinions and much more
- www.oyez.org is a law school-based website designed for the public. It includes short, easy-to-read summaries of each decision, the briefs, case announcements and audio recordings of oral arguments
- www.supremecourtus.gov is the Court's official website
- www.streetlaw.org has more than 100 Supreme Court cases summarized in a case study format as well as a wide array of free lesson plans for teachers.

TAKING ACTION: LAW AND DEMOCRACY

Who Should Be on the Supreme Court?

PROBLEM 5.5 (p. 59)

There is little question that U.S. Supreme Court decisions have wide-ranging impact on people throughout the country. The justices are not elected, nor are they accountable to any person, only the U.S. Constitution. Some argue that the judiciary has become the strongest of the three branches of government. For these reasons, there is much debate and popular discussion of who should be appointed to the Court.

Presidential nominations to the Court have become a significant issue in presidential campaigns. The role of the Senate in confirming nominations, which can act as a check on the appointment power of the president, has also become more visible. The Robert Bork and Clarence Thomas hearings were particularly controversial, prompting subsequent appointments of more mainstream candidates (Bork's nomination was not confirmed; Thomas's was). Ask students what issues should be explored in nomination hearings and if any should constitute "litmus tests" (as abortion has in recent years). Ask students to describe the moral values a Supreme Court justice should possess. Should justices be held to a higher moral standard than other government officials? Why or why not? What social values do Americans seem to be imposing on nominees? Are they relevant to the responsibilities of a justice?

a. This problem presents an excellent opportunity to integrate writing into social studies. Answers will vary. Students' suggestions will include a variety of favorable characteristics to consider, including a reputation for fairness, intellectual power, an unblemished personal record, good health, substantial legal experience, political views in sympathy with the president's, and writing and communication skills. The president may also consider whether the potential judge is of a particular racial group, ethnic group, or gender that could provide balance and a broad experience base to the Court. Age might also be a factor. Since justices serve a life term, the president might wish to nominate someone who will be able to serve on the Court for many years in the future to carry on the president's legacy.

b. Students' opinions will vary about whether these characteristics are important. The characteristics should provide for a lively class discussion, "take a stand" activity, or small-group exercise.

c. Answers will vary. This question poses a core dilemma for elected officials: should their votes reflect the wishes of the people they serve or should they vote according to their own best (experienced) judgment? If this particular senator is personally opposed to abortion (while his or her constituents support the right to choose an abortion), the dilemma becomes even more complicated. As students reach their own conclusions, be sure they weigh how important the judge's overall reputation is compared to the judge's potential influence over this issue of abortion rights.

INTERNATIONAL COURTS (P. 60)

CAPTION ANSWER (P. 60) The International Court of Justice may settle any dispute based on international law.

ACTIVITY—RESEARCHING INTERNATIONAL COURTS

Students may be interested in learning about international courts and the cases before those courts.

Information about the International Court of Justice including jurisdiction, pending cases, and important documents of international law can be found at https://www.icj-cij.org/en. Similar information the about the International Criminal Court is available at https://www.icc-cpi.int/.

NOTES

(1) "Dane County Court Grant to Improve Jury Diversity," *Wisconsin Lawyer*, March 2001.

(2) *Batson* v. *Kentucky*, 476 U.S. 79 (1986).

(3) *J.E.B.* v. *Alabama Ex Rel T.B.*, 511 U.S. 127 (1994).

(4) Thomas Henderson, "Helping Swamped State Courts Cope With Change," *Washington Post* (January 1, 1994): A4.

(5) R. William Ide, III. "ABA 'Public Jury' to Consider Reforms in Legal System," *Washington Post* (January 1, 1994): A4.

(6) U.S. Constitution, Art. III, Section 2.

(7) 25 U.S.C. 1301.

(8) *Strate* v. *A-1 Contractors*, 520 U.S. 438 (1997).

(9) *U.S.* v. *McBratney*, 104 U.S. 621 (1882); *Oliphant* v. *Suguamish Indian Tribe*, 435 U.S. 1919 (1975).

(10) *Gideon* v. *Wainwright*, 372 U.S. 335 (1963).

(11) *Argersenger* v. *Hamlin*, 407 U.S. 25 (1972).

networks™

One of the goals of *Street Law* is to help students learn to identify ways they can avoid legal problems and resolve some legal problems on their own. Still, in the course of a lifetime, many people will need to hire a lawyer to help them understand and navigate the legal system. This chapter provides an introduction to deciding when you need a lawyer, how to find the right one, how to work most effectively with a lawyer, the professional and ethical rules lawyers must follow, and how people become lawyers.

ADDITIONAL RESOURCES

Teaching this chapter provides an excellent opportunity to bring a lawyer or judge into your classroom to co-teach lessons in law. Street Law, Inc., strongly recommends that you ask these resource persons not to prepare a lecture, but instead to engage students in interactive activities. If you or a lawyer in your community are interested in interactive lessons written specifically for lawyers, judges, and law school students, visit www.streetlaw.org.

WHEN DO YOU NEED A LAWYER? (PP. 61–63)

Learning Outcomes

After completing this section, students should be able to:
1. name at least five situations in which a person might wish to consult an attorney;
2. analyze a situation to determine whether or not a person involved should hire a lawyer; and
3. define the terms *litigator* and *bar association*.

BACKGROUND—USING LEGAL SERVICES

Students should not confuse helpful advice from trusted friends or teachers with legal advice from a trained and licensed attorney. Certain situations require the assistance of legal counsel. When it is essential to seek professional advice, it is important to do so early enough to avoid aggravating a problem.

This section introduces strategies for careful consumer shopping for legal services. Just as consumers sometimes have problems with goods they purchase, they may also experience problems with services such as legal assistance. The material in this section should make students more careful, effective, and assertive consumers of legal services.

CAPTION ANSWER (P. 62) A lawyer could help someone involved in a car accident, especially if injury and damages are significant, by explaining the person's legal rights and responsibilities. If a lawsuit results from the accident, a lawyer could represent either the defendant or the plaintiff.

a. As long as your insurance company agrees to handle the cost of all personal injuries and property damage, there is no need to retain counsel. However, if you are sued for more than the amount of your insurance coverage, you may wish to hire an attorney.

b. This problem can probably be resolved informally if your friend agrees to explain the situation to the police. However, if you are arrested and booked before the situation is clarified, you may need an attorney to help you expunge (erase) your arrest record.

c. The law implies a warranty that may still be in effect beyond the dates of the written guarantee. The buyer in this case can seek assistance from local consumer protection agencies or sue in small claims court. An attorney is probably not required to resolve this problem and hiring one may cost more than the price of the laptop.

d. Car buyers need good advice, but not necessarily from an attorney. Your bank may be able to provide assistance in reading the contract of sale and the financing agreement. A good mechanic's advice is also invaluable.

e. You would definitely want an attorney in this situation, since you will probably be charged with a serious crime. Even though you did not take part in the robbery, if the charges are true, you may be liable for criminal conspiracy or as an accessory to the crime.

f. Before hiring an attorney, you could contact the Equal Employment Opportunity Commission (EEOC) or a local human rights commission. They may be able to mediate a resolution. If not, an attorney who specializes in employment or discrimination law may be able to help you determine whether and how to bring suit.

g. You should hire a lawyer who specializes in wills. He or she can help you spell out in a legal document to whom you want the contents of your estate to go. If you do not have a valid will specifying where you want the money to go, your estate will be distributed according to your state intestacy laws (laws that deal with how to manage a person's estate if he or she dies without a will), which may result in your family inheriting your savings.

h. If there are contested issues that involve such matters as child support, custody, alimony, or property division, you should consult an attorney. If there are no contested issues, you may wish to handle the divorce yourself. You should ask your local family court clerk about whether you can file the divorce papers pro se (on your own behalf). Chapter 32, "Separation, Divorce, and Custody," provides a detailed discussion of divorce.

i. You usually do not need a lawyer to file your federal income tax return. Individuals with complex tax-planning issues (often involving estates and trusts) may wish to consult a tax lawyer. However, a tax accountant or bank can also assist with this type of planning. If you have questions about preparing and filing your tax return and want free assistance, you can contact the Internal Revenue Service (IRS). In addition, many private businesses or organizations offer tax return preparation assistance for a fee. If you are audited and cannot satisfactorily resolve a tax problem on your own, you may wish to hire a tax lawyer.

HOW DO YOU FIND A LAWYER? (PP. 63–64)

Learning Outcomes

After completing this section, students should be able to:

1. assess the positive and negative effects of advertisements by lawyers;
2. evaluate whether or not advertising by lawyers is proper or improper in given case scenarios;
3. explain how to find and retain suitable legal counsel; and

(p. 63) To find local and state bar associations, have students visit the American Bar Association at www. americanbar.org. Students who are interested in minority bar associations can click on "National Minority Bar Associations." Another useful part of the ABA website at https://www.americanbar.org/groups/legal_services/ provides a national directory of lawyers, referrals, and information about how to get free legal help.

CAPTION ANSWER (P. 64) Many people claim that the best way to find an experienced lawyer is through the recommendation of someone who had a similar legal problem that was resolved to his or her satisfaction.

BACKGROUND—LAWYERS AND ADVERTISING

Considerable controversy surrounds the issue of lawyers and advertising. The history of legal advertising dates to 1908 when the American Bar Association banned an advertisement, ruling it was unethical and undignified. In the 1977 case of *Bates v. State Bar of Arizona*,[1] the U.S. Supreme Court held that while the First Amendment prohibits bar association policies from suppressing all attorney advertising, regulations could limit advertising in certain instances. The Court found that reasonable time, place, and manner restrictions may be placed on attorney advertisements. For example, ads that are false, deceptive, or misleading can be banned. Since then, an increasing number of attorneys have used advertising in newspapers, on television, on the radio, and on the Internet to attract clients. The trend toward targeted online advertising is rapidly growing. As a group, lawyers spend millions of dollars each year on advertising.

Some people feel that consumers profit from legal advertising. It not only makes them more aware of the services offered, but it enables them to price services, in turn encouraging lawyers to keep their fees competitive. Despite its advantages, most lawyers agree that the best way to find a good attorney is through referral by a trusted friend.

PROBLEM 6.2 (p.64)

Ask students to analyze the advertisements they find using the following questions.

1. What claims does the attorney make about his/her services?
2. Does the advertisement give information about the attorney's fees?
3. Are graphics or photos used? If so, in what way? Are they effective?
4. Who is the intended audience for this advertisement?

When students have finished analyzing the advertisements, use the following questions to conduct a class discussion:

- What overall impressions do you have of the advertisements?
- Are your impressions good? Bad? Mixed?
- Do any of the advertisements motivate you to hire one particular lawyer or law firm over another? If so, what were the compelling features of the advertisement?
- If you were a lawyer, would you advertise? Why or why not?

Ask students to compile a list of advantages and disadvantage to advertising. Answers will vary, but some advantages of advertising might be that it makes consumers aware of the services offered and perhaps the fees, keeps fees competitive, allows consumers to compare law firms. Some disadvantages might be that advertising turns attorneys into sales people giving them an incentive to exaggerate their claims. Advertising also might encourage consumers to choose the attorney with the slickest advertisements instead of the best attorney for their situation.

BACKGROUND—LEGAL SERVICES FOR INDIGENT DEFENDANTS

As noted in Chapter 5, the U.S. Supreme Court has ruled that indigent criminal defendants are entitled to counsel in felony cases[3] and in misdemeanor cases in which a prison term can be imposed.[4] However, free legal counsel is not constitutionally required in civil cases or in criminal cases where no prison time is possible (fine only).[5]

In 1974 President Richard Nixon signed a law creating the Legal Services Corporation (LSC). Congress funded the LSC at the minimum access levels of two full-time poverty lawyers for every 10,000 poor people in need. This action recognized special needs populations with unique barriers to the justice system, including migrant workers, Native Americans, and people confined in institutions. There have been numerous attempts to eliminate all federal funding for civil legal services and to limit the types of cases handled (e.g., class action lawsuits).

ACTIVITY—FIELD TRIP OR LEGAL RESOURCE PERSON

Locate and visit the organizations in your community that offer free or reduced-cost legal services. If that is not possible, invite an attorney from a legal services organization to address your class. Students should interview the attorney to obtain answers to these questions: Who is eligible for these services? What kinds of cases do they handle? How long must one wait to get an appointment? Will they provide representation equal to that provided by privately paid attorneys? If a client feels that the attorney provided by the office is not doing a good job, what can he or she do?

Many people are concerned about the quality of representation provided for people entitled to public defenders. Because so many public defenders have such large caseloads, some people fear they do not have as much time to devote to each case as they would if they were working for a private client who could pay more. Discuss with students whether the premise is true, that is, whether we are facing a system of justice in which defendants who can pay are more likely to be found innocent or to face lesser penalties.

In 2004, the National Committee on the Right to Counsel was formed to examine whether the U.S. criminal justice system provides adequate lawyers and legal representation to defendants who cannot afford to hire and pay lawyers themselves. This bipartisan national committee also makes recommendations for system improvements. The committee includes judges, prosecutors, legal aid lawyers, law enforcers, and policy makers. To learn more about the extent of the problem and recommendations for various states and localities, visit the websites of two organizations who are helping to lead the project: The Constitution Project (www. constitutionproject.org) and The National Legal Aid and Defender Association (http://www. nlada100years.org).

BECOMING A LAWYER (P. 65)

Learning Outcomes

After completing this section, students should be able to:
1. Describe the path to becoming a lawyer in the United States;
2. Explain the importance of state bar exams; and
3. Use resources such as the Law School Admission Council's website to find more information on applying to law school.

DISCUSSION – DIVERSITY IN LAW SCHOOLS

Many law schools encourage diverse applicants, and make it a goal to increase diversity in classes. Ask students to explain what groups might offer diversity. Answers should include racially and ethnically diverse candidates, LGBTQ candidates, candidates from various ages, geographical areas, career backgrounds, socioeconomic statuses, and candidates with disabilities. Ask students why it might be important for law schools to have a diverse student body. Answers might include that diverse students bring diverse perspectives, life experiences, and skills.

Ask students what opposition might be raised if a law school gave preference to diverse candidates in admissions. Students might reference "reverse discrimination" and cases in which less diverse students with higher GPAs and LSAT scores were not admitted. You may wish to explain the case of *Grutter* v. *Bollinger* (2003) brought by a white student who was denied admission to the University of Michigan Law School alleging that the school's policy favored diverse students in violation of the Equal Protection Clause. In this case the Supreme Court ruled that the law school did not violate the Constitution in using its narrowly tailored system of giving preference to diverse applicants because it had a compelling interest in increasing diversity.

ACTIVITY – LSAT PRACTICE QUESTIONS

Students can explore the types of questions on the LSAT exam by visiting the Law School Admissions Council's website at https://www.lsac. org/lsat. There are short videos on each type of question (reading comprehension, analytical reasoning, logical reasoning, and the writing sample) as well as general LSAT prep. There is also a sample test available. Consider selecting a few questions of each type and having students attempt them first individually, and then in pairs. Review the correct answers. Afterward, discuss why these types of questions might be used to assess a student's likelihood of succeeding in law school.

ACTIVITY – FINDING THE RIGHT FIELD OF LAW

Explain to students that not all careers in law require law school and that not everyone may be interested in law as a career. However, for this activity, ask students to assume that they are planning on pursuing law. There are many fields of law they may choose from. Instruct students to take the interest quiz at https://www.lsac.org/discover-law/pathways-legal-career/quiz. The quiz results will suggest fields of law the student might be interested in. After seeing their results, ask students to investigate their top three matches and any others on the list that interest them at https://www.lsac.org/discover-law/pathways-legal-career/fields-law. Discuss as a large group the accuracy of the interest quiz in identifying their true interests. Conclude by having students write a journal entry about the field/s of law they would most like to pursue and their reasons why.

PROBLEM 6.3

a. People who graduate from law school and pass the bar exam can work in many areas of law, business, government, academia and more. Some examples include: public defender, prosecutor, private practice criminal defense or civil attorney, jury/trial consultant, agent, real estate attorney, patent attorney, judge, immigration attorney, government employee (EPA, EEOC, Department of Justice, etc.), judicial clerk, human rights or civil rights advocate, arbitrator/mediator, congressional aide, lobbyist, teacher or professor. This is not an exhaustive list. A short video entitled "Discover what a law degree can do for you" is available at https://www.lsac.org/discover-law.

b. Some obstacles to becoming a lawyer can be getting into law school, paying for law school, and passing the bar exam. Depending on the year, somewhere between 50% and 60% of law school applicants are accepted. In general, a high undergraduate GPA and LSAT scores are necessary. According to U.S. News and World Report in 2018, three years of law school at a public-school costs $26,264 for in-state students, a private institution costs on average of $43,020, and just one year at a top 10 law school was $60,293. Less than three-fourths of law school graduates pass a state bar examination on their first attempt.

NOTES

(1) *Bates* v. *State Bar of Arizona*, 433 U.S. 350 (1977).

(2) *Shapero* v. *Kentucky Bar Association*, 486 U.S. 466 (1988).

(3) *Gideon* v. *Wainwright*, 372 U.S. 335 (1963).

(4) *Argersinger* v. *Hamlin*, 407 U.S. 25 (1972).

(5) *Lassiter* v. *Department of Social Services*, 452 U.S. 18 (1981).

UNIT 2
Criminal Law and Juvenile Justice

networks™

Unit 2 provides an overview of criminal law. It explores the nature of crime; current issues in criminal law, including gangs, guns, and computer crimes; and a variety of crimes and defenses. Students learn about the criminal justice process from the investigation phase through sentencing and corrections. The unit also explores the juvenile justice system and the debate over whether juveniles should be treated differently than adults.

CHAPTERS IN BRIEF

CHAPTER 7
Crime in America
Chapter 7 provides an overview of crime in the United States, describing the nature and causes of crime and looking at the relationships between gangs, guns, alcohol, drugs, and crime.

CHAPTER 8
Introduction to Criminal Law
Chapter 8 introduces students to the study of criminal law. It also discusses categories of crimes such as state and federal crimes, crimes of omission, preliminary crimes, misdemeanors, and felonies.

CHAPTERS 9–10
Crimes Against the Person
Crimes Against Property
Chapters 9–10 contain information on crimes against persons and crimes against property, including computer crime.

CHAPTER 11
Defenses
Chapter 11 describes the defenses available to people accused of a crime.

CHAPTERS 12–15
Criminal Justice Process
Chapters 12–15 deal with the criminal justice process—from the rules that police must follow when conducting arrests, through the proceedings that occur before trial and the constitutional protections that shape the trial itself, to issues dealing with sentencing and corrections.

CHAPTER 16
Juvenile Justice
Chapter 16 looks at the operation of the juvenile justice system and the special challenges it faces in dealing with young people who commit serious and violent crimes. The chapter also describes each step in the process as offenders move through juvenile court.

SERVICE LEARNING AND SPECIAL PROJECTS

1. **Court Visitation:** Arrange for students to observe judges, lawyers, defendants, witnesses, and juries in court. Ask students to note their impressions of each of the participants in the criminal procedures and whether those procedures represent what the students expected. For example, did they observe the rights of the victims and defendants being protected in the trial? This activity can be done as an introduction to the unit or as a summary activity at the end of the unit of study.

2. **Research Project:** Students could conduct crime and victimization surveys to determine whether other young people are taking measures to prevent crime.

3. **Interview:** Students could interview legal resource persons about their jobs, including qualifications, educational requirements, application process, salary, duties, rewards, and challenges. After students complete their interview, ask them to report back to the class about what they learned.

4. **Service Learning:** While community service is educational and meaningful on many levels, service learning takes it to "the next level" by connecting service with classroom learning and reflection. The following activities are suggested to help students enhance what they learn in Unit 2 by serving their communities.

   • Students can start a school crime watch program or a neighborhood watch program. For guidance, they might want to speak to their school resource officer or to a community-based police officer who specializes in neighborhood watch programs.

   • Students can participate in crime prevention education programs and teach their peers, younger students, neighbors and/or elderly people the skills to help them avoid becoming victims of crime.

   • Students can work with an advocacy group that reflects their own views about the rights of people who are crime victims and/or the rights of people who are accused of crime.

   • Students can develop and distribute a pamphlet or poster that lists contact information for local organizations that help victims of crime.

   • Students can start an anti-graffiti campaign to bring attention to the costs of graffiti to the community, to replace graffiti with (sanctioned) art from students, and to restore property that has been vandalized.

   • Students can present a mock trial of a criminal law issue for younger students. Older students might also help younger students conduct their own mock criminal trials. One popular method is to put fairy-tale characters (characters that most young children would know) on trial.

   • Students can establish a youth court or volunteer with an existing youth court in their school or community.

UNIT RESOURCES

Using Legal Resource Persons

One of the "best practices" in law-related education is to invite outside resource people to co-teach lessons in your classroom. These guests should not be asked or expected to lecture on a topic, but to engage students in interactive activities that showcase student work with the guidance of an expert. It is ideal to ask a particular resource person to work with the same group of students repeatedly.

1. Police officers and school resource officers can lead students in activities about crime, law enforcement policies, and the criminal justice process, in particular arrest, search, and interrogation. They can also assist in acting out some of the role-plays that appear in this unit.

2. FBI agents or other federal officers, such as drug enforcement agents, border patrol, or secret service agents, can assist students in activities which include the elements, enforcement, and prosecution of federal crimes.

3. Invite local public defenders to discuss the defense of accused criminals, including plea bargaining, trials, and sentencing. An assistant district attorney could discuss the prosecution of criminals. Other attorneys with criminal and/or juvenile justice experience are also valuable resources.

4. Juvenile and criminal probation and parole officers can describe the probation and/or parole process.

5. Correctional personnel can describe the theory and practice of local adult and juvenile facilities, jails, and prisons.

networks™

THE NATURE OF CRIMES (PP. 68–73)

Learning Outcomes

After completing this section, students should be able to:

1. explain who determines what constitutes a crime and the goals for designating crimes;
2. debate the seriousness of various actions to determine what should be designated a crime;
3. interpret trends in the number of crimes reported, arrests made, and who are the victims of crime in the United States;
4. compare various theories about the causes of crime;
5. evaluate methods of reducing crime; and
6. define the terms *crime, incarceration,* and *community policing.*

A crime is the violation of a law established to protect people and maintain an orderly society. People everywhere are affected by crime; however, certain factors such as age, gender, and location influence the likelihood of becoming a victim of crime. Authorities disagree over the causes of crime. Some argue that poverty, unemployment, lack of education, gangs and gang activity, drug and alcohol abuse, and inadequate police protection are to blame. They believe that working to end these problems would lead to a decrease in crime rates.

PROBLEM 7.1 (p.69)

This problem does not have a correct answer because it asks students to express their opinions. The problem provides an opportunity to examine the sometimes unclear line between legal—though perhaps immoral—behavior and a criminal act. Have students work in groups of three or four to place each act on the continuum from the most serious to least serious crimes (see 7.1 TM Figure). Remind them to place the crimes on the continuum based on how serious they think each one should be, not on how serious the law says it is. Each group should be prepared to explain its placements.

As students are working in their groups, project or post a spectrum like the one in **7.1 TM Figure** below. Invite a representative from each group to put their placements on the class continuum. Ask the groups to analyze and compare the responses of other groups. Ask students to explain their reasons for the relative placement of acts along the spectrum.

You can also use this activity to further explore the relationship between the law and morality. For example, leaving the store with too much change (**f.**) or observing a friend committing a crime but not reporting it (**k.**) may both be immoral but not necessarily illegal.

Tie students' reasons for their rankings to the policy considerations that legislators make. Facilitate a discussion among students about the relationship between community standards and criminal laws. For example, recreational marijuana use may be illegal because most people in a community think it is wrong, but there are some communities where it is not illegal. To conclude the activity, you may wish to have students research whether or not each act is a crime in your state and the penalty each crime carries. A prosecutor, criminal defense lawyer, or police officer, could all serve as resources for this part of the assignment.

a. Larceny/theft was the most commonly reported crime in 2017.

b. Arrests occurred in approximately 20 percent of the total reported crimes in 2017.

c. Murder and non-negligent manslaughter are the crimes for which people were most likely to be arrested. Motor vehicle theft is the index crime for which people were least likely to be arrested. Students' answers will vary about why certain crimes result in arrest more or less often. It may be because more resources are expended solving the most serious crimes against people than solving property crimes.

d. Citizens can help police improve arrest rates by reporting crimes they observe, taking notice of people and things that are out of place in the community, and being willing to come forward to serve as witnesses. Also, citizens can support police efforts to be involved in the community, organize neighborhood watch programs, and support funding issues for law enforcement.

FIGURE

7.1 TM Figure

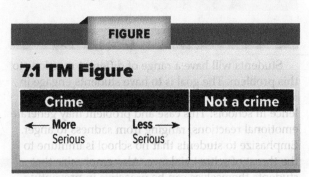

Crime		Not a crime
← **More** Serious	**Less** → Serious	

CAPTION ANSWER (P. 71) Students' answers will vary but may include neighborhood watch programs, improving street lighting, cleaning up vandalism, and increasing community policing.

DISCUSSION—CRIME STATISTICS

Two general factors influence the accuracy of crime statistics: (1) the degree to which victims and others in the community are willing to report crimes, and (2) the ability of the police to keep accurate records. For example, a slight increase in a community's reported crime rate could be caused by greater public trust in the police, resulting in an increased willingness to report crime, and/or better police record keeping, as opposed to an actual increase in crimes committed. Ask students to explain why victims sometimes do not report crimes or cooperate fully with police and prosecutors. Have

students brainstorm consequences for individuals and society when victims and witnesses fail to report crimes.

BACKGROUND—UNDERSTANDING CRIME CLOCKS (WITH FIGURE 7.2)

It is important to emphasize to students as they read a crime clock that they should not infer that a particular crime actually occurs at the given time intervals. The clock simply illustrates the average frequency with which a particular type of crime occurred during a given year. For example, the crime clock in Figure 7.2 says one murder occurred every 30.5 minutes in 2017. This does not mean that someone was killed every 30.5 minutes. It means that during the year, the number murders averaged out to one every 30.5 minutes. Have students consider why statistics might be presented in this way.

The data in Figure 7.2 were collected from the most recent year's Uniform Crime Report available at the time of publication, based on information from the U.S. Department of Justice at http://www.fbi.gov/ucr/ucr.

This site contains more data, including the most recent information about changes in violent crime and property crime; crime volume and rates by region of the country; arrest data; information on crime clearances (i.e., crimes solved); specific data on the index crimes (murder, forcible rape, motor vehicle theft, robbery, aggravated assault, burglary, and larceny); information on hate crimes; and information on the number of sworn law enforcement personnel.

Use the statistics in Figure 7.2 as the basis for a discussion on the causes of crime.

Encourage students to:

1. hypothesize about the reasons people commit the crimes identified by the statistics;

2. identify how each kind of crime harms both individuals and communities; and

3. brainstorm ways to decrease crime rates for each category.

a. On the whole, crimes occurred less frequently in 2017 than in 2009. The most significant decline was burglary which changed from one every 14.3 seconds in 2009 to one every 22.6 seconds in 2017. The most evident pattern is that crime is occurring less frequently.

b. Students' answers will vary. Traditionally, victims of rape are less likely to report the crime than victims of other crimes. However, the increased reporting of rape may reflect that greater resources are being committed to educating the public about rape and to assisting rape victims with greater sensitivity. These factors may encourage more victims to report the crime of forcible rape.

c. Student responses will vary based on where they live. If students are basing their impressions about the rate of crime on media and news coverage, they will likely learn that the media tend to focus on the more serious crimes, although they occur less frequently.

PROBLEM 7.4 (p.73)

A local, state, or federal legislator, police officer, or prosecutor could add interest and insight to the discussion of this question.

a. Students' opinions will vary. Criticism of the National Council on Crime and Delinquency (NCCD) might include that it is "soft" on crime, there should be harsher penalties (i.e., more confinement) for criminals, and that it is unrealistic to expect all communities to have the resources to accomplish NCCD goals.

b. Students' answers will vary. To extend this activity, have students conduct a survey of their family members, other students, police officers, judges, social workers, and other members of the community asking them to rank the causes of crime.

c. Students should discuss the role that each level of government (local, state, and federal) should play in reducing crime and what types of efforts are appropriate for each level of government. For example, local regulation is more appropriate for jaywalking, whereas federal regulation is better suited for dealing with issues such as international terrorism. In many cases, several levels of government may be involved in controlling a particular type of criminal activity. For example, drugs sales in a school might be a local and state issue and part of a larger ring of drug trafficking that requires federal intervention.

CRIME ON CAMPUS (PP. 73–74)

Learning Outcomes

After completing this section, students should be able to:

1. describe the concerns regarding campus safety;
2. explain how the use of drugs and alcohol is related to crimes on campus; and
3. identify the issues related to the adequacy of campus and local services that deal with students.

CAPTION ANSWER (P. 74) Schools may install metal detectors, video surveillance cameras, and use guards and police to monitor the actions of students, teachers, and visitors in the school.

THE CASE OF...

Weapons on Campus

PROBLEM 7.5 (p.75)

Students will have a range of different reactions to this problem. The goal is to have students engage in a thoughtful conversation about the problem of violence in schools. This case and problem may generate emotional reactions, ranging from sadness to anger. Emphasize to students that no school is immune to the threat of school violence. Also emphasize that students themselves can be proactive in preventing violence by reporting suspicious activity, even if they think other kids are joking or would never carry out their threats.

Students may benefit from discussing this problem and their answers to it with leaders in your school. Consider inviting a school counselor, child psychologist, school resource officer, security officer, and/or a school administrator to join the discussion. For additional resources about school violence and bullying, see Chapter 9.

a. Samuel's decision to commit this crime may have been motivated by his feelings of alienation, loneliness, anger, academic failure, and depression.

b. The school could make greater efforts to educate teachers and parents about the warning signs for at-risk youth and provide activities that encourage greater sensitivity among all students. Signs of Samuel's problems included his lack of friends, time spent alone playing violent video games and surfing the Internet, shoplifting, being the object of teasing by other students, and being withdrawn. It could be argued that the counselor had a responsibility to intervene or to contact the parents when efforts to make an appointment failed. Where counseling offices are understaffed and overworked, it may be the school's responsibility to concentrate more resources in this area, particularly given the increase in school violence and disaffected young people. Some schools offer a "newcomers" group, where students who are new to the school can meet friendly peers and adults. These groups can also monitor students' academic progress and attendance. Although many students might not resort to the violence planned by Samuel, many adolescents have similar emotional needs that require professional help.

c. Students' answers will vary.

GANGS AND CRIME (PP. 74–78)

CAPTION ANSWER (P. 76) Gangs in the nineteenth century were composed mainly of adults. They were interested in protecting turf, reputation, and cultural heritage.

ACTIVITY—RESEARCH AND DISCUSSION ABOUT GANGS

Have students visit www.nationalgangcenter. gov, a website hosted by the National Gang Center (which is funded by the U.S. Department of Justice). Direct students to the "Frequently Asked Questions" section (www.nationalgangcenter.gov/FAQs) as well as to the analysis of the latest youth gang survey (https://www.nationalgangcenter.gov/Library/#survey). Ask students to explore the site and to report on the following questions:

- How are youth gangs today different from gangs in the past?
- What factors contributed to the growth of gangs in the past?
- What proportion of crimes can be attributed to gang activity?
- Are females joining gangs in larger numbers than in the past?
- What is the racial and ethnic composition of youth gangs?
- What are the consequences of gang membership? Is it true that they provide protection?
- Why and how do youth leave a gang?

After students conduct their research, invite resource people to hear about and to discuss the student's research. These local resource people could be police officers involved in gang units, prosecutors, defense lawyers, and juvenile correctional institution administrators. Debrief the students' research by asking them if their research is consistent with their own observations or experiences. Ask in what ways gangs affect individuals and communities.

CAPTION ANSWER (P. 77) Several factors put young people at risk for gang involvement: poverty, failure in school, feelings of alienation, substance abuse, family dysfunction, and domestic and community violence.

PROBLEM 7.6 (p.78)

a. Students should share their opinions or observations about whether there is a local gang problem or not. Signs that might indicate that gangs exist in a community include graffiti; people passing coded notes; people using hand signals; and groups of people with symbolic tattoos, clothing with similar symbols, sports team insignia, and distinctive colors.

As students suggest ways to deal with gang problems, they should refer to the list of successful strategies on pages 77–78 of the Student Edition. Additional prevention efforts might include providing extracurricular activities for young people so they are supervised after school; organizing sports teams that provide students with a sense of belonging and family; delivering parenting classes for those who lack the skills necessary for rearing children; conducting drug and gang awareness programs in the schools; and having local professionals come into the schools and describe their careers so that students are exposed to legitimate employment opportunities.

Other responses might include passing and enforcing laws that make it illegal to be a member of a criminal street gang, tougher drug laws, gun control, parental responsibility laws, lowering the age at which a child can be tried as an adult, and confiscating money gangs earn illegally and using it for anti-gang programs. Ask students to evaluate each of these ideas and decide which might violate the Constitution. Emphasize that one difficulty of designing laws targeting gang activities is that it is difficult to define a gang. The definition should not be so inclusive that people's First Amendment rights to express themselves and to associate with others are infringed upon.

The solutions to gang problems require the involvement of every aspect of the community: law enforcement, businesses, community groups, schools, parents and family, and citizens. Examples of cooperative efforts include "positive loitering" by community members to combat gang presence, neighborhood foot patrols, community members videotaping gang activities for the police, community members confronting gang members, identifying gang members to police, or calling police when gang members are present in the area.

In many communities early-intervention has been used successfully. After being charged with his or her first offense, the gang member might be placed in a rehabilitation program to learn about alternatives to gang life. Practical law is sometimes taught to first offenders (not necessarily gang members) in lieu of criminal charges.

b. Students may say that gangs today have a broader age range, more members with prison records or ties to prison inmates, and more technologically advanced weapons. In addition, studies show that gang members commit a disproportionate share of crimes—both violent and nonviolent. Gang members use alcohol and drugs more extensively and are more likely to be involved in drug trafficking.

Gangs operate in a hierarchy with a leader who provides protection and a sense of belonging. There are gang traditions and culture, much like those a family might have. Gangs can provide support, a sense of identity, and pride.

Youths are both pushed and pulled into gangs. Gang membership can enhance prestige or status among friends and provide companionship that pulls in members. Social, economic, and cultural forces push many adolescents into gangs. Protection from other gangs and perceived safety are key motivators for some young people. The

underclass status of minority youth may make gangs particularly appealing for some youth. Feeling socially marginalized, some adolescents join gangs for social relationships that give them a sense of identity. For some young people, gangs provide a way of coping with social adjustment problems. In some communities, young people are recruited or coerced into gangs. Impoverished youth are attracted to the money they can make from gang illicit activity such as selling drugs. A few people are born into gangs as a result of neighborhood traditions and/or their parents' prior gang participation.

c. Students' opinions will vary, depending on whether they accept the stereotypes of gang membership. The definition of gangs on page 76 of the Student Edition does not limit gang membership to people from a certain socioeconomic group. The hypothetical description in this question suggests that teenagers who hang out together to the exclusion of others, who engage in illegal activities, and who encourage one another to commit criminal acts might be considered a gang regardless of their wealth. Encourage students to think critically about what is and is not a "gang" and what the consequences of that label might be. What opportunities to prevent gang activity might be lost if people define gangs too narrowly?

d. Students' answers will vary, but students may debate the extent to which popular culture reflects behavior and to what extent it influences behavior. It is also important to discuss how the media treat images of violence. Are these topics handled in ways that sensitize or desensitize the community to the issues? Are the acts of violence glorified or deplored?

Students who see the media's portrayal of violence or violent computer games as a problem may favor a variety of ways of addressing it. Some people would censor violent material. Other people see this as a restriction of free speech. This group of people might prefer an approach that puts parents, teachers, and community leaders in the role of determining what is appropriate. Some people might advocate requiring label ratings or filtering devices so that parents can make informed decisions about the computer games their children download or play and what their children watch and listen to. Other people see the media as driven by market forces and advocate boycotting products, programs, or sponsors of programs that display violence in an insensitive manner. Still other people believe the federal government must take a more active role through laws passed by Congress or regulations declared by the Federal Communications Commission (FCC).

ACTIVITY—MOOT COURT

Help students conduct a moot court about the case of *Chicago* v. *Morales*,[1] which concerned a city ordinance against loitering that was intended to reduce gang activity. The case was heard by the U.S. Supreme Court in 1998. For suggestions and guidelines about conducting mock trials and moot courts, see the introduction in the front of this Teacher Manual. You may also want to refer to *Street Law's Classroom Guide to Mock Trials and Moot Courts*. It is available from Street Law, Inc. at https://store. streetlaw.org/publications/.

GUNS AND THE LAW (PP. 78–80)

Learning Outcomes

After completing this section, students should be able to:
1. explain the meaning of the Second Amendment to the U.S. Constitution;
2. describe how the U.S. Supreme Court has interpreted gun-control laws in relation to the Second Amendment; and
3. describe various state and federal laws that regulate firearms.

CAPTION ANSWER (P. 79) Laws can control gun possession by imposing reasonable restrictions such as requiring background checks and licenses, but banning guns is a violation of the 2nd Amendment.

THE **CASE** OF...

The Gun Control Law

PROBLEM 7.7 (p.80)

a. There are several schools of thought about what the Second Amendment means. One school of thought focuses on collective rights. According to this interpretation, the Amendment protects the rights of the states to have a militia. If you adopt this interpretation, the D.C. law does not violate the Constitution. Another school of thought

focuses on individual rights. According to this interpretation, the Amendment protects the rights of individuals to bear arms. In June 2008, the U.S. Supreme Court decided the case of *District of Columbia* v. *Heller*,[2] on which the facts of problem 7.7 are based. The Court held that the Second Amendment guarantees an individual right to bear arms. This means that citizens have the right to own guns independent of membership in a state-regulated militia. The opinion struck down D.C.'s complete ban on handguns, but also held that reasonable regulation of gun ownership (like prohibiting guns in government buildings and requiring licenses for gun owners) is not unconstitutional.

b. The requirement that rifles and shotguns be kept disassembled or bound by a trigger lock is a regulation but not a ban. The other part of the law—dealing with handguns—is a ban. Many argue that the state might have power to reasonably regulate arms but not to ban them entirely, as the D.C. law does with handguns.

c. The strongest arguments for the law are the interpretation of the Second Amendment that protects militias, which the D.C. law obviously does not infringe, and that local lawmakers, elected by the people, should be able to make decisions about community safety and criminal justice.

d. The strongest argument against the law is that it violates an individual right that is protected by the Constitution. Even if the majority (through its elected representatives) wants to ban handguns and regulate rifles and shotguns, this should not overrule a specific right protected by the Constitution.

PROBLEM 7.8 (p.80)

Invite pro- and anti-gun-control advocates to serve as resource persons. They can add interest and depth to expand this discussion. As with all resource people, obtain approval from n administration before inviting them to participate.

a. Students' opinions will vary. Supporters of laws requiring gun registration might argue that it would assist police in solving crimes involving weapons; it would help keep guns out of the wrong hands, such as children, convicted felons, and people who are known to be dangerous to themselves or to others, as was the case of the shooter in the 2012 massacre at Sandy Hook Elementary School and appears to be the case of the shooter in the Aurora, Colorado, movie theater shooting in 2012. Critics argue that gun-control laws are the first step toward government confiscation of all weapons, so that individuals cannot protect themselves from crime. Each side of the debate has interpreted the Second Amendment of the Constitution to support its position. Those against gun control believe the Second Amendment gives individuals the right to carry guns, which cannot be limited by the government. Supporters of gun control say that the Second Amendment gives the states the right to have their own militias but does not prevent the government from limiting individual possession and ownership.

b. Students' answers will vary. Consider using a continuum activity in which students stand along a wall marked "support" on one end and "oppose" on the other. As you ask each of the questions in the problem and the additional questions below, students can move to show the extent to which they support or oppose those restrictions. Ask students why they "stand" where they stand on whether to:

- restrict certain designs of weapons that make them easily hidden (e.g., snub-nosed revolvers);
- require safety devices, such as trigger locks and mechanisms that show the gun is empty when both the clip and chamber are empty;
- prohibit the manufacture of certain bullets, such as those that can pierce a police officer's bulletproof safety vest;
- impose fines and put out of business gun sellers who repeatedly sell weapons to ineligible persons or sell to "straw buyers" who in turn resell the weapons out of car trunks in high-crime neighborhoods;
- allow victims of gun violence and their families to hold gun manufacturers liable in tort suits; or
- require gun owners/possessors to complete a gun safety course prior to ownership/possession.

c. Students' answers will vary. Following the horrific shooting of 26 children and adults at Sandy Hook Elementary School in 2012, there was much public discussion about creating stricter regulations for semiautomatic weapons. The Senate considered extending a previous ban on assault weapons that had expired in 1994. The Senate bill was defeated. President Obama called for the creation of a gun violence task force and issued a series of executive orders aimed at addressing gun violence. Many of the executive orders addressed issues involving

background checks for gun purchasers. They also recommended more training and support for first responders, getting armor piercing bullets off the street and other initiatives. Following the mass shooting at Marjory Stoneman Douglas High School in Parkland, Florida, students created Never Again MSD and led a nationwide call for increased gun control. President Trump suggested arming teachers.

d. To research the gun laws in their states, students should visit the federal Bureau of Alcohol, Tobacco, Firearms, and Explosives site at www.atf.gov/ content/firearms which lists laws in each state as well as U.S. Territories.

Investigating the Law Where You Live

(p. 80) The federal Bureau of Alcohol, Tobacco and Firearms site at www.atf.gov/ content/firearms includes a publication that lists laws in each state as well as U.S. Territories. Ask students to search using the terms "state laws and published ordinances firearms" and look at the search results to pick the most recent report. Note that some students may find the reading level of the actual state statutes challenging.

Two websites that use "plain English" could be helpful. Have students visit the sites of two groups with competing views on gun laws. (For the sake of balance, we do not recommend using only one of these sites.) For state laws according to the Brady Campaign to Prevent Gun Violence, go to https://www.bradyunited. org/. For gun laws according to the National Rifle Association, visit www.nraila.org/ gun-laws/.

SUBSTANCE ABUSE AND CRIME (PP. 81–87)

Learning Outcomes

After completing this section, students should be able to:

1. describe the relationship between alcohol and violent crimes;
2. describe the legal penalties and human costs of driving while under the influence of alcohol;

3. explain implied consent laws and the possible consequences of refusing to take an alcohol test;
4. describe the purposes of drug courts;
5. weigh the merits of various approaches to the drug problem;
6. evaluate plans to legalize illicit drugs; and
7. define the terms *substance abuse*, *drunk driving*, *driving while intoxicated*, *driving under the influence*, *implied consent law*, and *recidivist*.

Investigating the Law Where You Live

(p. 83) Many websites provide the public access to state laws or statutes. A particularly helpful site for the question of state laws dealing with underage drinking is published by the Federal Trade Commission. Students can search "Alcohol Laws by State" by visiting https://alcoholpolicy.niaaa.nih.gov/underage-drinking/state-profiles.
The Cornell Law School site at www.law.cornell.edu/states/listing.html might also be helpful. When the students click on their state, have them click on "statutes" and then try various search words, including "drinking," "underage," and "alcohol."

BACKGROUND—PENALTIES FOR DRIVING UNDER THE INFLUENCE (DUI)

A national campaign is underway against drunk driving. One of the most important pieces of federal legislation is the *Anti-Drug Abuse Act of 1988*.[3] This legislation provided $125 million in grants to states over a three-year period for more stringent enforcement of laws against drinking and driving. As a result, arrests for DUI increased dramatically.

The general trend toward tougher laws for drunk drivers has resulted in a continuing decrease in alcohol-related fatalities, more license revocations and suspensions, more states requiring jail sentences as part of a criminal conviction, and widespread awareness of the risk of civil liability for serving alcohol to someone either in a home or in a bar who then drives and gets into an accident.

Law enforcement officials say most people whose licenses are suspended or revoked keep on driving regardless. In response, many states now have laws that allow officers to confiscate vehicles when drivers are known to be driving under the influence, some for 30 days or longer and some permanently.

Congress has endorsed this confiscation approach in a law requiring the states to enact tougher minimum penalties for drivers convicted two or more times for alcohol-related violations. One way for states to meet the requirement is to enact a vehicle-impoundment law. Other ways include mandatory license suspensions of at least a year. States that do not pass such laws have some of their federal highway construction funds diverted to safety programs.

The easy availability of alcohol to teens is a factor. According to nationwide survey conducted by the Insurance Institute for Highway Safety in 2018, 86 percent of high school seniors believed it "fairly easy" or "very easy" to get alcohol.

The National Highway Traffic Safety Administration conducted a study in Maryland. Maryland law states that individuals who are under 21 years of age and have a blood alcohol concentration (BAC) level as low as 0.02 are illegally intoxicated. Maryland also restricts night driving by youths. The study found that the Maryland law, "when combined with a public information and education campaign, resulted in a nearly 50 percent reduction in underage alcohol-related crashes over a two-year period, 1989–1990."

As you share information about initiatives aimed at reducing the number of drunk drivers, ask students to speculate about each method's potential for success. Students might then conduct research to determine the effectiveness of each method and identify other possible strategies.

BACKGROUND—IMPLIED CONSENT TO DUI TESTS

One well-established exception to the warrant requirement is when a person freely and voluntarily consents to the search by giving the officer permission, usually verbally. A derivative of that exception is that the state may, under certain circumstances, require people to submit to warrantless searches as a condition of receipt of a government benefit. All 50 states have these laws known as "implied consent" laws. These laws typically provide that, by driving on the state's roads, a person consents to testing of their breath, blood, or urine if they are arrested for drunken driving. When a police officer arrests a person and requests a sample for testing, that person can withdraw their consent. However, if they do, then they are subject to certain penalties, such as automatic revocation of their drivers' license. The implied consent laws of 29 states additionally provide that if the person is unconscious at the time the police officer requests a sample for testing, then the person is presumed not to have withdrawn their consent to the test. In those cases, the laws authorize the police officer to take a sample (usually of blood) from the unconscious person.

In 2019, the Supreme Court decided *Mitchell v. Wisconsin*[4], a case involving the taking of blood samples from an unconscious DUI suspect. In a 5-4 decision, the Supreme Court ruled that performing "implied consent" blood tests on an unconscious driver was constitutional based on the exigent circumstances exception to the Fourth Amendment. The exigent circumstances exception applies when there is no time for the police to get a search warrant but they need to conduct the search immediately to protect public health and safety or to prevent the destruction of evidence, in this case alcohol dissipating in the blood stream.

THE **CASE** OF...

The Graduation Party

PROBLEM 7.9 (p.84)

The range of penalties for parents who host parties where minors consume alcohol varies. In one case, parents were fined $3,000 for hosting a party in which there was one underage drinker, even though they had collected and labeled car keys from all 100 guests and expected anyone who had too much to drink to spend the night. Just miles away across a state line, a parent and step-parent were convicted of hosting an underage drinking party, and both were sentenced to jail time of 27 months. As this comparison suggests, the range of criminal and civil penalties is quite inconsistent, which may reflect a lack of consensus about the proper role of parents in these situations. Some parents think their children will drink "no matter what," so having them drink in their own homes is safest, particularly if they take away the car keys. However, as this problem illustrates, drunk driving is not the only risk associated with underage drinking. Being under the influence of alcohol also reduces reaction time and judgment, which leads to a significant increase in the likelihood a person will become a victim of crime, particularly sexual assault and date rape.

a. Students will study civil law in Unit 3 of the *Street Law* text. At that time, they will learn about negligence. One way to look at the issues of liability and negligence is to ask whether the people being sued acted reasonably. One could argue that by providing nonalcoholic drinks and snacks and remaining in the house, the parents did act reasonably. Others might say that parents have an obligation to monitor this kind of party more closely and should have been circulating during the party.

b. As students will learn throughout this criminal law unit, most crimes involve both an act and a guilty mental state (mens rea). In the United States, people are not often found criminally liable for failing to act. However, police are concerned about parents who do not adequately supervise this kind of party, and it is possible that they could be charged. In some instances where the parents have served alcohol, they have been charged.

c. Students' answers might include having the parents circulate throughout the party all night, having Sandra express her concerns about possible drinking to her parents or to other responsible party-goers who could have walked the drinking students home or given them rides.

d. Students' answers will vary. Lawmakers in favor of such laws believe lives could be saved if people who call for help do not fear getting in trouble themselves. For example, Maryland passed a law protecting Good Samaritans from getting in trouble if they summon aid for another person who is or may be overdosing. So, if a teen calls for help because they fear a friend is in danger, neither he or she will be arrested for underage drinking (even if the underage caller was drinking, too). Most states have such laws. If students want to learn whether their own state has such a law, direct them to: http://teens.drugabuse.gov/blog/post/good-samaritan-laws-save-lives.

BACKGROUND—ONLINE RESOURCE ABOUT DRUGS AND ALCOHOL

Drivers under the age of 21 represent 10 percent of licensed drivers. However, they are responsible for 17 percent of fatal alcohol related accidents. For more information visit http://dui.drivinglaws.org/resources/dui-and-dwi/dui-basics/the-sobering-facts-underage-duis.htm or https://madd.org/the-problem/.

The National Institute on Drug Abuse (NIDA) is a subdivision of the National Institutes of Health, a part of the federal government. NIDA has devoted a portion of its website for use by teachers and students. A good resource for drug abuse statistics can be found on the NIDA site at www.drugabuse.gov.

Health information and data referring to cigarettes, e-cigarettes, and other tobacco products can be found in the section, "Health Effects of Specific

Drugs." The NIDA also provides further information, publications, and resources on youth trends in the daily use of drugs, alcohol, cigarettes, and smokeless tobacco in a survey called the Monitoring the Future study. This study can be found online at www.drugabuse.gov. The NIDA also provides free resources, activities, and lesson plans for high school teachers at https://teens.drugabuse.gov/teachers/lesson-plans#/questions.

ACTIVITY—CONDUCTING A DEBATE

The 1988 *Anti-Drug Abuse Act*[5] requires mandatory life sentencing for those convicted of major drug trafficking offenses and a mandatory 30-year prison term for using a machine gun during a drug trafficking offense. A mandatory minimum prison sentence for drug offenses was also enacted. The law is intended to deter drug use and distribution by increasing the severity of punishment.

Critics contend that only low-level drug offenders are sentenced to jail, while the high-level offenders trade information for a less severe sentence or no sentence at all. Furthermore, the resources needed for rehabilitation, counseling, and drug treatment programs are being exhausted by the costs of incarcerating marginal offenders.[6]

On the other hand, those who favor mandatory minimum sentences argue that we do not know how many potential offenders they deter. Despite the costs and flaws in the justice system, they believe that taking more criminals off the street will be helpful.

Ask students to learn more about this controversy and then to debate the topic.

BACKGROUND—MINIMIZING THE USE AND SALE OF ILLEGAL DRUGS

Law enforcement authorities have used a variety of methods to halt the sale and use of illegal drugs. Such methods include "clean sweeps" in which hundreds of police officers force dealers out of certain areas. Enforcement techniques aimed specifically at young people have involved random searches of students and school lockers, drug testing of students involved in athletics and extracurricular activities, and curfew laws barring teenagers from public places after certain hours. Drug Free Zones, especially near schools, have been established, and extra penalties have been enacted for those caught selling or possessing drugs in these areas. Ask students whether they think these methods are effective. You might also ask a school resource officer or community police officer to join the discussion.

Investigating the Law Where You Live

(p. 84) The Cornell Law School website at www.law.cornell.edu/states/listing.html can help in answering this question because it links to state laws. As students click on their state, suggest that they click on "statutes" and then try various search words, including "illegal drugs," "dangerous drugs," and "illicit drugs."

CAPTION ANSWER (P. 86) Drug courts offer nonviolent offenders a simple deal: submit to drug testing on a regular basis, enroll in court-supervised drug treatment, stay off drugs, and they can stay out of jail.

PROBLEM 7.10 (p.86)

Use this problem to help students prepare for a classroom debate on the proposal to legalize drugs.

Although the questions focus on drug legalization, it is important to realize that there are actually three positions in the current national debate: (1) prohibition of some or all drugs; (2) decriminalization of some or all drugs; and (3) legalization of some or all drugs.

The *prohibition of all drugs* (also known as criminalization) reflects the current effort to control the harmful effects of using drugs by making it a crime to possess, buy, or sell certain drugs, often with heavy penalties attached. The purpose of criminal prohibition is to sharply reduce the availability and access to drugs, but critics argue that this approach is ineffective.

Decriminalization generally means reducing or eliminating criminal penalties for personal use, possession, and cultivation of drugs. For example, possession of a small amount of marijuana or cocaine might result in a simple citation, the equivalent of a traffic ticket or littering fine. Advocates of such policies argue that this is a compromise that stops short of the government sanctioning drug use, but others argue it is hypocritical to allow drug possession while prohibiting drug sales.

Legalization of drugs goes one step further and seeks to control the effects of drugs by regulating, instead of criminally prohibiting, their sale and use. Depending on the drug in question, legalization might require a medical prescription or a minimum age for purchase. Even if drugs are legalized, the government could criminalize certain drug-related activities, such as selling to minors or driving while intoxicated. In this way, drugs would be treated much like alcohol and tobacco.

a. Students' responses will vary.

b. Arguments favoring the legalization of drugs include: (1) prohibition has had no substantial impact on illegal drug use; (2) prohibition increases illegal drug use or encourages the use of harmful legal drugs; (3) legalization would eliminate the black market for drugs and related crime; (4) legalization would allow drugs to be regulated through enforceable standards established for use, sale, and taxation; and (5) drug prohibition and enforcement waste government resources.

c. People who are against legalizing drugs argue that it would lead to increased drug use, addiction, and related crime. Even some people who believe marijuana is not addictive believe it must be banned because it is a "gateway" drug that eventually leads users to more harmful drugs.

In order to have an informed debate on the issue of drug legalization, frame the issue to students in the following way: Do drug laws do more harm than good? This will provide a more sophisticated and thoughtful discussion than examining whether drugs are good or bad.

TAKING ACTION: LAW AND DEMOCRACY

Drugs in the City

PROBLEM 7.11 (p.87)

This problem can be answered in a number of ways. Students could simply answer the questions independently or you could set up a mock legislative hearing and conduct it before students answer the questions in Problem 7.11. Suggestions for conducting mock legislative hearings appear below the answers in this problem. Additional general suggestions for using and teaching mock legislative hearings are in the front of this Teacher Manual.

a. Students should rank the effectiveness of the represented viewpoints and give reasons for their rankings. It may be wise to have students revisit question a. after they complete questions b. and c., as further analysis of pros and cons may alter their rankings.

b. If students have trouble considering the costs and benefits of each option, discuss the

background notes provided below that correspond to each expert's testimony.

c. Answers will vary. Students might investigate the costs of the various proposals, and then work within a realistic budget for their community to draft a plan, using two or more approaches.

d. Students can express their opinions and give reasons.

As you prepare for the legislative hearing, invite resource persons such as police officers, legislators, drug education and treatment advocates, judges, prosecutors, and defense attorneys to coach each group prior to testifying, to observe the hearing, and to debrief students after the simulation.

Roles for a Mock Legislative Hearing

The six student "experts" who will testify should prepare their testimony based on the points of view listed in the Student Edition. Their testimony should, however, be in their own words. Additional information about each of these strategies is presented in the background notes below. If time permits, assign roles to students ahead of time and give them information about their strategy so that they can prepare more substantive testimony.

Other students should serve as members of a city or county council or a state legislature that has power to change the law. Council members should question those who testify and reach a decision after they hear all of the testimonies. The students who are neither participating in the testimony nor acting as legislators could evaluate the effectiveness of testimony or write news stories on what transpired in the hearing.

Law Enforcement Approach (represented by Police Chief Anderson):

Costs: the expense of hiring and training 100 additional police officers and equipping them with the latest weapons; the risk that increased firepower of police could provoke a similar response from drug criminals, escalating the violence; increased arrests might place more cases on court dockets and further burden the already overcrowded jails and prisons. **Benefits:** increased security for private citizens; deterrence effect on drug dealers; the probability of quick results as measured in arrests and an increase in jail sentences for convicted criminals

Restrict Civil Liberties Approach (represented by District Attorney Fisher):

Costs: Innocent people as well as the lawbreakers will have to sacrifice individual rights (i.e., teenagers'

loss of privacy at schools, citizens' loss of privacy at checkpoints, teenagers restricted after 9 P.M.) resulting in more of a police state; could increase tension between citizens and police if people think the police are overstepping their authority; more laws will require more police and corrections officers and more prison cells; courts may rule some searches unconstitutional and exclude evidence from trials (see exclusionary rule section later in this unit), reducing or eliminating the chance for conviction.

Benefits: In the short-term, there will be more arrests and convictions if courts go along with this approach, sending a message to drug dealers; additional spillover effect will reduce related crimes if guns and other items are found during searches.

Drug Treatment Approach (represented by Terry Blade):

Costs: would require opening many new drug treatment centers; would take some time before its effects (fewer addicts and reduced demand for drugs) would be felt; emphasis on treatment may give the message that the city is not "tough on crime."

Benefits: Treating and curing drug addicts of their addiction would be less expensive than incarceration; it would produce long-term results; and the product—concerned and committed citizens like Terry Blade—would be preferable to ex-convicts. The problem might be framed as a health problem and a criminal problem combined. If the demand for drugs is reduced, drug-related violence will decline too.

Preventive Education Approach (represented by School Superintendent Lee):

Costs: There are no short-term results; does not reach existing addicts; initial investment is expensive; some may doubt it will work; some will say that the people who are selling drugs will not be able to find jobs that pay as much, so they have little incentive to stop.

Benefits: Prevention is cheaper in the long term than imprisonment; stops problem before it starts; saves on law enforcement and treatment costs; better for the city as a whole (more employment among teenagers).

Penalties Approach (represented by Prosecutor Horton):

Costs: great expense and further overcrowding of prisons; treating 15-year-old first offenders as adults would expose them to the adult system of justice and corrections, which could lead to more recidivist behaviors (see more in Chapter 16). Many judges,

even some who are considered "tough on crime," do not support an approach in which state legislatures create mandatory sentences, because those requirements take away the judges' discretion to impose penalties that reflect their experience and discretion as well as the particular situation in each individual case.

Benefits: Effects would be felt quickly; easier to apply; does not require new programs.

Legalization Approach (represented by Rocio Fuentes):

Costs: The proposed law's restriction of drug sales to people over 21 would allow the illegal drug industry to continue to target teenagers; the number of addicts would probably grow (at least initially) because drugs such as heroin and cocaine are more addictive than alcohol; no provision for price controls, so it may not succeed in eliminating drug-related theft or large profits for sellers; condones drug use and may result in increased drug usage; increased drug use might result in more school dropouts, more unemployment, and decreased productivity in some communities.

Benefits: It might reduce the black market in drug sales which would result in less profit for dealers and less violence among rival dealers; could make funds available for treatment and education that would otherwise be spent on enforcement, prosecution, and incarceration.

After the Hearing

The council should discuss the issues and vote on proposals. The class should decide whether or not it agrees with the council's action.

VICTIMS OF CRIME (PP. 88–90)

Learning Outcomes

After completing this section, students should be able to:

1. describe demographic patterns and trends in crime victimization including age, race, gender, and socioeconomic background;
2. describe methods used by victim assistance and advocacy groups to assist victims of crime;
3. explain the purpose of "Megan's Laws;" and
4. define the term *restitution*.

(p. 88) If students need assistance contacting their police department or prosecutor's office, suggest that they ask their school resource officer or check online.

The following extension activities might be interesting to students. Assign a different group of students to research and report back on each of the items below:

- Look into how federal, state, and local governments work with private groups. Research the *Victims of Crime Act* (VOCA), which established a federal office to assist and advocate for victims of crime. VOCA also provides funding to various federal, state, and local victims' compensation programs. For more information about the national office and initiative, have students visit http://ojp.gov/ovc/.
- Interview personnel at a local crime prevention or victim assistance program (such as a rape crisis center) to learn how they operate. Find out if there is a law in your state that compensates victims for their injuries.

CAPTION ANSWER (P. 88) Gender, socioeconomic status, and race are also factors that influence a person's likelihood of becoming a victim of crime.

PROBLEM 7.12 WITH FIGURE 7.4 (p. 89)

The best place to get the most recent crime statistics, including information on victimization, is at http://www.bjs.gov. Have students visit this website for the latest statistical findings about trends in violent and property crime victimization to update Figure 7.4. After students update the data, have them compare it to the data printed in the Student Edition to observe trends and changes.

a. Answers will vary but may include: there were less reported victims in 2016 than 2013. Males were slightly more likely to be victims of crime. Victims were most likely to be white. The most likely age group to be a victim of crime is 35-49.

b. The statistics on race and origin would be more meaningful if the percentage of the population of each race was calculated instead of total numbers.

BACKGROUND AND ACTIVITY—MEGAN'S LAW

In March 2003, the U.S. Supreme Court handed down decisions in two major challenges to state laws that require people convicted of sex offenses to register on public lists, a common feature of Megan's Law in many states. In one case, the plaintiff believed he had already served his sentence and should therefore not be subject to further punishment by making personal data about himself and his conviction available to the public without due process. His attorneys argued that he should not have to register without being given a hearing to determine if he was still "currently dangerous." The court ruled that his procedural due process rights were not violated and that states can, in fact, compel offenders to register.[7]

The second case addressed the idea of ex post facto laws. These are laws that make something a criminal act or punish someone for an act that was not a crime at the time it was committed. Such laws are prohibited by the Constitution. In this case, the plaintiffs argued that they should not be required to register with law enforcement because the law creating the state registry was passed after they had already completed their sentences. The Court ruled against them and said that the state's sex offender registry was not created for punishment, only as a way for the state to create a system to protect the public from harm. Since the purpose of the registry was not punitive, it could be applied retroactively.[7] Students can learn more about these cases online at FindLaw (www.findlaw.com) and Oyez (www.oyez.org).

Students could also check the databases for their own communities, but it is important to tell them that they should not rely solely on these lists to protect themselves. Such data can often become outdated.

PREVENTING AND REPORTING CRIME (PP. 91–92)

Learning Outcomes

After completing this section, students should be able to:

1. list ways of preventing crime;
2. weigh alternative responses of people who are about to become victims of crime;
3. state how to report a crime; and
4. define the terms *complaint* and *testify*.

BACKGROUND—GOOD SAMARITAN AND DUTY TO RESCUE LAWS

"Good Samaritan" laws protect people who offer aid to a victim (like CPR) from being sued for harming or even wrongful death a victim. Their purpose is to make the Good Samaritan less reluctant to offer assistance for fear of negative repercussions. Horror stories in which witnesses failed to act during muggings, rapes, and other crimes while the victims cried for help have caused some states to enact "Duty to Rescue" or "Duty to Assist" laws. One of the most publicized cases occurred in 1983. In a New Bedford, Massachusetts, bar a woman was raped on a pool table while customers looked on. Because of the law at the time, the observers were not held criminally responsible, though some of those involved in the rape were convicted. Duty to Assist laws now require witnesses to summon the police or medical help or to offer "reasonable assistance." Some laws allow for civil lawsuits, criminal fines, or even jail terms against bystanders who do not help. These laws are criticized as difficult to enforce. The laws' proponents argue that they will encourage people to act more responsibly. While acting as a Good Samaritan may aid a victim of crime, it may also put the Samaritan at risk of injury or lawsuit if something goes wrong. For this reason, many people hesitate to get involved. Ask students:

1. Are you aware of cases in which a Good Samaritan saved the day?

2. What would you do in such a situation?

3. Why would you react that way?

4. Do you think laws should require witness action?

ACTIVITY—CRIME PREVENTION AND FIGHTING BACK

This activity is designed to help students reflect on their own experiences as crime victims or on the experiences of people they know. Since this is a very personal topic and can be sensitive for some people to talk about, you might consider asking the following questions as journal entries. If you choose to ask them in a discussion format, you should remind students to avoid using names to protect people's privacy. You should also consider inviting a school resource officer, community police officer, or a person who works in a victim assistance program.

1. Have you or someone you know been a victim of crime? If so, what was the crime and how did it affect the person and his or her family and friends? This question is designed to help students think about crime and how it affects people. Crime victims include not only the individuals personally harmed by the crime, but also the families and friends of those individuals. Victims of crime often suffer economic loss due to medical bills, loss of wages, and court costs, and they endure physical and emotional pain.

2. List and discuss at least four things you can do to protect yourself from becoming a victim of crime. This question tests students' understanding of crime prevention techniques. Students may list any of the techniques mentioned in the Student Edition or other crime prevention methods. You should stress to students the importance of reporting crimes. You may wish to extend this activity by asking students to create a poster or public service announcement to be broadcast on school or local radio stations to give other teens crime prevention strategies.

3. Have you ever witnessed a crime? What happened? What did you do? If it happened again, would you do the same things? If students say that they have witnessed a crime but did not report it, explore the reasons. Stress the importance of reporting crime. Discuss other reasons for not reporting crime and what might be done about this. Respect the privacy of students who may not wish to discuss their own victimization. Note that reporting crime and confronting criminals directly are quite different. If a police officer is present, ask him or her to discuss whether and how students and other citizens can report a crime anonymously.

NOTES

(1) *Chicago v. Morales*, 527 U.S. 41 (1999).

(2) *District of Columbia v. Heller*, 128 S.Ct. 2783 (2008).

(3) *Anti-Drug Abuse Act of 1988*, Pub. L. No. 100-690, 102 Stat. 4181 (1988).

(4) *Mitchell v. Wisconsin*, 139 S.Ct. 2525 (2019).

(5) *Anti-Drug Abuse Act of 1988*, Pub. L. No. 100-690, 102 Stat. 4181 (1988).

(6) *Common Cause News* (January 1990).

(7) *Connecticut Department of Public Safety et al.* v. *Doe, individually and on behalf of all others similarly situated*, 271 F.3d 38, reversed (2003).

(8) *Smith et al.* v. *Doe et al.*, 259 F.3d 979, reversed and remanded (2003).

networks™

CHAPTER **8**
Introduction to Criminal Law

Crimes are characterized by three elements: the act itself; a guilty state of mind, meaning the act was done intentionally, knowingly, or willfully; and a motive, or the reason for performing the act. Each of these three elements must be proven at trial in order to obtain a conviction.

Criminal laws at both the federal and state levels cover different classes of crimes. Felonies are serious crimes punishable by more than one year in prison. Misdemeanors are less serious and can result in one year or less in prison.

INTRODUCTION (P. 93)

Learning Outcomes

After completing this section, students should be able to:
1. name three elements of a guilty state of mind;
2. describe the difference between motive and state of mind;
3. identify an example of a strict liability offense;
4. explain how a strict liability offense differs from other crimes; and
5. define the terms *state of mind, mens rea, motive, strict liability,* and *statutory rape.*

DISCUSSION—INTENTIONS AND CRIME

Before students read the introductory section, ask them to respond in writing to this question: Should a person's intentions matter in deciding if he or she committed a crime? For example, should it matter if an act was done on purpose? If it was done when a person was being reckless? If it was done when a person was enraged? Discuss students' answers briefly, and then compare them to the text's introduction.

GENERAL CONSIDERATIONS (PP. 94–95)

Learning Outcomes

After completing this section, students should be able to:
1. describe the elements of a crime and the requirements that prosecutors face in proving guilt;
2. explain how a single act can be tried in both a criminal court and a civil court; and
3. define the term *elements.*

ACTIVITY—ELEMENTS OF CRIME

Give examples of crimes broken down into elements, and organize students into small groups to identify each element as either an "act" or a statement about "mental state." Contact your local clerk of the court to request jury instructions. These instructions are a useful resource for this activity.

PROBLEM 8.1 (p.95)

Before assigning students this problem, review the differences between crimes and torts.

a. Anton has violated both civil and criminal laws prohibiting assault and battery.

b. Derek decides whether or not to make a complaint to the police. The owner of the diner or other patrons may also call the police. The police report then goes to the prosecutor, who decides whether or not to charge Anton with a crime. Derek decides whether or not to bring a civil action. A civil action is the most common way for a person who has suffered damages to recover money. Even without a lawsuit, if Anton is convicted in either an adult or juvenile criminal court, he would usually be required to pay restitution to Derek as part of his sentence or disposition. Derek could also ask the police department or prosecutor if his community has a fund for reimbursing some of the costs associated with being a victim of crimes. Many jurisdictions have such programs.

c. No. Civil courts and criminal courts are entirely separate. A civil action and a criminal charge can never be tried in one case. In a criminal case, the government's prosecutor brings the case to court and argues that the accused person committed a crime that is an offense against the state. In a civil case, a private party brings a lawsuit. There are also differences in the rules of evidence and procedure for civil and criminal cases. The most important difference is the burden of proof facing the person who brings the case to court. In a criminal case each element of the crime must be proven beyond a reasonable doubt. In a civil action the plaintiff need only convince the judge or jury by a preponderance (greater weight) of evidence.

d. Encourage students to think creatively about alternatives to formal legal action. Derek could negotiate with Anton privately about compensation for lost wages and medical bills. If Derek and Anton can agree to settle their dispute and reach an agreement about fair reimbursement without a lawsuit, both would save the legal expenses involved in a lawsuit. Many areas have neighborhood justice centers or other types of mediation services where a neutral third party would be available to serve as a mediator between Anton and Derek.

STATE AND FEDERAL CRIMES AND CLASSES OF CRIMES (P. 95)

Learning Outcomes

After completing this section, students should be able to:

1. identify two or three crimes typically prosecuted only in state courts;
2. identify two or three crimes prosecuted only in federal courts;
3. identify two or three crimes that may be prosecuted in either state or federal courts; and
4. define the terms *felony* and *misdemeanor.*

ACTIVITY AND RESOURCE PERSON— STATE AND FEDERAL CRIMES

Invite a federal prosecutor, also called an assistant U.S. attorney, to discuss what constitutes a federal crime.

Ask students to work with a partner to brainstorm a list of crimes. After a few minutes, ask volunteers to write these crimes on the board. Then ask students to deduce which crimes would be tried in state courts, which would be tried in federal courts, and which could be tried in both. Have students give their reasons about why they would classify the crimes in these ways. Discuss whether federal crimes are more serious.

If students have already studied the concept of federalism in their government or civics courses, they may be able to predict how crimes are typically divided between federal and state courts. If not, students may not be able to identify whether a crime is a state or federal crime (unless it occurs on federal property) without consulting the federal criminal statutes. Take time to clarify any misconceptions that students have.

BACKGROUND—STATE AND FEDERAL COURTS AND DOUBLE JEOPARDY

Students may question whether or not it should constitute double jeopardy to be prosecuted for the same crime in both federal and state courts. Since they are separate court systems, the U.S.

Supreme Court has consistently held that it does not constitute double jeopardy. In 2019, the Supreme Court decided the case *Gamble* v. *United States*[1]. Gamble, a man prosecuted by both the state of Alabama and the federal government for being a felon in possession of a firearm, claimed double jeopardy. The Supreme Court upheld it's long standing precedent that the "separate sovereigns" or "dual sovereigns" doctrine permits a person to be charged with and prosecuted for a state crime as well as a federal crime resulting from the same conduct.

PARTIES TO CRIMES AND CRIMES OF OMISSION (PP. 95–96)

Learning Outcomes

After completing this section, students should be able to:

1. distinguish between a principal and an accomplice in a crime;
2. compare legal consequences for principals and accomplices;
3. distinguish between and give examples of an accessory before the fact and an accessory after the fact;
4. identify the legal consequences for those convicted as accessories before or after the fact;
5. define the terms *principal, accomplice, accessory before the fact, accessory after the fact*, and *crime of omission*; and
6. describe and give examples of crimes of omission.

DISCUSSION—PARTIES TO CRIMES

It is vital that students understand that if they are present when a crime is committed by someone else, they are potentially liable in criminal or juvenile courts. Ask students to develop a hypothesis to explain why the law does not ignore those who are present when a crime is committed. Ask students how they think society's failure to penalize those who are parties to crime or who are guilty of crimes of omission would endanger public safety and thwart justice.

CAPTION ANSWER (P. 96) An accessory before the fact is the person who orders the crime or helps the principal commit the crime, but who is not present during the crime. An accessory after the fact is the person who, knowing that the crime has been committed, conceals the crime, or helps the principal escape or avoid capture.

PROBLEM 8.2 (p.96)

Encourage students to begin this complicated problem by creating a chart like the one in **8.1 TM Figure**. This chart lists the cast of characters, their varying degrees of involvement, and the charges they may face. Once students have completed their charts, have them discuss their answers with the class.

THE **CASE** OF...

The Drowning Girl

PROBLEM 8.3 (p.97)

This case presents an opportunity to analyze a problem involving criminal responsibility.

a. Abe, the drowning child's father, has both a legal and a moral obligation to attempt to save his child's life if he is able to do so without harm to himself. Should he fail to act, he could be charged with criminal homicide. Kristi is criminally liable. If she intended to kill the girl, she could be charged with murder; if not, she could be charged with involuntary manslaughter or negligent homicide. Chin appears to be innocent of any criminal wrongdoing. Hannah may have a moral obligation to act, since she would probably be able to save the drowning girl at no risk to herself, but in many states there is no legal duty to rescue a stranger.

b. Students' answers will vary.

PRELIMINARY CRIMES (PP. 97–99)

Learning Outcomes

After completing this section, students should be able to:

1. explain the purpose or function of criminalizing certain behaviors that occur before a crime is committed;
2. define the terms *inchoate crime, solicitation, attempt, conspiracy,* and *overt,* giving examples of each;
3. describe the relationship between an overt act and a conviction for conspiracy; and
4. develop a hypothesis to explain why it is illegal to fail to inform authorities about illegal activities.

8.1 TM Figure

Character	Involvement/Actions	Possible Charges
Harold	Harold planned the burglary, broke into the jewelry store, removed the items from the safe, and fled from the jurisdiction.	Harold is the principal and will be charged with burglary (and possibly conspiracy).
Marci	Marci also planned the burglary and drove the getaway car.	Marci is an accomplice and can be legally charged with the same crimes as the principal.
Carl	Carl told Harold and Marci the location of the vault. It is not clear whether he knew their intentions when he told them or whether he was present during the burglary.	If Carl knew of their intention to steal, he is an accessory before the fact and can be charged as a principal in most states. In some states, if Carl told of the vault location and knew of their intention, he would have to go to the police or take active steps to thwart the crime in order to be relieved of criminal responsibility.
Shawn	Shawn learned of the crime afterward and helped Harold to flee.	Shawn is an accessory after the fact and can be punished for the separate crimes of harboring a fugitive and obstruction of justice. The critical fact for Shawn is that he knew about the burglary and then helped Harold get away. He cannot be charged with burglary.
David	David witnessed the crime and recognized the perpetrators but did not report it.	David may have had a moral obligation to take some action, but he is not criminally responsible for failing to report the crime. However, if he is subpoenaed as a witness, he must go to court or risk being found in contempt of court. Ask students what they think about this.

PROBLEM 8.4 (p.98)

a. Martin would not be guilty of the crime of attempt. Although he has engaged in considerable preparation, he has not taken any concrete, substantial steps toward embezzlement.

b. Gilbert would be guilty of attempted larceny. The victim's lack of money does not matter, except that the crime might be attempted grand larceny rather than petty larceny if the wallet had contained a substantial sum of money. The legal analysis here focuses on the perpetrator's mental state (Did he intend to commit the crime?) and his physical act (Did he go beyond mere preparation?).

c. In this situation both Rita and Anwar have taken steps beyond mere preparation. However, their acts to this point are likely not enough to prove their intent to commit the crime of robbery. While this is a rather close case, it is unlikely that they would be charged with attempted robbery. It appears that Rita has not yet committed an illegal act (except perhaps conspiracy to commit robbery), while Anwar could be arrested and charged with automobile tampering or attempted auto theft.

d. Amy would be guilty of attempted arson. She has done everything except get the matches and light the gasoline. Spreading the gasoline was a substantial step and a clear indication of her intent to commit arson.

BACKGROUND—CONSPIRACY

Conspiracy charges are often criticized because of the inherent vagueness, due process, and free speech problems they raise. In a famous conspiracy case, Supreme Court Justice Robert Jackson referred to the crime of conspiracy as "an elastic, sprawling and pervasive offense . . . so vague that it almost defies definition."[2] The government has sometimes used conspiracy prosecutions in political cases; however, because of First Amendment problems, these prosecutions have seldom resulted in convictions.[3] Conspiracy has also been used frequently in recent years to prosecute people involved in the drug trade. Large-scale drug dealers who plan activities to import and sell drugs have been convicted and sentenced to long prison terms under conspiracy statutes.

CAPTION ANSWER (P. 98) Some people believe charging a person with conspiracy violates the constitutional rights of freedom of speech and association.

PROBLEM 8.5 (p.99)

a. In most states, once Johnson, Hector, and Rajana agree to burn down the school and take some action that furthers that commitment (such as buying kerosene, loading it into the truck, and driving to school), they could be charged with conspiracy.

b. They could be charged with attempted arson once they have performed all the elements of the crime (pouring kerosene near the school and lighting a match), even if the fire did not start.

c. Johnson could be charged as an accessory before the fact and with conspiracy.

ACTIVITY—CREATIVE WRITING

Challenge students to apply their understanding of the terms in this chapter by asking them to write a creative story that includes as many vocabulary words as possible. As an option, students could make two copies of their stories. The first would have blank spaces where the vocabulary terms would go. For example: "Alex was charged with being an _____ because Officer Scott caught him driving the getaway car." This copy could be given to a classmate for him or her to read and to fill in, testing their own knowledge of the terms. The second copy would contain the entire story—including the terms—and could be turned in to the teacher.

NOTES

(1) *Gamble* v. *United States*, 139 S. Ct. 1960 (2019).

(2) *Krulewitch* v. *United States*, 336 U.S. 440, 445–6 (1949).

(3) *United States* v. *Dellinger*, 472 F.2d 340 (7th Cir. 1972); *United States* v. *Berrigan*, 482 F.2d 171 (3d Cir. 1973). In *Dellinger*, the Supreme Court denied certiorari in 1973. No appeal to the U.S. Supreme Court was made in *Berrigan*.

networks™

Crimes against the person are crimes directed at people. They include homicide, kidnapping, assault, battery, and rape. (Robbery is also a crime against a person, but it is dealt with in Chapter 10 because it is also a crime against property.) All of these are serious crimes, and a defendant found guilty of any one of them could receive a harsh sentence. State laws define the elements of these crimes quite specifically.

INTRODUCTION AND HOMICIDE (PP. 100–103)

Learning Outcomes

After completing this section, students should be able to:
1. differentiate between first-degree murder, felony murder, and second-degree murder;
2. differentiate between voluntary and involuntary manslaughter;
3. cite examples of negligent homicide;
4. list examples of noncriminal homicide; and
5. define the terms *homicide, malice, first-degree murder, felony murder, second-degree murder, voluntary manslaughter, involuntary manslaughter, negligent homicide,* and *negligence.*

ACTIVITY—COMPARING MURDER STATISTICS

The U.S. Department of Justice's Bureau of Justice Statistics compiles statistics from the Uniform Crime Reports about various crimes and makes them available to the public. Ask students to visit www.bjs.gov/index.cfm?ty=dcdetail&iid=245, http://www.fbi.gov/about-us/cjis/ucr/ucr to learn about different trends and statistics involving homicide, or the National Center for Injury Prevention and Control at the Centers for Disease Control and Prevention (CDC) www.cdc.gov/ViolencePrevention/index.html.

The goal of the research should be to give students a general sense of the frequency, trends, and other factors associated with homicide. Ask students to find out:

- the most recent homicide rate and whether the rate has remained stable, increased, or decreased since 1976;
- how the homicide rates have compared by race, age, and gender over time;
- the difference between whether male and female murder victims of crime knew their assailants; and
- which types of weapons were most often involved in murders over time.

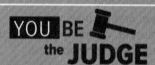

YOU BE the JUDGE

Homicide Cases (p. 102)

a. Walt would most likely not be charged with the jogger's death. Assuming he called the authorities and remained at the scene after realizing the jogger was dead, this appears to be a case of noncriminal homicide.

b. Depending on state law and whether her actions are seen as the product of negligence or gross negligence, Belva will likely be charged with involuntary manslaughter or negligent homicide. In this case, gross negligence might be the charge because Belva was using the car as a dangerous instrument with the intention of doing harm, even though murder was not the harm intended. Belva would not be charged with felony murder because an attempted collision is not a felony.

c. In determining whether he should be charged with negligent homicide or noncriminal murder, Gordon's actions would be viewed in the context of the appropriate conduct for a security guard. It appears that Gordon responded to the best of his ability under emergency circumstances, and he would most likely not face any criminal charges. However, if this occurs in a state that recognizes the felony-murder rule, both Alison and Brad could be charged with first-degree murder.

SUICIDE (PP. 103–104)

Learning Outcomes

After completing this section, students should be able to:

1. describe the legal consequences for those who assist someone else in committing suicide;
2. identify statistics that underscore why teen suicide is of serious concern;
3. identify resources that are available to people who feel suicidal; and
4. define the term *suicide*.

BACKGROUND—SUICIDE RISK FACTORS

Invite a school counselor or community member who works at a suicide prevention program to co-teach this information with you. Ask him or her to explain the complexity of suicidal behavior, that it is often a response to a combination of risk factors, what those risk factors are, and that many people with those risk factors do not attempt or commit suicide.

Ask students to consult the CDC's National Center for Injury Prevention and Control "Fast Facts," available at https://www.cdc.gov/violenceprevention/suicide/fastfact.html to learn to what extent suicide is a leading cause of death and how that changes with age, race and ethnicity, and gender.

Encourage students to learn about how issues of sexual identity and sexual orientation factor into suicide rates. According to PFLAG (Parents, Families, and Friends of Lesbians and Gays), the risk of suicide is three times higher for gay, lesbian, transgender, or questioning youth than of their peers. PFLAG attributes these alarming statistics to young people's internalization of society's negative, hostile, and degrading attitude toward gay, lesbian, bisexual, and transgender individuals which lead to feelings of despair, low self-image, low self-esteem, substance abuse, and depression. These risk factors are usually more profound within these groups.

DISCUSSION AND OPTIONAL RESOURCE PERSON—WHEN SOMEONE TALKS TO YOU ABOUT SUICIDE

It is highly advisable that you invite a counselor or community advocate who works with a suicide crisis center to assist you as you teach about this topic.

Tell students about the warning signs that might indicate that someone could be considering suicide. (These were compiled by the Trevor Project but are fairly widely accepted.)

- A tendency toward isolation and social withdrawal
- Increasing substance abuse
- Expression of negative attitudes toward oneself
- Expression of hopelessness or helplessness
- Loss of interest in usual activities
- Giving away valued possessions
- Expression of a lack of future orientation: "It won't matter soon anyway."
- For someone who has been very depressed, when that depression begins to lift, the individual may be at increased risk of suicide, as the individual will have the psychological energy to follow through on suicidal ideation.

Talk to students about strategies to use if they suspect that someone they know is considering suicide. The following are some points to emphasize in dealing with a person who is suicidal:

- Always take a person who talks about suicide seriously.
- Do not enter into any secret pacts. If a friend asks you not to tell anyone, respond that you care too much not to tell someone. If you are afraid that telling someone about the friend's problem might ruin your friendship, remember that not having the friend around at all would be far worse.
- Tell someone. This could be a teacher, counselor, parent, or other trusted adult. Students must realize that they are not trained to handle this kind of situation, so it is best to put it into the hands of someone who is.
- Encourage the person who is considering suicide to make concrete plans for the future, including the next time you will see each other. Making plans with him or her for a future date will provide the person with comfort, hope, and direction. It may also provide some time for the person to get professional help.
- Above all, remember that a friend, loved one, or even a professional can only do so much. If a person truly wants to take his or her life, the final decision is that of the individual.

In addition to discussing these facts and strategies, post suicide hotline phone numbers in the classroom, including 1-800-273-8255, the number for the National Suicide Prevention Lifeline. For students who might be uncomfortable making a

phone call, www.imalive.org offers a network of trained crisis counselors who are available for online chat. Additionally, the Trevor Project, a hotline for gay, lesbian, transgender, and questioning youth, is available at www.thetrevorproject.org or at 1-866-488-7386. The Trevor Project also offers posters, wall-sized hotline cards, and a teacher's guide as part of its Trevor Survival Kit.

CAPTION ANSWER (P. 103) Safeplaces provide guidance and support to teens in crisis. People working at the safeplace discuss issues and provide referrals to mental health professionals.

THE **CASE** OF...

The Dying Cancer Patient

PROBLEM 9.1 (p. 104)

Suicide among elderly people is an increasing health and societal risk. Some reasons often cited by older people considering suicide include the loss of a loved one, illness, financial problems, loneliness, depression, feeling unneeded or unwanted, and not wanting to be a burden on others. In addition, some elderly people feel a loss of purpose once they have retired from their jobs. Counselors recommend that there are effective ways to decrease the number of suicides among the elderly through involvement in community activities and other programs that enable the elderly to interact with others.

Inform students that there are actually two forms of euthanasia: active and passive. The type referred to in this problem is active euthanasia. In passive euthanasia, medical help is withheld; that is, the person is not hooked up to life-sustaining equipment.

a. Yes; Wilfred was requesting the pills in order to end his life.

b. Students' answers will vary, but should include reasons for their decisions. Although Wilfred took the pills himself, Martha could be charged as an accessory to manslaughter or for the crime of assisting a suicide. Murder charges would probably not be filed because Martha's actions were not done with malice. However, manslaughter charges could be filed because her actions were intentional. If the assisted suicide was highly publicized, which most are not, the district attorney may want to bring charges against Martha to deter others from assisting loved ones in their own death.

c. The important part of this question deals with the reasoning behind students' votes. If they voted to convict Martha, students may cite her involvement in her husband's death, the fact that her actions were deliberate, and society's interest in protecting human life. On the other hand, students who voted not to convict might reason that Wilfred wanted to die, that his condition was incurable and painful, that he was the one who took the pills willingly, and that Martha's actions were done without malice. Sentencing recommendations will also vary. A reduced sentence might reflect the unique circumstances and the defendant's motive; a harsher sentence could set an example to deter others.

d. Encourage students to discuss their opinions. If a doctor had given Wilfred the pills knowing he would use them to end his life, the doctor might be guilty of a crime as well as an ethical violation. If Wilfred took the pills without others knowing he would do so, then no one else would be held liable. Students may focus on the potentially conflicting responsibilities of doctors to ease suffering but to do no harm.

e. Note that students' reactions to assisted suicide laws may be emotional, particularly based on experiences in their own families. Students should also discuss state statutes regarding assisted death. Most states have statutes relating to the rights of the terminally ill and have similar language. They state that death resulting from the withholding or withdrawal of life-sustaining treatment does not constitute a suicide or homicide. The statutes are clear, however, in saying that the state does not condone, authorize, or approve of mercy killing or euthanasia.[1] (California, Colorado, District of Columbia, Hawaii, Maine, New Jersey, Oregon, Vermont, and Washington are exceptions because those states have each passed a *Death with Dignity Act* that allows for assisted suicide for the terminally ill.) Mercy killing or euthanasia involves any affirmative or deliberate act or omission to end an individual's life that prevents the natural process of dying.

ACTIVITY—DEBATE OR MOOT COURT: PHYSICIAN-ASSISTED SUICIDE

Have students debate whether they agree with laws that make it illegal for doctors to assist a person in committing suicide. Does a state have a right to protect its citizens from suicide by criminalizing

physician assistance? Or do the terminally ill have a right to commit suicide that should not be infringed by the states? For suggestions about conducting an effective policy debate, see the front of this Teacher Manual.

Instead of a debate, you might consider conducting a moot court or mini-moot courts in which students explore the legal and constitutional issues presented in the case of *Washington* v. *Glucksberg*.[2] (For suggestions and strategies about conducting effective moot courts and mini-moot courts, see the front of this Teacher Manual.) The information below is provided for the teacher, but you can adapt portions to help students prepare for their case. Further information is available at https://www.oyez.org/cases/1996/96-110.

Dr. Harold Glucksberg—along with four other physicians, three terminally ill patients, and a nonprofit organization that counsels individuals contemplating physician-assisted suicide—challenged the state of Washington's ban on physician-assisted suicide, saying it denied competent terminally ill adults the liberty to choose death over life. The U.S. Supreme Court had to decide whether or not the Constitution (specifically the due process clause of the Fourteenth Amendment) permitted the state of Washington to ban physician-assisted suicide.

The Court held that the right to assisted suicide is not a fundamental liberty interest protected by the due process clause because its practice has been, and continues to be, offensive to our national traditions and practices. Moreover, the state of Washington has a legitimate interest in protecting medical ethics, shielding disabled and terminally ill people from prejudice that might encourage them to end their lives, and preserving human life. This decision means that a state legislature may choose whether or not it wants to ban physician-assisted suicide. (Compare this to abortion, which the Court has ruled cannot be prohibited by law.) Therefore, Washington may ban physician-assisted suicide, and Oregon may legalize it. The result is that a doctor's actions would be legal in some states and illegal in others. Point out that Washington State enacted a *Death with Dignity Act* in 2008.

Ask students their opinions about the fact that different states may have differing laws related to this issue. How does this issue of physician-assisted suicide reflect the goals of the Framers of the Constitution in creating a system with some power delegated to the federal government and some retained by the states (federalism)? Why might this be treated as a state rather than a national issue?

KIDNAPPING (P. 104)

Learning Outcomes

After completing this section, students should be able to:

1. define the terms *kidnapping*, *unlawful imprisonment*, and *abduction*; and
2. explain how the charges relating to kidnapping change if the abductor brings a person across state lines.

ASSAULT AND BATTERY (PP. 105–106)

Learning Outcomes

After completing this section, students should be able to:

1. describe the significance of actual injury in the crimes of assault and battery;
2. show how differing degrees of seriousness are reflected in legal classifications of types of assault and battery; and
3. define the terms *assault*, *battery*, *stalking*, *sexual assault*, *cyberstalking*, and *bullying*.

LEGAL RESOURCE PERSONS

Since the number of young victims of sexual assault and stalking is high, encourage students to learn about the impact of stalking and sexual assault by inviting a counselor, police officer, or lawyer with experience in this area of crime to talk to the class. Students should learn about self-protection techniques and where they can go for help if they are concerned for their safety.

Investigating the Law Where You Live

(p. 105) There are several ways to find out how your state defines and classifies the crimes of assault and battery. One way, of course, is to ask a local expert, such as a school resource officer, community police officer, lawyer, or judge. Students can also visit the Cornell Law School site at www.law.cornell.edu/wex/state_statutes2. Note, however, the reading level may be challenging for some readers.

BACKGROUND AND ACTIVITY— BULLYING AND CYBERBULLYING IN SCHOOLS

The crime of cyberbullying is a relatively new and rapidly evolving crime characterized by someone using a phone, the Internet, or another digital technology to torment, harass, humiliate, or otherwise target another person. It is different from other kinds of bullying in a number of ways, including the perpetrators' ability to remain anonymous, which can be even more distressing. Whereas victims of "regular" bullying at school might feel safe elsewhere, cyberbullying finds victims everywhere— even places they feel safe. Also, due to the technological nature of cyberbullying, the harassing or embarrassing messages or images can be spread on a huge scale and with lightning speed.

Cyberbullying is also a crime whose frequency is increasing. According to a 2018 poll by the Pew Research Center, 59 percent of teens in the United States who use the Internet say they have been targets of cyberbullying including annoying and potentially menacing online activities. In some cases, cyberbullying has tragic outcomes, including suicide.

Several organizations offer resources to help teachers and students understand and prevent cyberbullying. One group, based in the United Kingdom, offers a free video and lesson plans that can be downloaded at www.digizen.org/cyberbullying/. The official United States site is StopBullying.gov.

CAPTION ANSWER (P. 105) Students' answers will depend on the laws of the state in which they live.

RAPE AND SEXUAL ASSAULT (PP. 106–107)

Learning Outcomes

After completing this section, students should be able to:

1. distinguish between forcible rape and statutory rape;
2. explain the reason consent is not relevant in cases of statutory rape;
3. explain the purpose of rape shield laws;
4. describe proof that may be required for a rape conviction;
5. explain why victims of rape, including acquaintance rape and sexual assault, may be hesitant to report the crime; and
6. define the terms *rape*, *statutory rape*, *criminal sexual assault*, *acquaintance rape*, and *date rape*.

BACKGROUND—THE SENSITIVE TOPIC OF RAPE AND SEXUAL ASSAULT

Young people are more likely to be victims of rape than most people realize. According to RAINN, 15% of rape and sexual assault victims are under the age of 18, of that 15 percent, 66 percent are aged 12–17. Over 90 percent of juvenile victims of rape or sexual assault knew their attacker (www.RAINN.org). Keep those statistics in mind as you teach this important subject. Express to students that rape is a sensitive but important topic for classroom discussion. Tell students to be sensitive to others and avoid making inappropriate comments or jokes when the topic of rape is discussed. A rape crisis counselor or victim's advocate is a very valuable resource person for this topic.

DISCUSSION—INVESTIGATING AND PROSECUTING RAPE

Rape is believed to be one of the least reported crimes. (Male rape victims have been even more reluctant than female victims to report this crime to the police.) Ask students to hypothesize why so many rape victims do not report their crimes to the police. Their answers may include ideas similar to the following:

- Many people feel embarrassed or ashamed after being the victim of rape.
- Some people fear that they will be treated insensitively by those who investigate their claim. In response, many police departments have created special units to investigate sex crimes and to refer victims to social services agencies that can offer the support needed after such crimes.
- Some people believe the criminal justice system has a poor record regarding rape prosecutions. Many times prosecutors are reluctant to pursue a case in which the victim knows the assailant because they do not believe they can win the case.
- Some people worry that a trial might bring back difficult memories and subject them to invasive questions. In some states, victims may be subject to tough cross-examination by defense attorneys, including questioning about their prior sexual conduct. Attorneys do this in an attempt to establish that a victim's past sexual relations with other persons are relevant to whether or not the victim consented in the case in question. The trend, by court decision and statute, is to rule evidence of past sexual relations with persons other than the defendant as irrelevant. As indicated in the student text, many states have enacted rape shield laws to protect victims from this type of questioning.
- Some people feel further victimized because, to obtain a conviction, some state laws also require other evidence, called corroboration, in addition to the testimony of the victim. These laws have been criticized by those who argue that it should not be more difficult to get a conviction for rape than for any other crime.

Some questions to raise may include: Can the adversarial legal system discover the truth in cases dealing with rape? How? Discuss state rape shield laws that protect against questions about the complainant's past sexual activity. Are these laws fair? Can students suggest changes that would make it more likely that victims of rape would report the crime and seek the help they are entitled to receive?

CAPTION ANSWER (P. 106) Rape shield laws limit or prohibit defendants from introducing evidence concerning the victim's past sexual behavior.

PROBLEM 9.2 (p. 107)

a. The woman's suggestion that a condom be used does not constitute consent. This man should be prosecuted for rape.

b. This problem is based loosely on the Mike Tyson case. At the time of the case, Tyson, the heavyweight boxing champion, was a guest at the Miss Black America pageant where he met one of the contestants. One night, about 2:00 A.M., the two took a limousine ride, and then returned to Tyson's hotel room where the incident occurred. The contestant claimed she was raped, while Tyson claimed she had consented to sex. Tyson was convicted and sentenced to prison.
   If students express different views on whether the female in this problem implied her consent to sex when she agreed to go to his hotel room, use that situation to clarify the law. Consent to visit a person's room does not equate with consent for sex. In fact, legally, a person can agree to some sex acts but if forced to do any sex act against his or her will, it is a sexual assault.

c. If the age of consent is 16 and the girl is 15, then this is a violation of law. Many states have moved from applying statutory rape laws to applying sexual assault laws, also the prosecutor has some discretion about whether or not to charge or to prosecute this offense. The fact that the male involved in this scenario is in a group in his school that appears to be encouraging sexual assault would be a reason in favor of a prosecutor taking some action. The fact that this was consensual would be a reason for the police or prosecutor to handle this situation more informally.

In some states, the law applies only against males who have sex with underage females. The U.S. Supreme Court, which addressed the issue of statutory rape in 1981, held that a law punishing only males for this crime was constitutional.[3] Many states have changed their laws so that males and females can be prosecuted for sexual assault. Students may be surprised to learn the law regarding statutory rape: neither the minor's consent nor a mistake—even a reasonable one—as to age is a good defense. In some jurisdictions, a person can be prosecuted for having sex with a minor even if he or she did not know the minor was underage.

d. Remind students that there cannot be consent if a victim is unconscious, mentally incompetent, or if the victim's judgment is impaired by drugs or alcohol.

Acquaintance rape is a significant problem that should be discussed with students. Statistics on acquaintance rape, or date rape, are difficult to compile because it often goes unreported. Many people do not realize that being forced into sexual relations by a person they know, and may even have been dating, is a serious criminal act. These victims may tolerate such an assault because they do not know their rights or are unwilling to bring criminal charges against someone known to friends and family. If people become more aware of the prevalence and serious nature of this crime, more victims might report the crimes and get assistance, and perpetrators might be stopped before they harm others.

Investigating the Law Where You Live

(p. 107) There are several ways to find out how your state defines criminal sexual assault and how that crime is punished in your state. One way, of course, is to ask a local expert such as a school resource officer, community police officer, lawyer, or judge. Students can also visit the Cornell Law School site at www.law.cornell.edu/wex/state_statutes2. These statutes can help students learn how their state defines the legal age of consent as it relates to statutory rape.

DISCUSSION—DATE RAPE OR ACQUAINTANCE RAPE AND DATING VIOLENCE: HOW TO PROTECT YOURSELF

According to the Centers for Disease Control and Prevention, (CDC), about eight percent of high school students report having been hit, slapped, or physically hurt—on purpose—by their boyfriend or girlfriend. There are numerous programs and resources available to help young people prevent violence, build healthy relationships, and get assistance if they become victims. Direct students to: https://www.ncjrs.gov/teendatingviolence/ to learn more about effective prevention and assistance programs.

The CDC also tracks sexual violence against teens—boys and girls. It supports multiple programs to prevent sexual violence, many of which have been proven to be effective. Encourage your students to learn about the risk factors (especially alcohol and drug use) and prevention strategies. See: http://www.cdc.gov/violenceprevention/sexualviolence/prevention.html

NOTES

(1) Ark. Code Ann. § 20-17-210 (Michie 1992); Ala. Code § 22-8A-10 (Michie 1992); 20 Pa. Cons. Stat. Ann. § 5402 (West 1993).

(2) *Washington* v. *Glucksberg*, 521 U.S. 702 (1997).

(3) *Michael M.* v. *Superior Court of Sonoma County*, 450 U.S. 464 (1981).

INTRODUCTION AND ARSON (P. 108)

Learning Outcomes

After completing this section, students should be able to:
1. describe steps people can take to help reduce the incidence of property crimes;
2. define the term *arson;* and
3. identify two crimes related to arson.

BACKGROUND—PROPERTY CRIME STATISTICS

According to the National Crime Victimization Survey, the rate of property crime victimization is at its lowest point since 1973. This is true for the specific crimes of theft and motor vehicle theft. The victimization rate for burglary is also down significantly, although it has remained stable in the last few years. (Visit https://www.bjs.gov/content/pub/pdf/cv18.pdf for detailed statistics from the 2018 report.)

Students and teachers who are interested in property crime statistics should look for the most recent version of the FBI's Uniform Crime Report at www.fbi.gov/ucr/ucr.htm. Another useful website is the Bureau of Justice Statistics at www.bjs.gov. Using data from these reports, students can look for trends and answers to the following types of questions:

- How many property crimes were estimated for the most recent reported year? Is that an increase or decrease over previous years? If so, by what percentage?
- How many robberies and how many burglaries were estimated in the most recent reporting year? How do these figures compare to the previous five years?
- What is the estimated dollar amount lost due to robbery in the most recent reported year? What is the estimated dollar amount lost due to burglary in the most recent reported year? What is the average dollar amount lost per incident?
- How many motor vehicle thefts were reported? Is that an increase or decrease over previous reporting years? What is the estimated total dollar lost from motor vehicle theft? How much is the average loss?
- How many incidents of arson were reported? What is the average property value lost per incident?

This chapter focuses on crimes in which property is destroyed, such as arson and vandalism, and crimes in which property is taken against the will of the owner, such as larceny. Cybercrimes such as identity theft and cyberstalking are also included, along with laws and strategies that are used to prevent and address computer crimes.

VANDALISM AND LARCENY (PP. 109–110)

Learning Outcomes

After completing this section, students should be able to:

1. define the terms *vandalism*, *larceny*, *shoplifting*, and *concealment*;
2. identify types and consequences of vandalism;
3. identify the synonym for vandalism;
4. identify two classes of larceny; and
5. describe the relationship between larceny and keeping lost or misdelivered property.

DISCUSSION—VANDALISM: HOW BIG IS THE PROBLEM AND WHO ARE THE VANDALS?

Some people think of vandalism as simply a game with no victims. This perspective ignores the fear and outrage people feel when their homes, businesses, or communities are deliberately damaged for someone else's entertainment. It also ignores the enormous costs involved in repair, cleanup, and replacement of vandalized property, which is estimated to cost more than $1 billion nationwide each year.

According to the National Report of Juvenile Offenders and Victims published by the U.S. Department of Justice, an estimated 108,100 juveniles were arrested for vandalism in 2017. Of those arrested, 14 percent were female and 81 percent were male.

BACKGROUND—THE BROKEN WINDOWS THEORY AND ZERO TOLERANCE FOR VANDALISM

Some criminologists, politicians, and police believe that when communities do not react strongly to crimes like vandalism, panhandling, and prostitution, worse crime will follow. The "broken windows theory," originally suggested by Dr. James Q. Wilson and Dr. George Kelling, and made popular by then New York mayor Rudolph Giuliani in the 1990s, suggests that when one broken window is not repaired, other windows will be broken. By analogy, when there is no response to "low-level crime" by law enforcers, criminals will assume that crime is tolerated in that community and crime will

therefore escalate. Theorists also believe that vandalism begets other social and economic problems. As one restaurant owner said, "I look at it from the financial end of it. Do [people] want to go to eat on [that street] where it's all pretty and nice? Or do [they] want to go to eat someplace where it looks like thugs hang?"[1] City leaders and police chiefs who agree with the broken windows theory direct law enforcement to focus their efforts on catching people who commit vandalism and other low-level crimes. In many places, this policy has developed into a zero-tolerance policy that calls for punishing first-time offenders for these low-level crimes swiftly and significantly.

People who support this policy say that communities are cleaner, residents feel safer, and the general quality of life improves. Many people believe that zero-tolerance policies contributed to a significant drop in the crime rates of cities that adopted the broken windows theory. In New York City during Mayor Giuliani's eight-year term, the overall crime rate dropped 38 percent to its lowest level in 25 years.

The success of zero-tolerance policies, however, requires a certain level of cooperation from the community, and there is a limit to how much the public will accept when it comes to the enforcement of "quality of life" laws. For example, in the spring of 2003, there was public outcry from the residents of New York City when police ticketed a man who was sitting on a milk crate for "unauthorized use of a milk crate," a tourist who fell asleep between subway stops for occupying more than one train seat, and a pregnant woman for sitting on public stairs. These examples demonstrate that law enforcers need to make reasonable judgments when attempting to set safe community standards through the law; otherwise the public will protest.

People who disagree with these types of policies believe that police and community leaders should focus their resources on more serious crimes. They contend that the crime rate was already dropping for other reasons before these policies went into effect in New York City and in other places.

Some critics are concerned that zero-tolerance policies have a disproportionate effect on the poor, because many instances of vandalism and crime take place in poverty-stricken areas. They claim that these types of fines often target the people who are least able to pay them. They add that in some communities, the relationships between residents and police officers are already strained and are made worse when residents feel like they are harassed for minor offenses by police officers who are simply "doing their jobs." In many cities, the number of complaints against police rose after zero-tolerance policies went into effect. While some critics agree that these policies might reduce crime, they say that the trade-offs are too great.

Ask students if they support the idea of zero-tolerance policies for crimes like vandalism. Have them explain their answers.

PROBLEM 10.1 (p.109)

a. Students' opinions may differ. Vandalism is often the result of alcohol or drug use, group or peer pressure, a desire for attention, thrill seeking, anger, or disdain for private property.

b. Some possible solutions to school vandalism include publicizing the problem; applying firm, fair, and consistent discipline within the school; conducting social programs and acquiring increased funding to deal with youth gangs; and taking steps to instill pride in the local school and community.

c. Students' answers will vary. The question is designed to elicit student feelings about common situations involving vandalism. Students may consider factors like the age of the vandals, whether the property damaged was public (school) or private (home), and their relationships to the parties involved. If students would report the vandals in one case and not the other, you should probe the reasons for this inconsistency. Discuss the issue of legal versus moral or ethical behavior.

ACTIVITY—FINDING POLICY SOLUTIONS TO VANDALISM

As an extension of Problem 10.1 and the discussion of the broken windows theory, ask students to determine the best policies for reducing vandalism in and around their school.

Begin this activity by asking students if they think vandalism is a significant problem in their school. If they cannot think of examples, suggest the following scenario. Ask students to suppose vandalism is a nagging problem at your school. Graffiti—including gang tags and obscene words—covers the back wall of the school. Student property is stolen from the hallways and even from locked lockers. Landscaping efforts are continuously destroyed. Recently, a teacher's car tires were slashed. Gum and scribbling on desks and in the bathrooms are the norm.

Draw a spectrum on the board that looks like the diagram in **10.1 TM Figure** below. Then ask students to consider each of the following solutions and decide whether they think each strategy would be effective or ineffective at reducing vandalism in their school. Students should also explain why they placed each strategy where they did on the spectrum. This activity can be done in a large group or with individual students recording their own responses.

1. When vandals are caught, they should be required to remove or pay for the repair of any damage.

2. The school should focus on more serious crimes than vandalism.

3. Whether or not the vandals are caught, graffiti should be cleaned up immediately even if it costs the school money.

4. School staff should find out who engages in graffiti and encourage them to become involved in art projects or other activities that display their art in a positive manner.

5. The principal should forbid students from bringing anything to school besides schoolbooks.

6. Surveillance cameras should be placed in hallways and around the outside of the building.

7. Students should organize volunteer activities to clean up vandalism on school grounds.

8. School resource officers should be stationed at areas where vandalism is a problem. If necessary, more such staff should be hired.

FIGURE

10.1 TM Figure

◄——— Not Effective	Somewhat Effective	Effective	Very Effective ———►

PROBLEM 10.2 (p.110)

a. Answers will vary. Students should know that many shoplifters steal because they are unable to pay for the things they need or want. Others do so compulsively, taking things for which they have little real desire or use. Sometimes young people shoplift in groups, and their actions may be caused by peer pressure or the need for attention. Ask students why they think this crime is so common among high school students.

b. Answers will vary. Highly visible protective measures in stores, such as security guards, surveillance cameras, and magnetic door barriers, may deter people from risking an arrest for shoplifting. Signs or other media publicity that threaten shoplifters with prosecution and stiff penalties may also deter them. Shoplifting may be a symptom of a psychological disorder that can be addressed through treatment. Education about the issues involved may also help students who shoplift understand their motives and avoid repeating the crime in the future.

c. Encourage students to imagine themselves in the situations described. If their responses would vary for someone they knew or a close friend, they should explain why. Discuss the issues of legal versus moral or ethical behavior and loyalty to a friend versus acting as a good citizen in these types of situations.

d. This question refers to the 2002 case in which actress Winona Ryder was accused, tried, and convicted of felony grand theft and felony vandalism after shoplifting more than $5,500 worth of merchandise from a Saks Fifth Avenue store in Beverly Hills, California. She was sentenced to three years of probation and 480 hours of community service. Ryder's sentence also required that she undergo drug and personal counseling and pay $6,500 in restitution to Saks Fifth Avenue as well as $2,700 in fines.

Ask students if they think famous people receive special treatment in the criminal justice system. Topics for discussion include whether it is possible for celebrities to receive a fair trial by members of their community and whether their ability to pay for high-priced lawyers gives them an advantage over those who must rely on appointed lawyers to make their way through the criminal justice system.

EMBEZZLEMENT AND ROBBERY (P. 111)

Learning Outcomes

After completing this section, students should be able to:

1. define and distinguish between the terms *embezzlement* and *robbery*;
2. list an example of embezzlement; and
3. identify two harms associated with robbery.

DISCUSSION AND RESOURCE PERSON—EMBEZZLEMENT

Invite a prosecutor and/or defense attorney to help clarify your state laws regarding embezzlement and theft. A person with experience prosecuting or defending "white collar crimes" would be especially interesting and helpful. Students could ask him or her questions such as:

- What is the average dollar amount taken in embezzlement cases compared to the average in other types of theft in our state?
- Are there any trends in the types of victims and the types of offenders for embezzlement compared to other types of property theft in our state?

The teacher or resource person could ask students:

- Which is worse? The crime of embezzlement or the general crime of theft?
- Why do you hold that opinion? What factors influence your thinking about that? Does the scope of the problem matter? Is there a moral difference in your mind between taking something from a stranger and taking something you were entrusted with?

EXTORTION, BURGLARY, AND FORGERY (PP. 111–113)

Learning Outcomes

After completing this section, students should be able to:

1. define the terms *extortion, burglary, forgery, identity theft,* and *uttering;*
2. identify the synonym for extortion;
3. list three threats that extortion laws generally cover;
4. identify examples of forgery and uttering; and
5. explain the potential impact of identity theft on a person and the steps one can take to protect his or her identity.

ACTIVITY—ROBBERY, BURGLARY, AND LARCENY

Many people confuse the terms *robbery, burglary,* and *larceny.* Ask students to create a graphic organizer that helps them learn the differences between these crimes. To do this, they will probably need to review the elements of a crime discussed in Chapter 8 and think about how these crimes differ and how they are the same.

ACTIVITY—UNDERSTANDING EXTORTION

To apply the crime of extortion to practical situations involving students, you might use the following scenario.

Rita is a quiet, hard-working student who always does her homework. Madlyn is much more interested in her social life than school, but her parents put a lot of pressure on her to do well. After spending all evening on the phone and instant-messaging her friends, Madlyn forgets to do her math homework. The next morning while riding the bus to school, Madlyn asks to copy Rita's homework. When Rita refuses, Madlyn threatens to tell everyone that Rita is sleeping with a teacher.

Ask students the following questions.

- Is this extortion?
- What should Rita do?
- Can you think of any situations you have been involved in that could be considered extortion?
- Is extortion a problem at your school or in your community?

- Is this the kind of crime that might typically be underreported?

Outline with students the elements that constitute extortion. Because extortion involves the use of threats (Madlyn does threaten Rita) to obtain the property of another (Rita's homework—it is her intellectual property), one could argue that the crime of extortion is being committed in the scenario above. Although extortion usually involves physical threats, it can also include threats to injure someone's character or reputation. Rita's reputation is likely to be harmed if Madlyn spreads this rumor.

Extortion is a common problem in schools, particularly in lunchroom and on school busses. Ask students if extortion takes place in your school, where it is most likely to occur, how it takes place, and what recourse the victim might have. If students indicate that it is a problem, have them brainstorm ways the school might discourage it. Some schools, for example, now maintain computerized student accounts for their cafeterias in which students use PIN numbers rather than cash to purchase food. While this does not eliminate the problem, it may discourage extortion for money by reducing the need to bring cash to school.

BACKGROUND—IDENTITY THEFT

A 2016 Department of justice report found that 10 percent of people 16 years old or older (28 million) were victims of identity theft during the prior 12 months. This crime has the potential to (and often does) victimize all sorts of people, regardless of age, gender, income, race, or country of origin. Types of identity theft include:

- unauthorized use or attempted use of existing credit cards,
- unauthorized use or attempted use of other existing accounts (like bank accounts), and
- misuse of personal information to obtain new accounts or loans or to commit other crimes.

Identity theft can be devastating. Victims have had their credit histories damaged, been denied phone and utility service, arrested for crimes they did not commit, been denied medical treatments, lost jobs, and had possessions taken away—all because a criminal stole their identity.

The federal government has created several initiatives to help identify the extent of the problem, to prevent it, and to prosecute offenders. Among those efforts were the creation of the National Computer Security Survey (www.bjs.gov/index. cfm?ty=dcdetail&iid=260), which is intended to estimate the extent of cyber-security crimes against business and industry.

Since 1972, the federal government has conducted an annual National Crime Victimization Survey (NCVS) to measure violent and property crime victimization. In 2004 questions about identity theft were added to the survey.

To find the results of the latest National Crime Victimization Survey, go to www.bjs.gov and enter the search words "identity theft."

Criminals often target children for identity theft. If the thief can get access to a child's social security number or other personal information, his or her resulting crimes may not be detected until the child is much older and applies for a credit card, attempts to use a driver's license, or gets a credit report.

The methods thieves use for identity theft change constantly. At the time of this publication, the FTC reports that the most common methods of identity theft are:

1. **Dumpster Diving:** Thieves rummage through trash looking for bills or other paper with your personal information on it.

2. **Skimming:** Thieves steal credit/debit card numbers by using a special storage device when processing your card.

3. **Phishing:** Thieves pretend to be financial institutions or companies and send spam or pop-up messages to get you to reveal your personal information.

4. **Changing Your Address:** Thieves divert your billing statements to another location by completing a change of address form, therefore gaining access to your accounts and information.

5. **Old-Fashioned Stealing:** Thieves steal wallets and purses; mail, including bank and credit card statements; preapproved credit offers; and new checks or tax information. They steal personnel records or bribe employees who have access.

6. **Pretexting:** Thieves use false pretenses to obtain your personal information from financial institutions, telephone companies, and other sources.

For more information about identify theft, students could visit https://www.identitytheft.gov/ or www.consumer.gov. Both are federal government websites that contain information about the extent of the crime and the steps the government is taking to prevent and prosecute the crime.

CAPTION ANSWER (P. 113) The person you gave the check to could fill in other information, such as a dollar amount that you did not agree to. However, because your signature is on the check, the check will be honored by the bank.

RECEIVING STOLEN PROPERTY AND UNAUTHORIZED USE OF A VEHICLE (PP. 113–114)

Learning Outcomes

After completing this section, students should be able to:

1. define the terms *receiving stolen property, unauthorized use of a vehicle*, and *carjacking*;

2. distinguish between joyriding and larceny; and

3. describe the legal consequences of carjacking.

PROBLEM 10.3 (p.113)

a. The facts of this situation suggest several possibilities. If the car belongs to Anthony or he has the owner's permission to use it, then there is no crime. If Anthony has taken the car without the owner's permission but intends to return it later, then he is guilty of unauthorized use of a vehicle. If Ivan should have known that Anthony was not authorized to use the vehicle, then Ivan could be charged as an accomplice. If Anthony stole the car with no intention of returning it, then he committed auto theft, which is a type of grand larceny. Because Ivan did not participate in the planning, commission, or concealing of the crime, he would most likely not be charged with a crime. However, Ivan could be fined for his failure to report this crime. If the phone does not rightfully belong to Anthony, then this is also a case of larceny. If Ivan chooses to purchase the phone from Anthony knowing that it was stolen, then Ivan could be charged with receiving stolen property upon taking possession of it.

b. Students' answers may vary. The main reason for criminalizing the receipt of stolen property is to deter theft by making it difficult for a thief to find willing buyers. Also, a general belief exists that no one should benefit from a crime, neither the thief who sells the things he or she has stolen, nor the buyer who gets a great deal on the items.

c. Students' answers will vary. Ask students to think about their moral and/or legal responsibilities in the type of situation posed in this problem. It may be difficult to know with certainty whether or not something has been stolen, but students should be aware that the law holds them responsible whenever they knew or should reasonably have known that an item was stolen.

CYBERCRIME (PP. 114–117)

Learning Outcomes

After completing this section, students should be able to:

1. define *cybercrime* (also known as computer crime).
2. describe the criminal and commercial consequences of piracy;
3. state the requirements for public libraries and public schools under the provisions of the *Children's Internet Protection Act of 2000*; and
4. describe steps teens (and others) can take to protect themselves from becoming the victims of cybercrime.

LEGAL RESOURCE PERSONS

For this section, local online bulletin board operators, computer user groups, and law enforcement officials would make excellent resource persons.

BACKGROUND—CYBERCRIME

In the case of *Elonis* v. *United States*[2], discussed on page 115 of the Student Edition, the Supreme Court ruled for Elonis, but did not address the First Amendment issue in the case. Examining the federal law Elonis was convicted under, the Court said that the judge in his case had not told the jury the proper rule to use when deciding whether he was guilty. The Court said the government had to prove more than just that a reasonable person would have felt threatened by his words—that "wrongdoing must be conscious to be criminal." The Court sent Elonis's case back down to a lower court to apply a different standard under the federal law.

Incidents of cybercrime rose dramatically in 2014 and now cost the U.S. economy hundreds of billions a year. Cyber criminals have developed elaborate ways to invade our personal as well as corporate cyberspace environments. Not only are cyber criminals hacking and phishing, they are using malware, spyware, viruses, and worms to steal personal data. It is also becoming a serious national security issue

as more and more cyber criminals operate in jurisdictions outside the United States. The law in cybercrime grows more complex each year as computer investigators, law enforcement officials, legislators, and court officials try to keep up with this growing field of crime. Many computer crimes do not fit into traditional criminal laws or typical law enforcement methods. For example, the FBI and Secret Service have had to restructure themselves to address the growing problem of hacking.

Ask students to speculate about what motivates hackers and phishers. Their answers will likely vary. When asked why hacking appeals to so many young males, one young hacker who served jail time for hacking into computers at NASA and at the Department of Defense said, "Well, it's a power trip. It's intellectual. Everybody likes to be in control... It's just harmless exploration." However, the prosecutors involved did not see it as harmless.

In response to the claim that they are crusaders, the Department of Justice's Chief of the Intellectual Property and Computer Crimes Section says: "It seems to me that thanking hackers who violate the privacy of networks or network users for pointing out to us our vulnerabilities is a little bit like sending thank-you notes to burglars for pointing out the infirmity of our physical alarms. That's silly."

BACKGROUND—PRIVACY AND POLICE SEARCHES OF EMPLOYEE COMPUTERS

The *Electronic Communication and Privacy Act of 1986*[3] offers protection to individual computer users by requiring the federal government and law enforcement officials to obtain a search warrant before seizing or reading any email. This requirement, however, does not apply to private employers. Many employees are concerned because their email accounts contain private messages. Also, the controversial *USA PATRIOT Act of 2001* gives government and law enforcement officials broader powers to access a suspect's Internet communications than has typically been permitted by the Fourth Amendment. For more information about the *USA PATRIOT Act* and law during wartime, see Chapter 44, "Law and Terrorism."

CAPTION ANSWER (P. 114) The federal government has passed several laws to address the issue of computer crime. These include the *Electronic Communication and Privacy Act of 1986*, the *USA PATRIOT Act of 2001*, the *Children's Internet Protection Act*, the *Computer Fraud and Abuse Act of 1986*, and the *National Information Infrastructure Act of 1996*.

BACKGROUND—CYBERBULLYING AND CYBERSTALKING

Another area of concern regarding computers and crime is the Internet's role as a venue where people meet. Cyberbullying has developed as an issue related to the use of electronic and social media. The 2017 School Crime Supplement indicates that 15 percent of students in grades 6–12 experienced cyberbullying.[4] Laws and policies are being developed to address the issue, but at a slow pace. Of the 50 states that have passed anti-bullying laws, 48 include cyberbullying.[5] Schools and communities struggle to balance the free speech rights of young people with the need to protect young people from a form of bullying that can be difficult to monitor.

Cyberstalking has also become a major problem, to which young people are particularly vulnerable. They may meet kidnappers or pedophiles online and inadvertently reveal personal information that makes them easy prey for such criminals. The challenge is to find ways to protect children from people who abuse the Internet without overly restricting access and discussion groups for the majority of adults who use the Internet for lawful, constitutionally protected uses.

This section offers an opportunity to alert students to risks associated with cyberbullying and cyberstalking. Stress to students that they should alert a parent or another trusted adult if they receive invitations to meet someone with whom they have come into contact online.

For more information on cyberbullying and ways to address it visit www.stopbullying.gov/cyberbullying/index.html.

BACKGROUND—INTERNET PORNOGRAPHY

Child pornography and minors' access to adult pornography online also are forms of computer crime. Actions aimed at effectively curbing these illegal uses of computers often threaten to infringe upon important First Amendment rights concerning freedom of speech, expression, and association, as well as access to information. Child pornography is always illegal in the United States, and the use of the Internet to promote such images is also illegal. However, since the Internet is an international tool, access is available to child pornography that is shot in places where it is not illegal. The United States has no jurisdiction over these websites.

The First Amendment does not protect the right of any minor to access pornography, and laws that prevent sales and rentals of such materials to minors have been upheld as constitutional. Minors are generally not viewed as enjoying the full range of rights as adults, and infringements on constitutional rights are acceptable where there is an important government interest. The government has an interest in restricting minors' access to pornography. While it is not difficult to pass and enforce laws that prevent businesses from selling pornographic magazines to anyone under the age of 18, it is much more difficult to limit access to this information on the Internet.

CAPTION ANSWER (P. 115) Concerned about minors' access to obscene material on the Internet, Congress passed the *Children's Internet Protection Act* in 2000. This act requires that public libraries install filtering software on all of their computers. Failure to do so could result in losing federal technology funding.

DISCUSSION—POLICY ANALYSIS OF SCREENING SOFTWARE AT SCHOOLS AND LIBRARIES

Ask students to weigh the responsibility of a school or library to provide access to information versus the responsibility of a school or library to protect young people from harmful and potentially harmful sites.

A case that is particularly relevant to this discussion and will most likely affect your students directly is *United States, et al.* v. *American Libraries Assn., Inc., et al.* (2003).[6] In 2000 Congress enacted the *Children's Internet Protection Act (CIPA)* to address what it saw as a national problem of minors using computers in public libraries to access pornography. The legislation makes federal funding for public libraries contingent upon a library installing specific antipornography screening software. The American Libraries Association (ALA) sued the government, arguing that this law violated First Amendment rights. The association argued that decisions about the most appropriate ways to limit child access to pornography are better left to the discretion of individual libraries. The ALA argued that individual libraries are in a better position to establish restrictions tailored to the use of computers at their particular library. Although the Supreme Court had struck down similar laws on two previous occasions, the Court held that *CIPA* was specific enough to serve the important government interest of preventing child access to pornography.

Have students consider the effectiveness of the screening software used in your school. As students may recognize from their own experiences, overinclusion and underinclusion are problems that occur often with screening materials. Often students are able to gain access to inappropriate sites (underinclusion) but may be restricted from sites that feature artwork or the word "sex," even in the context of a term such as *sex discrimination* (overinclusion). Ask students about the use of proxy sites to evade the screening technology. Librarians are concerned that mandated filters might impair their patrons' ability to conduct useful research using the Internet. The government's response is that librarians can disable the software on a case-by-case basis to allow an individual's research to proceed.

Ask students whether they think *CIPA* unfairly restricts the rights of adults who want to use library computers to access information or pornographic websites. Many adults use public computers because they cannot afford their own. This law imposes more limitations on adults using public computers than adults using their own private computers. Is this simply the cost of using public resources, or is this law inequitable because it gives greater protection to people who can afford their own computers?

CAPTION ANSWER (P. 116) Copyright laws are broken when someone illegally copies music. A person who purchases music agrees to play the music on their registered devices only. Sharing widely without the publisher's permission, is illegal and violates copyright laws.

PROBLEM 10.4 (p.117)

This problem (**a.–g.**) asks students to give their opinions about what *should* be a crime, not about *what is* a crime. It also asks them to rank the actions described in situations **a.–g.** from most serious to least serious.

You may choose to do this problem as a "continuum activity" in which you post a sign on one corner of the wall saying "most serious" and a sign on the opposite corner saying "least serious or not a crime." As you read each of the situations, have students move to the place along the wall that best represents their views. Be sure to ask students to explain their reasons.

Use each situation to review the content of this section of the chapter, including what constitutes a computer crime (**a., c., e., f.**), steps students can take to be safe from cybercrime (**d., e.**), respecting intellectual property laws (**a., f., g.**), and that employers have the legal right to track the online activities of employees using computers owned by the employer (**b.**).

NOTES

(1) David A. Fahrenthold, "Taggers Torment District Businesses: Owners Fear Graffiti Will Lure Crime," *The Washington Post*, September 2, 2003, page B1.

(2) *Elonis* v. *United States* (2015).

(3) *The Electronic Communication and Privacy Act*, 18 U.S.C. §§ 1367 2232 et seq. (1986).

(4) *Facts About Bullying*: 2019, StopBullying.gov, https://www.stopbullying.gov/media/facts/index.html#stats.

(5) Sameer Hinduja, Ph.D., and Justin W. Patchin, Ph.D., *State Cyberbullying Laws: A Brief Review of State Cyberbullying Laws and Policies*, Cyberbullying Research Center, November 2018, www.cyberbullying.us/Bullying-and-Cyberbullying-Laws.pdf.

(6) The *Electronic Communication and Privacy Act*, 18 U.S.C. §§ 1367 2232 et seq. (1986).

(7) *United States, et al.* v. *American Libraries Assn., Inc., et al.* 539 U.S. 194 (2003).

networks™

For a conviction to occur in a criminal case, two requirements must be met. The prosecutor must establish beyond a reasonable doubt that the defendant committed the act in question and that the defendant committed the act with the required intent. The defendant does not have to present a defense. He or she can simply force the government (the prosecutor) to prove its case. Several defenses are available to defendants in criminal cases.

INTRODUCTION (P. 124)

Learning Outcomes

After completing this section, students should be able to:
1. state what a prosecutor must prove for a conviction to occur in a criminal case; and
2. identify what a defendant is not required to do in a criminal case.

NO CRIME HAS BEEN COMMITTED AND DEFENDANT DID NOT COMMIT THE CRIME (PP. 118–119)

Learning Outcomes

After completing these sections, students should be able to:
1. describe how a defendant may establish reasonable doubt that he or she did not commit a crime; and
2. define the terms *alibi* and *DNA evidence*.

BACKGROUND

The DNA case referred to on page 119 is *District Attorneys Office v. Osborne*, 2009[1]. If students want to learn about this case, they may want to visit www.oyez.org and search for the case name. In addition, this topic may be a good one to collaborate with a science teacher to co-teach.

CAPTION ANSWER (P. 119) A defendant may also use DNA evidence to prove that he or she did not commit the crime by ruling them out as the perpetrator.

DEFENDANT COMMITTED THE ACT, BUT IT WAS EXCUSABLE OR JUSTIFIABLE (PP. 119–120)

Learning Outcomes

After completing this section, students should be able to:

1. describe circumstances under which the law recognizes the right of a person to use reasonable force in self-defense;
2. describe when the use of force in self-defense becomes unreasonable;
3. describe the extent to which force can be used in defense of one's property; and
4. explain how some states' Stand Your Ground laws vary from the typical standard for the use of force in defense of property.

PROBLEM 11.1 (p.120)

a. Many students will feel that Ms. Urbanski's actions are completely justified. However, she cannot legally claim that she acted in self-defense. When Ms. Urbanski fired the gun, the intruder was already fleeing. The intruder presented no direct threat to her. In most cases, deadly force cannot be used to protect property; it can only be used when an individual reasonably fears imminent death or serious injury. However, in such circumstances, prosecutors are reluctant to prosecute and juries are reluctant to convict. Some people argue that the experience of a burglary or robbery is so traumatizing that it is hard to rationally distinguish whether your person or just your property is in danger.

Ask students to state their opinions about whether it would matter if Ms. Urbanski's state had a "Stand Your Ground" law. Some states either have or are considering laws that make it legal to shoot an intruder in one's home. Discuss whether this is sound public policy.

b. Students' answers will vary. The key legal issue is whether the officer had reasonable cause to believe the suspect posed a significant threat of death or bodily harm to the officer or to others.

This problem is based on an actual case. In December of 2014, Cleveland, Ohio, police responded to a call of a "young black male" pointing a gun. The person was twelve-year-old Tamir Rice. Police arrived and ordered Rice to hold up his hands. Rice then reached for his waist, with the toy pellet gun in his hand. Within seconds, an officer shot Rice, who died the next day. The death was ruled a homicide by the Cleveland medical examiner.

Following the shooting, there were several inquiries into what went wrong and whether the officer involved used excessive force or had reasonable cause to believe that this suspect posed a significant threat of death or bodily harm to the officer or to others.

The parents of Tamir Rice filed a wrongful death lawsuit, arguing that the officer used excessive force when he shot their son and did not provide adequate emergency care to the victim.

This shooting occurred just weeks after Michael Brown was fatally shot by a Ferguson, Missouri, police officer, sparking weeks of national protests and efforts in police departments across the country to review their training and procedures. The shooting deaths also prompted the Obama administration to set up a task force to make recommendations for community policing and police procedures. Since then, there have been several high profile police shootings that garnered national attention.

DEFENDANT COMMITTED THE ACT BUT IS NOT CRIMINALLY RESPONSIBLE (PP. 120–123)

Learning Outcomes

After completing this section, students should be able to:

1. describe how the defense of infancy can be applied;
2. distinguish between circumstances that make intoxication a valid defense and those that make it an invalid defense;
3. identify the basic idea behind the insanity defense;
4. differentiate between when the insanity defense does and does not apply;
5. state the three distinct times the question of the sanity of a defendant is relevant for criminal convictions;
6. explain how a defendant's lawyer may attempt to prove his or her client's insanity, and explain who makes the determination whether a defendant is insane or was insane at the time of the crime;

7. contrast circumstances that are and are not considered entrapment;
8. explain when duress and necessity are not allowable defenses; and
9. define the terms *infancy, intoxication, insanity, entrapment, duress,* and *necessity.*

DISCUSSION AND REVIEW—MENS REA AND GUILTY STATE OF MIND

Before teaching this chapter, it may be helpful to review the term *mens rea* and the basic idea of a guilty state of mind. Explain that almost all crimes require an act accompanied by a guilty state of mind. This means that the person who did the act did so intentionally, knowingly, or willfully. Ask students how those requirements might explain the defenses of infancy, intoxication, and insanity.

DISCUSSION—APPLYING THE INFANCY DEFENSE

The idea behind the infancy defense is similar to the insanity defense: people should not be convicted or punished if they do not know right from wrong. Ask students: if a three-year-old child plays with matches, starts a fire, and the house burns down, is it arson? What if the child was eight years old? Eleven years old? Sixteen years old? Ask students how their answers would differ if children of the same ages were fighting and one shot the other.

Like most areas of criminal law, the infancy defense can be used in various ways in different states. Ask students whether they think these various standards are fair and appropriate. Is an eight-year-old in New Jersey different from an eight-year-old in Mississippi, for example?

For additional information about the differences between the adult and juvenile justice systems, see Chapter 16.

CAPTION ANSWER (P. 121) Many states adhere to some version of the notion that children under age seven are legally incapable of committing a crime. Children between the ages of 7 and 14 are presumed to be incapable of committing a crime, although this presumption could be proven wrong. Other states provide that children under a specific age cannot be tried for their crimes but must instead be turned over to juvenile court. Children under the specified age may use the defense of infancy.

Investigating the Law Where You Live

(p. 121) There are several ways to find out about how your local law enforcement officials deal with very young defendants. One way, of course, is to ask a local expert such as a school resource officer, community police officer, lawyer, or judge. If students prefer to search the Internet, have them visit the Cornell Law School site at www.law.cornell.edu/wex/state_statutes2. Note, however, that the reading level may be challenging for some readers.

In addition, later in Chapter 16, students will consider the debate about whether juvenile offenders should be considered adults and therefore tried and punished in the adult criminal system.

DISCUSSION—THE INTOXICATION "DEFENSE"

It is critical that students understand that being drunk or high on drugs is not an acceptable defense to a crime, but it might be considered a "mitigating factor" that results in lesser charges or a more lenient sentence. After students have read this section of the Student Edition, ask them to propose a rule for how a claim of intoxication should be factored into defendants' charges, convictions, and sentencing.

DISCUSSION—HIGH-PROFILE INSANITY DEFENSE CASES AND INCARCERATIONS IN MENTAL HEALTH FACILITIES

Point out the difference that exists in some states between "not guilty by reason of insanity" and "not competent to stand trial." In the latter, the accused is not tried until, if ever, he or she is deemed able to understand the proceedings and participate in his or her defense.

Explain that John Hinckley, Jr., who attempted to assassinate President Ronald Reagan in 1981, was found not guilty by reason of insanity. Prior to the Hinckley case, the burden of proof fell on the prosecution to prove that the defendant was sane. After the Hinckley case, the burden of proof shifted in many states so that if a defendant wanted to use the insanity defense, the defense team had the burden to prove he or she was insane at the time of the crime.

In the fall of 2003, the Hinckley verdict again raised controversy when a judge allowed Hinckley unsupervised visits away from the mental health facility to which he had been committed in 1982.

In another high-profile case, Andrea Yates confessed to drowning her five young children in a bathtub. The jury convicted her and rejected her insanity defense and sentenced her to life with the possibility of parole after serving time for at least 40 years. She appealed the case, which was re-tried, and she was found not guilty by reason of insanity upon appeal.

Ask students: if the courts have determined that a person was not guilty by reason of insanity and that the person must be confined to a mental health facility, should that person ever be allowed to reenter society? If so, under what circumstances? Who should make that decision? Should people confined in psychiatric institutions be allowed to contest their confinement? Should they be confined for more time than they would have served in prison?

Investigating the Law Where You Live

(p. 122) If students need help finding your state's criminal code defining *insanity*, direct them to Find Law at https://criminal.findlaw.com/criminal-procedure/the-insanity-defense-among-the-states.html.

Before they click on the option to see how the insanity defense is applied in your state, they should first read a very brief history of the insanity defense and trends in the use of the insanity defense. Most importantly, students should read and understand the basic definitions regarding the various "rules" or "tests" used in different states to determine how insanity defenses may be used. These are important background topics because the chart of state laws refers to terms students might otherwise not understand.

CAPTION ANSWER (P. 122) Students' answers will vary but should reflect an understanding of the possible sentences discussed on page 128 in the Student Edition.

PROBLEM 11.2 (p.122)

a. The insanity defense can be used if the accused was insane at the time the crime was committed, or if he or she is insane at the time of trial and unable to understand the charges or to defend himself or herself against them. If the accused can prove an inability to understand what he or she was doing as a result of a mental disease or disorder, an inability to tell the difference between right and wrong, or an inability to conform his or her conduct to the requirements of the law, then the accused will be found innocent or found guilty but mentally ill.

b. Students should explore their own ideas about the insanity defense and explain their reasons.

PROBLEM 11.3 (p.123)

a. Entrapment would be very unlikely to succeed as a defense in this case. In fact, it does not work very often. The key thing courts look for is whether the police set a trap for an unwary criminal or for an unwary innocent person. Courts also look at predisposition: did the police in this case give Edward an opportunity to commit a crime he was already going to commit? Or did the police make a person who was not predisposed to commit this crime into a criminal? The facts given in this problem do not indicate whether or not Edward was predisposed to the crime. In the cases where courts have overturned convictions based on entrapment, there was usually persistent police conduct. The facts in this case do not appear as though the police engaged in persistent conduct to specifically target Edward.

b. This is not entrapment. Jan made the offer; the police simply provided the opportunity for the sale. A key issue in entrapment cases is whether or not the defendant was predisposed to commit the crime. If so, the entrapment defense will not be successful.

c. This is likely entrapment if Sammy can prove that he would not have entered the illegal gambling ring without the constant pressure from the police officer. If Sammy has no history of gambling, and therefore is not predisposed to involving himself in this illegal activity, a jury might believe that the officer took advantage of Sammy's recent unemployment and enticed him into committing the crime.

SUMMARY AND REVIEW ACTIVITY— OVERVIEW OF DEFENSES

Ask students to make a chart comparing the defenses highlighted in this chapter. Their graphic organizers should include the name for the defense, a basic definition in the students' own words, and a reference to the crimes it may not be used for.

NOTES

(1) *District Attorney's Office for the Third Judicial District* v. *Osborne*, 557 U.S. 52 (2009).

networks™

The criminal justice process includes everything that happens to a person from arrest through prosecution and conviction to release from control by the state. This chapter deals with the investigation phase, which includes arrest, search and seizure, interrogations, and confessions. To build a case against the accused, the police gather information about a crime and collect evidence against suspected criminals. This chapter also outlines the constitutional rights of suspects during the investigation phase, including how the U.S. Constitution limits what police can do.

INTRODUCTION AND ARREST (PP. 124–131)

Learning Outcomes

After completing this section, students should be able to:
1. identify when an arrest takes place;
2. describe the Fourth Amendment rights a person has during an arrest;
3. identify steps on a diagram of the criminal justice process;
4. describe what an arrest warrant must contain and how it is obtained;
5. list factors that show probable cause;
6. explain the debate over the use of drug courier profiles in light of the requirement of "individualized suspicion";
7. know the powers of the police and the rights of the individual when police stop and question those suspected of a crime;
8. describe guidelines concerning the amount of force officers may use;
9. describe what a person should and should not do if arrested; and
10. define the terms *arrest, arrest warrant, probable cause, drug courier profile, corroborate, reasonable suspicion,* and *stop and frisk*.

ACTIVITIES AND DISCUSSION WITH POLICE OFFICERS

This chapter provides an excellent opportunity for students to connect with police officers serving in their school or community. It can also help improve relations between students and the police as both groups better understand the perspectives and experiences of the other group.

Invite one or more police officers to your class to discuss various issues relating to police investigations. Questions an officer could address include how officers can and should interact with people who are cooperative—and who are not—and what constitutes "professional behavior" by a police officer.

BACKGROUND—SEQUENCE OF EVENTS IN THE CRIMINAL JUSTICE PROCESS

Direct students to Figure 12.1 in the Student Edition: "Sequence of Events in the Criminal Justice Process." Take time to review each step and to define various terms that may be new or confusing to students. Remember to return to this page at several points throughout the unit to help students understand the terms and the significance of each step.

Inform students that great discretion can be exercised by criminal justice personnel at each step of the process, from the police to the prosecutor to the sentencing judge to the correctional system. Many of the most critical events of a case happen before the trial (e.g., at a pretrial hearing, when the defendant may attempt to suppress certain evidence), and relatively few cases actually result in a trial.

ACTIVITY—RESEARCHING CRIMINAL PROCEDURE RIGHTS

In some states, such as California, an accused person's rights under state constitutions are interpreted in the same way as they are by the federal Constitution. In other states, the rights granted by the state constitution may be greater than those provided by the U.S. Constitution. For example, in the state of Washington, arrests based on information from informants require a credible informant and reliable information. At an appropriate point in your study of criminal procedure, you might invite a law professor who specializes in your state's constitution to discuss with the class how rights protected by your state's constitution compare with rights under the U.S. Constitution. He or she might also discuss the discretion that is involved at every step of the criminal process and the tension between the crime-control model and the due-process model of law enforcement.

BACKGROUND—ARRESTS, WARRANTS, AND PROBABLE CAUSE

Because of the way police arrests are portrayed on television, where warrants are rarely seen and probable cause is seldom discussed, few people understand the role of arrest warrants. In fact, some felony arrests are made legally without a warrant. The chart in **12.1 TM Figure** can be recreated or copied to help students understand terms and the level of proof required for each type of police encounter. It can be useful throughout the chapter.

After students are familiar with the chart and with probable cause, make sure they understand that judges and/or juries—not police officers—determine whether a defendant is convicted or acquitted. A higher level of proof than probable cause is required for criminal conviction. Convictions require that the accused be found guilty beyond a reasonable doubt.

PROBLEM 12.1 (p.127)

a. The arrest appears to be based on probable cause. The facts are based loosely on those of *Draper* v. *United States*.[2] In that case the Court held that if an informant is known to be credible and the police can corroborate the information, probable cause for arrest can arise from an informant's tip. In this problem, when the police saw that the time of arrival and the appearance of the person fit the informant's description, they had the required corroboration.

In 1983, the Court adopted a standard called "totality of the circumstances," which reviewing courts could use when analyzing a judge's decision to issue a warrant based on an informant's tip. This standard requires judges to look at all surrounding circumstances in deciding whether or not the tip is reliable.[3]

b. There are two possible answers to this question. The police could seek an arrest warrant based on the detailed information from the reliable informant or, more likely, they could make an arrest without a warrant, arguing that probable cause existed once the information was corroborated by the person's appearance.

c. This version of the problem involves using a drug courier profile, which is a controversial practice. The police do not have probable cause to stop and search the 16-year-old. However, courts are split on the use of drug courier profiles. Some courts make allowances to help police in the so-called war on drugs.

Emphasize that adherence to the probable cause standard, as set out in the Fourth Amendment, does not ensure that police will always arrest the right person. Police sometimes have probable cause to arrest people who are innocent of any wrongdoing. The criminal justice process is designed to correct such errors at various points.

12.1 TM Figure

Police Action	What Is It?	When Can Police Do It?
Consensual encounter	An officer talks with an individual. The individual is free to leave at any time.	An officer can do this at any time. No information is required prior to an informal contact. (Examples: an officer asks a pedestrian if she saw the person who broke a store window, or an officer talks to students about safety.)
A stop (also known as an investigative detention)	A brief period of questioning during which no charges are made. The person is not free to leave at any time.	If an officer, based on his or her experience, has a *reasonable suspicion* that a person is involved in a crime that is taking place or being planned, then the officer can stop the person to ask for identification and an explanation. Reasonable suspicion is more than a hunch and is based on specific details or facts. The person may be detained for a reasonable amount of time. One U.S. Supreme Court decision held that 20 minutes was reasonable.[4] If the person is forced to go to a police station, courts have usually held that an arrest has taken place. (Example: an officer sees a person pacing in front of a store window, picking up rocks, and looking up at the window.)
Stop and frisk	An officer "pats down" the outer garments of an individual to check for weapons in order to protect the officer's safety.	In the case of *Terry* v. *Ohio* (1968), the U.S. Supreme Court sanctioned stopping and frisking a suspect to search for weapons when there was *reasonable suspicion* that a crime was about to be committed and that the suspect might be armed and dangerous.[4] If an item is felt during the frisk and the officer believes the item to be dangerous, the item will be taken, or seized. If the item taken provides the police with probable cause to arrest the person, the officer may then do a full search (such as pockets and socks).
Arrest	A person suspected of a crime is taken into custody. A person is not free to go and must remain with the police.	An officer needs *probable cause* to make an arrest. Probable cause is the reasonable belief that a person has committed a crime. In some cases, prior to the arrest, officers must request an arrest warrant from a judge, who will determine whether there is probable cause to believe that the person named has committed a crime. In other cases, officers may not need a warrant. See pages 141–143 in the Student Edition. (Example: an officer sees a person throw a rock through a store window.)

BACKGROUND—THE USE OF DEADLY FORCE

Before students start to answer question 12.2, part **f.**, it may be helpful to review the ideas and limits of deadly force that appear in the Student Edition.

The 1985 U.S. Supreme Court case involving use of deadly force mentioned in the Student Edition changed the law in many states.[5] In this case, a Memphis police officer shot a young person as he fled behind a house that the officer suspected him of burglarizing. The officer did not know whether the youth was armed (he was not), but Tennessee law allowed use of deadly force if a suspect continued to flee after notice of intent to arrest. The Court ruled this law, as well as the practice of using deadly force against people whom officers did not have probable cause to believe were dangerous, to be an illegal seizure under the Fourth Amendment. Even before the decision, a survey found that 87 percent of police departments allowed use of deadly force only against dangerous, fleeing suspected felons. Discuss with students their opinions about circumstances in which the use of deadly force would be justified. This might also be an interesting topic for a visiting police officer to discuss.

If students wish to learn more about the topic of "use of force by police," have them use those search words for a basic Internet search or a search on the website of the American Civil Liberties Union at www.aclu.org. Students can also view reports from the U.S Department of Justice at http://www.bjs.gov.

THE **CASE** OF...

The Unlucky Couple

PROBLEM 12.2 (p.128)

Be sure students read the entire section on arrest in the Student Edition before completing this problem. You may also want to discuss the background notes about deadly force found on the previous page.

This problem presents another excellent opportunity to invite a police officer to help students understand police procedure. Rather than lecturing, the officer can "coach" students through these answers and through the role-play in question **d**.

a. This question gives students an opportunity to put themselves in the place of both Lonnie and Officer Ramos. Students may say that Officer Ramos should pursue Lonnie's speeding car. While they may feel that Lonnie's actions are understandable under the circumstances, they should understand that fleeing from the scene provides the officer with reason to stop and question him.

b. Officer Ramos certainly has reasonable suspicion to stop the car and investigate further. This is known as an investigatory detention, during which Lonnie and Melissa would not be free to leave for a limited period of time, generally a few minutes to half an hour. If the officer fears the occupants are armed, she may have them step out of the car to do a pat-down search for weapons.

In addition, Officer Ramos has probable cause to issue a speeding citation. Speeding does not generally involve a full custodial arrest and does not justify a full-blown search of the car.[6]

Depending upon what the officer sees in plain view in the vehicle, observes in Lonnie's demeanor, and smells on Lonnie's breath, the officer may have probable cause to arrest Lonnie for driving under the influence (DUI). DUI does involve a custodial arrest and would justify searching the car. Depending upon their ages, the officer may be able to arrest Lonnie and Melissa for underage drinking and perhaps also for an open-container violation.

Because Lonnie and Melissa did not commit the burglary, Officer Ramos would discover no evidence of the burglary in their car. Therefore, there would be no probable cause to arrest either of them for the burglary.

c. Students' opinions will vary. Practical tips for dealing with the police in such situations should emerge from the discussion. Refer students to the *Steps to Take* feature, "What To Do If You Are Arrested," in the Student Edition for more tips.

d. The role-play is designed to build empathy for police and citizens, as well as to help students develop skills that are useful in police-citizen contacts. A police officer could visit the class, observe the role-play, and participate in the discussion. Have the officer explain how the police handle such situations.

e. It is unlikely that Lonnie and Melissa would have a valid tort or civil lawsuit for false arrest if they were arrested for the burglary. If Lonnie and Melissa were abused or mistreated by Officer Ramos, they could make a complaint at police headquarters or file a tort or civil rights lawsuit. If they chose to lodge a formal complaint for police abuse, they would need to provide as much detail as possible about the incident, including:

- the date, time, place, and nature of the incident;
- the name, badge number, and/or physical description of the officer;
- their names, addresses, and telephone numbers, as well those of any witnesses to the incident;
- a detailed summary of the incident;
- any available physical evidence, such as pictures, videotape, or a medical record of any injuries.

f. According to the Supreme Court, a police officer can use deadly force only if his or her life is being threatened or if it is the only way to stop a suspected felon from escaping.[7] Waving the bat would not be sufficient to justify using deadly force unless Officer Ramos believed her life was in danger. If Lonnie were about to use the bat to attack the officer, the officer would be justified in using enough force to repel the attack.

THE **CASE** OF...

The Dangerous Car Chase

PROBLEM 12.3 (p.130)

Note: This problem is based on the case of *Scott v. Harris*[8] which was decided by the U.S. Supreme Court in 2007.

a. Harris could argue (and did) that his rights were violated by the police who used excessive force. He claimed speeding is an ordinary crime and does not justify the use of deadly force. He also argued that the police did not have to "seize" him at the time of the chase—they could have stopped chasing him and tracked him down later. Harris also argued that there were no bystanders in the nighttime chase and that most cars had moved to the side of the road after hearing the sirens. (This was confirmed by videotape of the incident.) Finally, Harris argued that it was unnecessary to use deadly force in this situation because there was no indication that the suspect was a threat to others.

b. In the actual case, Officer Timothy Scott argued that he did not violate Harris's rights when he rammed the back of his car—he applied the appropriate amount of force for the situation. Harris had, in fact, threatened to harm innocent pedestrians and motorists by speeding down the two-lane road, running red lights, and swerving past cars. This would justify the use of deadly force. He further argued that Scott was guilty of speeding and ignoring officer's commands to stop. Scott also argued that by ramming the back of Harris's car, he exercised reasonable force—after all, he did not shoot Harris or even hit Harris's car on the side, forcing him to spin out. Finally, Scott argued that courts must look at what is objectively reasonable from the perspective of the officers at the scene, because officers have to make split-second decisions about what type of force to use. The Court should not second-guess those decisions.

c. Students' answers will vary. Be sure they support their answers with reasons. In *Scott* v. *Harris* (2007), the Supreme Court ruled in favor of Officer Scott, stating that an officer's termination of a high-speed car chase that threatens the lives of innocent bystanders does not violate the Fourth Amendment, even if it might seriously injure or kill the driver. The Court based its decision largely on videotapes of the car chase that showed Harris driving "shockingly fast," running multiple red lights, and swerving around cars. They said this "Hollywood-style car chase" put innocent bystanders in danger and that it was reasonable for Scott to ram Harris off the road. (This is different from a previous ruling in *Tennessee* v. *Garner* (1985)[9] in which a suspect's rights were violated when the officer shot him while he was running from a chase. In that case, the suspect did not pose a significant threat of death or serious physical injury to the officer or others, so the officer's use of force was not reasonable.)

d. Encourage students to brainstorm what an effective, fair, and constitutional policy might be. You might also suggest that they contact their school resource officer or their local or state police to see if such a policy already exists. How does the student policy compare?

Investigating the Law Where You Live

(p. 131) Students should search the name of their local police force and "excessive force complaint" or "community relations." You may want them to compare the local process to the United States Department of Justice procedures at https://www.justice.gov/crt/addressing-police-misconduct-laws-enforced-department-justice to evaluate if they are adequate.

SEARCH AND SEIZURE (PP. 131–143)

Learning Outcomes

After completing this section, students should be able to:

1. state how the Fourth Amendment limits the power of the government;
2. explain how the exclusionary rule protects individuals against the unreasonable use of police power;
3. describe how a search warrant is obtained and what it must specify;
4. describe the notion of "reasonable expectation of privacy";
5. list and describe situations when searches are considered reasonable and may be conducted without a warrant;
6. evaluate situations to determine whether police violated the Fourth Amendment and whether evidence would be admissible;
7. describe the *New Jersey* v. *TLO* decision and other U.S. Supreme Court decisions related to students' Fourth Amendment rights and drug testing;
8. compare the role of internal affairs units, civilian complaint review boards, police commissions, special prosecutors, and offices of professional accountability in handling complaints of police misconduct;
9. evaluate various policy solutions to the problem of racial profiling; and
10. define the terms *exclusionary rule*, *search warrant*, *bona fide*, *affidavit*, *contraband*, and *racial profiling*.

LEGAL RESOURCE PERSON

Invite a school resource officer, community police officer, or judge to discuss search warrants and probable cause. Ask him or her to bring a blank search warrant so students can see the type of information a judge weighs when evaluating probable cause and deciding whether to issue a search warrant.

DISCUSSION—THE FOURTH AMENDMENT

Ask students to read the excerpt of the Fourth Amendment that appears in the Student Edition. Confirm that students understand the vocabulary of the amendment, and then ask:

- What is protected?
- Whose actions are limited?
- What kinds of searches are prohibited? What kinds are permitted?
- What is a warrant? How is one obtained?
- Are warrantless searches ever permitted? If so, in what circumstances?
- What values are protected?

BACKGROUND—SEARCH AND SEIZURE LAW

Search and seizure laws balance the citizens' right to privacy with the government's need to gather information for law enforcement purposes. Explain the Fourth Amendment's historical antecedents to students (i.e., it arose from the colonists' reaction to the British writs of assistance).

Like other Bill of Rights protections, the right to privacy is not absolute. Only "unreasonable" searches and seizures are prohibited. What makes a search unreasonable is the subject of a large and sometimes conflicting body of judicial opinions.

The Fourth Amendment protects people from the government and those acting with the authority of the government. To illustrate this point, tell students that in the 1980s, a man rented out his trained Labrador so that concerned parents could have the dog sniff their children's rooms for drugs. Because the Fourth Amendment was designed to protect citizens from unreasonable intrusions by the government and not searches by parents, no Fourth Amendment violation existed in that case.

In analyzing search cases, it is helpful to ask: Did the person complaining of the search have a reasonable expectation of privacy in these circumstances? This approach helps explain why one's privacy rights are usually greater in the home than on the street.

Since the mid-1990s, the U.S. Supreme Court has issued several decisions that set out rules for police officers conducting searches when issuing traffic citations. In one case, the Court ruled that a full search of a car belonging to a man stopped for speeding constituted an unreasonable search and

invalidated the state law allowing such searches.[10] In another case of a man stopped for speeding, the Supreme Court upheld the officer's full search of the car—in which drugs were found—because the driver consented to the search. The Court refused to require that a defendant be advised that he or she is free to go before recognizing the consent as voluntary.[11]

The Court also upheld a stop for a traffic violation that was a pretext for determining whether drug crimes were being committed. The stop was reasonable where the police had probable cause to believe that a traffic violation had occurred. When the officers observed drugs in the hands of one of the passengers, the search was considered a plain-view search.[12] The Supreme Court ruled that a police officer making a traffic stop may lawfully order the driver and all passengers out of a vehicle during the stop.[13]

In April 2015, the Court ruled in *Rodriguez* v. *United States*.[14] This case is about whether the police can extend a traffic stop in order to have a dog sniff a car for drugs even after the original purpose of the stop (to give a ticket or a warning) has been completed. The Court decided that while a previous Court decision (*Illinois* v. *Caballes*, 2005) allows for a dog sniff during a traffic stop, this case was different. They said that a driver may not be held for longer than the actual traffic stop took or a reasonable traffic stop would have taken. By holding Rodriguez after the purpose of the initial stop had been concluded, the officers violated his Fourth Amendment rights. The Court sent this case back to a lower court to determine if the police officer had separate reasonable suspicion of criminal activity from his interactions with Rodriguez and the passenger. That would have allowed him to conduct the dog sniff after the traffic stop concluded.

Recent cases have also explored the nature of the "knock and announce" rule, which requires officers to knock on the door and announce their identity and purpose before attempting a forcible entry.[15] The law usually requires that special reasons be given for permitting the search at night between the hours of 10 P.M. and 6 A.M. This lessens the chances that a search will be an unreasonable invasion of a citizen's privacy. Searches are generally limited to daylight hours to avoid the trauma of the "midnight knock." In addition, it may be more dangerous for police to execute search warrants at night.

The cases mentioned in the Student Edition that deal with searches are *Maryland* v. *Buie*,[16] the "protective sweep case," *Minnesota* v. *Dickerson*,[17] the "plain feel case," *Hudson* v. *Michigan*[18] about the "knock and announce" requirement, and *Georgia* v. *Randolph*[19] about whether a spouse can consent to a search if the other spouse is present and objects.

PROBLEM 12.4 (p.132)

If you assign this problem to students before they have read through pages 134–139 of the Student Edition, they are not likely to know the correct answers. This could still be a useful activity because it could be a good "pretest" to the topics of warrants and searches without warrants. If you want students to know the correct answers before they attempt the problem, wait until they have read through page 139.

a. A person's mere presence in a high-crime area is not enough to establish reasonable suspicion to justify stopping and questioning that person against his will. There must be some level of individualized suspicion; there is none here.

b. As mentioned in the Student Edition, the Court has ruled that gathering information from garbage is neither a search nor seizure for purposes of the Fourth Amendment, because an individual does not have a reasonable expectation of privacy for items discarded in a trash can.[20] Because this is not a search, probable cause is not necessary.

c. Assuming Jill's former boyfriend was neither acting as a government official nor as the agent of one at the time that he broke into Jill's apartment, the evidence would be admissible. The Fourth Amendment protects individuals only from unreasonable search and seizures by the government. However, Jill's former boyfriend could be criminally liable for breaking and entering or civilly liable to Jill for the torts of trespass and conversion.

d. There are two Fourth Amendment issues in this problem: (1) Pam's arrest and (2) seizing stolen merchandise found in her apartment. Pam's arrest was reasonable because she was observed committing a crime. However, the stolen merchandise would be admissible as evidence only if police first obtained a warrant to search her home. Although police appear to have probable cause for the search, this probable cause must be validated by a judge-issued warrant prior to the search, because this scenario does not fall under one of the warrant exceptions. As long as Pam was outside her apartment door when she was caught by police in hot pursuit, the area inside her apartment was beyond her immediate control and therefore beyond the permissible scope of the search.

e. This search is probably unlawful. Claire could consent to the search of common areas of the apartment, such as the living room or kitchen. However, Sandi would retain a reasonable expectation of privacy in her bedroom. Even if the bedroom were shared, she retains a privacy interest in the dresser, as long as she has exclusive control of that dresser drawer.

BACKGROUND—ISSUES IN SEARCH AND SEIZURE LAW

The cases mentioned in the Student Edition on page 141 are *Georgia* v. *Randolph* (2006)[21] and *Fernandez* v. *California* (2014)[22]. In the *Georgia* case, the Court ruled that one spouse cannot give consent for a warrantless search of her home when the other spouse is present and objects to the search. In the *Fernandez* case, the Court ruled a co-resident could give consent to a search if the objecting resident had been removed from the property for a reasonable purpose such as an arrest.

Ask students: Is it possible for police to conduct a search of your house that violates your Fourth Amendment rights without ever entering your home or touching anything? As a result of modern technology and the Supreme Court's decision in *Kyllo* v. *United States*,[23] the answer is yes.

In the *Kyllo* case, federal agents were suspicious that marijuana was being grown in Danny Kyllo's home and used a thermal imaging device to determine the amount of heat emanating from the home. The amount of heat was consistent with the high-intensity lamps that are often used for growing marijuana indoors. The scan showed that Kyllo's garage roof and a side wall were relatively hot compared to the rest of his home and substantially warmer than neighboring homes. On the basis of this evidence, a judge issued a warrant to search Kyllo's home, where agents found marijuana growing. After he was indicted on a federal drug charge, Kyllo challenged the use of the thermal imager without a warrant as an unlawful search under the Fourth Amendment.

This case raised new issues for the Court. Under the expectation-of-privacy test, it could be argued that Kyllo had no expectation of privacy in the heat emanating from his home because he had done nothing to conceal it or keep it private. However, under the circumstances, this test seemed unfair. Because Kyllo did not know that technology could allow detection of heat waves outside his home, he saw no reason to conceal them. He assumed his actions were private. In a 5-to-4 decision authored by Justice Scalia, the Court agreed with Kyllo that a warrant is required if the government uses advanced technology that is not common in everyday use to obtain information about activities within a home or other settings for which the defendant has an expectation of privacy. However, a warrant would not be necessary if officers used binoculars to see inside someone's home, because binoculars are in common use. The dissenting opinion argued that officers should be allowed to draw inferences from information that is available in the public domain, in this case heat waves.

TAKING ACTION: LAW AND DEMOCRACY

Policing the Police

PROBLEM 12.5 (p.133)

a. The phrase "blue wall of silence" usually refers to the idea that some police officers (blue uniforms) treat their colleagues as such a tight-knit and unified group that they would never say or do anything that might get another officer in trouble.

b. Students' answers will vary. The strength of the Internal Affairs Model is that the people doing the investigation are trained officers, so they are more likely to understand the proper procedures and realities of the job. One negative about Internal Affairs investigations is that some officers may be overly sympathetic to fellow officers. The Civilian Complaint Review Board Model is generally more open to the public and therefore may do more to increase public trust of the police. However, it may also include members who know little about police work and lack the experience or judgment necessary to fairly judge a situation. The Civilian Complaint Review Board may also lack adequate funding to carry out its responsibilities. Some officers may fear that investigations into police wrongdoing that are conducted by civilians will not be kept as private as would an investigation through Internal Affairs.

Both the Police Commission Model and the Office of Professional Accountability Model are strong because they involve a combination of people with expertise "inside" the police department and from the community. However, both are also likely to be influenced by politics

because they are headed by people who are appointed by mayors and confirmed by city councils.

The Special Prosecutor Model has the advantage of being totally independent from the law enforcement officials it would investigate. While the process for appointing special prosecutors varies widely from state to state, they are generally used when either a conflict of interest exists or the situation is politically charged or controversial. With that said, some might be concerned that other political forces might unduly influence a criminal investigation.

ACTIVITY—RIDE-ALONG PROGRAMS

In some places, the police allow students to accompany an officer on patrol. Students can note their observations and report them to the class. (**Note:** Students and their parents may be required to sign a waiver of liability that relieves the police of responsibility.)

ACTIVITY—TAKING A FIELD TRIP

To learn about police procedures, take the class to a police department or arrange for police officers to visit your class to demonstrate procedures such as frisking for weapons, fingerprinting and photographing a suspect, and searching for and gathering evidence. If there is a police crime lab in your community, try to arrange a visit or have one of their experts visit your class.

CAPTION ANSWER (P. 134) Search warrants are used most often for searches of a person's home, to obtain a warrant police must convince a judge that the search is justified (i.e., that there is probable cause to believe evidence of a crime will be found).

BACKGROUND—PLAIN VIEW

The plain-view exception to the search warrant has been expanded to include plain hearing, plain smell, and plain feel. Plain hearing allows officers to listen to conversations taking place in private areas where they have a right to be. So, if officers can hear a conversation from a motel room next to one occupied by the suspects, they have a right to listen in. Police may seize objects based on their odor when the odor establishes probable cause. For example, police can search for and seize marijuana based on the odor coming from a car. Plain feel applies to situations in which a pat-down search immediately reveals the felt object is contraband or other evidence of a crime.

THE **CASE** OF...

Fingers McGee

PROBLEM 12.6 (p 136)

"The Case of Fingers McGee" provides a good opportunity for a role-play and for using police officers to assist in the resulting discussion. The problem raises the issues of arrest, searches, interrogations, and confessions. You may wish to assign it to students after they complete the section "Interrogations and Confessions" in the Student Edition.

The role-play has two scenes: first, the street encounter in which McGee speaks with the police, and second, the investigation of Johnson's house. The role-play will be more realistic if you provide a few simple props to use in the second scene. You could use a sack full of play money (or crumpled newspapers) placed in the corner of the room where Johnson is sitting, a cardboard cutout of a knife placed in plain view, simulated drugs (such as small balls of tinfoil) placed on Johnson's person, and a cardboard cutout of a gun placed out of sight but within Johnson's reach, perhaps in a desk drawer. (**Note:** Check with your administrator to find out if toy guns and toy knives are banned at your school.) You may wish to equip students acting as the police with a *Miranda* card.

Ask the students who are playing the role of the police to leave the room after scene one. Explain that the classroom door is the door to Johnson's house. Close the door after they leave, put Johnson and the props in place, and then signal to the students outside to proceed with scene two, starting with their arrival at the closed door. If you have invited an actual officer to help with this role-play, he or she should lead the discussion at the end of the role-play. The officer should analyze each step—street scene, entry into the house, arrest, interrogation, seizure of evidence, etc.—to note the appropriate legal restrictions and describe typical police procedure for each.

a. During the role-play the officers should try to get specific information, such as a description of the person's clothing, exactly where Johnson lives,

and so forth, as well as to determine how McGee got his information.

b. If the police learn where they can find Johnson, they should probably proceed to his residence, although in practice they would also likely phone for a backup unit.

c. The police may proceed to the house to investigate further. There is not time to obtain a warrant, and they do not yet have enough information to get one. Even if at some point the police have probable cause to arrest Mark Johnson, they must first make sure the person they are arresting is actually Mark Johnson.

d. In most instances, police will knock first and announce their purpose and authority. If there is no response, it would be illegal to enter without Johnson's consent at this point. The law allows police to enter a house to arrest or search only where probable cause has been established and where an announcement could result in harm to police or other citizens or in the destruction of evidence. If a police officer is assisting with this activity, ask him or her to explain how entry into a house to arrest or search should be conducted to make it legal, safe, and effective.

Forcible entry into homes by police is governed by the knock-and-announce rule of the Fourth Amendment. This rule requires police to knock and announce that they are police and that they are there to execute an arrest or search warrant. If there is no response, the police may enter using force, if necessary. Police may be excused from following the law under emergency circumstances (for example, if the officer is genuinely in danger or contraband is being destroyed). In 1997, the U.S. Supreme Court ruled that the Fourth Amendment does not permit a blanket exception to the knock-and-announce requirement.[24] However, under the facts of that case, the officers had a reasonable suspicion that the individual might destroy evidence if given further opportunity to do so. The no-knock entry into the accused's hotel room by officers executing a warrant was held to be reasonable under the circumstances.

In 1995, the Supreme Court ruled that the knock-and-announce rule forms part of the Fourth Amendment reasonableness test.[25] That is, one element in determining if a particular arrest or search was reasonable is whether or not the police first knocked and announced their presence. In 2006 the Court allowed the use of evidence obtained after police entered a house without following "knock and announce" rules.[26]

e. If the entry is lawful, police can seize any evidence that is in plain view. Whether or not police can arrest Johnson may depend on the exact description provided as well as Johnson's actions at the house. If the informant described Johnson as having a knife, or if Johnson acts in a way that might endanger the officers, they can frisk him for weapons (under the *Terry* precedent). If they make a lawful arrest, they can search him and the area within his immediate control. Once they see the knife, gun, bag of money, and/or drugs, they will have probable cause, as long as they had a right to enter and see those items in the first place. If they did not have a right to enter, the search and any items seized will be inadmissible.

The extent to which Johnson can be questioned is discussed in the next section of Chapter 12, "Interrogations and Confessions." Based on reasonable suspicion, Johnson can legally be questioned or shown to the liquor store owner as part of an investigatory detention, for an approximate period of a few minutes to roughly 30 minutes. Once Johnson is in custody, police must give the *Miranda* warnings before questioning him. Otherwise, any confession or incriminating statements cannot be used directly against Johnson at his trial.

ACTIVITY—CONDUCTING A ROLE-PLAY ABOUT PUBLIC SCHOOL SEARCHES

Note: The following activity will help students explore the extent to which the Fourth Amendment applies to students in schools. This activity is based on the precedent-setting case *New Jersey* v. *TLO* (1985) mentioned in the text.[27] You should anticipate strong disagreement among students about how these issues should be handled legally and fairly. Consider inviting a school administrator, security officer, school resource officer, community police officer, and/or attorney to hear student opinions, share their own perspectives, and to help facilitate the activity and subsequent discussion.

Before class begins, select four students to role-play two short scenes in front of the class. Meet with these students briefly to describe the scenes (explained below) and assign roles. One student will play a teacher, two students will play high school students (one should be a female), and the fourth student will play a school principal.

Ask the students to role-play a scene in which the teacher catches the two students smoking and takes the students to the principal's office. The

principal should ask the students if they had been smoking. The female student should deny that she was smoking and that she ever smoked. Then the principal should ask the female student for her purse, and she should give it to the principal. When the principal opens the purse, he or she sees cigarettes and rolling papers. The female student should deny that these items belong to her. Knowing that rolling papers are often associated with marijuana, the principal further searches the purse and finds marijuana, drug paraphernalia, $40 in one-dollar bills, and written notes about the female student's sales of marijuana to other students. This scene could be made more engaging by giving the female student a purse containing a box or deck of cards labeled cigarettes, small pieces of paper to represent rolling paper, play money, and some notes listing the names of fictitious students and amounts of marijuana they have purchased. If necessary, remind students to play their roles respectfully, especially if guests will be helping to facilitate the activity.

When class begins, introduce the resource person if one is present and begin the role-play in front of the class. After the role-play, use the questions below to generate a class discussion.

a. Should the exclusionary rule apply to searches of students in high school by school officials? Why or why not?

Students' answers will vary. Be sure to ask for their reasons. In the 1985 case, the state of New Jersey argued that the exclusionary rule should not apply to schools at all. New Jersey argued that school officials were not agents of the state like police, who must follow the exclusionary rule. Instead, they argued, school officials were standing in for the students' parents (a doctrine called in loco parentis) and the escalating problems of drugs and violence in the schools justified the exclusionary rule not being applied in school settings. The Court rejected these arguments. It held that the rule should apply because students are citizens who should have the same basic rights as citizens on the street, although a lower standard of proof may be required. The Court also ruled that public school officials were agents of the state.[28]

Note: This ruling does not apply directly to private or parochial schools (where there is no state action), though these schools may have their own rules giving students rights, including freedom from unreasonable searches. Make sure students understand that if school resource officers or community police officers are involved in a search, they are agents of the state, so they must follow the probable cause standard, and the exclusionary rule does apply.

b. How much evidence should a school official have before searching a student's purse or locker? Should the standards of probable cause or reasonable suspicion be required?

Students' answers will vary. Be sure to ask for their reasons. The Supreme Court ruled that the standard of probable cause required for searches outside school did not apply to school officials searching a student's person or purse. There has not been a Supreme Court ruling on searching student lockers, but most courts have allowed such searches by school officials on reasonable suspicion, which is less than probable cause. These searches are usually on the basis that the lockers are owned by the school and that students do not have a reasonable expectation of privacy in their public school lockers. In this case, the Court ruled that the students, known as TLO, could be searched if the school official had "reasonable grounds for suspecting that the search will turn up evidence that the student has violated, or is violating either the law or rules of the school." (Violating a "no smoking" rule can justify a search. Also, the exclusionary rule applies only to court proceedings. Even if evidence is improperly seized, it can be used against a student at a school disciplinary hearing.) The dissenting justices thought the normal probable cause standard should be required for school searches, and that the reasonable grounds standard constituted an inappropriate watering down of the Fourth Amendment as it applied to schools.

c. Do you believe that the principal had the right to open the student's purse? Could the marijuana and drug paraphernalia be used against her in court?

Students' answers will vary. Be sure to ask for their reasons. In the actual case, the Supreme Court found that the fact that the student had been observed smoking in violation of school rules provided reasonable suspicion. This justified the principal's decision to open her purse and to look for cigarettes. In addition, seeing the rolling papers in the purse gave rise to a reasonable suspicion that she possessed marijuana, which justified further search of the purse. The dissenting justices argued that there was no need to open the purse because the teacher had

observed the students smoking. Even if the purse could be opened, once the cigarettes were found the principal had no right to look for other items.

Note: The general rule on searches of student property such as book bags and purses is that the principal or designee must have reasonable suspicion to start the search, and the scope of the search must also be reasonable. It could be argued that upon finding cigarettes, it was reasonable for the principal to continue searching for matches or a lighter, which would help to determine whether or not this student had actually been smoking. In a lawful search, it is permissible to seize anything that is illegal to possess.

d. Should high school students have fewer rights or the same rights as adults in the community? Explain your answer.

Students' answers will vary. Be sure to ask for their reasons. Some people argue that students' rights should be restricted because of their age, lack of maturity, and the fact that schools are special places of learning that should not be compromised by the distractions that stem from problems such as drugs and violence. Others argue that students cannot be taught the principles of the Constitution or other civic values if these principles do not apply to them as well. They may also argue that if a school provides students fewer rights than adults, the message is that the rights of students are not important.

The case mentioned in the Student Edition was a Supreme Court ruling that helped to clarify what the limits are for public school officials when searching students. In *Safford Unified School District* v. *Redding (2009)* the Court held that a student's Fourth Amendment rights were violated when school officials searched a student's underwear for non-prescription medication.[29] Justices noted that the search procedures used by school officials must be "reasonably related to the objectives of the search and not excessively intrusive in light of the age and sex of the student and the nature of the infraction."

CAPTION ANSWER (P. 137) The Court has allowed schools to search student lockers on the theory that the lockers belong to the school and students do not have a reasonable expectation of privacy in school property. Courts have also allowed drug-sniffing dogs to enter schools to search for drugs.

a. The Oregon case mentioned in the text is *Vernonia Sch. Dist. 47J v. Acton*.[30] Both cases involved students' privacy interests regarding urine samples. However, the Oregon case affected only student athletes at a school that had a serious drug problem, whereas the Tecumseh High School[31] case affects all students who are involved in any type of extracurricular activities at a school that did not have the same pervasive drug problem. In *New Jersey v. TLO*, which also involves the Fourth Amendment issue of searching a student's belongings, there was some individual suspicion that led the principal to search the purse of a student caught smoking, whereas at Tecumseh there is none.

b. Students' arguments may include that students have the right to be free from unreasonable searches. Part of what constitutes a reasonable search is that there is a specific suspicion directed toward the individual being searched. The Tecumseh school policy does not require individualized suspicion but implies that participation in school extracurricular activities requires giving up the right to be free from unreasonable searches. Other cases held that people have a reasonable expectation of privacy over their bodily fluids (e.g., urine), so the testing procedure should be considered a search. Consent is not really voluntary where students need extracurricular involvement for college admissions and scholarships. The interest of the school district in reducing drug usage does not outweigh the students' constitutional right to privacy, particularly where there is little evidence of a drug problem. Other less intrusive methods of investigation would adequately serve the school's interests in preventing drug use. The program lacks adequate safeguards against abuse of discretion by school officials. The testing program is too broad because urine samples may be tested for a variety of conditions, such as pregnancy and use of birth control. The fact that the program requires the disclosure of confidential information, including use of prescription medication, in order to rebut a positive test result is in violation of the students' right of privacy.

c. The school's arguments may include that the school is responsible for the custody and education of the children. In school settings, students' privacy expectations are reduced because they are routinely required to submit to various physical examinations and required vaccinations against serious diseases. No individualized suspicion should be required because teachers must be able to resort to swift and informal procedures. The reasonableness of searches should be judged under a totality of the circumstances test. Students have no legitimate expectation of privacy over their urine because it is a waste product. The consent form indicates that students have voluntarily consented to these searches, and extracurricular activities are not a required part of the school program. The searches are conducted for non-punitive purposes—law enforcement is not involved in any way. If students test positive, they have adequate notice and an opportunity to rebut the test. Therefore, their due process rights are protected. Finally, there is no police involvement in the case, which makes for less need for elaborate due process protection.

d. Answers will vary. Following is a summary of the Court's opinion in the case *Pottawatomie County v. Earls* (2002)[32]

In an opinion written by Justice Thomas, the majority held that individualized suspicion was not necessary in order to require drug testing of students participating in activities, nor was a warrant required because public schools fall under the special needs exception. The Court found that this was one of the limited circumstances, like a sobriety checkpoint to catch drunk drivers, in which the need to discover hidden conditions or prevent their development is sufficiently compelling to justify the privacy invasion. This is consistent with the precedent that a student's privacy interest is limited in a public school environment because the state is responsible for maintaining discipline, health, and safety. The Court compared it to schoolchildren being required to submit to physical examinations and receive vaccinations. The Court said that securing order in the school environment sometimes requires that students be subjected to greater controls than those appropriate for adults.

The Court quoted Justice Powell's concurrence in the *TLO* case: "Without first establishing discipline and maintaining order, teachers cannot begin to educate their students. And apart from education, the school has the obligation to protect pupils from mistreatment by other children, and also to protect teachers themselves from violence by the few students whose conduct in recent years has prompted national concern."

Justice O'Connor dissented, as she did in *Vernonia*, arguing that individualized suspicion that a particular student is using drugs should be necessary before the student is required to submit to drug testing. Justice Ginsberg, who agreed with the Court's decision in *Vernonia*, also dissented in this case. Justice Ginsberg distinguished between requiring athletes to submit to drug testing (*Vernonia*) and requiring students in all extracurricular activities to submit to drug testing (*Earls*). In Justice Ginsberg's view, there was a relationship between drug use and athletics that did not exist between drug use and, say, chess club.

e. This case dealt with students' consent to drug testing based on their decision to participate in certain activities. Therefore, this decision does not authorize the testing of all students, faculty, and staff. However, such a case could be presented in the future.

YOU BE the JUDGE

Police Searches and Technology (p. 140)

For both **a.** and **b.**, remember to ask students to give their opinions about whether the Court should uphold the search or not. They should also give their reasons for their conclusions.

a. These are the facts of the case *United States* v. *Jones*.[33] The Court held that installing a Global Positioning System (GPS) device on a vehicle and then using that device to track the vehicle constitutes a search under the Fourth Amendment. In this particular case, police had obtained a warrant to place a GPS device on Jones' car. However, the court that issued the warrant had specified that the GPS could only be installed in Washington, D.C. It was installed in Maryland and had expired at the time of installation. Authorities then used the data collected from the device to convict Jones. Because the evidence was collected as part of a "warrantless search," it should not have been admitted as evidence.

b. This problem is based on the case of *Riley* v. *California*.[34] The Court held that police may not, without a warrant, search digital information on a cell phone seized from an individual who has been arrested. This search did not fall under a lawful "search incident to a lawful arrest" because the data on the phone did not present any risk and did not warn of any impending danger. The decision was a unanimous one. Chief Justice Roberts stated in the opinion that "the fact that technology now allows an individual to carry such information in his hand does not make the information any less worthy of the protection for which the Founders fought."

Another landmark Supreme Court case dealing with high tech searches was *Carpenter* v. *US* (2018)[35]. In this case the government accessed the cell-site location records from Carpenter's wireless provider without a warrant. Using this location data, law enforcement was able to place him at the scene of criminal activity. In a 5-4 decision, the Supreme Court ruled that the warrantless search of Carpenter's location data violated his Fourth Amendment protection from unreasonable search and seizure.

ACTIVITY—RESEARCHING RACIAL PROFILING IN POLICE INVESTIGATIONS

Complaints of racial profiling have increased in recent years. African Americans are becoming more willing to protest being stopped just because they are black. African Americans sometimes say they are treated as if it is a crime to be "driving while black," "walking while black," or even "shopping while black." Many Latinos, Arabs, Muslims, and people of Southeast Asian decent have also lodged similar complaints.

Much of the racial profiling discussion centers on traffic stops. In December 1998, a federal judge reduced an African American defendant's criminal sentence on the grounds that his lengthy prior record may have been skewed by race-based traffic stops. In 1992, the Maryland American Civil Liberties Union (ACLU) successfully won a lawsuit against the Maryland state police, and the court ordered the state police to monitor traffic stops. As a result of *Wilkins* v. *Maryland State Police*,[36] many studies on racial profiling were conducted throughout the United States, with alarming results.

Students who are interested in learning about the results of those studies, problems of police profiling, statistics relating to the problem, or recommendations about how to reduce racial profiling may be interested in checking out the resources compiled by the National Criminal Justice Reference Service. These resources contain numerous reports about race-based stops, perceptions of police among various ethnic communities, and even international perspectives on the problem. For more information, visit www.ncjrs.gov, and use the search terms "racial profiling" or "police profiling." Other excellent sources include the federal office of Community Oriented Policing at www.cops.usdoj.gov, the National Urban League at www.nul.org, and the American Civil Liberties Union at www.aclu.org.

After the terrorist attacks of September 11, 2001, many Arab Americans, people of Middle Eastern descent, Muslims, and people who simply "looked Arab" complained that they were being detained or questioned by police or by security guards at airports for no reason other than their appearance, clothing, or because they were carrying a religious symbol or book.

The law prohibits racial profiling, as it requires that most stops, arrests, and searches made by police officers be based on some sort of individualized suspicion.

However, it is sometimes difficult to prove why a police officer stopped or arrested a person. The frequency of the problem has been viewed as serious enough in some states that governors, mayors, police chiefs, and legislatures have implemented measures to track instances of racial profiling, punish those police officers guilty of racial profiling, and ultimately reduce racial profiling. As of 2008, 25 states had passed legislation requiring data collection to learn more about the extent of racial profiling, and an additional 22 states were collecting data voluntarily.

CAPTION ANSWER (P. 141) In certain situations, police officers may use race as one factor among others in deciding whom to stop. If an eyewitness provides a specific description that includes a racial description, then a police officer can reasonably use race as one of the factors.

TAKING ACTION:
LAW AND DEMOCRACY

Should Anything Be Done About Racial Profiling?

PROBLEM 12.8 (p.142)

This exercise presents a great opportunity to include community members such as police officers, school resource officers, citizen groups, or state and local legislators. This problem should be presented as a legislative simulation in which students play the roles of the six legislators and defend their positions. Each legislator should state a possible solution to the problem of racial profiling.

a.–b. Students' answers will vary. Students should give their reasons. If members of the community are present, engage them in a discussion or in the legislative hearing about these issues.

Following are some considerations regarding each solution:

Gomez: Most people would agree that police need training on cultural diversity and that being unfamiliar with people of different races may breed suspicion or stereotypes. However, some people might question whether training alone will really overcome existing bias.

Wu: Students could argue that this remedy would change the dynamic between the police officer and the person stopped and perhaps reduce the instances of racial profiling. Police would be more aware of the reasons for their actions, and they would realize that the people they stop can hold them accountable. In addition, this solution might encourage more individuals who feel they have been victimized to come forward. Others would argue that the police officers might only be going through the motions of fairness while continuing to practice racial profiling. Another argument against this solution is that it might create adversarial feelings on the part of police toward citizens, because police officers might feel they are being blamed before they do anything wrong.

Letaliano: Some governors and state legislatures have mandated data collection, but the data still might not reveal the true reason for individual stops. This solution could only encourage police officers to "fudge" their reasons for stopping people. In addition, if the data show that certain minority groups commit more crimes than other groups, some people may argue that racial profiling is not wrong and that members of minority groups should be stopped and searched more.

Reynolds: This argument ignores the fact that recent studies have shown that many members of minority groups feel that police are biased and racial profiling does occur. These individuals are not likely to be satisfied with bringing their grievances to a panel of police officers whom they already see as biased.

Al-Aziz: The video idea might be the most effective way to document abuses. However, it is expensive, and some would argue that it would take money from already strapped police departments that could be spent on solving other crimes. Some jurisdictions have implemented this solution, although some police officers argue that videotaping puts unfair pressure on them; that being constantly watched makes it difficult to do their jobs; that it is unfair to treat every officer as if he or she is doing something wrong with no evidence of it; and that it creates negative feelings and an adversarial atmosphere in every encounter with citizens.

Debouche: The idea of citizen complaint boards has been tried in some places, but they are often opposed by police who believe citizens will too often take the side of the person bringing the complaint.

ADDITIONAL RESOURCES

Street Law, Inc., has written a number of lesson plans to help school resource officers teach lessons about law, including a lesson about racial profiling. For more information about Street Law's *Police & Teens* program, visit streetlaw.org/programs/police-and-teens.

PROBLEM 12.9 (p.143)

a. It would not be considered profiling to stop this driver because he was, in fact, speeding. Whether the officers properly searched the car is a different matter. The facts presented do not seem to indicate that the officers had probable cause to conduct the search of the trunk.

b. This actually occurred after the attacks of September 11, 2001, and civil liberties groups criticized the practice as racial profiling. The U.S. Justice Department defended its actions on the grounds that there was an emergency situation and that the terrorists had been Muslims. Though no court has yet decided the issue, students may say that reasons other than religion would be needed to target areas where there are mosques. Before the passage of the *USA PATRIOT Act*, such wiretaps would have required a warrant based on probable cause, which is not present here. The law—criticized by some—gives the government wide discretion in using wiretaps for investigations relating to terrorism. See Chapter 44 for additional background.

  In a separate case dealing with possible religious profiling and a stop and search at the border, the U.S. Second Court of Appeals considered the case of five Muslim U.S. citizens who were detained when they returned from Canada. They had been to Canada to attend a three-day conference called "Revising the Islamic Spirit," a gathering of roughly 13,000 people. Despite the fact that these men had no prior criminal records and were not individually suspected of terrorism, they were fingerprinted, frisked, had their cars searched, and were questioned for several hours. They were not informed of the reason for their stop and search. In their

suit against the U.S. Customs and Border Control, they claimed their privacy and religious rights were violated. They tried to require the government to expunge all records of previous similar searches and to prevent the government from conducting similar future searches. The Court found that their constitutional rights were not violated. According to the decision, the U.S. Customs and Border Control had received intelligence that the conference might be a meeting place for terrorists and ordered special searches of attendees returning to the United States. The Court said, "We agree...that the government has a compelling interest in protecting against terrorism."[37]

c. The police officers questioned the two men partly because of their appearance, but also because they were sitting outside a store that the officers had good reason to believe would be robbed that day. This scenario appears to be an appropriate use of ethnicity because the witness was able to give specific information about the number of people involved, their gender, the language they spoke, and the exact jewelry store they intended to rob. Because ethnicity was not the sole factor in questioning them, the incident is not profiling. Also, this is just an informal field stop, not an arrest or search.

d. To question a person solely because of her nationality may seem unfair, but a court might uphold this stop for national security purposes. This view is based on the increased hostility toward the United States that would be expected from citizens of an international enemy. On the other hand, the question says "recently at war" rather than "currently at war," so a court might hold that national security is no longer a compelling reason to allow the detention.

INTERROGATIONS AND CONFESSIONS (PP. 143–145)

Learning Outcomes

After completing this section, students should be able to:

1. identify rights of an individual being interrogated that are stated in the Fifth and Sixth Amendments to the Constitution;
2. explain the legal principle upon which the protection against self-incrimination is based;
3. state when a confession is not admissible;

4. identify police conduct that would render a confession inadmissible;
5. describe how the *Miranda* and *Escobedo* cases clarified terms of a defendant's right to counsel; and
6. define the terms *interrogate, self-incrimination*, and *custodial interrogation*.

DISCUSSION—MIRANDA WARNINGS

As a way to introduce this section to students, ask them what rights people have when they are arrested. If they do not know, prompt them by saying "You have the right to...." Many students will be able to recall the elements of Miranda warnings, but they may not know their common name or their origin in the *Miranda* case. Then ask students to look at the sample *Miranda* warning card on page 150 of the Student Edition. Ask students why they think police officers might put the waiver in writing. Why might police officers ask a defendant to sign the waiver? Explain that these procedures came about because of the landmark case *Miranda v. Arizona* in 1966.[38]

ADDITIONAL RESOURCES

For additional lesson plans, primary source materials, and resources relating to *Miranda v. Arizona*, visit https://www.landmarkcases.org/. This site contains materials developed by Street Law, Inc., in partnership with the U.S. Supreme Court Historical Society.

CAPTION ANSWER (P. 144) Recent cases have altered the original effect of the *Miranda* case. In one case, the Court held that police may ask questions related to public safety before advising suspects of their rights. The Court also limited the impact of the *Miranda* ruling by requiring that the person be in a condition of custodial interrogation before the *Miranda* warnings are needed.

BACKGROUND—CUSTODIAL INTERROGATION AND CONFESSION LAW

The law in the area of interrogations and confessions is widely misunderstood. Many students think that *Miranda* warnings must be given at the time of arrest or the case will be thrown out. While *Miranda* warnings often are given at this point, they are not a requirement of a lawful arrest. They *are* required once a defendant is in custody or otherwise deprived of his or her freedom in some significant way and is being interrogated. This taking into custody might actually precede an officer's statement,

"You are under arrest." The key question is: when did *custodial interrogation* begin? Giving or not giving the *Miranda* warnings is not related to the validity of the arrest. If the warnings are not given, the arrest itself is still considered valid if it is supported by probable cause if the officer has begun interrogation, although the state will not be able to use any improperly obtained confession against the defendant at the trial. Depending on other evidence that the state has, this could—but might not necessarily—result in charges being dropped.

In *Standbury v. California*,[39] the U.S. Supreme Court further explained what is meant by custodial interrogation. If, during questioning, an officer begins to suspect the person of a crime but does not tell the person, then a reasonable person would feel that he or she was free to leave and therefore not in custody. At this point, *Miranda* warnings are not required until the suspect is in custody.

In a 1980 case, a robbery suspect was given the *Miranda* warnings several times and replied that he wanted to consult a lawyer. On the way to the police station, one officer said to another that he was afraid a missing shotgun (believed to have been used in the robbery) would be found by a student from a nearby school. The other officer made similar comments. Overhearing, the defendant then said he would show them where the gun was located. The U.S. Supreme Court held that the police comments were "offhand remarks" and not an interrogation that the officers would have expected to evoke an incriminating response.[40]

The Supreme Court has also held that the *Miranda* case does not apply to a police officer stopping a motorist suspected of driving while intoxicated. The Court said that no *Miranda* warnings need to be given until the person is "in custody."[41] The case referred to in the Student Edition, which created the public safety exception to *Miranda*, is *New York v. Quarles*.[42] *Miranda* warnings also need not be given in the exact form described in the *Miranda* case. This interpretation of the *Miranda* decision occurred in the 1989 case *Duckworth v. Eagan*.[43] The defendant was informed that if he could not afford a lawyer, one would be appointed "if and when you go to court." The Supreme Court held that this form of the *Miranda* warnings was adequate because it conveyed the necessary information to the defendant.

The *Miranda* warnings continue to raise difficult questions. Even when they are given, how must the police determine whether or not they are understood? According to a 1981 decision involving a deaf defendant, *Miranda* rights must be understood by a suspect in order for any of his or her subsequent statements to be used in court.[44] Interpreters for the police department were unable to accurately communicate the *Miranda* warnings to the defendant. Ask students how they think cases should be handled with non-English-speaking defendants. Some urban police officers carry a card with the warnings written in both English and Spanish.

The *Miranda* rights apply to juveniles and people arrested for misdemeanors as well as felonies. Many people, however, question whether or not juveniles can adequately understand the meaning of the warnings. Ask if students think young people should be given a more simplified version of the *Miranda* warnings. Perhaps juveniles should not be questioned at all without an attorney or their parents present. In some places, before questioning begins, parents are called and asked whether or not they waive their child's *Miranda* rights.

In one state, the *Miranda* warnings for juveniles have an additional warning: "If you are under 18, anything you say can be used against you in a juvenile court prosecution for a juvenile offense, and can also be used against you in an adult court criminal prosecution if the juvenile court decides that you are to be tried as an adult."

An interesting anecdote is that Miranda was subsequently retried after his victory in the U.S. Supreme Court, convicted based on evidence other than the original confession, and sent to prison. Years later, after his release from prison, he was found dead near a courthouse. In his pockets were packs of cards containing the *Miranda* warnings that he had been selling to defendants at the courthouse.

THE **CASE** OF...

The Juvenile and Miranda Warnings

PROBLEM 12.10 (p.145)

Students will likely be very interested in how Miranda Warnings and the decision in the *Miranda* case do or do not apply to juveniles.[45] Before asking students to complete this problem, be sure they have read the entire section about interrogations and custody. This problem is based on the case of *Yarborough* v. *Alvarado*, which was decided in 2004.[46]

a. Students' answers will vary. Alvarado can (and did) argue that a reasonable person would not have felt free to leave the interrogation room. His mother had brought him to the station at the request of the police. The interview was more than two hours long, and his mother's request to be with him during questioning was denied. Given this, Alvarado was in custody and should have been informed of his rights under *Miranda* before the interview took place.

The second major consideration was Alvarado's age. He argued that police should consider a suspect's age. Juvenile justice experts have long acknowledged that compared to adults, teens are less mature, are more submissive in the face of police authority, and lack critical knowledge and experience. Police officers should know that younger suspects may feel less free to leave and, therefore, may think they are in custody before an adult might. Younger suspects should benefit from a different application of *Miranda*.

b. Students' answers will vary. Yarborough could (and did) argue that Alvarado was not in custody at the time of the interviews, so the officer was not required to inform him of his Miranda rights. He was transported to the station by a parent. His mother was just outside the interview room. He was offered breaks, and he was free to leave (and did) after the interview.

Regarding age, Yarborough argued that it would make law enforcement efforts much more complicated if police had to change their Miranda procedures because of a suspect's possible age. A new Miranda rule for juveniles might undermine the clarity of the original *Miranda* ruling and make arrest and interrogation procedures more confusing and ineffective for all.

c. Students' answers will vary. The Court ruled that Alvarado was not in custody, and therefore the warnings were not required at the time of the interview. However, it was a split decision (5-4). The majority said it was impractical and unreasonable to ask that police consider age and experience when determining the need to give Miranda warnings. Justice O'Connor wrote in a concurring opinion that the age of the suspect could be relevant to determining custody in certain cases. The dissenting opinion, written by Justice Breyer and joined by three others, concluded, "What reasonable person...brought to a police station by his parents at police request, put in a small interrogation room, questioned for two solid hours, and confronted with claims that there is strong evidence that he participated in a serious crime, could have thought to himself, 'Well, anytime I want to leave I can just get up and walk out'?"

d. Students' answers will vary. Besides giving police officers their names, if they are asked questions by police officers that they do not wish to answer because the answers might be incriminating to them, they should remain silent and request a lawyer. This applies to juveniles and to adults. According to the Court, the officer did nothing wrong. However, some might argue that he should have read the *Miranda* warnings at the time of the interview to honor the spirit and intent of *Miranda*.

NOTES

(1) *Draper* v. *United States*, 358 U.S. 307 (1959).

(2) *Illinois* v. *Gates*, 462 U.S. 213 (1983).

(3) *U.S.* v. *Sharpe*, 470 U.S. 675 (1985).

(4) *Terry* v. *Ohio*, 392 U.S. 1 (1968).

(5) *Tennessee* v. *Garner*, 471 U.S. 1 (1985).

(6) *Knowles* v. *Iowa*, 525 U.S. 113 (1998).

(7) *Tennessee* v. *Garner*, 471 U.S. 1 (1985).

(8) *Scott* v. *Harris*, 550 U.S. (2007).

(9) *Tennessee* v. *Garner*, 471 U.S. 1 (1985).

(10) *Knowles* v. *Iowa*, 525 U.S. 113 (1998).

(11) *Ohio* v. *Robinette*, 519 U.S. 33 (1996).

(12) *Whren* v. *United States*, 517 U.S. 806 (1996).

(13) *Maryland* v. *Wilson*, 519 U.S. 408 (1997).

(14) *Rodriguez* v. *United States*, 135 S.Ct. 1609 (2015).

(15) *Richards* v. *Wisconsin*, 520 U.S. 385 (1997); *Wilson* v. *Arkansas*, 514 U.S. 927 (1995).

(16) *Maryland* v. *Buie*, 494 U.S. 325 (1990).

(17) *Minnesota* v. *Dickerson*, 508 U.S. 366 (1993).

(18) *Hudson* v. *Michigan*, 547 U.S. 586 (2006).

(19) *Georgia* v. *Randolph*, 547 U.S. 103 (2006).

(20) *California* v. *Greenwood*, 486 U.S. 35 (1988).

(21) *Georgia* v. *Randolph*, 547 U.S. 103 (2006).

(22) *Fernandez* v. *California*, 571 U.S. 292 (2014).

(23) *Kyllo* v. *United States*, 533 U.S. 27 (2001).

(24) *Richards* v. *Wisconsin*, 520 U.S. 385 (1997).

(25) *Wilson* v. *Arkansas*, 514 U.S. 927 (1995).

(26) *Hudson* v. *Michigan*, 547 U.S. 586 (2006).

(27) *New Jersey* v. *TLO*, 469 U.S. 325 (1985).

(28) *New Jersey* v. *TLO*, 469 U.S. 325 (1985).

(29) *Safford Unified School District* v. *Redding*, 557 U. S. ____ (2009).

(30) *Vernonia Sch. Dist. 47J* v. *Acton*, 515 U.S. 646 (1995).

(31) *Board of Educ. of Independent School District No. 92 of Pottawatomie County* v. *Earls*, 536 U.S. 822 (2002).

(32) *Board of Educ. of Independent School District No. 92 of Pottawatomie County* v. *Earls*, 536 U.S. 822 (2002).

(33) *United States* v. *Jones*, 565 U.S. 400 (2012).

(34) *Riley* v. *California*, No. 13–132 (2014).

(35) *Carpenter* v. *United States*, 138 S.Ct. 2206 (2018).

(36) *Wilkins* v. *Maryland State Police*, Civ. No. MJG-93-468 (USDC MD 1993).

(37) Christine Kearney, "Border Search of Muslims Was Lawful, Court Says," *Reuters*, November 27, 2007.

(38) *Miranda* v. *Arizona*, 384 U.S. 436 (1966).

(39) *Standbury* v. *California*, 511 U.S. 318 (1994).

(40) *Rhode Island* v. *Innis*, 446 U.S. 291 (1980).

(41) *Berkemer* v. *McCarty*, 468 U.S. 420 (1984).

(42) *New York* v. *Quarles*, 467 U.S. 649 (1984).

(43) *Duckworth* v. *Eagan*, 492 U.S. 195 (1989).

(44) *State* v. *Mason*, 2012 – Ohio – 5463.

(45) *Miranda* v. *Arizona*, 384 U.S. 436 (1966).

(46) *Yarborough* v. *Alvarado*, 541 U.S. 652 (2004).

BOOKING AND INITIAL APPEARANCE
(PP. 146–147)

After the arrest of a criminal suspect, but before the criminal case reaches the courtroom, several preliminary proceedings take place. Most of these proceedings are standard for every case. Depending on the specific circumstances and the result of these preliminary proceedings, the charges may be dropped or the defendant may plead guilty. If either of these two things occurs, there will be no trial.

Learning Outcomes

After completing this section, students should be able to:
1. identify two circumstances during preliminary proceedings that may result in no trial;
2. list steps involved in booking a person;
3. identify four things that may occur at an initial appearance in court;
4. identify the most important part of the initial appearance; and
5. define the terms *booking* and *arraignment*.

BACKGROUND—PROCEEDINGS BEFORE TRIAL

Some interesting court cases involving pretrial issues have dealt with taking fingernail clippings,[1] handwriting specimens,[2] and blood samples from defendants.[3] The cases raise the question of whether or not such actions violate a defendant's right to be free from self-incrimination and from unreasonable searches and seizures. The U.S. Supreme Court has held that these procedures do not violate the self-incrimination clause of the Fifth Amendment because they do not extract evidence of a testimonial or communicative nature. However, the Court found that pumping a defendant's stomach against his will in order to recover drugs swallowed during a police raid is "shocking to the conscience" and unreasonable.[4]

An important pretrial issue is the precise point at which the defendant is entitled to representation by counsel. Should the defendant have an attorney brought to the place of his or her arrest? The Court has held that the accused is entitled to counsel at any "critical stage of the prosecution," such as the preliminary hearing or arraignment.[5] Defendants are entitled to an attorney at a post-indictment lineup[6] but not a pre-indictment lineup[7] or when a handwriting sample is taken.[8] In practice, poor defendants often have an attorney appointed for them at the bail hearing or initial appearance.

ACTIVITY—TAKING A FIELD TRIP

In some communities, police will walk students through the booking process at the local police department. It might also be possible to arrange with the police department to have students sit in on a lineup while a police officer describes what occurs.

BAIL AND PRETRIAL RELEASE
(PP. 147–149)

Learning Outcomes

After completing this section, students should be able to:

1. identify the purpose of bail;
2. describe cases in which bail may not be granted;
3. describe the process of posting bail;
4. state the relationship between bail and the Eighth Amendment;
5. describe circumstances in which the accused may be released on personal recognizance;
6. list additional methods courts use to ensure that a defendant returns for trial;
7. weigh the merits of arguments for and against pretrial release; and
8. define the terms *bail* and *personal recognizance*.

DISCUSSION—BAIL

Ask students why they think we have a system of bail in our society. How does bail relate to our basic ideas of justice and to our Bill of Rights? Students' answers will vary but should include the notion that the right to bail is based on the idea that a person is presumed innocent until proven guilty. The protection from "excessive" bail is contained in the Eighth Amendment.

BACKGROUND—BAIL AND PREVENTATIVE DETENTION

Many people continue to criticize the release of those who have been arrested for serious crimes before their trials. Others state that the Eighth Amendment protection from "excessive" bail is based on the notion that a person is presumed innocent until proven guilty. Under a federal criminal law passed in 1984—the *Bail Reform Act*—persons charged with federal crimes may be held without bail if they are found to be "dangerous to the community."[9] The law also presumes dangerous a person arrested for a drug offense that carries a possible sentence of more than ten years. Someone who previously committed a violent crime while released pending trial is also presumed dangerous.

Defense lawyers in a 1987 U.S. Supreme Court case challenged the constitutionality of the *Bail Reform Act*. They charged that holding people

without bail before their trial amounted to punishment before any finding of guilt. The Court rejected this argument—noting that the purpose of the law was to protect the public, not to punish the accused person—and the law remains in effect in federal courts today.[10]

For more information about the *Bail Reform Act of 1984* and the Supreme Court's rulings about it, encourage students to read the legislation and decision. (Citations for each are listed at the end of this chapter.) All 50 states allow this type of "preventive detention" for defendants considered to be a threat to the community.

CAPTION ANSWER (P. 147) Operating a bail bond company is a risky business. If a defendant flees before trial, the company must pay the bond to the court unless the defendant can be found. A defendant who is found might not willingly accompany the bail bond company employee to court.

DISCUSSION—BAIL FOR POOR DEFENDANTS

Many judges are criticized for imposing de facto preventive detention by setting high bail for indigent defendants. Discuss with students the factors judges weigh when determining bail or release, and discuss other issues involving bail, preventive detention, and crimes committed by persons released before trial.

A challenging bail problem involves people mistaking the nature of bail. In several cases, people, such as immigrants who may not have understood the language or the culture, have paid bail, believing it to be payment of the fine (or the required bribe to the judge) and then have been confused when arrested for failure to appear at trial.[11]

Because poor people have greater difficulty raising bail money than others, they are more likely to remain in jail during the pretrial period. This makes it more difficult for them to prepare for trial, and they sometimes must wear prison clothes in court. Wealthy defendants, including some drug dealers, are more likely to have bail funds. Ask students if they believe the poor are treated unfairly by the bail system. How might wearing prison clothes in court affect the outcome of a trial? How else might the system try to ensure that defendants show up for their trials? Ask students if the the term *excessive* in the 8th Amendment should be interpreted in the same way for every defendant of the same crime or adjusted based on their financial resources.

CAPTION ANSWER (P. 148) Judges should consider factors such as the nature and circumstances of the offense and the accused's family and community ties, financial resources, employment background, and prior criminal record.

a. These questions encourage students to think about the rationale for bail. Bail is based on the presumption of innocence balanced against the need to ensure that the defendant shows up for trial. In discussing the questions, encourage students to imagine an ideal system and how such a system could be achieved.

b.–c. Students' opinions should be supported by reasons.

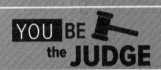

YOU BE the JUDGE

Bail Hearing (pp. 150)

The bail hearings in this feature are designed to expose students to some of the problems involved in applying the standard of "equal justice." Have students work in small groups. Each group should simulate a bail hearing in which both an attorney for the state and a defense counsel prepare arguments recommending a bail option. A judge for each group should make a judgment in the five cases. In the class discussion that follows, each judge should explain how he or she decided each case. Were the reasons behind the decisions consistent within groups? Among different groups? Was any form of sexual, economic, or other bias detected in the decisions?

Students may wish to learn more about the bail system in their area before doing this exercise. Invite an attorney, a representative of the pretrial services program, a bail agency, or a bondsperson familiar with the local bail system to make the activity more authentic.

INFORMATION AND PRELIMINARY HEARING (PP. 149 AND 151)

Learning Outcomes

After completing this section, students should be able to:

1. identify the purpose of a prosecutor's information;
2. define the term *information* as it applies in this context;
3. identify the purpose of the preliminary hearing;
4. state three rights defendants in most states have in a preliminary hearing; and
5. define the term *preliminary hearing*.

ACTIVITY—LEARNING TERMINOLOGY

Many people confuse the terms *information, preliminary hearing,* and *grand jury*. After students read these three sections in the Student Edition, have them create a chart that compares the three terms. Questions they should try to answer include:

- Is this procedure used for felonies, misdemeanors, or both?
- Is this procedure a formal hearing?
- Is this procedure used in all states? Is it used for federal crimes?
- What is the main purpose of the procedure?
- Can defendants appeal decisions made in this procedure?
- Do defendants have the right to an attorney during this procedure?
- Can defendants call and cross-examine witnesses in this procedure?
- Who makes the decision here? A judge? A jury?
- Is this procedure called for in the Bill of Rights?
- What happens to a defendant after this procedure, assuming the charges are dropped? Assuming the case moves forward?

GRAND JURY (PP. 151–152)

Learning Outcomes

After completing this section, students should be able to:

1. explain the purpose of a grand jury;
2. state how the rights of individuals may be protected by the grand jury system in the United States;
3. describe the roles (if any) of the prosecutor, defendant, defense attorney, judges, and witnesses in a grand jury proceeding; and
4. define the terms *grand jury* and *indictment*.

BACKGROUND—THE GRAND JURY SYSTEM

The prosecution controls the grand jury system in part because the prosecution controls the presentation of witnesses and evidence. As with preliminary hearings, many people criticize the grand jury system. Some feel that grand juries are rubber stamps for prosecutors. Proponents of grand jury reform feel that the media often shape grand juries' opinions and cause them to indict despite lack of evidence.

The defense attorney is not allowed in the grand jury room but can wait outside. During proceedings, the defendant can leave the room to obtain advice from his or her attorney. Grand juries sometimes choose not to indict because of insufficient evidence to support the charges. Proponents of the grand jury system see a legitimate refusal to indict as an example of citizens protecting their peers from oppressive government action.

In 1998, the U.S. Supreme Court ruled on discrimination in the makeup of the grand jury. In that case, a white defendant had been indicted by a grand jury for the murder of another white person. The defendant proved that no African American had served as a grand jury foreperson in that judicial district for the last 17 years, suggesting that the grand jury process was unfair. In this case the Court extended protection against racial discrimination in the composition of petit juries to include grand juries as an element of due process and receiving a fair trial.[12]

PROBLEM 13.2 (p.152)

Student responses will vary. Many people say the main advantage of the grand jury system is that it allows prosecutors to see if they have enough evidence to take a case to trial, kind of like a "test run." By giving prosecutors this opportunity, the government might avoid the costs of an unnecessary trial. Critics of the grand jury process contend that the process itself lacks transparency and the necessary safeguards of a criminal trial, such as the right of a defendant to appear before the Grand Jury, the right to an attorney to advocate for him or her, and evidence rules that are much less strict.

FELONY ARRAIGNMENT AND PLEAS (P. 152)

Learning Outcomes

After completing this section, students should be able to:

1. describe the steps in criminal procedure that follow a guilty plea;
2. describe the steps in criminal procedure that follow a not-guilty plea;
3. describe the benefit of pleading nolo contendere; and
4. define the term nolo contendere.

BACKGROUND—PLEA BARGAINING

Point out to students that when a defendant first appears in court, he or she almost always pleads not guilty. This occurs even when the defendant will later agree to plead guilty. The not-guilty plea, however, gives the defense attorney time to make sure that any guilty plea is based on an informed choice and may make it possible for the defendant to plea-bargain with the prosecutor. Plea bargaining often allows the defense attorney to work out the best deal possible for the defendant.

PRETRIAL MOTIONS (PP. 152–154)

Learning Outcomes

After completing this section, students should be able to:

1. describe the general purposes of pretrial motions the defense may file;
2. explain the purpose of the exclusionary rule;
3. state the relationship between the Fourth Amendment and the exclusionary rule;
4. describe how Mapp v. Ohio affected the rights of the accused in cases at the state level;
5. weigh the merits of arguments for and against the exclusionary rule and judicial integrity and deterrence;
6. describe the relationships between the exclusionary rule, judicial integrity, and deterrence;
7. identify the "good faith" exception to the exclusionary rule and the reason for its existence; and
8. define the terms pretrial motion, exclusionary rule, judicial integrity, and deterrence.

BACKGROUND—HISTORY OF THE EXCLUSIONARY RULE

The U.S. Supreme Court held in Mapp v. Ohio (1960)[13] that the exclusionary rule was applicable to the states. Thus, illegally seized evidence is not allowed at any trials. Ms. Mapp was convicted of "knowingly having had in her possession and under her control certain lewd and lascivious books, pictures, and photographs...." The police "unlawfully seized these items during an unlawful search" of Ms. Mapp's home following a forced entry. Additionally, the existence of a search warrant for Ms. Mapp's home was in question.

As indicated in the Student Edition, in the years since the *Mapp* decision, courts have reevaluated the exclusionary rule and have modified it somewhat. For example, in 1988, the U.S. Supreme Court held that evidence initially discovered during an unlawful, warrantless search may be used in court if the same evidence is rediscovered by a subsequent lawful search.[14] This was another step toward limiting, while not revoking, the impact of the exclusionary rule on criminal prosecutions.

In 1989, the Court reaffirmed the breadth of the exclusionary rule. Under certain circumstances, an exception to the rule allows prosecutors to introduce illegally obtained evidence for the limited purpose of impeaching (calling into question) the defendant's credibility.[15]

The exclusionary rule applies not only to illegally obtained evidence from searches (Fourth Amendment), but also to confessions obtained in violation of the *Miranda* rules (Fifth and Sixth Amendments).

For more information and lesson plans about the exclusionary rule as well as *Mapp* v. *Ohio*, visit www.landmarkcases.org/, a free teacher resource developed by Street Law, Inc., with support from the Supreme Court Historical Society.

CAPTION ANSWER (P. 152) Media attention may influence jurors' perceptions of the defendant and the case.

CAPTION ANSWER (P. 153) If an important piece of evidence is excluded from trial because it was obtained illegally, the defendant could go free. Many claim that the exclusionary rule is a legal loophole that allows dangerous criminals to be released.

PROBLEM 13.3 (p.154)

a. Students' answers should include the fact that the exclusionary rule holds that any evidence illegally seized by law enforcement officers cannot be used at trial as substantive evidence against the accused. The rule is used by criminal defense lawyers when filing a motion to suppress evidence. The motion asks the court to exclude from the trial any evidence illegally obtained. Hearings are often held on this type of motion. Students should also understand that the illegally obtained evidence may still be used to discredit statements made by the defendant and are admissible in other court proceedings, such as hearings to determine probable cause, sentencing, and parole and probation revocation.

b. The Supreme Court adopted the exclusionary rule "to put teeth into the Fourth Amendment." The rule is designed to deter police from illegal conduct, to keep the state from benefiting from illegal behavior, and to preserve the integrity of the court system.

Critics of the rule claim it does not work. They argue that it does not deter the police, who they say are more concerned with arrests than convictions and often do not understand the complexities of the Fourth Amendment. Critics also say the rule hurts the public more than it does the police by letting guilty criminals go free.

Students should give their ideas about the rule and explain the reasons for their positions. Attorneys and police officers may also be good resource persons to help with these discussions.

c. The good faith exception to the exclusionary rules makes it possible for the evidence to be admitted in court even if the search warrant that led to that evidence was later found to be invalid. In the case of *U.S.* v. *Leon*, The U.S. Supreme Court determined that the police had been reasonable when they acted in accordance to the warrant that was later found to be invalid.[16] In the *Sheppard* case, the Court found that although the magistrate used the wrong form, the exclusionary rule did not necessarily apply, because the police had acted in good faith.[17]

The *Leon* and *Sheppard* cases involved "mistake of fact." In 2014, the Court ruled on a case which involved a "mistake of law," not fact. In the case of *Helen* v. *North Carolina*, the Court ruled that evidence is admissible even if the officer conducting the search made a "reasonable" mistake about what the law said as long as the officer obtained the evidence after establishing a reasonable suspicion.[18]

PLEA BARGAINING (PP. 154–155)

Learning Outcomes

After completing this section, students should be able to:

1. explain why most defendants who are convicted never go to trial;
2. describe concessions typically granted to a defendant in exchange for a guilty plea;
3. evaluate arguments for and against the use of plea bargaining; and
4. define the term *plea bargaining*.

PROBLEM 13.4 (p.155)

a. Students' answers will vary. Recent studies on plea bargaining conclude that it benefits the prosecutor more than the defendant. The studies found that, for the most part, defendants did not receive lighter sentences when they pleaded guilty than when they were convicted at trial. It was also found that without plea bargaining there would be more dismissals and the cost to the criminal justice system would be higher. A study of the California courts estimated that, on average, a jury trial costs the state $3,000, while a guilty plea costs about $215. The advantages of plea bargaining are that it saves considerable court time and money and speeds up the overall court process, and many people say that the entire criminal justice process would break down without it.

A possible disadvantage may be that some people who would not be convicted at trial plead guilty anyway. Their decision is based on either poor advice from their attorneys or fear of what might happen at a trial. Plea bargaining may also result in lighter sentences for defendants who deserve more punishment.

b. Students should state their opinions on this issue. Consider inviting a local defense attorney to discuss cases where this might happen. The *New York Times* reported that police interrogation techniques have become so savvy that the vast majority of suspects waive their rights to trial. While many guilty criminals have given confessions, police have also extracted confessions from innocent people. DNA evidence has cleared some criminal defendants who had originally confessed to the crimes. Psychologists say there are certain personality types that are more likely to make false confessions (for example, some unstable people who are drawn to the lurid glamour of notorious cases). At other times suspects confess to protect the real criminal. Many suspects are mentally unstable, delusional, or otherwise highly susceptible to suggestion. Finally, some suspects simply believe that the police have uncontestable evidence against them and that a confession will persuade the police to be lenient, so they might confess in order to get that leniency.[19]

Investigating the Law Where You Live

(p. 155) Students could contact local legal officials such as prosecutors, defense attorneys and judges to better understand the plea bargaining guidelines in your state.

BACKGROUND—IMMIGRANTS, NONCITIZENS, AND PLEA BARGAINS

People who are not U.S. citizens who plead guilty to crimes in state court generally are unaware of the immigration consequences of this plea. Possible consequences include loss of lawful status, mandatory deportation, or permanent inadmissibility. During the 1990s, Congress rewrote immigration laws a number of times. Notably, Congress enacted two major pieces of legislation in 1996 to expand both the kinds of criminal behavior that trigger immigration penalties and the severity of those penalties.[20] Encourage interested students to explore this issue. For additional information about law and immigrants, see Chapter 42.

ACTIVITY—BUILDING VOCABULARY

This chapter includes a number of terms most students will not be familiar with before they encounter them in the text. Make a list of all the terms you want them to know. Jumble the order of the words, and then have students write a creative story in which they incorporate all the terms. A fun way to vary this assignment is to have students write their stories but leave numbered blanks where the terms should go and then write their answer keys on a separate page. Have them exchange stories with a fellow student and let the other student try to complete the story.

NOTES

(1) *Cupp* v. *Murphy*, 412 U.S. 291 (1973).

(2) *Gilbert* v. *California*, 388 U.S. 263 (1967).

(3) *Schmerber* v. *California*, 384 U.S. 757 (1966).

(4) *Rochin* v. *California*, 342 U.S. 165 (1952).

(5) *Coleman* v. *Alabama*, 399 U.S. 1 (1970).

(6) *United States* v. *Wade*, 388 U.S. 218 (1967).

(7) *Kirby* v. *Illinois,* 406 U.S. 682 (1972).

(8) *Gilbert* v. *California,* 388 U.S. 263 (1967).

(9) *Bail Reform Act,* 18 U.S.C.A. § 3141 (1988).

(10) *U.S.* v. *Salerno,* 481 U.S. 739 (1987).

(11) Joanne I. Moore and Margaret Fisher (eds.)
Immigrants in Courts (Seattle and London:
University of Washington Press, 1999).

(12) *Campbell* v. *Louisiana,* 523 U.S. 392 (1998).

(13) *Mapp* v. *Ohio,* 367 U.S. 643 (1961).

(14) *Murray* v. *U.S.,* 487 U.S. 533 (1988).

(15) *James* v. *Illinois,* 367 U.S. 643 (1961).

(16) *United States* v. *Leon,* 468 U.S. 897 (1984).

(17) *Massachusetts* v. *Sheppard,* 468 U.S. 981 (1984).

(18) *Heien* v. *North Carolina,* 574 U.S. 54 (2014).

(19) Jan Hoffman, "Police Refine Methods So
Potent, Even the Innocent Have Confessed,"
New York Times (March 30, 1998): A1.

(20) *Illegal Immigration Reform and Immigrant
Responsibility Act of 1996,* Pub. L., No. 104-208,
110 Stat. 3009 (1996).

Many of the basic rights set forth in the U.S. Constitution apply to people who have been accused of a crime. Accused people are entitled to have a public jury trial without undue delay. They are entitled to be informed of their rights and of the charges against them, to confront and cross-examine witnesses, to require witnesses to testify on their behalf, to refuse to testify against themselves, and to be represented by an attorney. These rights together constitute the overall right to a fair trial.

INTRODUCTION AND RIGHT TO TRIAL BY JURY (PP. 156–157)

Learning Outcomes

After completing these sections, students should be able to:

1. summarize the rights to which people accused of crimes are entitled;
2. state how the Sixth Amendment protects people accused of crimes;
3. identify circumstances in which a jury trial is not required;
4. state how the U.S. Supreme Court has ruled when attorneys attempted to exclude jurors because of their race;
5. develop a hypothesis to explain the phenomenon of jury nullification; and
6. define the terms *due process, waive, voir dire, for cause challenge, peremptory challenges*, and *jury nullification*.

Note: For additional information about trials, including trial courts, steps in a trial, the roles of judges and jurors, and jury service, review the materials in the Student Edition and Teacher Manual for Chapter 5, "The Court System."

ACTIVITY—IDENTIFYING THE QUALITIES OF IDEAL JURORS

Show some help-wanted advertisements or online postings to students before you begin this activity with the class. The ads or posts should describe the type of candidate the employer is seeking. The particular jobs do not matter.

After sharing the ads with students, ask the following questions:

- How many of you have ever read a help-wanted advertisement? What do help-wanted ads look like? What kinds of things do they say? *Students' answers will vary, but they will probably mention that most ads include the job title, salary, skills and experience required, whom to contact, etc. If many students have never seen a help-wanted ad, you may want to pass a few around the class for reference.*
- What do you think are the most important qualities of an effective juror?

Give students the following directions and have pairs of students spend a few minutes planning and writing a help-wanted ad for an ideal juror. This person should be the kind of juror the students would want if someone they care about had to face a jury.

1. Imagine that you are getting ready to write an advertisement to recruit new jurors.

2. What are the skills, values, and experiences you are looking for in an effective juror? (Explain that the term *skills* describes things jurors should be able to do. The term *values* describes things jurors should believe in. The term *experiences* describes what jurors have gone through or observed to give them their unique perspectives.)

3. Besides skills, values, and experiences, what are you looking for in a juror?

4. Write a help-wanted ad for a juror.

When students have completed the assignment, invite four student volunteers to the board to record answers. Assign each volunteer a different word or column, so that each time a student in the class mentions a *skill*, that recorder writes down the skills. The other students will be assigned *values*, *experiences*, and *other qualifications*. Ask two or three pairs of students to read their want ads aloud. Then lead a "call-out" session, in which you ask students who have not yet shared to call out other skills not yet mentioned. Have them do the same for values, experiences, and other qualities.

When that part of the discussion is finished, ask students:

- If you were a prosecuting attorney, do you think you would look for the same kind of juror that the class just described? Why or why not? What might a prosecuting attorney look for that would be different from what a defense attorney might want? *Answers will vary, but students may mention that a prosecutor might look for someone who is "tough on crime" or who will relate to the victim, while defense attorneys might look for someone who can relate to and sympathize with the accused.*

At the conclusion of the activity, review with students the selection process for juries, using the jury selection background notes provided here.

BACKGROUND—HOW ARE PETIT JURIES SELECTED?

Petit jurors are people who hear evidence in a trial and determine whether or not a defendant is guilty. In some states, petit jurors also decide the punishment a guilty person receives. (This is in contrast to grand jurors.) The Student Edition provides a brief overview of the selection process for petit juries and explains peremptory challenges. Additional background follows.

The Summons

The first step in selecting a jury is to call a group of potential jurors to the courthouse for jury duty. Most people asked to serve on juries get a letter in the mail called a summons. The summons tells them where and when they should report for duty. Those who receive summonses are usually picked from a list of people who have registered to vote in that state. Some states also use lists of licensed drivers or recipients of other state-issued identification to determine potential jurors. Anyone whose name is on the designated lists is considered part of the jury pool and could be summoned for jury duty at any time.

The Jury Venire

Most people who appear for jury duty are not actually picked to serve on a jury. The court sends summonses to more people than it needs. Once a person shows up for jury duty, he or she is officially in the jury venire, or panel, from which the jury is chosen. In most court systems, a large group of people are summoned to appear on the same day. Each is assigned a number. The clerk then calls for jurors by number to go to a particular courtroom. Once a person is sent to a courtroom, the chances of being selected for duty are much higher. Depending on how many juries are needed that day, the rest of the people who were summoned will be sent home.

The Voir Dire

To narrow down the group even more, lawyers representing the defendant and lawyers representing the prosecutor or plaintiff question potential jurors. Through the questioning process, lawyers try to determine whether a potential juror holds biases or prejudices that would affect his or her ability to be impartial. This questioning process is called voir dire, which means to "speak the truth" in French. Typical voir dire questions are: "Do you know the defendant or the victim personally? Have you seen media coverage about this case? Have you made up your mind about whether the defendant is guilty?" In some places, the voir dire process is done by a judge instead of by the attorneys.

Removal for Cause

If, based on answers given in voir dire, lawyers can cite reasons that a potential juror would be biased against their side of the case, they can request that the juror in question be removed from the pool. The judge will make this determination. This is called removal for cause. As potential jury members are eliminated, the venire gets smaller.

Peremptory Challenges

Remind students that in the adversarial system of justice, lawyers want jurors who will be sympathetic to their side of the case. In addition to removing jurors for cause, it has been a long tradition to allow lawyers to remove certain potential jurors from the venire without stating a reason. This is called peremptory challenge. When lawyers use peremptory challenges, they may base their requests on intuition and probability. As mentioned in the Student Edition, the U.S. Supreme Court has ruled that judges and lawyers cannot use peremptory challenges to remove potential jurors because of their race,[1] gender,[2] or national origin.[3] Each side may use only a limited number of peremptory challenges, which varies from trial to trial.

Seating (or Empanelling) the Jury

Once the voir dire is finished and potential jurors are removed for cause or through peremptory challenges, a jury is empaneled. In most criminal trials, 12 people serve on a jury and may be joined by one or two alternates. Some civil trials—cases involving lawsuits—use 12 jurors, while others use 6 jurors.

BACKGROUND AND DISCUSSION— IMPROVING THE JURY SYSTEM

The right to a jury trial in criminal cases was the only explicit guarantee to appear in both the original U.S. Constitution and in the Bill of Rights. In fact, while the Framers of the Constitution disagreed on many points, they consistently agreed on the need to safeguard the right to a trial by jury.[4]

The role of the jury in both civil and criminal trials has been the subject of much debate. One argument is that U.S. trials should become more inquisitorial, meaning the judge should play a more dominant role, as is the case in some European countries. Another argument is that the jury should be more actively involved in the case, which would improve the jury's ability to interpret information and determine the facts. Some specific suggestions to improve the jury system include:

- looking to a wider variety of sources from which to draw potential jurors to provide a more diverse jury pool;
- eliminating or cutting back on peremptory challenges and extensive lawyer-conducted voir dire;
- retaining the rule of unanimity and the 12-member jury;
- drafting clear and concise jury instructions and presenting the instructions to the jury before the trial starts;
- giving jurors the right to communicate with each other, to ask questions of the witnesses and the judge, and to take notes during trial;
- allowing for greater jury participation in sentencing; and
- requiring the jury to give reasons for its verdict in a written decision.

Discuss proposed reforms with students. Students might conduct research to determine whether the courts in their state have adopted any of these proposed reforms. They might also attempt to interview judges in the local area to find out what they think of the proposed reforms and to identify other possible ways to improve the system.

The U.S. Supreme Court has held that juries in state courts need not be composed of 12 persons. For non-petty cases using a 6-person jury, the Supreme Court has ruled that conviction must be unanimous.[5] In some states smaller juries are permitted so long as the jury is large enough to promote group deliberation and provides a possibility for obtaining a cross section of the community.[6] A jury of fewer than 6 persons for a non-petty offense is deemed to violate the constitutional right to trial by jury.[7] The Supreme Court has permitted a 9-to-3 verdict in a noncapital state criminal case.[8]

BACKGROUND—A JURY OF YOUR PEERS

The right to a jury trial helps guarantee judgment by one's peers and provides for community participation in the criminal justice system. These ideas are considered basic to the American notions of fairness and justice.

To illustrate the legal difficulties involved in peremptory challenges, you can use the following example of jury exclusion. In *Batson* v. *Kentucky*, an African American defendant was convicted by an all-white jury in Kentucky. The defendant argued that the jury should be dismissed on the grounds that the prosecution's removal of African American jurors violated the defendant's rights under the Sixth and Fourteenth Amendments. These amendments guarantee the defendant a jury drawn from a cross section of the community and guarantee that each defendant receives equal protection under the law.

The U.S. Supreme Court held that the equal protection clause of the Fourteenth Amendment prohibits the prosecution from excluding potential jurors solely on the basis of race. The Court also held that the clause forbids the prosecution's exclusion of African American jurors based on the state's assumption that African American jurors as a group are unable to impartially consider a case against an African American defendant. The Court found that this type of exclusion not only denied the rights guaranteed to the defendant under the Sixth and Fourteenth Amendments, but also discriminated against the excluded juror. Moreover, the Court noted that discriminatory selection procedures undermine the public's confidence in the fairness of our justice system.[9]

In a much earlier case, the Supreme Court ruled that a state law exempting women from jury service solely because of their gender deprives a defendant of his or her Sixth and Fourteenth Amendment rights to an impartial jury. The Court said that excluding identifiable segments of the population cannot be squared with the constitutional concept of trial before a jury composed of a fair cross section of the community.[10]

The *Americans with Disabilities Act (ADA)*[11] prohibits discrimination against an individual with a disability. The *ADA* plays a role in the jury selection process because jurors and potential jurors must be given reasonable accommodations that enable them to serve, rather than being excluded outright.

DISCUSSION—THE COMPOSITION OF JURIES

Ask students the following questions:

- Should every juror have the same skills? Experiences? Values?
  Students' answers will vary.

- What is diversity? If you were looking into a room that was full of a diverse group of people, what would you see?
  Students' answers should include attributes or characteristics that people are born with (gender, race) and things people can acquire (education). Most people agree that a diverse group would include people from different ethnicities, religious backgrounds, sexual orientations, physical qualities, ages, economic backgrounds, political perspectives, and experiences.

- Is it good to have a diverse jury? Explain.
  Students' answers will vary.

- What would be the advantages of having different perspectives on a panel of jurors, if any? What might be the disadvantages?
  Students' answers will vary.

Explain to students that when the jury system first began in the United States, the only people allowed to serve on juries were white men who owned property. Over time, the property, race, and gender requirements were dropped. In the late 1870s, the U.S. Supreme Court ruled that states cannot prevent any citizen from having the opportunity to serve on a jury because of his or her race. The Court also said that a state denies an African American defendant equal protection when it puts him or her on trial before a jury from which members of his or her race have purposely been excluded. The Court wrote: "The very idea of a jury is that it is a body of men (or women) composed of the peers or equals of the person (who is on trial)."[12] Remind students that despite this decision, many juries remained segregated well into the 1950s.

Some people remain concerned about the composition of juries and how it affects justice today. Tell students that the questions they answered concerning whether juries should be diverse and how they could be more diverse have been debated among legal scholars and people involved in the justice system for years.

Ask students the following questions:

- What do you think the phrase "a jury of your peers" means?
  Students' answers will vary.

- If the jury was all male and the defendant was female, do you think the proceeding would be fair? Why or why not? What are the benefits of having a jury that includes female jurors? What are the drawbacks? *Students' answers will vary.*

- Should the jury be from the same part of town or same neighborhood as the defendant? Why or why not? What are the benefits of having the jury and defendant be from the same community? What are the drawbacks? *Students' answers will vary.*

- If the jury was composed of Latinos and the accused was Asian, do you think the proceeding would be fair? Why or why not? What are the benefits of having a jury match the ethnicity and race of the offender? What are the drawbacks? *Students' answers will vary.*

- If it is a right to have "a jury of your peers," where could you find it written down? Where are most of our legal rights written? *The words "a jury of your peers" does not appear in the U.S. Constitution, however it has been interpreted that a defendant is guaranteed one based on several provisions.*

Direct students to examine the following sections of the U.S. Constitution: Article III, Section 2; the Sixth Amendment; the Seventh Amendment; and the Fourteenth Amendment, Section 1, to find out if these sections guarantee a right to a jury of one's peers. As you help students analyze the document, please note:

Article III, Section 2: This does *not* guarantee a jury of one's peers. It says we have a right to a jury from the state in which the crime was allegedly committed.

The Sixth Amendment: This amendment focuses on the rights of people who have committed crimes, including the right to a jury. In modern times, the U.S. Supreme Court has said adults charged with felonies or misdemeanors for which they could receive jail time of six months or more are entitled to a jury. People accused of misdemeanor traffic violations that would be punishable by a fine or jail time of less than six months are not entitled to a jury. The Sixth Amendment does *not* say we have a right to a jury of our peers. It does say we have the right to a jury that is impartial. Tell students you will come back to this idea of impartiality shortly.

The Seventh Amendment: This amendment focuses on the rights people have in civil trials. Like the Sixth Amendment, it also does *not* guarantee a jury of one's peers. It does guarantee that defendants and plaintiffs involved in lawsuits may request a jury trial for cases involving a significant amount of money.

The Fourteenth Amendment, Section 1: While the word *jury* does not appear in the Fourteenth Amendment, the U.S. Supreme Court and many legal scholars have interpreted this amendment's due process clause and equal protection clause to give defendants the right to a fair trial and the chance for a jury that is representative of a defendant's community. In fact, most legal challenges concerning jury diversity and representative juries center on the Fourteenth Amendment.

Stress to students that the Constitution does not literally and specifically guarantee a diverse or "representative" jury of a defendant's peers; however, it does guarantee the right to an impartial jury. Ask students the following questions:

- What do you think it means for a jury to be impartial? *Answers will vary, but students will probably suggest that impartial means unbiased or unprejudiced.*
- Ask students to think about whether they have any prejudices against anyone in any of the following groups. (Students should not answer aloud.)

- Older people or younger people
- Women or men
- Highly educated or less educated people
- People in any racial or ethnic group
- People with disabilities (physical, mental, or educational)
- People of different religions or those who are not religious
- People who are heterosexual, homosexual, bisexual, or transgender
- People from any part of the world other than the United States
- Attractive or unattractive people
- People who are politically liberal, conservative, or not political
- People with a criminal record or people who have never been caught or convicted of engaging in criminal behavior

- If it is true that everyone or nearly everyone holds some sort of bias or prejudice, how can any defendant ever hope to have an impartial jury? *Discuss student responses briefly, and then remind students that the American legal system is set up in such a way as to give defendants (through their attorneys) the opportunity to screen potential jurors for bias. They can do this through the voir dire process, removal for cause, and peremptory challenges.*
  In a legal setting, the concern is not that jurors are free of every bias and prejudice, but that the jurors are willing and committed to decide a particular case on the basis of the evidence presented in the courtroom and to not judge the defendant or case based on their own preconceptions.

- Why do you think the Framers of the Bill of Rights (the first 10 amendments to the Constitution) included the guarantee that juries would be from the state and district where the crime took place?
  Possible answers: A jury from the place where the crime was committed helps to ensure that the people on the jury can understand the perspective of people in the community that was harmed by the crime. It also makes it more likely that the jury will be able to view the defendant fairly because the jurors may know people who are similar to the defendant.

- How does jury service fit with citizenship? Is it a right? A responsibility?
  Students' answers will vary.

ACTIVITY—*TWELVE ANGRY MEN*

The popular film *Twelve Angry Men*, starring Henry Fonda, is a brilliant film that illustrates the complexities of the jury system and why juries should include people with a variety of experiences. After showing the film, ask students how the composition of that jury influenced the verdict they reached. *Each person in the jury had something in his own background that helped him make a careful decision about the defendant. When the jurors shared their stories, they showed their own biases and eventually worked to eliminate those biases.*

ACTIVITY—JURY DIVERSITY AND POLICY ANALYSIS

If you have not done so already, discuss with students the advantages of jury diversity. Students should also be familiar with the process for selecting jurors outlined in the background notes on pages 111–112 of this Teacher Manual.

Explain that many people are looking at ways to make adult juries more diverse, particularly due to historical cases like the rape trial known as the *Scottsboro* case and the murder trial after the assassination of Emmett Till.

More recently, some Americans have been skeptical of high-profile and racially charged cases, such as those involving O.J. Simpson, Rodney King, George Zimmerman, several law enforcement officers tried for the death of minority suspects, and others.

If students want to learn more about these cases, encourage them to conduct research about one or two of them and report back to the class about the effect of the composition of the juries on the level of justice some people perceived in those cases.

For this activity, explain that the class has been selected to serve on an important citizens' committee or to advise a panel of state officials about the best way to improve diversity on their community's juries.

Organize students into groups of three to five. Tell one group of students they will be the panel to make the final decision after the other groups make recommendations. List the five policy options provided below. Then explain the following directions to students:

1. Discuss the policy options within your group. The panel making the final decision should not complete steps 2–4 until after the other groups have presented their recommendations.

2. After you have discussed each option, rank them on a scale of 1 to 5, with 1 being the best option.

3. Once you have selected the best option, write one or two sentences about why your group feels it is the best solution.

4. A member of your group should be ready to explain your recommendation to the decision panel.

Policy Options

A. **Use driver's license lists and registered voter lists.** Some states summon only potential jurors who are registered to vote. Analysts who have studied juries say that this group of people tends to be more civic minded (more likely to feel jury duty is an important responsibility of citizenship) than average. This group also tends to be less diverse than the general public. Many people want states to also use lists of all people who are licensed to drive or who have state identification cards. Analysts say this group tends to be younger and less affluent than most registered voters. They are also more likely to be angry about being called for jury duty and more likely to have criminal records than people on registered voter lists.[13]

   Possible concerns about this option: Are the driver's license and state identification lists accurate? Do these lists include enough people and enough of a variety of people? Should there be additional lists to draw from for the jury pool?

B. **Invest time and money to be sure voter registration lists and driver's license lists are accurate.** Obviously, people who do not receive their summonses do not show up for jury duty, so it is essential that addresses be up to date. For example, in one Wisconsin county, court officials found that 50 percent of the summonses sent to minorities were undeliverable. In comparison, only 17 percent of summonses sent to nonminorities were undeliverable. Of all the potential jurors summoned to serve, 3 percent were minorities. However, minorities comprised nearly 9 percent of the county's total population and 37 percent of that county's jail population.[14]

   Possible concerns about this option: Where would the money come from to do the ongoing research and data collection? Would it require expensive new computers or software? Is it worth it?

C. **Pay jurors more money and provide day care for jurors who need it.** Most people who serve on juries are paid less than minimum wage for their time. Many people try to get out of jury duty because they cannot afford to take off from work, and their employers will not pay for their time on a jury. Other potential jurors have difficulty finding someone to care for their children while they serve on a jury.[15]

Possible concerns about this option: Where would the money come from to implement this option? Our government does not require much of us—jury duty is our way to participate in a democratic justice system. We should be willing to serve on juries for little or no compensation.

D. Require that juries reflect the composition of their communities. Several states are considering ways to be sure that a minimum number of minorities serve on each jury so that the composition of juries reflects the composition of the community. For example, one county asks potential grand jurors to complete a questionnaire asking them if they would like to be identified as a minority. Then 21 of the 23 grand jurors are picked at random. If that group contains at least two minorities, the remaining jurors are picked randomly. If the original group does not contain at least two minorities, the remaining jurors are picked exclusively from the self-identified minority pool.[16]

Possible concerns about this option: Some legal scholars think it is unconstitutional to use racial quotas in jury selection. They say the U.S. Supreme Court has established strict standards about when the government can consider race as a factor in any government action.

E. Do not change the system. If the composition of juries is manipulated by considering race, gender, religious background, age, or other factors, the assumption is that people of various groups cannot be fair. Manipulating the composition of juries by considering such factors would also constitute using discrimination to achieve the goal of diversity. The goal is not to assemble juries that "look like America," but rather to empanel jurors who "look beyond looks."[17]

Possible concerns about this option: Many Americans view the justice system with suspicion and even antagonism. They perceive the system to be biased against people like them. If proactive steps are not taken to ensure that all types of voices can be heard in jury boxes, the general public might lose confidence in justice altogether, resulting in fewer people being willing to testify as witnesses, to report crime, or to participate in any of the processes of justice.

When the groups have finished ranking the policy options, ask if any group selected option A as the best option. If so, ask a representative of that group to explain why they selected it. If more than one group selected option A, ask the second group if it had different reasons for doing so. Follow the same steps for each of the options. Following the presentations, ask each member of the decision panel to vote on the options and to give a brief explanation about why he or she was most persuaded by that option.[18]

ACTIVITY—TAKING A FIELD TRIP

Field trips to observe parts of criminal court proceedings are an ideal way to generate student interest and to enhance instruction about the trial stage of the criminal justice process. Call the judge's law clerk or the clerk of the criminal court in advance to arrange for the class to sit in on proceedings. Students may wish to see any or all of the following proceedings: an arraignment, a motion to suppress, a preliminary hearing, the *voir dire* process, a trial (a misdemeanor trial will normally be shorter than a felony trial), and/or a sentencing. If possible, arrange for the judge or attorneys involved in the cases to speak separately with the class about what they observed.

Following the field trip, ask students to reflect on what they observe. Questions may include:

- What roles did the judge and the jury play in the proceeding?
- Based on what you observed, did you think the jury took its job seriously?
- Did the procedures seem fair to both the defendant and the victim?

PROBLEM 14.1 (p.157)

a. Students' answers will vary. Juries were used for several centuries in England as a protection against arbitrary rule. This practice was first brought to the United States by the colonists and later incorporated into the U.S. Constitution. A person may choose not to have a jury in cases where a judge would be better able to understand a complicated legal defense or where there is reason to believe that community sentiment may prejudice a jury against the defendant.

b. Students should give their opinions, supported by reasons. Some people contend that allowing less-than-unanimous verdicts waters down the standard requiring proof beyond a reasonable doubt. They argue that more innocent people may be convicted if unanimous verdicts are not required. Others suggest that since the Constitution does not require juries in state courts to be unanimous, the conclusion of a clear majority of jurors should suffice.

c. Students' answers will vary. Proponents of public deliberation argue that this approach could reduce doubts about the process and allow for better analysis of the jury system at work. Critics argue that it would greatly inhibit jurors in the important process of deliberating, allow unfair scrutiny by persons not in the jurors' difficult positions, violate privacy interests of jurors and others involved in the trial, and may even put jurors in danger or at risk of retaliation.

BACKGROUND—JURY NULLIFICATION

The Fully Informed Jury Association (https://fija.org/) which seeks to pass a law requiring judges to discuss the possibility of nullification when they give their standard instructions to a jury. Clearly, many people oppose their efforts. Encourage students to research both sides of the debate and to reach their own conclusions about jury nullification.

RIGHT TO A SPEEDY AND PUBLIC TRIAL (P. 158)

Learning Outcomes

After completing this section, students should be able to:
1. state how the rights of people accused of crimes are protected by the Sixth Amendment requirement for a speedy trial; and
2. identify how a person who is denied a speedy trial might be harmed.

ACTIVITY—CONDUCTING RESEARCH

Explain to students that in *Barker* v. *Wingo*[19] the U.S. Supreme Court announced the four factors that courts must use when determining whether or not the right to a speedy trial has been violated: (1) the length of the delay; (2) the reason for the delay;

(3) whether or not the defendant asserted his or her right to a speedy trial; and (4) the prejudice resulting from the delay.

Check to see whether your state has a speedy trial act, which specifies how soon after an arrest a case must be brought to trial. Have students conduct research on a few other states to compare their rules for speedy trial, and then ask students whether they think it is fair that states can vary in their approach to the issue. A helpful resource for this research is the collection of state laws compiled by Cornell Law School at www.law.cornell.edu/states/listing.html.

BACKGROUND—PUBLIC TRIAL

The constitutional guarantee to a public trial can be a source of confusion. Explain to students that public trials, along with freedom of the press to cover trials, are meant to limit the power of government to deprive accused people of their rights.

While the Student Edition does not deal explicitly with the right to a public trial, students should be aware that this right, like others in the Constitution, is not absolute. Check to see what kinds of trials are not public where you live. For example, some jurisdictions close all juvenile and domestic relations court proceedings. Judges (or one or both parties) in some high-profile cases have attempted to exclude the press from preliminary proceedings based on the theory that pretrial publicity makes it impossible to select unbiased jurors. Problem 36.1 in the Student Edition deals with this issue.

PROBLEM 14.2 (p. 158)

a. Students' answers will vary. A speedy trial is important because it permits both sides to locate and call witnesses before time dims witness recollections. Additionally, in cases where the defendant is held in jail before his or her trial, a speedy trial minimizes the defendant's liberty infringement without due process. It reduces the conflict between the concept of "innocent until proven guilty" and the need to imprison people before trial to protect the community. Some also believe that swifter (and more certain) trials are more likely to serve as a deterrent to crime.

b. Students' answers will vary. Speedy trials may bring on more accurate convictions or acquittals because events are still fresh in the minds of those who testify. Speedy trials also increase the perception among the general public that there are consequences to criminal behavior.

Additionally, defendants who must spend lengthy pretrial time in confinement suffer from being separated from their families, their jobs, and other responsibilities. Moreover, for an innocent defendant, a lengthy wait for a trial would constitute punishment for a crime he or she did not commit and would violate the presumption of innocence until proven guilty.

On the other hand, there must be sufficient time before the trial for each side to prepare its case. If the crime is particularly violent, people's emotions may be running high, and a longer period before trial gives the potential jury pool time to "cool off."

In criminal trials, time limits are based on the seriousness of the offense. While defendants are guaranteed the right to a speedy trial, the time allowed for the prosecution to prepare its case may be extended in situations where the crime has been concealed, the suspect has fled the jurisdiction, or on other specifically defined grounds.

c. Students' opinions will vary. Some states, such as Florida, open all criminal trials to television cameras. Although the presence of cameras may make it more difficult for the judge, attorneys, and witnesses to perform their tasks, public education and information about the criminal justice system is deemed desirable. For a complete list of states and their rules about media coverage, send students to the website of the Radio-Television News Directors Association at www.rtdna.org/content/cameras_in_court.

Of course, the U.S. Supreme Court does not hold criminal trials, but the issue of television coverage at their proceedings is also a subject of intense debate. The Court currently releases transcripts of its hearings as well as audio recordings of arguments in selected cases, but the timing of the release of those transcripts and recordings varies. There have been several bills introduced in Congress that would require the Court to televise its hearings, but at the time of publication, none has become law, perhaps because the move is strongly opposed by all nine sitting justices. To follow that bill, go to www.congress.gov and use the search term "Supreme Court televising."

RIGHT TO COMPULSORY PROCESS AND TO CONFRONT WITNESSES (P. 159)

Learning Outcomes

After completing this section, students should be able to:

1. explain why being able to subpoena witnesses is important to people accused of crimes;
2. state how courts may modify the right to confrontation for child witnesses; and
3. define the terms *subpoena* and *contempt of court*.

BACKGROUND—CONFRONTATION

The issue of the right to confrontation has been the focus of special attention in child and sexual abuse cases. Although the Supreme Court has rejected state statutes that afford blanket protections for traumatic child abuse cases, the Court has allowed the use of closed-circuit television for witness testimony where a case-specific determination is made that the child witness would be traumatized by the presence of the defendant.[20] Still, the Court has expressed "a preference for face-to-face confrontation" between witnesses and defendants where feasible. This idea derives from the traditional concept that persons are less likely to fabricate testimony when forced to look squarely at the person they are accusing.

THE CASE OF...

The Tape-Recorded Witness Statement

PROBLEM 14.3 (p.159)

This problem is based on the case of *Crawford* v. *Washington*, which was decided by the U.S. Supreme Court in 2004.[21]

a. Students' answers will vary. Be sure they explain their reasons. People who agree with Crawford's point of view might cite the Fifth and Sixth

Amendments. The Fifth Amendment provides due process rights for all people who may be deprived of life, liberty, or property. By extension, the Sixth Amendment guarantees that when a person is being tried for a crime, he or she has the right to challenge the person (witness) whose evidence may lead to a conviction and a sentence that would deprive him or her of liberty, for example, by going to prison. In addition, if the state already has a law prohibiting a spouse's testimony without the defendant's consent, that law was violated. Crawford might also argue that if a witness is not in the courtroom and therefore is not subject to cross examination, the judge and jury will not have the ability to gauge the credibility of the witness by her demeanor while testifying.

b. The best arguments for the state might be that when the prosecution introduced the recording of the wife's statement to police, it was following procedures that had been allowed for more than 25 years. In a 1980 ruling of *Ohio* v. *Roberts*,[22] the Court decided that out-of-court testimony could be admitted in trial if that testimony is considered "reliable." In this case, the police and prosecutors determined that the wife was a reliable witness concerning the question of whether her husband had acted in self-defense.

c. Students' answers will vary. In the actual case, the Court sided 9-0 with Michael Crawford and overruled the earlier ruling in the *Roberts* decision. In the majority opinion, Justice Scalia wrote a long history of the Sixth Amendment right to confront witnesses and concluded: "Dispensing with [the right to confront a witness] because testimony is 'obviously reliable' is akin to dispensing with a jury because a defendant is obviously guilty."[23]

FREEDOM FROM SELF-INCRIMINATION (P. 160)

Learning Outcomes

After completing this section, students should be able to:

1. explain the meaning and importance of freedom from self-incrimination;
2. explain how immunity laws protect witnesses, what witnesses must do, and the circumstances in which prosecutors may use immunity; and
3. define the term *immunity*.

BACKGROUND—SELF-INCRIMINATION

Some leading self-incrimination cases, such as *Miranda* v. *Arizona*,[24] were mentioned in Chapter 13, "Criminal Justice Process: Proceedings Before Trial." Freedom from self-incrimination is a controversial constitutional protection. Critics argue that self-incrimination is no protection for innocent defendants; rather, it keeps criminals from being convicted. Others say that its importance is not to protect "the innocent from conviction, but rather to preserve the integrity of a judicial system in which even the guilty are not to be convicted unless the prosecution shoulders the entire load."[25]

PROBLEM 14.4 (p. 160)

a. Students' answers will vary. A defendant who is articulate, presentable, and without prior convictions can be an extremely convincing witness on his or her own behalf. A defendant lacking these qualities may be a detriment. A defendant taking the stand opens the door for the prosecution to introduce evidence of prior convictions. Evidence may also be given of prior statements inconsistent with the testimony given at trial. The prosecution will also cross examine the defendant who will be under oath to tell the truth, although he may also invoke the 5th Amendment if the answer to the question will incriminate him.

b. Students' opinions will vary. Some people feel that, despite the judge's warning, jurors consider the defendant's failure to take the stand as evidence of guilt. If a prosecutor makes remarks suggesting that the jury infer guilt from the defendant's failure to testify, this may be grounds for a mistrial.

c. The right against self-incrimination applies to testimonial evidence, not to physical evidence. The persons in a lineup can be asked to repeat some words or phrases that the observer heard the defendant say. This can help facilitate the identification process and does not violate the privilege against self-incrimination.

Defendants cannot, however, be forced to take lie detector tests. Also, most courts still do not admit lie detector results as evidence because they have not been scientifically validated. In contrast, drivers may be required to take alcohol breath tests, and refusal to do so is often inferred as a sign of guilt.

d. Students will express their views. It would take a constitutional amendment to make this change.

RIGHT TO AN ATTORNEY (PP. 160–161)

Learning Outcomes

After completing this section, students should be able to:

1. describe the meaning and importance of the right to counsel;
2. summarize how Supreme Court rulings on the Sixth Amendment right to counsel have evolved since 1937;
3. state why a trial might not be fair if a defendant had no attorney; and
4. explain concerns over the fairness of the public defender system.

BACKGROUND—RIGHT TO AN ATTORNEY AND EFFECTIVE CONTROL

The case of *Gideon* v. *Wainwright*[26] is a landmark decision that changed criminal procedures dramatically. For more information about this case, including lesson plans and primary source materials, visit www.landmarkcases.org/. This website was created by Street Law, Inc., with support from the U.S. Supreme Court Historical Society.

See Chapter 13, "Criminal Justice Process: Proceedings Before Trial" for more information about the right to counsel, the point in the legal process at which the right to an attorney may be exercised.

The right to an attorney has been held to mean that people have the right to "effective" assistance of counsel. If this is not provided in a criminal case, defendants may be able to appeal and ask for a new trial. This does not mean that a person must have an "excellent" or even a "good" lawyer. In *Strickland* v. *Washington*, the Supreme Court ruled that in order to prevail on an appeal, a defendant must show reasonable probability that the result would have been different, but for the attorney's unprofessional conduct.[27] To prove "ineffective assistance of counsel," one must show a serious error by the attorney that affected the outcome of the case. This is often difficult to prove, particularly by simply reading a transcript of the trial, so the Court has been reluctant to take many cases of this type.

CAPTION ANSWER (P. 161) Criminal defense counsel will advise clients in most cases not to confess and will also assemble evidence and identify witnesses to help present a defense. At trial, the lawyer for the defendant will also provide an opening and a closing statement, cross-examine the government's witnesses, and examine witnesses for the defense.

PROBLEM 14.5 (p. 161)

a. Students' answers and opinions will vary. In *Faretta* v. *California*, the Supreme Court held that defendants have a constitutional right to defend themselves if they have voluntarily and intelligently waived the right to counsel.[28] A defendant who represents himself or herself is required to follow all the normal procedural rules. While it is legally permissible, it is almost always a bad idea for a defendant to handle his or her own defense. Lawyers are warned against this by the saying, "A lawyer who represents himself has a fool for a client."

b. Students' answers and opinions will vary. A lawyer may feel that his or her client is morally guilty, but legal guilt must be determined through the adversarial process. Criminal defense counsels are bound by the Canons of Ethics to defend their clients zealously and within the bounds of the law. The right to effective assistance of counsel would lose its meaning if lawyers assumed the role of judge and jury. However, the American Bar Association (ABA) Code of Professional Responsibility prohibits a lawyer from putting a client on the witness stand if the lawyer knows the client is going to lie. See Chapter 6, "Lawyers," for more information on this topic.

Investigating the Law Where You Live

(p. 161) Findlaw.com has a number of resources related to public defenders, including a data base of defense resources by state. Students may go to https://criminal.findlaw.com/criminal-legal-help/public-defenders-by-state.html to search through these resources. To evaluate how well the system works to ensure justice, students may want to conduct their own research about who defends and who criticizes the public defender system. Using that information, students can prepare for a class discussion, debate, or deliberation on the topic.

CRIMINAL APPEALS (PP. 161–162)

Learning Outcomes

After completing this section, students should be able to:

1. identify the options defendants have if they think they have been wrongly convicted;
2. explain various reasons a defendant who is appealing a conviction or sentence may wish to hire a new lawyer;
3. describe what an appellant or petitioner must convince the appeals court of; and
4. define the terms *double jeopardy*, *mistrial*, *petitioner*, *appellant*, *writ*, and *habeas corpus*.

BACKGROUND AND DISCUSSION— CRIMINAL APPEALS

To refresh students' memories about the appeal process, review the end of Chapter 2 and all of Chapter 5. Ask students:

- Can people appeal a verdict because they think the jury made a mistake? *No, usually an appeal is possible only when someone claims the trial court made an error of law, not an error of fact.*
- Assume a judge made an error during the trial that involved law. Will the case automatically be granted an appeal? *No, the trial court's decision will not be reversed if the judge's error is considered so minor that it would not affect the outcome of the case.*
- Are appeals heard by a jury of citizens? *No, typically, appeals are heard by a panel of three or more judges.*

ACTIVITY—COMPARING THE APPEAL PROCESS IN FEDERAL AND STATE COURTS

Review with students how the appeal process works. Then share the following statistics with the class. These statistics are for federal crimes and reflect the most recent data available at the time of publication. For updated statistics, visit the Bureau of Justice Statistics online at www.bjs.gov. Once you are on the BJS site, use the search term "appeals" to find the most recent data.

One of the more compelling issues surrounding the appeal process is how people who are indigent are served. There are significant differences among the states regarding whether a poor person can get assistance with the costs associated with appeals, such as lawyer fees, filing fees, transcript costs, etc. Have students find out what assistance is available to indigent people in their own state and compare it to several other states. Students can use the following website to conduct their research:

- The Bureau of Justice Statistics site has a section dedicated to information on indigent defense, including the Sixth Amendment right to counsel, services and methods used to provide counsel to indigent defendants, case proceedings/characteristics of state and federal indigent defendants, and other related information. The information is available at www.bjs.gov/index.cfm?ty=tp&tid=28.

When students complete their research, ask students to defend or refute the following quote from former Attorney General Janet Reno, presented at the First National Symposium on Indigent Defense:

"I believe that all of us, regardless of our position in the criminal justice system, have the responsibility to work to improve the quality of criminal defense for the poor. Our system of justice will only work, and will only inspire complete confidence and trust of the people, if we have strong prosecutors, an impartial judiciary, and a strong system of indigent criminal defense. When the conviction of a defendant is challenged on the basis of inadequate representation, the very legitimacy of the conviction itself is called into question. Our criminal justice system is interdependent: if one leg of the system is weaker than the others, the whole system will ultimately falter."

ACTIVITY—TAKING A FIELD TRIP

Observing an appeals trial will give students a clearer understanding of the process and procedures involved in criminal justice. If possible, arrange ahead of time for the attorney and/or judges involved in the case to speak to students during a break or before or after the trial.

NOTES

(1) *Batson* v. *Kentucky*, 476 U.S. 79 (1986).

(2) *J.E.B.* v. *Alabama ex rel T.B.*, 511 U.S. 127 (1994).

(3) *Hernandez* v. *New York*, 500 U.S. 352 (1991).

(4) Albert W. Alshuler and Andrew G. Deiss, "A Brief History of Criminal Jury in The United States," *University of Chicago Law Review*, Summer 1994, p. 2.

(5) *Burch* v. *Louisiana*, 441 U.S. 130 (1979).

(6) *Williams* v. *Florida*, 399 U.S. 78 (1970).

(7) *Ballew* v. *Georgia*, 435 U.S. 223 (1978).

(8) *Johnson* v. *Louisiana*, 406 U.S. 356 (1972).

(9) *Batson* v. *Kentucky*, 476 U.S. 79 (1986).

(10) *Taylor* v. *Louisiana*, 419 U.S. 522 (1975).

(11) Pub. L. No. 101-336, 104 Stat. 327 (1990).

(12) *Strauder* v. *West Virginia*, 100 U.S. 303 (1879).

(13) William R. Levesque, "Prosecutors Object to New Method of Jury Selection," *St. Petersburg Times*, December 28, 1998.

(14) "Dane County Court Grant to Improve Jury Diversity," *Wisconsin Lawyer*, March 2001.

(15) "Arizona Supreme Court Committee on More Effective Use of Juries: Summary of Recommendations," *The Power of Twelve*, Arizona Supreme Court, January 8, 2002.

(16) Deiss, Andrew G. Dwyer, "Negotiating Justice: The Criminal Trial Jury in a Pluralist America," *University of Chicago Law School Roundtable*, 1996, and McNulty, Jennifer, "Sociologist Testifies About How to Overcome Racial Bias in Jury Selection," *Currents*, University of California, Santa Cruz, March 3, 1997.

(17) Randall Kennedy, *Race, Crime, and the Law* (foreword), Pantheon Books, New York, 1997.

(18) This activity, the help-wanted activity, and the discussion notes about jury selection and a jury of your peers were all adapted with permission from *Street Law for Youth Courts: Educational Workshops*, by Lena Morreale Scott, Washington, D.C., 2002.

(19) *Barker* v. *Wingo*, 407 U.S. 514 (1972).

(20) *Coy* v. *Iowa*, 487 U.S. 1012 (1988).

(21) *Crawford* v. *Washington*, 541 U.S. 36 (2004).

(22) *Ohio* v. *Roberts*, 448 U.S. 56 (1980).

(23) *Crawford* v. *Washington*, 541 U.S. 36 (2004).

(24) *Miranda* v. *Arizona*, 384 U.S. 436 (1996).

(25) *Tehan* v. *United States ex rel. Shott*, 382 U.S. 406, 415 (1966).

(26) *Gideon* v. *Wainwright*, 372 U.S. 355 (1963).

(27) *Strickland* v. *Washington*, 466 U.S. 668 (1984).

(28) *Faretta* v. *California*, 422 U.S. 806 (1975).

Sentencing and corrections are the final phases of the criminal justice process. If found guilty, a defendant will be sentenced by a judge or a jury, depending on individual state law. The sentence is the most critical decision in the process, as it can determine a defendant's fate for years or even life. Several sentencing options exist, ranging from a suspended sentence and probation to imprisonment or even death. Criminal sentences serve a number of purposes, including retribution, deterrence, rehabilitation, and incapacitation.

After the defendant has been sentenced, he or she enters the corrections system. Several treatment or punishment options are available, including community corrections, halfway houses, jails, and prisons. The convict's entry back into society after his or her sentence has been served can be a difficult adjustment. To ease this transition, the government and many nonprofit and religious organizations have developed programs to ease re-entry.

SENTENCING OPTIONS (PP. 163–166)

Learning Outcomes

After completing this section, students should be able to:

1. list and explain eight sentencing options judges may exercise;
2. describe factors that affect sentencing decisions;
3. evaluate criticisms of using judicial discretion in determining sentences;
4. summarize the arguments in support of and in opposition to Three Strikes Laws; and
5. define the terms *suspended sentence, probation, home confinement, fine, restitution, work release, imprisonment,* and *presentence report.*

BACKGROUND—SENTENCING

In response to public concerns about judges who were "soft on crime," some states have moved toward determinate sentencing. This approach does not allow the broad discretion formerly allowed to judges in sentencing criminal defendants. Under the determinate sentencing approach, criminals are sentenced on the basis of an offender score. Rather than tailoring the sentence to the individual circumstances of the offender and considering the potential for rehabilitation, the judge sentences offenders within a limited range of punishment based on the seriousness of their present offense and their prior criminal record. Judges can go outside the range of punishment only if specific mitigating or aggravating circumstances are found. Some judges, lawyers, and others are critical of sentencing guidelines and determinate sentencing. They say it takes away from judges the discretion that they need to make fair sentencing decisions.

States have also passed:

- mandatory prison terms for crimes such as narcotics and firearm offenses and murder;
- sentence "enhancements" for specific situations (such as when guns are involved in the crime);
- habitual offender laws that give mandatory minimum sentences to habitual offenders;
- Three Strikes Laws such as those described in the Student Edition; and
- laws creating a civil commitment process for those sexual offenders determined to be sexual predators, in which the convicted are confined in a locked treatment facility once their criminal sentence has been served.

In addition, federal and state laws have lengthened confinement times for violent, sexual, and drug crimes. These statutes have all contributed to prison overcrowding.

The 2012 Supreme Court decision described on page 166 of the Student Edition is the case of *Miller* v. *Alabama*.[1] In that case, the Court held that mandatory life sentences without the possibility of parole were unconstitutional for juvenile offenders. Students will learn more about juvenile justice in chapter 16.

CAPTION ANSWER (P. 163) The advantages to a sentence of home confinement are that the offender does not have to spend time behind bars and can maintain his or her job or school responsibilities. This approach may be less expensive than imprisonment. The disadvantages to such a sentence are that the offender cannot leave his or her home except for essential purposes (work, school, doctor's appointments) and that he or she must wear a monitoring device. Depending on the jurisdiction, offenders may be required to pay for the device and monitoring.

THE CASE OF...

The Three Strikes Law

PROBLEM 15.1 (p. 165)

This case is based on the case of *Lockyer* v. *Andrade*,[2] decided by the U.S. Supreme Court in 2003.

a. The California legislature most likely passed the law in response to public outrage over the murder of Polly Klaas at the hands of a repeat offender. These laws have become popular based on the belief that mandatory sentences will deter crime and from frustration with the prison system's perceived inability to rehabilitate convicted felons.

b. Students' answers will vary. The most convincing arguments for upholding Andrade's sentence are that it was given lawfully by a judge and supported by the people of California. In addition, the long sentence ensures that the defendant will not repeat the offense.

c. Students' answers will vary. Arguments against the sentence imposed by this law include that it virtually eliminates judicial discretion, imposes sentences that are disproportional to the severity

of the crime, and threatens to overcrowd the prisons with nonviolent offenders such as Andrade. This approach also directs state resources into corrections instead of programs that work to prevent crime.

d. Students' answers will vary but should reflect the arguments made in answers **b.** and **c.** In the actual Supreme Court case, Justice O'Connor, writing for the majority, found no Eighth Amendment violation because the sentence was not grossly disproportionate to the seriousness of the crime for which Andrade was convicted. Therefore, the sentence was upheld. Four justices dissented on the grounds that the sentence was grossly disproportionate to the crime, thereby rising to the level of cruel and unusual punishment, which is proscribed by the Eighth Amendment.

e. Students' opinions will vary. Ask students to consider why this law was so appealing to voters, emphasizing that the law was adopted through the referendum process in California. Information that would be helpful for reaching a decision includes the number of crimes that are committed by repeat offenders, the effect of mandatory sentencing laws on crime rates in the states in which they have been adopted, the costs to taxpayers, and possible alternatives that may more effectively deter and rehabilitate repeat offenders.

ACTIVITY—TAKING A FIELD TRIP

An excellent and often sobering destination for a criminal law unit field trip is a sentencing hearing. You may be able to arrange for students to attend a sentencing hearing for someone convicted of a specific kind of crime, such as DUI or an offense related to substance abuse. Some courts have programs in which ex-offenders speak to students about their own histories as part of such a field trip.

LEGAL RESOURCE PERSON

Legal resource persons could include parole board members, judges, prosecutors, or members of state commissions on sentencing. Ex-offenders can raise awareness of the nature of life behind bars.

Note: Specify with your resource person the topic focus and discussion parameters prior to such a visit in order to avoid discussions that may be too graphic or otherwise inappropriate.

(p. 166) If students need help finding out whether their state has special laws relating to repeat offenders, suggest that they contact a lawyer or police officer. They could also conduct an online search using the term "repeat offender laws + (the name of their state)." They might also search their state criminal code, available from Cornell Law School at www.law.cornell.edu/wex/state_statutes2.

PURPOSES OF PUNISHMENT AND PAROLE (PP. 166–168)

Learning Outcomes

After completing this section, students should be able to:

1. describe four theories regarding the purposes of punishment and the assumptions on which each theory is based;
2. list and evaluate the factors that determine whether or not parole will be granted to a convicted person; and
3. define the terms *retribution, deterrence, rehabilitation, incapacitation,* and *parole.*

CAPTION ANSWER (P. 167) Students' answers may vary, but they should show an understanding of the range of educational, vocational, and counseling programs that are available to prisoners in many rehabilitation programs.

(p. 167) Student answers will vary depending on where they live. Students should justify their answers about whether parole should be abolished.

PROBLEM 15.2 (p. 168)

Students' responses will vary. Supporters may say that the high rate of incarceration keeps criminals off the streets and makes society safer. Some might argue that this also acts as a deterrent to criminal behavior. One of the biggest disadvantages with the high rate of incarceration is the expense.

Some critics say that more effort and spending should be dedicated to helping people avoid crime rather than to be locked up for it. They also see the disproportionate sentences for inmates of different races who are convicted of the same crimes as a human rights and civil rights issue.

CAPITAL PUNISHMENT (PP. 168–171)

Learning Outcomes

After completing this section, students should be able to:

1. summarize how views on capital punishment have evolved throughout American history;
2. state how U.S. Supreme Court rulings have influenced the imposition of the death penalty;
3. describe how due process applies to persons sentenced to death;
4. evaluate the merits of using the death penalty for defendants who are minors or who had an intellectual disability at the time of their alleged crime;
5. weigh arguments for and against the use of the death penalty; and
6. define the terms *capital punishment, aggravating circumstances,* and *mitigating circumstances.*

BACKGROUND—CAPITAL PUNISHMENT

Technically, *capital punishment* means imposition of the death penalty or life imprisonment. However, we tend to think of capital punishment only in terms of the death penalty.

The U.S. Supreme Court typically hears several cases each term on the death penalty. As stated in the Student Edition, courts must look at aggravating and mitigating circumstances before imposing the death penalty. The capital punishment cases mentioned in the text are *Furman* v. *Georgia* and *Lockett* v. *Ohio.*[3] In *Buchanan* v. *Angelone,*[4] the Supreme Court ruled that the trial judge's failure to instruct the jury on the concept of mitigation in general, as well as about specific mitigating factors, did not violate the defendant's rights.

The Court has also considered the issue of whether someone who did not actually pull the trigger of the gun can receive the death penalty. In *Enmund* v. *Florida* (1982) the defendant had driven the getaway car after his cohorts robbed and shot to death an elderly couple.[5] Under state law, this was felony murder punishable by life imprisonment or death. The Court reasoned that Enmund's lack of intent and his physical absence during the killings would make the death sentence cruel and unusual punishment.

The Student Edition refers to two Supreme Court cases relating the constitutionality of lethal injections. In the first case, *Baze v. Rees* (2008),[6] a death row inmate challenged Kentucky's method for lethal injections that use the common four chemicals combination. The inmate objected to the method on several grounds, including the argument that one of the chemicals paralyzes the prisoner so if he experiences unreasonable pain it would not be noticeable by the people who are in charge of the executions. (In an earlier case, *Gregg v. Georgia*,[7] the Supreme Court ruled that prison officials violate the Eighth Amendment if they create an unnecessary risk of pain for inmates.) The inmate also raised the point that the procedure using those same chemicals had been botched in other states causing considerable pain. The Court disagreed with the inmate and held that Kentucky's lethal injection method did not violate the Eighth Amendment. They noted that when administered correctly, the procedure is humane. They said the inmate failed to prove the incorrect administration of the drug combination amounted to cruel and unusual punishment. However, the Court also suggested that a state may violate the ban on cruel and unusual punishment if it continues to use a method without sufficient justification in the face of superior alternative procedures.

The second case referenced on page 169, *Glossip v. Gross*, 2015,[8] also involved constitutional questions about lethal injections for the death penalty. The case involved three Oklahoma death row inmates who challenged the state's protocol, and more specifically the state's use of the drug midazolam as the first step in the lethal injection. The drug was intended to put the inmate into a deep coma-like state so that the two fatal drugs could be administered humanely. The inmates contended that there was considerable debate as to whether midazolam would reliably achieve that result. The questions before the Court were: Is it constitutional for a state to execute inmates using a three-drug protocol when (a) there is significant scientific consensus questioning the efficacy of the first drug in inducing a coma-like state for the inmate, and (b) if the first drug is ineffective, the state's protocol would subject the inmate to considerable pain and suffering. Further, the Court was to decide whether the inmate must prove the availability of an alternative drug protocol even if the state's current protocol violates the Eighth Amendment. The Court ruled that the Oklahoma drug protocol did not violate the Eighth Amendment. The Court said that the inmates

challenging the drug protocol had not shown that midazolam was "sure or very likely to result in needless suffering." Further, they said, in order to challenge a method of execution, an inmate must show the state has a better available alternative.

In a separate case, *Kennedy v. Louisiana*,[9] the Court ruled that the death penalty is not constitutional as a punishment for the crime of child rape.

Explore with students what effect, if any, cost should have on a state's decision to have a death penalty statute. Critics argue that those resources should instead be put into crime prevention programs such as education, increased lighting in high crime areas, or victim compensation programs.

The cost of keeping a prisoner on death row typically exceeds the cost of that same person serving a life sentence for murder. The cost is higher because they require more time: the preparation time for capital cases is usually longer; there are usually more pretrial motions, more experts to be hired, and the defense may be entitled to additional (state-paid) defenders; juries in these cases are more likely to be sequestered, and there is likely to be a second phase of the trial sentencing; the jails and prisons where capital suspects are held during trial and where convicts are sentenced are usually more secure and therefore more expensive.

According to a 2014 report by the state of Nevada, the costs of death penalty cases are double those of other murder cases where a lesser penalty is sought.[10]

For current and state-specific information visit The Balance (www.thebalance.com/comparing-the-costs-of-death-penalty-vs-life-in-prison-4689874) and the Death Penalty Information Center (https://deathpenaltyinfo.org/policy-issues/costs).

Investigating the Law Where You Live

(p. 169) If students need help finding information about whether their state provides for the death penalty, direct them to the website of the Death Penalty Information Center at www.deathpenaltyinfo.org/states-and-without-death-penalty.

In addition, it offers teacher resources and curriculum about the topic as well as a Student Resources section. To find out how states without the death penalty punish those convicted of serious crimes, students can access their state penal codes through the Legal Information Institute at the Cornell Law School website (http://www.law.cornell.edu/wex/state_statutes2).

The Death Penalty for Defendants with Intellectual Disabilities and Juvenile Defendants

PROBLEM 15.3 (p. 171)

This problem is based on two cases decided by the Supreme Court. The first case, involving a patient with an intellectual disability, was *Atkins* v. *Virginia*.[11] The second case, involving a juvenile sentenced to death, was *Roper* v. *Simmons*.[12]

a. Atkins was convicted and sentenced to the death penalty for robbing and murdering Eric Nesbitt. Atkins also had a history of felony convictions. Simmons was convicted and sentenced to death for a first-degree murder he committed and confessed to when he was 17 years old.

b. Students' answers will vary. Those who oppose the death penalty for individuals with an intellectual disability may argue that the punishment must be directly related to the defendant's personal culpability. Thus, defendants who have emotional and mental issues may be less culpable than defendants without such problems. Because they are deemed less culpable, some say their respective punishment should be less severe. It may also be argued that imposing the death penalty for defendants with intellectual disabilities is cruel and unusual punishment because such a defendant is unable to comprehend the ramifications of his or her actions.

Proponents of capital punishment for individuals with intellectual disabilities may argue that the inability to comprehend the extent of their actions makes them a continuing threat to society. Therefore, executing such defendants is seen as a means of protecting society from future harm. An example rests in the vast number of inmates with intellectual disabilities that jurors have placed on death row.

c. Students' answers will vary. It is quite rare for the Supreme Court to acknowledge that public opinion influences its decisions. However, cases involving the Eighth Amendment are among those in which the Court does consider it. In the *Atkins* decision, the Court referred to "society's evolving standards of decency." In the *Roper* case, the majority opinion cited a "consensus against the juvenile death penalty among state legislatures."

d. Students' answers will vary. Just as the Court rarely considers domestic public opinions, it rarely considers international law or opinion, but Eighth Amendment cases are sometimes the exception. For example, in the *Roper* case, the majority opinion pointed to "overwhelming" international opinion against the juvenile death penalty.

e. Students' answers will vary. In the actual *Atkins* case, the Court voted 6-3 and stated that executing people with intellectual disabilities was unconstitutional. In the *Roper* case, the Court voted 5-4 that evolving standards of decency now make the execution of minors "cruel and unusual punishment" prohibited by the Eighth Amendment.

DISCUSSION—WHO'S ON DEATH ROW

Ask students to look at the information in the Student Edition about the number of prisoners on death row. Ask students to consider the implications of the statistics relating to the gender, race, and ethnicity of people on death row. Then ask them the following questions:

- How does the number of people on death row from each group compare to that group's proportion of the general population? How does it compare to the total number of people from that group arrested and/or convicted of the same crime?

  This information can be found in U.S. Bureau of the Census statistics at www.census.gov.
- To what extent do you think the race of the victim should matter in death sentences? According to a report by the U.S. General Accounting Office, "In 82% of the studies [reviewed], race of the victim was found to influence the likelihood of being charged with capital murder or receiving the death penalty, i.e., those who murdered whites were found more likely to be sentenced to death than those who murdered blacks." For current statistics on race and capital punishment visit the Death Penalty Information Center (https://deathpenaltyinfo.org/policy-issues/race).
- What could explain the differences in treatment by judges and juries among racial and ethnic groups? Do some groups have a better chance of being placed in prevention programs or of receiving competent legal representation?

  The American Bar Association (ABA) Death Penalty Representation and Due Process

Review Projects are designed to reverse the United States' "fatally flawed" administration of the death penalty. Through the project, the ABA seeks to establish a national standard of practice that ensures that every capital defendant in every state receives a fair trial and competent legal representation. For more information on the lack of adequate representation for death row inmates in the United States, visit https://www.americanbar.org/groups/crsj/projects/death_penalty_due_process_review_project/.

ACTIVITY—TAKING A STAND ON CONTROVERSIAL ISSUES

Post the following signs at opposite ends of the room: "The Death Penalty is RIGHT!" and "The Death Penalty is WRONG!" Have students stand in a location between the signs that they feel best represents their position on the death penalty.

1. Ask volunteers to explain *why* they chose to stand in that location.

2. Have students talk to those who "took a stand" nearest them to determine why they placed themselves where they are. Students should then adjust their positions on the continuum if necessary.

To extend the discussion, pose the following hypothetical circumstances and ask students whether their views might change depending on the crime.

- Would the number of victims matter?
- Would the age of the victims matter?
- Would the type of violent crime matter? For example, should murderers be more likely to receive the death penalty, as current law reflects?
- Would the mental capacity of the victim matter? Or the mental capacity of the defendant?
- Would the "type" of victim matter? For example, should someone who murders a police officer be sentenced differently than someone who murders a fellow criminal?
- Would it matter if the defendant was the victim of extreme abuse since childhood?
- Would it matter if the defendant had prior convictions?
- Would it matter if the defendant wanted to receive the death penalty?
- Would it matter if the defendant has recently found evidence that may prove someone else did the crime but he or she has run out of habeas corpus appeals?

- Would it matter if you personally know the victim? Or the defendant?

DISCUSSION—THE INNOCENCE PROJECT

The Innocence Project's website may be a great place for students to do further research. Send students to www.innocenceproject.org and suggest that they read the Fact Sheets for background information on legal issues such as post-conviction DNA exonerations, preservation of evidence, compensation for people who are exonerated, and false witness testimony.

After they have read the Fact Sheets, ask students to discuss why these issues are important in a just society, what individuals or groups might oppose these reform efforts, and why they might oppose them. Students can also do a separate search for examples of opposition to the Innocence Project's work. Finally, students can click on "National View" and then choose one of these subject areas to find out how their state compares to others on questions such as the following:

- What (if anything,) do my state laws say about access to post-conviction DNA testing?
- Does my state compensate people who have been wrongly convicted and later proven innocent?
- Does my state have a law requiring the preservation of DNA material and other physical evidence? If so, for how long must it be kept?

CORRECTIONS (PP. 172–175)

Learning Outcomes

After completing this section, students should be able to:

1. distinguish between jail and prison;
2. contrast life behind bars with life in open society;
3. describe how views of prisoners' rights have evolved;
4. identify the benefits of and reasons for an increase in prison population since the 1990s;
5. identify problems caused by the increased prison population and costs associated with it; and
6. explain how reentry programs work to reduce recidivism.

BACKGROUND AND DISCUSSION— DISPROPORTIONATE MINORITY CONTACT (DMC) AND CORRECTIONS

The issue known as disproportionate minority contact (DMC) is complicated and is relevant in any discussion regarding public policy, law, and corrections. The concern is that a disproportional percentage of racial and ethnic minorities enter the juvenile and criminal justice systems, with different outcomes for minorities in every stage of the system—from racial profiling during stops and arrests through charges, plea bargaining, jury verdicts, sentencing, the death penalty, and even in access to reentry programs. The reason it is called "disproportionate" is that data show that even when people of various racial or ethnic groups commit the same crimes at the same rates, they are often treated differently in the system. For example, according to a study published in July 2007, African Americans are incarcerated at more than five (5.6) times the rate of whites, and Hispanics are incarcerated at nearly double (1.8) the rate of whites.[13]

The federal government and many states have attempted to study the problem and to develop solutions to make the entire system more balanced and fair. Some people point out that certain laws need to be reconsidered, such as drug laws that punish users and dealers of powdered cocaine much more leniently than the users and dealers of crack cocaine. Others say that Three Strikes Laws disproportionately hurt African Americans.[14] Still others cite the problems mentioned previously that indicate that more minorities are sentenced to death than whites who commit the same crimes.

The issue of disproportionate minority confinement presents many critical issues for the criminal justice system and for society as a whole. For example, if people perceive they will not be treated fairly, they may be less likely to cooperate at various stages of the criminal justice process—from coming forward and testifying as witnesses to serving on juries. "The problem also threatens the validity of judicial decisions among members of minority and majority communities alike.... [It] challenges the basic American assumption that everyone receives 'equal justice under law.'"[15]

For statistics and more information on DMC, visit the websites of The Sentencing Project at www.sentencingproject.org, The Justice Policy Institute at www.justicepolicy.org, and the federal government's Office of Juvenile Justice and Delinquency Prevention at www.ojjdp.gov.

PROBLEM 15.4 (p. 174)

It is obvious that when people are incarcerated, they lose some of their freedoms and some of their privileges. The realities and necessities of orderly institutional operations justify further restrictions. The challenge for the courts is to balance the inmate's rights against legitimate interests of the institution.

Students may ask why prisoners do not lose all of their rights. Explain that the federal courts, beginning in the late 1960s, stated that if the government is going to operate a prison, "it is going to have to be a system that is countenanced by the Constitution of the United States,"[16] and that "there is no iron curtain drawn between the Constitution and the prisons of this country."[17]

a. Students' answers will vary. Students may list rights to free speech such as mail, phone calls, and visitors; freedom to practice their religion and to obtain needed items for religious practice (e.g., religious diets, jewelry, sacred items); freedom from establishment of religion; and basic human needs of food, space, personal safety, medical care, privacy, sanitation, shelter, due process, and access to attorneys. Students may also list parole, work, education, social activities, lottery tickets, conjugal visitation, color television, films, and tobacco. Inform them that the latter have been deemed *privileges* by courts.

b. Students' answers will vary. Prison wardens might read and censor mail that poses a security threat; tape telephone calls (except attorney calls); limit the number of visitors and types of visits (noncontact, contact, conjugal); restrict various religious practices that conflict with security or the orderly running of the facility (such as requiring Native Americans to display contents of their medicine bag to security staff for search); provide fair procedures before taking away "good time" or early release credits; provide inmates and their attorneys a place to speak confidentially and open attorney mail only in the presence of inmates to inspect for contraband; create rules against fighting and penalties for those who break the rules; and prohibit insubordination to correctional officers.

c. Students' answers will vary. Students may say that since several states have legalized or decriminalized medicinal or recreational marijuana use that no states should imprison a person for mere possession. Students may say that only criminals who present an immediate threat to public safety should be behind bars. Other students may take the position that anyone who breaks a law that carries a prison sentence should be incarcerated.

d. Students' opinion will vary. Some students may be an advocate of both tough sentencing and treatment and prevention programs. This may lead to a discussion of limited resources and the need to prioritize policies for budgetary reasons.

ACTIVITY—TAKING A FIELD TRIP

Arrange to visit the adult jail, local or state prison, or juvenile detention facility in your community where students can meet with correctional officers and inmates to discuss the criminal justice process. Note: this field trip might be prohibited or need special approval from school administration. Before you go, prepare students for what they might see, hear, and experience on the field trip. Discuss with students how to dress appropriately for the setting. Determine beforehand if there are prohibitions on minors entering correctional institutions. During the field trip, students should find out why people are sometimes held before trial; what daily life is like for inmates in the institution; what rights inmates have; and what rights are limited.

BACKGROUND—REENTRY

Ask students what components they think effective reentry programs should include. Would those program components change depending on whether the offender was an adult or a juvenile? Then ask students who should take the lead regarding responsibility for reentry programs. Should it be a government initiative? A community initiative? An initiative from a religious group?

Law-related education programs can play a significant role in helping offenders return to society. Some programs, such as Street Law's Legal Life Skills program may include practical legal education designed to help young people negotiate the rules and laws of communities. Specific lessons might feature employment, housing, child abuse and neglect, police procedures, or community problem solving. Reentry programs can and should utilize community resource people such as lawyers, judges, and police officers in order to help youths build trust and learn how to access resources in their

communities. For more information about programs for juveniles in correctional settings, visit https://www.streetlaw.org/programs/?catid=127.

Government-sponsored reentry programs often include support for reentering people with transitional housing, job training and job placement, and mentoring. In some cases, the government provides those services directly. In other cases, private groups, including faithbased groups, can receive government funding to carry out reentry programs that they provide. Additional statistics, publications, links to federal and state resources, training and technical assistance opportunities, and other reentry initiatives are available online at www.bjs.gov/content/pub/pdf/reentry.pdf.

Investigating the Law Where You Live

(p. 174-175) Student answers will vary depending on location.

CAPTION ANSWER (P. 175) Ex-offenders face the challenges of reconnecting with the outside world. They must rebuild the trust of their friends and families, find a place to live, find a job, and learn how to live as law-abiding citizens.

PROBLEM 15.5 (p. 175)

Several advocacy groups offer resources relating to reentry and the rights of ex-felons. For more information on reentry issues, check The Center for Equal Opportunity at www.ceousa.org/voting/voting-news/felon-voting and The Sentencing Project at www.sentencingproject.org/template/page.cfm?id=133 which provides a map illustrating felony disenfranchisement by state.

a. Students' answers will vary. The arguments in favor of restoring voting rights to felons who have completed their sentences include:

- "The more people who vote, the better democracy will be."
- Because of racial and economic disparities in the criminal justice system, nonwhites and poor people are most affected by the ban on voting, which unfairly affects the democratic process.
- If Americans are going to fight and die overseas to promote democratic principles, we should be consistent and try to expand democracy here by extending voting rights to more people.
- Very few countries around the world permanently bar felons from voting. We should not be in their company.

- Ex-felons (who have completed their sentences) have already paid their debt to society and should be treated as full citizens with the right to vote.

The arguments against restoring voting rights to felons may include:

- We are a country based on the rule of law, therefore people who break the law should not have the privilege of giving their voice to government.
- Ex-felons may be more likely than others to vote in ways that harm the country.
- The problem of disproportionate minority contact with the criminal justice system and corrections cannot and should not be solved by giving lawbreakers more political rights. That problem should be solved in the criminal justice community.

b. Students' opinions will vary and should be supported with reasons. Those who agree with the idea that voting may help to rehabilitate ex-felons may say:

- People who vote (and who are allowed to vote) are more likely to feel they have a voice and stake in their own communities and in the country.
- Allowing ex-felons to vote makes them a part of the democratic society.

Arguments against the idea that voting could help to rehabilitate ex-felons might include:

- There is no evidence that voting will make people less likely to re-offend.
- People who want to improve the rehabilitation of ex-felons should concentrate their efforts on other things that are more likely to work, such as job training and placement, education programs, and mentoring.

ACCESS TO MEDICAL CARE FOR INMATES (P. 175-176)

Learning Outcomes

After completing this section, students should be able to:

1. identify the constitutional provision that guarantees inmates "adequate care";
2. debate what level of care is necessary for "adequate care"; and
3. explain the pros and cons of allowing prisons to charge co-pays for inmates' medical care and medicines.

DISCUSSION – WHAT IS "ADEQUATE CARE"?

To introduce this section, ask students to come up with a definition of "adequate" and post in the front of the room. Next, ask students to think about their own health care, dental care and mental health care. In small groups, ask students to generate a list of what they consider adequate care for themselves. Have groups report their answers and make a master list for the class. Then ask students to consider whether this list should be amended if the recipient of the "adequate care" was a prison inmate whose health care is funded by the state or federal government. Refocus students on their definition of "adequate." Strike or add services to the master list. If students are having difficulty or there is classroom disagreement over what qualifies as "adequate care" inform them that this is such a contested issue that a case, went to the Supreme Court in 1976 to decide.

Next explain the relevant facts of Estelle v. Gamble(18) (1976) to the class: J.W. Gamble was an inmate in a Texas prison. Estelle was the director of the Texas Department of Corrections. Gamble was assigned to a job in a textile mill and sustained a work-related back injury when a 600-pound bale of hay fell on him. He asked to go to the prison hospital. He was given a checkup and sent back to his cell. Later that night, his back was is so much pain he asked to go back to the prison hospital and was given some painkillers, re-examined, but did not receive any treatment. He was returned and confined to his cell. Gamble was soon put back on light work duty, but he refused to work because of the pain. He was put in solitary confinement for refusing to work during which time he continued to express that his back was in as much pain as the day of the accident. Almost a month later, a different doctor examined Gamble. He was diagnosed with high blood pressure. He also began having chest pains on a regular basis. He continued to refuse to work, was held in solitary confinement, and has hospitalized 17 times.

Gamble claimed that the lack of medical treatment he experienced and the punishment he received for refusing to work due to the pain amounted to cruel and unusual punishment in violation of the Eighth Amendment. After going through the lower courts, Estelle (director of the Texas Department of Corrections) petitioned the Supreme Court, and they agreed to hear the case.

Have students discuss this question in their small groups: Did Gamble suffer cruel and unusual punishment as a result of a lack of medical care from the prison? Remind them to consult their list of "adequate care" if that term comes up in their discussion. Groups may not reach consensus on this issue. After small group discussions, come back to a large group. Ask students to raise their hand if they would have found for Gamble in this case ("yes" to the discussion question) or Estelle ("no" to the discussion question). Ask for volunteers to give reasons for their decisions. Ask students what factors they considered when deciding this case. Did their small group discuss what the definition of "adequate care" means for inmates?

Conclude by telling students the resolution in Estelle v. Gamble: In an 8-1 decision, the Supreme Court found for Estelle. They wrote that the prison's treatment did not amount to cruel and unusual punishment because "negligent or inadvertent failure to provide adequate care did not constitute medical mistreatment." In simple terms, malpractice isn't cruel and unusual punishment just because the victim is an inmate. However, they went on to state the if there was evidence of "deliberate indifference to serious medical needs" on the part of the prison, that would be cruel and unusual punishment. So, although Gamble lost, the decision in this case protects inmates who need serious medical care while incarcerated.

ACTIVITY – STATE HEALTH CARE SPENDING COMPARISON

Health care spending varies widely from state to state. The four states that spend the most money on health care per inmate (California, New Mexico, Vermont and Wyoming) spend almost three times as much as the states that spend the least (Alabama, Indiana, Louisiana, Nevada, and South Carolina). In small groups, have students visit the Pew website article "Prison Health Care Spending Varies Dramatically by State": https://www.pewtrusts.org/en/research-and-analysis/articles/2017/12/15/prison-health-care-spending-varies-dramatically-by-state.

Ask students to find their state in the list and note what the health care cost per inmate was in 2015. Have students calculate what percentage their state's spending was of the top spending, median spending, and lowest spending. Ask students to hypothesize why their state is high, low, or average in spending. Then have students compare the spending in their state from 2010 and 2015. Ask students why they think the spending per inmate either increased or decreased in their state. As a whole group, discuss whether your state should consider increasing or decreasing spending per inmate.

PROBLEM 15.6 (p. 176)

a. Student answers will vary. Some students may feel that since many inmates are very poor, charging

them co-pays may in effect deny them medical coverage. This may contribute to the spread of disease or higher medical costs later. Others may feel that it is reasonable to charge inmates co-pays to offset the high cost of health care and discourage unnecessary procedures and costs.

b. Access to health care may influence other aspects of incarceration. Prisons must consider health care costs when budgeting for other programs. Re-entry of inmates into society may be complicated by health issues caused by a lack of preventative care while incarcerated.

NOTES

(1) *Miller* v. *Alabama*, 567 U.S. 460 (2012).

(2) *Lockyer* v. *Andrade*, 538 U.S. 63 (2003).

(3) *Furman* v. *Georgia*, 408 U.S. 238 (1972); *Lockett* v. *Ohio*, 438 U.S. 586 (1978).

(4) *Buchanan* v. *Angelone*, 522 U.S. 269 (1998).

(5) *Enmund* v. *Florida*, 458 U.S. 782 (1982).

(6) *Baze* v. *Rees*, 553 U.S. 35 (2008).

(7) *Gregg* v. *Georgia* 428 U.S. 153 (1976).

(8) *Glossip* v. *Gross*, 152 S. Ct. 2096 (2015).

(9) *Kennedy* v. *Louisiana*, 128 S. Ct. 2641 (2008).

(10) Lavender, Paige. "This State's Review of the Death Penalty Reveals the Shocking Cost of Executing a Prisoner," *Huffington Post*, December 3, 2014. http://www.huffingtonpost.com/2014/12/03/death-penalty-cost_n_6261778.html, accessed 3/17/15.

(11) *Atkins* v. *Virginia*, 536 U.S. 304 (2002).

(12) *Roper* v. *Simmons*, 543 U.S. 551 (2005).

(13) Mauer, Marc and Ryan S. King, "Uneven Justice: State Rates of Incarceration by Race and Ethnicity," *The Sentencing Project* (2007).

(14) Ehlers, Scott, Vincent Schiraldi, and Eric Lotke, "An Examination of the Impact of California's Three Strikes Law on African-Americans and Latinos," *Justice Policy Institute* (2004).

(15) Constitutional Rights Foundation Chicago, "Disproportionate Minority Confinement," www.crfc.org/dmc.html.

(16) *Holt* v. *Sarver*, 309 F. Supp. 362, 385 (E.D. Ark. 1970).

(17) *Wolff* v. *McDonnell*, 418 U.S. 539, 555–556 (1974).

(18) *Estelle* v. *Gamble*, 429 U.S. 97 (1976).

CHAPTER 16
Juvenile Justice

Juveniles who break the law are treated differently than adults. However, this has not always been the case. In earlier times, children were housed in the same jails as adults. Long prison terms and corporal punishment were common, and some children were even sentenced to death. Today, there is a separate justice system for juvenile offenders, although in some cases juveniles can still be tried as adults. Sentencing options for juvenile offenders range from counseling and probation to time spent in juvenile correctional facilities.

INTRODUCTION AND HISTORY AND OVERVIEW OF JUVENILE COURTS (PP. 177–180)

Learning Outcomes

After completing these section, students should be able to:

1. describe how the treatment of juveniles involved with the law has evolved during American history;
2. explain how the philosophy of *parens patriae* influences the way juveniles are treated in juvenile courts;
3. list and describe three groups of juveniles involved in juvenile courts;
4. describe steps taken to protect children who are found to be abused or neglected; and
5. define the terms parens patriae, *delinquent offender, status offender, neglected children,* and *abused children.*

CAPTION ANSWER (P. 178)   In addition to truancy, running away from home, violating curfew, refusing to obey parents, and engaging in certain behaviors such as underage consumption of alcohol are considered status offences.

PROBLEM 16.1 (p.179)

a. Reformers felt delinquency was caused by parents' failure to teach their children proper values and respect for authority. In addition, many felt that it was unduly harsh to punish children in the same manner as adults. As a result, reformers in the mid-nineteenth century instigated the creation of a separate juvenile court. The first was established in 1899.

   Note: Juvenile courts were created at roughly the same time as child labor and welfare laws and mandatory school attendance. These reforms came during the Progressive Era in U.S. history.

b. *Parens patriae*, a Latin term meaning "parent of the country," is the concept that the state has the right to intervene in the life of a child. This means the court can act as the ultimate parent or guardian for a child. It can attempt to rehabilitate a child by taking a moralistic approach and trying to help him or her learn community values. Some critics believe *parens patriae* is no longer valid today because society's views on adolescence have changed. Students should decide whether they support the idea of *parens patriae* or not. Was it a good idea in 1899? Is the concept still a good idea today?

c. Status offenders are youths who have committed acts that would not be crimes if committed by adults. Running away from home, skipping school, and refusing to obey parents are examples of status offenses. Many people feel that status offenders should not be

Criminal Law and Juvenile Justice   **133**

sent to institutions but should instead be sentenced to perform community-based service or other services. Delinquent offenders are youths who have committed acts that would also be crimes if committed by adults under federal, state, or local law. Ask students if there is a difference between the two types of offenders and if they should be treated differently.

d. Students' answers will vary. If time permits, organize students into small groups to discuss this topic. After group discussion, bring the class together and ask a spokesperson from each group to report his or her group's ideas. Some people believe that some young people cannot be rehabilitated and should therefore be punished. In response, many state legislatures have enacted mandatory minimum sentences for youths who have committed certain violent or drug-related offenses. In addition, many states transfer more serious juvenile offenders to adult courts.

e. Child neglect occurs when a parent or guardian fails to provide adequate food, clothing, shelter, education, or medical care for a child. Child abuse occurs when a child is sexually, physically, or emotionally violated. In both situations, a judge is responsible for deciding whether the child needs the protection of the court. A judge also determines whether the child should remain with the family while under court protection.

Investigating the Law Where You Live

(p. 179) Student answers will vary depending on location.

BACKGROUND AND DISCUSSION— PARENTAL RESPONSIBILITY LAWS

Some people believe that parents should be held responsible for crimes committed by their children. Those in favor of these parental responsibility laws believe they are particularly appropriate in cases in which parents know or should know that their children are using or selling drugs or belong to juvenile gangs. In some cases, parents may also be charged with contributing to the delinquency of a minor. Numerous states have laws that can hold parents responsible if their minor children gain access to a gun. In some states, parents can also be held responsible if their minor children engage in unlawful computer and Internet activities. Some states require parents to pay fines and restitution for crimes committed by their minor children.

Ask students whether they agree or disagree with parental responsibility laws. Ask students who agree with these types of laws to give three examples of situations in which parental responsibility should apply.

To learn more about parental responsibility laws, visit https://family.findlaw.com/parental-rights-and-liability.html. Students will also learn more about parental liability in Unit 5, "Family Law."

STATUS OFFENSES (PP. 180–182)

Learning Outcomes

After completing this section, students should be able to:

1. identify the types of charges that fall within the category of status offenses;
2. describe the national network established to help runaways; and
3. evaluate arguments for and against teen curfews.

CAPTION ANSWER (P. 181)   Runaways in need of help can turn to a national network of runaway shelters, which include counseling centers, shelters, and a nationwide toll-free telephone number. The National Runaway Safeline is 1-800-RUNAWAY.

BACKGROUND AND DISCUSSION— STATUS OFFENSES

Although the number of status offenders in institutions has declined, females still disproportionately outnumber males by a 10-to-1 ratio. Discuss this discrepancy with students. Ask them why the difference is so great. Some people claim that the courts try to play the role of father and are therefore more restrictive of female behavior. Others point to the obvious biases in laws governing juveniles. Still others claim that females are simply more likely to commit status offenses, while males more often commit delinquent acts. Propose these positions to students for discussion.

Investigating the Law Where You Live

(p. 181) If students need help finding runaway programs in their area, suggest that they ask a guidance counselor or visit the website of the National Runaway Switchboard at 1-800-RUNAWAY or at www.1800runaway.org. This organization offers special resources for teachers.

a. Students' answers will vary but should be supported with logical reasoning.

b. Students' answers will vary. Ask students to review their school's attendance policy or write their own. The policy should include reasons for the attendance rules. If the policy provides an attendance requirement, it should detail implementation procedures. It should also describe what will be done about chronically absent students. Should measures be punitive? Rehabilitative?

    Students could also role-play a debate on this topic between students, teachers, administrators, parents, employers, police officers, and adults who dropped out of school.

TAKING ACTION:
LAW AND DEMOCRACY

Hearing on a Curfew for Teens

PROBLEM 16.3 (p.182)

The topic of curfews typically has high interest for teens. This role-play allows students to explore a range of views on curfews. This activity becomes more authentic if students interview representatives from some of the groups whose testimony will be presented. This interaction will help students determine their own positions on the issue. Groups can be added to or deleted from the activity, and testimony can be altered from what is presented in the Student Edition. In lieu of interviews, you could invite representatives from your city council, police department, merchant association, or school board to advise students and to help facilitate this activity. At the conclusion of the activity, students may want to learn about their own community's curfew ordinances and to formally present their own proposal as an alternative.

JUVENILE JUSTICE TODAY
(PP. 183–194)

Learning Outcomes

After completing this section, students should be able to:

1. list rights to which juveniles are entitled as established by the *Gault*, *Winship*, and *McKeiver* cases;

2. compare and contrast rights to which adults and juveniles accused of crimes are entitled, including the right to appeal;

3. describe how "get tough" attitudes have influenced handling of juveniles accused of crimes;

4. given hypothetical cases, evaluate whether cases involving juveniles should be tried in juvenile or adult courts;

5. describe the types and purposes of diversion programs for youthful offenders;

6. explain the philosophy of restorative justice;

7. describe various dispositions juvenile offenders may receive;

8. describe how having a juvenile record can affect an individual after reaching adulthood and the steps to take to get a juvenile record expunged; and

9. define the terms *transfer (or waiver) hearing, age of majority, intake, initial hearing, preventive detention, adjudicatory hearing, disposition,* and *aftercare*.

THE **CASE** OF...

Gerald Gault

PROBLEM 16.4 (p.183)

This problem is based on *In re Gault* (1967).[2]

a. The unfair things that happened to Gerald Gault might include arrest on less-than-probable cause; not being informed of his *Miranda* rights; not being allowed to contact his family or an attorney upon being taken to the police station; not being informed of the nature of the hearing and not being represented by counsel; not having the opportunity to confront and cross-examine his accuser (Mrs. Cook); no record made at the hearing, making an appeal nearly impossible; not having a jury; being found guilty and sentenced by a judge using a standard of a "preponderance of the evidence" rather than "beyond a reasonable doubt"; and receiving a much harsher sentence than that for an adult convicted of the same offense.

A list of fair case proceedings might include that his parents were informed of the hearing and that Gault was given an opportunity to prove his innocence.

b. Applying most adult due process requirements would improve the fairness of the procedures (e.g., arrest based on probable cause, *Miranda* rights, right to an attorney, notice of the charges, right to confront and cross-examine witnesses, making a record of the hearing, the right to appeal, applying "beyond a reasonable doubt" as the standard of proof, and a sentence bearing some relation to the severity of the crime). Note that the U.S. Supreme Court's decision did not require all these procedures for juveniles. Discuss with students why each change would result in a more just procedure.

c. Adults have a constitutional right to bail, a right to a trial by jury, and a right to a trial record for appeal. None of these rights were granted in *Gault*. While *Gault* did not provide juveniles with rights equal to those of adults, it did attempt to inject procedural orderliness into the juvenile court system. The *Gault* decision sought to reverse the trend whereby "the child receives the worst of both worlds" (i.e., none of the adult procedural protections and all of the severity of punishment).[3] Remind students of the rights extended and denied to juveniles in the *Winship* and *McKeiver* cases, summarized in the Student Edition.[4] Despite the *Gault* decision, many advocates claim that youths often waive their right to counsel without being properly informed of such a right or its potential significance. (Also see notes in the juvenile court reform section below.)

d. Students should give opinions that are supported by reasons.

BACKGROUND—JUVENILE COURT REFORM

The Juvenile Law Center (www.jlc.org) and numerous child legal advocacy groups have also raised concerns about juveniles' access to quality legal representation in delinquency proceedings. They say the "spirit and promise of the *Gault* decision has been largely unfulfilled."[5]

A study by the American Bar Association, focused in the state of Maryland but intended to serve as a nationwide model, identifies the following concerns:

- Children who live in poverty do not have equal access to counsel because they often waive their right to counsel without understanding the significance of doing so.
- For those low-income respondents who do exercise their right to counsel, it is not offered at every step of the juvenile process, which undermines the case of the child.
- The majority of youths in detention were incarcerated without effective representation.
- Many attorneys representing young people are not adequately prepared to help their clients in transfer (waiver) hearings as well as in hearings about delinquency and disposition (sentences).
- Minorities are overrepresented in the juvenile justice system.
- Girls present unique issues in the juvenile courts because the rehabilitation services typically provided for the charges they commonly face (nonviolent offenses, status offenses, and parole violations) are often ineffective.

ACTIVITY—CONTROVERSIAL ISSUES CONTINUUM

Create a continuum by posting the following signs at opposite ends of the classroom: "Should be treated as a juvenile" and "Should be treated as an adult." Present each of the cases below and then have students decide where each should be adjudicated. They should answer by moving to the appropriate place on the continuum in the room. Be sure to ask students to explain their reasons for each decision.

- A 16-year-old is accused of skipping school.
- A 15-year-old is accused of assaulting a classmate.
- A 14-year-old is accused of committing murder.
- A 9-year-old is accused of committing murder.
- An 11-year-old is accused of committing rape.
- A 13-year-old is accused of shoplifting in a department store.

Note: This teaching strategy could also be used with the You Be the Judge questions in the Student Edition.

BACKGROUND—WAIVERS

All states allow juveniles, under certain conditions, to be tried as adults by way of one or more transfer mechanisms. Since the early 1990s, nearly every state has modified its laws to make it easier to prosecute juveniles in adult court. Legislatures also added many offenses for which juveniles could be tried in adult court and lowered the age at which certain juveniles could be tried in adult court. One of the more common changes gives prosecutors the option of filing charges in adult courts instead of juvenile courts. Many defense attorneys and judges disagree with the way this shifts the decision from judges to prosecutors.[6]

There are three types of waivers. A *legislative waiver* sends the youth to adult court based on certain objective criteria set by the state legislature. A *prosecutorial waiver* gives the prosecutor the discretion on how to charge the youth. A *judicial waiver* is the traditional method of allowing a judge to use subjective criteria in making the decision. Studies have shown that youths charged as adults suffer more physical abuse in jail and have a higher recidivism rate than those similarly charged in juvenile court. The minimum age for waiver to adult courts has been lowered to 14 in some states.

In the case of *Kent v. United States*,[7] the U.S. Supreme Court suggested nine factors for determining whether to use a transfer:

1. the seriousness of the offense and protection of the community;

2. whether the offense was committed in an aggressive, violent, premeditated, or willful manner;

3. whether the crime was committed against a person or against property;

4. the likelihood that the complaint would lead to indictment;

5. whether or not associates were being charged in adult court;

6. the sophistication and maturity of the child with respect to his or her home environment, emotional attitude, and pattern of living;

7. the child's previous record, if any;

8. the prospects for adequate protection to the public; and

9. the likelihood of successful rehabilitation.

Some say that today's juvenile justice laws place the burden on juveniles to prove that they can benefit from the protections of the juvenile court, thereby undermining the purpose of the juvenile

court. Discuss with students the laws of your state and the issue of treating juvenile offenders as adults.

For current state laws regarding transfer of juveniles to adult courts, visit the National Conference of State Legislatures website (http://www.ncsl.org/research/civil-and-criminal-justice/juvenile-age-of-jurisdiction-and-transfer-to-adult-court-laws.aspx). For information about the impact on juveniles who have been sentenced as adults, see the American Bar Association's website (http://www.ncsl.org/research/civil-and-criminal-justice/juvenile-age-of-jurisdiction-and-transfer-to-adult-court-laws.aspx).

YOU BE the JUDGE

Determining Juvenile Status (p. 185)

The idea here is not necessarily to decide how the juveniles *would* be tried under your state's laws, but rather how they *should* be tried. Ask the students to determine what criteria they would use in deciding whether or not to transfer a juvenile to adult court. Also ask students what other facts about the juvenile would be helpful in making this decision. For all scenarios students may need additional information such as family background, school performance, immediate environment, previous record (if any), maturity level, IQ, and/or strength of evidence against the minor.

a. Students' answers will vary. Marshall is only 15, but his record suggests that he is a repeat offender who might not respond to treatment in the juvenile justice system. He also appears to pose a threat to his community. Students might argue that he should be tried and, if convicted, punished as an adult. Others might feel that no 15-year-old should be tried as an adult and that he should be rehabilitated. His attitude toward the victim may also affect students' decisions.

b. Students' answers will vary. Leigh's action caused the death of another person. Many students may believe she must be punished as an example to others and that she should be held accountable for her actions. However, others may say that her age, her lack of prior involvement with the law, and her remorse suggest that perhaps she should be treated as a juvenile.

c. Students' answers will vary. Some students will probably argue that a 14-year-old under the influence of his brother should be tried as a juvenile. Others will be in favor of holding teenagers equally accountable with adults, noting that Carter made the decisions himself to sell drugs and stab the customer.

d. Students' answers will vary. Some students will argue that Angela should be kept in juvenile court despite the fact that this is her second weapons offense. Her motive for carrying the weapon is based on her perceived need to defend herself. Perhaps Angela could benefit from a juvenile diversion program designed for weapons offenders. Some students may point out that her prior experience in the juvenile system has done nothing to change her behavior. They may also argue that carrying a weapon is a violent offense.

DELIBERATION

Should violent juvenile offenders be treated as adults? (pp. 186-187)

An overview of the deliberation method is discussed in the front of this Teacher Manual. For free deliberation materials, student handouts, and an instructional video visit https://store.streetlaw.org/deliberations/.

If this is your first deliberation, consider devoting significant time to establishing norms for deliberations and civil discourse. Introduce the process of deliberations, including careful reading, clarification, preparing and presenting initial positions, reversing positions, free small group discussion, search for common ground, and whole-class discussion.

Begin class by introducing the deliberation issue: the treatment of violent juvenile offenders. Ask students when children develop a full understanding of right and wrong? Ask students to what extent are juveniles responsible for their actions? What factors should be used to determine when juveniles should be held responsible for crimes they commit in the same ways as an adult? Explain to students that this deliberation will help students explore whether juveniles should be treated as adults by the justice system. Students will strive to reach consensus on some aspect of the issue, but are not required to agree on an answer to the deliberation question.

Take students through the deliberation steps as outlined in the front of this Teacher Manual.

Debrief by instructing students to:

- Raise your hands if you changed your position on the issue.
- Raise your hand if you considered a new opinion that you had not considered before today.

- Raise our hand if you felt listened to during the deliberation.
- Follow up by asking students, how they might translate this activity to conversations outside the classroom.

Consider having students perform a self-assessment on the process and their contribution to it.

For the most recent information on trying juveniles as adults, see the following suggested resources:

- Office of Juvenile Justice and Delinquency Prevention (https://www.ojjdp.gov): Publications, research, data, and more from the U.S. Department of Justice.
- Juvenile Justice: Should teens who commit serious crimes be tried and sentenced as adults or children?" (http://www.aila.org/ https://www.pbs.org/wgbh/pages/frontline/shows/juvenile/): A PBS website that explores the stories and sentencing of four kids who committed crimes.
- Kids Behind Bars (https://www.youtube.com/watch?v=xQJYEB-E4e8): A 45-minute documentary from Bancroft TV about a juvenile unit located inside an adult prison.
- National Conference of State Legislatures—Juvenile Justice (http://www.ncsl.org/research/civil-and-criminal-justice/juvenile-justice.aspx): A collection of reports, news, and databases from a bipartisan organization.
- Inside Look at a Juvenile Justice Facility (https://www.youtube.com/watch?v=jMh-JCWblf8o): A two-minute YouTube video of a CBS News report about a small juvenile justice facility believed to be a "new wave" of reform.
- Inside Juvenile Detention (https://www.youtube.com/watch?v=C-0bURq6wBo): A ten-minute YouTube video from *The Atlantic* detailing life inside a Virginia juvenile facility.

CAPTION ANSWER (P. 188) After taking a juvenile into custody, the police have the authority to release or detain the juvenile. If the offense is minor, police may choose to give the juvenile a warning, release the juvenile to his or her parents, or refer the case to a social services agency.

DISCUSSION—REVIEWING VOCABULARY AND THE JUVENILE JUSTICE PROCESS

Use Figure 16.1 in the Student Edition as an introduction to the section about the juvenile justice process or as a tool for reviewing the terms and procedures students learn in this section. In either case, it is important to point out to students that the process outlined in the diagram is a general one, and the states vary significantly in how they handle juvenile proceedings. For this reason, it would be beneficial to have an attorney, judge, or child law advocate co-teach this topic. He or she can identify the ways in which your state differs from the process outlined in the Student Edition.

CAPTION ANSWER (P. 189) After a juvenile is taken into custody, he or she may be released, referred to youth court, or sent to juvenile court. Although not shown on the chart, for more serious offenses juveniles may be transferred to adult court for prosecution.

FYI For Your Information

Alternative Programs

PROBLEM 16.5 (p.190)

Youth courts are one of the fastest-growing intervention and prevention programs in the United States. To learn more about the national movement of youth courts, also known as teen courts, peer courts, or student courts, contact the National Association of Youth Courts. The center is sponsored by the Office of Juvenile Justice and Delinquency Prevention (OJJDP) and offers publications, training, and technical assistance to youth court administrators and to the young people with whom they work. The national association also maintains a database of all registered youth courts in the country. You can find more information about The National Association of Youth Courts at www.youthcourt.net. Young people who want to volunteer at a youth court can obtain information by clicking on the option called "Youth Volunteer Resources."

Restorative justice (sometimes known as balanced and restorative justice, or BARJ) is not exclusive to youth courts or programs designed for young people. In some places, its principles are applied to adult offenders. BARJ describes a judicial philosophy that emphasizes identifying and repairing harm. It is a systematic approach aimed at healing the damage done to victims, the community, and to the offender. Programs reflecting the aims of restorative justice attempt to involve all the important "stakeholders." For example, a youth court that strives to meet the goals of balanced and restorative justice might establish a process in which victims and members of the community are invited to explain to jurors how they were affected by the crime. Youth jurors, judges, and attorneys carefully structure questions to discover what prompted the offender to make the poor choice and what might motivate him or her to choose better next time.

To illustrate BARJ in a traditional courtroom, tell students that a young person brought in for vandalism might be required to fix the damage and complete a certain number of community service hours. For more information on BARJ, visit www.restorativejustice.org.

a. Students' answers will vary. Possible answers include that the youth involved have admitted their offenses and are willing to take responsibility for their actions. In addition, their individual issues are addressed through a community-based system that reinforces community standards and offers alternatives to crime. Young people may respond better to the judgments and recommendations of their peers than they do to adult judges. Finally, because young people can volunteer to play the parts of lawyers, judges, jurors, and other court officials, youth courts give young people a chance to learn about the justice system in a way that promotes a positive experience with the law. In fact, many respondents choose to volunteer and stay involved with youth courts after their disposition is complete.

b. Some youth courts have a lower rate of repeat offenders, and they encourage multilateral approaches to community problems. Many advocates claim youth courts help to clear otherwise clogged juvenile court dockets, allowing judges to focus on the most serious cases. They can also save the court and juvenile justice system money. However, youth courts require a coordinated effort among police officers, probation officers, court officials, and community leaders, which can be difficult to establish and to maintain. Youth courts are typically not used for more serious crimes such as felonies, so their impact is limited. Some observers perceive that young people tend to be tougher on respondents than juvenile court judges might be. Critics also claim that more research is needed to prove that youth courts really work and to determine what youth court programs must "look like" for them to be successful. In other words, poorly designed youth courts are a waste of resources and opportunities.

c. Students' answers will vary.

d. Students' answers will vary. If necessary, review the debates over "zero tolerance" and the Broken Windows Theory described earlier in this Teacher Manual.

e. Students' answers will vary. Teachers or their students could contact their local court, public defender, or prosecutor's office to find out about alternative programs. In some places *Street Law* lessons are used as part of alternative programs.

<hr>

PROBLEM 16.6 (p.191)

While the notion of preventive detention for juveniles has been upheld by courts, it is still controversial in some circles. Adults have a right to bail under the Eighth Amendment, though many who are poor and cannot pay the bail remain in jail before trial. Juveniles do not have a constitutional right to bail, yet they are usually released to their parents' or guardians' custody. A U.S. Supreme Court case, *Schall* v. *Martin* (1984) involved initial hearings in juvenile courts.[8] This case dealt with a New York law that allowed judges to order that juveniles be held in pretrial detention. When the judge determines that the juvenile is a "serious risk" and that the juvenile is likely to commit a crime before the next hearing, this is called preventive detention. It is more commonly used for juveniles than for adults. In *Schall*, the Court upheld the New York law, stating that it served the legitimate purpose of protecting the community and the juveniles themselves from the consequences of future crime. The Court held that the state's interest in promoting juveniles' welfare was paramount.

a. Students' opinions will vary. Critics could argue that preventive detention violates the equal protection clause. There is no evidence that juveniles are more likely to commit pretrial crimes than are adults. Adults receive more protection by the mere virtue of their age. However, as students will see in Chapter 41, "Discrimination," classifications based on age are almost always upheld by courts.

Supporters of preventive detention argue that the practice adequately protects youths from unnecessary deprivations of liberty. They are afforded notice, a hearing, and/or statement of the facts prior to any detention. Moreover, preventive detention serves the legitimate state objective of protecting the juvenile and society from pretrial crime.

b. Students' answers will vary. Most states and the federal government have laws requiring separate facilities for juveniles and adults to prevent corruption and abuse of juveniles by adult prisoners. Contact with adult offenders may also inhibit rehabilitation, which is the acknowledged goal of the juvenile system. Point out to students that many young people tried as adults are held in adult prisons and jails.

CAPTION ANSWER (P. 192) Conditions of probation may include that the juvenile attend school regularly, hold down a job, attend counseling sessions, submit to regular drug testing, and avoid contact with certain people.

ACTIVITY—DETERMINING THE APPROPRIATE DISPOSITION

Juvenile detention/correctional centers usually offer a variety of programs to the juveniles they house. Ask students to identify the types of programs they think should be offered in a juvenile center. Some typical programs available at juvenile facilities include Positive Peer Culture (P.P.C.) in which youths apply positive peer pressure to one another, psychological counseling, family therapy, job training, and educational training. Some even offer Street Law or other law-related education courses. Invite the director of a juvenile justice program to discuss with students some effective approaches to rehabilitating juveniles.

As an alternate activity, contact your local juvenile court and ask for a list of disposition (sentencing) options that judges use when making disposition decisions. Ask students to study those options along with the options described in the Student Edition. Then give students a sample case such as the one below and have them make disposition recommendations. Have students explain why they chose the recommendation they did.

Sample Case: Lynn is 16 years old. After a fellow student bumped Lynn in the hallway, an argument ensued and Lynn was charged with assaulting the person that bumped her. At the adjudication hearing, the judge found Lynn delinquent. The assault was fairly brutal, and Lynn is known to have an explosive temper. There were several witnesses present. Her temper has also created problems at home, at school, and in local businesses. Lynn does not obey family rules. Both of her parents work long hours and have little time to give her personal attention.

In the first disposition hearing, the judge required that Lynn make restitution to the victim, submit to weekly drug screening, meet with her juvenile counselor every two weeks, and write a letter of apology to the victim. However, Lynn did not comply with these terms, so there will be a second hearing to determine appropriate follow-up measures. (This is the point where students make their recommendations.)

To adapt this activity, organize students into groups of four. Ask one student in each group to play the part of a judge. The other students should play the parts of a probation officer, a social worker, and the prosecutor, who all make different recommendations to the judge.

CAPTION ANSWER (P. 193) For a person to be eligible to have a juvenile record expunged, most states require that several years have passed since the offense and that the person has committed no further offenses during that time.

PROBLEM 16.7 (p.194)

This problem gives students an opportunity to synthesize some of their feelings about the juvenile justice system. Where should the balance be in the juvenile justice system? Students who believe that the system should focus on protecting and rehabilitating youth might argue that if juvenile court records are available to employers, it could damage a juvenile's chance to get and keep a job—important steps to becoming a more responsible member of the community. Students who think the juvenile justice system should focus on protecting the rest of society from young criminals might argue that employers should be able to know whether a potential employee has a record of a crime that could affect the workplace. They already have the right to ask adults about their criminal records. Regardless of their opinions, students should support their views with reasons.

DISCUSSION—JUVENILE COURT RECORDS

Ask students whether they think it is "right" or "just" or "fair" that juveniles do not have criminal records. Their answers will likely reflect their feelings about the efficacy of the juvenile justice system. Students who think the system should seek to rehabilitate are more likely to support this practice than those who think the juvenile corrections system is too soft on crime.

While many students may already know that juvenile delinquents do not have a *criminal* record, some may be unaware of the extent to which a *juvenile* record can follow them through life. Ask them if this is "right," "just," or "fair." Confirm that students understand the process for getting juvenile

records expunged, and ask whether they think the process is appropriate or whether there is a better alternative.

For more information about expunging juvenile records, students may be interested in the work of the Juvenile Law Center (JLC). The Center is a public interest law firm that does a variety of work relating to child welfare and juvenile justice. Information about expunging records can be accessed at www.jlc.org, using the search term "juvenile records."

CHALLENGES FACING THE JUVENILE JUSTICE SYSTEM (P. 195)

Learning Outcomes

After completing this section, students should be able to:
1. describe the trend in disproportionate minority contact with the juvenile justice system and hypothesize why it is occurring;
2. analyze criticisms of the current juvenile justice system; and
3. identify an imporvement from the past in the current juvenile justice system.

BACKGROUND—JUVENILE JUSTICE REFORM

The Juvenile Justice Reform Act of 2018 was passed which reauthorized an the *Juvenile Justice and Delinquency Prevention Act of 1974* and added protections for juveniles involved in the justice system. The law reduces the placement of juveniles in adult jails before trial, requires decreases in racial and ethnic disparities to ensure equity, and promotes alternatives to incarceration among other provisions. The full text can be read at https://www.congress.gov/bill/115th-congress/house-bill/6964/text.

PROBLEM 16.8 (p.195)

Student answers will vary. Students should search their state in the Office of Juvenile Justice and Delinquency Prevention's "Juvenile Justice State Profiles" at https://www.ojjdp.gov/ojstatbb/special_topics/stateprofile.asp. To spark ideas about improvements, you can suggest students consult the National Council of State Legislature's article, "Improving the Juvenile Justice System" at http://www.ncsl.org/research/civil-and-criminal-justice/improving-the-juvenile-justice-system.aspx.

NOTES

(1) U.S. Census Bureau, "Mean Earnings by Highest Degree Earned: 2009" http://www.census.gov/compendia/statab/2012/tables/12s0232.pdf

(2) *In re Gault*, 387 U.S. 1 (1967).

(3) *Kent v. United States*, 383 U.S. 541, 556 (1966).

(4) *In re Winship*, 397 U.S. 358 (1970); *McKeiver v. Pennsylvania*, 403 U.S. 528 (1971).

(5) "Maryland: An Assessment of Access to Counsel and Quality of Representation in Delinquency Proceedings," American Bar Association Juvenile Justice Center and Mid-Atlantic Juvenile Defender Center, et al. (October 2003).

(6) Patricia Torbit and Linda Szymansi, "State Legislative Responses to Violant Juvenile Crime: 1996–97 update," *OJJDP Juvenile Justice Bulletin* (November 1998).

(7) *Kent v. United States*, 383 U.S. 541 (1966).

(8) *Schall v. Martin*, 467 U.S. 253 (1984).

UNIT 3
Torts

Unit 3 provides an overview of tort law—the largest branch of civil law. This unit highlights the differences between tort law and criminal law; describes how torts developed historically; presents various circumstances under which a person can sue or be sued; outlines the processes by which torts are adjudicated; and discusses the role of insurance in tort law. Tort law is also closely related to economics and to public policy issues. The final chapter in this unit introduces students to several cutting-edge issues, including tort reform.

CHAPTERS IN BRIEF

CHAPTER 17
Torts: A Civil Wrong
Chapter 17 defines *tort law* and identifies the parties in a civil lawsuit. It also helps students apply basic concepts such as liability, settlement, and damages.

CHAPTER 18
Intentional Torts
Chapter 18 defines the two general types of intentional torts—actions taken to deliberately harm another person and actions taken to harm property. The chapter also discusses how the judicial system treats intentional torts. Defenses to intentional torts are described.

CHAPTER 19
Negligence
Chapter 19 explains the concept of *negligence*. The chapter then explores the legal elements of negligence: duty, breach of duty, causation, and damages. The defenses a person charged with negligence might use are also outlined.

CHAPTER 20
Strict Liability
Chapter 20 describes torts in which defendants are held to strict liability standards because they engaged in extremely hazardous activities. The chapter explains how this area of law may serve as an incentive for careful and safe practices at work and at home.

CHAPTER 21
Torts and Public Policy
Chapter 21 reviews the function of the tort law system as it relates to public policy. Then the chapter challenges students to evaluate the importance and fairness of the tort system as they assess current tort reform efforts.

SERVICE LEARNING AND SPECIAL PROJECTS

1. **Court Visitation:** Arrange for students to attend a civil trial or hearing. Ask students to take notes identifying the parties involved and the roles played by attorneys, judges, witnesses, plaintiffs, etc. If students have already seen a criminal trial, ask them to observe differences in procedures between criminal and civil trials. If possible, have students observe the voir dire process and identify reasons why some prospective jurors were not included in the final panel. Students might also outline procedures they observed and make judgments applying their knowledge to the case (e.g., the reasonable person standard, intentional wrong, negligence, strict liability, damages, and the like). Attorneys involved in the trial might be willing to speak with students afterward.

2. **Field Trip:** Take a field trip to your state's legislature and meet with a legislator who is involved in an area of tort reform.

3. **Mini-Tort Trials:** Assign students to groups and have them select a story that illustrates a situation that could result in a tort. (For example, could the three bears sue Goldilocks? Should Chicken Little be liable for the emotional distress he caused his neighbors when he repeatedly claimed the sky was falling?) Ask students to identify potential plaintiffs and defendants, whether the defendant can show the required elements of that tort claim, and the defenses that might apply to the defendant. Finally, have students act out a brief mock trial featuring their "tort stories," with representatives from other groups serving as the jury. The jury should determine what damages, if any, should be awarded to the plaintiff.

4. **Service Learning:** While community service is educational and meaningful on many levels, service learning takes it to "the next level" by connecting service with classroom learning and reflection. The following activities are suggested to help students enhance what they learn in Unit 3 by serving their communities.

   - Students can write and distribute a pamphlet for high school students about car insurance. The pamphlet should include basic definitions of the terms *insurance* and *deductibles*. It should also explain why each of the various types of auto insurance is important and how they differ.

   - Students can write, produce, and perform a play or video about negligence to be viewed by younger students.

   - Students can research people in their community with various viewpoints about tort reform and ask them to serve on a panel to debate the issues in a community forum.

UNIT RESOURCES

Using Legal Resource Persons

One of the "best practices" in law-related education is to invite outside resource people to co-teach lessons in your classroom. These guests should not be asked or expected to lecture on a topic, but to engage students in interactive activities that showcase student work with the guidance of an expert.

1. Law students or attorneys with experience in the civil litigation arena could discuss their work.

2. A doctor could speak on issues of malpractice insurance and jury awards.

3. A representative from a consumer protection agency could discuss manufacturers' responsibilities, fraud, and issues of liability to the consumer.

4. Hold a question-and-answer session with an insurance salesperson or a claims agent. Discuss insurance fees, how they are determined, and how they are adjusted after an accident or traffic citation.

5. Invite a reporter from a local magazine, newspaper, or television station to discuss defamation, privacy, and freedom of the press. Learn how the reporter takes care not to commit a tort while writing a news story.

6. Find out what the dram shop laws are in your state. Invite a legislator who voted for the bill to answer questions, or invite a representative from Mothers Against Drunk Driving (MADD) or Students Against Destructive Decisions (SADD) to discuss the dangers, as well as the tort liabilities, of drinking and driving.

7. Two lawyers might make a presentation of tort reform: one should be a plaintiff's lawyer and the other should be an insurance company's or defendant's lawyer.

8. Judges might address topics from Unit 3, including tort reform; the relative merits of the U.S. tort law system compared to that of Europe; or special issues for teens in relation to torts, including consequences of negligent behavior and of substance abuse.

CHAPTER **17**
Torts: A Civil Wrong

Civil law deals with torts, or civil wrongs, against individuals. In civil law, the injured person (plaintiff) can sue the person accused of causing the harm (the defendant). If a defendant loses a judgment, he or she may be responsible for paying monetary damages to the plaintiff and may be ordered to stop the behavior complained of in the suit. Torts and crimes are different legal categories, but the same activity can be both a crime and a tort.

THE IDEA OF LIABILITY (PP. 198–201)

Learning Outcomes

After completing this section, students should be able to:
1. define the terms *tort, plaintiff, judgment, defendant, damages, liable, remedy, liability,* and *settlement;*
2. identify the parties involved in tort action case scenarios;
3. explain the concept and purpose of tort law and liability;
4. analyze a series of situations in order to determine whether the actions of the persons involved are reasonable or unreasonable; and
5. describe the general ways in which tort actions are resolved.

BACKGROUND—THE STUDY OF TORTS

The overall purpose of this unit on torts is to provide students with practical information about the largest body of civil law—torts. The study of torts should emphasize:

- the dynamic nature of law (tort law changes over time depending on how society calculates the benefits of permitting certain behaviors versus the costs of those behaviors to other individuals or to society);
- that civil law exists to help society settle disputes fairly, efficiently, and with certainty by making wrongdoers (or, in some instances, the parties in the best position to absorb the loss) pay money to the person(s) harmed; and
- that antisocial behavior can be deterred by assigning a cost (liability) to civil wrongs (torts).

In a sense, tort law emphasizes responsibility. Tort law is the vehicle by which wrongdoers pay for their misdeeds. A thorough study of this area of law should inspire students to become more careful, responsible persons.

In addition to providing compensation to victims, one major purpose of tort law is to promote responsible behavior on the part of citizens. The deterrent value of civil law is based on a desire of society's members to avoid paying for losses. This aspect of civil law might be explored in the following activity, which is designed primarily as a catalyst for discussion.

ACTIVITY—ANALYZING THE DETERRENT VALUE OF TORTS

Provide students with the following scenario: Nancy's mother asks her to shovel the snow off the driveway. Nancy refuses to do so. Walking up the slippery driveway after work later that day, Nancy's father slips and breaks a leg. Because Nancy failed to respond to her mother's request, she is grounded for one month. Tell students to assume that Nancy's parents have absolute power to impose and enforce the "sentence" (i.e., she cannot sneak out, negotiate an exception, or in any other way circumvent the wishes of her parents). During this time, Nancy is not allowed to talk on the telephone, watch TV, use the Internet, or receive or send any e-mail. She must come home right after school and stay in her room, eat her meals in solitude, and not communicate with anyone.

Ask students the following questions:

- Do you think the consequences Nancy is facing are punishment?
- If you were in Nancy's situation, would this experience convince you to shovel the snow the next time you are asked?

Answers will vary. Some students will say they would absolutely shovel the snow the next time. Others may reply that they would not be pressured no matter what their parents threatened to do to them.

Now change the scenario. This time, tell students that when Nancy refuses to shovel the driveway, her parents take $2,000 out of the $4,000 in her savings account to pay her father's medical bills and his salary for the days he missed work. Because Nancy is a minor, she has no legal recourse. She cannot get the money back from her parents. She has been saving this money for years. Her parents inform her that should she fail to conform to the rules of the house again, they will confiscate the remaining $2,000 in the account.

Ask students the following questions:

- Do you think the removal of money from the bank account constitutes punishment?
- If you were in Nancy's situation, would you conform to the wishes of your parents next time given their threats of taking your money?

Most students will agree that taking someone's money is indeed a form of punishment and a very heavy deterrent. Point out that though the purposes of civil and criminal law are different—the former providing compensation to those injured by other people or organizations, the latter imposing punishment for crimes against society—the deterrent value of torts rests with the desire of defendants to avoid paying damages in a civil suit. Discuss whether the inclination of many students is to view the loss of money as a greater punishment than incarceration. Ask students who share this view to explain their reasoning. In both scenarios, Nancy's parents were clearly seeking to enforce norms of acceptable behavior, as well as provide consequences for Nancy's recalcitrance.

PROBLEM 17.1 (p.200)

This problem gives students an opportunity to consider the notion of reasonable behavior and the issue of liability. Sometimes, there are a number of possible defendants. However, typically, lawyers try to sue a defendant with "deep pockets"—someone with either the assets or the insurance to pay a judgment if the plaintiff prevails. There are a variety of possible right answers to the situations described in this problem.

a. The plaintiffs are Jill's parents, on behalf of Jill, since Jill is a minor. The defendant is Carrie, the babysitter. Carrie's behavior might be considered reasonable if she went into the kitchen to answer a phone call, or if she were making a very brief call, perhaps to arrange for her ride home. Since she left the child alone to make a lengthy call to her boyfriend, however, this would probably be considered unreasonable. Babysitters should know that the safety of the child they are caring for is their primary concern. Could Jill's parents be considered unreasonable if they did not give Carrie clear instructions or did not find out beforehand whether she was an experienced babysitter? Another way to look at this—especially after students have learned the elements of negligence—is to ask whether or not Carrie's conduct caused harm to the child. Under negligence law, if the child would have fallen even if Carrie had been in the room, then her leaving the room to make the phone call should not result in liability.

b. The plaintiff is the teammate. The defendant is Ben. The action is reasonable. While students will learn later that tackling a person is considered battery, football players on the field give implied consent to be tackled. However, there have also been numerous successful lawsuits against coaches and school systems involving interscholastic and intramural sports. For example, a football coach who runs a full contact practice without pads and other necessary equipment might be engaging in unreasonable conduct.

c. The plaintiff is Mrs. Gonzalez. The defendants are Mr. Ghosh and the janitors. One would assume that Mr. Ghosh has "deep pockets." Therefore, if Mrs. Gonzalez chooses to file a suit she may want to consider focusing her efforts on

Mr. Ghosh (as opposed to the janitors). In any case, Mr. Ghosh would probably be liable for the janitors' actions, by way of the legal concept called *vicarious liability*. Vicarious liability means that, by reason of some relationship between two people (employer/employee), the negligence of one (the employee) is to be charged against the other (the employer), even though that person played no direct part in the tortious act or did nothing to encourage it. Mr. Ghosh's liability for conduct that is not his own (waxing the floor and placing the sign) extends to any and all tortious conduct of his employees who are acting within the scope of their employment. Presumably, waxing the floor would be part of the janitors' job description.

The decision as to whether the action is reasonable depends on whether or not the sign gave sufficient notice of the dangerous condition of the floor. Should the sign have been larger? Should it have been placed outside the front door? Is it necessary to rope off wet or recently waxed areas of the floor? Should such maintenance work be restricted to hours when there is very little traffic by residents? If some tenants do not speak English, must the sign be written in the languages of the tenants? What constitutes careful behavior in this situation? These are some of the considerations involved in determining the reasonableness of the conduct. Of course, Mrs. Gonzales is also obliged to be careful in entering the building. If she was carrying the grocery bags in such a way that she would not have seen the sign, she may not be able to recover damages. Consider using this scenario as an opportunity to introduce the concepts of contributory negligence and comparative negligence.

d. The plaintiffs are the neighbor's parents, on behalf of their three-year-old son. The defendant is Corina. Students may view this as a pure "accident" in which Corina's behavior and actions were reasonable, so there is no liability. However, does Corina have a duty to ensure the safety of the children she invites over to play with her daughter? Given the circumstances, was Corina's behavior reasonable? While the tort system is designed to provide compensation, not all harm is caused by tortious conduct. A jury could decide, in a case such as this, that the defendant was not at fault and therefore not liable. On the other hand, a jury could conclude that this harm to children was foreseeable and that Corina should have taken care to anticipate and avoid it. Home owners' insurance generally covers injuries such as this.

e. The plaintiffs are the parents of the injured students. The defendant is Jamal, perhaps his doctor, and the school district. Again, students should discuss several alternative points of view regarding reasonable behavior. If Jamal was told by his doctor that the heart condition could interfere with safe driving, or if Jamal should have inferred that from what his doctor did say, his conduct could be considered unreasonable. If the doctor knew that Jamal was a school bus driver and did not make his warning clear enough, his conduct could be viewed as unreasonable. Some students may even suggest that school districts should take certain care in assuring that their bus drivers are healthy and capable of safely operating a school bus. Most school districts require that buses be inspected; should the same requirement apply to the bus drivers? If the school district did not require a physical exam, perhaps its conduct (by omission) was unreasonable.

Even if the school district did not act unreasonably and had no idea of Jamal's condition, it could still be held liable under the doctrine of vicarious liability. More specifically, the doctrine of *respondeat superior* states that an employer is liable for the acts of employees performed within the scope of their employment. Since driving the bus was clearly within the scope of Jamal's employment, the plaintiffs can receive compensation from the school district—the "deep pocket"—based on *respondeat superior* if they can prove that Jamal was negligent.

f. The plaintiff is Matt. The defendant is the player, team owner, or the owner/operator of the stadium where the baseball game was played. Hitting a foul ball is not unreasonable conduct, so the player could not be sued successfully. This problem provides an opportunity to introduce to students the defense of assumption of risk. People who attend baseball games take a known risk of being hit by a ball. Of course, the team must take reasonable steps to make the stadium safe for spectators. All stadiums in which major league baseball teams play have a wire mesh screen behind the batter, covering at least the first deck of seats. If the stadium and/or team provides such a safety net but fails to repair any holes that develop, then the stadium owner (or team) might be guilty of unreasonable conduct. That was not the case in this scenario, however. Again, given all of the circumstances, did any of the defendants fail to exercise due care? Not surprisingly, there have been a number of lawsuits against sports teams for injuries suffered by spectators. Usually the spectators lose, as courts find that the spectators assumed the risk by attending the game.[1] Ask students to bring in a ticket stub from a professional sporting event, if possible. Point out that in many instances, a warning is printed on the back of the ticket noting that the purchaser assumes all risks in attending the event.

g. The plaintiff is the bicyclist. The defendant is Jess. Jess's behavior would be unreasonable only if her failure to fix her brakes was the cause of the harm. Depending on the exact facts proven at the trial, a jury might conclude that the accident was caused by bad driving conditions and that Jess was not at fault. Students may discuss whether or not the bicyclist was also engaged in unreasonable conduct. Laws regarding bicycles vary from state to state. Generally, riding one foot from the right-hand curb is considered reasonable. Riding at night without reflectors or some form of lighting may not be reasonable. Riding in the rain may seem foolish, but bicycles are a primary form of transportation for some people. You may want to refer students to the negligence defenses section in Chapter 19 of the Student Edition to briefly introduce the ideas of contributory and comparative negligence.

BACKGROUND AND DISCUSSION— WHAT IS REASONABLE?

In the Evan and Martha case on page 201 of the Student Edition, the issues are:

- Who acted reasonably or unreasonably?
- Who should be responsible?
- How much money represents reasonable settlement?

Go over this case and encourage discussion. You could alter the scenario a number of times and ask students to apply the issues in the case to different fact patterns to see how the outcome of the case would differ under other circumstances. Suppose, for example, that the set of stairs on which Evan was walking had ice on them, or that Evan was wearing new shoes with slippery soles. Ask students how the outcome might differ in each case.

This exercise can also be used to illustrate common law, which is explored in more detail in the next section of this chapter. Have students form a general rule or principle as they decide each hypothetical case. For example, "When one person shoves another, he or she must pay for all injuries." As you change the facts, tell students that they are still bound by the old rule. They may attempt to distinguish the new case from the others based on the facts to form a

different principle, such as "When someone shoves another person, he is not responsible for injuries resulting from the carelessness of the victim."

CAPTION ANSWER (P. 200) When determining liability, four factors are generally considered: duty of care (a responsibility by the defendant to use reasonable care), breach of duty (the defendant did not used reasonable care), causation (the plaintiff's harm was caused by the defendant's action or inaction) and injury (real harm suffered by the plaintiff). Contributory negligence on the part of the plaintiff may also be considered.

CAPTION ANSWER (P. 201) The injured party might be able to negotiate a settlement with the wrongdoer's insurance company in some cases. There might also be a remedy using workers' compensation.

THE IDEA OF TORTS: YESTERDAY, TODAY, AND TOMORROW (PP. 202–203)

Learning Outcomes

After completing this section, students should be able to:

1. define the terms *common law*, *precedent*, and *statutes*; and
2. explain how tort law attempts to strike a balance between preserving individual choice, determining the usefulness of a product, and protecting people from harm.

ACTIVITY—ANALYZING COSTS AND BENEFITS

Have students complete the following activity, which develops the issue of how tort law has evolved, with specific reference to the usefulness of products versus their potential harm. The Student Edition gives the examples of drugs for cancer patients and cigarettes. Students may want to examine the following products or inventions using a cost-benefit analysis: cell phones, nuclear energy, semi-automatic weapons, X-rays, and police radar detectors. Organize students into groups of four. Within each group, two students should compile a list of the advantages of each product while the other two members list the potential harms. Give groups ten minutes to brainstorm, then list the costs and benefits of each product on the board. Once the list is complete, present hypothetical tort cases that may arise from use of the products. For example, a nurse who spends the day giving X-rays develops cancer; a driver speeding while using a radar detector is involved in an accident which killed his passenger. Tally student responses for how each case should be decided to see if there is any relationship between the cost-benefit analysis of each product and the question of liability for the product manufacturers. Have students analyze whether or not the products' usefulness influenced their decision. Ask students what the consequences would be if all persons injured by the product were able to win lawsuits against the manufacturer. *The product would have to be redesigned for greater safety or perhaps withdrawn from the market.*

CAPTION ANSWER (P. 202) Students' answers will vary.

THE **CASE** OF...

The Lung Cancer Death

PROBLEM 17.2 (p.203)

When similar cases were first litigated in the 1960s, there was no consistent pattern among lower-court decisions.[2] With the advent of widespread knowledge about the relationship between lung cancer and cigarette smoking and prominent warnings on packages and billboards, it became more difficult for plaintiffs to win this type of case.[3] Smokers know and understand the risks associated with the product. To decide these cases in favor of the plaintiff would make the cigarette manufacturer liable for the personal habits of millions of Americans.

Significantly, recent reports state that cigarette smoking kills more than 1,000 Americans a day. Some students may know about the tobacco settlement in which several states joined together to sue the tobacco industry for their Medicaid costs for treating patients with illnesses due to smoking. In 1998, 46 states settled the case for $206 billion, payable over the next 25 years. However, many advocates charge that the states have not fully kept their promises to use the settlements for anti-smoking campaigns. For more information about the tobacco industry's settlement with the states, and statistics on tobacco use in the United States and the world visit www.tobaccofreekids.org.

Ask students how they feel about similar products. What other products call for individual choice and protection from harm? Does society put restrictions on any of these products? Should e-cigarettes be regulated the same as traditional cigarettes? What types of restrictions exist? Some examples are alcohol, e-cigarettes, prescription drugs, foods high in fat and calories, and pornography. You may want to invite a legal resource person to speak to the class or organize a field trip to attend a hearing that focuses on product liability.

a. The Garrett family's attorney could argue that ABC Tobacco Company was familiar with research on the dangers of smoking and continued to advertise and sell its products. The attorney could introduce ABC's advertisements, sales records, studies of the harmful effects of smoking tobacco, and expert witnesses on this topic. He or she could also argue that the ads did not adequately warn of known dangers and addictive nature of cigarette smoking.

b. ABC Tobacco Company's attorney could argue that Mrs. Garrett assumed a known risk. She had adequate warnings of the potential health risks of smoking, and she exercised free choice by smoking anyway. ABC Tobacco Company's attorney could also argue that the company had no knowledge of the health dangers when they first marketed the product and that other factors may have caused Mrs. Garrett's cancer. The attorney could introduce his or her own experts and their studies.

c.–d. These questions do not have a definitive answer and should be debated by students. Discuss the impact of various possible jurors: nonsmokers; smokers; those who at one time smoked; those who are employed by or hold stock in tobacco companies; etc. Note that there is a trend toward requesting a jury when an individual sues a large corporation. Lawyers believe that there is a natural tendency for jurors to identify with the individual over a large company in a case like this.

ACTIVITY—CONDUCTING A DEBATE

Students can use this activity to explore how tort law can be used to regulate the safety of products or even to effectively ban a product or activity. The e-cigarette example is valuable because it can be used in two ways. For adults, most people in society have determined that the individual choice of vaping or not vaping outweighs society's interest in banning an untested and potentially harmful product. However, for minors, the interest in preventing harm outweighs the choice of the minor regarding vaping.

Ask students to research and take part in an informal policy debate on this statement: *It should be illegal for U.S. e-cigarette companies to manufacture vape pens in flavors that attract minors.*

Questions raised might include the issue: Do minors have the right to make decisions about what they put into their bodies? Should tobacco companies have details of their manufacturing and sales regulated by the government? Have students research and discuss the matter and participate in a class debate.

TYPES OF TORTS (PP. 203–204)

Learning Outcomes

After completing this section, students should be able to:

1. define the terms *intentional wrong, negligence,* and *strict liability;*
2. distinguish among the three main categories of torts: intentional wrongs, acts of negligence, and activities for which strict liability is imposed; and
3. given a case scenario, identify the type of tort, if any, that occurred.

BACKGROUND—STRICT LIABILITY

Strict liability can be a difficult concept to grasp. For both intentional torts and negligence, students can readily see that the plaintiff must prove some kind of fault, as we commonly understand that term. On the other hand, strict liability is actually liability without fault, or at least without the legal requirement to prove fault. Remember that a primary purpose of tort law is to compensate plaintiffs for their injuries. The doctrine of strict liability allows plaintiffs to recover damages from defendants engaged in unusually dangerous activities where the risk of harm cannot be eliminated by exercising reasonable care (for example, demolishing a building or using explosives in an urban area).

PROBLEM 17.3 (p.204)

a. This is an accident; there is no tort.

b. Courts find this type of case troublesome. Some courts have held pharmaceutical manufacturers liable using the theory of strict liability.[4] These decisions hold that the business of producing drugs involves dangers that cannot be totally eliminated even with extraordinary care. Also, the manufacturer is typically in a better financial position to absorb the loss—through insurance and by spreading the cost among all its customers—than is the plaintiff. Other courts would not find liability unless the company had been negligent—for example, by not testing the product sufficiently or by not providing adequate warnings or directions. This lower standard may also encourage companies to develop new drugs for diseases such as AIDS without fear of liability for rare reactions that cannot be anticipated even through comprehensive testing.

c. Chen was negligent because he failed to use due care by driving while intoxicated (also a crime). His supervisor might be considered negligent for letting him drive when she knew that he was impaired. However, a court might ask whether Ruth had the duty to supervise Chen at (or after) an office party.

TAKING YOUR CASE TO COURT (PP. 205–208)

Learning Outcomes

After completing this section, students should be able to:

1. define the terms *civil law, standard of proof, preponderance of the evidence, deep pockets, minor, immune, waive, class action,* and *contingency fee;*
2. distinguish between who brings a civil (tort) suit and who files criminal charges;
3. explain the differences between the standard of proof used to determine guilt in a criminal prosecution and the standard used to determine liability in a tort suit;
4. describe who can be sued and explain the term *deep pockets;*
5. determine which groups of people have protection (immunity) from certain types of tort suits; and
6. describe class action suits.

DISCUSSION—COMPARING THE CRIMINAL AND CIVIL PROCESSES

Comparing criminal and civil processes may be useful to help illuminate the differences between them. The general steps for each type of case are listed here. Point out to students that criminal and civil cases are tried separately and can never be combined.

Criminal Process

1. **Arrest.** Police take a person into custody. Booking and fingerprinting take place.

2. **Initial appearance**

   a. **Misdemeanor case.** The defendant is given a copy of the complaint and asked to enter a plea. A trial date is set, and the judge either imposes bail or releases the defendant.

   b. **Felony case.** The defendant is informed of the charge and is advised of his or her right to a preliminary examination or presentation of the case to a grand jury (or both). No plea is entered.

3. **Indictment or information.** The prosecutor, or government's attorney, either presents evidence to a grand jury to get an indictment or has sufficient evidence from police that an information can be filed.

4. **Pretrial proceedings.** Hearings are held on motions to dismiss the case, to have evidence ruled inadmissible, or to permit discovery. The defendant may enter a plea of guilty with the hope of receiving a lesser sentence.

5. **Trial.** Presentation of evidence is made by the prosecution and the defense.

6. **Decision.** The verdict is made by the trier of fact, which may be a jury or a judge.

7. **Sentencing.** A penalty, which may be a prison term, probation, fine, or other punishment, is imposed on the defendant.

Civil Process

1. **Complaint filed by plaintiff.** The plaintiff files papers claiming a civil wrong done by the defendant.

2. **Answer by defendant.** The defendant files papers stating the defense in the case and responding to the factual allegations contained in the plaintiff's complaint.

3. **Pretrial proceedings.** Motions (requests by the parties to the court) are filed requesting discovery (an exchange of information between the parties).

4. **Trial.** Presentation of evidence is made by the plaintiff and defendant.

5. **Decision.** The verdict is made by the trier of fact, which may be a jury or judge.

6. **Judgment.** Pronouncement by the judge is made in favor of either the plaintiff or defendant.

7. **Enforcement of judgment.** The court forces the person against whom a judgment was pronounced to pay damages or do something to otherwise compensate the person to whom the harm was done.

BACKGROUND—WHO CAN BE SUED?

This section introduces the idea that a plaintiff may sue an employer for some harms caused by one of his or her employees. This is called the doctrine of

respondeat superior. Basically stated, it means that an employer is responsible for the torts of its employees that are committed within the scope of their employment. *Respondeat superior* is a type of vicarious liability. Vicarious liability means that, by reason of some relationship between two people (for example, employer and employee), the negligence of one (the employee) may be charged against the other (the employer), even though he or she played no direct part in the tortious act or has done nothing in particular to encourage it.

Generally, parents are not held vicariously liable for their children's torts. There must be some negligence on the part of parents (such as inadequate supervision) for the parents to be held liable.

The majority of states have abolished interspousal immunity, which prohibits spouses from suing each other, and a smaller number have abolished parent-child immunity. Other states give partial immunity in these cases, allowing lawsuits in certain circumstances, such as for willful or wanton intentional torts.

Although the *Federal Tort Claims Act*[5] allows plaintiffs to sue the United States, there are several procedural restrictions. For example, the claim must be presented to the "appropriate federal agency" before it is filed; a judge, rather than a jury, must hear the suit; and the contingency fees lawyers may collect on such suits are strictly limited.

One form of immunity is stated in Article I, Section 6, of the U.S. Constitution: "The Senators and Representatives . . . shall in all cases, except Treason, Felony and Breach of the Peace, be privileged from Arrest during their attendance at the Session of their respective Houses, and in going to and returning from the same; and for any Speech or Debate in either House, they shall not be questioned in any other place."

Presidential immunity comes from the 1982 case of *Nixon* v. *Fitzgerald*[6] in which A. Ernest Fitzgerald brought a civil suit against President Nixon for firing him for illegitimate reasons from his government position as a management analyst with the Air Force. The U.S. Supreme Court held that presidents are immune from civil suits arising from their public duties because the president might be a vulnerable target for numerous suits, and this would interfere with his or her ability to perform presidential duties. However, in the case of *Clinton* v. *Jones*[7] the Court held that a sitting president does not have even temporary immunity from a civil suit arising from actions unrelated to the president's official duties. Paula Jones sued President Clinton for alleged sexual harassment that occurred while he was governor of Arkansas, before Clinton became president.

BACKGROUND—CLASS ACTION SUITS

A class action suit provides a means by which a large group of people who feel they have been harmed by the same wrong may be represented by an individual or a small group of people. The representative individual or small group may file a suit without having to join every member of the class. An example of a class action suit involved a case filed by female employees of the Department of Social Services and the Board of Education of New York City in 1977.[8] In this case, the women had identical complaints, and so they filed their claims together in a class action suit. The policies of both organizations compelled pregnant employees to take unpaid leaves of absence before medical reasons required such leaves. Although the courts decided in favor of the plaintiffs, calling the mandatory leaves of absence unconstitutional, they denied the plaintiffs' claims for back pay.

THE **CASE** OF...

The Spilled Peanut Butter

PROBLEM 17.4 (p.206)

a.–c. It appears that Jenny committed the wrongful act. However, a suit against a child, or even against her father (for failing to supervise his child or for failing to report the problem immediately to the supermarket), may not result in Mrs. Hightower receiving enough money to pay for her expenses and damages. For this reason, plaintiffs often sue a corporate defendant who has deep pockets (i.e., the ability to pay a court judgment). The managers and employees at Foodland Supermarket may have an ongoing duty to inspect the store and keep it safe for its customers. Within ten minutes, a store employee should have discovered or been notified of the problem. Mrs. Hightower could also argue that the display was not set up in a proper and safe way.

Mrs. Hightower also had a duty to use reasonable care while in the supermarket. For example, the defendant could argue that a reasonably careful person would have both seen and avoided the broken glass and peanut butter in the aisle.

d. Mrs. Hightower might prefer mediation, dispute resolution, or even two-way communication with Foodland Supermarket, as these options could result in a faster settlement and no legal fees. Her decision may depend upon whether she believes she will receive a larger settlement by going to court.

CAPTION ANSWER (P. 206) Although minors can be sued for damages, most do not have deep pockets, so plaintiffs often sue the minor's parents.

THE **CASE** OF...

The Steering Wheel Failure

PROBLEM 17.5 (p.208)

a. Sarah could bring a civil action against Town and Country Motors, the service department supervisor, the service department technician who worked on her car, and the manufacturer of the car.

b. Students' answers will vary but should be supported with reasons. It appears from the facts that Sarah has a good case against Town and Country Motors for negligence. Sarah should engage an expert witness to help establish the existence of a negligent repair.

c. In this case, the potential recovery is quite large. The lawyer's share of the settlement might be greater with a contingency fee than with an hourly fee. A fixed fee or hourly fee might be best for Sarah. However, a lawyer might not accept such a case unless it is on a contingency-fee basis (a practice criticized by some). Under a contingency-fee arrangement, Sarah would also have the advantage of not paying if she loses and of not paying until after the case is over even if she wins. However, even in contingency-fee cases, Sarah would have to pay court costs and litigation costs, including filing fees, copying, witness fees, etc.

d. Sarah might prefer mediation, dispute resolution, or perhaps direct negotiation and communication with Town and Country Motors. These options may result in a faster settlement and no legal fees.

THE CASE OF...

PROBLEM 17.6 (p.208)

NOTE: This problem is based on the downing of Flight 103 over Lockerbie, Scotland in 1988. Families of victims filed a class action suit against the government of Libya.

a. This tragic case scenario is exactly the type of situation where a class action suit would be appropriate. Class actions are brought by a group of individuals whose interests are sufficiently related so as to justify the adjudication of their rights in a single court action rather than several individual proceedings. Here, the families of the deceased passengers and crew all have similar interests. They all should be compensated (to the extent they can be) for the possible wrongful death of a loved one stemming from a single event. It would also be more efficient and less expensive to bring one class action instead of 270 separate actions.

b. There are many potential defendants: (1) the terrorist who smuggled the bomb on board; (2) the sponsoring terrorist organization; (3) the commercial airline itself for allowing a terrorist with a bomb to get on the plane; and (4) the owner/operator of the airport in Frankfurt, Germany, charged with the responsibility of providing security checks and screening for passengers leaving on flights.

c. This determination would, of course, depend on the specific facts brought out at trial. However, it is safe to say that the parties responsible for the security and screening of passengers on the ill-fated flight would be likely candidates for liability. Presumably, this would be the commercial airline, the entity in charge of security at the airport, and possibly the manufacturer of the security system used at the airport. It might be difficult to identify the sponsoring terrorist organization and to locate and obtain any assets held by the organization.

d. Students will have varying opinions about how much a human life is worth in terms of monetary compensation and whether the civil law system is the appropriate avenue through which victims should seek redress for their harms. Students may be interested to know that the Lockerbie case was eventually settled out of court for $2.7 billion or approximately $10 million per family.

INSURANCE (PP. 209–214)

Learning Outcomes

After completing this section, students should be able to:

1. define the terms *liability insurance, contract, premiums, malpractice, medical coverage, collision coverage, deductible, comprehensive coverage, uninsured* and *underinsured motorist coverage,* and *exclusive remedy;*
2. explain the purpose of liability insurance and its role in American society;
3. describe why doctors and other professionals purchase malpractice insurance and why the premiums can be so costly;
4. identify different types of auto insurance and discuss the types of accidents that are covered by each;
5. describe how the workers' compensation system operates; and
6. analyze the advantages and disadvantages of the workers' compensation system.

LEGAL RESOURCE PERSONS

Insurance is a mystery to millions of Americans and certainly to many high school students. Teachers and insurance agents acting as resource persons might find it helpful to emphasize the practical applications of insurance for students, as well as explaining the purpose of local laws which may require the purchase of insurance.

THE CASE OF...

The Expensive Insurance Premium

PROBLEM 17.7 (p.209)

Due to the rising cost of malpractice insurance, many doctors have changed their specialties. Obstetricians have been among the specialists hardest hit by the high cost of insurance. As a result, fewer medical students enter this field, and many of the doctors within this specialty have left for more lucrative, less dangerous areas, such as liposuction and plastic surgery, where insurance premiums cost less. The net result is that patients may suffer as it becomes more difficult to find doctors and obtain appointments. Discuss the trade-offs with students, and ask for possible suggestions that might improve this situation.

Another issue involving medical malpractice is the residency program that physicians are required to undergo before they can be licensed. These programs place medical school graduates in hospitals to train for their specialties. For many years, it was routine for residents to work more than 100 hours a week and to rotate "on call," which requires the resident to work for 24 to 36 consecutive hours. These training programs have been criticized as causing overtired residents to provide inadequate medical care, which may result in medical mistakes. Critics also argue that hospitals impose long hours as a means of keeping labor costs low.

In July 2003, after highly publicized errors involving residents working long shifts, the Accreditation Council for Graduate Medical Education (ACGME), which accredits training programs for medical doctors, issued a regulation that reduces the number of hours that medical residents can work. The new regulations require a limit of 80 hours per week, a workday lasting no more than 24 hours, a break of at least 10 hours after every shift, and several other restrictions. While these regulations are applauded by many people, others criticize the remaining loopholes and exceptions. Others cite continuing pressure on residents to under-report their hours and threats of punishment for whistle-blowers.

To learn more about this issue, as well as federal and state legislation, visit the American Medical Student Association at www.amsa.org. Discuss this issue with the class. Do students feel the current medical residency program is a wise system? What alternatives do they propose? You might want to invite a physician or hospital administrator to visit the class and discuss this topic.

a. Dr. Akiba could be sued if a patient thought that he committed malpractice. If he did not have insurance to protect him, the loss of money from legal fees and a possible award might put him out of business or even bankrupt him.

b. Students' answers will vary. There are several possible reasons that account for why Dr. Akiba's insurance premiums are so high. When a surgeon makes an error, it tends to be costly. If Dr. Akiba has been sued many times, that makes him a poor insurance risk, so the insurance

company might charge him more than other surgeons practicing in the same area. Finally, insurance companies often make substantial profits, which further adds to the cost of malpractice insurance policies.

c. Initially Dr. Akiba pays his own insurance premiums. However, medical fees are calculated in the same way that a business calculates its prices. The cost of malpractice insurance to the doctor is a cost of doing business, and this cost is passed on to patients in the form of higher fees for medical services.

d. Students' answers will vary. This question raises the problem of medical malpractice, a topic treated in greater detail in Chapter 21. Some argue that malpractice is committed by relatively few doctors and that the profession should monitor practitioners more stringently to prevent harm to patients. Getting these few negligent doctors out of medical practice would substantially lower the cost of insurance for all. Others argue that many frivolous suits are brought by patients who hope a sympathetic jury will award them a large sum of money. So-called tort reforms limiting the ability to sue for medical malpractice—or placing a cap on judgments—could also reduce insurance costs.

PROBLEM 17.8 (p.211)

Students' answers will vary. This question helps students apply what they have learned about the different types of auto insurance. For most people, purchasing *collision* insurance is a question of economics. Although some people might think paying $500 a year to insure a car worth $4,000 is expensive, if a collision causes $2,500 worth of damage, in the end, it is more economical to spend the $500 per year and pay any required insurance deductible to have the car fixed than to pay all repair costs out of pocket. Once the value of a car is less than $1,000 or so, most individuals do not purchase collision insurance. However, all car owners and drivers should carry *liability* insurance, which pays for injuries to other people and property if you are responsible for the accident. In fact, most states require car owners to carry liability insurance.

Consider inviting an insurance salesperson or claims agent for a question-and-answer session with students.

THE **CASE** OF...

The Nonstop Car

Note: Students will revisit this case and answer additional questions about it in Problem 17.10 in the Student Edition.

a. Students could argue that the person at fault should be responsible for paying the medical bills and car repairs for all parties. Terrell is at fault, according to the facts presented.

b. Students should understand that determining fault is complicated. In most cases, the insurance company of the party at fault pays for the repairs resulting from auto accidents. If the party at fault does not have insurance, then the not-at-fault party's insurance company will pay most expenses, provided there is coverage for uninsured drivers. Some states have no-fault insurance, meaning that each party's own insurance will pay regardless of who is at fault.

CAPTION ANSWER (P. 212) A deductible is an amount of money the insured person must pay toward repairs before the insurance company pays for anything.

Investigating the Law Where You Live

(p.212) There are two ways students can learn about the types of auto insurance required in their state. One way is to invite an insurance salesperson to discuss insurance with the class. If students prefer to look for information online, direct them to www.carinsurance.com. From the home page, tell students to click on the "Car and Insurance By State" tab and then scroll down to the section called "All Other States." Here they will find an interactive map that shows minimum insurance requirements for each state. Please note that this site is commercial, so students should know that the hosts of the site are trying to sell insurance.

a. Terrell's insurance company would pay Candace's car repair bills, up to the limits of his policy. Because it is a no-fault state, Candace's insurance company would pay for her personal injury damages. However, she could sue Terrell's insurance company if the damages were higher than the limits on her policy.

b. Assuming that Terrell had collision and medical coverage, Terrell's insurance company would be responsible for paying his bills up to his policy's limits.

c. Candace would likely sue to recover damages from Terrell, who would be held personally responsible for any amount in excess of his coverage.

d. Terrell would have to pay only the deductible ($250) as set out in his policy. Note that Terrell's insurance premiums will likely go up.

ACTIVITY—COMPARING INSURANCE COSTS

Ask students to research car insurance. Tell them to assume that they want to purchase a new car. Ask them to consider both their dream car and a more practical choice, such as a less expensive model or a used car. Have them find out the selling price for these cars. Then tell students to contact several insurance companies to compare and contrast costs for insuring each car. Students should also ask about how insurance rates might change if they have an accident that is their fault or if they get a speeding ticket.

BACKGROUND—WORKERS' COMPENSATION

An argument can be made that the workers' compensation system is quicker, more efficient, and administratively easier than litigation. It follows that the system saves both time and money. It is cheaper for employers and does not raise the question of fault. An opposing argument stresses that the system hurts employees by not allowing them to sue when they have been victims of negligence. Victims cannot recover all the damages incurred and may receive less income while they recover, all for the sake of administrative convenience. Ask students whether they think the court system could handle the many suits that would arise if there were no workers' compensation statutes. Which is a better system—workers' compensation or litigation?

Workers' compensation is not always an absolute bar to employees suing employers. In a few states, an employee can sue an employer when the injury is a result of fraudulent conduct by the employer. The employee can sue an employer in some states under the *dual capacity doctrine*. This is a situation in which the employee is injured, not necessarily within the scope of his or her employment, but because of the nature of the business. For example, suppose a nurse works for a doctor and is injured by that doctor while being treated as a patient. The fact that she is employed by the doctor does not necessarily preclude her from suing the doctor for medical malpractice.

CAPTION ANSWER (P. 213) Students' answers will vary. As a matter of good public policy, students might argue that the law should contain incentives for following safety rules, for example, by not paying for injuries to workers who fail to follow safety rules.

THE **CASE** OF...

The School Slip and Fall

PROBLEM 17.11 (p.214)

a. The school's maintenance staff member, possibly his or her supervisor, and the school are responsible for their injuries.

b. Dale can recover damages from the school, which has vicarious liability for all acts of its employees within the scope of their employment. He will be able to recover the amount of damages that he is able to prove in court or through a settlement with the school. The school probably has liability insurance to cover this claim.

c. As an employee, Mrs. Braun will be eligible to receive workers' compensation, and she will probably have to file a workers' compensation claim. She is limited to the amount established through the workers' compensation schedule.

d. Students' answers will vary. This question provides an opportunity to discuss the strengths and shortcomings of the workers' compensation system. A local resource person who knows how the system works where you live would be an excellent addition to this discussion.

Discuss with students the conflicting views surrounding workers' compensation. For an overview of these conflicting views, see the section "Background—Workers' Compensation" on the previous page.

NOTES

(1) *Shaw* v. *Boston American League Baseball Co.*, 325 Mass 419, 90 N.E. 2d 840 (1950).

(2) The plaintiffs who won in these early cases tended to prevail against manufacturers on a breach-of-implied-warranty theory. (See the consumer law material in Unit 4 of the Student Edition.) *Cooper* v. *RJ Reynolds Tobacco Co.*, 214 F. 2d 170 (1st Cir. 1956).

(3) Plaintiffs in the 1980s lost many of their cases as courts ruled that cigarettes were not defective or unreasonably dangerous and that the federal law requiring a warning label preempted any claim that the warning was inadequate. *Palmer* v. *Liggett Group, Inc.*, 85 F. 2d 620 (1st Cir. 1987).

(4) *Sindell* v. *Abbott Laboratories et al.* v. *Rexall Drug Company*, 607 P.2d 924 (1980) (the drug DES); *Ferrigno* v. *Eli Lilly and Co.*, 420 A 2d 1305 (1980); *Reyes* v. *Wyeth Laboratories*, 498 F. 2d 1264 (5th Cir. 1974) (polio vaccine unavoidably unsafe and manufacturer did not adequately warn about the dangers); *Brochu* v. *Ortho Pharmaceutical Corp.*, 642 F. 2d 652 (1st Cir. 1981) (oral contraceptives were defectively designed and inadequate warnings were given to the prescribing doctors).

(5) *Federal Tort Claims Act*, 28 U.S.C. § 2671 et seq.

(6) *Nixon* v. *Fitzgerald*, 457 U.S. 731 (1982).

(7) *Clinton* v. *Jones*, 520 U.S. 681 (1997).

(8) *Monell et al., Petitioners* v. *Department of Social Services of the City of New York et al.*, 436 U.S. 658 (1978).

networks™

TYPES OF DAMAGES (PP. 215–216)

Learning Outcomes

After completing this section, students should be able to:
1. identify the two different classes of intentional torts; and
2. define the terms *intentionally, intentional tort, compensatory damages, nominal damages,* and *punitive damages.*

Actions taken that deliberately harm another person or their property are called intentional torts. There are two general types of intentional torts: those causing injury to persons and those causing harm to property. Torts that injure persons are battery, assault, infliction of emotional distress, false imprisonment, and defamation. Two different types of property—real property and personal property—are protected by tort law against interference with the owner's exclusive use of the property. Tort law also protects property against being taken or damaged. There are several defenses to intentional torts, with the most common being self-defense.

THE **CASE** OF...

The Mischievous Child

PROBLEM 18.1 (p.216)

a. Jeremy can be said to have committed a battery (intentionally causing a harmful or offensive touch) because he was aware that she would almost certainly land on the ground when he pulled away the chair. The child's youth is certainly a factor in determining whether or not he had the cognitive ability to understand that pulling the chair would result in Helen hitting the ground. There is no per se rule that children under a certain age are incapable of committing an intentional tort. This contrasts with the historical rule in criminal law that children under a certain age (usually seven years old) are incapable of forming criminal intent. On remand, the trial judge in this case found that Jeremy did act with the requisite intent.[1]

b. If Jeremy had not pulled the lawn chair away, Helen would not have fallen and fractured her hip. Therefore, Jeremy can be said to have caused the fall.

c. Children may be sued for the torts they commit. In most states, parents are not vicariously liable for the torts committed by their children. Therefore, in order to successfully sue the parents, Helen would have to have shown some kind of negligence on the part of the parents, such as failure to adequately supervise their child. The facts of this case do not necessarily support such a result. Some states' laws place liability up to a certain dollar amount (e.g., $5,000) on parents for intentional torts.

d. The intent necessary to commit a battery is intent to cause a touch. Even if Jeremy honestly did not mean to cause any harm to the woman, as long as he intended for her to touch the ground, he committed a battery and he is liable for all resulting damages.

e. The legal outcome would be different because Jeremy would not have intended to cause a touch and therefore would not have committed a battery.

TORTS THAT INJURE PERSONS (PP. 217–222)

Learning Outcomes

After completing this section, students should be able to:

1. distinguish between battery and assault;
2. given case scenarios, determine whether or not the tort of assault and/or battery occurred;
3. define the tort of emotional distress and, given case scenarios, determine whether or not this tort occurred;
4. define the tort of false imprisonment and, given case scenarios, determine whether or not this tort occurred;
5. define the two types of defamation and describe appropriate defenses for them; and
6. define *battery, assault, intentional infliction of emotional distress, false imprisonment, defamation, slander,* and *libel.*

ACTIVITY—BUILDING A DEFINITION OF BATTERY

Students will have a better grasp of the definition of the term *battery* if they build the definition themselves. This activity should be completed before students read the section of the text that defines battery. To prepare, write out a definition of battery on a piece of paper or create a Power Point slide, which you will later reveal to the class. A possible definition is, "Battery occurs when a person intentionally causes an unwanted touch that is harmful or offensive to another person." Give students ten minutes to search online or print news sources for stories about a physical touch. Alert them that their stories will be read aloud.

Have students share each article's facts with the larger class. After each, ask: "Should this touching be a tort (battery)?" Discuss students' reasons and ask the class to come up with a definition of when a touch should be considered a tort. Write the first definition on the board. After each story, allow revision of the class definition. The definition should be refined with each new story until a final definition is arrived upon through consensus. Then reveal the actual definition of when a touch constitutes a tort (battery).

Students should compare their class definition to the actual law, identifying and discussing elements that are the same and those that are different.

Students may include the concept of privilege in their definition of battery. As discussed in "Defenses to Intentional Torts" in the Student Edition, certain persons may have privilege, or authority, to touch another in a way that the person touched may consider harmful or offensive. For example, police may touch an arrestee to place handcuffs, pat search, and place the arrestee in a police vehicle. The arrestee may view this as offensive touching that is intentional, but it is not a battery because it is deemed "privileged touching."

Another example that may arise is the issue of teachers touching students. Such touching is generally permitted when the student is younger and the teacher is comforting the student.

Different communities have different rules when it comes to inappropriate touching that is sexual in nature. In the case of *Gebser* v. *Lago Vista Schools District*,[2] a male teacher and a female student had a sexual relationship that began when she was in eighth grade and continued until they were caught by police when she was in ninth grade. Later, the student sued the school district, saying it was liable for the sexual harassment of the student under *Title IX of the Education Act Amendments*. The case went to court and was appealed. In 1998, the U.S. Supreme Court issued a decision that set guidelines for whether and when schools can be "vicariously liable" for the sexual harassment of a student by a teacher. The Court ruled that the plaintiff (student) must prove that a school district official "with the ability to institute corrective measures" against the teacher knew of the "forbidden conduct" and failed to respond in a proper manner.

CAPTION ANSWER (P. 217) Because the tort of battery deters intentional touching without consent, it recognizes the autonomy of each person regarding his/her body.

a. Assault is defined as an intentional threat, show of force, or movement that causes a reasonable fear of or an actual physical contact with another person. Assaults can be a crime or a tort. The issue is whether the fear is reasonable. It was reasonable for Cynthia to fear that she would be shot when Lenny pointed the gun at her. She did not know it was unloaded. Lenny would be liable for assault. There is no requirement that the wrongdoer must actually be able to carry out the harmful or offensive contact. As long as the victim reasonably fears that such a contact will imminently occur, an assault has occurred.

b. A battery can be committed against an unconscious person because there is no requirement that the victim be aware of the harmful or offensive touch. However, an element of the tort of assault is that the victim fears a touch, and this cannot occur when the victim is unconscious. Therefore, if a person sneaked up from behind someone who was standing on the edge of a cliff and pushed that person over the edge, a battery would have been committed, but not an assault.

THE CASE OF...

The Funeral Protest

Although the definition is less precise than most intentional torts, generally there are four elements that define intentional infliction of emotional distress (IIED): (1) the distress is intentionally inflicted; (2) the behavior is extreme and outrageous; (3) the behavior causes the emotional distress; and (4) the emotional distress is severe. The vulnerability of the victim and the relationship of the parties can be critical.

Courts often focus on the second and fourth elements. Although there is no objective standard, mere rudeness and offensiveness are not enough. Often an emotional distress claim is joined with other tort claims and generally prevails where a plaintiff's other remedies at law are insufficient.

a. The strongest argument in favor of Mr. Snyder is that protesters' outrageous behavior satisfied all the elements of IIED. They intended to upset attendees of the funeral and the general public, the behavior was extremely hateful and repugnant, easily satisfying the requirement for "extreme and outrageous" behavior. Finally, the messages of the protesters caused Mr. Snyder severe emotional distress such that he became physical ill, while in the weakened state of bereavement.

b. Some students may argue that Mr. Snyder did not even see the protester's signs while attending his son's funeral and that the protesters were not directing their messages to him. However, the strongest argument in favor of the church is that, regardless of how distasteful the speech is for most people, it is protected by the First Amendment.

c. Students' answers may vary. Because the speech is so hurtful in this case and clearly intended to cause severe distress, many students will likely decide that Mr. Snyder should prevail.

When this case, *Snyder* v. *Phelps*[3], was decided by the U.S. Supreme Court in 2011, the Court ruled in favor of Fred Phelps, the leader of the Westboro Baptist Church. The Court explained that despite the extremely outrageous nature of the speech, it is nonetheless political speech which is protected under the First Amendment.

ACTIVITY—DEALING WITH ANTISOCIAL BEHAVIOR IN SCHOOL

This activity gives students an opportunity to see how bullying and the law intersect. It can also be used to take a thorough look at their own school policies about bullying.

Ask students to read and analyze each of the cases below. You may want to divide up the scenarios and have groups of three to five students consider each case and report their findings to the class.

Instruct students to read the cases carefully. If an intentional tort has been committed, they should name the tort. In addition, ask students to consider what remedies the victim might seek through the civil justice system. Finally, ask students to consider whether there are school policies that could help the victim in each case. The answers are provided here for the teacher to use during the class discussion.

Before students begin to answer this problem, be sure they each have a copy of their school's bullying and/or discipline policy.

a. Evan's family has just moved from a large urban area to Smallville. Evan is a quiet boy with purple spiky hair. A group of students led by Shawn and Jason constantly make fun of Evan calling him embarrassing names. Four times in the last month Shawn and Jason have thrown Evan into a trash dumpster behind school. The last time, Evan broke his arm. Evan has become withdrawn and scared to go to school.

(Answer) Shawn and Jason have committed the torts of battery and intentional infliction of emotional distress. When they threw him into the dumpster, they met the requirement that they touched Evan or came into contact with him in a harmful way. Evan's emotional distress appears to be caused by his fear of injury. Direct students to the previous section on assault and battery to evaluate Evan's claim fully.

Ask students what their school policy says about name calling and harmful physical contact. According to the policy, how can/should victims or bystanders report allegations such as these? Do students think the policy is clear and applied in a way that reduces bullying?

If no policy exists or if it is not implemented well, how would students write or rewrite the policy or change the way it is applied?

b. Tiana is a very shy high school sophomore who always wears black. She is not performing well in school and has few friends. She wants to drop out. Some of her classmates taunt her and call her rude names. Tiana wants to be a poet and she keeps a journal where she writes about how lonely she is at school. She stores it in her locker. One morning she receives an anonymous email entitled "Ghoul Girl Speaks Out," and the email contains entries from her journal. Tiana leaves school immediately and never goes back.

(Answer) Tiana can make a reasonable claim of intentional infliction of emotional distress to collect damages for the invasion and exploitation of her personal property. Ask students what privacy interests they have in their school lockers. Ask students what their school policies say about lockers, privacy, and mass e-mail blasts. If no policies exist or if they think the existing policy could be improved, what would students do to improve them?

c. Ramon is a senior on his high school's varsity football team. He suffers from a speech impediment that causes him to stutter when he is upset or nervous. Speech therapy has allowed him to control his stutter but he is still self-conscious about it. In the final seconds of an important and very close game, Ramon fumbles the ball. For the next several weeks, two of his teammates, Diego and Kyle, harass Ramon, blaming him for the team's loss and making fun of his stuttering. He tries to defend himself but begins to stutter which makes his teammates taunt him even more. As a result of his stress, Ramon's stuttering has gotten worse.

(Answer) Diego and Kyle committed the tort of intentional infliction of emotional distress. Courts have consistently found that, regardless of any special sensitivities that may have preceded the tort action (such as Ramon's stuttering), defendants are responsible for any injury that they may cause.

Like a. and b., this problem also provides an opportunity for discussing how teachers, administrators, school resource officers, and students handle bullying at your school. Do victims and bystanders tolerate bullying behavior? Who has a responsibility to create a bully-free school?

For additional materials relating to bullying, visit www.stopbullying.gov/ or if you work with a school resource officer, he or she may be interested in teaching the lesson about bullying in Street Law's *Police & Teens* curriculum available at www.streetlaw.org.

PROBLEM 18.4 (p.220)

Clarify the meaning of the term *infliction of emotional distress*. Discuss why our legal system takes infliction of emotional distress seriously. Keep in mind that students may assume that emotional injury is not as serious or as punishable as physical or property injury.

Ask students to complete Problem 18.4 individually, but ask them not to name actual victims or bullies in their school. After they have written their dialogues, ask student volunteers to read them. Then ask the class to vote to determine if damages are warranted, and if so, to decide the appropriate amount of damages in each case. Focus the discussion on the need to protect individuals from outrageous behavior versus the impracticality of suing every rude person for every insult.

ACTIVITY—FALSE IMPRISONMENT

Explain that false imprisonment includes situations in which individuals are imprisoned without legal authority. For example, if a prisoner's scheduled release date is April 3, but she is not released until May 3 due to an error in record keeping, false imprisonment has not occurred. As indicated in the Student Edition, however, it occurs when someone intentionally and wrongly confines another person against his or her will.

Four elements are necessary to prove false imprisonment. First, the defendant's action or failure to act must have resulted in the confinement or restraint of a person in a bounded area. Second, the defendant's actions must have been wrongful (without a legal justification). Third, the defendant's actions must have been carried out with the intent to restrain or confine. Finally, the confinement must have been caused, directly or indirectly, by the defendant's actions. You may want to list these elements on the board and then describe the case below. As you describe the case, ask students to identify each of the elements of false imprisonment and to predict the court's decision in the case based on whether all four elements are present.

In *Drabek* v. *Sabley*,[4] a child throwing snowballs at oncoming cars was grabbed and restrained by the driver of one of the cars he hit. The driver of the car took the youth to a police officer in the village. The child sued for false imprisonment for being taken and kept in the car. Ask students to develop the best arguments for both sides of this dispute. Then ask them to predict the outcome of this actual case. After their discussion, inform students that the Court rejected the child's claim. The court said that when a child is taken into custody, his or her parents shall be notified "as soon as possible" but found the driver's conduct to be reasonable in this case.

THE **CASE** OF...

The Captured Shoplifter

PROBLEM 18.5 (p.220)

a. Students should work in small groups to rank the options and facilitate discussion. Remind students that reasonable options are those in which the shopkeeper uses no more restraint than is necessary to protect his property.

b. Situations 2 and 3 would likely qualify as false imprisonment. This activity provides an

opportunity to use a resource person from your community who works in the area of store security. Shoplifting is a major problem in many areas, and there are many people who specialize in this line of law enforcement.

LEGAL RESOURCE PERSONS

Invite a police officer or a security guard to discuss what is considered reasonable detention of shoplifters. An attorney with experience representing plaintiffs in these cases may also be invited. These resource people would also be helpful advisors as students answer Problem 18.5.

DISCUSSION—TORTS RELATED TO DEFAMATION AND REPUTATION

Issues related to defamation present another good example of legal values in conflict. Plaintiffs in these cases want to protect their reputations, and defendants want to protect the exercise of their rights of expression in a free society. When the state or federal government is involved in limiting speech, these cases get into First Amendment jurisprudence. Students may already be familiar with some of the public-figure cases, especially those involving the more sensational tabloids. A key question is: Should celebrities be able to recover damages from the tabloids when outrageous (and false) stories are printed, or have they waived their right to privacy to some degree? Public figures must prove malice by clear and convincing evidence when trying to sue for libel.[5]

Another point to discuss with students is: Who is a public figure? An actor? A politician? A popular musician? An amateur athlete? An Olympic athlete? A writer? A student who wins an all-city or all-state competition? An airline pilot who was the victim of a hijacking? The daughter of a local television celebrity? A high school student who organizes a citywide food drive? A winner of a lottery? Students should decide whether any of these people should be considered public figures. If so, they will have to prove malice or reckless disregard for the truth if they are defamed by the press and try to recover damages. A private citizen would simply have to prove falsity and harm. Tell students to consider whether an individual chooses to become a public figure. According to *Gertz* v. *Welch*,[6] people are considered public figures if they "voluntarily inject themselves into" or are "drawn into" a public controversy, or if they have achieved "pervasive fame or notoriety."

LEGAL RESOURCE PERSON

Invite a reporter from a local newspaper, magazine, or television station to discuss defamation, privacy, and freedom of the press. Students should ask questions to determine how reporters write accurate and informative news stories without committing torts.

THE **CASE** OF...

The Very Unpopular Photographer

PROBLEM 18.6 (p.221)

After students answer the questions below, explain that the story is based on a series of allegations involving actress Nicole Kidman, photographer Jamie Fawcett, and an Australian newspaper.[7]

a. Before students decide what the photographer has to prove in his defamation suit, they should first decide whether he is a public figure, because public figures have additional requirements when they are suing the media. If the photographer was not famous, he would have to simply prove that the newspaper statements were made, that they were false, that they were communicated to a third party, and that they caused harm to his reputation. However, in the facts given, the photographer is explicitly described as famous, so he would likely be considered a public figure by the courts. The photographer therefore would have to prove the requirements above and that the statements were made with actual malice, that is, with knowledge of their falsity or with reckless disregard for whether the statements were true.

b. Students' answers will vary. Some students may say that the photographer may have difficulty getting people to consent to be photographed in the future or that other news media may be less inclined to purchase and run his photos in the future. Other students may say that since he seems to be famous for his candid, unauthorized photos, his reputation will not be hurt.

c. Students' answers will vary. Students may suggest that the newspaper can defend against the defamation claim by proving that the

photographer had, in fact, installed the listening devices. They might also claim that their statement that the photographer is the "most hated" is merely an opinion and is, therefore, protected.

d. Students' answers will vary and should be supported with reasons.

TORTS THAT HARM PROPERTY (PP. 222–224)

Learning Outcomes

After completing the following section, students should be able to:

1. explain how tort law can protect property owners from people who trespass or create a nuisance;
2. evaluate claims to determine whether the defendant unreasonably interfered with another person's property;
3. explain the types of remedies available to victims of torts that harm property; and
4. define the terms *real property, personal property, trespass, nuisance, injunction,* and *conversion.*

CAPTION ANSWER (P. 222) Tort law protects property against interference with the owner's use of the property. It also protects against the property being taken or damaged.

Real Property and Reasonable Interference (p. 223)

a. Students should consider and recognize the concerns of both parties. Darrell enjoys and has a right to listen to his music. The damage is that the noise awakens Mr. Iwamoto who, unlike most people, goes to sleep in the morning when he comes home from work. Rather than filing a lawsuit, the parties should try to work out a compromise through informal dispute resolution. Students will come up with a variety of remedies. One possible solution is for Darrell to turn down his music when he passes Mr. Iwamoto's house. There may be a noise ordinance that, if broken, could result in a fine or an injunction against Darrell.

b. The passenger's action may be viewed as a public nuisance if his cell phone use unreasonably interferes with the public's right to enjoy quiet on a train car. Although the passenger may find it efficient to conduct business on his cell phone during his daily commute, his volume could interfere with other passengers who desire a quiet environment to read or sleep during their commutes. Possible remedies may include establishing a "quiet car" on the train or regulating the volume of passengers' activities. Legal action would most likely not be successful because the interference is not permanent or long lasting.

c. The refinery is useful to the community for the products it produces. However, the damage is twofold: people are getting sick from the gases, and the restaurant is losing business. In an actual state court decision, Morgan won the case because she proved that the refinery intentionally allowed the gases to escape, resulting in the diminished use and enjoyment of her property.[8] This case occurred more than 50 years ago, well before EPA regulations.

d. Irritating pop-up ads may be a necessary cost of using the Internet. Although these ads may interfere with your intended Internet use, such advertising offers businesses a different medium to attract consumers and provides businesses with the profit needed to provide Internet service. The courts may not be the best remedy, but economic pressure, such as boycotting products advertised on pop-ups or sites that allow them, may prove to be a more successful alternative. Suggested remedies include regulations requiring "opt-out" features for spam and criminalizing deceptive practices used by spammers, such as disguising the origin of e-mail.

e. Larry and Meg have a right to run their business. However, they are doing so in a residential area and disturbing other residents. This may be a nuisance, and the neighbors may be able to stop Larry and Meg from running their shop out of their garage. Additionally, there may be a zoning ordinance prohibiting a commercial enterprise in a residential area. If there is no zoning problem, the parties may be able to come to an agreement by which Larry and Meg limit their evening work hours in an effort not to disturb the neighbors.

f. The use of the airport by the local and national community is important to commerce, travel, and employment. The damage to local residents occurs in their daily use and enjoyment of their property as well as in depreciated property values. However, most courts would not stop an airport from conducting its business. RAMP could try to contact local organizations such as newspapers, television stations, lobbying groups, local legislators, and airport officials for publicity and support. Citizen action groups have had some success in influencing airline landing patterns and the hours at which take-offs and landings occur.

DEFENSES TO INTENTIONAL TORTS (PP. 224–226)

Learning Outcomes

After completing this section, students should be able to:

1. define *consent, privilege, self-defense,* and *defense of property;*
2. analyze the amount of force that may be used to protect property and/or protect an individual;
3. explain the "Castle Doctrine"; and
4. explain how people can apply the defenses of consent, privilege, and defense of self and property to defend against intentional tort claims.

CAPTION ANSWER (P. 225) It is not battery when a child knocks another child down during play because consent is assumed when they begin playing. While a certain amount of touching is assumed to be consented to, this does not absolve a child (or the child's family) from liability in the event of a vicious assault on another child.

PROBLEM 18.7 (p.225)

Before you assign this problem, you may want to review the "Castle Doctrine" or "Stand Your Ground law" that is exists in some states.

In this case, the issue is whether having the dog would be considered using deadly force and therefore excessive and unreasonable. It is probably not considered deadly force, but there are many factors students could debate—for example, the breed and size of the dog or whether the dog was restrained. Students may identify additional factors that would either make this a deadly situation or show that it was not.

Would this case be decided differently if the burglar had broken in during hours in which the store was open and the Kings were present? Can more force be used to protect a person than to protect property?

Ask students what distinctions, if any, should be made between protecting people and protecting their property.

Ask how they think the following case should have been decided: In *Katko* v. *Briney,*[9] some young men broke into an uninhabited farmhouse to steal antiques.

Because of earlier burglaries, the owners of the farmhouse set up a 20-gauge spring gun in the bedroom of the house and rigged it to the doorknob so that when the door was opened the gun would fire at an intruder's legs. The gun was not visible from outside the room. The plaintiff was hit as he entered the room and much of his leg was blown away. The plaintiff sued the owners of the farmhouse for excessive use of force—and won.

Other people have employed electrical fences, spring guns, and other types of "booby traps" to protect their property. Courts have held that these methods are illegal when they can cause death or serious injury to a trespasser. As noted in the text, deadly force can be used to protect property only under severely limited circumstances or when a state has a Castle Doctrine in place. However, deadly force may be used to protect a person.

One may be justified in using deadly force against a burglar or trespasser if the occupants of the property are at home and in danger of serious harm. If the homeowner can successfully argue that he or she was protecting his or her family, the use of deadly force may be justified.

YOU BE the JUDGE

Intentional Torts and Legal Defense (p. 226)

a. There was no tort here since the pitcher did not intentionally hit the batter. If the pitcher had intentionally thrown at the batter, he could try to defend his actions by claiming that there is implied consent involved in playing baseball. One might argue that the pitcher's action goes beyond implied consent. Note that even implied consent must be informed consent. The plaintiff must be aware of the risks involved, otherwise there cannot be consent—explicit or implied.

b. Josh has given consent only to having one tooth removed. Students could discuss whether or not this implied the consent to remove the other teeth. Many cases in state courts have dealt with this general problem of exceeding consent in a surgical procedure. Surgeons often lose these cases unless they can establish that there was an unforeseen emergency that was so critical in its nature that it justified the surgeon's act.[10] Other cases are decided in the surgeon's favor if a later operation would be needed to correct the problem and the situation was life-threatening.[11] Finally, some cases are decided based on what a reasonable person (patient) would have decided had he or she not been under anesthesia.[12] This case raises a question, beyond the law, of

following proper medical procedures. With X-ray technology, it might be argued that the dentist should have known *before* the surgery that the other teeth were coming in crooked.

c. Sandy has committed the tort of battery. The fact that Sandy was throwing the snowball at someone else is not a defense. Torts use the same rule of "transferred intent" as criminal law. Remember that a battery requires an act intended to cause a harmful or offensive contact with another. The elderly man would not have to prove that Sandy intended to harm him in particular, only that the snowball was thrown with the intent to strike someone.

d. The prisoner has committed a battery on Maya. Maya has the privilege of using self-defense and can use enough force to protect herself. In this case Maya would be entitled to get up and control the prisoner, but kicking the prisoner once she is down may exceed this privilege of self-defense. Self-defense is not designed to teach the initial wrongdoer a lesson or to counterattack with equal force, only to repel the attack.

e. Wendy's action could be considered the tort of conversion, and Amy's actions could be considered assault. Amy's action most likely would not be considered self-defense because the facts given do not indicate that she or another person was in danger.

ACTIVITY—INTENTIONAL TORT REVIEW

Students should be able to identify intentional torts in real-world situations. To help students practice this skill, split the class into several small groups and give each group a copy of a daily newspaper or ask students to access local news online. Instruct the groups to find and cut out or print out pictures or descriptions of intentional torts. Students may use any section of the paper, including sports and cartoons. At the end, have each group report to the class the articles it found, why each describes the situation in the article it found an intentional tort, and what possible defenses may be available for each. Lead a class discussion evaluating the acceptability of each article or picture.

A variation of the activity is to use a ten-minute clip from an action movie. Ask students to record as many possible intentional torts as they can find in the clip, who the plaintiff would be, who the defendant would be, and possible defenses. Then discuss as a class each possible intentional tort found in the film clip. Award a prize to the student who finds the most acceptable examples.

NOTES

(1) *Garratt* v. *Dailey*, 46 Wash. 2d 197, 279 P.2d 1091 (1955).

(2) *Gebser* v. *Lago Vista Schools District*, 524 U.S. 274 (1998).

(3) *Snyder* v. *Phelps*, 131 S. Ct. 1207 (2011).

(4) *Drabek* v. *Sabley*, 142 N.W. 2d 798 (Wis. 1966).

(5) *Anderson* v. *Liberty Lobby*, 477 U.S. 242 (1986).

(6) *Gertz* v. *Welch*, 413 U.S. 323 (1974).

(7) Welch, Dylan, "Kidman snapper to appeal," *The Sydney Morning Herald*, February 27, 2008. www.smh.com.au/news/national/nicole-kidman-snapper-to-appeal/2008/02/27/1203788394066.html.

(8) *Morgan* v. *High Penn Oil Company*, 238 NC 185, 77 S.E. 2d 682 (1953).

(9) *Katko* v. *Briney*, 183 N.W. 2d 657 (Iowa 1971).

(10) *Guin* v. *Sison*, 552 So. 2d 60 (1989).

(11) *Sagala* v. *Tavares, M.D.*, 533 A. 2d 165 (1987).

(12) *Cheung* v. *Cunningham, M.D.*, 520 A. 2d 832 (1987).

INTRODUCTION AND ELEMENTS OF NEGLIGENCE (PP. 227–228)

Learning Outcomes

After completing these sections, students should be able to:
1. list the four elements that must be proven by a plaintiff in a negligence claim; and
2. define the terms *negligence* and *elements*.

BACKGROUND—IDENTIFYING ELEMENTS OF NEGLIGENCE

The Student Edition explains elements of negligence and provides cases and problems students may use to master each of the elements. Students should be able to do the following in relation to the four elements of negligence as they analyze problems:

- State the duty.
- Identify the breach of duty.
- Evaluate whether or not the defendant's conduct was the direct and proximate cause of the plaintiff's harm.
- Determine the damages caused by the defendant's conduct.

Students will learn to identify legal defenses to negligence later in the chapter. Some states have developed case law that distinguishes among degrees of negligence (for example, gross negligence, recklessness, etc.). When higher levels of negligence are proven, it may be possible for plaintiffs to recover punitive damages. Check with an attorney to learn whether your state recognizes various degrees of negligence.

Tort law establishes standards of care that society expects from people. These standards protect people against unreasonable risks of harm. When conduct falls below these standards, negligence has occurred. Tort law analyzes such negligence as it relates to a person's conduct. People accused of negligence can offer reasonable defenses if they can show that the plaintiff contributed to the problem or assumed a risk that led to the harm. Plaintiffs who prevail in negligence claims may be entitled to a number of different types of damages.

DUTY AND BREACH (PP. 228–233)

Learning Outcomes

After completing this section, students should be able to:

1. define the terms *duty*, *breach*, and *attractive nuisance*;
2. identify the duty of care in a given situation;
3. identify breach of duty in a given situation;
4. explain the reasonable person standard and its special applications for minors and for professional experts; and
5. apply the reasonable person standard to sample cases.

BACKGROUND—REASONABLE CARE

While specific duties sometimes exist as a result of a law, the emphasis here is on the general duty of reasonable care that people are bound by at all times. You may wish to have students read the section on the reasonable person standard at this point. In order to understand the defenses, students should remember that plaintiffs and defendants both have the same duty to act with reasonable care.

THE **CASE** OF...

The Spilled Coffee

PROBLEM 19.1 (p.229)

a. The plaintiff is Stella Liebeck. The defendant is the fast-food restaurant.

b. The defendant may have been wrong in selling coffee that was too hot for consumption. The plaintiff may have been wrong in two ways: by not waiting until the coffee cooled before attempting to remove the lid and by removing the lid while the cup was balanced in her lap rather than on a sturdy surface. Discuss with students whether or not it is unsafe to eat while driving and whether or not fast-food restaurants with drive-through windows act negligently by encouraging such a practice. Does the consumer who eats fast food while driving act negligently?

c. The defendant did not cause injury to the plaintiff on purpose; however, the defendant was in a position to recognize the dangers posed by extremely hot coffee and to protect customers from those dangers. In fact, there were many claims filed against the company previously. According to the jury award (note the punitive damages), the corporation breached its duty of care to customers.

d. The restaurant has a duty to exercise reasonable care in providing its products to the public for consumption. This means that it must consider the likelihood that its coffee will harm a customer if it is spilled and how seriously the customer could be hurt. The restaurant, if acting reasonably, must then conform its actions to avoid highly risky actions. Students may disagree about whether the restaurant upheld its duty, depending on the level of risk the restaurant took compared to the burden of avoiding that risk.

e. Students' answers will vary. Some students may agree with the outcome of the case but feel that the damages were excessive. Many critics charged that the case was frivolous. Students should evaluate whether or not they think the tort system has created an overly litigious society in which every accident ends up in a long, expensive lawsuit.

f. Students' answers will vary. Possible arguments for awarding punitive damages: The restaurant knew that its coffee was dangerously hot and that it presented a risk of injury. The restaurant disregarded the danger. The company has engaged in a cost benefit analysis and determined that it is in the company's financial best interest to disregard safety even though it would have to pay for lawsuits by injured customers. The award of punitive damages may drastically change the cost-benefit analysis. Finally, in some cases, punitive damages help to offset the legal fees paid by the plaintiff.

Possible arguments against awarding punitive damages: The level of damages seems out of proportion with the severity of the damage or harm. In fact, many wrongful death judgments do not result in such large awards. Also, if the plaintiff has been fully compensated for her injuries, why should she also receive punitive damages? Large punitive damages may encourage others to bring frivolous suits in hopes of finding a sympathetic jury and collecting a windfall. In the end, customers will absorb the costs of such excessive judgments.

BACKGROUND AND DISCUSSION—THE REASONABLE PERSON STANDARD

The reasonable person standard applies in negligence cases and considers what an ordinary or reasonably prudent person would think is reasonable. This involves balancing the interests of reasonable behavior versus the risk of harm. Ask students to balance the likelihood and seriousness of harm versus the burden of avoiding harm in the following scenarios:

- A landlord fails to repair a faulty common stairway in an apartment building. The stairway collapses, injuring a tenant.[1]
- A landlord repairs a common stairway, which later collapses when some tenants try to move a grand piano into their apartment.

Review with students the application of the reasonable person standard to minors and to experts. Are these rules fair? What reasons can students give for these distinctions?

Another interesting area of negligence law concerns the liability resulting from failure to properly or efficiently remove snow from one's sidewalks or driveways. Many communities have ordinances that place the duty on the property owner to remove snow from these areas. Some ordinances state time limits within which sidewalks and driveways must be shoveled. Homeowners are protected up to the time limits in their homeowner's insurance policy if a walkway is not properly cleared and someone gets hurt as a result. Under proper circumstances, the homeowner may use the assumption of risk defense (discussed later in the Student Edition). Homeowners may still lose money if the award is more than the amount of their coverage.

In order for a property owner to be subjected to a lawsuit in these types of situations, three criteria must usually be present:

- The property owner was aware that the snowstorm occurred.
- The owner had reasonable time to clear the walkways.
- The owner breached these duties.

Point out that children, and in some instances their parents, can be liable for negligence if they clear others' walkways in a careless fashion. Although children are less likely to be the target of such suits due to their lack of deep pockets, a party

could file a claim against the homeowner. The homeowner could, in turn, file a claim against the child, depending on the child's age. Generally, children over 13 years of age are considered able to anticipate the consequences of their actions, and therefore could be liable for negligence.

Another area of negligence law concerns child safety seats in automobiles. Many states require that parents place their young children in state-approved car seats to ensure their safety. State laws differ as to age requirements.

For example, in one state, parents may have to put their children in car seats while traveling until the children reach five years of age. In other states the age requirement may be three or four years of age and/or a certain weight.

Failure to place a child in a car seat may establish that the parents have breached their duty to act reasonably. Child restraint laws are listed for each state at https://www.ghsa.org/state-laws/issues/child%20passenger%20safety.

CAPTION ANSWER (P. 231) In most states, you have a legal duty to warn guests of any known danger on your property.

THE **CASE** OF...

The Unfenced Swimming Pool

PROBLEM 19.2 (p.231)

a.–b. When a trespasser is a child, the property owner is often liable for injuries sustained even if the owner takes all reasonable steps to protect and warn.

Because of the child's immaturity and lack of judgment, he or she may be incapable of perceiving risks that accompany trespassing. The landowner is in a better position to protect a straying child.

Teenagers, however, should be aware of the dangers associated with trespassing and swimming, and therefore, if the trespasser were a teenager, the landowner would not be held liable. The landowner may want to consider posting a "No Trespassing" sign and erecting a fence around the pool. Some localities may have ordinances requiring fencing around open water sources.

THE **CASE** OF...

Liability for Serving Alcohol

PROBLEM 19.3 (p. 231)

This is an important issue to discuss with students because a disproportionate number of drunk driving deaths involve teenagers. The dangers of drinking and driving cannot be overemphasized.

Teens should also know that adults can be held responsible for serving minors and/or visibly intoxicated persons. Such statutes are called *dram shop statutes*. They date back to the nineteenth century when widows successfully sued tavern owners for permitting their husbands to get intoxicated and wander out of the tavern (or dram shop) onto railroad tracks. Under dram shop laws, restaurant owners in some jurisdictions may be held liable if their employees serve an intoxicated person who subsequently commits a tort.

"The Case of Liability for Serving Alcohol" was adapted from several cases in which bartenders, hosts, and bar owners were held liable for the damage caused by unreasonably intoxicated customers. In *Adamian* v. *Three Sons, Inc.,*[2] the owner of a bar was held liable for negligently continuing to serve an intoxicated customer in violation of his duty to members of the general public who use the highways. The court held that the defendant knew or should have known that the customer had arrived by automobile. The intoxicated customer subsequently collided with another automobile in which the plaintiff and a passenger were riding. In *Michnik-Zilberman* v. *Gordon's Liquor, Inc.,*[3] the defendant liquor seller/supplier was held liable for serving alcohol to a minor who later drove into and killed the plaintiff's husband. The plaintiff did not have to prove that the minor had been intoxicated, only that he or she had been served alcohol.

A majority of states and the District of Columbia currently hold tavern owners and other liquor licensees responsible for injuries caused by a customer if the licensee serves an intoxicated customer. Some states hold private individuals (social hosts) liable for the injuries sustained by a third party if a guest drinks and then causes a car accident. Most courts that use host liability apply the principles of common law negligence. Therefore, serving alcohol is seen as a proximate cause of harm to an injured third party by an intoxicated driver because intoxication and injurious behavior are foreseeable consequences of serving alcohol. For up to date

information about state social host liability laws, visit https://injury.findlaw.com/accident-injury-law/social-host-liability.html.

a. The driver of the other car may be able to sue Abby, Stefan, Lance, and even Lance's parents if Lance lives in a state that has host liability. Stefan's ability to recover damages from Abby may be limited by his own negligence if he drank with Abby or knew she had been drinking before he allowed her to drive and became a passenger in her car.

b. Lance had a duty to not serve alcohol to minors and to not allow Abby to drive if he knew she was intoxicated. If Lance lives in one of the states that imposes social host liability, he may be liable for allowing a driver to leave his home intoxicated or for allowing other minors access to his parents' liquor. Remember that minors are liable for their torts. The standard for minors is to act with the care of the ordinarily prudent minor of the same age, intelligence, and experience.

c. Should parents who were not at home be held responsible? Remind students that the purpose of tort law is to encourage people to make their private activities less likely to cause injury to others. Would holding parents to a legal duty induce them to make sure their children are better supervised? Some states have tried to make clear that parents are responsible for parties or other activities of their children while parents are away. For more information, refer to pages 52–55 of this Teacher Manual.

Courts have more readily imposed liability where parents were present and knowingly served minors who later became involved in drunk driving crashes. Courts have been much more reticent to hold adults to such a duty at a social function involving only other adults. What is the difference between serving minors and adults where either may be involved in a drunk driving incident? Few state courts have imposed this type of social host liability, and where they have, legislators have quickly responded by reinstating immunity for hosts (California) or granting social hosts strong protection (New Jersey).[4] Explore whether this is a good idea and the possible legislative intent. Ask students to identify the implications of imposing social host liability for adult gatherings.

d. The driver of the car could sue Abby, Lance, or the owner of the bar. Stefan may be able to sue the same people, although his ability to recover damages may be limited by his own negligence. Lance, the bartender, had the duty to stop serving alcohol once Abby and Stefan were visibly intoxicated, and he violated that duty if he continued to serve them. This duty is spelled out in state dram shop laws, which make it a misdemeanor to serve alcohol to a person who is obviously intoxicated. In all likelihood, the suit would be brought against the owner of the bar because of the deep pockets concept. Therefore, Lance's negligent conduct would be imputed to the bar owner through the previously discussed theory of vicarious liability.

e. Tell students to revisit the difference between a moral or ethical duty and a legal duty introduced in Chapter 1 in the Student Edition. Have them consider the differences between the legal obligations imposed on minors and the obligations imposed on owners of businesses who provide alcohol to the public.

f. Some restaurants and bars now participate in designated driver programs and have installed Breathalyzers in order to keep their liability insurance.

Perhaps social host liability will result in alternatives to drunk driving becoming a part of the planning of social events such as making arrangements for taxis, designated drivers, or key collection. Ask students if they think imposing social host liability would discourage people from hosting social events, as many state courts and legislatures fear, or if it would encourage hosts to act more responsibly in planning their events.

LEGAL RESOURCE PERSONS

You may wish to invite a school resource officer or police officer who works with community relations programs related to drinking and driving to discuss related laws. Students can discuss various designated driver programs in their community and suggest ways to strengthen these programs.

ACTIVITY—ADVOCACY PROJECT

Students may choose one of the following research projects:

1. Collect data about accidents and deaths associated with drunk driving in your area.

2. Investigate whether your community has dram shop laws. If so, what do the laws require?

3. Collect statistics to determine whether strengthened dram shop laws have decreased rates of alcohol-related accidents.

4. Locate and interview a legislator—possibly via e-mail—who was involved in drafting or sponsoring the local dram shop law.

5. Locate a state chapter of Mothers Against Drunk Driving (MADD) and request to speak with an outreach worker about its work in your community, or request materials explaining the goals of the organization and reasons why it was created.

6. Find out whether your school has a chapter of Students Against Destructive Decisions (SADD). If not, consider forming one. If a chapter does exist, consider joining and participating in the group's activities. Many chapters become especially active during prom season.

7. Find out if your state has social host liability laws and to what extent parents in your state can be held liable for drinking that happens in their homes.

THE CASE OF...

AIDS Liability

PROBLEM 19.4 (p.233)

Many states have passed legislation making it both a crime and a tort not to inform a sexual partner of a sexually transmitted disease (STD).[5] In other states, court decisions may differ on the legal duty to inform someone of the disease, but the trend seems to be toward holding someone like Tyler liable. The bulk of STD cases have been herpes claims made primarily by partners who were infected by former companions. The majority of AIDS claims have so far addressed behavior that created a risk of infection, whether or not transmission occurred.

In fact, the bulk of AIDS court cases that address risky sexual behavior have not been civil suits but criminal state prosecutions. In the early years of these AIDS prosecutions, defendants were tried under traditional felony statutes such as attempted murder and assault with a deadly weapon. Such cases were hard to win because prosecutors had trouble demonstrating intent, a key element in these crimes. Newer statutes have eliminated the requirement of intent to inflict harm and instead require a demonstration of recklessness.

States eventually began to craft criminal laws that specifically prohibited reckless sexual behavior by a person infected with the AIDS virus. Under a 1990 law, the federal government put a condition on its funding for the care of AIDS patients. It would release the funds on the condition that a state had adequate laws to prosecute HIV-infected people who intentionally exposed others to the virus. For up to date information on HIV and STD criminal laws visit the Centers for Disease Control and Prevention website at https://www.cdc.gov/hiv/policies/law/states/exposure.html.

a. Students should say that Tyler had a duty to tell Audrey. This problem is designed to alert students to the possible legal ramifications and health hazards of engaging in casual sex. In addition to specific duties set out in statutes or in court decisions, all persons have a general duty not to subject others to an unreasonable risk of harm. In this case Tyler had the burden of exercising this duty by simply telling Audrey of his disease. The cost of not telling her is extremely high—she may get AIDS and she might die.

Plaintiffs have successfully used several different tort theories to recover damages for diseases they contracted through sexual contact with a person who knowingly did not disclose the existence of HIV/AIDS or other sexually transmitted diseases.

The tort of battery involves an intentional act with offensive or harmful touching. Consent is generally a defense to battery. Ask students if, assuming that Audrey consented to have sex with Tyler, was it knowing consent if she did not have the information about his disease?

"Negligent failure to warn" has also been used successfully by plaintiffs seeking damages. Persons who engage in sexual contact have a duty of care to inform their partners of any communicable diseases they have. If they fail to disclose their disease and pass on the disease to their partner, they are liable for negligent failure to warn.

Courts have allowed recovery of damages in this situation for the tort of fraud. The diseased person misrepresented the situation (by silence or by denial) and the unknowing sexual partner relied on misinformation in consenting to sexual contact.

Defendants have tried to use their right to privacy as a defense, stating that the government cannot require them to reveal such personal health information. This defense has been uniformly rejected, with courts stating that the right of privacy should not insulate a defendant who has negligently or deliberately infected another.

b. While the damages would be less if the disease were easily curable, Tyler would still have a duty to tell Audrey about the disease.

c. The damages Audrey recovers would depend on the extent of her harm. She could recover lost wages, medical expenses, pain and suffering, and possibly money for intentional infliction of emotional distress. Some courts also allow recovery for loss of consortium. Consortium is the fellowship between husband and wife or parent and child and the right of each to the company, affection, and aid of the other in a relationship. Damages for loss of consortium are often sought in wrongful death actions.

BACKGROUND—PARENTAL NEGLIGENCE

Under common law, parents are not automatically held liable for torts committed by their children. Similarly, most state statutes do not impose parental liability for torts of their minor children merely because of the parent-child relationship.[6] Some statutes, however, do impose liability when the child commits an intentional tort (which in many instances is also a crime), but these statutes generally place a cap on the financial liability.[7] Some state courts have found parents liable for torts their child committed while acting as an agent for the parents. For example, the parents could be held liable if their child commits a tort while running an errand for his parents.

Some states have also held parents liable for their own negligence in dealing with their children. Parents may be held liable for injuries that result from negligently or unreasonably giving their children an instrument or item which is foreseeably dangerous.[8] The New York courts have held that even if the parents do not own the dangerous instrument, they can still be held liable if they knew the child had the instrument and permitted the child to use it.[9] The parents of a three-year-old child were found liable for injury to a one-year-old child when the car their child was playing in rolled down the driveway and struck the one-year-old child. The court held that the parents allowed the three-year-old to use a "dangerous instrument" by leaving the car doors unlocked and the windows open, despite their knowledge that the emergency brake was easy to operate and that the car had rolled down the driveway on a previous occasion.[10]

State courts have held that a parent can be held liable if the parent knows of the child's propensity for engaging in a specific dangerous activity and fails to prevent the child's action.[11] The parents of a child who hit another child with a croquet mallet were not liable for injury. The court determined that there was no evidence that the child had previously engaged in the particular act.

Additionally, parents in New Hampshire were not held liable for the actions of their child who set fire to a barn, as there was no evidence that the parents should have known of the child's dangerous propensity.[12]

Other state courts have held that parents may be liable if they know, or should know, that they have the ability to control the child and there is a necessity and an opportunity to exercise control.[13] Parents were held liable for injuries caused by their minor child when the child pushed a grocery cart into a customer. The court found that the parents had the ability to control the child and prevent the accident.[14]

CAUSATION (PP. 233–234)

Learning Outcomes

After completing this section, students should be able to:
1. define the terms *causation, cause in fact, and proximate cause;*
2. differentiate between cause in fact and proximate cause; and
3. analyze a situation in order to determine whether or not a given harm was foreseeable.

THE **CASE** OF...

The Great Chicago Fire

PROBLEM 19.5 (p. 234)

a. Mrs. O'Leary breached her duty of care by placing the lantern too close to the rear leg of the cow. Her breach was the direct cause of the Chicago fire.

b. The public policy question that arises is how far the courts should go in holding someone liable for damage, at least some of which was not foreseeable at the time of the negligent act. Even if a court held Mrs. O'Leary responsible for the fire, she would clearly not have the funds or the insurance to rebuild large sections of the city of Chicago. Have students discuss how much

responsibility a person should have for his or her negligent act. If the wrongdoer is not totally responsible, who should be? Students may say that Mrs. O'Leary should probably be held responsible for the damage to the shed and to the area immediately surrounding it, as those damages were foreseeable.

DAMAGES (PP. 234–235)

Learning Outcomes

After completing this section, students should be able to:
1. define the term *damages*;
2. identify the basic idea behind damages; and
3. cite examples of the types of losses plaintiffs can recover in court.

BACKGROUND AND LEGAL RESOURCE PERSON—HOW DAMAGE AWARDS WORK

The concept of damages revolves around responsibility. Traditionally, society has tried to hold people responsible for their actions by requiring those responsible to pay money for the harm they cause. Consider inviting a lawyer who handles tort cases to discuss how damage awards work in your state.

Some people question whether money damages are always the best way to compensate plaintiffs for the harm they suffer. For example, assume a teenager riding a bicycle strikes an elderly person walking home from the store carrying groceries. Ask students whether it would be better to require the teen to bring this person his or her groceries for some period of time rather than to make the teen pay damages. Invite students to raise other hypothetical situations in which damages other than money would be appropriate.

PROBLEM 19.6 (p. 235)

a. Carolyn's prank of removing a stop sign is a crime as well as the tort of conversion. The issues of duty and breach are clear. The problem is causation. Was the removal of the sign the direct cause of the accident? Could the motorist have missed the sign even if it had been at the intersection? Is that fact relevant? Is the damage that occurred foreseeable? That is, was Carolyn's prank the proximate cause of this serious harm to the motorists and their cars? It seems reasonable to assume that the foreseeable harm of removing a stop sign is that a motorist would drive into the intersection without stopping first.

b. Students' answers will vary. The plaintiffs might be able to collect for: replacement of autos, medical bills, pain and suffering, lost wages, etc. Unless Carolyn is very wealthy, the plaintiffs are unlikely to be able to recover all these damages. One possible way to access deeper pockets might be to sue the college and claim it failed to stop these types of pranks.

DEFENSES TO NEGLIGENCE SUITS (PP. 235–240)

Learning Outcomes

After completing this section, students should be able to:

1. list and describe the most common defenses in negligence suits;
2. analyze negligence scenarios to determine whether or not a good defense exists; and
3. define the terms *contributory negligence*, *comparative negligence*, *counterclaim*, and *assumption of risk*.

BACKGROUND—DEFENSES

Use the following case to introduce the concept of defenses to a negligence suit. In *Janifer* v. *Jandebeur*,[15] the estate of a passenger killed in a car accident brought suit against the intoxicated driver. The court found that the passenger, Mr. Redman, voluntarily exposed himself to an unreasonable risk when he agreed to ride with the intoxicated driver. Thus, Mr. Redman knowingly assumed the risk of injury and/or death. Accordingly, the court did not award his estate damages from the driver.

The defenses of contributory negligence and assumption of risk are similar but not identical. Contributory negligence occurs when the plaintiff's own negligence played a part in causing the plaintiff's injury.[16] Assumption of risk occurs when the plaintiff voluntarily takes on the risk of loss, injury, or damage. The following example may clarify this distinction for students.

Tell students to suppose a group of teenagers are playing a game in which they run out in front of speeding cars. Arguably, these teenagers know of

and appreciate the danger of engaging in such risky actions. If Todd is struck by a car and sues the driver, the driver/defendant may be able to use the defense of assumption of risk. On the other hand, assume Todd is talking on a cell phone while crossing a street and is struck by a speeding car. In this scenario Todd failed to use ordinary care in crossing the street. Thus, the driver could argue that Todd failed to act reasonably and contributed to the negligence because he breached his duty of care.

Hotels provide unusually rich opportunities to study torts. Hotel bathrooms typically have railings and/or other protection against falling in bathtubs, and maintenance crews usually vacuum the lobby between 3:00 and 6:00 A.M. when guests are less likely to trip over the electrical cords. Also, hotel pools are surrounded with warnings. "Swim at Your Own Risk" signs do not, however, relieve a hotel of all liability. For example, a defective diving board, defective ladders in the pool, or any other malfunction with the pool equipment or surrounding area can cause injury. In these situations, the hotel may be liable for the injuries because of its failure to properly maintain equipment. The sign simply protects the hotel from injuries one could sustain due to the lack of supervision. This is also true for some other signs that attempt to disclaim responsibility. A person injured in such places should consult an attorney to determine if there is a viable civil claim.

FYI For Your Information

Cigarettes and the Law (p 236)

After students have read the *For Your Information* feature in the Student Edition, ask them to debate the fairness of placing liability on cigarette companies. This topic should naturally stimulate debate, and several issues concerning government regulation and commercial speech are worth exploring. Questions for debate include:

1. **Is it fair to the cigarette companies to subject them to liability when they had been manufacturing a legal product that contained a notice printed on the package that contained a health warning?**

   An inadequate warning can be more harmful than no warning at all. Misleading information can be equally harmful when consumers are evaluating the risk of a particular product or activity. If a company is negligently or intentionally deceptive about the nature of its products, does this infringe on an individual's ability to make personal choices? On the other hand, in a country that has regulatory procedures for the production and sale of food and drugs, should a company be held liable where the federal government allows the sale of the product?

2. Should it make a difference that the product, though legal, caused great harm?

Remind students that the product not only caused great harm, but was highly addictive. Also, the harm was caused not only to those who chose to smoke, but also to others who were forced to inhale secondhand smoke and to taxpayers who bear the brunt of medical bills associated with smoking-related illnesses.

One study actually concluded that the government saves money from the public's use of cigarettes because smoking shortens life expectancy, reducing payouts for Social Security and Medicare. Ask students to list the ramifications of the government's choosing not to ban tobacco use, based on such a study.

3. Should the federal government regulate cigarettes?

In 2009, Congress passed historic legislation granting the FDA the authority to regulate the manufacturing, sale and marketing of cigarettes.

To learn more about both sides of the debate, students should do general media searches and visit the websites of tobacco companies such as RJ Reynolds at www.rjrt.com and the Campaign for Tobacco-Free Kids at www. tobaccofreekids. org to read their position papers about the regulation legislation.

As students form their opinions, encourage them to consider various issues. Should people be free from government interference when it comes to choices about their bodies, even if those potential choices could do great harm? Is smoking simply a matter of individual choice if the public has to bear the medical costs of smoking-related illness and is exposed to the pollution and health risk from cigarette smoke?

One possible compromise would be for the government to regulate information rather than regulating the product. The public would still have access to the product but would receive ample information to make informed choices about its use. Ask students to consider why the government is in a better position to compel cigarette manufacturers to provide such information than individual consumers are. These issues touch on the difference between commercial

speech and political speech that will be further explored in Unit 6, "Individual Rights and Liberties," in the Student Edition. Companies can be required to put certain messages on their products or can be punished for making misleading statements about their products.

4. Should it make a difference that tobacco companies withheld information about the harmful effects of their products?

In May 1995, documents of a major tobacco company (Brown and Williamson) revealed that tobacco executives discovered risks of smoking before the Surgeon General of the United States did. Additionally, claims that the cigarette companies manipulated the nicotine levels in cigarettes to increase their addictiveness appeared to be substantiated. These revelations may have influenced the outcome of the tort cases against cigarette makers.

5. Should a bartender who never smoked but was exposed to secondhand smoke for years while working in a bar that permitted smoking be able to recover damages against cigarette manufacturers?

One theory is that people are compensated for the risks inherent in their employment by receiving higher wages for riskier jobs. (However, studies suggest that the higher wages do not match the level of risk.) For example, the bartender may decide that the higher risk of lung cancer is worth the tips she earns. However, if the company is misleading its employees about the harmfulness of its product, the bartender will not be able to accurately balance the cost of her position (the health risks) versus the benefits (her salary or enjoyment of her work).

The cigarette company might argue that there is no causation between the plaintiff's lung cancer and its product. Lung cancer can come from many sources. Also, if secondhand smoke were the cause, the industry could argue that the smoking patrons caused the injury and not the cigarette company. They might further argue that the bartender knowingly assumed the risk by continuing to work in the bar.

6. Should states and/or the federal government restrict vaping manufacturers from using packaging and flavors to attract minors and young adults to their products?

Currently there are regulations at both the national, state, and local level. For up to date information on state regulations and laws visit

CAPTION ANSWER (P. 237) The property owner could claim that the injured person was aware of the known risk and voluntarily accepted the risk of danger. However, the property owner could still be held liable if the injured party was hurt on a faulty piece of equipment.

DELIBERATION

Should a sports league be held liable for brain damage in its former players? (pp. 238–239)

An overview of the deliberation method is discussed in the front of this Teacher's Manual. For free deliberation materials, student handouts, and an instructional video visit https://store.streetlaw.org/deliberations/.

If this is your first deliberation, consider devoting significant time to establishing norms for deliberations and civil discourse. Introduce the process of deliberations, including careful reading, clarification, preparing and presenting initial positions, reversing positions, free small group discussion, search for common ground, and whole-class discussion.

Begin class by introducing the deliberation issue: the liability of sports leagues for brain damage in former players. Ask students who play sports how their teams/school try to limit the risk of injury in players. Ask students why athletes might risk injury to play sports in both amateur and professional settings. Does it matter whether the player is an amateur or a professional? Ask students to what extent athletes consent to the risk of injury by voluntarily playing the sport? Does their answer to that question vary based on the sport involved? Explain to students that this deliberation will help students explore to what extent a sports league should be liable for brain injuries of former players. Students will strive to reach consensus on some aspects of the issue but are not required to agree on an outcome.

Take students through the deliberation steps as outlined in the front of this Teacher Manual.

Debrief by instructing students to:
- Raise your hands if you changed your position on the issue.
- Raise your hand if you considered a new opinion that you had not considered before today.
- Raise our hand if you felt listened to during the deliberation.
- Follow up by asking students, how they might translate this activity to conversations outside the classroom.

Consider having students perform a self-assessment on the process and their contribution to it.

For the most recent information on traumatic brain injury legislation and litigation, see the following suggested resources:
- National Conference of State Legislatures – Traumatic Brain Injury Legislation (http://www.ncsl.org/research/health/traumatic-brain-injury-legislation.aspx): State laws on Traumatic Brain Injury.
- "NFL & Sports Concussions Litigation Update: What's Happening?" (https://brain-law.com/brain-injuries/nfl-concussion-2/).

YOU BE the JUDGE

Determining a Defense to Negligence (p. 240)

a. The plaintiff is Olivia. The defendants are the amusement park owner(s), the designer of the ride, and the operator of the ride. Student answers may vary regarding whether the defendants have legal defenses. The plaintiff will probably lose her case because she contributed to her own injury when she unhooked the safety bar. The amusement park owner(s) took the step of buying a ride that included a safety bar, the designer of the ride included a safety bar, and the ride operator secured the riders. However, students might discuss whether rides should be designed in such a way that a passenger cannot unhook the safety bar. For example, if Olivia could prove that the amusement park operator showed a lack of reasonable care by choosing safety bars that could be unhooked, she might be able to recover damages. Olivia might also try to prove that there was a design defect in the bar that allowed it to be unhooked while the ride was in operation.

b. The plaintiff is Howard's family. The defendants are the state, the city or some other entity responsible for the beach, and the lifeguard. Student opinions will vary about whether the defendants have legal defenses. In general, beach owners are not responsible for providing a lifeguard, but if there is one, he or she must perform the job in a nonnegligent manner. However, this does not mean that Howard's family will automatically win the case. The defendant(s) will argue that Howard assumed the risk in spite of the warning sign and buoys or showed negligence by swimming beyond the sandbar, based on the information on the sign. The plaintiff will argue that the lifeguard should have been watching swimmers who wandered out too far and should have issued a warning. It is unclear whether the defendants will have a strong legal defense in this case.

c. The plaintiff would be the parent of the injured minor student, and the defendants might be the manufacturer of the Bunsen burner, the teacher, and possibly the school. Assuming that the Bunsen burner manufacturer included instructions and safety features, the manufacturer of the burner would have met its duty of care and should be free from liability. The teacher should have discussed safety issues with students before engaging in a potentially dangerous activity. There is also the possibility that the spill resulted from a lack of care on the part of the student. If so, the damages being sought from the teacher or the school by the student would be reduced.

d. The plaintiff would be Shayna, the parent of the minor child who was injured. The defendants might be the city, the government entity that maintained the park, and the manufacturer of the monkey bars equipment. In this problem, the court will look at the duties of Shayna, the manufacturer of the playground monkey bars, and the city, and determine the extent of each party's liability accordingly. The court will examine Shayna's failure to adhere to the clearly posted warning, the duty of the manufacturer of the monkey bars to build safe playground equipment for children, and the duty of the local town or city to routinely inspect and maintain a safe playground for children. If the mother was more than 50 percent at fault, she will not be able to recover any damages.

e. The plaintiff would be Eric (or his parent if he is a minor.) The defendant would be the management of the office building, which could be a private individual, company, or government entity. Here, the court will consider the duty of care of Eric, and the duty of care of the office building management. The office building management has a duty (set out in state law) to keep sidewalks reasonably safe. During a snow or ice storm, however, it is impossible to have clean sidewalks at all times. In addition, running on ice will probably result in Eric's not being able to recover any damages at all.

f. The plaintiff would be Amy, and the defendant would be the drunk driver. In this case, each party's behavior fell short of the duty of care. Remember that young drivers are held to the adult standard of care. The finder of fact (judge or jury), if the case goes to trial, will have to determine which side was more at fault. If Amy was equally at fault or more at fault, she will not be able to recover damages. If her fault was less than the fault of the drunk driver, her recovery will be reduced by the amount of her fault. As a practical matter, these kinds of cases usually do not go to court and are negotiated between insurance companies.

g. Since Jake is a minor, his mother would be the plaintiff on behalf of her minor child. The defendant would be the owners and management of the sporting equipment store. Here, the court will have to further examine the specific facts of the situation to address questions that this fact pattern does not answer. For example: Did the store post a warning sign to its customers on the treadmill? Should Jake have known that the treadmill would be plugged in? What standard of care would a reasonable person exercise in such a situation? If there was no warning sign, the store may be found liable for failing to warn customers of this foreseeable danger. There is also the possible defense for the store that Jake acted in a dangerous manner and that damages should be reduced.[17]

ACTIVITY AND LEGAL RESOURCE PERSON—ANALYZING WAIVERS AND LIABILITY

Ask students whether they have ever been asked to sign a waiver or release from liability before participating in certain potentially dangerous activities. Ask students why they might have been asked to sign such a waiver. *Waivers are designed to release the person(s) sponsoring the activity from liability if the signer is injured through the negligence of the sponsor.*

Ask student volunteers to record the following notes on the board:

- In most states, waivers or releases are enforceable as long as they are clear and understandable to a layperson.
- If the conduct of the party asking someone to sign the waiver is worse than negligent, and this causes damage to the signer, then the waiver will not protect the activity sponsor from liability.
- Some states do not allow some businesses (typically those regulated by government) to use waivers to protect themselves from liability for their negligence.

Ask students to bring in sample waivers or releases. They might find them in the school's athletic department if student athletes must sign a waiver. Another place to find them might be with an adventure sports company such as those that offer white-water rafting or bungee jumping. Ask students to analyze each waiver or release to interpret its limits and the extent to which liability has been released. Emphasize that a lawyer would need to provide a definitive statement regarding what the waiver means in your state. Consider inviting a lawyer to help with the analysis of the waivers.

NOTES

(1) *Banks* v. *District of Columbia*, 551 A. 2d 1304 (D.C. App. 1988).

(2) *Adamian* v. *Three Sons, Inc.*, 233 N.E. 2d 18 (Mass. 1968).

(3) *Michnik-Zilberman* v. *Gordon's Liquor, Inc.*, 453 N.E. 2d 430 (Mass. 1983).

(4) *Morella* v. *Machu*, 563 A.2d 881 (N.J. 1989).

(5) 24 Houston L. Rev. 957 (1987).

(6) *Hanks* v. *Booth*, 736 P.2d 1319 (Kan. 1986).

(7) *Pierre* v. *Watervliet*, 465 N.Y.S. 2d 685 (1985).

(8) *Len* v. *City of Cohos*, 534 N.Y.S. 2d 505 (1988).

(9) *Acquaviva* v. *Piazzolla*, 472 N.Y.S. 2d 704 (1984).

(10) *Jackson* v. *Moore*, 378 S.E. 2d 726 (Ga. App. 1989).

(11) *Snow* v. *Nelson*, 475 So. 2d 225 (Fla. 1985).

(12) *Clark* v. *McKerley*, 126 N.H. 778, 497 A.2d 846 (1985).

(13) *Campbell by Donnellan* v. *Haiges*, 504 N.E. 2d 200 (Ill. App. 1987).

(14) *Cashman* v. *Reider's Stop-N-Shop Supermarket*, 504 N.E. 2d 487 (Ohio App. 1986).

(15) *Janifer* v. *Jandebeur*, 551 A.2d 1351 (D.C. App. 1989).

(16) *Blacks Law Dictionary* (pocket ed., West 1996): 48, 434.

(17) *Finney* v. *Rose's Stores, Inc.*, 120 N.C. App. 843 (1995).

networks™

In tort law, there is usually some degree of fault on the part of the defendant, which makes him or her liable to the plaintiff. However, strict liability—liability without fault—is one exception to this requirement of fault. In some strict liability cases, the defendant is liable to the plaintiff regardless of who is at fault, even if the defendant acted in a reasonable and prudent manner. Strict liability is applied to hazardous activities involving the storage and transportation of dangerous substances, the use of explosives, the harm caused by dangerous animals, and the harm caused by the manufacture and sale of defective products.

CHAPTER **20**
Strict Liability

INTRODUCTION (P. 244)

Learning Outcomes

After completing this section, students should be able to:
1. define the term *strict liability*; and
2. explain how and why strict liability differs from negligence.

DANGEROUS ACTIVITIES (PP. 242–243)

Learning Outcomes

After completing this section, students should be able to:
1. list some of the dangerous activities for which strict liability applies;
2. define the term *toxic torts;* and
3. explain why applying the standard of strict liability to certain activities creates an incentive for careful and safe practices.

BACKGROUND—WHEN STRICT LIABILITY IS IMPOSED

This section presents some of the major activities for which the law imposes strict liability. Students should differentiate between this type of tort and negligence. In strict liability cases, unlike negligence cases, the plaintiff does not have to prove that there was a duty and a breach. Once it is determined that strict liability should apply, the plaintiff has to show only causation and damages.

Some people say that the most important area of strict liability is product liability. Manufacturers, sellers, and others in the chain of distribution of consumer products are held strictly liable for injuries sustained from an unreasonably dangerous product. The injured party does not have to prove that the manufacturer was at fault or negligent, simply that the product caused the injury.

DISCUSSION—CONSUMERS AND NEGLIGENCE

Post the following questions.

- Is an ultrahazardous activity being performed?
- Was damage incurred?
- Should the company be responsible for the injury? Was the harm foreseeable?

Then tell students to use these questions as criteria to evaluate the hypothetical cases **1.–3.** below.

1. Rob buys a gaming console. As he hooks it to his television, its wires short-circuit, and he is severely burned.

2. Francesca buys a curling iron. While she is using the iron, it overheats, her hair catches fire, and she is burned.

3. Brett buys a football to play catch. As he catches the ball, it explodes in his face.

In each of these three cases, the consumer can recover damages without having to prove negligence. Strict liability for manufacturers is a relatively new development in tort law and is closely related to public policy considerations. A defendant whose "fault" is not proven may have to pay the plaintiff for harm suffered because the defendant is in a better position to pay for the loss—either through insurance or by spreading such costs among all consumers through increased prices. Students should explore fairness issues in this section as they have throughout the unit. Is it fair to require a company to pay even if it took precautions? Is strict liability necessary to protect society from people who engage in hazardous activities, own vicious animals, or make and sell defective products?

LEGAL RESOURCE PERSON

Ask an attorney specializing in strict liability to speak to the class. Ask students to develop scenarios in which they believe strict liability would apply. Then question the attorney as to how a court would apply the law to each case. This will help students learn the meaning of strict liability and its application.

You could use this activity to test students' understanding of negligence. Ask students to develop a scenario in which strict liability would apply, and then have them change the scenario so that negligence would apply. Alternatively, teams could create and trade scenarios for analysis. An attorney could assist by evaluating students' scenarios.

PROBLEM 20.1 (p.242)

a. Operating a large water treatment plant may be considered a dangerous activity. If so, the families could recover damages using the claim of strict liability. However, if a court concluded that taking reasonable care would eliminate the risk of harm (i.e., that operating such a plant is not

unreasonably dangerous), then the plaintiffs would have to prove negligence, such as a failure to inspect regularly for leaks, in order to recover damages. In either case, the families affected could bring a class action suit, but they still must prove either strict liability or negligence.

b. Operating an auto repair shop is not an unreasonably dangerous activity. However, the mechanic can see the oil and can keep clean the area where customers walk. Strict liability should not apply, but negligence may. On the other hand, perhaps spilled oil is a danger that a consumer should expect; Anita should have been on the lookout for spilled oil. Negligence may apply to her as well, in which case she may not be able to recover damages.

c. Blasting in an urban area is unreasonably dangerous. Since there is no way to totally eliminate the possibility of harm, strict liability applies, and Donna can recover damages if she sues.

d. Kyung Lee can probably win damages, but not based on strict liability. This is a case of negligence. A waiter's work is not unreasonably dangerous.

CAPTION ANSWER (p. 242) Parties injured from industrial pollution must establish causation before they can recover damages. This can be difficult because toxic torts often result in injuries that have a long latency period.

PROBLEM 20.2 (p.243)

a. Under the concept of strict liability, a person who engages in an abnormally dangerous activity does so at his own peril and is responsible for any damages which result from that activity, even if the activity has been carried out with great care. In determining whether strict liability should apply, a court will examine whether or not the nature of the activity in question presented a high risk of harm to person, land, or property of others. The court will also consider whether Mattingly could have eliminated the risk of harm by exercising reasonable care, or whether the activity is one that cannot be carried out safely even when reasonable care is used. Using this standard, strict liability would apply here because courts have generally held that crop dusting and spraying are unavoidably hazardous.

For a claim of negligence, the neighbor's argument would focus on Mattingly's failure to use reasonable care in protecting her neighbor's bees from the effects of the pesticide. Of course, the neighbor would have to prove all the elements of negligence.

b. Mattingly may first contend that she should not be held strictly liable for the use of the pesticide. She could argue for a public policy exemption to strict liability on the theory that her fruit trees and the pesticides they require serve an important societal function, or she could argue that she should not be held liable for such unforeseeable effects of nature as a gust of wind.

   If Mattingly is successful and is held to a negligence standard instead of a strict liability standard, she could defend herself by showing that she took all foreseeable precautions to prevent harm to another's property. She could also possibly raise the defense that her neighbor did not properly protect the bees from reasonable harm.

c. Students' opinions will vary. The case presents an excellent opportunity for students to attempt to prove each type of tort (strict liability and negligence). Ask students whether the crop duster could be held liable. Under what tort theory? Should he have checked weather reports before beginning the dusting? Should he have insurance to cover this type of accident?

ANIMALS (PP. 243–244)

Learning Outcomes

After completing this section, students should be able to:
1. summarize how courts have decided liability for harm caused by untamed animals and household pets; and
2. describe the relationship between pet-owner negligence and liability.

BACKGROUND—STRICT LIABILITY AND ANIMALS

The section of the chapter on strict liability and animals has obvious appeal to students because many of them have responsibility for their family's pets. Also, cases involving pit bulls have been in the news with some frequency. Ask students to investigate whether or not your community has a leash law or any other laws about specific breeds of animals.

THE **CASE** OF...

The Dangerous Dog

PROBLEM 20.3 (p. 244)

Many states have passed "dog bite" laws that impose strict liability on dog owners for injuries caused by their dogs. In some cases, states or local communities have also passed breed-specific laws that require owners to take extra steps if they own a breed that has been suspected of being particularly dangerous, such as pit bull terriers, Rottweilers, and Presa Canarios. Those extra requirements might include bans on breeding, requiring liability insurance coverage of up to $100,000, requiring registration of the dogs with the city animal warden, or requirements to keep the dogs securely confined or on particularly short leashes. Some cities ban entire breeds from their city limits. Some pet advocates oppose breed specific laws (BSLs) and claim they are misguided. They say that laws should "punish the deed, not the breed," meaning that if a specific dog bites someone, that dog's owner should be held accountable, but the owners of other dogs in that breed should not be punished. To learn more about the debate from multiple perspectives, visit

- FindLaw's section on animal attacks and dog bites at https://injury.findlaw.com/torts-and-personal-injuries/dog-bites-animal-attacks.html;
- a site that gives advice on dog bite law at http://dogbitelaw.com/breed-specific-laws/breed-specific-laws;
- the American Kennel Club has a site on responsible dog ownership at www.akc.org/dogowner/responsible_dog_ownership/index.cfm; and
- the National Animal Interest Alliance, which opposes laws banning specific breeds of dogs at www.naiaonline.org.

a. Arguments for Matthew's parents include that this type of animal has a well-known record of being dangerous and that the owners knew or should have known that allowing a pit bull to roam freely in the yard created an unreasonable risk.

b. Arguments for the owners include that Matthew trespassed and that this particular dog did not have a record of vicious behavior. Therefore, the dog's owners could not have been on notice that the dog was dangerous. Another possible argument is that Matthew's parents were negligent when they failed to properly supervise him.

c. Students' opinions will vary. The case of Matthew's parents is strengthened by the fact that the child was too young to know that he was trespassing. However, Matthew's parents may also be held responsible to the degree that they allowed their unsupervised child to wander into their neighbor's yard.

d. If Matthew were older, the case would be much weaker because he would be held to a higher standard of responsibility. The law treats the 15-year-old more like the 35-year-old than the 5-year-old.

As an extension of this problem, explore the issue of animal rights. Students may have strong feelings about this issue. Survey their beliefs by asking whether animals that have attacked humans should be euthanized. Ask who should be held liable for any subsequent attacks if the animal is not euthanized.

DEFECTIVE PRODUCTS (PP. 244–245)

Learning Outcomes

After completing this section, students should be able to:

1. describe the role of the U.S. Consumer Product Safety Commission in protecting consumers from defective products;
2. discuss product liability and describe the way it relates to strict liability; and
3. define the term *product liability*.

DISCUSSION—PRODUCT SAFETY

Ask students to recall the extent to which product safety could be assumed during the Industrial Revolution, before regulation offered consumers any meaningful protection. Ask how holding product manufacturers to a strict liability standard provides an incentive to produce safer products. What types of safety tests, warning labels, directions, and protective parts are needed to make products safe? Discuss these issues as they relate to everyday household appliances, power tools, poisonous

chemicals, children's and infants' toys, and other products.

DISCUSSION AND SMALL GROUP ACTIVITY—DANGEROUS PRODUCTS

Ask students to work with a partner to create a list of five items that are or can be dangerous, making note of how each could be dangerous. For each item, the partners should list the product's benefits. Then, the partners should decide whether the government should ban it, regulate in some way (such as requiring warnings), or take no action at all. Students should be prepared to report to others about their lists, their decisions about government involvement in the product, and their reasons.

If students need help, consider offering the following example analyzing an iron. An iron can be dangerous to use. The manufacturer should probably place warning labels in easy-to-see areas and provide very clear directions to alert users. An iron is a popular appliance, so its usefulness and popularity may outweigh its potential dangers. There are some serious dangers associated with incorrect use of the iron, such as burns and electric shock; thus, the manufacturers should adequately warn of the iron's dangers.

THE **CASE** OF...

The First Responders

PROBLEM 20.4 (p.245)

Before students answer these questions, be sure they have read the entire section about defective products.

a–b. Although students' answers may vary about whether a vaccination company should be held liable if a person contracts a disease, drug companies usually assume they will be held responsible and figure the cost of compensation into the price of their product. Generally, companies engage in cost-benefit analysis to see whether the costs entailed in compensating one person in a million outweigh the profit to be made from the other 999,999 who use the product with no serious ill effects. Such analysis is a little tricky because it assumes that statistics are completely accurate. In a well-known case, a large automobile manufacturer seriously miscalculated the cost-benefit analysis of one of its products and knowingly placed a dangerous automobile on the market. The gas tank of this automobile exploded upon a slight rear-bumper impact, causing many injuries and deaths. It would have cost the company just a few more dollars per automobile to correct the fatal defect.

Liability would also turn on whether the company had adequately warned users of the potential dangers of the product.

c. If the company's estimates are correct, it is preventing 999,999 people from contracting smallpox, 30 percent of whom may have died from it. Therefore, the product serves an important public health function. If the company would have to cease manufacturing the drug or impose a sharp increase in price under a strict liability requirement, the company may be held to the lesser negligence standard, because there is a strong state interest in not hampering vaccination programs. Also, although "assumption of risk" is not generally a defense in product liability cases, there are some exceptions when the risks are inherent to the activity and the activity serves an important social function or is in common usage. The adequacy of the warning of the vaccination's risks would be an issue.

d. The government is generally immune from lawsuits when it makes a decision according to what it believes to be in the best interest of public health. However, it may be problematic that Gabriella's individual choice about a personal medical decision is limited by government involvement. Ask students whether and why the government should have wide latitude in this area.

DEFENSES TO STRICT LIABILITY (P. 246)

Learning Outcomes

After completing this section, students should be able to:

1. describe defenses to strict liability cases; and
2. explain the relationship between causation and damages in strict liability cases.

BACKGROUND—DETERMINING STRICT LIABILITY

While few defenses to strict liability exist, courts do not assume or impose liability automatically. The court must first decide whether it is appropriate to apply strict liability. Misuse of a product, if unreasonable or unexpected, can also limit a plaintiff's chance at winning damages. The relevant law for strict liability is decided on a state-by-state basis, so it is important to use local resource persons and materials. Consider inviting a manager of a manufacturing company or a lawyer to discuss this issue with students.

Under strict liability, plaintiffs usually must prove that some defect in the product caused the injury. The defect can be due to design or manufacturing. A design defect is present in some products that roll off the assembly line. For example, a toy with small parts that children may choke on contains a design defect. A manufacturing defect is a flaw in one individual unit of the product that is not present in the rest. For example, a chair that is missing a bolt has a manufacturing defect. The defect does not have to be the result of carelessness or fault, and the fact that the product caused an injury probably means that it was defective. According to some legal theorists, "defective" means the product could possibly have been made safer.

If a manufacturer can prove that its product was misused, the plaintiff may not be able to win the lawsuit. However, the misuse must be unforeseeable by the manufacturer.

Generally, assumption of risk is also a defense to strict liability. Assumption of risk occurs when a consumer is aware of a dangerous defect in a product and voluntarily takes the risk anyway.

THE CASE OF...

The Exploding Tire

PROBLEM 20.5 (p.246)

a. The best arguments for the wife are that the tire manufacturer produced a defective tire, and the tire store mounted the defective tire on Myra's car. The plaintiff's attorney can support her argument with police reports, driving records, or other evidence that show Myra's careful driving. The attorney can also hire an expert witness in auto safety to inspect the vehicle and testify about the tire's defects. The case must show that Myra was killed as a result of the defective product and through no fault of her own, so the tire manufacturer and tire store should be held responsible.

b. The defendants' best argument is to try to prove that their product did not cause Myra's death, but that Myra's own negligence caused her death. For example, if it can prove that Myra herself overinflated her tires by 15 pounds, then she would have been negligent.

c. Students can deliberate about the two standards discussed: negligence and strict liability. Students should be able to recognize that a strict liability standard is more beneficial to the plaintiff (and more harmful to the defendants). A strict liability case is easier to prove because plaintiffs need only provide evidence of causation and harm. Students should also recognize that a negligence standard, rather than a strict liability standard, is more beneficial to the defendants, because it gives them an opportunity to refute the existence of a standard of care and breach of that standard.

It is likely that the court will consider this to be a strict liability case. Therefore the plaintiff need only prove causation (i.e., that the tire blowout caused Myra's death) and actual harm or damages (i.e., that Myra died). Myra's death will be easy to prove, but it may be more difficult to argue causation.

If negligence must be proven, the plaintiff's best evidence would be to present national auto safety standards for tires presented in published

laws, consumer regulations, or other publications. If such standards are in fact adopted and published, then the defendants would be legally bound to them, and would be found negligent for violating a duty of care to consumers. The defendant's best argument is to deny that such standards are the industry standard and that they had no such duty to manufacture and sell tires according to such standards.

d. Students' answers will vary, especially because the facts of the case as given leave several questions open to interpretation. This question gives students the opportunity to discuss the merits of the case and the arguments in questions a.–c.

Students who believe that the manufacturer and the tire store should be held responsible for Myra's death should be able to cite as evidence some or all of the following: the fact that the tires were new; the fact that the store installed the tires; the dry driving conditions; the fact that Myra was driving the speed limit (or that nothing is mentioned about Myra's driving negligence); and that the defendants should be held strictly liable.

Students who believe that the defendants should not be held responsible for Myra's death should be able to support their argument with the following: the fact that the tire was overinflated by 15 pounds and that Myra could have overinflated it; and just because Myra was driving the speed limit does not mean that Myra was driving carefully. Supporters of the defendants should also be able to argue that a negligence standard should be adopted.

According to public policy, the tort law system should do three things: (1) compensate harmed persons promptly, (2) allocate benefits to victims and costs to wrongdoers fairly, and (3) deter conduct that is unreasonably risky or dangerous. Critics of the system, however, claim that the amount of money awarded to victims is often too high, that going to court takes too long, and that tort law is so complicated that it is often difficult to determine who is really at fault.

As a result of such claims, the tort reform movement has developed. Various efforts in the reform movement target each of these criticisms. Because tort reform is a part of public policy debate, questions about whether and how the system should be changed is the source of significant debate.

CHAPTER 21
Torts and Public Policy

INTRODUCTION AND TORT REFORM (PP. 247–249)

Learning Outcomes

After completing these sections, students should be able to:
1. identify purposes of the tort law system;
2. summarize common criticisms given of the tort law system;
3. provide examples of states' tort reform efforts that target the process and the outcome of tort cases;
4. compare the benefits of the British tort system with those of the U.S. tort system; and
5. define the terms *tort reform, statute of limitations,* and *frivolous lawsuits.*

ACTIVITY—GREAT BRITAIN AND THE UNITED STATES: WHO PAYS THE ATTORNEY FEES?

This activity describes differences in the way lawyers are paid for handling tort cases in the United States and in Great Britain. The issue of who should pay attorneys' fees is of serious concern. Some argue that the U.S. system, which makes both parties to a tort pay their own legal fees, floods the legal system with frivolous cases. Some reformers argue that a British approach, in which the loser pays the fees of both parties in addition to any damages, would discourage frivolous litigation.

Have students form teams representing the U.S. and British systems of tort law and brainstorm arguments to support the use of their system. Next, have the teams informally debate the merits of the two systems. Next, choose three students to read aloud or role-play the dialogue that follows. You will need a moderator, a U.S. attorney, and a British attorney. The class should compare the arguments in the prepared dialogue with those they came up with on their own.

Four questions and background follow the prepared dialogue below; use them for class discussion. Expect that students' opinions will differ. Some will argue that the U.S. approach results in too much litigation and that some modification is needed to reduce the number of cases brought. Others may argue that the U.S. system ultimately provides greater protection to citizens and consumers by forcing those who provide goods and services to do so with great care.

Moderator: William Smith stepped off a curb into the street, where he was struck by a car driven by Mary Minow and seriously injured. One witness said Minow was exceeding the speed limit of

25 mph and should have seen Smith and stopped. Another said that Smith should have been more careful when crossing the street.

If Smith hires a lawyer and files a lawsuit asking Minow to pay his medical bills, who will pay his attorney fees? Let's listen to two lawyers describe how Great Britain and the United States differ on the issue of attorney fees in a tort case:

British lawyer: "In Great Britain (and most European countries), if Smith sues Minow and proves she was at fault, Minow will have to pay Smith's medical bills and attorney fees. Since the idea is to make the injured party whole, it would not be fair if Smith won the case and still had to pay his own attorney fees. If Smith loses, however, he will have to pay both his and Minow's attorney fees."

U.S. lawyer: "In the United States, Smith and Minow are each responsible for their own attorney fees. We believe that going to court is everyone's right, and the British rule would discourage people from filing lawsuits. In the United States, most lawyers and clients agree to a contingency fee agreement, which says that the lawyer does not get paid by the hour (or how much work he or she does) but will be paid a percentage of the settlement if the client wins. Typically, Smith would be allowed to pay his attorney through a contingency-fee arrangement, with the attorney receiving one-third of the amount the court orders Minow to pay Smith."

British lawyer: "If Smith wins and is required to pay his attorney one-third of the money awarded to him, either he won't be able to pay all his medical bills or the jury will recognize his high attorney fees and give him a very high money award, which occurs too often in the United States. You also encourage frivolous lawsuits by not requiring the loser to pay the winner's attorney fees."

U.S. lawyer: "Smith and Minow's case is a close one in that neither party is totally right or wrong. To make the loser pay the winner's attorney fees would be unfair. To discourage Smith from bringing the case for fear he will have to pay Minow's attorney fees is also unfair."

British lawyer: "Under your system, people with small claims of less than $2,500 or so will not file cases because their attorney fees may end up being $3,000 or more. Also, poor people and others will not file public-interest cases."

U.S. lawyer: "On the contrary, we have small claims courts where people can file small lawsuits without lawyers; we also make available free lawyers for poor people, and there are laws which allow attorney fees to be awarded to the plaintiff in civil rights, environmental, and other public-interest cases."

British lawyer: "To us, paying attorney fees should be a necessary part of losing a lawsuit. On what principle can a person wrongfully run down someone on a public highway and have to pay that person's doctor's bills but not his or her lawyer's bills?"

Discuss the following questions with the class:

- Describe the differences between the British and American rules on who pays attorney fees in civil cases. *In Great Britain (and most European countries) the losing party is required to pay the prevailing party's attorney fees as well as his or her own attorney fees. This principle is commonly referred to as the "English Rule" or the "Loser Pays Rule." In the United States, on the other hand, each party is responsible for his or her own costs, including attorney fees. There are two general exceptions to the "American Rule": (1) The parties can agree in a contract that one particular party will pay the other's attorney fees if a suit is ever filed. This is common in leases and other agreements. (2) A state or federal statute can also require one party to pay the attorney fees of the prevailing party. The Americans with Disabilities Act and other civil rights laws are common examples.*

- What are the three best arguments for the English Rule, or the Loser Pays Rule? What are the three best arguments for the American Rule? Do you think one rule is better than the other? Explain. *Those who support the U.S. approach may argue that each party should be responsible for paying all the costs associated with bringing a suit because these costs are a necessary consequence of creating litigation. Additionally, people would be less likely to file legitimate claims if they knew they had to pay the other party's fees if they lose. Moreover, many citizens find it difficult enough to pay their own attorney, let alone the opposing party's attorney.*

  The British would argue that their rule discourages frivolous lawsuits and requires the party to thoroughly research his or her case before burdening the court with a filing. Another argument in support of the English Rule is that it provides full compensation for the winning party. British attorneys would also argue that under the American Rule, many just claims are never adjudicated because the expense of engaging a lawyer is greater than the amount which can be recovered.

ACTIVITY—TAKING A FIELD TRIP

Take students to observe a civil trial. If possible, arrange for the judge or the opposing attorneys to speak to students during a recess in the proceedings. After the field trip, ask students whether the process seemed fair and whether they believe that the lawsuit was reasonable or a waste of time and resources.

LEGAL RESOURCE PERSONS

Invite two lawyers to debate tort reform. One should be a plaintiff's lawyer and the other should be an insurance company or defense attorney.

ACTIVITY—EVALUATING WEBSITES OF GROUPS SUPPORTING AND OPPOSING TORT REFORM

Encourage students to learn more about the viewpoints of those who support and those who oppose tort reform. Send them to the websites of several groups that oppose and support tort reform, such as:

- Consumer Watchdog at www.consumerwatchdog.org
- American Association for Justice at www.justice.org/what-we-do/advocate-civil-justice-system
- American Tort Reform Association at www.atra.org
- Institute for Legal Reform at www.instituteforlegalreform.com
- American Medical Association at www.ama-assn.org Use the search term "medical liability reform."

Ask students to determine for each group:

1. What is the group's mission? What is their view about tort reform?

2. What issues are most important to them right now? What are they working on?

3. Who supports this group? What can you learn about the membership of this group from the website?

4. If someone wanted to support this group or "get involved" what are three actions that person could take?

5. How can visitors to this website determine whether the information presented is accurate or credible?

6. What is your assessment of this group's website? Is it easy to navigate? Convincing? Visually appealing?

Depending on time, you may assign all students to visit each site, or you could break students into teams and have them report their findings to other teams, like a "jigsaw" activity. Conclude the activity by asking students to create a blog or post to a class discussion board explaining their own opinions about whether tort reform is necessary.

Investigating the Law Where You Live

(p. 249) A list of current medical malpractice award cap legislation by state is available at https://www.nolo.com/legal-encyclopedia/state-state-medical-malpractice-damages-caps.html. The National Conference of State Legislatures has information at http://www.ncsl.org/research/health/medical-malpractice-reform-health-cost-brief.aspx. An infographic with state information can be found at https://www.theexpertinstitute.com/medical-malpractice-damages-caps-a-state-by-state-comparison/. Students may also research by searching the term *tort damage limits* and their state name.

THE CASE OF...

The New Car That Was Used

PROBLEM 21.1 (p. 249)

This problem is based on the case of *BMW of North America, Inc.* v. *Gore*.[1]

a. Mr. Gore bought a car that he thought was new. When he learned that the BMW dealership had simply repainted it and claimed it was new, he sued the dealership, claiming it had committed fraud by selling it as new. The dealership admitted its policy to sell "as new" cars that could be fixed for a small percentage of the car sales price. The dealership lost the suit, and Mr. Gore won $4 thousand in compensatory damages (the lost value of the car) plus $4 million in punitive damages. Upon appeal, the state supreme court said the punitive damages were not excessive, but it lowered the amount to $2 million.

b. The Supreme Court had to decide whether the punitive award was excessive, unfair, and/or violated the due process clause of the Fourteenth Amendment.

c. Students' answers will vary. Students who believe the punitive damages violate the Fourteenth Amendment might say that BMW could not have reasonably anticipated such a penalty because there was no notice or state law indicating that BMW might face such a stiff fine. (The applicable state law would have imposed a $2,000 fine.) Supporters of BMW's case might also say the ratio between actual damages and punitive damages is so large that it is unreasonable. Supporters of Mr. Gore's case might argue that BMW should have anticipated that it would be charged with fraud and should have avoided taking such fraudulent actions. They might also argue that the jury awards are not a constitutional issue and that states, their courts, and their juries have the right to set penalties as they see fit.

d. Students' answers will vary.

e. This position was argued by lawyers on behalf of Mr. Gore. Students should reach their own conclusions and support their answers with reasons.

NOTES

(1) *BMW of North America, Inc.* v. *Gore*, 517 U.S. 599 (1996).

UNIT 4
Consumer Law

netw✦rks™

Unit 4 introduces students to the practicalities of consumer and housing law. It covers a host of topics—such as contracts, consumer protection laws, and credit—that will inevitably affect students directly in their daily lives. The unit emphasizes both rights and responsibilities of consumers, giving students the tools they need to protect themselves and to manage their finances effectively. The features and problems throughout Unit 4 guide students in developing the skills that will make consumer and housing law work for them.

CHAPTERS IN BRIEF

CHAPTER 22
Contracts
Chapter 22 examines contracts and their elements. It also distinguishes between written and oral contracts and describes the merits of each. Illegal contracts are also discussed.

CHAPTER 23
Warranties
Chapter 23 describes express and implied warranties and disclaimers.

CHAPTER 24
Credit and Other Financial Services
Chapter 24 introduces the topics of credit and other financial services. It provides insight into the costs and risks of credit and discusses the importance of managing money wisely and building good credit.

CHAPTER 25
Deceptive Sales Practices
Chapter 25 exposes common deceptive sales practices, such as telemarketing scams and bait-and-switch techniques, to help consumers avoid becoming victimized. Laws to protect consumers are also discussed.

CHAPTER 26
Becoming a Smart Consumer
Chapter 26 describes federal, state, and local laws and agencies that regulate sellers and protect customers.

CHAPTER 27
Major Purchases
Chapter 27 presents issues of consumer awareness when making major purchases related to cars, housing, paying for college, and health care.

SERVICE LEARNING AND SPECIAL PROJECTS

1. **Field Trips:** Students might attend a hearing at a small claims court or a hearing in their state or local legislature that addresses a consumer or housing issue. Students should identify the issue and the interests of the parties involved and evaluate arguments made by both sides. After returning to class, students might act as judges, a jury, house of representatives, or city council and decide the issue among themselves.

2. **Internet Activity:** Have students create a Consumer's Guide to the Internet. They can share it with each other, with other students in the class and with their parents and guardians. Students could search for and compile a list of sites that:

   - rate services and goods;
   - assist with budgeting;
   - calculate mortgage amortization schedules;
   - locate local apartments for rent;
   - function as consumer or housing advocates; and
   - protect consumers, promote home ownership, and work to halt housing discrimination.

3. **Debate:** Students could research and debate controversial issues related to housing and consumer law. Such issues include:

   - rent control;
   - regulation versus deregulation of specific products or industries;
   - restrictions on advertisements for alcohol and tobacco products;
   - appropriate responses to housing discrimination; and
   - appropriate responses to problems of homelessness.

4. **Student Advocacy and Service Learning:** While community service is educational and meaningful on many levels, service learning takes it to "the next level" by connecting service with classroom learning and reflection. The following activities are suggested to help students enhance what they learn in Unit 4 by serving their communities.

   - Students can write a consumer law pamphlet on how a particular consumer problem is handled in their state.
   - Students can work with groups that help low-income people with credit problems, housing discrimination, or legal issues related to landlord-tenant conflicts.
   - Students can make videos illustrating how to handle consumer problems, show the videos to other young people, or post them on a social networking website.
   - Students can write a play or public service announcement about minors and contracts. They can play it on your school's morning announcements or at a youth-oriented meeting.
   - Students can develop a list of consumer phone numbers and publish it in the school paper or in a consumer newsletter.
   - Students can write a consumer help column in the student newspaper.
   - Students can develop a coloring book for younger students that demonstrates smart shopping strategies.
   - Students can research companies that operate sweatshops and consider the most effective ways to protest those companies and end this practice.
   - Students can assist Habitat for Humanity in building a house for a local family, and then report what they have learned.
   - Students can conduct research about homelessness and its causes and identify ways to help homeless people.

UNIT RESOURCES

Using Legal Resource Persons

1. Invite judges, attorneys, and law students to assist with mock trials, legislative hearings, or debriefings after a court visit. They might also speak about consumer and housing-related issues, such as class action suits, bankruptcy, or housing discrimination.

2. A physician could speak to the class about consumer safety issues related to prescription and nonprescription drugs and the FDA drug-approval process.

3. Invite a representative from your state's legislature to assist with or evaluate testimony at a mock legislative hearing on a consumer or housing-related issue.

4. A representative of a local consumer group could address consumer issues, interests, and resources in the local area.

5. A local housing inspector might discuss reasons for codes, landlord and tenant responsibilities and common sources of conflict, and safety steps every homeowner and tenant should implement.

6. A bank officer could assist students in building hypothetical budgets and discuss mortgage discrimination, criteria used to evaluate consumers who apply for credit, problems associated with excessive use of credit cards, and the importance of saving money to prepare for long-range goals such as college education and home ownership.

7. Representatives of landlord and tenant organizations could assist with debates or discussions about housing discrimination or rent control.

Other useful websites include:

- Consumer Product Safety Commission at www.cpsc.gov. This site links to all federal consumer agencies.
- The Federal Citizen Information Center at www.pueblo.gsa.gov. This site provides answers to questions about a wide range of consumer issues and government services.
- FIRSTGOV For Consumers at www.consumer.gov. This site is a "one-stop" link to a broad range of federal information resources available online.

- The Federal Health Insurance Marketplace at www.healthcare.gov. This site provides information on the different types of health insurance available and enables consumers to enroll in health insurance programs.
- U.S. Postal Inspection Service at https://www.uspis.gov/. This site provides information about the postal inspection service, which investigates sweepstakes, lotteries, and fraud.
- Sites about consumer and housing law include Nolo: Law for All at www.nolo.com, the Legal Information Institute at Cornell Law School at topics.law.cornell.edu/wex/Consumer_credit.
- The Better Business Bureau is available online at www.bbb.org.
- A multilingual consumer resources site is available at www.consumer-action.org.

networks™

The law of contracts reaches into many aspects of our daily lives. A contract is a legally binding agreement between two or more parties to exchange something of value. For example, when you agree to buy something you usually form a legal contract. There are three elements to a legally binding contract: an offer must be made by one party, the offer must be accepted by another, and an exchange of consideration must be made—meaning that something of value is given in return for something else of value. A contract is breached when a party fails to live up to the promise he or she set forth in the agreement. There are specific laws that pertain to minors and contracts, as well as to written versus oral contracts. Illegal contracts, such as an agreement to commit an unlawful act or an agreement based on fraud, are unenforceable in court.

INTRODUCTION (P. 252)

Learning Outcomes

After completing these sections, students should be able to:
1. explain the general functions of consumer law; and
2. define the terms *contract* and *breach*.

ELEMENTS OF A CONTRACT (PP. 252–253)

Learning Outcomes

After completing this section, students should be able to:
1. describe elements of a legally binding contract;
2. explain why it is unwise to enter into a contract without careful consideration; and
3. define the terms *offer, acceptance, consideration,* and *competent*.

ACTIVITY—READING CONTRACTS AND IDENTIFYING ELEMENTS OF A CONTRACT

This chapter provides a chance to talk with students about the importance of careful reading and understanding of all legal documents. A variety of activities could be used, either in isolation or in combination, to illustrate the importance of reading contracts and to identify essential elements of a contract.

- A legal resource person could visit your class and bring examples of the kinds of contracts that students are likely to encounter and may have difficulty understanding. Ask the resource person to explain the recent movement toward requiring the use of "plain English" for legal documents. Students could conduct research to determine whether your state legislature is considering requiring that plain English be used by regulated industries such as banks.
- You or the resource person could ask students whether they have ever encountered a website that requires them to "agree" to the terms of the site before they use it. Then ask students whether they are in the habit of reading those agreements and what might result if they do not agree to the terms.

- Assign pairs of students the task of identifying six examples of offers, acceptances, and considerations that they encounter in their daily lives. Ask students to compare and contrast their examples in a class discussion. After they discuss oral contracts, show students written contracts and ask them to identify the important elements. Ask students:

  - Are these documents written in "plain English"?
  - Should these documents be rewritten in "plain English" to make them easier for consumers to understand?
  - Are there any clauses or terms in the documents that seem unfair?

PROBLEM 22.1 (p.253)

a. No contract has been made because there has not been an acceptance by the auctioneer. "Do I hear a bid ..." is an invitation to make an offer. The $300 bid is only an offer and nothing more. Once the auctioneer says "sold," a contract is made.

b. No contract has been made. Although Basil tried to make an acceptance, a valid offer was not made. Yukiko said she was "going to sell" her car for $500, but she did not state that she was offering it for sale at that amount to Basil. The offer had to be made to a specific person.

   If Yukiko had said, "I am willing to sell you my car for $500," and Basil replied he would buy it, then there would have been a contract.

c. Use this problem to explain the idea of "preexisting duty to act." There was not a valid contract between the citizens of the town and the sheriff for the reward money. The sheriff already had an obligation to attempt to capture the suspect as part of his job, so he had a preexisting duty to act. He could not accept the offer because there could be no consideration given by him.

d. This is not a valid contract because there is no consideration (i.e., something of value was not given in exchange for something else of value). Megan would have turned 18 whether or not she had been promised $1,000 so the fact that she turned 18 is not, in itself, something of value.

e. This is a valid contract because certain kinds of offers can be accepted either by words or by performance (or deeds). Even though Lynn did not verbally accept the offer, her action was sufficient to indicate acceptance. It might be argued that walking across the bridge was not something of value, and consequently there was

no consideration. However, because walking across the bridge is something that she might not have done in the absence of the offer, and because Shelly was willing to pay Lynn $5 to do so, there was consideration.

f. This is not an enforceable contract because it is an agreement to commit an illegal act. Even though there is an offer, acceptance, and consideration, no court will enforce contracts that call for the commission of a crime. This is known as an "illegal contract" and is discussed in more detail later in the chapter.

MINORS AND CONTRACTS (P. 254)

Learning Outcomes

After completing this section, students should be able to:

1. compare and contrast contractual obligations of adults and minors;
2. cite two examples of when a minor may be held to a contract; and
3. define the terms *cosign* and *ratify*.

BACKGROUND—ENFORCING CONTRACTS WITH MINORS

The law concerning minors and contracts provides an opportunity to discuss the relationship between rights and responsibilities. As the Student Edition indicates, minors have less responsibility than adults to fulfill their obligations under most contracts, but their rights are also limited; they usually need an adult to cosign before merchants will make contracts with them.

A contract has been ratified when a minor continues making payments on the contract after reaching the age of majority. (The age of majority is set by state laws and differs from state to state. State legal age laws including age of majority, eligibility for emancipation, contracts by minors, ability to sue, and consent to medical treatment may be found at https://statelaws.findlaw.com/family-laws/legal-ages.html.) Once a contract has been ratified, it may no longer be voided by the person who was a minor when the contract was made.

Some state laws may create other situations where contracts entered into by minors are enforceable and cannot be voided. For example, if a minor tells the seller that he or she is 18 and it is reasonable to believe that he or she is 18, the minor may not be able to get out of the contract agreement.

Educational loans entered into by someone age 16 or older may not be canceled in some states. Minors in some states may not be able to cancel contracts for life or disability insurance for themselves if they are a certain age.

a.–b. The fairness issue raised in this case is useful for class discussion. Ask students to explain why sellers want minors to have an adult cosign the contract before they enter into finance agreements. Who is protected by an age requirement for entering into a contract? Ask students whether or not this is fair to Kara. The manager's actions were legal and prudent since such a large purchase was involved. In fact, if the manager had agreed to sell her the computer, Kara may have been able to refuse to recognize the contract or make payments under the contract at a later time, because a contract with a minor is invalid. Ask students if it would be fair to require the merchant to sell the computer to a minor without requiring that an adult cosign the contract.

CAPTION ANSWER (P. 254) Minors may make a contract, but as a general rule they cannot be forced to carry out their promise to honor the contract.

WRITTEN AND ORAL CONTRACTS (P. 255)

Learning Outcomes

After completing this section, students should be able to:
1. identify which contracts must be in writing to be enforceable; and
2. cite two reasons why written contracts are more desirable than oral contracts.

BACKGROUND—WRITTEN CONTRACTS

The requirement that certain contracts be made in writing derives from the "statute of frauds." This law was originally enacted in England in 1677 to prevent fraud, which often occurred when the only proof of a contract was oral evidence.

This problem provides an opportunity to discuss and apply the statute of frauds.

a. Assuming that Ruth is at least 18, she has legally entered into a contract with Mike but not with Paul. She made an offer that Mike accepted. They exchanged promises—Ruth to deliver a bicycle and Mike to pay $400. A written contract was not necessary between Mike and Ruth because the item was to be sold for less than $500. Of course, it may be difficult to prove Ruth's oral promise to sell the bicycle to Mike. In her later agreement with Paul, she has broken her word, but she has not breached a contract because the statute of frauds requires that an agreement for more than $500 be in writing.

The court will require Ruth to reimburse Mike for any damages, but Mike is obligated to try to minimize his damages—that is, to find another similar bicycle that fits his needs for as close to the original contract price ($400) as possible. Ruth will be responsible for any additional reasonable costs that Mike incurs in replacing the bicycle. However, if Mike can find another similar bicycle for $400 or less, Ruth will not owe him any damages. (For more information about the buyers' obligations and damages, see the "Breach of Contract" section in the Student Edition.) Only in extremely rare circumstances could one party to a contract force another party to sell them the item in question. The item would have to be unique, like the Hope Diamond or Barry Bonds's record-breaking baseball, for a court to force the breaching party to deliver the item instead of paying damages.

b. In debating whether or not Paul should be able to enforce the contract, ask students whether they agree with the law requiring contracts over $500 to be written in order to be enforceable in court. Emphasize the difference between moral obligations and legal obligations. Some students may believe that Ruth should be morally obligated to honor both promises. Ask students if it is fair that the law does not hold Ruth to the same standards.

c. If Paul's agreement were in writing, Ruth would be legally obligated to pay damages to both Paul and Mike. Again, the amount would be the difference, if any, between what each had intended to pay her for the bicycle and the cost of each purchasing different bicycles.

ILLEGAL CONTRACTS (PP. 255–257)

Learning Outcomes

After completing this section, students should be able to:

1. cite examples of illegal contracts;
2. define the terms *unconscionable* and *fraud*;
3. describe characteristics of contracts that are considered unconscionable (as opposed to those that are just a "bad deal" for one of the parties involved); and
4. explain why it is easy for consumers to fall victim to fraud.

BACKGROUND—ENFORCING CONTRACTS

In addition to refusing to enforce illegal contracts, courts may also refuse to enforce an agreement that violates an important public policy or is unduly oppressive to one of the parties. Courts generally presume that all parties read, understand, and agree to each provision of their contracts. Someone is unlikely to win in court simply because he or she did not, in fact, read, understand, or agree to each provision. Remind students that courts "allow" consumers to make bad deals.

CAPTION ANSWER (P. 255) Courts will refuse to enforce a contract if it is considered unconscionable—that is, if it is unfair, harsh, or oppressive. Fraud and misrepresentation are also grounds for courts to invalidate a contract. Courts will also not enforce illegal terms of an otherwise valid contract.

THE CASE OF...

The Unfair Contract

PROBLEM 22.4 (p.256)

Before students read and answer this problem, read the first two paragraphs of the case aloud to them. Then ask students to discuss the following questions:

- What arguments might the seller make to support his or her position?
- What arguments might the consumer make to support her position?
- Is the fact that the woman is unemployed and on public assistance important?

- What would be a fair result in this case?
- Should the store be able to take back only the couch?

After students have answered these questions, direct them to the problem and have them read the third paragraph that contains the court's decision. Then ask students to answer questions **a.–c.**

a. Normally, when a consumer defaults on a secured loan, the lender can take back the item(s) that secured the loan. However, "The Case of The Unfair Contract" involves an "add-on" type of contract in which the store owned every item she purchased at the store until all the items were fully paid for.

The problem is based on the case of *Williams* v. *Walker-Thomas Furniture Co.*,[1] which involved this add-on type of contract. The court in *Walker-Thomas* called such a contract grossly unfair and refused to enforce it. The decision may have been influenced by the fact that the store continually pressured Ms. Williams into making expensive purchases despite the fact that they knew she had a low income and was probably unable to understand the agreement. The court felt that the contract was unconscionable.

b. Students' opinions will vary. Ask them to explain their reasons.

c. This question gives students an opportunity to consider issues of fairness in contracts made between parties with unequal power. Ask students to brainstorm ideas about what will protect a consumer with limited resources and what terms will protect creditors and sellers from consumers with poor credit.

BREACH OF CONTRACT (PP. 257–258)

Learning Outcomes

After completing this section, students should be able to:

1. describe and differentiate between various remedies a buyer can use if his or her consumer contract has been breached;
2. explain the law's requirement that sellers take reasonable steps to mitigate damages after a buyer breaches a contract; and
3. define the terms *expectation damages*, *rescission, restitution, specific performance,* and *duty to mitigate.*

PROBLEM 22.5 (p.258)

a. Jeanine's best remedy is damages. However, the amount of damages could be a problem. Jeanine should ask for the replacement value of the dress, but the cleaners would probably argue that she was entitled only to the market value of a used dress. Rescission and restitution might also be helpful in this situation.

Students may be surprised to learn about a bizarre case that made national news in 2007.[2] In that case, a sitting administrative judge sued a dry cleaning business for $54 million, claiming that the dry cleaners lost a pair of pants he had brought in for alterations. Before the case went to trial, the dry cleaners offered $3,000 in compensation, then $4,600 in compensation, and then $12,000 in compensation. Each offer was refused. The plaintiff based his $54,000,000 claim on a little-known law in the District of Columbia that indicates he was entitled to $1,500 per violation. He interpreted that to be $1,500 per day the situation was unresolved because the store had signs that said "Satisfaction Guaranteed" and "Same Day Service." He also filed for $1 million in emotional damages and legal fees. In the end, the court found in favor of the dry cleaners. Months later, the dry cleaning business went out of business, blaming the years of legal fees, the influence the lawsuit had on their credit and the stress of the lawsuit. While some claim this case is an example of why the tort system should be reformed, others, including a spokesman for the American Association of Justice (formerly the American Trial Lawyers Association) disagree, saying this case was so bizarre and outrageous that it bears no resemblance to the many "ordinary people—who are seeking real justice for real cases of negligence and wrongdoing."

b. The Zhous' best remedy is specific performance (getting the spraying done) on some modified schedule, or perhaps rescission and restitution of the money already paid.

SUMMARY ACTIVITY— UNDERSTANDING CONTRACTS

Have students interview their parents or other adults to clarify how consumers are affected by contracts. Students should ask the following questions:

- Have you signed any contracts that are legally binding on you now? (Common examples might include mortgages, automobile loans, and credit card agreements.)
- Have you ever known someone who was a victim of fraud? What happened? Was the situation resolved? How?
- Have you ever known someone who was a victim of an unfair contract? What happened? Why was it unfair? Was the situation resolved? How?

NOTES

(1) *Williams v. Walker-Thomas Furniture Co.* 121 U.S. App. D.C. 315, 350 F.2d 445 (1965).

(2) Avila, Jim, Chris Francescani and Scott Michels, "Judge Rules in Favor of Dry Cleaners in $54 Million Pants Lawsuit" *ABC News*, June 25, 2007.

networks™

A warranty is a promise or guarantee made by a seller that goods for sale are not defective and will perform properly. Many warranties also include a statement of what the seller will do to remedy the situation in the event of a problem with the product. Not all warranties are the same, so it is important to compare warranties while shopping. Express warranties and implied warranties are two types of guarantees. An express warranty is a statement—written, oral, or by demonstration—concerning the quality or performance of goods offered for sale. An implied warranty is an unwritten promise, created by law, that a product will do what it is supposed to do. Consumers should also be aware of disclaimers—clauses or statements in a warranty that attempt to limit the seller's responsibilities should any problems arise with the product.

196

INTRODUCTION (P. 259)

Learning Outcomes

After completing this section, students should be able to:
1. define the term *warranty*; and
2. list at least three important questions that warranties should answer for consumers.

BACKGROUND—BASIC CONSUMER QUESTIONS

Warranties give consumers important rights, and therefore are probably the most basic form of consumer protection. Remind students that warranties answer several essential consumer questions:

- What parts and repair problems are covered?
- Are any parts or repairs excluded from coverage?
- How long does the warranty last?
- What will you have to do to get repairs?
- What will the company do if the product fails?
- Does the warranty cover "consequential damages," that is, other losses caused by the product's failure? For example, if your freezer breaks and all your food spoils, the loss of the food would be consequential damages.
- Are there any conditions or limitations on the warranty?

Encourage students to compare warranties when making purchases to see what is best for them.

EXPRESS WARRANTIES (PP. 259–261)

Learning Outcomes

After completing this section, students should be able to:
1. describe characteristics of express warranties;
2. list three requirements of written warranties according to the *Magnuson-Moss Warranty Act*;
3. distinguish between full and limited warranties; and
4. define the terms *express warranty* and *puffing*.

ACTIVITY—IDENTIFYING EXPRESS WARRANTIES

After students have a basic understanding of express warranties and puffing, ask them to bring in advertisements or labels from merchandise and determine if express warranties are made.

Students should be able to easily identify statements that are merely puffing. Remind students that this type of "seller's talk" does not create an express warranty. Students should try to determine if the warranty is full or limited and search for an effective disclaimer. They might also evaluate the language of the warranty to decide if it is written in "plain English" and if any clauses or terms in the warranty seem unfair.

BACKGROUND—WARRANTY LABELS

The *Federal Consumer Product Warranties Act*, commonly known as the *Magnuson-Moss Warranty Act*, requires warranty labels on most products carry the words "Full Warranty" or "Limited Warranty."[1] Explain to students that this law requires that the warranty be written in plain language so that a person can understand it. A wise consumer should carefully read and compare warranties or find someone else who can do so. For example, in comparing two like items at the same price, one with a full warranty and the other with a limited warranty, the full warranty may not be better. A one-year full warranty might be less valuable than a 20-year limited warranty. It depends on what each warranty promises.

Purchasers almost always need to provide proof of purchase in order to receive warranty service. A dated check, a receipt from the seller, a credit card statement, and warranty registration cards are three ways to prove date of purchase. This topic provides an opportunity to introduce another basic skill of effective consumers: record keeping. Even if students do not develop elaborate methods of tracking the items they buy and the money they spend, they should develop the habit of scanning, saving and filing receipts, warranties, and other pertinent purchasing information.

PROBLEM 23.1 (p.261)

a. The manufacturer, Excellent Digital Cameras, is making the warranty. The seller, an authorized service center, or the service department of the manufacturer can make all repairs.

b. The warranty is for one year from the date of purchase. The buyer does not have to do anything to make the warranty effective, although the buyer will need to prove the purchase date because of the one-year limitation. Mailing the enclosed registration card is one way of proving the purchase date. Students should note that it is important to save receipts, canceled checks, or credit card receipts and statements as evidence of the purchase date.

c. The third paragraph of the warranty lists all the limitations and exclusions. It is a limited warranty. With a full warranty, removal and

reinstallation would be free. The warranty covers the entire product. The warranty promises either repair or replacement at the option of the warranter (the company). The consumer is responsible for postage and any other charges involved in delivering the item to the place of repair.

IMPLIED WARRANTIES (PP. 261–263)

Learning Outcomes

After completing this section, students should be able to:

1. distinguish among three types of implied warranties: warranty of merchantability, warranty of fitness for a particular purpose, and warranty of title;
2. explain how consumers can seek remedies if products harm them;
3. explain why consumers should carefully inspect cars and other products before making a purchase; and
4. define the terms *implied warranty, warranty of merchantability, warranty of fitness for a particular purpose, warranty of title*, and *strict liability*.

BACKGROUND—CONSUMER PROTECTION

The implied warranty of merchantability, as codified in the *Uniform Commercial Code* and adopted in some form by the legislatures in all 50 states, terminates the common-law idea of caveat emptor,[2] or "let the buyer beware." In fact, in response to the growth of government regulation, some critics of consumer protection describe the contemporary marketplace with the somewhat tongue-in-cheek paraphrase "let the seller beware."

CAPTION ANSWER (P. 262) Courts usually do not interpret the implied warranty of merchantability to provide much protection in used-car sales. Consumers should shop carefully for an express warranty when buying a used car.

PROBLEM 23.2 (p.263)

a. There has been no warranty created here. The warranty of merchantability does not apply to sales between casual sellers such as friends or acquaintances. However, courts have had difficulty determining how long a particular used car of average quality should run. Before purchasing any used car, a consumer should always have the car checked carefully by a qualified mechanic. Also, beware of buying a used car "as is." This phrase usually serves as a legally sufficient disclaimer. Try to bargain with the seller for an express warranty in writing.

b. In this case, a warranty of fitness for a particular purpose has been created. Deidre told the sales clerk that she planned to machine-wash the dress and the clerk said that would be fine. Because the dress shrank in the washer, the warranty has been breached and she should be able to get her money back. She will, of course, have to prove that the conversation took place. The sales clerk's statement may also create an express warranty concerning the washable nature of the material.

c. There is an implied warranty of merchantability, but the words "it will last for years" are not an express warranty. They constitute puffing. Therefore, the issue is whether or not a camera's advance button that breaks after eight months is of ordinary quality.

d. Scott breached the warranty, which was an implied warranty of title. This is the only type of warranty that applies to merchants as well as to casual sellers.

e. An advertisement with a picture and a written description creates an express warranty that the product purchased will be as it appears in the advertisement. In this case, the warranty has been broken, and Trina can exchange her paperback book for a copy in hardcover.

However, a company is given some leeway for a mistake that should have been obvious to the consumer or where an honest mistake was made. The bookstore could argue that "hardcover" was a clerical error in the advertisement and that the price was obviously well below the price of a hardcover book. Generally the picture that accompanies a book advertisement is the same for both hardcover and paperback. Still, the bookstore may decide it is a better business strategy to honor the advertisement or at least offer some compensation for its mistake.

f. In this case, the implied warranty of merchantability has been created by the sale. A new sofa of average quality should not have a leg fall off two weeks after delivery, so the warranty has been broken.

DISCLAIMERS (P. 264)

Learning Outcomes

After completing this section, students should be able to:
1. define the term *disclaimer*;
2. explain how sellers can disclaim the implied warranty of merchantability of an item for sale; and
3. explain how sellers use disclaimers to limit consumers' remedies.

BACKGROUND—WARRANTY LAW

Tell students that warranty law does not guarantee perfect products. However, consumers who avoid impulse buying, comparison shop, and carefully inspect products before purchasing them are more likely to be satisfied with their purchases. A disclaimer attempting to exclude a seller's liability for physical harm caused by consumer goods is considered unconscionable.

If you have not yet taught, or do not plan to teach Unit 3, "Torts," you may wish to introduce students to the concepts of negligence and strict liability from that unit. From a consumer's standpoint, recovering damages for harm caused by a defective product is best accomplished by bringing a lawsuit based on strict liability.

THE CASE OF...

The Guitar That Quit

PROBLEM 23.3 (p.264)

a. Shari should bring the guitar back to the store to get it repaired or replaced. Three hundred dollars is a substantial purchase, and Shari should be able to expect the guitar will last far longer than three uses.

Even though the store receipt disclaimed an express warranty, the store was not clear in disclaiming a warranty of merchantability because the receipt did not use specific, easy-to-understand language like "as is" on the receipt. Unless the store owner has evidence that

Shari misused the guitar, and therefore caused it to break, the store should fix the guitar free of charge or replace it with a new one. Otherwise, the owner and the business could suffer the negative effects of a reputation for faulty products and bad business practices.

b. Students' answers will vary. This question gives students a chance to consider that numerous factors, not just price, should influence their purchasing decisions. Discuss the importance of factors such as warranty terms, limits, brand reputation, and the reputation of the seller.

c. When consumers see signs like these, they should carefully investigate the company and its products before making a purchase there. Consumers should consider: Have I evaluated the risks of this purchase? Have other customers been satisfied with their purchases at the store? Is it possible that it may fall apart? Consumers should also express their concerns to the sales-person, in the presence of others if possible. By doing so, they may be able to get a warranty, preferably in writing. Often, salespeople have some room to negotiate where a large purchase is involved.

NOTES

(1) *Federal Consumer Product Warranties Act*, 15 U.S.C. section 2301 et seq. (1988).

(2) *Uniform Commercial Code* section 2–314. The implied warranty of fitness for a particular purpose is found at *U.C.C.* section 2–315 and the warranty of title is found at *U.C.C.* section 2–312 (1987).

networks™

There are three primary ways in which consumers can pay for goods and services: cash, bank accounts (including savings and checking), and credit. Although most sellers accept it, paying with cash is not always convenient. Bank accounts offer convenient alternatives—such as ATM and debit cards—to paying with cash. Using credit to pay for goods and services means making a promise to pay in the future. There are important issues that all consumers should be aware of when purchasing things on credit, such as annual fees, interest rates, repayment cycles, and so forth. Failure to repay debt can result in default and/or collection practices, such as repossession or court action, from creditors.

INTRODUCTION AND THE BASICS ABOUT BANK ACCOUNTS (PP. 265–269)

Learning Outcomes

After completing these sections, students should be able to:
1. compare the advantages of using checking accounts and automatic teller machine (ATM) cards over using cash;
2. explain what overdraft protection is and why consumers should find out the costs and terms of those services before they accept the protection;
3. list common fees associated with many checking accounts;
4. describe why it is important to quickly notify your bank if your checkbook, ATM card, or debit card is stolen;
5. distinguish between an EFT (or ATM) card and a debit card; and
6. define the terms *credit* and *stop payment*.

CAPTION ANSWER (P. 266) Overdraft protection is like a line of credit and assures the account holder that checks written on and debits made from a bank account, up to the limit of the overdraft protection, will be honored.

CAPTION ANSWER (P. 267) ATM cards offer the convenience of making purchases without worrying about whether you have enough cash or taking the time to write a check.

ACTIVITY—COMPARISON SHOPPING FOR CHECKING ACCOUNTS, ATM CARDS, AND DEBIT CARDS

Ask students to create a chart that lists in each row the common fees associated with checking accounts, ATM cards, and debit cards. Then ask students to write the names of several local banks across the top of their chart in each column. Have students contact those local banks or consult their websites and complete their chart by filling in dollar amounts for each fee. Many banks publish these fees online, though in some cases, students may need to speak with a customer service agent at the bank.

Students should share the results of their research with the class, making it clear that these fees are all subject to change.

Note: Explain to students that some people rely on check cashing stores to cash payroll and other checks. However, some of these stores charge high fees. In fact, the fee to open a basic checking or savings account at a bank, savings and loan, or credit union may be less than the cost of cashing one check at a check cashing store. Tell students that some states are considering legislation that would regulate such stores. As an extension of the activity above, ask students to add a column to their chart to note the fees for their local check cashing stores. Students can also investigate to find out if their state imposes limits on bank or check-cashing store fees.

THE **CASE** OF...

The Lost Wallet

PROBLEM 24.1 (p.269)

The goal of this problem is to help students understand the differences between credit cards and debit cards. In addition, the problem serves as a reminder for students about the importance of being diligent in maintaining these cards and reporting their loss.

a. Bridget's liability for the unauthorized charges on her credit card is $50, no matter when she reports the card stolen. In the interest of maintaining good consumer relations, many credit card companies do not charge their customers anything for unauthorized purchases if the losses are reported in a timely manner.

b. Whether Bridget reports the stolen card and the loss of funds on that day or within 60 days, she can be liable for up to $500 because she did not notify her bank of the stolen card within two business days (the following Tuesday after her ill-fated trip to the beach). That means that of the $755 withdrawn from her bank account, the law entitles her to receive only $255 back from her bank. Had Bridget notified the bank within two business days, she would have been liable for only up to $50 (like her stolen credit card). Like credit card companies, however, banks may voluntarily limit their customers' liability for losses incurred as the result of lost or stolen debit cards or ATM cards.

c. Students' answers will vary and should be supported with reasons. Ask students to consider the differences between the two types of cards. Credit cards offer greater protection in exchange for charging high interest rates that benefit the credit card company. On the other hand, banks generally offer debit cards primarily for their customers' convenience. Debit cards may automatically protect people from spending more money than they have in their bank accounts. Although debit cards may offer less compensation if stolen and used, it is less likely that a debit card will be used fraudulently because a PIN number is often

required for extra protection. Where debit cards can be used for purchases without requiring a PIN, banks generally use a policy for those purchases that is identical to their credit card policy.

d. Students' answers will vary and may focus on customer service, competition, loyalty, and fairness.

AN INTRODUCTION TO CREDIT (PP. 270–273)

Learning Outcomes

After completing this section, students should be able to:
1. explain what it means to use credit;
2. describe the basic roles of creditors and debtors;
3. contrast the consequences of defaulting on secured credit and unsecured credit;
4. list the types of information a consumer should investigate when comparing credit card offers;
5. describe how interest is calculated;
6. explain what a consumer can do if a credit card is lost or stolen;
7. describe steps a consumer should take if there is a billing error on his or her statement;
8. state how consumers can determine if they are using too much credit; and
9. define the terms *creditor*, *debtor*, *finance charge*, *interest*, *unsecured credit*, *secured credit*, *collateral*, *default*, and *annual percentage rate (APR)*.

BACKGROUND AND DISCUSSION

Use the "wise shopper" theme in conjunction with credit. Tell students that most car buyers, for example, would visit several dealers before buying a car, but many consumers do not comparison shop for credit. In introducing the subject of credit, it is useful to discuss the many ways in which consumers use credit. For example, using bank charge cards is a form of credit, even when the monthly bill is paid in full and no interest is charged. The merchant offering the convenience of bank credit card sales pays a percentage to the company issuing the card. Studies suggest that the widespread use of credit cards has caused an increase in retail prices.

After discussing types of credit, ask students where credit is available in their community and why people use credit.

During an inflationary period, many consumers feel that "buying now and paying later" is good consumer economics. They expect price tags to be even higher in the future, so they reason that it makes sense to buy at today's prices and pay with tomorrow's cheaper dollars. However, millions of consumers who have followed this strategy have become overextended, and personal bankruptcy has increased. The debt-counseling business experiences a boom when many consumers abuse easy credit.

CAPTION ANSWER (P. 270) The annual percentage rate (APR) is calculated in the same way by all lenders and is the percentage cost of credit on a yearly basis.

BACKGROUND—CONSUMER CREDIT RESOURCES

The Federal Trade Commission's website at www.consumer.ftc.gov provides a wealth of information for consumers about credit and also data about government publications related to this issue. Consumers Union, the publisher of Consumer Reports, also makes a wide variety of useful information available online at https://advocacy.consumerreports.org/. Use the search term "credit" to find out about recent legislation concerning consumer credit as well as the group's efforts to keep credit information safe from those who might use it for computer crimes.

BACKGROUND—CALCULATING INTEREST

The goal of federal regulation in the area of credit, as in much of consumer law, is disclosure or notification to consumers. Starting in 1980 and continuing today, major credit card companies—certain large retailers and many banks—began to change the way in which they calculated interest. While in many cases, no interest is charged if the statement balance is paid in full within 30 days, an increasing number of lenders are eliminating this grace period and charging interest from the date of a purchase or cash advance. Also, some creditors allow consumers 30 days to pay off their balance before assessing interest, but if a consumer does not pay in 30 days, the company charges interest beginning on the date of the purchase rather than the date payment was late. The impact of this change is to increase the cost of using credit cards for those card holders (estimated at nearly two-thirds of the total number)

who do not pay monthly bills in full. Consumers need to carefully read disclosure notices included with their monthly statements to keep abreast of these types of changes.

CAPTION ANSWER (P. 271) Consumers should consider annual fees, percentage rate charged on money owed, and whether interest is charged from the date of the transaction or only on balances unpaid at the end of the billing period.

CAPTION ANSWER (P. 272) As a general rule, if a consumer spends more than 20 percent of their take-home salary to pay off debts (excluding mortgages), they are using too much credit.

LEGAL RESOURCE PERSON

Invite a local banker or credit counselor to visit your class to discuss:

- how the bank decides who qualifies for a credit card;
- if minors qualify for credit cards;
- how credit limits are set;
- if the bank collects a fee from merchants who accept the bank's credit cards;
- steps consumers should take if a credit card is lost or stolen; and
- why many consumers have concluded that it may be too risky to use credit cards.

PROBLEM 24.2 (p.273)

If you think your students will have difficulty reading the billing statement connected to this problem, consider projecting it so you can circle relevant digits and show the math as you work through the problem together.

a. United Virginia Bank Card is the creditor. John Q. Consumer is the debtor.

b. The new balance is $668.72. The creditor arrived at this figure by taking the previous balance, $425.00, and subtracting the payment, $100.00, leaving $325.00. The finance charge of $4.88, and the new transactions, totaling $338.84, were added to $325.00 for a total of $668.72.

c. The credit available is $1,831.28. This figure is determined by subtracting the new balance, $668.72, from the credit limit, $2,500.

d. An acceptable example is shown in **24.1 TM Figure** on the next page. The consumer should keep a copy of the letter as well as the original receipt.

FIGURE

24.1 TM Figure

February 19, 2019

United Virginia Bank Card Center
7818 Parham Road
P.O. Box 27182
Richmond, VA 23270

Dear United Virginia Bank Card:

I believe there is a billing error of $48.00 in my statement which closed 2/12/19. I was charged $125.67 for the item from Snap Shot Camera, reference number 22161982. However, the actual cost of the item was only $77.67. I am enclosing a copy of the receipt from the store, along with a copy of your bill to me.

Please make the necessary adjustments in my next statement. Also, please be certain that I am not charged interest for the amount in error.

Sincerely,

Name
Address
Account Number 4366-040-878-000

THE COST OF CREDIT (PP. 274–277)

Learning Outcomes

After completing this section, students should be able to:

1. explain why comparing the APR of credit is an effective way to compare rates;
2. describe the risk involved in taking out loans with variable interest rates;
3. list and describe four charges that may be added to the price of credit;
4. describe what the *Credit Card Accountability, Responsibility, and Disclosure Act* and the *Truth in Lending Act* requires of creditors; and
5. define the terms *usury, variable interest rate, credit property insurance, credit life/disability insurance, service charge, penalty charge, loan sharking, balloon payment, acceleration clause,* and *bill consolidation.*

PROBLEM 24.3 (p. 274)

a. Students' answers might include banks, credit unions, and savings and loan associations. Some merchants also offer financing.

b. The creditors may charge interest, require minimum payments, penalties, insurance fees for the property or to cover the payments if the creditor dies or becomes disabled, or other fees. Direct students to the Student Edition to clarify those possible fees.

c. Students' answers will vary but should include a comparison of interest rates, fees, terms, and other elements of the agreement with each institution.

PROBLEM 24.4 (p.277)

a. With the $50 down payment and $600 in monthly payments ($50 × 12 months), Linda will pay a total of $650 for the washing machine. If the washing machine costs $500, then $150 of the $650 is considered interest, resulting in an annual interest rate of 30 percent. A typical interest rate for an installment payment program for consumer goods is approximately 17 to 21 percent. Students will have various reactions to this credit plan and should raise questions about fairness, adhesion contracts, and the imbalance between creditors and consumers.

b. Linda may be at a significant disadvantage if she misses a payment to The Washer Mart because there is no clear statement of what the penalties might be. Possibilities include: The Washer Mart might assess additional finance charges; it might report Linda to a credit agency, which will affect her credit rating in the future; or it may repossess the washing machine.

c. Eighteen percent interest annually is $90, making the total cost $590. Students should discuss Linda's options, including making the purchase with a lower-interest credit card, finding a different merchant, trying to negotiate a better deal, and signing a written contract that defines her liability for missed payments.

ACTIVITY—ILLUSTRATING COSTLY CREDIT ARRANGEMENTS

Challenge students to devise visual methods—for example, creating cartoons, graphs, flowcharts, Venn diagrams, or sketches—to illustrate loan sharking, balloon payments, acceleration clauses, and bill consolidation. Students should share their finished work with the class and discuss what each image depicts.

BACKGROUND—CONSUMER-RELATED LEGISLATION

The *Truth in Lending Act*,[1] like most other consumer-related legislation, requires accurate disclosure of information. If consumers do not or cannot read and understand the various forms, the protections are ineffective. The nature of this legislation suggests the importance of classroom activities to clarify common—yet complicated—legal forms.

WHAT LENDERS WANT TO KNOW (P. 277)

Learning Outcomes

After completing this section, students should be able to:
1. list four kinds of information about borrowers that lenders want to know before extending credit;
2. describe how the *Equal Credit Opportunity Act* protects consumers; and
3. identify three federal regulatory agencies that protect borrowers from discrimination.

Investigating the Law Where You Live

(p. 277) Students can search for information about their state's consumer protection agency at https://www.usa.gov/state-consumer. This website provides links to state, regional, and local consumer protection offices.

BACKGROUND—APPLYING FOR CREDIT

Creditors sometimes speak of the three Cs of credit:

- *capacity* (Can you repay the debt? What is your income? What are your expenses?)
- *character* (Will you repay the debt? What is your credit history?)
- *collateral* (Will the creditor be fully protected if you fail to repay the debt? Can you secure the loan with something of value?)

Emphasize to students that the *Equal Credit Opportunity Act* does not guarantee a person credit.[2] Applicants must still pass the creditor's test of creditworthiness. However, this law requires the creditor to apply these tests fairly and without discrimination based on the factors listed in the Student Edition. The "source of income" factor is designed to protect applicants whose income is from welfare or Social Security. While an application cannot be denied just because of the source of income, this factor may legally have some bearing on creditworthiness. For example, the age of any dependents can be considered when a welfare recipient applies for credit, as benefits may be lost when a dependent reaches a certain age. Similarly, age can have some bearing on creditworthiness. An older person might not qualify for a large loan with a small down payment, but might qualify for a smaller loan, with a larger down payment, secured by good collateral.

Several other important protections are not discussed in the Student Edition:

- Generally, creditors may not ask for gender information on an application form.
- Women need not use *Miss, Mrs.,* or *Ms.* on forms, but in some cases creditors may legally ask about marital status.
- Creditors may not ask about birth control practices or whether an applicant intends to have children. Nor can they make any assumptions about childbearing plans.
- Creditors must count all income, including money from part-time employment, child support, and alimony. Applicants do not have to disclose child support and alimony payments, but if they do, creditors must count it.
- Creditors may not consider whether applicants have a telephone listed in their name, as this would discriminate against people whose home phone is listed under their spouse's name.

WHAT IF YOU ARE DENIED CREDIT? (PP. 278–279)

Learning Outcomes

After completing this section, students should be able to:

1. identify rights that the *Equal Credit Opportunity Act* and the *Fair Credit Reporting Act* guarantee to borrowers; and
2. describe steps borrowers should take if they discover that their credit file contains inaccurate information.

BACKGROUND—FEDERAL LAW AND CREDIT

Students should be familiar with federal laws governing consumers, creditors, and credit because

it is likely that most will apply for credit at some point in their lives. The *Equal Credit Opportunity Act* protects not only against credit refusal based on unlawful reasons, but also prohibits discouraging applicants or delaying the processing of applications on those same grounds. As the Student Edition notes, consumers who are refused credit are entitled to an explanation of the creditor's reasons. Consumers have a right to receive this notice in writing, and they have a right to a credit decision within 30 days of the filing of a credit application.

The *Fair Credit Reporting Act (FCRA)*[3] also provides substantial protection to consumers. The FCRA is aimed at three potential problems in the credit reporting industry:

1. inaccurate or misleading information in the files of consumer reporting bureaus or agencies;
2. irrelevant information in credit files; and
3. lack of public standards to ensure that an individual's credit file is confidential and used only for the intended credit information purposes.

The stated purpose of the FCRA is to require credit bureaus to "adopt reasonable procedures for meeting the needs of commerce for consumer credit, personnel, insurance, and other information in a manner which is fair and equitable to the consumer, with regard to the confidentiality, accuracy, relevancy, and proper utilization of such information."

Explain to students that it makes good sense to occasionally check their credit history to make sure that all the information in their file is accurate and relevant. In most cases, obtaining a credit report costs very little and, in some instances, it may be free. Two websites that offer free credit histories are www.creditkarma.com and www.annualcreditreport.com.

Tell students that to dispute the accuracy or relevancy of information in their credit file they may register their concern in writing with the credit bureau. The credit bureau must then investigate the disputed information. If they still dispute the content of their credit file after the investigation, they may contact the Federal Trade Commission (FTC) or the Consumer Financial Protection Bureau (CFPB) to file a complaint or file a civil action in court. They may also file their own version of the disputed information. The credit bureau must then include the consumer version in any subsequent report.

PROBLEM 24.5 (p.279)

a. Although her income is low, it is steady, so Erika appears to be a reasonable credit risk. The creditor must consider her income to be $1,120 per month. She appears to have income of $170 per month in excess of her expenses. Therefore, she should have the capacity to repay the debt. (A $1,100 loan for two years at 15 percent APR would require monthly payments of only about $53.) If she has not defaulted on past loans, her character and credit rating would be sound. She may have to pledge the refrigerator as collateral.

b. Jerry is not a very good candidate for a loan. His monthly expenses, not including food, are $900, compared to his seasonal take-home pay of $1,200 per month. With outstanding credit card debt and no money in the bank, there is some question as to his willingness to budget. If he has made all payments in a timely manner on his two other installment purchases, that would work in his favor. Still, his seasonal unemployment might worry creditors.

c. This situation presents the problem of getting a first loan without a credit history, income, or property. On traditional grounds, Barbara's application would be very weak. However, the government recognizes the dilemma facing young persons and has established programs that guarantee loans from lending institutions. With a federal or state guarantee, the bank should make the loan. Other government programs provide assistance directly to students. Barbara should discuss alternatives with the financial aid officer at her college. Her excellent grades and apparent commitment to medical school will make her a somewhat more attractive risk to a lender because most doctors earn substantial salaries.

CAPTION ANSWER (P. 278) To find out if there is a *payday lending law* in your state visit the National Conference of State Legislatures website at http://www.ncsl.org/research/financial-services-and-commerce/payday-lending-state-statutes.aspx or the Consumer Federation of America's website at https://paydayloaninfo.org/state-information.

BACKGROUND—PAYDAY LENDING LAWS

Approximately 19,000 payday loan stores operate across the country and are currently regulated by individual states. Payday lending stores are often concentrated in lower-income and minority neighborhoods. In 2016, twelve million Americans took out payday loans paying approximately $9 billion in fees. Some states have specifically exempted short-term loans from their usury laws (which ban excessive interest rates), thereby allowing lenders to charge as much as they want. Other states have enacted legislation that bans payday lending or caps

the size of payday loans and/or the interest rates that payday lenders can charge. The federal government has enacted legislation that caps the interest rate that lenders can charge military personnel at 36% APR.

Those in favor of more payday lending regulation argue that payday loans are generally made to (and advertised to) low-income consumers. Payday lenders advertise how easy it is to get a loan but often fail to mention the extremely high interest rates and strict terms. Many people who borrow from payday lenders end up trapped in a cycle of debt, paying far more in interest than they initially borrowed. Those against more regulation argue that payday lenders provide loans to high-risk borrowers when other financial institutions will not. This service is expensive because it's more expensive to make small short term loans. More information about payday lending laws is available from the Consumer Federation of America at www.paydayloaninfo.org/state-information and from the Center for Responsible Lending at http://stopthedebttrap.org/.

ACTIVITY—A TYPICAL PAYDAY LOAN

You may wish to begin this activity by showing a short student-friendly video explaining payday loans available at https://www.youtube.com/embed/XUqyyJSoM_s?&enablejsapi=1&origin=https://www.consumerfinance.gov. Share the following scenario with students by either reading it aloud and asking students to keep track of the numbers, posting them on the board, or creating a handout:

Ron works at a store and earns $1,600 per month. His rent, utilities, food, and other expenses usually total $1,450–$1,600 each month. He has $200 in his savings account.

Last fall, Ron's car broke down, and the mechanic told him it would cost $400 to repair it. He was trying to figure out how to scrape together the money for his car repairs when he saw an ad on TV for CashToday, a local payday lender. The ad promised that, "As long as you have a job, you can walk out with cash! No credit checks! Apply in only 15 minutes!" That sounded perfect to Ron. He went to CashToday and applied for a $200 loan. CashToday gave Ron a $200 loan until his next payday—two weeks away—for a fee of $20 per $100 borrowed.

He used the $200 from CashToday and the $200 from his savings account to get his car fixed right away. When his next payday rolled around, Ron only had $40 extra to pay back the loan. Ron paid the $40 toward the loan and CashToday rolled the loan forward for another two weeks. Two weeks later, Ron had saved up another $40. He went into

CashToday but was surprised that his balance was still $240—the original $200 loan plus another two weeks' fee of $40. So Ron paid another $40 to roll the loan forward. Two weeks after that, Ron finally had the full $240, and paid off the loan. Ask students:

- What is the total amount of fees Ron paid to borrow the $200? *In the end, Ron paid $120 in fees to borrow $200 for six weeks.*

- What is the annual percentage rate for this loan? *It was an APR of 521%.* If your students would like more information on calculating annual percentage rates (APR), they can visit www.calculatorsoup.com/calculators/financial/apr-calculator.php.

- What other options might Ron have had for getting the money to have his car fixed? *Ron could have tried to work out a payment plan with the mechanic who fixed his car. If Ron had a credit card, borrowing the same amount as a cash advance on a credit card probably would have cost Ron between $14–$20 (a 50–75% APR).*

- What was "fair" about the scenario and what was "not fair"? *Students may say it was "fair" because the lender disclosed information regarding repayment of the loan even if Ron did not understand it or that onus was on Ron to ask how the loan worked. Students may say it is "unfair" because the lender gave the loan to Ron without making it clear that he would be paying an exorbitant percentage rate.*

ACTIVITY—LEGISLATIVE COMMITTEE HEARING ON PAYDAY LOANS

The objective of this activity is to give students the opportunity to take a position related to payday loan regulation and create arguments in support of that position. Before you begin, review the following vocabulary terms with students:

Interest: money paid for the use of someone else's money; the cost of borrowing money.

Annual percentage rate (APR): the interest rate paid per year on borrowed money.

Loan sharking: lending money at high, often illegal, interest rates.

Default: failure to pay back a loan.

Put students in 3, 6, or 9 groups of 3–5 students each, assigning groups to the following roles:

a) **Payday Lenders Association** They will testify on behalf of payday loan companies in favor of loose or no regulations.

b) **Consumer Watchdog Organization** They will testify on behalf of consumers who feel that payday loans are predatory and want strict regulations.

c) **State Senators** They will listen to testimony and ask questions.

Present the bill that the state senate is considering in this activity. Sample: A bill to cap the APR on short term loans at 36%, to require short term lenders to accept installment payments, or to require lenders to disclose their APR in advertisements.

Give each group 15 minutes to prepare. The senators should prepare questions to ask the interest groups. The interest groups should create a list of arguments in support of their position.

If students need assistance preparing their arguments, you might share the following:

- Arguments in favor of regulation:

   1. Very high interest rates on payday loans often trap borrowers in a cycle of debt.

   2. Many payday loans are "rolled over" multiple times, thus increasing fees.

   3. Payday lenders tend to market to consumers who live paycheck to paycheck and who tend to be located in low-income neighborhoods.

   4. Payday lenders advertise how easy it is to get a loan but fail to mention the excessively high interest rates and strict terms.

- Arguments opposed to regulation:

   1. Many low-income consumers do not have large savings accounts or access to traditional bank loans or credit cards.

   2. Payday lenders provide loans to high-risk borrowers when other lenders will not.

   3. Payday lenders are willing to lend smaller amounts to consumers, meeting the needs of the consumers they serve.

   4. Introducing regulations of payday loans would stifle competition and do little to protect consumers from excessive debt and high-cost lending because borrowers would just seek out illegal loan sharks.

When 15 minutes have passed, hold mini-committee hearings. Match each State Senators group with one Consumer Watchdog Organization group and one Payday Lender Association group. You will have 1–3 mini-committee hearings in the room, depending on the number of students in your class. Provide the instructions for the committee hearings:

- The state senators should call the hearing to order and invite one group to testify first.
- The first interest group has 3–5 minutes to make an opening statement, and then the second interest group has 3–5 minutes for their opening statement.
- The state senators should then begin asking their questions. Allow a 10 or 15 minute limit on the questions. Questions may be directed to a specific group or to both groups.
- After the questioning period, the state senators should each describe their current position on the law and note what other information they would need to finalize a position.
- You may want to conclude the activity by asking students to find out if your state has regulations on payday loans. Students can then write their state lawmakers proposing a new regulation or proposing to amend or end the existing regulation.

DEFAULT AND COLLECTION PRACTICES (PP. 280–283)

Learning Outcomes

After completing this section, students should be able to:

1. define the terms *default, bankruptcy, repossess, default judgment, garnishment,* and *attachment;*
2. describe four options consumers should consider if they have problems paying their bills;
3. explain the short-term and long-term consequences of declaring bankruptcy; and
4. describe four methods creditors use to collect debts.

BACKGROUND AND DISCUSSION— BANKRUPTCY

The U.S. Constitution vests full power in Congress to establish all laws on the subject of bankruptcy.[4] Bankruptcy laws must be uniform throughout the country and must not deprive a debtor of his property without due process of the law. Bankruptcy is a procedure, authorized by federal law,[5] by which a debtor who cannot pay his or her debts on time is relieved of total liability by participating in a court-approved plan to make partial repayment. In many cases, the creditor gets only a small portion of the amount owed. In some cases the creditor may get absolutely nothing.

Over time, the federal bankruptcy law has been amended to prevent persons seeking bankruptcy from discharging certain debts. These include taxes, alimony, child support payments, and student loans.

Remind students that filing for bankruptcy is a serious decision with long-lasting implications. An attorney should almost always be consulted before taking this step.

CAPTION ANSWER (P. 280) Bankruptcy is a procedure in which a person who cannot make all of his or her payments places assets under the control of the federal court in order to be relieved of debt. Chapter 13 bankruptcy requires the person to make an arrangement, supervised by a federal court, to pay off some or all of what is owed over an extended period of time. Chapter 7 bankruptcy is more severe and requires that the federal court take control of most of the debtor's assets, sell them, and use the money to pay the creditors.

Investigating the Law Where You Live

(p. 280) There are many agencies and nonprofit organizations that provide financial counseling services. If your students have difficulty finding them using the usual search methods, send them to www.usa.gov/directory/stateconsumer/index.shtml, which has a directory of state, county, and city consumer protection offices. Students should also learn about the credit counseling resources at www.moneymanagement.org.

BACKGROUND—CREDITOR COLLECTION PRACTICES

The *Fair Debt Collection Practices Act of 1978*[6] has an important loophole. While providing substantial protections against unsavory actions by professional debt collectors, creditors collecting their own bills are not regulated at all. Some state laws close this loophole.

THE CASE OF...

The Missed Payment

PROBLEM 24.6 (p.282)

a. Assuming that Orlando had paid $3,000 toward the principal when the car was repossessed,

Orlando still owes $2,000 plus interest. He will also be responsible for the reasonable expenses incurred in the repossession and sale. Therefore, he would owe a total of at least $2,300 ($2,000 on the contract plus the $300 in expenses). The resale price of $2,000 is applied to what he owes; therefore, he would still owe Top Value $300, even though he no longer had use of the car.

b. Although professional debt collectors have the right to make phone calls and send letters to a debtor in order to collect a debt, calling every hour and contacting the debtor at work would probably be considered unreasonable. Orlando is protected from the debt collection agency by the *Fair Debt Collection Practices Act (FDCPA)*, the federal law regulating third-party collection businesses (i.e., the collection agency hired by the creditor). The law forbids repeated harassment by bill collectors and gives victims the right to sue for violations and to receive punitive damages in some cases. It is illegal for bill collectors to call a debtor repeatedly or to contact a person before 8 A.M. or after 9 P.M. Also, they cannot phone a person at work if the employer prohibits such calls. They cannot use obscene or profane language, threaten to use violence, fail to identify themselves as bill collectors, claim that property will be seized, or send a paper that looks like a legal document. Violations can be reported to the Federal Trade Commission (FTC) or the Consumer Financial Protection Bureau (CFPB), but evidence is required. These limitations do not apply to creditors who try to collect debts themselves. Students should consider what recourse a debtor has, including contacting the FTC, CFPB, or the phone company to file a complaint against the collection agency. Students' opinions will vary about contacting a debtor at work or calling a debtor's employer.

c. Students' answers will vary, but they should consider the expense and inconvenience for Top Value to go to small claims court. Students can brainstorm options, starting with the least invasive methods to the most aggressive actions a creditor can or should take to collect a debt.

DISCUSSION—CREDIT AND SMALL CLAIMS COURT

Ask students whether they think people in civil courts are entitled to a court-appointed attorney if they cannot afford to hire one themselves. Students may be confused about the right-to-counsel

guarantee in relation to debtors. The Sixth Amendment's guarantee of right to counsel applies only to criminal cases. The Constitution does not guarantee legal assistance in civil cases, though in some instances the federal government, through the federally funded Legal Services Corporation, or other local agencies may provide representation in civil cases.

ACTIVITY—TAKING A FIELD TRIP

Court action by creditors, especially for small debts, often takes place in small claims courts. A field trip to the small claims court in your area may help students understand the difficulties faced by some debtors as well as some creditors.

ACTIVITY—REVIEWING THE CHAPTER

Ask students to summarize (in list or bullet form) the main advice they would give others based on what they learned in this chapter. Have students post their lists around the classroom and then walk around and look at each others' lists.

NOTES

(1) *Truth in Lending Act*, 15 U.S.C. sections 1601 et seq. (1988).

(2) *Equal Credit Opportunity Act*, 15 U.S.C. sections 1691 et seq. (1988).

(3) *Fair Credit Reporting Act*, 15 U.S.C. sections 1681 et seq. (1982).

(4) U.S. Constitution, Article I, Section 8.

(5) 11 U.S.C.A. Sections 101 et seq., titled the *Bankruptcy Reform Act of 1978*.

(6) *Fair Debt Collection Practices Act*, 15 U.S.C. sections 1692 et seq. (1988).

The Student Edition also mentions several other consumer credit laws. They are:

- *The Electronic Funds Transfer Act*, 15 U.S.C. § 693a–1693s (2000).
- *The Fair Credit Billing Act*, 15 U.S.C. § 1666 (2000).
- *The Fair and Accurate Credit Transactions Act of 2003 (FACTA)*, Pub. L. No. 108–159, 117 Stat. 1953.
- *Wage Garnishment Act*, 15 U.S.C. § 1671–77 (2000).

Consumers make purchases and conduct business in a variety of ways—in person, over the phone, and online. Although most sellers are honest, some are not. Therefore, consumers should be aware of the possibility of deceptive sales practices. Door-to-door and telephone sales can involve high-pressure sales and smooth talk to get consumers to buy things they would otherwise not buy.

Advertising is everywhere and has become more persistent and intrusive in recent years. Although advertising is regulated by local, state, or federal laws, instances of puffing and illegal advertising still mislead consumers. Making purchases online presents consumers with potential pitfalls. Careful research and shopping practices can help consumers avoid problems caused by deceptive sales techniques.

TELEMARKETING SALES (PP. 284–285)

Learning Outcomes

After completing this section, students should be able to:

1. describe steps consumers can take to be sure they are buying from a trustworthy telemarketer;
2. define the term *telemarketing;* and
3. summarize how state laws and two federal agencies—the Federal Trade Commission and the Federal Communications Commission—protect consumers.

DISCUSSION—THE NATIONAL DO NOT CALL REGISTRY

Ask students whether they have ever received calls from telemarketers in their homes, where they work, or on their cell phones. Have they ever called a phone number they saw in a print or online advertisement? Have they ever bought anything from a telemarketer? Have they ever been the victim of a scam or suspected a scam artist was calling? Do students find calls from telemarketers useful, or do they consider them a nuisance?

Tell students that in 2003, after years of complaints from consumers, the federal government established the National Do Not Call Registry. The registry, run by the Federal Trade Commission (FTC) and the Federal Communications Commission (FCC), allows people to prevent most telemarketers from calling any phone numbers they register. The free registration process takes about five minutes and, following the *Do-Not-Call Improvement Act* of 2007, is effective permanently. For more information, refer students to www.donotcall.gov or 888-382-1222.

Remind students that many fraudulent schemes are conducted over the phone. Consumers should be particularly careful if a telephone salesperson asks for their credit card number. This person may not only fail to send you your order but may also make additional purchases using your credit card number. Identity theft (discussed in Chapter 10) is also a potential problem.

DOOR-TO-DOOR SALES (P. 286)

Learning Outcomes

After completing these sections, students should be able to:
1. Summarize the circumstances when the "cooling off" rule allows customers to cancel a contract to purchase something;
2. explain steps to take if you regret signing a contract with a door-to-door salesperson for more than $25.00; and
3. describe rules door-to-door sales people must follow.

DISCUSSION—DECEPTIVE SALES PRACTICES

There are special problems associated with door-to-door and telephone sales. These types of sales offer consumers no chance to comparison shop, and many people encounter high-pressure sales tactics and problems obtaining warranty service. To illustrate these problems, ask students the following questions:

- How are these sales situations different from a buyer-initiated encounter at a store?
- Is there some psychological coercion present in the home setting?
- Is there a need for a special law to regulate door-to-door sales?
- How do you feel about telephone solicitation?
- Should the law treat telephone solicitation sales and door-to-door sales the same?
- What kinds of consumers might be most vulnerable to the deceptive sales practices used by some telephone solicitors? (Explain that the elderly may be especially at risk as they may be lonely and also fearful of consequences if they refuse to listen to the solicitor's sales pitch.)

Note: Many students may have the mistaken idea that the three-day cancellation period applies to any contract. Make sure they understand that it is limited to contracts entered into away from the seller's place of business (e.g., door-to-door sales, sales parties, exhibitions, or "home shows"). The sale must be for more than $25. Some state laws extend the three-day cancellation period to other sales.

Encourage students to take the necessary steps to learn about the quality and reputation of products and those selling them before making a purchase.

Information on specific products is available from the Consumers Union (which publishes *Consumer Reports* magazine) at www.consumerreports.org and www.consumersunion.org.

Students can also contact the Better Business Bureau (BBB) to learn about companies that have had complaints filed against them. Access the BBB online at www.bbb.org.

BACKGROUND—SWEEPSTAKES

According to the U.S. Postal Service, consumers hoping to make a quick financial gain spend about $50 million each year in response to offers of instant wealth in magazines, on television, and over the phone. A common advertising technique is the use of sweepstakes. The lure of winning thousands or even millions of dollars is used by publishers and other companies to entice consumers to respond to their advertisements. Although people must be able to enter contests without buying anything, sweepstakes advertisements are skillfully designed to increase sales and benefit the company.

Companies that employ sweepstakes techniques must deliver exactly what is promised. Unethical companies often promise great prizes for a small fee; however, the products received are often not what were expected. Pseudo-sweepstake techniques include sending potential victims notice via letter, phone, or e-mail that they have already won a prize. All the winner has to do is call the company and confirm that he or she is the winner by providing a credit card number. The result is that large charges may later appear on the card for products the victim never purchased. These and other pseudo-sweepstake methods are illegal.

Carefully reading the rules of any promotion is the best way for consumers to protect themselves from fraudulent mail schemes. If no rules are included, the promotion is apt to be a sham. When a game of chance involves the food, retail, or gasoline industries, the FTC requires the following information to be disclosed:

- a list of prizes being offered;
- the retail value of the prizes;
- who is eligible to enter and who is excluded;
- how and when the winners will be notified;
- if the grand prize is cash, whether it is awarded over a period of years or all at once;

- when the contest begins and ends;
- odds of winning each prize;
- whether or not winners are expected to be part of an advertising campaign;
- a mailing address where people can write for a list of winners;
- when the drawing takes place; and
- whether or not taxes related to the prize are the responsibility of the winner.

Prior to entering a contest, consumers can call their local Better Business Bureau (BBB) to inquire about the legitimacy of a promotion and the company. Tell students they should contact their local post office or the BBB, if they or anyone they know have fallen victim to any kind of fraud.

Encourage students to bring in sweepstake offers they have received in the mail or have seen online. Have students examine the offers to determine whether or not the required information has been disclosed.

ADVERTISING AND THE CONSUMER (PP. 286–289)

Learning Outcomes

After completing this section, students should be able to:

1. distinguish between puffing and illegal advertisements;
2. describe circumstances in which the Federal Trade Commission may order corrective advertising;
3. identify restrictions the federal government has imposed on advertisements for liquor and tobacco; and
4. define the terms *substantiated, corrective advertising* and *puffing*.

CAPTION ANSWER (P. 287) Students' answers will vary. Encourage students to share their answers with the class.

LEGAL RESOURCE PERSONS

Invite someone who works for an advertising agency or a consumer advocacy group to describe how advertisements are designed and how the law affects—or should affect—advertising. Bring in ads from newspapers and magazines (in particular, ads targeting teens) or have students view ads online. Ask students to analyze them with the aid of the resource person.

ACTIVITY—TEEN SMOKING AND TEEN VAPING

Encourage students to learn more about the problem of teen smoking and vaping. Students should choose one issue related to the problem, conduct research about it, and present their findings to the class in an oral report.

Ample information about teen smoking and vaping is available on the Internet at:

- National Center for Tobacco-Free Kids at www.tobaccofreekids.org.
- The American Cancer Society at www.cancer.org, which provides information about cancer in English, Spanish, Chinese, Vietnamese, and Korean.

Since e-cigarettes hit the U.S. market in 2007, there has been significant debate over the effect of vaping and the appeal it has to teens. There are no federal regulations that limit how the makers of e-cigarettes can advertise. However, in 2016 the FDA finalized a rule extending restrictions on the advertisement and sale of tobacco products to e-cigarettes that contain tobacco as well. Consumer watchdog and health advocates concerned about any type of smoking claim advertisers are targeting teens. According to a study in Pediatrics magazine, there was a 256 percent increase in the number of television commercials about e-cigarettes between 2011 and 2013, and most of those commercials aired on cable shows popular with teens.[1]

Ask students to find advertisements for e-cigarettes. These could be ads that appear in print or online. Ask students to report on the messages that are obvious and more subtle in the ads. Do they appear to be targeting teens? In what ways? Where did they find the ads? On a television show, social media site, news outlet, or some other place? Is that a place teens are likely to be exposed to?

Then, ask students to look for credible research that indicates whether advertisements (in general—not just the ads they found) for e-cigarettes have increased the number of teen smokers. You may suggest the American Cancer Society's website at https://www.cancer.org/latest-news/report-more-and-more-teens-seeing-e-cigarette-ads.html, the FDA's website at https://www.fda.gov/tobacco-products/products-ingredients-components/vaporizers-e-cigarettes-and-other-electronic-nicotine-delivery-systems-ends or Campaign for Tobacco Free Kids website at https://www.tobaccofreekids.org/.

Finally, ask students to decide if they think there should be limits on advertising e-cigarettes to teen audiences. Students can complete a culminating project with a letter to their state and federal law makers recommending limits or recommending no limits on such ads.

Students' answers will vary depending on the advertisements brought to class. Use this problem to confirm the difference between illegal advertising and puffing. Remind students that consumers should not rely on the promises they see in advertisements.

ACTIVITY—ANALYZING ADVERTISEMENTS AIMED AT CHILDREN

Children's advertising has been an important issue in recent years. The Federal Trade Commission (FTC) at www.consumer.ftc.gov and groups such as the Parents Television Council at w2.parentstv.org contend that such ads entice children to ask for products (e.g., heavily sugared cereals) that are unhealthy choices. The advertisers claim that as long as it is not untrue, children's advertising is protected by the First Amendment. Under pressure from advertisers, Congress passed legislation in 1980 that allows FTC regulation of false or deceptive advertising. Any proposed regulation of children's advertising now must be passed directly by Congress.[2]

Ask students to analyze ads aired during cartoons or other television shows aimed at children. Students should examine the use of symbols, color, movement, and music. Ask students to also identify the emotional appeal of each ad. For example, does the ad suggest that the child will be more popular with peers? Does it imply that the child will feel more powerful if he or she owns the item? Does it suggest that he or she will have the physical capabilities of the action figure?

Ask students to write their own ads for specific toys or child-oriented products. They should present their findings in a written report. Have students use the following websites to conduct their research:

- National Association of Broadcasters at www.nab.org
- Children, Youth and Family Consortium at www.cyfc.umn.edu. This site includes addresses of television and cable networks and guidelines for writing letters of complaint about television advertising and programming aimed at children.
- Federal Communications Commission at www.fcc.gov
- Center for Media Literacy at www.medialit.org

a. To find laws regarding the sales of tobacco and e-cigarette in their state, students may use this interactive map at https://tobacco21.org/state-by-state/. Students may also search their state legislature's website using the key term *tobacco*.

For e-cigarette sales information by state visit the Public Health Law Center's website at https://www.publichealthlawcenter.org/resources/us-e-cigarette-regulations-50-state-review.

To see the progress of laws raising the age of tobacco sales and use to 21 years old visit the American Lung Association's website at https://www.lung.org/our-initiatives/tobacco/cessation-and-prevention/tobacco-21-laws.html.

b. Answers will vary, however students may offer the following as groups that would support such legislation:

American Lung Association, Campaign for Tobacco Free Kids, CDC, Tobacco 21, the FDA, and parents. Groups that might oppose the legislation are tobacco growers, tobacco products manufacturers and retailers, e-cigarette manufacturers and retailers, vape store owners and employees, tobacco and e-cigarette users between the ages of 18 and 21.

THE CASE OF...

Easy Money

a. The advance-fee loan described in this problem is an example of a fraud commonly perpetrated on consumers. Operators promise to issue a loan once a consumer pays a fee that ranges from $200 to $1,000. The operator takes the fee and disappears, never delivering the promised funds.

Clearly, the company is using deceptive advertising and appealing to consumers who are desperate to obtain money at a low cost. Because the operator never intends to deliver the loan, the whole proposal is a criminal fraud.

b. Consumers like the Johnsons should be alert to offers that seem too good to be true. When they encounter the phenomenon of "boiler room" operators—people operating from unidentified locations and/or organizations—they should be alert to the possibility of fraudulent practices.

Consumers should be particularly careful when they are in dire need of money and should only conduct business with lending institutions that can be verified by a consumer agency. They could have contacted the Better Business Bureau to inquire about complaints others may have made about Easy Money.

The Johnsons also could have requested written information from Easy Money, Inc., explaining the terms of the loan arrangement before sending their money order. In all likelihood, the Johnsons would never have received the requested information, thereby raising their suspicions.

c. The Johnsons could contact the FTC, which coordinates the efforts of local and state agencies to battle this type of fraud. They may also want to contact the local prosecutor's office to see whether the office is aware of these fraudulent activities. This is a clear case of criminal fraud. The office of the state's attorney general should also be notified.

States can fight this type of fraudulent practice by enhancing the penalty for these crimes. For example, 100 advance-fee companies operated in Florida until the state passed a law that made charging an advance fee for a loan a felony. As a result, most of the Florida operators shut down or moved to other states.

BAIT AND SWITCH (P. 290)

Learning Outcomes

After completing these sections, students should be able to:

1. explain the purpose of the bait and switch advertising and sales technique;
2. distinguish between bait and switch and loss leaders;
3. describe requirements online sellers must comply with under the *Mail Order Rule*; and
4. identify strategies consumers can use to protect themselves when they make purchases online.

BACKGROUND—BAIT AND SWITCH TECHNIQUES

Bait and switch is a commonly used technique, especially in stores selling big-ticket items such as major appliances, audio equipment, and televisions. The line between aggressive selling and bait and switch is not always clear. Stores commonly advertise loss leaders—items advertised at low prices in order to attract customers to the store. This practice is legal, and a salesperson who merely shows a customer a better-quality, more expensive item has not committed an illegal act. However, when the seller either disparages or has no supply of the advertised item and tries to switch the consumer to another product, then bait and switch has occurred, and the seller's actions are illegal.

Legal selling techniques having the effect of bait and switch can be very subtle. For example, one major appliance store purposely connected the inexpensive units (the advertised items) incorrectly so they provided poor reception; the expensive televisions had crystal-clear pictures and were located in a comfortable viewing room.

Tell students that while not required by law, rain checks are often offered by reputable stores for advertised items that they do not have in stock. The rain check allows the consumer to purchase the item at a later date for the advertised price.

PROBLEM 25.4 (p. 290)

a. The best way to handle an aggressive seller is to comparison shop at other stores. Tell the salesperson that if you need assistance, you will ask for help. Salespeople sometimes back off if you inform them that you are just looking and not planning to buy anything yet.

b. This appears to be a bait-and-switch situation. The salesperson has disparaged the advertised product and directed Kara and Aaron to a higher-priced product. If the product was simply a loss leader, the salesperson would not have "talked down" the advertised product. Kara and Aaron may have a right to buy the 250 cc cycle at the sale price if it was not advertised as being in limited supply.

c. Although Big Wheel may be engaging in puffing ("Come to Big Wheel for the Best Deals on the Slickest Wheels in Town!"), it is not illegal to sell the bike at a higher price than a competitor. Kara and Aaron should read the store's return policy to determine whether they can return the bike for any reason. If they can, and the bike has not been ridden, they may be able to return the bike and purchase the same model at the other store. Some merchants will give price adjustments to meet or beat a competitor's price, but they are not required to do so. If the store refuses to give them a refund or offer a price adjustment, then they are probably stuck with the bike they bought at the higher price.

INTERNET COMMERCE (PP. 291–292)

Learning Outcomes

After completing this section, students should be able to:

1. explain the online fraud of phishing;
2. describe the rights that buyers have if a seller does not ship within 30 days;
3. describe requirements online sellers must comply with under the Mail Order Rule; and
4. identify strategies consumers can use to protect themselves when they make purchases online from unscrupulous Internet-based merchants.

CAPTION ANSWER (P. 291) Consumers can protect themselves when making purchases online by getting the company's permanent, real-world location and address.

BACKGROUND—SAFETY AND THE INTERNET

In general, consumers should exercise the same caution in making purchases online as they would elsewhere. A consumer who makes an online purchase may be unable to later locate the vendor to return a defective product or to pursue a claim regarding a product ordered but never received. For these reasons it makes sense to make purchases from Internet sites that have established reputations. Established Internet sales sites can offer consumer protections such as guaranteed returns and refunds.

This topic provides an opportunity to raise a significant issue related to student safety. Discuss risks students may face as they surf the Internet, noting not only consumer issues addressed in Chapter 25 but personal risks as well. Students should be cautioned never to give their actual name, address, or phone number to anyone over the Internet unless they have initiated contact in order to make a purchase. Tell them that some adults pose as teens in order to lure teens into sexual or other exploitative relationships. Students should immediately inform a parent or another adult if they encounter any suspicious offers or inquiries online.

Consumers should be particularly skeptical when organizations reach out to them via email. Never give out personal information when responding to an email, no matter how authentic the email seems. Rather, go to the originating website to check to see if the request for information was valid. If the email is a "phishing" attempt, delete immediately. Never open attachments associated with such emails.

ACTIVITY—ANALYZING INTERNET ADS

Ask students to conduct an online search and analyze the advertising they encounter. Students should examine placement of ads, note whether they have to reject an offer (e.g., click "no thanks") in order to proceed further in their search, and note similarities and differences between online ads and ads on TV or in magazines.

PROBLEM 25.5 (p.292)

Direct students to a portal to online auction sites such as eBay or to the Federal Trade Commission's guide to auction buyers and sellers at www.consumer.ftc.gov.

REPAIRS AND ESTIMATES (P. 293)

Learning Outcomes

After completing this section, students should be able to:

1. identify problems consumers may face as they seek repairs and estimates; and
2. describe steps consumers should take to exercise caution as they seek repairs and get estimates.

BACKGROUND—AVOIDING AUTO REPAIR FRAUD

Auto repair fraud is one of the most common traps into which consumers can fall. Ask students to locate articles in local publications that rate repair shops. A local consumer protection agency may be able to refer students to such publications.

Students might also check to see if Angie's List (angieslist.com), Craig's List (www.craigslist.org/about/sites), or Consumer Checkbook (www.checkbook.org) serve their communities. These groups offer customer-to-customer referrals and reviews of a variety of service providers. Consumer Checkbook also publishes the results of surveys and consumer-related investigations conducted by professional researchers.

It might be helpful to bring some auto repair receipts into class so that students can become familiar with the language of the "mechanic's lien." A lien is a claim against property (in this case, the consumer's auto) which arises as a result of some legal obligation of the owner (here, to pay the mechanic).

Consumers should also note odometer readings when they drop off their car so they will be able to determine whether or not the car was test-driven to check the adequacy of the repair. Finally, most reputable repair shops provide a warranty on their work, usually lasting from 30 to 90 days. However, consumers will need to keep appropriate documentation (the work order, proof of payment, etc.) in order to enforce the warranty.

THE **CASE** OF...

The Costly Estimate

PROBLEM 25.6 (p. 293)

Nicole should have asked for a written estimate, and she should have directed the shop that no work be done if it would exceed the estimate. She may have some legal protection if the jurisdiction in which City Repair Shop is located has a repair and estimate law. If there is no such law, Nicole will have to pay the bill. If she fails to pay the bill, City Repair Shop will probably be able to keep the car until she does pay it, because most repair agreements include a mechanic's lien.

ACTIVITY—SUMMARIZING THE CHAPTER

To summarize the material covered in this chapter, have groups of students review the chapter and create a "Consumer Self-Defense Tactics" brochure detailing what every wise consumer should know. Students' brochures could be copied and made available to students outside of the Street Law class.

NOTES

(1) Glum, Julia. "Teens Smoking E-Cigarettes: Marketing May Be to Blame for Increase in Number of Vaping High School Students" *International Business Times.* November 14, 2014. http://www.ibtimes.com/teens-smoking-e-cigarettes-marketing-may-be-blame-increase-number-vaping-high-school-1724105 Accessed March 25, 2015.

(2) 15 U.S.C. sections 41–58 (1988).

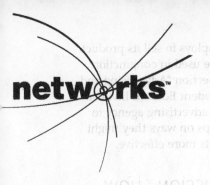

CHAPTER 26
Becoming a Smart Consumer

INFLUENCES ON CONSUMERS (PP. 294–296)

Understanding advertising techniques and how they influence shopping habits, knowing the difference between wanting and needing a product, and deciding whether one can afford the product all work together to make a smart consumer. In addition, learning about federal, state, and local laws that protect consumers enables people to find solutions to consumer problems. There are also practical steps to take before and after making a purchase that will help avoid or remedy consumer problems.

Learning Outcomes

After completing this section, students should be able to:
1. explain why sellers try to appeal to buyers' emotions through advertising; and
2. identify the advertising techniques of association, bandwagon, celebrity appeal, and claims of authorities.

PROBLEM 26.1 (p.295)

a.–c. This problem is designed to make students aware of their role as consumers and to introduce students to the forces that influence consumer decision making, such as advertising, peer pressure, and specific wants or needs. Online advertising has grown tremendously in the last decade. Many websites are funded entirely by online advertisements, and many online merchants create pop-up ads that appear when specific websites are opened by the consumer. The placement of these online ads is not random; rather, advertisers employ research methods to determine what websites their target audiences are visiting in order to reach the maximum number of people interested in their products and services. Students should also consider the benefits and drawbacks of researching consumer products online.

CAPTION ANSWER (P. 296) The use of celebrities in ads brings perceived style, glamour, and an implied endorsement by the celebrity to the ads and the products they are advertising. However, remind students that this does not necessarily mean the products are of high quality.

PROBLEM 26.2 (p.296)

a.–c. Students' answers will vary based on the ad they brought to class. Advertisers use market analysis to identify the type of consumer most likely to purchase their product or service and to find the best medium to reach potential consumers. Analysts investigate various types of media prior to placing an ad to determine the type of audience it reaches. Advertising strategies are designed to reach the greatest possible number of potential customers. Traditionally, television ads directed at teens appear during prime-time programming and after-school hours. Household products are usually advertised on television during the daytime to reach homemakers, whereas children's toys are advertised primarily during children's programming and Saturday morning cartoons. In addition, many adult education training programs are advertised during daytime hours to reach

Consumer Law   **217**

unemployed individuals. However, now that many people watch recorded or streaming television and movies on their phones or computers, the time of day is less of a factor. So, advertisers focus more on who would watch that show at any time.

d. Although answers will vary according to the product or service selected, relevant information would include the usefulness, cost, and any warranties offered. Many television advertisements created by manufacturers do not include the price because it may vary from seller to seller. Consumers may gather further information about the product or service by calling the appropriate retail stores, asking others who have purchased the product or service whether they are satisfied, and reading consumer reporting magazines.

e. Ads employ a variety of techniques to encourage or manipulate consumers to purchase the advertised product or service, including scientific research, appeals to authorities, and consumer surveys. Other ads appeal to emotion by implying that a product or service will elicit a specific emotion or reaction in others. Some ads use famous spokespeople to endorse a product. The promise of popularity, health, safety, wealth, success, good looks, and sex appeal are also used to sell products or services. The Student Edition provides additional details about these techniques.

Point out any sexist language or images evident in ads directed at men or women. Ads aimed at male audiences often portray men as being powerful, rough, and rugged, while women are depicted as attractive sex objects or as being submissive and dependent on men. Ask if students have encountered ads they find demeaning or offensive. Do ads help to perpetuate sex role stereotypes or do they merely reflect society's common attitudes?

f. Encourage students to consider the products that they often buy or would most like to buy and evaluate how advertising shapes their wish list. They may even want to conduct their own "market research" to find out what products appeal to other students their age. A little research about the advertising business can show them how their strategies compare to those of professionals.

Organize students into groups of three to five students to collaborate on this task. Give groups time to create a television advertisement for a product. After each group presents its ad to the class, have the remaining students identify the

techniques the group employs to sell its product. This activity could also be used in conjunction with Chapter 25, in the section "Advertising and the Consumer" of the Student Edition. Invite a resource person from an advertising agency to offer suggestions to groups on ways they might make their advertisements more effective.

ACTIVITY AND DISCUSSION—HOW DOES ADVERTISING AFFECT CONSUMERS?

Ask students to carefully examine advertisements aimed at teens as well as advertisements for tobacco, beer, and liquor. As students analyze the different elements of those advertisements, ask them the following questions:

- What does the physical environment in the ad look like?
- In what way is it appealing?
- What makes the people in the ad attractive?
- Examine their clothing and facial expressions. Do the men appear to be macho? Are the women made to look sexy?
- Is there an implication of fun or rebelliousness within the group? How do the people in the ad appear to be relating to each other?
- Does the ad imply that the product will produce fun, happiness, or romance?
- Is there any suggestion (beyond any required warnings) that it is risky to use this product?

Ask students to describe how ads manipulate teenagers and how they feel about being the targets of manipulation. What specific characteristics common among teens do advertisers exploit (e.g., the desire for independence, the desire to be different, especially from adults)? To what extent do students consider substance abuse problems among teens as being a product of such advertisements? To what extent do advertisements featuring thin people contribute to problems with self-image, self-esteem, and eating disorders among people of all sizes?

Students might also wish to debate the tension between the First Amendment right to free speech and the need of society to protect vulnerable citizens from being manipulated. Ask whether it is appropriate that banners advertising alcoholic beverages be displayed in the background of televised basketball games and other sporting events. Would it be appropriate for the government to ban such sponsorships? Would it be appropriate for the government to limit the ways in which sponsors display their products and logos?

CONSUMER PROTECTION (PP. 297–300)

Learning Outcomes

After completing this section, students should be able to:

1. describe the purpose and powers of the Federal Trade Commission (FTC) and the Consumer Product Safety Commission (CPSC);
2. name and explain several federal laws designed to protect consumers;
3. describe remedies consumers can seek in order to stop unfair and deceptive sales practices; and
4. define the terms *class action*, *remedy*, *cease and desist order*, *consent decree*, and *restitution*.

DISCUSSION—FEDERAL PROTECTION FOR CONSUMERS IN HISTORY AND ECONOMICS

Ask students to recall from their studies of American history the consequences for consumers of laissez-faire policies during the industrial era. Discuss the meaning of the phrase *caveat emptor*, (let the buyer beware) and ask students to what extent this is an adequate means of protecting consumers. To make clear why the federal government began acting to protect consumers, read a selection from Upton Sinclair's *The Jungle*. Students might also debate the appropriate balance between promoting a market economy and the need to protect consumers. How much regulation is too much? What kinds of costs do producers and consumers face because of regulation? What are its advantages? What kinds of costs might we face following deregulation? What are advantages of deregulation?

DISCUSSION, SURVEY ACTIVITY AND RESEARCH—REGULATIONS REQUIRING NUTRITION LABELS

As mentioned on page 297 of the Student Edition, the federal government now requires that chain restaurants provide calorie information on their menus. Ask students if they pay attention to the calorie information they see and if it makes a difference in the choices they make at chain restaurants. Ask them to predict if there is evidence to

prove that the regulations have changed other consumers' habits. Help students develop a poll to gather data from friends and family members. Once the information is gathered, have them analyze their data and compare it to data they find published by the government or from reputable news sources.

CAPTION ANSWER (P. 297) The *Nutrition Labeling and Education Act* requires that all food labels list ingredients and nutritional information to help consumers make more informed dietary choices by considering serving size, calories, percentage of suggested daily value of vitamins, sodium, fat, and more.

DELIBERATION

Should we further regulate unhealthy foods and drinks? (pp. 298–299)

An overview of the deliberation method is discussed in the front of this Teacher Manual. For free deliberation materials, student handouts, and an instructional video visit https://store.streetlaw.org/deliberations/.

If this is your first deliberation, consider devoting significant time to establishing norms for deliberations and civil discourse. Introduce the process of deliberations, including careful reading, clarification, preparing and presenting initial positions, reversing positions, free small group discussion, search for common ground, and whole-class discussion.

Begin class by introducing the deliberation issue: further government regulation of unhealthy foods and drinks. Ask students how they make decisions about what they choose to eat and drink? Do they consider the potential health effects of their choices? Would they make different choices if the price of those items was significantly higher? Would they be upset if the government made it more difficult to purchase items it deemed "unhealthy"? Explain to students that this deliberation will help students explore to what extent the government should regulate unhealthy food and beverage choices. Students will strive to reach consensus on some aspect of the issue, but are not required to agree on an answer to the deliberation question.

Take students through the deliberation steps as outlined in the front of this Teacher Manual.

Debrief by instructing students to:
- Raise your hands if you changed your position on the issue.
- Raise your hand if you considered a new opinion that you had not considered before today.

- Raise our hand if you felt listened to during the deliberation.
- Follow up by asking students, how they might translate this activity to conversations outside the classroom.

Consider having students perform a self-assessment on the process and their contribution to it.

For the most recent information on government regulation of foods and beverages, see the following suggested resources:

- Tax Foundation – State taxes on candy bars and soda by state. (https://taxfoundation.org/sales-taxes-on-soda-candy-and-other-groceries-2018/)
- Center for Disease Control and Prevention – "State and Local Programs" https://www.cdc.gov/nccdphp/dnpao/state-local-programs/index.html
- The Tax Policy Center – "The State of State (and Local) Tax Policy" https://www.taxpolicycenter.org/briefing-book/how-do-state-and-local-soda-taxes-work

DISCUSSION—CLASS ACTION SUITS

Describe circumstances in which a class action suit might be used to remedy consumer grievances. Some examples include suits by dieters and athletes who used ephedra products and consumers who had defective automobile tires. Ask students to identify the advantages and disadvantages of bringing a lawsuit collectively rather than individually. Students might also identify groups, such as manufacturers, who might oppose such suits, as well as those who believe consumers should have this remedy as an option. Interested students should look into the role of class action suits in controversies related to the Legal Services Corporation, a government-subsidized organization that provides free or low-cost legal representation to Americans who otherwise could not afford it.

Investigating the Law Where You Live

(p. 300) Students can use search terms "consumer action agencies" paired with the name of the student's city, town, county, or state to find information suggested in this feature. To find out which consumer protection activities are handled by the state's attorney general, students can simply use the search term "attorney general" preceded by the name of their state, or they can search www.usa.gov/directory/stateconsumer/index.shtml.

PROTECTING YOUR RIGHTS AS A CONSUMER (PP. 300–309)

Learning Outcomes

After completing this section, students should be able to:

1. describe what consumers should consider (besides the list price) when they comparison shop;
2. list steps consumers should take before signing a contract;
3. describe steps consumers should take if they have purchased defective products;
4. describe characteristics of effective oral and written consumer complaints; and
5. name government and private groups that consumers can contact to learn about methods used to resolve consumer problems.

PROBLEM 26.4 (p 300)

A good way to approach this problem would be to ask pairs of students to quickly brainstorm lists of things that they would want to know before buying the bicycle and where they could get the information. Post each pair's ideas on the board.

Before buying the bike, students should want to know how long the bicycle can be expected to last; how to take care of it; where to take it for service or repair; whether parts and repairs will be available along the route they expect to take on their bike trip; how much the bicycle costs; and whether or not it has an express warranty. The Student Edition also emphasizes the importance of finding a seller with a good reputation for price and service. In addition, consumers should inquire about the terms and duration of any warranty.

In this case, the purchaser would want to compare the listed prices at two or more local bicycle shops. Students may wish to research buying the bicycle direct from the manufacturer's website, but then need to consider the shipping and handling costs as well as potential assembly costs. He or she could talk to salespeople to find out when the items might go on sale. Dealers could provide valuable information on what types of bicycles would be most appropriate for a trip across the state. The consumer should also ask whether the dealer will service the bicycle and, if so, for how long.

Students can find useful product comparisons and information through the Consumers Union (www.consumersunion.org), in *Consumer Reports* magazine (www.consumerreports.org), or in *Consumer's Bulletin*. Consumers can also find product information by contacting the dealer or manufacturer of the product directly, as well as through industry magazines and websites that offer customer ratings or "expert" comparisons. (Students should evaluate how neutral or objective any source is that rates consumer products.) Federal, state, and local government agencies also provide information on many goods and services.

ACTIVITY—COMPARISON SHOPPING

To help students practice comparison shopping, ask them to design a "basket of goods" study. Ask students to brainstorm a list of 10 or 15 commonly purchased grocery store items.

Explain that the size and quality of the items must be specified in order to do the study. Tell students they should use unit prices where size and quantity are not identical. Students should visit a variety of grocery stores (major chains, warehouse or wholesale stores, independent stores, small neighborhood stores, and 24-hour convenience stores) in a variety of neighborhoods (urban, suburban, rural) if possible to obtain prices for each item in the basket. In a class discussion, students can determine which stores appear to provide the lowest prices. Ask students why they think prices are different at different types of stores and in different neighborhoods. Ask students to develop hypotheses to explain the differences.

CAPTION ANSWER (P. 301) Consumers should always compare prices and products before buying a big-ticket item such as a camera. In addition, a smart consumer should read and understand the warranty before making a final decision.

THE **CASE** OF...

The Cheap Vacation Home

PROBLEM 26.5 (p.303)

a. The Cole family could have researched the company through the Better Business Bureau and checked with their state's office of consumer affairs. No one should ever buy property without inspecting it and reviewing public records for the title. They also could have requested printed literature on the seller and the property. Consumers should never give out their credit card number on a phone call initiated by an unknown seller.

b. Possible remedies include criminal prosecution for consumer fraud, a cease and desist order, a consent decree with the seller, and/or restitution. Depending upon the number of injured consumers, a class action suit possibly could be brought against the seller.

c. Organize students into groups to draft the law. Ask groups to first brainstorm what the law might say or require. Their ideas will vary, but may include a provision that prohibits sales over a certain amount of money by phone or require phone solicitors to register with a government agency designed to investigate consumer fraud. The law could also call for a required cooling-off period.

CAPTION ANSWER (P. 304) When returning an item, the consumer should identify the item, present the receipt, give the date and location of purchase, describe when and how the problem with the item arose, and explain how he or she would like the problem resolved.

PROBLEM 26.6 (p.305)

Before students complete this problem, review the suggestions for writing a consumer letter of complaint listed on pages 302–303 in the Student Edition.

a. This role-play is designed to teach students the skill of making a verbal complaint and negotiating a solution. For purposes of the role-play, assume that the Burts received no written warranty from the seller. As students learned in Chapter 23, the law implies a warranty of merchantability—that the item will be of at least ordinary quality—in every commercial sale.

The Burts should be polite but firm in their demand for a TV that works. They might say they had heard that Tally's was a reliable store and that if they are not helped they will have to take other action. How they deal with Mr. Foxx should be analyzed to determine the most effective tactics. Students should also analyze whether or not the way Mr. Foxx responds is best for the reputation of the store in the community. Most businesses care about this, and some follow the philosophy that "the customer is always (or at least usually) right."

b. If Mr. Foxx refuses to help, the Burts could write to the president of the company that manufactured the television. They should send a certified letter and should keep a copy for themselves. The Burts' letter should include the date on which they bought the TV; whether it was new or used; its brand, description, serial and model numbers, and cost; whether or not there were any guarantees; what happened to the picture tube; their efforts to redress the problem (including a copy of the service mechanic's repair estimate and a description of their meeting with Mr. Foxx); and the remedy or remedies they are seeking. The Burts should also note that they expect a television of ordinary quality to last longer than a few weeks. They might also consider sending copies of the letter to regulatory enforcement agencies. A sample letter is shown in **26.1 TM Figure** on the next page.

c. They could contact the manufacturer by phone. If they are still unsuccessful, they could contact consumer groups, consumer protection agencies, and the media, which sometimes can negotiate complaints for consumers. A final resort might be to contact an attorney or consider going to small claims court.

CAPTION ANSWER (P. 306) Students' answers will vary. They may volunteer that they have used online consumer product reports such as www.consumerreports.org/.

Investigating the Law Where You Live

(p. 306) Students will find the Better Business Bureau at www.bbb.org. From this link, they can enter their zip code and find local bureaus.

ACTIVITY—FIELD TRIP OR CLASSROOM VISIT

Plan a visit to the local office of the Federal Trade Commission (FTC) or the office of a state or local consumer protection agency. Students should prepare questions in advance. Those questions might include:

- How can this agency or office help consumers?
- What kinds of complaints are received by the office?
- What is the most common type of complaint?
- How long does it take to process a complaint?
- What can consumers do to make it more likely their claim will be resolved successfully?

If a field trip is not possible, invite resource persons from these agencies could also to visit the class. Find out what, if any, consumer education literature is available from these agencies. In many instances, you can obtain free class sets of some items.

CAPTION ANSWER (P. 307) State licensing boards set rules and standards for the occupation, prepare and give licensing and certification exams, issue or deny licenses, and handle complaints from consumers.

ACTIVITY—"CONSUMER HELP" COLUMN

Students might coordinate with the school newspaper sponsor and staff to write a "consumer help" column for the school newspaper, develop a list of important consumer phone numbers for the school paper, or create and distribute their own consumer newsletter.

Note: Remind students that any written criticism of merchants must be based on fact, or they could face possible libel action.

PROBLEM 26.7 (p.308)

a.–c. This problem requires students to conduct independent research on a service in their community. Students should use resources listed in the Student Edition, as well as the telephone, the library, and the Internet, to help them find the information. Have students share their findings with the class.

ACTIVITY—UNDERSTANDING CONSUMERS' OPTIONS

Use this exercise to further students' understanding of the various organizations and services available to disgruntled consumers. Although it is designed to test student comprehension of federal agency descriptions in the text, state and local agencies may also be helpful in handling some of these problems. Ask students how they would handle each of the problems described. Have them identify which agencies or organizations would be able to help and what types of assistance the agencies would provide. Please note that the answers suggested here list only pertinent federal agencies.

1. You become ill after eating a can of tuna purchased from a local supermarket. You know several friends who also became ill from eating this particular brand of tuna. You protest to the supermarket, but they do nothing. *You should contact the Food and Drug Administration (www.fda. gov). The FDA is responsible for regulating the safety of food and drugs.*
2. You apply for a charge account at a local department store. You are over 21 and have a good job

26.1 TM Figure

December 1, 2020

Ms. Emily Featherstone, President BTR
Television Corporation
42 Forest Avenue
Paramus, New Jersey 07652

Dear Ms. Featherstone:

During the second week of October 2020, we purchased one of your 42-inch color television sets at Tally's Electronics Shop, an authorized BTR dealer. We paid the $1,000 purchase price in full (see the attached copy of my canceled check). Mr. Foxx, the salesperson there, told us that we would be pleased with our new purchase.

Around Thanksgiving, the set completely lost the picture while watching the Thanksgiving Day parade the picture became so blurry that we had to shut off the set. Appliance Repair, Inc., advised us that the power supply had malfunctioned and repairs would cost $600 (see attached copy of their November 30 estimate).

We returned to Tally's Electronics Shop on November 30 and spoke with Mr. Foxx. At that time he refused to either repair or replace the set, telling us that the store had made no warranties and could not help us.

In initially selecting a BTR television, we had relied on our prior experience with a BTR (which was virtually trouble-free for six years) and on your extensive nationwide advertising. It seems to us that in good faith you should either repair or replace the set or refund the purchase price. Surely a television of ordinary quality should NOT break after just two months of use.

As you can see from the list of organizations that have received copies of this letter, we are prepared to pursue this matter further. If we do not hear from you within ten days, we will assume that you refuse to stand behind your product, and we will be forced to proceed with further action.

Sincerely,

Jeff and Kristin Burt
1415 16th Street, N.W.
Washington, DC 20011

cc: Tally's Electronics Shop
George Washington University Consumer Help Washington
Star News Action Line
Better Business Bureau

but are turned down anyway. You receive no reason for the rejection. *The Federal Trade Commission (www.consumer.ftc.gov) and the Consumer Financial Protection Bureau (CFPB)(www. consumerfinance.gov) handle credit-related problems. There may also be a local agency which could handle* this problem. *If a similar problem had arisen in connection with a bank credit card, the consumer should complain to the Federal Reserve Bank.Consumers are entitled to the reasons why they are being denied credit.*

3. You buy a new set of radial tires. Three weeks later, one of them blows out. You run off the road, causing minor damage to your car. The dealer offers to replace the tire, but you are not satisfied. *The National Transportation Safety Board (www.ntsb.gov) might be helpful since they set standards for vehicle safety. You could also contact local consumer agencies. Again, to receive damages you would have to bring a civil suit.*

4. You buy some furniture on a time payment plan. When you get your first bill, you discover the total cost of the payments is over $850, while the price of the furniture was only $700. You call the seller and they tell you that the interest amounts to 20 percent a year. You would not have bought the furniture on the merchant's credit plan had you known it would cost so much. *Contact the Federal Trade Commission, since it appears that you were not fully informed about the full cost. The FTC is concerned with all unfair trade practices. Though the FTC may be able to end the practice, you may have to file a separate case in state court to get the money returned (if you paid the total bill). If the interest charges violated your state's usury law, you should contact the local prosecutor's office.*

CAPTION ANSWER (P. 309) The United States Postal Service investigates mail fraud and other mail problems.

PROBLEM 26.8 (p.309)

a. On the local and state level, the Consumer Protection Agency or Consumer Affairs Bureau may be helpful in advising you regarding safety measures. At the federal level, you may want to contact either the Office of Consumer Affairs or the Consumer Product Safety Commission for information relating to exercise bikes. Remember, it is always a good idea to call your local Better Business Bureau before making a major purchase. They would have information relating to complaints by previous customers regarding retailers in your area or particular products.

b. The Department of Transportation's Office of Aviation Enforcement and Proceedings (www.dot.gov/airconsumer) handles complaints involving overbooking or bumping.

c. The Office of Consumer Affairs and the Consumer Product Safety Commission should be able to provide relevant information or lead you to an appropriate source. Business, trade, and professional associations may also prove helpful.

d. Federal-level organizations such as the Federal Trade Commission may be helpful because they monitor false advertising. The Better Business Bureau, the local chamber of commerce, or the state consumer protection agency (in the office of the state's attorney general) may have information about these claims made by the vocational school.

DIRECT ACTION BY CONSUMERS AND TAKING YOUR CASE TO COURT (PP. 310–313)

Learning Outcomes

After completing these sections, students should be able to:

1. describe examples of direct action taken by consumers to influence an organization's business practices;
2. distinguish between criminal and civil consumer complaints;
3. compare the advantages and disadvantages of taking your claim to a small claims court versus a civil court;
4. identify procedures consumers should follow to file a suit in small claims court; and
5. define the term *direct action*.

DISCUSSION—TYPES OF DIRECT ACTION

As the Student Edition points out, there are many types of direct action that consumers can take. A good method of discussing each would be to pose a problem such as "Apartheid in South Africa," where a government discriminated against all citizens who were nonwhite and gave the worst treatment to those who were of African descent. Ask students to discuss each method of direct action and how it might be used in this situation.

- **Letter-writing campaigns:** *Letter-writing campaigns were used extensively during apartheid as people around the world wrote letters to their own governments, often asking them to impose sanctions against South Africa; to the South African government, asking for change including the freeing of Nelson Mandela; and to corporations, threatening to boycott them unless they pulled out of South Africa or at least used nondiscriminatory practices with workers in South Africa.*

- **Boycotts of goods produced in South Africa:** *Boycotts could be started by individual citizens or come in the form of a sanction against South Africa in which South African goods could not be imported into the country.*

- **Press conferences:** *Press conferences were used by the U.S. government in announcing sanctions or otherwise trying to pressure South Africa. Anti-apartheid groups also used press conferences to pressure the South African government. At the same time, the South African government used press conferences to defend its actions.*

- **Picketing or other types of demonstrations:** *Demonstrations were used extensively by anti-apartheid groups in the United States and other countries. They often targeted South African embassies and consulates and corporations doing business in South Africa.*

CAPTION ANSWER (P. 310) Consumers may be concerned about workers in sweatshops because low wages and dangerous working conditions often characterize these facilities.

CAPTION ANSWER (P. 311) Criminal fraud occurs when a salesperson or a consumer knowingly misstates or misrepresents some important fact with the intent to defraud another party, resulting in harm.

BACKGROUND—LOCAL CIVIL COURTS

In some large cities, the time lapse between filing a complaint and the beginning of the trial may be a year or more. The clerk of your court can give you this information for your jurisdiction. If there is a long time lapse, ask students how they might weigh the relative merits of bringing a civil suit as a means of remedying a consumer complaint.

ACTIVITY—TAKING A FIELD TRIP

Arrange for the class to visit a local small claims court. Contact the clerk of the court before the visit and obtain copies of the complaint form for your students to examine.

Before visiting the court, have students read the *Steps to Take* feature "Taking Your Complaint to Small Claims Court" in the Student Edition. This feature outlines for students the steps involved in filing a suit in small claims court. Ask students to identify the purpose of various sections of the form and then to comment on how easy or difficult it is to use. On the day of the field trip, ask the judge to spend a few minutes speaking with students. Discuss the following issues:

- Are attorneys allowed?
- What is the filing fee?
- How complicated is the paperwork?
- How long is the delay from filing the paperwork to court date?
- What is the largest sum of money that can be claimed?
- What happens if the loser refuses to pay what the judge ordered?
- Ask students whether the rules of the court seem fair and whether or not they seem designed to make this small claims court a "People's Court."

TAKING ACTION: LAW AND DEMOCRACY

Mock Trial: *James Phillips* v. *The Sound Shop*

PROBLEM 26.10 (p. 313)

a. The law involved in the mock trial is the implied warranty of merchantability. The effect of the mock trial will be heightened if James has a sales slip and a broken wireless earbuds to use as props. For further information on classroom mock trials, see *Street Law's Classroom Guide to Mock Trials and Moot Courts,* as well as the *FYI* feature "Steps in a Trial" in the Student Edition.

b. If students did not notice, point out that lawyers were not involved in this process. Ask students to consider whether the absence of lawyers improved the effectiveness of the process. Students may connect the absence of lawyers with the ability to constrain costs and simplify proceedings. Ask students to explain their reasons to support their opinions about whether this process is the most effective.

NOTE

(1) *The Federal Hazardous Substances Act,* Public Law 103–267, (1994).

networks™

BUYING A CAR (PP. 314–319)

Buying a car, renting a place to live, paying for college, and purchasing health insurance are four of the most important purchases students are likely to make. The credit history that young people establish through these transactions will be relevant for many years. Student loans are a special kind of credit and a common way to pay for college. Student loans are often the first encounter young people have with credit. Therefore, students must be aware of the complicated legal issues associated with these major purchases. Concepts already studied in this unit—contracts, warranties, comparison shopping, credit, and others—apply here as well.

Learning Outcomes

After completing this section, students should be able to:

1. describe five factors consumers should consider when purchasing an automobile;
2. list the costs of owning a car besides the purchase price of the car;
3. list questions borrowers should be able to answer before they finance the purchase of a car;
4. illustrate how interest rates (annual percentage rate) and terms of loans can affect the total finance charge and the total cost of a car;
5. compare the benefits of leasing a car to those of buying a car; and
6. describe what to do and what not do if you are involved in a car accident.

LEGAL RESOURCE PERSONS

Numerous people could help co-teach this chapter. Consider inviting local insurance agents, consumer advocates, loan officers, car dealers, car safety experts, attorneys, judges who hear small claims cases, motor vehicle representatives, and credit counselors to enliven and personalize the material throughout the chapter.

CAPTION ANSWER (P. 315) The "Buyer's Guide" window sticker—required by the Federal Trade Commission to be posted in all used cars—describes any warranty information for the car.

RESEARCH—FUEL EFFICIENCY, COST, AND POLLUTION

The Department of Energy's website at www.fueleconomy.gov allows consumers to research how cars impact the environment. Their database includes cars, vans, pick-up trucks, and SUVs being sold as new, as well as vehicles sold as new as far back as 1985. The site also allows buyers to do side-by-side comparisons of vehicles to see how they compare in their miles per gallon (fuel efficiency), estimated cost to drive, carbon footprint, and EPA pollution score. It is an excellent resource for consumers who are mindful of the environment and attentive to the costs of filling their vehicles.

DISCUSSION—HOW DOES THE LAW AFFECT AUTOMOBILE CONSUMERS?

Have students work individually to brainstorm a list of areas in which the law affects consumers who purchase automobiles (e.g., contracts, warranties, remedies for a defective automobile, insurance, licensing, registration, sales tax, personal property tax, gas tax, repairs, etc.). Discuss students' responses as a class and create a master list on the board. If students have difficulty identifying laws, encourage them to scan the textbook's table of contents and this chapter in particular to look for laws and regulations mentioned in the text. For example, in the Student Edition, students will find the *Truth in Lending Act*[1] and the *Consumer Leasing Act*[2].

ACTIVITY—IDENTIFYING THE BEST BUY

Ask students to identify three examples of new cars they would like to own. Then have them conduct research to complete a five-column chart on which they record data for each car about safety, price, quality, warranty, and fuel economy. Students might add columns for other criteria they consider important as well. Tell students to assume that their budgets are limited. Once they have completed their research, have students write a brief report about the car they conclude is the best buy. This activity could be done in conjunction with the activity in Chapter 17, in which students are asked to compare the costs of insuring various types of cars.

Remind students that when they are negotiating for the "best buy" or best price, they should carefully consider the vehicle's "options"—items that dealers often offer just before purchasers sign contracts. Students should ask themselves whether options such as undercoating, special floor mats, and other various appearance packages are truly worth the additional costs. Buyers should not be afraid to ask for more time to consider the options so they can avoid last-minute decisions they may regret. Or, better yet, before car buyers ever walk into a showroom or sales lot, they could research the various options that are available and the dealer's costs for those options. That prior knowledge may help buyers avoid impulse purchases.

PROBLEM 27.1 (p.316)

Costs to consider when purchasing a car include registration and tags, insurance, gas and oil, tune-ups, taxes, and inspection fees. Your state

department of transportation or Bureau of Motor Vehicles can give information on the fees for registration, tags, inspection, routine emissions tests required in some states, and license. Car insurance companies can provide information on the cost of insurance. The dealership or private mechanics can describe the cost of an oil change, tune-up, and maintenance. Gas prices are clearly posted at gas stations, but fluctuate widely over time.

BACKGROUND—CONSUMER RESOURCES

In order to successfully negotiate the price of a car, tell students it is useful to know the dealer's profit margin. Profit margin information on many new cars is available from guides such as *Edmund's New Car Prices* and *Buyer's Guide Reports*. Both are usually available at bookstores. Another source is *Consumer Reports* magazine (typically in the April issue), available in any library and at www.consumerreports.org. Most banks and credit unions also have used-car pricing guides. The American Automobile Association (AAA) provides concise resources at www.aaa.com to help people buy and sell their cars.

To compare insurance rates and to avoid becoming a victim of an automobile insurance scam, purchasers should review the materials on the websites of AAA at www.aaa.com, using the search term "car insurance scams," and the National Highway Traffic Safety Administration (NHTSA) at www.nhtsa.gov using the search term "vehicles and equipment." Students can also learn how to avoid becoming the victim of odometer fraud on the same NHTSA site using the search term "odometer fraud."

Ask students to review the steps consumers should take if something they purchased is defective. (For additional background, review Chapter 26.) In the case of defective automobiles, the Center for Auto Safety recommends several courses of action for car owners:

- Try to find out if other owners of this make and model car have had the same problem.
- Save all repair bills. If the manufacturer is forced to accept liability, receipts will enable you to collect reimbursement.
- Contact your state attorney general, inform the staff of the problem, and request that action be taken.
- Ask the Better Business Bureau (www.bbb.org) to arbitrate your claim. If the outcome is not legally binding, you may reject the decision and go to court.

- Consider going to small claims court to recover repair costs, car rental fees, and other expenses related to the defects.
- Write to your state senator or state representative to ensure that the FTC and the NHTSA are acting on the complaint you filed.

BACKGROUND—EXTENDED WARRANTIES

Sometimes it is not necessary to purchase an extended warranty when buying a car. Consumers should always read the factory warranty prior to entering into an extended warranty agreement. Generally, extended warranties will reimburse the car owner for towing, car rental, and other related expenses. Extended warranties can be classified as either a Vehicle Services Contract (VSC) or Mechanical Breakdown Insurance (MBI). Usually, auto dealers offer VSCs. With this type of warranty, the dealer agrees to repair or replace specific mechanical parts on the auto if they fail. An MBI, however, is typically offered by an insurance company. This warranty is the same as or better than a VSC and costs considerably less. Moreover, MBIs offer the consumer more protection than most VSCs in the event that the seller of the warranty becomes insolvent.

THE **CASE** OF...

The Used-Car Purchase

PROBLEM 27.2 (p.317)

a. Sasha should have thought about how much she could afford to pay for the car (total price and monthly payment), how much insurance would cost, what the most economical means of financing the car would be, and how she would pay for the finance charges. She also should have researched what kind of car would be best by looking at *Consumer Reports* and asking other knowledgeable people.

b. She should have had an independent mechanic inspect the car, and she should have test-driven the car. She also should have found out the interest rate, finance charges, and possible penalties on the loan, the cost of the insurance, as well as whether she would be provided with a written warranty.

c. The seller promised her a 30-day or 10,000-mile warranty (whichever came first) and a sale price

of $3,500. His statement that it was an "excellent car" that would give Sasha "many years of good service" was puffing.

d. The advantage of dealer financing and insurance is convenience, but sometimes financing and insurance can be less expensive if obtained elsewhere.

e. In this case, the warranty provided does not necessarily make this a better deal. Most states have laws that hold dealers responsible if they do not meet reasonable quality standards. Because the car was not sold "as is," Sasha would be well within her rights to return the car for repairs 30 days after purchase even without a warranty.

PROBLEM 27.3 (p.318)

a. 24-month term = $7,317.52
36-month term = $7,473.88
48-month term = $7,632.64

If students calculate a different number than these, remind them Nathan made a $1,000 down payment which must be included in the total cost of the car.

b. The 24-month credit arrangement is the least expensive in the long run. He will pay a little more each month, but the total cost will be less. However, the arrangement that is most desirable depends upon such factors as his income and the monthly payment he can best afford.

Ask students how much more Nathan will pay altogether if he takes a 48-month loan instead of a 36-month loan. *He will pay $158.76 more.* What if he takes a 48-month loan instead of a 24-month loan? *He will pay $315.12 more.* Ask students to assume they are facing the same options as Nathan. Would having lower monthly payments be worth the difference in the overall cost of the car? *Students' answers will vary.*

Investigating the Law Where You Live

(p. 318) Every state has an agency or department that issues drivers licenses and plates. They are usually called the Department of Motor Vehicles or something similar. If students have difficulty finding out the procedures they must follow to register a car and to obtain license plates in their community, you might suggest an Internet search that combines the terms "motor vehicles" and the name of their state. From that search, students should be able to find links to help them.

ACTIVITY—STEPS TO TAKE IN THE EVENT OF AN AUTO ACCIDENT

Have students read the *Steps to Take* feature "What to Do in the Event of an Auto Accident" in the Student Edition.

After students have read the feature and identified reasons for each of the steps in it, use the following activity to reinforce what students should and should not do in these circumstances. Read the following account to the class and then ask students to complete the steps that follow.

On a winter's evening after dinner, your car is hit in the right rear fender. The accident occurred as you proceeded through an intersection on a yellow light. No one seems to be injured. In speaking with the driver of the other car, you notice that his eyes are bloodshot.

1. Make a list of all the information about this accident that you would need in order to make a thorough report. *This question is designed to stimulate thinking about the various questions and issues that drivers should be aware of after an accident. In addition to the information listed in the* Steps to Take *feature, the report should include where the car was hit, the location of each car before impact, the time of day, the fact that there were no apparent injuries, and your observation that the eyes of the other driver were bloodshot. If possible take pictures of any damage to both cars, the license plates of those involved, and even the insurance card of the other driver.*

2. Role-play the conversation between the two drivers at the scene of the accident. *Use this role-play to stress to students the importance of exchanging information (name, address, phone number, license number, and registration number as well as insurance company, insurance agent, policy number, and agent's telephone number). However, emphasize to students that they should not tell the other driver the extent of their insurance, confess any guilt, sign any statement that they were not injured, or say that their insurance company will take care of things.*

   Consider adding to the role-play a police officer who arrives ten minutes after the accident. Invite an officer to class to assist in discussing the role-play.

3. Making reasonable assumptions about needed information that has not been given, draft a letter to your insurance company about your accident. *Share with students the sample letter in 27.1 TM Figure below. This example contains all of the important information that should be included in such a letter.*

FIGURE

27.1 TM Figure

Dear _____:

At 7:15 p.m. on the evening of _____, I was driving my _____ (year and type of car) north on _____ Street. There were no passengers in my vehicle. As I entered the intersection of _____ Street and _____ Street, the traffic light turned yellow. As I proceeded through the intersection, a _____ (year and type of car) heading west on _____ Street crashed into my right rear fender. There were no passengers in that vehicle. At the present time there appear to be no injuries. I noted that the other driver had bloodshot eyes.

His name, address, and license number follow: (name, address, and license number). His car registration number is _____. We exchanged information at the scene of the accident. His insurance agent is (name, address, and phone number). His insurance company is _____; _____ is his policy number. The police did not come to the scene, so there is no accident report on file with them. We did not identify any witnesses to the accident. I have attached pictures of the damage to my car taken at the scene of the accident.

Please inform me as to what steps I should take next. I would appreciate your contacting and handling correspondence with the other party and his insurer. Kindly send me copies of all letters exchanged.

Sincerely,

(Include your name, address, phone
and e-mail contact information,
and insurance policy number.)

Alternatively, have students draft talking points to use when they speak to their insurance agent on the phone or if they have to fill out a claim online.

RENTING A PLACE TO LIVE (PP. 320–336)

Learning Outcomes

After completing this section, students should be able to:

1. explain why it is important for buyers to carefully consider the type of mortgage they sign;
2. identify steps prospective tenants can take to protect themselves before they sign a lease;
3. explain why written leases are preferable to oral agreements between landlords and tenants;
4. explain the consequences of failing to meet requirements typically found in leases, including prompt and full payment of rent;
5. describe the landlord's obligations that are typically found in rental agreements and housing codes;
6. explain security deposits and the steps tenants should take to avoid losing their deposits;
7. identify the limits of landlord access and inspection;
8. describe the responsibilities and protections landlords have under subleases and the responsibilities the (original) tenants have under subleases;
9. describe various reasons why people become homeless;
10. describe how the Universal Declaration of Human Rights addresses the right to shelter; and
11. define the terms *mortgage, term, fixed-rate mortgage, adjustable-rate mortgage, foreclosure, tenant, landlord, lease, clause, lease application, month-to-month lease, tenancy at will, tenancy for years, rent control, warranty of habitability, eviction, waste, fixture, waiver of tort liability, waive, right of entry or access, sublease clause, release,* and *right to quiet enjoyment.*

DISCUSSION—BUYING A HOUSE

Clarify the basic vocabulary terms *mortgage, term, landlord,* and *tenant* for students. Then use the following questions to lead a class discussion.

- Why must most individuals or families obtain a mortgage in order to purchase a home?
- Why must most families obtain long-term mortgages?
- What is a down payment?

Explain that down payments are one of the biggest obstacles people face in buying a home. Discuss the importance of having a savings plan in order to make a home purchase possible. Discuss the fact that owning a home is an investment that may appreciate and, therefore, bring a profit. Tell students that savings will continue to be necessary after buying a home so that it can be maintained.

- Why should people shop carefully for the lowest possible interest rates for home mortgage loans?
- Why do most people rent a place to live before they buy a home?

RESEARCH—ONLINE RESOURCES FOR HOME BUYERS

After an initial discussion about the importance of finding the best available interest rate for a mortgage, ask students to visit www.mortgage101.com. Instruct them to select "mortgage calculators" and then click on "monthly payment." Students should enter a loan amount (such as an estimate of the average cost of a new home in their community), an interest rate (say, 4 percent initially) and term (30 years). Discuss each of the calculations provided by the website. Next, have students change the interest rate, raising it by 0.5, 1.0, or 2.0 percent, and recalculate the terms of their mortgage, using the same data for loan amount and term entered for the first calculation. For a detailed account of payments and balances, students should select the "Full Amortization" option under the input boxes. Follow up with a more in-depth discussion about interest rates and other loan costs.

You can also use this opportunity to discuss down payments. Have students calculate how much money they would have to save to make a down payment of 10 percent of the purchase price. Banks generally will not lend the down payment to the borrower. Some government programs help first-time home buyers by granting loans for the down payment. Fannie Mae, available online at www.fanniemae.com, provides excellent resources for individuals seeking to buy a home, as does Freddie Mac at www.freddiemac.com. In particular, the section "Homeowners & Communities" provides advice and resources for finding a mortgage, selecting a home, and achieving home ownership. Have students consider how the necessity for a down payment on a home in the future might influence how much they budget for rent when they move out of their family's home into their first apartment.

BACKGROUND—LEASES

Because a lease is a contract, it may be useful to review with students general contract principles discussed in Chapter 22. As in any contract, the rights of the makers—in this case the landlords and tenants—will be determined by what they agree to in the lease. However, in most localities certain rights and responsibilities are established by state or local law. Therefore, to have a good understanding of landlord-tenant law in your area, it may be necessary to find out what laws your state or local legislature has passed or how your state courts have ruled in important landlord-tenant cases. Contact your local government to ask for resources related to leases and landlord-tenant relations.

Leases are legal documents, so they are sometimes written in language that is difficult to understand. Their meaning, however, can be simplified and made understandable. The principal objective in teaching about leases should be to provide students with the knowledge and skills necessary to deal with leases.

It is important to emphasize that a renter may want to seek outside assistance from an attorney or other person experienced with leases before signing. Some localities have legal aid programs that can provide free assistance to low-income tenants.

Explain to students the issue of oral leases. In most places, oral leases for terms of one year or less are enforceable in court, but leases for more than one year should be in writing.

Many people believe oral leases do not provide them with any rights. In truth, the housing code, the duty to repair, and other rights apply to oral as well as to written leases. Under an oral lease, a landlord is usually required to give 30 days-notice that a tenant must vacate.

PROBLEM 27.4 (p.321)

This problem gives students the opportunity to brainstorm factors to consider before renting an apartment. A role-play of a meeting between the prospective tenant and the landlord may be appropriate.

a. Possible checklist items include the general condition of the building; adequate space and working appliances in the kitchen; adequate size and number of bedrooms; sufficient storage space; adequate lighting and workable windows (including screens); adequate heating and cooling systems; overall safety of the rental unit, parking areas, and surrounding area; adequate locks and other security systems; reasonable rent; a landlord who will make repairs; and adequate parking.

b. Possible questions to ask the landlord include:

- What is the exact rent to be paid?
- What is the due date of the rent?
- Are there any penalties for late payment of the rent?
- How much is the security deposit and what are the conditions for its return?
- What is the term, or the length, of the lease?
- What conveniences exist in the neighborhood? (shopping, transportation, schools, babysitters, playgrounds, childcare, etc.)
- Are there any rules against children or pets in the building?
- What security does the apartment building have?
- Will the landlord make needed repairs before I move in?
- May I contact the apartment's previous tenant?
- What type of neighborhood is the apartment located in?

In addition to talking to the landlord, it is important for potential tenants to visit the area at different times of the day and night. Are there persons loitering on street corners at night or other suspicious activity? Is traffic extremely loud at rush hour? Are there loud parties on weekends?

Potential tenants should also talk to at least three neighbors about the neighborhood, the building, the landlord, public transportation, neighborhood parking, the safety of the neighborhood, the other children in the neighborhood, childcare, and schools.

ACTIVITY—RENTING AN APARTMENT

Ask students to brainstorm things they would look for—and look out for—if they had an opportunity to inspect an apartment. Then have students virtually tour apartments for rent online. They can use websites such as apartments.com, apartmentlist.com, and rent.com. Students should make a list of their observations, as well as the monthly rental amount and any required deposits.

After completing their research, students should calculate how much income a person would need in order to afford the apartment they found. Tell students that their calculations should be based on the advice that financial experts give regarding budgets for housing: people should usually spend no more than 30 percent of their net (after-tax) income on housing.

THE **CASE** OF...

The Summer Rental

PROBLEM 27.5 (p.322)

Be sure that students have read the entire section before they attempt to answer these questions.

a. Remind students that a lease for less than a year need not be in writing to be legally binding. Therefore, the student is obligated to pay the additional two months' rent if the landlord is unable to find another tenant for the apartment during that period.

b. If the landlord succeeds in renting the apartment immediately, the student will likely be liable only for the landlord's cost of re-renting the apartment (such as the cost of the newspaper ads, etc.) and a pro-rated daily rate for any days the apartment was vacant.

c. The woman should have called the landlord in an effort to make arrangements and explained her situation. If the landlord would not let her out of the lease, she could have asked for permission to sublet the apartment to someone else.

d. This role-play should illustrate the importance of maintaining a courteous, respectful, and honest relationship between landlord and tenant.

DISCUSSION—GROUP LIVING ARRANGEMENTS

Because group living arrangements are common among college students, summer renters, extended families, and other people, this section of the "Major Purchases" chapter provides a good opportunity to discuss some of the complexities and potential risks involved. Students should understand that if several people sign a lease together and one person moves out, the remaining residents are still required to make the entire rent payment.

Alternatively, if only one person in a group signs the lease, that person is liable to the landlord for the duration of the lease, regardless of whether the other housemates stay or leave, even if he or she moves out. The landlord generally spells out in a lease the number of persons who may live in the rental unit, and sometimes the amount of rent varies with the number of residents. Adding additional residents without the landlord's knowledge and approval may constitute a violation of the lease.

Have small groups of students draft roommate agreements designed to anticipate the possibility of individuals moving in and/or out of the rental unit. Discuss the merits of oral versus written leases, including problems that might arise if no written agreement exists—both between landlords and tenants and between roommates.

CAPTION ANSWER (P. 323) A tenant might want to change a part of the lease before signing. Negotiating with the landlord before signing ensures that the lease states exactly what the tenant and the landlord have agreed to regarding the rental property.

PROBLEM 27.6 (p.324)

a. The key provisions of the lease include the term of the lease, the amount of the rent, the amount of any security deposit, conditions for raising the rent, who pays utilities, rules against pets or visitors, sublease provisions, and provisions for repairs and injuries in the building. The landlord is Randall Real Estate Company. The tenant is required to pay all utilities (Clause 2) and is prohibited from having a pet (Clause 10).

b. Students' answers will vary. Point out that this lease is not very favorable to the tenant. In addition to the regular rent and utilities, Clause 16 allows the landlord to raise the rent at any time to cover increased costs. Clause 11 states that the landlord is not responsible for any damages or problems in the building. A number of other clauses also are unfavorable to the tenant. Some may even be illegal and unenforceable. These will be pointed out later in the chapter.

c. Students' answers will vary. The landlord might want to increase the notice the tenant must give before vacating the premises (Clause 13). Emphasize the clarity with which any new clause must be written. Like most leases, a landlord wrote this one and, therefore, the provisions tend to favor the landlord.

CAPTION ANSWER (P. 326) According to the warranty of habitability, the landlord is responsible for making the repairs.

a. Students' lists will vary. Typically, landlords expect tenants to make minor repairs in the rental property. Two examples would be replacing light bulbs and unclogging drains. Some landlords allow tenants to paint or do other decorating.

b. Students' lists will vary. Typically, landlords are responsible for all major repairs in the rental property. Some examples are repairing broken heating or hot water systems, major plumbing and structural problems, broken appliances, or other major defects or problems. Generally, if tenants rent a house, they will be expected to mow the lawn and to take more responsibility for maintenance and repairs than in an apartment. Some landlords write a clause into the lease specifying which major appliances they will replace. They may also name certain appliances or features in the apartment that are offered "as is."

c. A warranty of habitability entitles tenants to livable, safe, and sanitary conditions. Any condition caused by the tenant is not a breach of the warranty and must be fixed by the tenant.

TAKING ACTION: LAW AND DEMOCRACY

Lease Negotiation

This role-play can be done by four students in front of the entire class or in several small groups. Have students prepare a list of issues to negotiate.

a. The Monicos should have asked questions about safety, recreational facilities, schools, stores, laundry, and parking. This question highlights the need for tenants to consider many issues before renting.

b. This activity points out the difficulty of trying to negotiate rent. Although some landlords may resent any attempt by a potential tenant to negotiate, the tenant must remain polite and respectful. In this situation the Randalls (landlords) are eager to rent the apartment because it has been vacant for two weeks. Therefore, they might be

willing to reduce their $900 rent request for a short time, such as three months. In reality, where demand for rental property is great, tenants can rarely negotiate a lower rent. Because of the possibility that the Monicos might have to move within a year, they may want to consider renting for one year, with an option to renew.

c. The Monicos should talk about the apartment's problems, such as the broken window, inadequate locks, peeling paint, and the inadequate stove. Because money is a concern, the Monicos could offer to fix the problems in exchange for a reduction in the amount of rent. It is best to discuss these points before—rather than after—the lease is signed. Landlords often will agree to make repairs, and tenants should get such an agreement in writing.

d. See answer **a**.

e. Leases often include a number of special rules that tenants may wish to negotiate to change. In this lease, the tenants may wish to revise Clause 6 (to have the landlord enter only at reasonable times), Clause 10 (to allow them to have a dog), Clause 11 (to make the landlord liable if the discontinuation or damage is not the result of the tenant's action), Clause 16 (tenant may not wish to pay fuel cost increases), and Clause 14 (tenants should not agree to clauses which may effectively sign away their rights). In some places such clauses are illegal and will not be enforced by a court. In that case, signing such a clause would not result in any real loss of rights. However, it is always best to check local laws before signing a lease.

f. This question raises the issue of whether or not tenants may lose the apartment by being too aggressive and assertive about their rights. This can happen and is an important consideration when the rental market is tight. However, one of the benefits of trying to negotiate is that the tenant becomes aware of how the landlord will react to requests in the future.

g. Since the Monicos will be responsible for their own utilities (clause #2), they will be responsible for their own Internet access. The lease has specific language limiting the use to a dwelling (clause #3). Traditionally this clause was included in leases to reduce the incidents of one renter interfering with the rights of other tenants in the same building. (For example, if they were to start a day care business in their apartment). Since the jewelry business would be conducted over the Internet, it might be acceptable to the landlord, as it would not disturb other tenants and would increase the Monicos' income and ability to pay the rent. The best strategy would be to get express (written) permission in the lease to conduct this business.

Note: Tell students that many state laws require landlords and tenants to walk through the apartment or rental unit together and complete a checklist of the condition of the unit, prior to signing the lease. Both parties should keep a signed copy of that list. Upon completion of the lease and when tenants move out, the landlord and tenants walk through the unit again with the checklist. Tenants are liable for any (new) damage beyond normal wear and tear.

DISCUSSION—USE OF THE PROPERTY

Ask students whether they think telecommuting will change laws regarding the use of property and whether it should. Ask students where they would draw the line regarding the use of property for business purposes. Could a neighbor run a catering business from his home? A hair salon? A dog kennel?

Tell students to suppose that they are married and live in a one-bedroom apartment and have just had a baby. The lease specifies a maximum of two residents. Ask students to determine their options in this situation. What would be fair to them? Fair to the landlord?

Have students consider how limits on the number of occupants in a rental property might be used to discriminate against families with children or against groups of people who tend to live with large extended families for cultural or economic reasons.

THE **CASE** OF...

The Unsavory Visitors

PROBLEM 27.9 (p.330)

a. Generally, tenants are responsible for what happens on the rental premises. Although the law varies in different localities, many judges will grant a landlord's request to evict a tenant who allowed criminal activity to occur. The fact that the criminal activity involved the tenants' friends rather than the tenants themselves usually would be considered irrelevant.

The government has regulations that make it easier to evict tenants of public housing projects for allowing drug use or drug activity on the premises. Some criticize this practice as just creating more homelessness, including innocent children of drug users. Others argue that strong action must be taken against drugs.

In an attempt to help public housing communities rid themselves of drugs and drug-related problems, the federal government enacted the *Anti-Drug Abuse Act of 1988*[3]. The law requires local public housing authorities to make their tenants sign new leases that made it explicit that the tenants could be evicted if they, their families, or their guests engaged in any criminal activity that threatened the "health, safety, or right to peaceful enjoyment" of the other residents or employees of the housing community. In 1996, the act was amended so that it applied to drug-related criminal activity "on or off" the premises, not just on or near the premises.[4] Between 1988 and 2002, numerous tenants were evicted under the law. Four similar cases went to the Supreme Court. They involved senior citizens who were evicted because of the drug-related activities of their children, grandchildren, or caretakers. In one case, the drug user was caught in a parking lot. In 2002, the U.S. Supreme Court upheld the law, ruling 8-to-0 that public housing tenants may be evicted if a guest or any member of his or her household is caught using illegal drugs. It does not matter if the tenant is unaware of the drug use.[5]

b. Students' answers will vary. The Larkins are responsibile for knowing and controlling what their friends do in their apartment. They are in the best position to do so, not the landlord or the police. Students should take note of the lesson implicit in this problem. (See notes in answer **a.**)

c. The first step any tenant should take when a problem involving his or her lease occurs is to speak with the landlord. It may be that an agreement can be worked out informally. Most localities require that a landlord give a tenant a "notice to quit," which is a written statement that the tenant has violated the lease and forfeited the right to occupancy. Notices to quit usually must contain a description of the violation and a statement of what the tenant may do to remedy the problem. Only after the tenant has failed to stop the behavior within a specified time, such as 30 days, can the landlord request the court to evict.

However, in the case of a criminal violation, such as drug possession occurring on the premises, there may be no requirement to allow the tenant to remedy the problem. The right to quit more often applies to situations where the tenant breaks a noncriminal provision of the lease, such as having a dog in violation of a "no pets" provision.

If the tenant does not remedy the lease violation within a specific time, he will receive a court summons. A tenant should never ignore such a notice but should appear as specified. Most landlord-tenant courts are operated on a fairly informal basis, and tenants may appear without a lawyer, but it is always a good idea to have one if possible.

d. Students' answers will vary. Some states have instituted a system for informing landlords of the names of tenants who have been evicted previously for possible drug use. Proponents argue that such a system is necessary to protect landlords and to prevent drug-related activity from simply moving from one apartment to another. Opponents point out that the system allows tenants to be blackballed and stigmatized without ever being formally charged or convicted. This, they say, is a violation of the right to due process.

BACKGROUND—SECURITY DEPOSITS

Many landlord-tenant disputes arise over tenants' use of the property and the return of their security deposits. If one of these disputes ends up in court, the answers to the following questions become important:

- What damage existed when the tenant moved in?
- Can the tenant prove the damage existed when he or she moved in?
- Who caused the damage?
- Did the landlord know about the damage?
- Was the damage normal wear and tear, which is the landlord's responsibility, or damage the tenant must pay for?

The *FYI* feature "Security Deposits" in the Student Edition is designed to help tenants avoid security deposit problems. As noted earlier, checklists created and signed before moving in and upon moving out can help with this.

Studies have shown that disputes over security deposits are the most common housing problem litigated in small claims courts.[6] Findings and recommendations of the studies include the following: (1) leases tend to be difficult to read and unclear regarding landlord and tenant obligations; (2) there should be walk-through inspections and signed

checklists of problems existing in an apartment at the inception and termination of the lease; (3) an impartial public fact finder should inspect apartments; (4) landlords often have difficulty locating tenants who move out after damaging the apartment or not paying rent; and (5) small claims courts may not be the best way to solve emotionally loaded landlord and tenant problems, and alternatives such as counseling, mediation, and arbitration should be considered first.

Investigating the Law Where You Live

(p. 330) If students have difficulty finding local or state laws about security deposits, they might speak to a lawyer specializing in housing law, to a representative of a tenant organization, or to a person in their local legal aid office. They will also find helpful information at www.rentlaw.com using the search term "security deposit."

CAPTION ANSWER (P. 332) Inspecting an apartment before signing the lease and moving in, then inspecting it again after moving out at the end of the lease, protects tenants from having to pay for damage (other than normal wear and tear) that they did not cause. Such inspections ensure that tenants will get the total amount of the security deposit back at the end of the lease.

PROBLEM 27.10 (p.332)

Be sure that students have read the entire section on security deposits before they try to answer these questions.

a. Because tenants have the responsibility to return the apartment to its original condition, the landlord will probably be able to deduct the reasonable costs of cleaning from the tenant's security deposit.

b. The damages involved in this case should be paid for by the tenant in the apartment with the overflowing toilet. As long as the tenant whose ceiling and carpet were ruined notifies the landlord promptly after the problem occurs, it is the landlord's responsibility to pay for it or try to get the money from the other tenant. However, if the tenant does not notify the landlord promptly of the damage, he or she may lose part of the security deposit.

c. The tenant must pay for cleaning the carpet stain regardless of whether or not the lease allows pets.

d. The landlord cannot keep the tenant's security deposit to pay for the faded paint on walls unless the tenant did something out of the ordinary to cause the fading. Fading is generally considered normal wear and tear.

e. The tenant would be responsible for paying for the damage to the hardwood floors since the tenant never told the landlord about the leak. The tenant should have informed the landlord by letter as soon as he or she became aware of the leak.

BACKGROUND—RESPONSIBILITY FOR INJURIES IN THE BUILDING

The main questions to consider in this section are whether the landlord has a duty to prevent harm and whether this duty was breached, resulting in injury. A landlord's duty to protect against injuries has increased in many states through new laws or court cases. The liability of landlords for injuries or damage has also increased. In most states, if landlords fail to repair something (e.g., a broken step) and someone is injured as a result, the injured person can sue the landlord for damages. The increase in crime in many areas has led to court cases and other actions by injured tenants who feel their safety was not protected.

CAPTION ANSWER (P. 333) Landlords can usually be held responsible—and forced to pay damages—if tenants or their guests are injured as a result of the landlord's negligence.

ACTIVITY—CASE STUDY OR MOOT COURT ABOUT SECURITY MEASURES

The following case will help students see to what extent landlords are responsible for tenant safety. The facts presented below could be used as either a case study or a moot court. For directions on both teaching strategies, see the introductory section in the front of this Teacher Manual.

Seven years ago, when Sara Kline moved into her apartment, the management locked the building each night at 9:00 P.M. There was also a doorman and a 24-hour desk clerk who sat in the lobby. Her written month-to-month lease, however, said nothing about the landlord providing security measures, and a few years later these services were discontinued. Since then, a number of tenants have been attacked in the building's common areas. One night about 10:00 P.M. recently, Ms. Kline was mugged and seriously injured in a hallway. She sues the landlord for damages.

Assume this case goes to trial. The following are two possible decisions of the court. Ask students which they agree with and why.

Opinion A

Landlords are not under a duty to provide police protection in their apartment buildings unless this is specifically promised in the lease. In this case, the lease said nothing about security or safety being provided by the landlord. To hold the landlord responsible for what is not in the lease would be both unfair and expensive.

The landlord's only duty is to make repairs and maintain common hallways and entrances. If a tenant is injured as a result of a landlord's failure to repair such items as a broken step or handrail, the landlord can be held responsible. However, landlords are not responsible for injuries caused by criminals or others over whom the landlord has no control.

If Ms. Kline was unhappy about the changes in services that occurred after she moved in or about the crime in the neighborhood, she was free to move to another apartment with better security. She had a month-to-month lease and could have easily moved out by giving the landlord 30 days notice.

Opinion B

Although courts have usually ruled that landlords are under no duty to provide security for tenants, this court believes that implied in every lease is a duty of the landlord to provide protective measures that are within the landlord's reasonable capacity.

In today's urban apartment building, there is no way the individual tenant can be protected in all the hallways at all times. Common areas, however, are under the landlord's control, and he has a duty to act reasonably in keeping them safe. In this case, the landlord knew that crimes had been committed in the building and still did nothing.

In addition, the tenant had come to expect a doorman, an employee at the desk in the lobby, and that the front door of the building was locked at 9:00 P.M. every night. Because these conditions existed when she moved in, the landlord had a duty to maintain the same or an equivalent degree of security for the duration of her lease.

As the text points out, whether the landlord would be liable in this situation depends first on whether or not there is a clause in the lease releasing the landlord from such liability and, second, whether or not the law in that state upholds such clauses as enforceable. The facts of the particular case study are based on *Kline* v. *1500 Massachusetts Avenue*.[7] The law in this case represents the trend in many states. In *Kline*, the court held that if a tenant is injured by a criminal act of another that results from the land-lord's negligence or failure to repair, the injured tenant may be able to sue the landlord for damages. (Opinion B is a summary of the court's actual opinion.) The landlord was not allowed to use the waiver of tort liability clause (Clause #17 in the lease in the Student Edition) as a defense. Most state courts will not enforce clauses attempting to waive liability for injuries.

THE **CASE** OF...

The Dormitory Rape

PROBLEM 27.11 (p.334)

After students have answered the questions and discussed the case, take the opportunity to coach students about questions they and their parents may want to ask officials at colleges where they are considering attending.

a. Although we usually do not think of them as such, colleges function as landlords when they rent out dormitory space to their students. Generally, landlords are not responsible for ensuring the safety of their tenants against criminals. However, there are certain basic precautions landlords must take on behalf of their tenants, such as providing adequate lighting and secure exterior doors.

In addition, a landlord who is aware that a particular danger exists has a duty to take reasonable steps to minimize that danger. For instance, if there have been parking-lot muggings outside an apartment building or school dormitory, the landlord or college probably would be required to provide extra lighting and to secure building entrances.

If a landlord advertises the security features of the premises, there is an added duty to provide such security. Many colleges tell parents, through brochures and orientation meetings, that they will take special measures to safeguard dormitory residents. In this case, there was a guard and a procedure for after-dark entrance to the dorm, but the system failed.

Although the student who left the door ajar was at fault, the college might have anticipated such problems. The guard neglected to check the door—a simple action that might have prevented the rape.

b. Some colleges have alarm systems that alert guards when a door is ajar. In this case, an alarm or other backup to the guard should have been

used. Dorm residents should be educated about the importance of securing the doors as well. Special procedures for weekends, when there are fewer students in the dorms, might be called for. A single, well-lighted main entrance to each dormitory is safer than numerous entrances, and there needs to be a sufficient number of campus police and security personnel.

- During the past three years, how many assaults, burglaries, rapes, and homicides were committed on school grounds?
- Are campus security personnel trained professionals or semi-trained students?
- What is the ratio of students living on school grounds to campus police and security personnel?
- Does the college vigorously enforce underage drinking laws and prohibit drug use?
- Is a registration log kept of all dormitory visitors and guests?
- Are security personnel stationed at the entrances to dormitories on a 24-hour basis?
- Do police and security personnel conduct regular foot patrols of the campus? Of dormitory hallways?
- Do all dormitory doors lock automatically?
- Are there electronic alarms to warn the security force if doors fail to lock?

DISCUSSION—RULES AND REGULATIONS

Landlords sometimes have rules that attempt to regulate a tenant's moral conduct, such as "No unmarried tenant may have overnight visitors of the opposite sex" or "No use of alcoholic beverages by tenants." Have students informally debate the fairness of such rules.

PROBLEM 27.12 (p.334)

One method of answering this problem is to have small groups develop the lists called for in questions a. and b., and then have groups join together and negotiate a compromise agreement.

a. Students' answers will vary. Rules the landlord might consider important include those regarding repairs, cleaning, and maintenance of the floors, walls, appliances, yard, plumbing, electrical system; rules about pets, visitors, noise, or moral conduct.

b. Students' answers will vary. Tenants would have to consider each rule and how much of an inconvenience or hardship it would present.

c. Tenants should discuss the rules they do not like with the landlord. Select one such rule and conduct a role-play to illustrate the manner in which such a discussion might be held.

CAPTION ANSWER (P. 335) Failure to follow the rules and regulations for the rental property could result in the loss of your security deposit or in eviction from the property.

PROBLEM 27.13 (p.335)

a. Most leases require the tenant to get the landlord's permission before subleasing because the landlord may want to personally select a tenant who will be responsible enough to pay the rent, respect the property, and not disturb other tenants.

b. Bimal is still liable for the rent because the sublease does not release him from his primary responsibility to pay the rent to the landlord. This is true even if the landlord approved the sublet. Bimal would also be responsible for any damage caused by his friend.

CAPTION ANSWER (P. 336) The answer would depend on how loudly and at what hours the music was played. In some instances, a tenant can play a musical instrument without violating the rights of other tenants as long as the noise level is acceptable and the other tenants can live in relative peace.

For example, a person could play an electric guitar and plug headphones into the amplifier. However, a group of people playing musical instruments (as shown in the photo) would most likely create too much noise, and therefore, violate the other tenants' right to quiet enjoyment. A tenant might be able to negotiate with neighbors for a band rehearsal from time to time.

PROBLEM 27.14 (p.336)

The answer to this question depends largely on state law. The tenants could argue that there has been a breach of the landlord's duty to ensure quiet enjoyment of the property. Many recent court decisions obligate the landlord to respond to these types of noise complaints.

Once the tenants have formally complained and the landlord has ignored their complaints, the tenants may be able to take another approach. For example, they could move out and claim that they were "constructively evicted." In states that recognize the doctrine of constructive eviction, the tenants might not be responsible for the remainder of the rent. However "constructive eviction" is sometimes difficult to prove.

PAYING FOR COLLEGE (PP. 337–338)

Learning Outcomes

After completing this section, students should be able to:
1. describe criteria college-bound students should consider before they decide to take out a student loan;
2. list the benefits of federal student loan programs; and
3. describe several long-term risks for college students who fail to make timely payments on their credit cards.

CAPTION ANSWER (P. 337) College-bound students should consider the total owed for tuition, fees, and books; how much living expenses will be; whether there will be other sources of income that can help pay expenses; and how they will pay back the loans after they finish school.

CAPTION ANSWER (P. 338) Federal student loans offer low interest rates, deferment of payments while the borrower is in school, grace periods, forbearance periods, and consolidation programs. They also offer graduated payment programs that allow the borrower to start out making low payments and increase the amount of the payments over time.

ACTIVITY—INVESTIGATING OPTIONS TO PAY FOR COLLEGE

Ask students to brainstorm a list of questions about paying for college. They can use the topics in the Student Edition if they are not sure where to begin. Contact a guidance counselor in your school or a financial aid officer from a nearby college or university if one is available. Ask that person to visit your class and to discuss options about paying for college. Together with that visitor, have students log on to one or more of the websites suggested in this section of the Student Edition. Students should search for answers and report their findings to their peers.

PROBLEM 27.15 (p.338)

a. There are significant advantages to taking out student education loans provided by the federal government and colleges and universities rather than using consumer credit cards to pay for college tuition. These loans are typically offered with interest rates far below those of consumer credit cards and regular bank loans. Also, the terms of these loans are usually quite favorable to borrowers. With student loans, repayment may be deferred as long as the student is enrolled in school. Student-loan lenders typically offer graduated payment schedules to account for a student's income level once the loans come due.

b. Students' answers will vary. Students will display varying levels of risk aversion to the idea of incurring debt for school. Some will believe that borrowing any amount of money is worth the cost of education and that the loans will pay for themselves as the result of increased earning power once they have a college degree. Some will feel that incurring debt will ultimately result in a greater burden, limiting their opportunities during and after college. Still others may favor borrowing a certain amount of money to pay for school, but will believe it is ultimately more responsible to earn money and pay for school as they attend.

Investigating the Law Where You Live

(p. 338) To find out whether their state offers two years of community college tuition free for some high school graduates, have students search scholarship sites using the search term "states with free community college tuition." Students can also research the requirements to receive the free benefit.

HEALTH CARE (PP. 338–341)

Learning Outcomes

After completing this section, students should be able to:

1. explain the purpose of health insurance and the advantages of being insured versus not being insured;
2. describe how the *Patient Protection and Affordable Care Act (ACA)* works to help make health insurance more accessible and affordable; and
3. define the terms *exchange, marketplace, individual mandate, subsidy, premium, deductible, copayment, coinsurance,* and *formulary.*

BACKGROUND—HEALTH CARE INSURANCE IN AMERICA

According to the Centers for Medicare and Medicaid, in 2017 U.S. health care spending reached $3.5 trillion, or $10,739 per person. The share of the economy devoted to health spending is 17.9 percent.[8] Congress created the *Patient Protection and Affordable Health Care Act* (2010) in an attempt to address the multiple issues associated with the U.S. health care and health insurance system, including out-of-control costs, ability to access affordable health insurance, and consumer protections. To better understand the need for health care and health insurance, reform, it might be helpful to understand how our employee-based health insurance system developed.

The idea of health insurance has been around for centuries, however, it was not until the early 20th century that the idea caught on with the general public. Included in the economic prosperity of the early 1920s was a dramatic increase in hospital construction. Expectant mothers realized that delivering babies in a medical facility was much safer than at home, and new hospitals quickly filled with new mothers and babies. The collapse of the U.S. economy in the late 1920s and early 1930s left hospitals empty and struggling financially. In 1929, a group of teachers at Baylor University and the University Hospital in Dallas, Texas, made arrangements to cover hospitalization at an annual premium of $6 per teacher.[9] This arrangement evolved into one of largest insurance companies in the country today, Blue Cross.

The idea of prepaying for medical care quickly spread. Soon similar plans developed across the nation. When companies struggled to find qualified workers during World War II because they were not able to increase wages due to government mandated wage freezes, offering health care coverage became a way to attract workers. By the 1950s, the idea of employee-provided health insurance was flourishing. The Internal Revenue Service ruled that employer-based health care should be tax-free, and Congress passed legislation in 1954 supporting this policy.[10] Employer-based health care plans were here to stay. With the creation of Medicare and Medicaid in 1965, affordable health care was now available to even more Americans. By 1968, 80.8% of Americans had some form of hospital insurance.[11]

In the 1980s, the situation started to change. Through the 1980s and into the 1990s, the number of Americans with health insurance began to decline. This placed a burden on a health care system that had grown dependent on health insurance companies to pay medical bills. As the baby-boomer generation has aged and medical costs have risen, health insurance premiums have risen in relation. This created an economic burden for employers and insurers. In an attempt to reign in premiums, health insurance providers responded by eliminating high-risk participants from their insured pool, specifically, denying health insurance coverage to those with pre-existing conditions.

Finally, as the American work place changes, many would argue that our employer-provided health insurance system no longer supports a more diverse American workforce. All of these factors have contributed to what some would call a health care crisis in the United States.

BACKGROUND AND RESEARCH ACTIVITY

In addition to the information presented about health care, students may be interested to compare health care in the United States to health care in other countries. In the United States under the *Affordable Care Act*:

- Insurance companies are prohibited from denying coverage to sick people or charging them more than others;
- All Americans are required to have health insurance either purchased by themselves or by their employers;
- Large companies are required to provide health insurance to their employees.
- People who meet certain income requirements may receive financial help from the government to purchase insurance.
- People who do not buy or have health insurance may be fined by the Internal Revenue Service.

Ask students to conduct research about how to get health insurance under the *ACA*. They might check out the federal government's website at www.healthcare.gov or they can explore the website of their own state's health care insurance program. They can find their state's site by starting at www.healthcare.gov and then choosing their state. They will be connected automatically.

Ask students to evaluate the information presented on the website(s). Is it easy to understand and to navigate? Is it available in multiple languages? Does it suggest additional people or resources that can help people who are just learning about the *ACA*?

Students can compile their research into a pamphlet, blog post, or presentation to inform other students or their parents.

BACKGROUND—THE SUPREME COURT CONSIDERS THE *AFFORDABLE CARE ACT*

Almost immediately after the *Affordable Care Act* was signed into law, individuals and several states

sued to get the law repealed. They claimed Congress did not have the power to require individuals to buy health insurance.

In June 2012, in a 5-4 decision, the U.S. Supreme Court affirmed in part and reversed in part the *Affordable Care Act*.[12] The Court ruled that the "individual mandate" provision of the act, which requires virtually all Americans to obtain health insurance or pay a penalty, is constitutional because Congress has the power to levy taxes (Article I, Section 8, Clause 1). The Court struck down the part of the law that required states to expand Medicare saying that the provision violates the Constitution by threatening states with the loss of their existing Medicaid funding if they decline to comply with Medicare expansion.

The House of Representatives continues to challenge the statute. By 2017 the House voted over 70 times to repeal or alter the *Affordable Care Act*. The sponsors have never had enough votes to force legislative changes.

By the end of 2014, the majority of *ACA* health reform provisions have been implemented, including the creation of health insurance exchanges and the individual mandate. Twenty-eight states and the District of Columbia have expanded Medicare coverage. Over 20 million Americans who did not have health insurance before the *ACA* was signed into law are now covered, bringing the total percentage of uninsured adults in the U.S. down from 18% before the *ACA* became law to 8.6%.[13]

PROBLEM 27.16 (p.340)

a. Although the $700 monthly premiums seem costly, John mad a bad health care choice when he chose not to enroll in health insurance. John is financially responsible for the $20,000 surgery and will have to pay "out of pocket." Young, healthy people need insurance for accidents and sudden illnesses.

b. Miguel made a good health care choice. High cholesterol can lead to heart disease and medical events such as stroke and heart attack. Treatment following a heart event can cost tens of thousands, compared to the $25 copay and subsequent preventative care.

c. Teresa made a bad health care choice. Hospital visits tend to be much more expensive than doctor visits. By avoiding her symptoms she is paying $200 more for probably the same treatment she would have received from her own doctor.

Student answers will vary. Information about existing health-care policies is available at the United States Heath Care page at healthcare.gov. News coverage of health-care reforms and policies from many different perspectives (left, center, and right) can be found at the AllSides website at allsides.com by using the search term "health care."

NOTES

(1) *Truth in Lending Act,* 15 U.S.C. sections 1601 et seq. (1988).

(2) *Consumer Leasing Act,* 15 U.S.C. § 1667 (2000).

(3) *Anti-Drug Abuse Act of 1988,* 42 U.S.C. § 1437d (1) (6).

(4) *Anti-Drug Abuse Act of 1988,* as amended in 1996, 42 U.S.C. § 1473d (1) (6).

(5) *Department of Housing and Urban Development* v. *Rucker et al.* and *Oakland Housing Authority et al.* v. *Rucker,* 535 U.S. 125 (2002).

(6) ABA Special Committee on Housing and Urban Development, "Housing Justice in Small Claims Court" (ABA, 1979).

(7) *Kline* v. *1500 Massachusetts Ave.* 439 F.2d 477 (D.C. App 1970).

(8) "National Health Expenditure Fact Sheet," United States Government, Centers for Medicare and Medicaid Services. http://www.cms.gov/Research-Statistics-Data-and-Systems/Statistics-Trends-and-Reports/NationalHealthExpendData/NHE-Fact-Sheet.html accessed October 18, 2019.

(9) Scofea, Laura. "The development and growth of employer-provided health insurance," *Monthly Labor Review,* March 1994, accessed through the Bureau of Labor Statistics, http://www.bls.gov/OPUB/MLR/1994/03/art1full.pdf. Accessed March 25, 2015.

(10) Blumberg, Alex, and Adam Davidson, "Accidents of History Created U.S. Health System," *National Public Radio,* October 22, 2009, http://www.npr.org/templates/story/story.php?storyId=114045132. Accessed March 25, 2015.

(11) Cohen, Robin, et al, "Health Insurance Coverage Trends, 1959-2007: Estimates from the National Health Interview Survey," *National Health Statistics Report,* Number 17, July 1, 2009, Centers for Disease Control and Prevention, http://www.cdc.gov/nchs/data/nhsr/nhsr017.pdf. Accessed March 25, 2015.

(12) *National Federation of Independent Business et al.* v. *Sebelius, Secretary of Health and Human Services, et al.,* 576 U.S. 519 (2012) 132 S.Ct 2566 (2012).

(13) ObamaCare Enrollment Numbers, ObamaCare Facts, (http://obamacarefacts.com/sign-ups/obamacare-enrollment-numbers/), October 2019.

UNIT 5
Family Law

networks™

Unit 5 introduces students to the numerous ways in which laws and government affect them as individuals and as members of families. In many ways, family life is private and the law is kept at a distance. For example, the law will not interfere when siblings disagree or when people decide whether or not to have children. At the same time, the law does impact some aspects of family life, such as when states set requirements for who may marry as well as how people divorce, divide property, and support children and former spouses. Local, state, and federal governments have rules about adoption and assisted fertility, and they provide resources for children who are abused, neglected, or in foster care. Governments also provide economic, health, and educational benefits to support individuals and families. This unit will challenge students to answer basic questions about what constitutes a family and how much government should be involved in families.

CHAPTERS IN BRIEF

CHAPTER 28
Law and the American Family
Chapter 28 explains how law affects Americans from the moment they are born until the end of their lives. The chapter also describes how the legal definition of *family* is changing as a result of social, economic, and political factors.

CHAPTER 29
Marriage
Chapter 29 discusses the legal issues related to marriage and to living together as a couple. It also explains the financial responsibilities of couples and issues related to property ownership in a marriage. Finally, the chapter highlights partner abuse and resources available to victims of abuse.

CHAPTER 30
Parents and Children
Chapter 30 outlines the legal implications of parent-child relationships, particularly their mutual rights and responsibilities.

CHAPTER 31
Foster Care and Adoption
Chapter 31 discusses the legal issues and resources devoted to foster care, adoption, and assisted fertility.

CHAPTER 32
Separation, Divorce, and Custody
Chapter 32 presents ways in which laws respond to family problems such as separation, divorce, child custody, alimony, property division, and child support.

CHAPTER 33
Government Support for Families and Individuals
Chapter 33 describes the many ways that federal, state, and local government programs provide economic, health, and educational benefits to families and individuals.

SERVICE LEARNING AND SPECIAL PROJECTS

1. **Debate:** Several controversial issues in this unit lend themselves to debates. Topics could include: (1) age requirements for marriage and how those requirements vary by state, (2) whether unmarried couples should have property rights when they live together, (3) welfare reform, and (4) whether adoption records should be open to adoptees.

2. **Survey on Controversial Issues:** Students could survey other students, parents, or community residents for their opinions on the issues described above and other questions raised throughout the unit.

3. **Service Learning:** While community service is meaningful on many levels, service learning takes it to "the next level" by connecting service with classroom learning and reflection. The following activities are suggested to help students enhance what they learn in Unit 5 by serving their communities.

   • Students can develop a guide for new parents about the requirements for immunizations and where they can get shots for their children.
   • Students can tutor, mentor, or simply spend time with children who are living temporarily in a shelter for children or battered women. They can also collect items to donate to those shelters.
   • Students can work with the guidance office in their schools to establish a welcome committee to mentor students who are new to the school, especially students who come to the school after the year has started. This group could include, but should not be limited to, students who are transient because they are in foster care.
   • Students can develop a pamphlet about state and federal benefits for people in need and make it available throughout the school and at Parents' Night.

UNIT RESOURCES

Using Legal Resource Persons

Remember that using resource persons to co-teach lessons in law is an excellent and proven way to increase student interest and retention of the materials. Used well, resource persons are not lecturing but co-teaching lessons with classroom teachers, as well as observing and co-facilitating student-centered activities.

1. Judges, attorneys, and social workers could discuss how laws affect people throughout their lives. They can also provide insights they have gained through their work in cases involving marriage, parenthood, adoption, family problems, wills and estates, and other family topics.

2. A physician or representative of a local victim's assistance group could speak to the class about domestic violence, child abuse and neglect as well as community resources available to help victims.

3. Representatives from your state's legislature could discuss public policy issues related to families, including assistance programs discussed in Chapter 33.

Useful websites include:

• Nolo: Law for All at www.nolo.com. This site includes sections on wills, estates, and planning; courts and mediation; parents and children; spouses and partners; and older Americans.
• The Legal Information Institute at Cornell Law School, www.law.cornell.edu/topics. This site includes specific segments covering topics including adoption, child custody, divorce, feminist jurisprudence, welfare, and a parents' directory.
• FindLaw at www.findlaw.com. Choose the option to "Learn About Law," and then click on "Divorce and Family Law." This site has links to family law websites, journals, databases, government documents, and law firms that specialize in family law.

CHAPTER 28
Law and the American Family

The law affects individuals and families throughout their lives through events such as births, deaths, marriages, divorces, and more. For example, when a child is born in the U.S., a birth certificate is issued by the state. Each state has a law requiring vaccinations for children entering public school. State laws may exempt parents from this requirement for medical or religious reasons. In addition, beginning at a certain age, children are required to attend school or provide proof that they are schooled at home. Families in the United States take a variety of forms as people make decisions about love, marriage, children, and with whom they will live.

INTRODUCTION AND LAW FROM BIRTH TO DEATH (PP. 344–346)

Learning Outcomes

After completing these sections, students should be able to:
1. identify examples of how state and federal laws affect individuals throughout their lives;
2. identify the benefits of having a will and the consequences of dying without a will; and
3. define the term *will*.

DISCUSSION—WHAT IS FAMILY LAW?

Before students begin reading this chapter, have them brainstorm a list of laws that affect families. This list could include every law that students identify, or it could be limited specifically to family law, including the principal areas of this unit (getting married; relations between husbands and wives, relations between parents and children; foster care and adoption; divorce, separation, child custody; etc.). Invite students to scan Unit 5 in the Student Edition for ideas. This should give students a good overview of what is meant by family law and why we study it.

You may also ask students to identify the benefits that families provide to their members and to society. Answers could include: (1) a socially accepted and orderly setting for sexual conduct; (2) stable and economically secure circumstances in which to raise children; (3) socialization and moral and physical development for children; (4) companionship and psychological support; (5) economic security and the potential to divide income, homemaking, and child-rearing responsibilities; and (6) long-range assurance that other members of the family will help each other in times of sickness, accident, old age, poverty, or other hardship. This list of benefits may also be useful in discussing the materials on marriage in Chapter 29.

CAPTION ANSWER (P. 345) A will states how a person wants his or her property distributed after death. If a person dies without making a will, then state law determines who receives that person's property. Having a will ensures that a person's estate, or property, goes to whomever he or she wishes in the amounts he or she chooses.

BACKGROUND—WILLS

Ask students to make a graphic organizer that summarizes the reasons for and against making a will. They should be able to create it based on what they read in the Student Edition. If students need additional prompting, remind them that the advantages of making a will include knowing who will get your property after your death and rewarding those who have helped you during your life. The disadvantages of making a will include the cost (although having a will drawn up is less expensive than students may think) and the time involved to work with an attorney and think about to whom your assets should go. In addition, some people avoid making a will because they do not want to consider the possibility of eventually needing one. Even if people own only personal items such as clothing and furniture, they still may wish to leave these to certain people. Emphasize the importance of using an attorney to be sure the will conforms to the laws in your state.

Note: A discussion of wills may be a sensitive issue. Writing a will and/or giving away prized possessions may be a warning sign that a teen may be suicidal. Statistics suggest that a substantial percentage of teens have these feelings at one time or another. Pay special attention to any student who displays an intense or unusual interest in wills. If you suspect a student may be suicidal, ask the student if she or he is considering suicide and then alert parents, the student's guidance counselor, and possibly the school nurse. Provide students with suicide hotline phone numbers and information about how to get assistance from those who are trained to provide counseling.

PROBLEM 28.1 (p.346)

Students' answers will vary but should be supported with clear examples and reasons.

WHAT IS A FAMILY? (PP. 346–348)

Learning Outcomes

After completing this section, students should be able to:
1. provide examples to show that the legal definition of *family* varies from one legal issue to another; and
2. describe ways in which American families have changed over the past 100 years and in the last 25 years in particular.

CAPTION ANSWER (P. 346) Examples of how family structure in the United States has changed over time include men and women who stay at home to raise children and maintain their jobs in the workforce by telecommuting. Other examples include the rise in the number of unmarried couples living together with children and the legalization of same-sex marriage.

PROBLEM 28.2 (p.347)

Students can answer this problem on their own or in small groups. Answers will vary for all questions, based on students' perspectives. If students need additional prompting, use the discussion points for guidance.

In discussing question **a.**, use the questions below to determine why students do or do not consider the groups represented in the various pictures to be families.

- Is a family a certain number of people?
- Is a family a group of people with a special relationship to each other? Is being a member of a family determined by blood? Marriage? Other factors or commitments?

For question **d.**, use the following questions to help students identify the characteristics of a family.

- What are the characteristics of the group represented in each photo?
- What characteristics must be present to call a group a family?
- What characteristics should a family relationship have? Marriage? Children? Duration? Commitment? Exclusivity? To what extent is each of these characteristics essential?
- How are decisions made in a family? Do families have a head or a leader? Should they?
- What is the purpose of a family? Is there more than one purpose?
- Are there other kinds of family arrangements not represented in the pictures?

Question **e.** raises the issue of how divorced parents should relate to each other after a divorce, and you should be sensitive to the fact that many students may have parents who have separated or divorced. Though the law does not treat divorced parents as "family," some individuals choose to continue their relationship with former in-laws in a family-like manner. Divorced parents also sometimes get together to deal with issues concerning raising their children or jointly attend significant events in their children's lives (e.g., graduations, weddings, etc.). You may discuss this issue with students now or defer it until Chapter 32, "Separation, Divorce, and Custody."

PROBLEM 28.3 (p.348)

a. Some of the larger changes are evident in the increased number of unmarried couples living together and greater numbers of unmarried couples with children. Ask students to develop hypotheses to explain this trend. One possible answer may be that people want to enter into relationships without any future need for divorce should they ever want to separate. Another possibility is couples living together on a trial basis prior to marriage. It has also become somewhat more socially acceptable for unmarried couples to live together, either prior to marriage or without plans for marriage, and for unmarried couples to have children.

The decline in numbers of "average household size" may be explained by changing values and lifestyles. As more women work outside the home and as costs for childcare, higher education, and other expenses increase, more couples may choose to have smaller families.

The growing number of families with both partners working reflects the increased presence of women in the workforce. This may reflect economic need, increased job opportunities for women, and/or changing values regarding the right of women to pursue careers outside the home. Discuss with students how changing roles of women have affected certain families or perhaps the institution of the family itself.

Current information on demographic trends is available online from the U.S. Census Bureau website at www.census.gov.

b. Students' answers will vary based on their personal experiences.

c. This is an open-ended question and answers will vary. If the pattern in the chart holds, there will be more unmarried couples with children and the average size of the household will decrease.

networks™

Marriage can be a relationship that involves personal, social, economic, legal, and, for some, religious issues. This chapter examines the legal aspects of marriage. It describes the steps that one must follow to get married, the requirements for a legal marriage, and the difference between formal and common-law marriage. This chapter also addresses marriage equality for same-sex couples who wish to marry. Married couples face financial responsibilities, as well as the issue of property ownership and other decisions, such as where to live and whether to have children. Sometimes marriages are threatened by domestic abuse, which may involve law enforcement and court intervention.

and age requirements, vary from state to state (State requirements to obtain a marriage license can be found at https://www.marriage and https://www.nolo.com/legal-encyclo-

GETTING MARRIED (PP. 349-351)

Learning Outcomes

After completing this section, students should be able to:
1. outline steps involved in legally getting married; and
2. define the term *marriage license*.

CAPTION ANSWER (P. 350)   Couples are required to obtain a marriage license so that the state has proof of their ages and a record of the marriage. Many states also check records to make sure the parties are not closely related nor currently married to someone else.

PROBLEM 29.1 (p.350)

a. Students' answers will vary. This question is designed to increase student awareness of the various factors and issues to consider when deciding whether or not to marry. It is also intended to emphasize the importance of such a decision. Additional considerations include where to live; whether or not to have children and, if so, when and how many; whether or not current finances are adequate to support a marriage; whether or not jobs and careers can be pursued in the same location by both partners; and whether or not the couple's personal and financial habits are compatible.

b. Students' answers will vary. Students should develop an appreciation for the complexity of a decision to get married and the role the law plays in that decision.

c. Students' answers will vary, particularly because each student is likely to have different religious or cultural traditions that may (or may not) require arrangements that reflect those family and social values. At a minimum, students should note that the legal arrangements prior to marriage include a marriage license, a wedding ceremony of some sort and in a few states, a blood test and/or a short waiting period.

ACTIVITY—ANALYZING MARRIAGE APPLICATIONS

Divide the class into groups of three or four students, and have each group create a marriage application containing questions they believe are most important. Then compare the questions posed by each group. Ask students to explain their reasons for asking each question.

To extend the activity and to develop skills in reading and understanding legal documents, obtain an actual marriage application and have students fill it out. A marriage bureau clerk could act as a resource person, questioning hypothetical student "couples."

BACKGROUND—MARRIAGE AND THE LAW

The law related to marriage has traditionally been a state issue. Marriage requirements, such as license and age requirements, vary from state to state (State requirements to obtain a marriage license can be found at https://www.law.cornell.edu/wex/table_marriage and https://www.nolo.com/legal-encyclopedia/chart-state-marriage-license-blood-29019.html.). However, legal marriages in one state are recognized by other states under the Full Faith and Credit Clause of Article IV of the U.S. Constitution.

Most state courts uphold marriages even if the couple fails to follow a technicality. Nevertheless, couples should strictly comply with all local requirements. With regard to age requirements, if a couple gets married under the legal age or without parental permission, the marriage usually becomes valid only when the couple reaches the required age or later obtains the required permission. In most states, the minimum age requirement can be waived by petitioning the court, particularly in the case of special circumstances such as pregnancy.

Discuss with students the age at which people get married. During the past 30 years, the average age at which people marry has risen in the United States. At the same time, a larger number of American children are being born into families in which their parents are not married. Ask students to develop hypotheses to explain these trends.

THE CASE OF...

Loving v. Virginia

PROBLEM 29.2 (p.351)

a. Students' answers will vary. The Commonwealth of Virginia argued that it was up to the state to regulate marriage, that interracial marriages created problems in society, that children of such marriages suffered, and that the law did not discriminate because it treated both blacks and whites equally.

The Lovings argued that they had a "liberty" interest under the Fourteenth Amendment which included a "right to marry" and that this right was being taken away without due process. They claimed that the terms of this law amounted to discrimination prohibited by the Equal Protection Clause of the Fourteenth Amendment.

b. Students' opinions will vary and should be supported with reasons. In *Loving* v. *Virginia*,[1] the U.S. Supreme Court decided that Virginia's marriage statute violated the Equal Protection and Due Process clauses of the Fourteenth Amendment. This meant that states could not pass laws regulating marriage according to race.

c. Students' answers will vary. Marriage has traditionally been subject to state regulation. As students answer the question of whether the state should regulate marriage, they must consider the balance between the state's interests in protecting individuals and protecting society. Students can give their opinions as to which, if any, of the listed areas should be subject to state regulation.

LEGAL ASPECTS OF MARRIAGE (PP. 351–353)

Learning Outcomes

After completing this section, students should be able to:
1. describe the legal requirements for marriage in most states;
2. list the grounds for annulment of a marriage; and
3. define the terms *incest*, *bigamy*, *consent*, *annulment*, *divorce*, *fraud*, and *polygamy*.

Investigating the Law Where You Live

(p. 351) If students have difficulty finding their state's laws regarding who may legally marry, suggest that they consult Cornell Law School's site at www.law.cornell.edu/wex/table_marriage.

DISCUSSION—MARRIAGE REQUIREMENTS

Note: This discussion could be used in tandem with the *Investigating the Law Where You Live* feature in the Student Edition or could stand alone. Discuss these and other marriage requirements by asking the following questions:

a. Why do you think states set minimum age requirements for marriage? *Two major reasons*

*for establishing a minimum age for marriage are:
(1) marriage entails legal and financial obligations
for which a minor may not be held responsible; and
(2) marriage involves a serious commitment that
requires a degree of maturity and judgment not generally found in young individuals. Therefore, minors
are often considered to be risky marriage candidates.
Students should discuss whether setting a minimum
age requirement for marriage helps to ensure these
legal and personal obligations. If students think there
should be a minimum age, have them state what they
think it should be and explain why.*

b. Do you think that allowing women to marry at
an earlier age than men is fair? Why or why not?
*This question should provoke student responses to
the different treatment of men and women under
some laws. This question can also provoke students
to contemplate how laws construct social norms and
practices. One reason females have had lower age
limits is that historically they were not held responsible for obligations concerning principal legal and
financial support, although customs and the resultant
laws in this area are changing toward more equal
responsibility. Some people also believe that girls and
women mature earlier than boys and men, and it has
been widely considered more acceptable for a male to
marry a younger woman than vice versa.*

*In Stanton v. Stanton,⁽²⁾ the U.S. Supreme Court
struck down a Utah law that established the age of
majority for males at 21 and for females at 18.*

CAPTION ANSWER (P. 352) Most states have the
following legal requirements that couples must meet before they
can marry: minimum age, not a close familial relationship, two
people, and consent.

DISCUSSION—INCEST, POLYGAMY, AND BIGAMY

Incest is a crime and grounds for an annulment.
Reasons for prohibiting incest include morality,
genetics, the danger of sexual exploitation within
families, and tradition.

Polygamy and bigamy are generally topics of
great interest to students. Ask students to develop
hypotheses to explain the following statements:

- Some cultures and communities practice
polygamy and bigamy.
- Some individuals support such practices.
- Other individuals oppose such practices.

This issue exemplifies a conflict between rights.
Have students debate the issue of when freedom of
religion should take precedence over religious practices based on beliefs that society condemns or that

might be harmful to children. *Reynolds v. United
States,*⁽³⁾ a Supreme Court case involving bigamy, is
discussed in the Student Edition.

COMMON-LAW MARRIAGE AND FINANCIAL RESPONSIBILITIES (PP. 353–354)

Learning Outcomes

After completing these sections, students should
be able to:

1. compare and contrast common-law
marriages and other legal marriages;
2. explain how common-law marriages can be
legally terminated;
3. describe how states that prohibit common-law
marriages treat such marriages when
common-law couples move from other states;
4. describe the financial responsibilities that
spouses have to each other; and
5. define the term *common-law marriage.*

BACKGROUND—COMMON-LAW MARRIAGE

Before you teach this topic, determine whether
your state allows common-law marriage. Students
should understand that common-law marriages are
subject to all the rights and duties of a formal marriage and that a court-ordered divorce is necessary
to dissolve them. There is no such thing as a common-law divorce. Even in states that do not recognize common-law marriages, cohabitation may give
rise to legal rights and responsibilities between the
partners. (See the Student Edition for more information about cohabitation agreements.)

THE **CASE** OF...

The Common-Law Marriage

PROBLEM 29.3 (p.353)

The problem does not indicate whether Rick and
Sarah are old enough to legally marry. In Montana,
people as young as 16 can marry with parental permission, and people as young as 18 can marry without parental permission.

a. The usual requirements for a common-law marriage are that a couple (assuming they are legally old enough to marry) decides to marry, live together (including having a sexual relationship), and hold themselves out to others as married.

b. The facts do not indicate or present a clear intention to marry (just "talking about it" is not enough to satisfy this requirement), so they may not have a valid common-law marriage. The other requirements—living together and holding themselves out as married—have been met.

c. Assuming that Sarah and Rick do not have a valid common-law marriage, Sarah can legally marry Dylan. If they do have a valid common-law marriage, Sarah and Rick must divorce before she marries Dylan. Otherwise, Sarah would be committing the crime of bigamy.

d. Students' opinions will vary.

DISCUSSION—FINANCIAL RESPONSIBILITIES IN MARRIAGE

To introduce this section, ask students whether they agree or disagree with the following statements. While there are no right or wrong answers in this activity, students should explain their positions and respond to the opinions of their classmates.

- Wives should take care of the house and children, and husbands should provide the family income.
- When a woman gets married, she should keep her own last name and not change it to that of her husband.
- Married women should work only if they have no young children.
- The husband should have the sole right to choose where the family will live.
- Husbands and wives should own everything equally, regardless of who earns more money or who pays for their shared property.

After the discussion, ask the class if any of their opinions have changed. Then discuss the ways laws have adapted to changing public attitudes about financial responsibilities in marriage.

To extend this activity, students might construct and tabulate public opinion polls to determine community opinions on these questions.

CAPTION ANSWER (P. 354) Traditionally, the husband was considered to be the head of the household. He had the duty to support his wife and children. The law reflected this view by giving husbands the legal right to make such decisions as where the family would live and how much money would be spent.

PROPERTY OWNERSHIP (PP. 354–355)

Learning Outcomes

After completing this section, students should be able to:

1. identify advantages and disadvantages of various property ownership laws relating to marriage; and
2. define the terms *separate property* and *marital property*.

CAPTION ANSWER (P. 355) Separate property is any property owned by either spouse before the marriage. Marital property is any property acquired during the marriage.

DECISIONS IN A MARRIAGE (PP. 355–357)

Learning Outcomes

After completing this section, students should be able to:

1. explain the purpose of a prenuptial agreement;
2. summarize how laws shape decisions regarding name changes, support, and inheritance;
3. identify three kinds of relationships that are considered privileged;
4. develop hypotheses to explain why the law protects the privacy and confidentiality of husband-wife relationships; and
5. define the terms *prenuptial agreement, privileged communications,* and *inheritance.*

CAPTION ANSWER (P. 356) A couple must decide how many children they want, when to have the children, and how to raise the children.

BACKGROUND—PRENUPTIAL AGREEMENT

In discussing decisions in a marriage, it may be appropriate to have students discuss the need for legal agreements before marriage, also called prenuptial agreements. Today, more and more people are putting these agreements in writing.

Some people see lawyers for advice or have lawyers review prenuptial agreements before signing. Ask students whether they think these agreements are necessary and whether the negotiation of such an agreement would be beneficial or cause unnecessary friction between the couple.

Prenuptial agreements most often pertain to property the partners owned individually before the marriage or how they will divide property acquired during their marriage. Such agreements usually answer the following questions:

- Does the couple wish to keep certain property separate and maintain separate bank accounts during the marriage, or do they wish all property owned before or acquired after the marriage to be owned equally by both?
- Will any inheritance one receives during the marriage become the property of both?

Prenuptial agreements may also be particularly important when one or both partners have been married before and have support obligations to a former spouse and/or children. Misunderstandings regarding property ownership often lead to problems, especially when a divorce occurs.

For a prenuptial agreement to be valid, there must first be a full and complete disclosure of each party's financial circumstances. If the couple divorces, some states allow the agreement to be overturned upon a simple showing of "unfairness and inequity"; others require that the agreement was "extremely unfair." For example, if an agreement results in one spouse being left by a wealthy spouse without any meaningful property, the courts may overturn it.

PROBLEM 29.4 (p.357)

a. In most states, Serena would not have to testify against her husband. In fact, one spouse may object to the other testifying against him or her. The reasons for this rule of evidence, called "marital privilege," are to protect family harmony and privacy and to encourage marital communication by forbidding either spouse from revealing statements made in confidence. As mentioned in the Student Edition, in federal criminal prosecutions, one spouse may choose to testify against the other without the defendant's consent.[4] Many states also allow this if the accused spouse consents. In some states, a spouse is considered the same as an ordinary witness and may be compelled to testify in any criminal case, including one where his or her spouse is being prose-

cuted. If Raul discussed his fault with his daughter instead of his wife, that information would not be protected by marital privilege.

b. If Liza and Brent live in a community property state, she would own half of all property acquired during the marriage. In all states, a spouse is protected by laws that provide what are called "dower" or "courtesy" rights, which state that one spouse must inherit one-half to one-third of the real and/or personal property of the other spouse. Some states have laws called "elective shares" in which a spouse who does not receive enough property through the will can elect to receive either a forced share (one-third to one-half) or what he or she would have received had there been no will—usually one-half of the estate.

c. Students' answers will vary. At one time, the laws of most states gave the husband the right to determine where his family would live. Today, the law does not specify which partner may make the final decision, and in this situation both partners are husbands. Suggest that students brainstorm options for James and Edward and then evaluate the pros and cons of each option. List these options, pros, and cons on the board so that students can see how they "add up." It is important that students realize, however, that a purely "mathematical" solution may not suit a particular couple. If a couple cannot agree and one partner moves without the other, the remaining partner can be charged with desertion. Some couples choose "commuter marriages," in which each lives in a different city and they visit on weekends and holidays, as their solution to the dilemma. A discussion of this lifestyle choice may help students examine their personal views of the meaning of marriage.

ACTIVITY—SIMULATING PARENTHOOD

In addition to the financial decisions couples must make in a marriage, one of the most significant decisions any couple should make before getting married has to do with children:

- whether or not both individuals want to have children;
- how soon they hope to have children;
- how many children they hope to have;
- how they will care for and support the children (i.e., whether both spouses will work outside the home or one will remain at home to care for the children).

Teens tend to romanticize parenthood. In order to "bring home" the relentless responsibilities of parenthood, divide the class into pairs of students who will hypothetically "marry." Couples should assume that they are planning to be married as they negotiate answers to the five questions listed above.

Next, have couples assume responsibility for a simulated "child" or "children"—raw eggs, which, like children, are fragile—for several days. Teachers should alert administrators and staff about this assignment so that misunderstandings do not occur. Parental notification and cooperation are also desirable for this activity. Explain that the couple must carry the egg (in a suitable, protective container) with them everywhere they go—including classes, after-school activities, at meals, and hanging out with friends. Students who hold jobs will need to arrange for childcare; they should find out how much it costs to hire a babysitter and find one who is available. Students should keep logs indicating which parent is responsible for the egg at which times.

Explain that any egg that is broken or left unattended for any period of time will bring legal consequences (as when a child is abused or neglected) that the teacher will determine.

You might also require students to conduct research to calculate the realistic economic costs of parenthood, including food, shelter, clothing, childcare, medical care, etc. Ask students to keep journals during the activity in which they record, several times each day, how having the egg is affecting their lifestyle.

After the experimental period, have couples revisit the questions at the beginning of this activity to see if any of their answers have changed. In a class discussion, have students:

- share insights gained from the experiment;
- identify the limits to insights one can gain from the experiment (i.e., raw eggs are not demanding and the exercise lasts for a limited period); and
- identify reasons why decisions related to children are probably the most significant decisions any couple can make before or during marriage.

Be sure to alert students to the legal ramifications couples may face if issues related to parenthood are not clearly understood or settled before marriage.

Learning Outcomes

After completing this section, students should be able to:

1. describe changing attitudes of police to cases of partner abuse and reasons for these changes;
2. identify ways in which the *Violence Against Women Act* has changed responses to partner abuse;
3. identify groups and resources that are available to help abusers change their patterns of behavior;
4. summarize the steps that victims of partner abuse should take;
5. identify groups that provide partner abusers with resources and help to change their behavior; and
6. define the term *protective order.*

BACKGROUND—INTIMATE PARTNER VIOLENCE

Given the prevalence of this problem, it is possible that some form of domestic abuse or intimate partner violence is taking place in the homes or social relationships of some students in your class. Approach the topic with caution and sensitivity, and be prepared to refer students to sources of assistance in your community (e.g., "hotline" phone numbers and counseling centers). Guidance counselors or school nurses generally can provide this information.

Consider inviting legal resource persons from organizations that assist victims of intimate partner violence abuse to speak to the class or to assist with some of the text questions or activities done in small groups. Point out that "domestic violence" includes incidents of abuse that occur among unmarried persons who are living together. Also discuss that men, as well as women, can be victims of intimate partner violence. For more information about domestic violence, visit the National Organization for Women (NOW) online at http://now.org/issues/stopping-violence-against-women and the National Domestic Violence Hotline at https://www.thehotline.org/.

It is important that students learn about domestic violence that occurs in families so that they:

- are sensitized to the seriousness of this issue;
- can recognize signs of such abuse in their own households or friends' homes;
- understand the patterns and dynamics of abusive relationships;
- become aware of persons and agencies to contact for help; and
- know what to do if abuse occurs.

Note: You might wish to teach this in conjunction with Chapter 9, "Crimes Against the Person."

As mentioned in the Student Edition, the *Violence Against Women Act*[5] created a federal office in the U.S. Department of Justice which describes its mission: "The mission of the Office on Violence Against Women (OVW) is to provide federal leadership to reduce violence against women, and to administer justice for and strengthen services to all victims of domestic violence, dating violence, sexual assault, and stalking. This is accomplished by developing and supporting the capacity of state, local, tribal, and nonprofit entities involved in responding to violence against women." Visit the office's website, www.justice.gov/ovw for more information, including publications, news, laws, and additional resources on violence against women.

Two other offices within the Department of Justice track statistics about crime to give law enforcement and the public an idea of the extent of various crimes. To learn more about domestic violence statistics, visit the National Institute of Justice online at www.nij.gov/topics/crime/intimate-partner-violence or the Bureau of Justice Statistics at www.bjs.gov.

There is a growing awareness of the crime's seriousness. Many experts believe that numerous future batterers begin exhibiting the initial signs of such behavior during their early dating experiences. The origins, in fact, may often lie in a child's observation of abusive behavior between his or her parents. It is important that students be given information concerning the extent of the problem and the most effective means of confronting it.

The song "Behind the Wall" by Tracy Chapman can be helpful in introducing the topic of domestic abuse. This song depicts an abused woman and the difficulties she encounters in getting help from police and other law enforcement authorities.

Investigating the Law Where You Live

(p. 357) Student answers will vary depending on location. Encourage students to conduct some research about domestic violence prosecution in other cities in your state.

CAPTION ANSWER (P. 358) Intimate partner violence rarely happens just once. Batterers typically repeat the act, often with increasing severity. Children who witness the abuse may grow up to carry on the cycle of violence with their spouses.

CAPTION ANSWER (P. 359) The economic, cultural, and personal barriers women and men face when leaving an abusive relationship can often be overwhelming to victims of abuse. Some may feel that staying in the abusive situation is easier than overcoming the barriers. They may have no safe place to go—particularly with children—to escape the violence. They may also feel (wrongly) that they have caused the problem.

PROBLEM 29.5 (p.360)

a. Students' answers will vary. Historically, the law was based on beliefs that: (1) husbands were entitled to expect and demand sexual relations from their wives, and wives were expected to submit regardless of their own wishes; (2) the common-law doctrine of interspousal tort immunity created a legal unity of husband and wife; (3) the state should not interfere in marital or family problems; (4) prosecution would cause more damage to the marriage; (5) it would be too difficult to prove marital rape, and (6) consent to sexual relations is implied by marriage.

b. Students' answers will vary. Students should remember that prosecutors do not file charges for every complaint that is received. They file charges in cases where there is enough evidence to prove to a judge or jury that a crime occurred. Once this particular case is investigated and the facts are known, the prosecutor can decide which charge—rape, assault, or no charge at all—is appropriate. A primary argument in favor of prosecuting is that it would deter future offenses by serving as an example to the husband and other men. In some states, interspousal rape can be prosecuted as a simple assault or as a misdemeanor. In these states, prosecutors may be more willing to prosecute and juries more willing to convict. Others maintain that rape by one's husband, since it involves a violation of intimate trust along with all the usual elements of rape, is *at least* as worthy of harsh punishment as when committed by a stranger.

c. Students' answers will vary. In some states, rape by one's husband is punishable only when the husband and wife are legally separated. The argument is that a legal separation ends many of the rights otherwise associated with marriage and that it is a public statement of a couple's intent not to continue living as husband and wife. Most people separate without filing a separation agreement with the court, however, so such an arrangement would not be considered a legal separation. In such instances, rape charges might not be brought or a conviction obtained.

THE CASE OF...

Partner Abuse

PROBLEM 29.6 (p.360)

As previously noted, teachers should remember that some students may find this topic difficult or uncomfortable. It is highly recommended that teachers ask a counselor or expert in family violence to co-teach this subject and to be available to such students.

a. Students' answers will vary. Like any other crime, an assault of this nature should be reported. However, many people believe that neighbors should not interfere in a family's problems. Others believe that the danger of abuse leading to serious injury or death necessitates action. Ask students what responsibilities they feel citizens have when they observe a crime being committed. Do those responsibilities apply in this situation, or is it somehow different?

b. Students' answers will vary. The purpose of this question is to sensitize students to the delicate role that police officers must play in domestic situations. Domestic dispute cases can be dangerous for police officers. Some feel that this potential danger justifies officers' reluctance to intervene in domestic violence cases. Critics of police inaction call this reluctance a way of sanctioning abuse against women. Point out to

students that answering drug-related calls also involves danger, but police still respond to such calls.

Domestic abuse calls can also be frustrating to police because some victims are reluctant to file complaints against their abusive partners. Some police departments have instituted policies giving an officer the authority to arrest if there is probable cause to believe that an assault has taken place. Ask students whether police need special training to handle this type of situation. If so, what kinds of training? Would the police be likely to react differently if the Darwins were an unmarried couple living together? Should they?

The police officers should find out what happened and why. They should try to learn of any previous history of abuse in the household. They must assess the extent of Ms. Darwin's injuries, whether any children are present, and whether Ms. Darwin and her children will be safe if they do not arrest Mr. Darwin. Departmental policy will determine whether they need Ms. Darwin's cooperation to arrest her husband. They also should inform Ms. Darwin of the options available to her, including shelters and counseling services.

c. Students' answers will vary depending on students' individual reactions to the situation. Encourage them to imagine the sorts of actions, attitudes, and beliefs that result in a person's using physical violence in the home. Remind them of some of the options both abusers and their victims have in altering their situations.

d. Students' answers will vary. A judge confronted with the Darwin case should consider many factors, including how badly Ms. Darwin was injured, whether her husband had abused her in the past, whether her husband was receiving counseling or was involved in Alcoholics Anonymous, whether Ms. Darwin wants to press charges, and whether a jail sentence is likely to improve the situation. The court could also order counseling for Mr. Darwin or the couple.

e. Ms. Darwin has a number of options, including moving out of the house or obtaining a lawyer and going to court to ask that her husband be ordered not to abuse her or be ordered to stay away from her altogether. Many areas have counseling services, women's shelters, citizen complaint centers, neighborhood justice centers, or mediation services. Her husband may also need treatment for mental illness or drug or alcohol problems.

Unfortunately, these options do not work in every situation. For example, if a woman moves out or obtains a restraining order, her abuser may come after her anyway. According to the U.S. Justice Department, more than 70 percent of assaults on women occur when they try to leave their batterers. Also, batterers often isolate their victims, taking control of finances and cutting them off from family and friends. This results in victims suffering from "waves of self-doubt and blame that cripple decision making" and "overwhelming distrust that strains or destroys relationships."[6]

ACTIVITY—WHAT TO DO IF PARTNER ABUSE OCCURS

After students review these steps, encourage them to learn about local resources and procedures. You could invite a police officer, counselor, or other representatives from the community who have expertise and resources regarding spouse abuse. These experts can explain how each of the suggestions made in the text works on a local level. If resource people are not available to visit the class, students can conduct research on their own or in groups. In either case, students should find out:

- policies of the local police department in responding to domestic abuse cases;
- hotline phone numbers and counseling resources for victims of domestic abuse in the community;
- steps victims must take to obtain protective orders;
- whether or not shelters for victims of domestic abuse exist in the community; and
- legal services that may be available to victims of domestic abuse in the community.

To conclude this activity, have students produce pamphlets that list and describe community resources. Students' pamphlets should include characteristics and patterns of abusive relationships, characteristics of abusers, and the impact of abuse on victims and children. Students can also draft policy recommendations for local and state government to improve responses to domestic abuse calls and services for victims of domestic abuse.

DELIBERATION

Should the government require health-care providers to report domestic abuse? (pp. 362–363)

An overview of the deliberation method is discussed in the front of this Teacher Manual. For free deliberation materials, student handouts, and an instructional video visit https://store.streetlaw.org/deliberations/.

If this is your first deliberation, consider devoting significant time to establishing norms for deliberations and civil discourse. Introduce the process of deliberations, including careful reading, clarification, preparing and presenting initial positions, reversing positions, free small group discussion, search for common ground, and whole-class discussion.

Begin class by introducing the deliberation issue: federal government requirements on health-care providers to report domestic abuse. Ask students why they think intimate partner violence goes so under reported in the United States. Ask why victims might not voluntarily report abuse to the police. Ask student who, other than the victim, might be in a position to know or suspect that abuse is happening. Explain that this deliberation will focus on whether the federal government should require one group of people, health care providers, to report domestic abuse. Students will strive to reach consensus on some aspect of the issue, but are not required to agree on an an answer to the deliberation question.

Take students through the deliberation steps as outlined in the front of this Teacher Manual.

Debrief by instructing students to:
- Raise your hands if you changed your position on the issue.
- Raise your hand if you considered a new opinion that you had not considered before.
- Raise our hand if you felt listened to during the deliberation.
- Follow up by asking students, how they might translate this activity to conversations outside the classroom.

Consider having students perform a self-assessment on the process and their contribution to it.

For the most recent information on government requirements for health care providers to report domestic abuse see:

- Find Law – "Mandatory Reporting of Domestic Violence" (https://family.findlaw.com/domestic-violence/mandatory-reporting-of-domestic-violence.html)
- The Administration for Children, Youth and Families, U.S. Department of Health and Human Services, "Compendium of State Statutes and Policies on Domestic Violence and Health Care (https://www.acf.hhs.gov/sites/default/files/fysb/state_compendium.pdf)
- AMA Journal of Ethics – "Mandatory Reporting of Injuries Inflicted by Intimate Partner Violence"

LEGAL ISSUES FOR SINGLE PEOPLE IN SERIOUS RELATIONSHIPS (P. 364)

Learning Outcomes

After completing this section, students should be able to:

1. describe how laws regarding palimony and single people who live together have evolved, especially since 1976; and
2. define the terms *cohabitation agreement*, *palimony, and civil union and domestic partnership.*

BACKGROUND—PROPERTY OWNERSHIP AND SURVIVORSHIP FOR UNMARRIED PEOPLE

Unmarried people may own property together in two ways: (1) they may be "joint tenants with right of survivorship," which means if one dies the other receives the deceased person's share of the property (this commonly occurs with joint bank accounts, jointly owned automobiles, and real estate); or (2) they may be "tenants in common," which means by express agreement they each own a share of the property (which need not be an equal share). If one of the tenants in common dies, the property does not automatically go to the other person unless he or she is specifically named in a will.

CAPTION ANSWER (P. 364) Legal issues that may arise between people who live together, whether or not they are married to one another, include how they want to deal with their money, property, and responsibilities both during their relationship and in the event that one partner dies or they decide to end the relationship.

BACKGROUND—PALIMONY

Palimony is a legal concept which has been adopted in some states and rejected in others. It allows a member of an unwed couple who lived together to claim property or support payments from the other member of the couple after the relationship ends, even though the property was not jointly titled in their names. The *Marvin* v. *Marvin* case mentioned in the Student Edition has served as precedent in many palimony cases since 1976.[7]

MARRIAGE EQUALITY AND THE MARRIAGE EQUALITY CASES (PP. 364–366)

Learning Outcomes

After completing this section, students should be able to:

1. describe the goals and impact of the *Defense of Marriage Act of 1996;*
2. explain the historical significance of the protections for same-sex couples offered in Vermont as part of its civil union law;
3. explain the difference between civil union, domestic partnership, and marriage;
4. describe the legal evolution of same-sex marriage law through court rulings, legislative action, and public referendum; and
5. explain the effect of the Supreme Court's decision in *Obergefell* v. *Hodges* (2015).

BACKGROUND—MARRIAGE EQUITY

One area of family law that has changed the most in the last decade is that of marriages between same-sex couples. The legal landscape that evolved is controversial to some people and cause for celebration for others.

CAPTION ANSWER (P. 365) Members of civil unions and domestic partnerships were not provided with: automatic inheritance; automatic rights to jointly accumulated property; automatic rights to seek support if the partnership is dissolved; automatic power of attorney; or the right to adopt the partner's surname. In 2015, *Obergefell* v. *Hodges* required all states to recognize same sex marriages and extended all the benefits of traditional marriages.

BACKGROUND—MARRIAGE EQUALITY

A dramatic change has occurred in marriage equality in the last decade through a variety of lawmaking avenues, including court rulings, legislative action, and public referendum. Analyzing the legal evolution of this issue could be an interesting way for students to explore the multiple ways laws are created.

Massachusetts and California were the first states to recognize same-sex marriage. In both states, same-sex couples brought discrimination suits to court claiming that it is unconstitutional for the state to deny them a marriage license or a valid marriage certificate. In the 2003 Massachusetts case of *Goodridge et al.* v. *Department of Public Health*,[8] the court found that the state's justifications for denying same-sex marriage were unconstitutional. In May 2008, the California Supreme Court struck down the state's ban on gay and lesbian marriages, citing the 1948 case *Perez* v. *Sharp*,[9] which invalidated the state law prohibiting interracial marriage—19 years before the U.S. Supreme Court issued its decision of *Loving* v. *Virginia*.

Just months later voters in California approved a ballot measure creating a state constitutional amendment banning gay marriage. Also in 2008, Connecticut's Supreme Court ruled that same-sex couples have the right to marry.

In 2009, the state legislatures in Vermont, New Hampshire, and Maine created laws to legalize same-sex marriage in their states. In Vermont the governor initially vetoed the law, however the state legislature overrode the governor's veto. In Maine, the governor signed a right to marry bill into law. However, just a year later, gay marriage opponents pushed through an anti-same-sex marriage ballot initiative, overturning the law created by the legislature. Also in 2009, the mayor of Washington, D.C. signed a freedom to marry bill into law after it passed the city council. New York was the next state to legalize same-sex marriage through legislative action in 2011.

In 2012, same-sex marriage appeared on the ballot again in Maine. This time the people voted on a measure in support of same-sex marriage. It passed, and Maine became the first state to legalize same-sex marriage through popular referendum. Months later, voters in Maryland and Washington state passed ballot measures legalizing same-sex marriage, while late in the year the U.S. Supreme Court announced it would hear a challenge to the federal *Defense of Marriage Act (DOMA)*, as well as California's ban on same-sex marriage. In 2013, Rhode Island, Delaware, and Minnesota become the next states to recognize same-sex marriage by passing laws through their legislatures.

Then in late June 2013, the U.S. Supreme Court announced its decision to strike down *DOMA* as unconstitutional. The petitioner, Edith Windsor, inherited the estate of her late spouse who died in 2009. The two were married in Toronto, Canada, in 2007, and their marriage had been recognized by New York state law. Because their marriage was not recognized by federal law as per the *Defense of Marriage Act*, Windsor was required to pay taxes on the estate. Had their marriage been recognized, the estate would have qualified for a marital exemption, and Windsor would not have been required to pay taxes on the estate. The Court held that the effect of *DOMA* was to impose a "disadvantage, a separate status, and so a stigma" on same-sex couples in violation of the Fifth Amendment's guarantee of equal protection. The case, *U.S.* v. *Windsor*,[10] was the first major Court ruling related to the issue of same-sex marriage.

The case, *Obergefell* v. *Hodges*[11], was the first case to be accepted by the Court for full review after *Windsor*. In a 5–4 decision, the Supreme Court ruled that states must license same-sex marriages and recognize those performed by other states. The Court noted that it has long recognized marriage as a fundamental right, and could no longer exclude same-sex couples from that definition. Marriage is of fundamental importance to our society and to rearing children, and the decision about who to marry is a private and personal one. These justifications for protecting the right to marry apply equally to same-sex couples as they do to heterosexual couples, according to the Court.

PROBLEM 29.7 (p.366)

a. As a counter argument to the dissenting justices, students might say that through the Supremacy Clause (Article 6, Clause 2) the Constitution supersedes the state laws. They might point to the Equal Protection Clause of the Fourteenth Amendment finding that states cannot construct definitions of marriage that do not provide equal protection to all citizens. They might also point to the Privileges and Immunities clauses in Article IV and the Fourteenth Amendment which would require states to recognize same sex marriages in other states.

b. Students answers will vary and will likely cite tension between the First Amendment Free Exercise Clause and the Equal Protection Clause. Students will be interested to know that this scenario is based on a real case, *Miller* v. *Davis*[12]. Kim Davis, a county clerk in Kentucky, refused to issue marriage licenses to all couples to avoid issuing them to same sex couples. Davis stated that she was opposed to same sex marriages for religious reasons. She also would not permit her deputies to issue the licenses because her signature appeared on them. Davis was ordered by a U.S. District Court judge to issue marriage licenses to all couples immediately. She appealed to the Sixth Circuit Court of Appeals and the Supreme Court of the United States to request a stay in the judge's order. Both courts denied her motion. She continued to refuse to issue licenses and was jailed for contempt of court until she complied with the order. She was released when her deputies began issuing licenses. Davis was allowed to return to work on the condition that she not hinder her deputies from issuing licenses. In 2015, the a new governor was elected in Kentucky. He issued an executive order that removed the county clerks' names from the marriage licenses thus avoiding the issue of signatures. This scenario also suggests one way this situation might be resolved.

c. Student answers will vary. Students might cite the fact that the Fourteenth Amendment extends protections in the Bill of Rights like the Free Exercise Clause in the First Amendment to the states. They might also point towards the Equal Protection Clause and the Privileges and Immunities Clause in the Fourteenth Amendment.

NOTES

(1) *Loving v. Virginia*, 87 S.Ct. 1817 (1967).

(2) *Stanton v. Stanton*, 421 U.S. 7 (1975).

(3) *Reynolds v. United States*, 98 U.S. 145 (1878).

(4) *Trammel v. United States*, 445 U.S. 40 (1980).

(5) *Violence Against Women Act*, Pub. L. No. 103–322, tit. 4, 108 Stat. 1902.

(6) Pam Maples, "Bringing Fear Home: U.S. Women Face Pervasive Threats of Violence, Often at the Hands of Husbands or Boyfriends," *Dallas Morning News* (June 16, 1993): 1A.

(7) *Marvin v. Marvin*, 557 P.2d 106 (Cal. 1976).

(8) *Goodridge et al. v. Department of Public Health*, 440 Mass. 309, 798 NE 2d 941 (2003).

(9) *Perez v. Sharp*, 32 Cal. 2d 711, 198 P. 2d 17 (Cal. 1948).

(10) *U.S. v. Windsor*, 570 U.S. 12, (2013). A2.

(11) *Obergefell v. Hodges*, 135 S.Ct. 2584 (2015).

(12) *Miller v. Davis*, 2015 WL 10692640 (6th Cir. 2015).

networks™

RESPONSIBILITIES BETWEEN PARENTS AND CHILDREN (PP. 367–375)

Being a parent involves many rewards and also many responsibilities. Parents have a legal obligation to care for, support, and control their children. When parents are unable or unwilling to fulfill their responsibilities, the legal system may intervene. Parents are legally responsible for their children; they must provide the necessities of life, including food, clothing, shelter, education, and medical care. Parents must also provide for the social and moral development of their children and must control and supervise their children's behavior. It is up to the parents to decide what is best for their children as long as they do not abuse or neglect them. However, if parents fail to exercise proper supervision and control over their children, they may be held legally responsible for their children's acts.

Learning Outcomes

After completing this section, students should be able to:

1. identify three basic obligations parents have to their children;
2. identify the legal responsibilities of fathers;
3. explain why some people resort to blood and DNA tests to prove paternity;
4. outline parents' legal responsibilities to children in terms of support, emancipation, education, medical care, care and supervision, discipline, responsibility for children's acts, and earnings and employment;
5. explain the goals and requirements of family responsibility laws;
6. identify the rights of public school students with disabilities under the *Individuals with Disabilities Education Act (IDEA);*
7. describe parents' legal options when their children continually disobey them or run away from home;
8. describe children's responsibilities toward parents; and
9. define the terms *paternity, emancipation, family responsibility laws, truant, contributing to the delinquency of a minor,* and *family car doctrine.*

DISCUSSION—PARENTS AND CHILDREN

Before students read this chapter, have them brainstorm a list of responsibilities of parents toward children and of children toward parents. Ask students to classify each responsibility as moral, economic, or legal. Expect a variety of opinions to emerge. Students might also debate the following questions concerning whether responsibilities should be contingent upon the conduct of others.

- Do children who have responsible parents have greater obligations to their parents than do children of irresponsible parents?
- If children become irresponsible and uncooperative as teenagers, should their parents be able to relinquish responsibility for these children?

CAPTION ANSWER (P. 368) The act requires all states to assist mothers and children in obtaining paternity testing and to allow paternity suits until the child is 18 years old.

Remind students that each state has its own paternity and child support laws. First, it is necessary to determine whether or not Michael is the father. Courts typically use DNA tests to prove paternity. However, DNA testing is often costly. If Michael is not the father, he has no legal obligation to Martha or her child. If he is the father, the state will not force him into marriage, but he can be legally compelled to support his child as prescribed by state law. It is irrelevant that Michael and Martha are minors.

Investigating the Law Where You Live

(p. 368) If students have trouble finding out which agency handles child support enforcement in their state, you might direct them to the website of the federal Office of Child Support Enforcement. It has links to each state office at www.acf.hhs.gov/programs/css/resource/state-and-tribal-child-support-agency-contacts.

BACKGROUND—CHILD SUPPORT

As mentioned in the Student Edition, the *Family Support Act of 1988*[1] requires all states to assist mothers and children in obtaining paternity testing to allow paternity suits until the child is 18 years old. Share with students the following statistics about child custody and support from the federal Office of Child Support Enforcement.

- In 2018, 14.7 million children were served by the child support system.
- Over one-quarter of all children under 21 years of age have one of their parents living outside of their household.
- In 2018, $32.3 billion in child support was collected by state and tribal child support programs.

To learn more about these statistics or to find more current statistics, go to www.census. gov and use the search term "child support."

The *Revised Uniform Reciprocal Enforcement of Support Act (RURESA)*[2] was enacted to help custodial parents collect child support payments from someone in another state. Under this act, the payment of child support is enforced when a court in the state where the parent who is owed child support lives contacts a court in the state where the nonpaying parent lives. In 1992, passage of the *Child Support Recovery Act*[3] made it a federal crime

to refuse to pay child support to a parent who lives in another state.

For more information about child support, visit the Office of Child Support Enforcement online at www.acf.hhs.gov/programs/css. This site offers general information in English and Spanish about child support and methods for collecting from delinquent parents. The site also includes valuable links to state offices of child support enforcement.

Tell students that each state has its own paternity and child support laws. State governments often encourage paternity suits, represent the custodial parent in court, and help locate any parent who does not want to provide support for his or her child. Many states have laws that allow for criminal prosecution of a parent who refuses to take responsibility for his or her child.

BACKGROUND—EMANCIPATION

Now that most states have lowered the age of majority to 18, emancipation is less of an issue than it used to be. When the issue does arise, one question is whether the minor is, in fact, independent of his or her parents. Does he or she have a place to live? Does he or she have a steady income? Typical situations where emancipation may occur include a minor joining the armed forces, becoming self-supporting, or getting married. Parental support obligations beyond the age of majority have become an important issue in recent years. For example, some question whether financially able parents should be required to pay their children's college expenses. In most states, there is no such legal obligation, but parents often do help pay such costs. Divorce decrees sometimes include orders for support to last through college or to age 21. Information about state emancipation laws is available at: https://www.law.cornell.edu/wex/table_emancipation.

THE **CASE** OF...

The Child with an Intellectual Disability

PROBLEM 30.2 (p.369)

Note: Students should complete this problem only after they have read the discussions under "Support" and "Emancipation" in the Student Edition.

a. Students' answers will vary. The tendency of courts in most states is to find that parents have an obligation to support children with disabilities who are unable to support themselves after they reach the age of majority.

This problem is based upon *Nelson* v. *Nelson*.[4] In that case, there was no law requiring child support payments after emancipation or majority. The District of Columbia Court of Appeals adopted a rule requiring parental support beyond majority for children with significant disabilities.

b. The general rule of common law is that the legal duty to support a child terminates when the child reaches the age of majority (usually age 18 or 21) or becomes emancipated. Students' opinions regarding support for children with disabilities will vary.

c. Students' opinions will vary. Various courts have found a parental obligation to support adult children with disabilities who have an intellectual disability, are emotionally ill, and/or are physically incapacitated. Ask students whether the parents should be legally required to support a child who develops the disability after reaching the age of majority. Some states hold that the duty to support these children exists whether the disability began when the child was a minor or after reaching the age of majority. The law generally does not require parents to support children while they are in college; ask students if they think it should.

Investigating the Law Where You Live

(p. 369) Answers will vary. Students should be able to support their answers with evidence.

CAPTION ANSWER (P. 370) Family responsibility laws require that adult children care for and support their elderly and/or needy parents. Individual states vary on family responsibility laws.

PROBLEM 30.3 (p.370)

Students' answers and opinions will vary. Point out that demographic studies show the American population is aging, and that the percentage of older Americans in the total population is increasing. A lower birthrate and medical advances that help people live longer explain this demographic shift.

It used to be a common custom that children took in and supported their needy parents. Today, many elderly Americans are in need, but their children often do not or cannot provide support for various reasons. This results in large programs to support the elderly, including the federal Social Security system, government-run or -supported homes for the elderly, and nursing homes. Many of these facilities and programs are criticized for maintaining substandard living conditions.

Laws in some states require that adult children support their needy parents, and in some states it extends beyond children to siblings of the needy person or to grandchildren. In many of these states, the support requirement exists only if the parents have themselves supported their children. Usually, the law requires only what the child can reasonably afford to contribute. However, collection costs often equal the amount of funds collected, and a number of states have repealed their family responsibility laws.

In addition to the questions posed in this problem regarding moral and legal obligations (about which students' opinions will vary), have students discuss the following:

- If the law does require adult children to support their needy parents, how should the amount of required support be determined?
- What standard should be applied to determine the parents' need?
- Some affluent (adult) children collaborate with parents to "spend down" the parents' assets so that the parents can qualify for free medical or nursing home care. Is this ethical? Who ends up paying for this care? Should elderly parents' savings be viewed as an expected inheritance or as the way to finance expenses incurred at the end of one's life? What role should the government play in answering these questions?
- Should affluent (adult) children be required to support parents who have been irresponsible in managing their finances?
- The lack of responsibility many children in the United States seem to feel toward their elderly parents has been regarded as an example of the individualistic culture and lack of a family-oriented society in the United States. Do you agree or disagree?
- How does your family's culture(s) treat the duty or obligations between adult children and their parents? Explain.

Investigating the Law Where You Live

(p. 371) The Home School Legal Defense Association maintains a website that shows homeschooling laws by state. It can be found at www.hslda.org/laws.

Before students answer this problem, ask them to reflect on a definition of *school* and the purposes of schools. Then share the following information about homeschooling with them.

Estimates vary as to how many students are homeschooled each year because some states do not require homeschools to register the number of their students, and in some cases, parents do not fulfill the requirement to report. In 2012, the U.S. Department of Education estimated that almost 1.8 million students were schooled at home,[5] up from 1.1 million in 2003 and 850,000 in 1999.[6] While the number of homeschooled students continues to grow, disputes still arise between parents and state or local officials over the enforcement of laws related to homeschooling. Most states require home-schooled students to have regular evaluations or to take regular standardized tests.

For current statistics, visit the National Center for Education Statistics website at https://nces.ed. gov/. Interested students may also wish to visit the website of the National Home Education Network, an advocacy group in support of homeschoolers, online at www.nhen.org.

a. Students' answers will vary. Students need to consider parents' interests in raising their children as they see fit and the state's interest in ensuring that all children receive enough education to eventually function independently in adult society and to be informed participants in the democratic process.

   This problem is based upon *Delconte v. North Carolina*.[7] The North Carolina Supreme Court held that the Delcontes' home was a school under its statute. The statute, it said, permitted a child to attend a nonpublic school if the school met any one of several requirements. The Delcontes met one of those requirements—that a private school receive no state funds. The courts and legislatures in several states have approved home instruction when parents have given religious reasons. Additionally, home instruction is permitted for children with an intellectual or physical disability. In *Delconte*, the supreme court of North Carolina did not discuss the parents' reasons for instructing their children at home. Their decision was based on the statutory definition of a school. The Delcontes did, however, present their religious views at an earlier phase of the trial.

b. Students' answers will vary. Supporters of homeschooling say it offers alternatives for parents who are concerned about violence, peer pressure, and poor academic quality in their community schools. For some supporters of homeschooling, religion plays an important role in the curriculum and in their motivation to teach their own children.

   Opponents of homeschooling say it lacks quality control measures and is a "dangerously unregulated industry." Some people believe students in homeschools miss out on important social lessons that being among other children provides. Other concerns are that parents may be keeping their children out of school because they do not want their children to mix with children from other races and cultures or because they want their children to work in a family business.[8]

c. Students' answers will vary. Encourage students to answer this question by considering what is required of professional school teachers. Should parents be expected to have similar experiences, credentials, personality characteristics, or work histories? Why or why not?

   In February 2008, a panel of three judges on the California state appellate court ruled that "parents do not have a constitutional right to home school their children" unless those parents or the tutors they hire have teaching credentials qualifying them to teach in public schools.[9] The decision sprang from a case in which an attorney for a child allegedly being abused by her father asked the court to require the family to enroll the girl in a public or private school rather than to have her homeschooled. The court refused, saying that it violated the parent's constitutional rights. In overturning that decision, the Court of Appeal of California based its decision on a rarely enforced state education law that most people did not know existed. California is the state with the largest number of homeschooled children, roughly 165,000 people. News of the ruling surprised many people, and the ruling spread quickly through the state and the country.[10]

   Advocates of homeschooling appealed the ruling, and the California Court of Appeals granted a motion to rehear the case, essentially vacating the ruling and putting the decision up to the state appeals court. The court ruled that homeschooling is permissible in California as a private school. This ruling reverses the decision requiring parents teaching in homeschools to have teaching credentials.[11]

d. Students' answers will vary. Some people believe that because the families of homeschoolers pay taxes that support public schools, they should be entitled to play sports or play in the band at those schools. Others say that it would be beneficial for homeschooled students to have the option of participating in sports or music programs so they can enjoy the social and physical rewards.

Those opposed say that since homeschooled students are not expected to meet the same state and county requirements that public school students must meet, they should not be allowed to compete on the same sports teams or music programs. Similarly, some say that homeschooled students might spend all day practicing their sports or instruments and gain an unfair advantage over other students. "... [K]ids who stay home all day (and work on their games) are nudging out the kids who have to go to school all day and do mundane things, like show up to class and learn."[12]

Many people believe that in order for homeschooled students to participate in public school sports, the state legislature would have to pass specific legislation to enable it. These laws are sometimes called "Tim Tebow laws" after a professional football and baseball player who was home schooled but played on the teams local schools. The laws in the state of Florida, where Tebow lived, permitted home schooled students to participate on teams in the school district in which they lived. Only a few states presently have such legislation. Interestingly, attempts to enact legislation in other states have failed, in part due to pressure from homeschoolers concerned that such legislation would open them up to increased regulation from the state.[13]

There are other options for athletes who are schooled at home. They may participate in community sports, attend sport camps, participate in individual sports such as running, or participate on special teams created by homeschoolers. In some places, students who are homeschooled can pay a fee to a local private school to participate on its team. Similar options may exist for musicians as well.

e. Students' answers will vary. Rules guiding educational officials in determining whether a home schooling family is in compliance with the state's compulsory education law should include state requirements such as required number of school days or hours, course completion or subject-area proficiency requirements and any state-level assessment requirements. For a comprehensive list with links to each states' high school graduation requirements, have students visit www.learningpath.org/article_directory/ High_School_Diploma_Info_by_State.html.

PROBLEM 30.5 (p. 372)

a. Student answers will vary. Students who support government funding of 2- or 4-year higher education might cite equity in educational opportunity, freedom from crushing student debt, and a need for a globally competitive workforce. Students who oppose these ideas may point out that taxes will have to be raised significantly, that money should be available for training for trades as well as college, and that these programs are not practical.

b. Student answers will vary. Students might hypothesize that if some states provided state-funded education and other did not, students and families would move to the states that fund college, therefore overburdening the system. In this case, a national system might be preferable. Students who support a state program may feel that voters within a state should decide if their state taxes should be used to fund higher education.

c. The strongest arguments for tuition-free higher education are equity in educational opportunity, freedom from student debt, and the creation of a globally competitive workforce. The strongest arguments against tuition-free higher education is an increase in taxes, lack of similar funding for training for trades, and the impracticality of such an extensive program.

BACKGROUND—PARENTS, CHILDREN, AND MEDICAL CARE

In some states, for certain areas of medical care, the parent cannot force a child to have certain treatments without the child's consent. For example, if a parent wishes to get dependency treatment for a child age 13 or older, the child must consent. If the parent consents, but the child does not, treatment cannot be provided unless involuntary treatment procedures are followed. Children age 13 years and older may consent to mental health treatment. A parent of a child age 13 years or older who wants to apply for the child's admission to a mental health evaluation and treatment center must have the child's consent or an order from a court. Also, reproductive prevention and care can be obtained without notice to the parent.

BACKGROUND AND DISCUSSION— THE *INDIVIDUALS WITH DISABILITIES EDUCATION ACT (IDEA)*

Please note that students with disabilities may or may not be comfortable discussing this issue. Also, other students may have preexisting negative or positive opinions about "special education." The purpose of this discussion is to provide accurate information and an opportunity to discuss the law related to this issue.

The *Individuals with Disabilities Education Act (IDEA)* was passed in 1997 to update an earlier law called the *Education for All Handicapped Children Act*.[14] Ask students to review the information in the Student Edition and summarize the protections offered to public school students with disabilities. (These protections are not provided to students with learning disabilities who attend private or home schools.)

If you teach in a public school, explain the services their school provides to students with disabilities. Tell students that the law requires students with disabilities to be taught in the "least restricted environment" that is educationally appropriate. In some cases, this requires that students be "main-streamed" in the same classes as other students. Explain the extent to which students with disabilities are mainstreamed in their school. Consider inviting a representative from your school's special education department to guide this discussion.

RESEARCH—CARE AND SUPERVISION: AT WHAT AGE CAN I BE LEFT HOME ALONE?

Students may be interested in their state laws concerning the age at which a child can be left home alone or in the care of other children. As mentioned in the Student Edition, these state laws vary quite a bit. To find out their own state laws or local ordinances, students can contact one or more of the following:

- The local police department or
- The local Child Protective Services offices. These offices can be found by contacting the national network Childhelp® 24 hours a day, seven days a week at its toll-free number 1-800-4-A-CHILD® (1-800-422-4453).

In addition, several organizations offer guidelines to help parents determine whether their children are ready to be left alone at home or under the care of another child. They are:

- FindLaw offers advice at http://family. findlaw.com/parental-rights-and-liability/ when-can-you-leave-a-child-home-alone-.html
- The American Academy of Child & Adolescent Psychiatry offers guidelines in *Home Alone Children* at www.aacap.org.

DISCUSSION—DISCIPLINE

Before students read the section "Discipline" in the Student Edition, have them answer the following questions in small groups, followed by a class discussion.

- Define *discipline*.
- What will happen if parents do not discipline their children?
- What kinds of discipline are most effective? Least effective? Why?

Introduce to students three basic styles of discipline—laissez-faire (characterized by loose rules and little enforcement), authoritarian (characterized by rigid rules and harsh enforcement), and authoritative (characterized by clear and humane rules, with firm enforcement). Ask students if they can think of any other discipline styles. Interested students may conduct research to determine why authoritative parenting is generally considered most effective. They could also compare and contrast various approaches to discipline by different cultural or religious groups.

- When is discipline reasonable? Unreasonable? When should the legal system become involved in determining what is reasonable?
- How should parents respond if their children continually disobey? Should the legal system become involved in this situation?
- How should parents respond if their children continually run away? Should the legal system become involved in this situation?

At the conclusion of the small- and large-group discussion, ask students to compare their opinions to the information in the Student Edition.

a. Students' answers will vary. Larry could argue that his father has a duty to pay for necessities, such as food and shelter. Some states have laws requiring financially able parents to assist their children with their college education. If Larry's father is not required to do so by state statute, most courts would not require such support, since Larry has reached the age of majority (18 in most states).

b. Students' answers will vary. If Hiroshi is a minor, the law gives his parents the right to determine where he lives. The arguments in favor of the parents are that his parents are supporting Hiroshi; that he is not financially independent and able to live on his own; and that the legal system should preserve family unity by not interfering in family affairs. The arguments in favor of Hiroshi are that his parents may be making a decision which is not in Hiroshi's best interests, and that he is close enough to legal adulthood to have a voice in the matter.

c. Students' answers will vary. Assuming psychiatrists agree with them, the Parhams will probably be able to have their daughter committed to a mental institution. Some state laws are changing to require that anyone who is committed to a mental health facility against his or her wishes be granted some due process rights. In *Parham* v. *J. R., et al.*, the U.S. Supreme Court upheld a Georgia statute that allowed the superintendent of a state hospital to observe and diagnose a child whose parents had sought to commit the child to a hospital for the mentally ill.[15] The Court said no hearing or separate representation of the child by an attorney was necessary.

DISCUSSION—PARENTAL RESPONSIBILITY FOR CHILDREN'S ACTS

Before students read the section "Parental Responsibility for Children's Acts," ask students to discuss the following questions in small groups, followed by a class discussion.

- Suppose a child does something illegal. Should his or her parents be held legally responsible? Under what circumstances?
- Suppose a teenager causes an automobile accident while driving under the influence of alcohol. Should the parents be held responsible? To what extent?

At the conclusion of the discussion, ask students to compare their opinions to the information in the Student Edition.

a. Students' answers will vary. It appears that Vanessa's parents failed to monitor her behavior adequately. If they suspected her involvement in drugs, they should have curtailed some of her freedom or kept a closer watch on her activities.

Some students may argue that parents' actions can affect the actions of their children in only a limited way. Others may say that parental guidance and being role models are important factors in determining a child's actions. It is possible that Vanessa's parents will be held negligent, which is a tort offense.

b. This question asks for student opinions. Students may believe that if Vanessa has the money, she should pay. Under parental responsibility laws, however, Vanessa's parents will have to pay, given her age.

c. Students' answers will vary. Some states do hold parents criminally responsible for the actions of their children, especially if they encouraged their children's illegal behavior. This does not appear to be the case in the fact pattern given.

DISCUSSION—EARNINGS AND EMPLOYMENT

Before students read the section "Earnings and Employment," ask them to answer and discuss the following questions with a partner.

- Do you have a job?
- Do you think your parents or guardians are entitled to part or all of the wages you earn?
- Are there any circumstances that would change your opinion about this issue? What if your family really needs those wages to pay its bills? What if your family is going to use your wages to offset the costs of your college expenses? What if your parents really need a vacation?
- In what ways do your parents or guardians support you financially?

As students brainstorm answers, record their answers on the board. Then ask students to categorize their responses as necessities or luxuries. For example, necessities include food, shelter, heat, basic clothing, and medical care. Luxuries include vacations, entertainment, fashion, games, etc.

- Should working children be expected to pay for their own necessities? For their own luxuries? To what extent should parents oversee spending?
- Under what circumstances is it reasonable for parents to take a child's earnings?
- When would it be unreasonable?
- For what other reasons might parents take a child's earnings?
- Should the legal system be involved in this issue, or should it be worked out by parents and their children?

Tell students that in 1998, Olympic gymnast Dominique Moceanu petitioned a court in Houston, Texas, to declare her a legal adult 11 months before her eighteenth birthday. She wanted the power to control her own finances, alleging that her parents had mismanaged her earnings. She further alleged that her parents had not worked in a long time and that they were living off money she earned.[16] The court granted her request after her parents agreed not to fight the petition.[17]

CHILD ABUSE AND NEGLECT (PP. 375–378)

Learning Outcomes

After completing this section, students should be able to:
1. describe forms and effects of child abuse;
2. identify forms and effects of child neglect;
3. list the job titles of professionals who are required by most states to report suspected cases of child abuse and neglect;
4. explain the short-term and long-term effects of child sexual abuse;
5. describe how to report suspected child abuse and/or neglect; and
6. define the terms *child abuse, child neglect* and *pedophile.*

BACKGROUND—TEACHING ABOUT CHILD ABUSE AND NEGLECT

Given the large number of reported child abuse incidents in the United States, it is possible that some students are or have been victims and may be reluctant to discuss the topic. Therefore, be extremely sensitive in presenting information about child abuse and neglect. At the same time, instruction about these issues may give students who are

victims the knowledge and perhaps the courage they need to seek help. This section can also help friends or relatives of victims identify appropriate ways to help people they care about.

Compile and distribute a handout that identifies local sources of help for abused and neglected children, including phone numbers for hotlines and local government resources (often found under the category of "protective services"). School nurses and guidance counselors should have access to this information. Contact the National Child Abuse Hotline at 1-800-4-A-CHILD or www.childhelpusa. org for additional resources.

The laws of most states make it a criminal offense for doctors, teachers, and certain other professionals to fail to report cases of suspected child abuse. Critics of these laws argue that they may result in innocent people being investigated. Others say that mandatory reporting laws shield these professionals from civil liability and help protect children.

Neglect can result in termination of parental rights. Because a termination hearing is not a criminal procedure, the U.S. Supreme Court has held that generally there is no right to counsel for parents who cannot afford to hire a lawyer.[18]

LEGAL RESOURCE PERSONS

Given the sensitivity, complexity, and possible immediacy of this topic for some students, legal resource persons are especially appropriate and helpful. Attorneys, social workers, school nurses, medical personnel, psychologists, guidance counselors, police officers, and others working in the field of child abuse and neglect would be good legal resource persons or facilitators.

CAPTION ANSWER (P. 375) The number of reported cases of child abuse increased by 3 million between 1976 and 2017.

According to the federal government report *Child Maltreatment 2017*, Child Protective Service agencies received an estimated 4.1 million referrals involving approximately 7.5 million children. Approximately 674,000 children were found to be victims of child abuse or neglect in 2017. As in prior years, the greatest percentages of children suffered from neglect (74.9%) and physical abuse (18.3%). A child may have suffered from multiple forms of maltreatment, and all maltreatment types were counted for each child. Victims in their first year of life had the highest rate of victimization at 25.3 per 1,000 children of the same age in the national population. The full text of *Child Maltreatment 2017* is available on the Children's Bureau website at https://www. acf.hhs.gov/cb/resource/child-maltreatment-2017.

In addition to the U.S. Department of Health and Human Services (www.acf.hhs.gov) which collects data and publishes the report named above, numerous agencies and groups provide additional key facts on their websites, including the Tennyson Center for Children (www.childabuse.org), the National Partnership for Women and Children (www.nationalpartnership.org), the National Crime Prevention Council (www.ncpc.org), and Childhelp® (www.childhelpusa.org).

Investigating the Law Where You Live

(p. 376) All states have a system to receive and respond to reports of suspected child abuse and neglect. If you suspect a child is being harmed, you should report your concerns to the appropriate authorities, such as child protective services (CPS), in the state where the child resides. Each state has trained professionals who can evaluate the situation and determine whether intervention and services are needed. Most states have a toll-free number to call to report suspected child abuse and neglect. Refer to the related organizations listing at www.childwelfare.gov/organizations for information about where to call to make a report in your state.

Another resource for information about how and where to file a report of suspected child abuse or neglect is Childhelp®. The organization runs the Childhelp® National Child Abuse Hotline, which can be reached 7 days a week, 24 hours a day, at its toll-free number 1-800-4-A-CHILD® (1-800-422-4453).

PROBLEM 30.8 (p.376)

a. Neither courts nor the majority of society would consider this child abuse. Grounding a child by not allowing him or her to attend social functions, watch television, talk on the telephone, etc., is usually considered reasonable discipline.

b. Shawn might argue that he is doing the best he can to support and care for his child. He might also say the child is not in danger because the child is asleep when he leaves for work—a job that he needs in order to support his child's well-being. Ask students to think about situations that could put Jeffrey in jeopardy if no one is there to protect or assist him. Even though his actions may not amount to abuse, every state

would find his actions at least negligent. A two-year-old is far too young to be left home alone even for a brief period of time, whether awake or asleep.

To extend this activity, ask students whether they think the following circumstances constitute abuse.

- Parents of a 16-year-old refuse to allow him to date or to go anywhere without them. *Courts would not consider this child abuse, but it may not be considered very good parenting. Many people would consider it unreasonable for parents to refuse to allow their teenage son to date or go anywhere unescorted, unless there were special reasons. Nonetheless, courts will rarely interfere in such parental decisions, as there may be some cultural or religious reason for the parents' actions.*

- Parents require a child to wear a sign for several days saying he is a liar. *An argument can be made that holding a child out for public ridicule on a continuing basis is emotional abuse because the result may be destruction of a child's self-esteem. Children who attempt suicide often relate stories similar to this scenario. The parents in the case upon which this scenario is based were prosecuted for child abuse.*

- Parents go away for the weekend and leave their 6-year-old son in the care of their 12-year-old daughter. *Local laws usually state the age at which children may be left alone without supervision. For example, a 6-month-old is too young to be left home alone for even a brief period of time. While not as irresponsible as leaving a 6-month-old alone, leaving a 12-year-old in charge for the weekend is considered negligent. Unfortunately, such cases rarely come to the attention of authorities unless the practice continues or some tragedy occurs. (For more information about this topic, see the section in the Teacher Manual called "Research—Care and Supervision: At What Age Can I Be Left Home Alone?")*

- Parents treat one daughter differently than they treat her brother and sister. They never buy her new clothes and they forbid her from participating in school and community activities. While the rest of the family eats dinner together, she must eat standing alone in the kitchen. *Sometimes just one child in a family is singled out for abuse. Occasionally he or she is different in some way, such as being more or less attractive than siblings or more or less intelligent. Often, however, there is no discernable reason why a particular child is singled out. Friends, teachers, and others to* whom the child reports this treatment may discount the child's story. Nevertheless, although it might be difficult to prove, habitually discriminating against a single child is emotional abuse and might also indicate the presence of other forms of abuse. It is not uncommon for children to blame themselves rather than their parents for the mistreatment.

- A parent spanks a 4-year-old boy for taking cookies out of the cupboard. The boy cries. *Unless the child is injured by the spanking, courts probably would not consider spanking to be child abuse because a parent has the right (within reasonable boundaries) to physically discipline his or her child. The fact that the child cried does not necessarily indicate the use of excessive force. Students might be interested to learn that Sweden has a law making it a crime to spank one's child. Ask them to identify possible reasons for Sweden's law.*

- A father tells his 14-year-old daughter that she can do anything she wants to do, including staying out all night, as long as she does not bother him. *Telling a 14-year-old child that she can do anything she wants, including staying out all night, might be considered failure to provide adequate care. However, this situation is unlikely to come before a court, unless the daughter becomes involved in some kind of illegal activity.*

THE **CASE** OF...

A Parent, Drug Use, and Neglect

PROBLEM 30.9 (p.377)

This is based on an actual case in Washington, D.C. In the initial family court proceeding, the judge ruled that Kimberly should remain with her mother, Cheryl Addy.[19] The judge decided that despite the evidence of drug abuse in the home, Kimberly was doing well in school and appeared to be well cared for. There was so much public outrage at the idea that a child would be returned to such an environment that police focused their efforts on proving the continued use of the apartment for drug purposes. After a second bust, Kimberly was removed from her mother's care by a different family court judge. The mother entered a drug rehabilitation program and focused her attention on regaining custody of her daughter. Unfortunately, the mother eventually

died of a methadone overdose. (Methadone is a controlled substance that is used to help heroin addicts overcome their addictions. It is not clear whether the mother was given too high of a dosage by the methadone clinic or whether she stole methadone and accidentally overdosed.) After the mother's death, Kimberly's father admitted that he had been responsible for the mother's drug addiction and for the drug use in the apartment. He also told of the mother's devotion to Kimberly and of her efforts to beat her addiction so that she could regain custody of her daughter.

a. Students' answers will vary. Arguments that find Kimberly neglected by Jenna could include the fact that Jenna permitted her daughter to be in a place where illegal and highly dangerous drug use was taking place, exposing Kimberly to both the physical and emotional harms of that situation. As a mother, Jenna has a responsibility to provide a safe and healthy environment for Kimberly. Additionally, she is liable for any illegal activity in her apartment.

   Those who argue that Kimberly was not neglected by her mother could point out that Kimberly is doing well in school and that Jenna is working to provide for her needs. Also, there is no evidence that Jenna is a current drug user. Jenna loves Kimberly and wants to continue to support and care for her.

b. Students' answers will vary. Have students carefully review the language of the statute given in the Student Edition. They should note that the statute indicates that both acts and omissions may constitute neglect. Jenna's failure to remove Kimberly from this situation could be such an omission.

c. Students' answers will vary. The judicial standard for removal of a child from the home is "the best interests of the child." Like judges, students may find it difficult to weigh Kimberly's wish to stay with her mother against possible damage she could face from the environment in her mother's apartment. The judge might order regular drug testing for Jenna and/or require that Jenna's boyfriend not enter the home she shares with Kimberly. As students brainstorm other orders the court might make, remind them that they should consider how the court will monitor whether or not the mother is complying with any orders it may make.

d. Students' answers will vary. Obviously, if the child is aware of the drug use, the parent is serving as a poor role model. However, whether the child is aware of the drugs or not, there will likely be negative effects on the child and on the family as a whole.

ACTIVITY—LEARNING HOW TO REPORT CHILD ABUSE AND NEGLECT

Note: This activity may be more effective and meaningful if one or more resource people are invited to facilitate. Attorneys, social workers, medical personnel, psychologists, police officers, and others working in the field of child abuse and neglect are good sources. A school nurse or guidance counselor could also assist with this discussion. Resource people may suggest additional scenarios similar to the one that follows for students to evaluate.

Ask students what steps they can take if they know someone who is being abused or neglected. Then ask students to refer to the Student Edition. Discuss with students the six steps outlined in the *Steps to Take* feature.

Have students consider the following situation, decide whether the action of the parent should be considered child neglect or abuse, and determine the appropriate steps to take. Be sure students explain their answers.

Assume you see the father of the family next door beating his 10-year-old son. The boy is screaming in obvious pain.

a. What, if anything, would you do? Do you think child abuse should be a crime? *Although people are understandably reluctant to become involved in the affairs of another family, child abuse is a serious matter that should never go unreported. If students have cause to believe that any adult is using excessive force against a child, most people would agree that there is a moral responsibility to contact the authorities.*

b. If the police are called to this home, what should they say and do? *This question is designed to make students more aware of the difficulty of involving state authorities in private family relations. Students should realize the delicate nature of this police work. The police must protect the child against physical abuse while respecting the parents' right to administer discipline. Officers should interview the parents and the children separately. Officers should take care to approach children and parents carefully and respectfully. Many police officers are trained to handle domestic and family violence, which helps them approach situations like this. If officers determine that a crime has been committed, they will proceed accordingly. They may also refer the child to protective services.*

c. If the father is taken to court for continually beating and injuring his son, what should the court do? What should happen to abusive parents? *If the father is taken to court for continually beating and injuring his son, most people agree that the court has a responsibility to protect the child. This may involve placing him in a foster home, shelter, or a state-run group home. Many courts order parents to undergo psychiatric counseling or therapy in cases such as this.*

Students may wish to investigate how child abuse cases are handled in your community. Are abusive parents punished? Provided with counseling? Both? Are there places where children can be removed by the state or county in an emergency situation?

d. Some say that children learn to be violent when they are victims of violence. Do you agree? *Studies show that victims of child abuse often grow up to be child abusers themselves. The reasons for this could be discussed with the assistance of a resource person.*

NOTES

(1) *Family Support Act of 1988*, Pub. L. No. 100–485, 102 Stat. 2343 (codified as amended in scattered sections of 42 U.S.C.).

(2) *Revised Uniform Reciprocal Enforcement of Support Act (RURESA)*, 9B U.L.A. 381 (1968).

(3) *Child Support Recovery Act*, Pub. L. No. 102–521, 106 Stat. 3403 (1992).

(4) *Nelson* v. *Nelson* 548 A.2d 109 (1988).

(5) "Parent and Family Involvement in Education, from the National Household Education Surveys Program of 2012," *The National Center for Education Statistics*, U.S. Department of Education.

(6) "1.1 Million Homeschooled Students in the United States in 2003," *The National Center for Education Statistics*, U.S. Department of Education.

(7) *Delconte* v. *North Carolina*, 313 N.C. 384, 329 S.E.2d.636 (1985).

(8) *Education Week* on the Web: www.edweek.org/ew/issues/home-schooling.

(9) *In re: Rachel L* Cal. App. 2 Dist., 2008.

(10) Surdin, Ashley. "California Parents Eager For Ruling On Home Schooling," *Washington Post*, April 20, 2008, A03.

(11) *Jonathan L. v. Superior Court*, 165 Cal.App.4th 1074 (Cal.App 2 Dist. 2008).

(12) Kasemen, Larry and Susan Kasemen, "Why the Question of Homeschoolers' Playing Public School Sports Affects All Homeschoolers," *Home Education Magazine*, May-June 2000. (13) Id.

(14) *Individuals with Disabilities Education Act*, Public Law 105–17, (1997).

(15) *Parham v. J.R. et al.*, 442 U.S. 584 (1979).

(16) "Moceanu Sues Parents, Alleging Mismanagement," *Washington Post* (October 22, 1998): E2.

(17) "Moceanu Is Declared a Legal Adult; Sorrowful Parents Opt Against Fight," *Washington Post* (October 29, 1998): E1.

(18) *Lassiter v. Department of Social Services*, 452 U.S. 18 (1981).

(19) Weiser, Benjamin. "A Child Living in a Heroin Gallery; Family Court Confronts Issue: Can Addicts Be Fit Parents?" *Washington Post*, December 3, 1988: A1.

CHAPTER 31
Foster Care and Adoption

Children do not always live with their biological, or birth, families. In situations of abuse or neglect, children may be removed from the family home and placed in foster care. Sometimes those children are placed for adoption. Parental problems such as abandonment, physical or mental illness, incarceration, substance abuse, and death may also result in children being placed in foster care. When a child is placed in the foster care system, the state becomes his or her temporary legal guardian and makes most decisions about the child's life.

The process of adoption also removes a child from the biological parents and makes another adult(s) the child's legal parent(s). If the parental rights of the parent of a child in foster care are terminated, then the child may be adopted by the foster family. Children are also placed for adoption when their birth parents make the decision to give them up at birth.

Note: Be aware that you may have students who are in or have been in foster care or who have been adopted. This likelihood will heighten both interest in and sensitivity about these issues. Also be aware that confidentiality laws limit the kind of information that can be shared about children who are in state care or have been adopted. Remain open to students' experiences, sensitive to their history, and cautious about revealing confidential information.

Because students are likely to pose detailed questions about laws in your state related to foster care and adoption, invite a social worker or an attorney who specializes in family law to coteach part or all of this chapter.

FOSTER CARE (PP. 379–380)

Learning Outcomes

After completing this section, students should be able to:
1. describe the circumstances that may lead to a state becoming a child's temporary legal guardian;
2. explain the goals of judges and courts in working with children and families involved in the family foster care system;
3. explain the requirements of the *Foster Care Independence Act of 1999*;
4. summarize the purposes of various court hearings related to removing a child from a family; and
5. define the terms *temporary legal guardian, family foster care, group home, kinship care,* and *terminate parental rights.*

BACKGROUND—THE FOSTER CARE SYSTEM

Being involved in the foster care system can be difficult and often comes as a result of very stressful experiences, including abuse. Youth in foster care often struggle to deal with their own emotions, insecurity about their lives, and being stigmatized by their peers. Still, young people are resilient and those in foster care are not significantly different, as a group, from youth in general. In fact, famous "alumni" of the foster care system include Simone Biles, Steve Jobs, Malcolm X, Eddie Murphy, Marilyn Monroe, John Lennon, Babe Ruth, Alonzo Mourning, and Daunte Culpepper. To learn more about these alumni or others, visit www.fosterclub.com.

According to the North American Council on Adoptable Children, in 2017, nearly 442,995 children were in foster care on any given day in the United States. There has been a 5 year consecutive increase with a 1.5 percent increase from 2016 and a 9.6 percent increase from 2013. However, the number is down from over 500,000 10 years ago. Children may be removed from their parents' home by a child welfare agency because of abuse or neglect and placed in foster care. Other reasons for foster placement include a variety of parental problems. These include abandonment, physical or mental illness, incarceration, AIDS, alcohol/substance abuse, and death. Most youth in foster care live in a family setting of some kind. Current statistics can be found at https://www.nacac.org/2019/01/18/foster-care-numbers-up-for-fifth-straight-year/.

As stated in the Student Edition, many children in foster care are ultimately reunited with their families. In fact, two out of five are reunited with their families within a few years. Other children may spend a longer time in foster care either waiting for an adoptive family or for the termination of their parents' parental rights.

CAPTION ANSWER (P. 380)   Placing children in the care of relatives maintains family bonds, makes adjustment easier, and provides stability and a sense of familiarity.

DISCUSSION—REMOVING CHILDREN FROM THE HOME

Foster care varies from state to state, as do child welfare processes. Thus, using a resource person for this section is especially helpful. Invite an attorney or social worker who works in the child welfare system to talk with the class on this topic.

The *FYI* feature "Removing Children From the Family," in the Student Edition, describes the general process for the removal of children from their homes. Have students research in greater detail the process, terms, and possible outcomes for this situation in their jurisdiction.

This discussion is a good follow-up to "The Case of A Parent, Drug Use, and Neglect," in the Student Edition. Some questions to ask a resource person regarding foster care could include:

- For what reasons can a child be placed in foster care?
- Who is eligible to be a foster parent in our community? How does someone become a foster parent?
- How much financial assistance do court-appointed foster parents receive to offset the costs associated with caring for a foster child?
- How much supervision does the state exercise over foster homes? Are all foster homes licensed?

- Are children represented by an attorney before being placed in foster care? If not, who should represent the interests of the child?
- After being placed in a foster home, how often does a child's case come under review by a court and/or social agency? Are the child's views considered?
- Do foster parents have the right to adopt a foster child following a successful period of foster care?

To conclude, have students review the hearings described in the *FYI* feature "Removing Children From the Family" in the Student Edition. Discuss ways in which hearings in their jurisdiction are the same as or different from those described.

BACKGROUND—THE *ADOPTION AND SAFE FAMILIES ACT OF 1997 (ASFA)* AND THE *FOSTER CARE INDEPENDENCE ACT OF 1997*

Federal and state laws, including the *Adoption and Safe Families Act of 1997 (ASFA)*,[1] require that the state make "reasonable efforts" to both prevent the removal of children from their homes and, if children have been removed, to eventually return them. The main goal of the child welfare system is to keep children safe but also to work toward family reunification.

When it is not possible to return a child to his or her home, the state may seek to terminate the rights of that child's parents, which makes the child available for adoption. *ASFA* changed child welfare law as it relates to termination. Under *ASFA* the state may seek termination of parental rights if a parent has subjected a child to aggravated circumstances that include serious bodily injury, sexual violence, aggravated physical neglect, or if the parents' rights have been involuntarily terminated with respect to another child. In addition, the state *must* seek to terminate parental rights if a child has been in placement for 15 of the previous 22 months or if parents have killed or seriously injured another child in the family. *ASFA* represents a change from a focus solely on family reunification to a primary focus on the safety of the child coupled with an attempt to move children out of foster care and into adoptive homes. After a parent's rights have been terminated, that child may be adopted—most often by his or her foster family.

ASFA also requires that every child have a hearing within 30 days of being removed from his or her home and subsequent hearings every six months after that. At these hearings, judges are required to make sure the child is safe, in the best placement available, and making progress in his or her "permanency plan." This plan outlines what needs to happen with the child and child's family while the child is in care. It describes the services that will be provided and lays out the goals for the child's "permanency." These permanency plans usually call for family reunification but may also include adoption, kinship care, or "independent living," if there are compelling reasons.

As stated in the Student Edition, the *Foster Care Independence Act of 1999* (also known as the Chafee Program)[2] gives older children who are in foster care the right to independent living services until they reach the age of 21. These services may include job training and assistance, life-skills programs, help paying for housing, and other services. Youth may also be eligible for health insurance through Medicaid. Some youth receive educational training vouchers to help pay for college. These programs vary from state to state.

For information about the Chafee Program in your state, contact your state's independent living coordinator. You can find your state coordinator by going to the website of the National Resource Center for Youth Services at www.nrcys.ou.edu and using the search term "independent living coordinator."

According to the Adoption Institute, *ASFA* has had tremendous effects on the number of children adopted from foster care. As a result of *ASFA* and earlier state initiatives, foster care adoptions increased 78 percent from 1996 to 2000, the last year that data was analyzed. In addition, *ASFA* requirements and incentives contributed to 34,000 adoptions from 1998 to 2000 which otherwise would never have occurred.

Furthermore, *ASFA* provides financial incentives to states that are able to exceed their previous years' total number of adoptions from foster care. Statistics for 2001 revealed that 26 states doubled the number of adoptions from foster care over four years, with Wyoming and Delaware tripling their foster care adoptions.

BACKGROUND—DISPROPORTIONATE MINORITY INVOLVEMENT IN FOSTER CARE

As a percentage, there are more children of color in the foster care system than there are in the general population. This is true despite the fact that rates of child abuse and neglect are about the same among all racial and ethnic groups. For more details

and statistics about race and foster care, go to www.fostercarealumni.org.

This problem mirrors similar disproportionate minority representation in the juvenile justice system. If possible, ask your resource person to discuss this issue with students.

ACTIVITY—EVALUATING INFORMATION

Ask students to survey the foster care resources offered on the websites listed below. As they gather data, ask students to evaluate which sites are most interesting and most useful for their purposes in investigating various topics. Students should present their findings in a written report.

- www.fosterclub.com is an interactive online community for youth in foster care. It includes articles, games, and information and resources in each state.
- www.nationalfostercare.org is the website for the National Foster Care Coalition, a national resource that provides information on foster care issues.
- www.nrcys.ou.edu is the online site of the National Resource Center for Youth Services, which has a wide variety of resources for youth in care and the adults with whom they associate.
- www.ylc.org is the website of the Youth Law Center, which has a wealth of information about legal aspects of the child welfare system.
- www.pewfostercare.org is the website for the Pew Commission on Children in Foster Care. The site features videos, statistics, and policy recommendations to improve the lives of children in foster care.

BACKGROUND—THE PROTECTION AND RIGHTS OF CHILDREN IN FOSTER CARE

The U.S. Supreme Court has held that convicted prisoners[3] and people with an intellectual disability[4] have a constitutional right to be free from harm while in state custody. However, despite the urging of many state officials, the Court has yet to determine whether children in foster homes enjoy the same right.[5] As federal circuit courts are split on this issue,[6] the Supreme Court may need to address it in the future. Courts prohibiting such claims against social workers or agencies have determined that case workers are entitled to immunity from damages.

After completing this section, students should be able to:

1. describe the process and legal steps involved in adoptions;
2. explain the types of contracts often signed by surrogate mothers and whether those contracts are enforceable everywhere;
3. summarize the arguments for and against interracial adoptions;
4. evaluate whether or not adoption records should be sealed; and
5. define the terms *adoption* and *surrogate mother*.

BACKGROUND—ADOPTIVE PARENTS' RIGHT TO INFORMATION

Several court opinions have said that adoptive parents may sue an adoption agency (including a governmental agency) for misrepresentation or nondisclosure of material facts about a child. In one case, despite medical reports to the contrary, an agency told adoptive parents that a child they were considering was healthy. After several years of medical problems and expensive tests, the adoptive parents learned that the child had a severe neurological disorder. Their doctor testified that if the child's birth records had been disclosed, he could have diagnosed the disorder earlier. The court in that case emphasized that an adoption agency did not have a duty to predict the future health of a prospective adoptee. What was required, the court determined, was "a good faith full disclosure of material facts concerning existing or past conditions of the child's health."[7]

BACKGROUND—CONSENT OF BIOLOGICAL PARENTS

Most states require the biological (or birth) parents' consent before an adoption can take place. Though some states do not require consent, the U.S. Supreme Court has held that the parents, even if unmarried, must at least be given notice of the adoption hearing and an opportunity to present their point of view.[8] At one time, some states required parental consent only by the mother before an adoption. The Supreme Court held this to be unconstitutional gender discrimination.[9] This ruling

contributed to an increasing number of lawsuits pitting birth parents against adoptive parents. Some birth fathers are now requesting custody of their child/children, claiming they never agreed to adoption. This has raised questions about the fairness of adoption procedures, specifically private ones.

A case exemplifying procedural concerns of adoption is the Baby Jessica case, which ended in July 1993. On February 8, 1991, Cara Clausen gave birth to Jessica. Cara knew Dan Schmidt was the father but claimed the father was another man. She and this other man signed a waiver of parental rights. Roberta and Dan DeBois won custody of Jessica, but before the private adoption was final, Cara changed her mind and told Schmidt that he was the father. The two married and were then awarded custody of Jessica.[10] "In cases such as this, judges are forced to juggle the rights of the biological parents, the adoptive parents, and the child's best interests, and case law is most often on the side of birth parents." As a result, national lobbying efforts are pushing for the enactment of a uniform federal adoption code that could be used as a model law for individual states.

A typical state law designed to regulate private adoption would require the following:

- a social evaluation to be completed before a child could be placed in any adoptive home (currently, only people working with the state or licensed placement agencies are scrutinized);
- a criminal background check of prospective adoptive parents to discover any history of child abuse; and
- prohibition of advertising for birth mothers by agencies that do not have licenses.[11]

Investigating the Law Where You Live

(p. 382) A professional resource person may be the best person to ask about whether your state allows adopted children to find out the identity of their birth parents. Students may also be able to find answers to these questions by going to the website of "Bastard Nation," (www.bastards.org) an advocacy group dedicated to adoptee rights. Their site includes a chart showing a variety of state-by-state laws regarding adoptee records.

CAPTION ANSWER (P. 383) Students' answers will vary but should be supported with evidence.

PROBLEM 31.1 (p.383)

Lead students in a discussion that allows them to examine whether race, religion, marital status, and sexual orientation should be considered in adoption. Have students consider the following questions: Do these considerations factor into whether or not a prospective parent is a fit parent? How do they affect the best interests of the child? Should the birth parents have any say in the matter? Make sure that students list the reasons for their opinions. Have students brainstorm and evaluate arguments that could be used by both supporters and opponents of such policies.

a. Laws or rules that forbid placing a child with an adoptive parent of another race have been held to violate the Equal Protection Clause of the Fourteenth Amendment. However, when race is considered as just one factor that may influence what is in the child's best interest, it has generally been allowed. The U.S. Supreme Court has not yet dealt with this issue. It declined to hear a case in which a federal circuit court decided that the Fourteenth Amendment was not violated when a state adoption agency used race as a factor in removing a child from his foster home.[12]

Of particular concern in such cases is placing children in homes in a timely fashion. African American children often remain in foster care longer than others, so delays are a relevant issue. Research suggests that African American children thrive in Caucasian adoptive homes, provided that parents address racial concerns and do not allow the child to become racially isolated.

Some states' laws forbid the mention of race, religion, or ethnic background in an adoption petition. Some argue that adoption is already difficult on a child; thus the added burden of having to adapt to parents who are of a different race, religion, or ethnicity may be too much for the child to handle. Others argue that as long as the couple loves and supports the child, they will make good parents regardless of race.

In 1994, the federal government passed the *Multiethnic Placement Act (MEPA) of 1994*,[13] and in 1996, it passed the *Removal of Barriers to Interethnic Adoption Provisions (IEP)*.[14] Both laws were designed to address the problems of the disproportionate number of African American children in foster care, that those children tended to stay in foster care longer than Caucasian children, and that there were far more African American children than Caucasian children waiting to be adopted. By making adoption policies more color-blind, children could move from foster care to adoption more quickly.

Fourteen years later, in May 2008, a leading adoption research and policy institute published a report called "Finding Families for African American Children: The Role of Race and Law in Adoptions from Foster Care" suggesting that *MEPA* and *IEP* deserve reconsideration. The report did not suggest limiting interracial adoptions, but it did call for major changes to better serve the needs of children of color and to improve their prospects of moving to permanent, loving homes. Among the study's findings are:

- *MEPA* and *IEP* intended to remove barriers to interracial adoptions but have not resulted in equity in adoption for African American children.
- The "color-blind" interpretations of *MEPA* and *IEP* run counter to widely accepted best practices in adoption.

The provisions of *MEPA* and *IEP* that called for "diligent recruitment" of prospective parents who represent the racial and ethnic backgrounds of children in foster care have not been well implemented or enforced.[15] To follow the impact of this report and to find a link to it, go to www.adoptioninstitute.org.

b. Some states require that a child be placed with adoptive parents of the same religion as the child and/or the biological parents. Where challenged, these laws have usually been upheld on grounds of religious freedom.

c. Students' answers will vary and should be supported with reasons. According to the National Adoption Clearinghouse, the number of single people adopting children has grown steadily and significantly since the 1970s, when most adoption agencies and even some states would not have permitted a single person to adopt a child. Approximately 33 percent of adoptions of children in foster care are by single parents, 25 percent of the adoptions of children with special needs are by single men and women, and it is estimated that about 5 percent of all other adoptions are by single people. Studies show that children adopted by single parents fair well, particularly younger children and older children who "need intense and close relationships."[16]

d. Students' answers will vary and should be supported with reasons. For more background on this topic, see the section below titled "Adoptions by Same-Sex Couples and LGBTQ Individuals."

You may want to continue the discussion this problem raises by asking students whether they think there is a certain age that is either too old or too young to become an adoptive parent. In a California case, the adoptive father was 70 and the mother was 55. The court of appeals ruled in favor of the California parents, who had had a long and successful marriage, financial security, and so on—known qualities that exhibited their stability as individuals and capability as a couple of caring for a child.[17] Ask students if they think there are ages beyond which people would be too old to adopt children.

BACKGROUND—ADOPTIONS BY SAME-SEX COUPLES AND LGBTQ INDIVIDUALS

According to the Census Bureau, between 2000 and 2009 the percentage of same-sex couples who have adopted children has nearly doubled from 10% to 19%. Some people argue that same-sex couples should not be allowed to adopt because the child will be adversely affected by the couple's nontraditional lifestyle. For example, other children may tease the child. Others argue that as long as the couple is loving and supportive of the child, they will make good parents, particularly in light of the high numbers of children in foster care and otherwise in need of a good, stable home.

There are advocacy groups on each side of this debate who can provide students with the various points of view. Encourage students to investigate those groups by searching the Internet or other sources. For a less biased perspective, students may consult the U.S. Department of Health and Human Services National Adoption Information Clearinghouse online at www.childwelfare.gov/topics/adoption/intro. This site offers various points of view about the potential impact on children who are adopted by LGBTQ (lesbian, gay, bisexual, transgender, queer or questioning) parents, including whether or not children will be teased or harassed, whether children raised in households with same-sex parents will become LGBTQ (studies suggest no link), or whether they are any more likely to be molested by their adoptive parents than they would be by heterosexual relatives (a child's risk of being molested by a heterosexual parent is 100 times greater than that of being molested by someone who is a member of the LGBTQ community).

Two types of adoptions relate to LGBTQ couples. In traditional adoption proceedings, a single person or a couple adopts a child. The other type of adoption is called second-parent adoption and is the equivalent of stepparent adoption because it allows a legal parent's partner to adopt the child. Roughly half of the states and the District of Columbia have laws allowing second-parent adoptions for same-sex couples. Court rulings about second-parent adoptions have been sharply divided nationwide. The state supreme courts of both California and Pennsylvania ruled that second-parent adoptions by gay and lesbian parents were legal.[19] As of 2019, the following states permit second-parent adoption: California, Colorado, Connecticut, District of Columbia, Idaho, Illinois, Indiana, Maine, Massachusetts, Montana, New Jersey, New York, Oklahoma, Pennsylvania, and Vermont according to the National Center for Lesbian Rights. The legalization of same-sex marriage nationwide has reduced the need for second-parent adoptions.

Like most issues related to families and children, the question of adoption—specifically adoption by same-sex couples or gay individuals—was tackled by state legislatures and courts with dramatically different results. However, the Supreme Court decisions in *V. L. v. E. L.* (2016)[19] and *Parvan v. Smith* (2017)[20] effectively struck down state same-sex adoption bans. Same-sex couples may now legally adopt in all states.

BACKGROUND—ARTIFICIAL INSEMINATION, SURROGATE MOTHERHOOD, AND ADOPTION

Note: Like other topics in family law, the issues surrounding assisted fertility may be sensitive ones for some students. Please consider which topics you are most comfortable teaching as well as which topics are worthy of stronger emphasis.

Advanced scientific developments have produced new reproductive techniques. One of these is in vitro fertilization, a technique in which a sperm is surgically implanted into an egg. In some cases, the sperm and egg belong to a couple trying to have a child and may be carried either by the female partner or another woman called a surrogate. In other cases, the sperm or egg may be donated and the resulting embryo may be carried by the female partner or by another woman. When the sperm and/or egg are donated or when the resulting embryo is carried by someone other than the woman trying to conceive, legal problems can arise regarding the rights and responsibilities of all parties involved. Courts differ on whether contracts between adoptive parents and surrogate mothers are enforceable.

One of the questions policymakers and prospective parents must consider is how sperm banks are monitored. The law in this area is still evolving. In fact, by some assessments, the law is being outpaced by medical and fertility advances. Questions that face legal and medical experts and ethicists include the safety and regulation of the assisted fertility industry; the rights to inheritance of donated frozen eggs, sperm, or embryos; the responsibilities of clinics that lose embryos or accidentally inseminate women with diseased sperm; and more.[21]

THE CASE OF...

Scarpetta v. The Adoption Agency

PROBLEM 31.2 (p.384)

Students' opinions will vary. Ask students whether there should be a presumption in favor of the biological mother. Should the mother's state of mind be considered? Is it important that she be aware of all the consequences when she makes this kind of decision?

This problem is based on an actual case in the early 1970s. The New York court ordered the baby returned to the biological mother, citing the arguments in Opinion B.[22] After learning the court's decision, the DeMartino family took their children and fled to Florida, where laws and courts are more sympathetic to the rights of adoptive parents. Olga went to Florida and again sued for the return of her baby. The Florida trial court, court of appeals, and state supreme court all decided against her, citing the arguments in Opinion A.[23]

The case raises a constitutional issue: Why didn't the Florida courts follow the decision of the New York court? Why didn't they give "full faith and credit" to the decision of another state court as required by Article IV of the U.S. Constitution? Tell students that this doctrine applies only to *final* decisions of a court. Because the New York court's custody decision could have been reviewed again at a later date, the Florida courts held that it was not entitled to full faith and credit.

NOTES

(1) *Adoption and Safe Families Act of 1997 (ASFA)*, 42 U.S.C. § 1305 (1997).

(2) *Foster Care Independence Act of 1999*, 42 U.S.C. § 677 (1999).

(3) *Estelle* v. *Gamble*, 429 U.S. 97 (1976).

(4) *Youngberg* v. *Romeo*, 457 U.S. 307 (1982).

(5) *LaShawn A.* v. *Dixon*, 762 F. Supp. 959 (D.D.C. 1991) (holding that children in foster care have constitutionally protected liberty interests), affirmed and remanded, 990 F.2d 1319 (D.C. Cir. 1993) (holding that decision should be based entirely on D.C. law), cert. denied, 510 U.S. 1044 (1994).

(6) *Eugene D.* v. *Karman*, 889 F.2d 701(6th Cir. 1989); *Doe* v. *Bobbitt*, 881 F.2d 510 (7th Cir. 1989); and *Babcock* v. *Tyler*, 884 F.2d 497 (9th Cir. 1989) prohibit foster children from pursuing claims against social workers and agencies. In contrast, *L. J. by and through Darr* v. *Massinga*, 838 F.2d 118 (4th Cir. 1988), *Del A.* v. *Edwards*, 855 F.2d 1148 (5th Cir. 1988), and *Taylor* v. *Ledbetter*, 818 F.2d 791 (11th Cir. 1987) found that foster children have a right to be protected from harm.

(7) *Michael J.* v. *Los Angeles County Dept. of Adoptions*, 247 Cal. Rptr. 504 (1988).

(8) *Stanley* v. *Illinois*, 405 U.S. 645 (1972).

(9) *Caban* v. *Mohammed*, 441 U.S. 380 (1979).

(10) Fields, Gary and Desda Moss. "Fight Over Tot Leaves Trail of Tears, Questions," *USA Today* (Tuesday, July 27, 1993): 2A.

(11) "Adoption Reform: Private Adoptions Need Tighter Regulation," *Dallas Morning News*, March 6, 1993, 30A.

(12) *Drummond* v. *Fulton County Department of Family and Children's Services*, 563 F.2d 1200 (1977), cert. denied, 437 U.S. 910 (1978).

(13) *Multiethnic Placement Act (MEPA) of 1994*, PL 103–382.

(14) *Removal of Barriers to Interethnic Adoption Provisions (IEP) of 1996*, as attached to PL 104–88.

(15) Smith, Susan Livingston, et. al "Finding Families for African American Children: The Role of Race and Law in Adoptions from Foster Care" *Evan B. Donaldson Adoption Institute*, May 2008.

(16) Shireman, Joan F. and Johnson, Penny R., "Single Parent Adoptions: A Longitudinal Study. *Children and Youth Services Review*, vol. 7 (1985): 333.

(17) *In re Adoption of Michelle Lee T.*, 117 Cal. Rptr. 856 (1975).

(18) The California case was *Sharon S. v. San Diego County Superior Court*, 2 Cal. Rptr.3d 699 (2003). The Pennsylvania case was *In re Adoption of R.B.F. and R.C.F.*, 803 A.2d 1195 (Pa. 2002).

(19) *V. L. v. E. L.*, 136 S.Ct. 1017 (2016).

(20) *Parvan v. Smith*, 137 S.Ct. 2075 (2017).

(21) Weiss, Rick, "Babies In Limbo: Laws Outpaced by Fertility Advances," *Washington Post*, February 8, 1998, A01.

(22) *Scarpetta, People ex rel. v. Spence-Chapin Adoption Service*, 28 N.Y.2d 185, 321 N.Y.S.2d 65, 269 N.E.2d 787 (1971).

(23) *Scarpetta v. DeMartino*, 254 So.2d 813 (Fla. App. 1971).

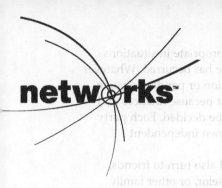
networks™

MARRIAGE PROBLEMS AND SEPARATION AND DIVORCE (PP. 385–390)

Problems in a marriage can sometimes be resolved with the help of family and friends, support groups, the clergy, or through counseling. In some instances, however, the couple may consider ending their marriage. When this occurs, it involves a variety of changes for the entire family, many of which have significant legal consequences. This chapter provides an overview of the legal procedures for ending a marriage through separation agreements or divorce decrees. Either of these two outcomes can also involve the issues of child custody, alimony, property division, and child support. If a parent remarries or finds a new life partner, children may have a new relationship with a step parent. All of these changes involve law.

Learning Outcomes

After completing these sections, students should be able to:
1. list the most common problems in marriages;
2. explain the purpose and protections of separation agreements;
3. state reasons why a waiting period before a divorce can be helpful;
4. list and explain the typical faults, or grounds, that are the basis for divorces;
5. evaluate the merits of no-fault divorces;
6. identify the benefits of using a family mediator; and
7. define the terms *marriage counselor, divorce, separation agreement, pro se, collaborative divorce, no-fault divorce, irreconcilable differences,* and *covenant marriage.*

Note: As with many issues in this unit on family law, be aware that some students may be personally familiar with the topic being covered. This holds especially true for students whose families are in the midst of divorce and custody disputes. Be especially sensitive to the intense feelings and the tendency of children to blame themselves when their parents divorce. Accordingly, strong reactions from students are possible, so to avoid putting anyone on the spot, do not ask students to share their personal experiences unless they volunteer to do so.

CAPTION ANSWER (P. 386) Separation and divorce are similar in that they are legal options for a couple whose marriage has broken down. A separation does not legally end the marriage. It can be temporary or permanent, but neither spouse is free to remarry during this time. A divorce legally ends a marriage. Once a divorce is final, each partner may remarry.

CAPTION ANSWER (P. 387) Divorcing couples face the task of dividing their property; financial obligations such as legal fees, alimony, and child support payments; the cost of maintaining two households; and, if children are involved, the continuing rights and responsibilities that parents must share.

PROBLEM 32.1 (p.388)

a. Students' answers will vary. There is no indication that the couple attempted to solve their marital problems before they considered divorce. Bill and Rachel could hire marriage counselors and/or mediators to help them work through their marital problems. Some government and community agencies provide free resources for people who cannot afford to pay for such services. Many couples in crisis also turn to family members, friends, or religious leaders for help. Many observers of the rising divorce rate believe that couples do not consider all the alternatives and try hard enough to save marriages and instead move too quickly to divorce. Before making the decision to divorce, Bill and Rachel should consider a trial separation as an option.

b. Students' answers will vary, depending on how they see the relationship between Bill and Rachel. A mediator or counselor could work to help the couple improve their communication and problem-solving skills, thereby strengthening the marriage.

If Bill and Rachel are determined to divorce, they might consider a pro se divorce kit and classes to better understand the divorce process. Like pro se divorces, mediation can be less time consuming and less expensive, and can promote better communication between the parties when compared to a more traditional, adversarial divorce involving lawyers. Those who support the use of mediation contend that couples are generally more satisfied with an agreement they reach by their own active decision making, rather than one imposed by a judge or settled by lawyers negotiating on their behalf. Students may also say that parents (with a mediator's help) can better determine issues involving their children than courts. Each party can still have an attorney review the final agreement so that neither party agrees to something illegal or unfair.

If they anticipate a dispute over child custody or property division, each may wish to get their own attorney or arrange for mediation in conjunction with their attorneys. Even if the couple works out an agreement on their own, an attorney should review it before it is signed. It is never a good idea to have the same lawyer represent both parties, as it could present a conflict of interest for the attorney.

Another option is a collaborative divorce or a traditional divorce, both involving lawyers. It may be necessary to use lawyers when couples are in extreme conflict and are unable to settle their own disputes. In addition, one spouse is often a more powerful negotiator than the other. In such instances mediation can be unfair because the other spouse will be at a disadvantage. Those who oppose mediation also argue that spouses who have stayed at home with children may be less likely to understand the legal issues involved, such as tax consequences and need lawyers to negotiate for them and protect their interests.

Mediation may be inappropriate in situations where domestic violence has occurred. Whatever the cause of the separation or pending divorce, legal advice is important because finances and property division must be decided. Each party should have his or her own independent attorney.

Bill and Rachel could also turn to friends, clergy, a marriage counselor, or other family members to help them work through their problems.

c. If Bill and Rachel choose to separate, they will have to decide: (1) who will have custody of their child; (2) what responsibilities each parent will have for child care and support; (3) whether either spouse will provide the other with financial support and, if so, how much; (4) whether one of them will keep the apartment and, if so, what each will pay for rent; (5) how they will divide their savings, car, furniture, and appliances, and (6) how they will handle their joint debts. It is possible for the couple to resolve these issues on their own or with the help of a mediator. However, they should still have an attorney review the agreement before they sign it to ensure that the document is fair and legally binding.

DISCUSSION—COVENANT MARRIAGES

Ask students to read the material on covenant marriages in the Student Edition. Then ask them whether their state should try to reduce the number of divorces by passing a law making covenant marriages possible. Ask students if they think covenant marriages are helpful in reducing divorce rates.

One reason covenant marriage contracts could reduce the number of divorces is that people who enter into a covenant marriage are required to go through more preparation before the marriage, thereby enabling them to evaluate whether they really want to get married and make a lifelong commitment. One reason the divorce rate may not have lessened as a result of the introduction of covenant marriage is that couples may still divorce—the only limitation is that no-fault divorces are prohibited. Divorce using the traditional fault grounds is still permissible.

BACKGROUND AND DISCUSSION— NO-FAULT DIVORCE

All states have some form of no-fault divorce. About one-third of the states have only no-fault divorce, and the other two-thirds of states allow the person filing for divorce to select either fault or no-fault divorce.

No-fault divorces make it much easier for couples to obtain a divorce than in the past, a factor that has contributed to the rise in the number of divorces. Discuss with students whether no-fault divorce laws should be repealed. The discussion might be more substantive if a judge, attorney, social worker, or representative of a women's advocacy organization joins in.

Investigating the Law Where You Live

(p. 389) If students need help finding out whether their state has no-fault divorces and how long divorces typically take in their state, direct them to the website of their state's Bar Association's, or at https://www.nolo.com/legal-encyclopedia/divorce-in-your-state-31013.html.

CAPTION ANSWER (P. 389) The shift to no-fault divorce occurred, in part, because of the difficulty of proving that one spouse was at fault and the embarrassment some people feel is associated with being divorced. In many cases, a finding that one spouse was at fault would preclude him or her from receiving any support after the marriage ended.

PROBLEM 32.2 (p.390)

a. Students' answers will vary. This question is designed to give students an opportunity to discuss an important sociological phenomenon—the decreasing divorce rate. Factors to consider could include:

- fewer people getting married to begin with;
- people waiting until they are over 25 years of age before they marry;
- improving economic conditions;

As noted in the Student Edition, the divorce rate for couples with college degrees is lower than the rate for people without them. Ask students to discuss why they think this is the case.

In 2014, the Huffington Post published an article that discussed 20 scientific studies about divorce that had been conducted in the previous five years. The studies looked at a variety of factors that seemed to impact the likelihood that a couple would get divorced. Not surprisingly,

many of the most significant factors had to do with stress. However, some of the specific stressors might surprise students, such as the length of a couple's commute or a significant difference in how much one person drinks than the other.

b. A fault divorce requires a person to prove one of the grounds listed in the Student Edition. A no-fault divorce usually means that the couple has to separate for a period of time (usually between six months and one year, depending upon the state), before they can get a divorce. State laws may require the couple to declare or prove irreconcilable differences. Partial no-fault divorce means that one of the parties must prove the breakdown and, if the other party disagrees, a trial may be scheduled to determine fault.

c. Students' answers will vary. Some of the reasons for allowing no-fault divorces are that it makes it easier for couples to obtain a divorce; a divorce can be obtained even if neither party is guilty of any specific wrongdoing; there is less stigma, and perhaps less trauma, attached to no-fault divorce because personal attacks on the character of the parties can usually be avoided; and forcing a couple to stay married until fault can be proven can perpetuate domestic violence. Some reasons for requiring a demonstration of fault by one of the parties include the fact that a couple can obtain a divorce more quickly by avoiding the waiting period required by many states before allowing a no-fault divorce; the party who is not at fault may acquire more in the property settlement; and not allowing no-fault divorce could lower the number of divorces by making divorce more difficult to obtain.

d. Students' answers will vary. Arguments for making divorce *more* difficult to obtain include: (1) marriage is a serious relationship that should not be easily undertaken or dissolved; and (2) a mandatory cooling-off period and counseling may decrease the divorce rate.

Arguments *against* making divorce more difficult to obtain include: (1) marriage is a private relationship between two people with which the state should not interfere nor unduly complicate; and (2) if a couple decide that their marriage is no longer viable, they should not have to endure any additional trauma.

CHILD CUSTODY (PP. 390–393)

Learning Outcomes

After completing this section, students should be able to:

1. list reasons custody decisions are among the most important issues settled in a divorce;
2. compare the characteristics and the merits of sole custody and joint custody arrangements;
3. identify factors judges consider in determining which parent is awarded custody; and
4. define the terms *custody, joint custody, tender years doctrine, best interests of the child,* and *kinship care.*

BACKGROUND—CUSTODY

At one time, some courts considered race when they determined custody. In 1984, a case came to the U.S. Supreme Court involving a Caucasian couple who divorced, and the mother was awarded custody of their child. Later, the father petitioned to change the custody order, in part because the mother had moved in with and then married an African American man. The father believed that the child would be harmed by living in a racially mixed household. Lower courts agreed with the father, but the U.S. Supreme Court disagreed, saying: "A core purpose of the Fourteenth Amendment was to do away with all governmentally imposed discrimination based on race.... The effects of racial prejudice, however real, cannot justify a racial classification removing an infant child from the custody of its natural mother. The Constitution cannot control such prejudice, but neither can it tolerate it. Private biases may be outside the reach of the law, but the law cannot, directly or indirectly, give them effect."[1] Today, interracial marriages and families are much more common.

CAPTION ANSWER (P. 391) Custody decisions are important because the parent with custody decides most aspects of the child's life. The judge must make his or her decision in the best interests of the child.

PROBLEM 32.3 (p.391)

Students should read the entire section on child custody before they answer these questions.

a. The advantages of joint custody include the following: (1) it will give the child a greater opportunity to develop a strong relationship with each parent; and (2) it will allow both parents to share in the rewards and responsibilities of child rearing. However, if the divorcing couple cannot work out a plan that is amenable and desirable to the child, it can add additional stress to the divorce and for the child.

b. The advantages of sole custody include the following: (1) the child will likely feel more secure living in just one home, with one parent making all of the major decisions; and (2) there will be less tension and fewer arguments between the parents if they do not have to interact regularly through a joint custody arrangement. The disadvantages of sole custody include: (1) the noncustodial parent may end up having less of a relationship with the child; and (2) the child could suffer from the emotional stress of prolonged separation from the noncustodial parent. Discuss what kind of arrangement students believe is preferable.

c. Additional information the court might want to consider before rendering a decision could include how strongly each parent desires custody; each parent's plan for providing child care; the time and travel demands of each parent's employment; the quality of each parent's relationship with the child; the emotional stability of each parent and the emotional stability and needs of the child; and possible effects of various custody arrangements. Generally, judges base their custody decisions on their view of what is in the best interest of the children and may even consider the input of older children.

d. Joint custody requires that both parents cooperate on a wide range of issues concerning their child, and the court requires an indication that cooperation is likely. Ultimately, if the parents cannot agree, the court will choose a custody arrangement. However, parents can negotiate the custody relationship (along with the other issues that need to be decided in a divorce) and present this arrangement to the court. Courts often ratify the arrangement that parents devise because they feel the parents have a better idea about what is best for their child and they are the ones who have to live with the arrangement. The court is unlikely to rule in favor of joint custody if the parents do not agree on this type of agreement.

CAPTION ANSWER (P. 392) Kinship care is an arrangement where a child is placed in the continuous care of relatives, such as grandparents, who are not his or her parents. Such placement often occurs when substance abuse, divorce, incarceration, or other family problems have prevented the parents from providing adequate care for the child.

ALIMONY, PROPERTY DIVISION, AND CHILD SUPPORT (PP. 393–397)

Learning Outcomes

After completing this section, students should be able to:

1. identify three economic issues that must be settled for a divorce to be finalized;
2. explain the purpose of rehabilitative alimony;
3. describe the factors that courts consider in awarding alimony;
4. define the terms *alimony, rehabilitative alimony, community property* and *equitable distribution*;
5. distinguish between alimony and property division; and
6. explain various ways the law helps parents enforce child support orders.

DISCUSSION—ALIMONY

Census Bureau data show that women tend to fare much worse economically than men after divorce. Following divorce, most women experience a decrease in available income while most men experience an increase in their economic well-being. In many cases this occurs because women have traditionally stayed home during their marriages to care for children while men pursued their educations and careers. Consequently, after divorce, women may have to restart their careers by accepting entry-level positions. Some also argue that discrimination against women in the job market and pay inequity contribute to this disparity. Students should remember that while these socioeconomic factors were the trend for many years (and are still true for many families), states may not restrict alimony payments to women only at the exclusion of men.[3]

Ask students whether a person should receive a greater share of the property in a divorce or larger alimony payments to compensate for not pursuing an education or a career during the marriage. Ask students whether the custodial parent should have a greater or lesser responsibility for alimony and/or child support than the noncustodial parent. Have students discuss whether they think alimony and/or child support payments should be equal or proportional to each parent's income or if the parent with the most income should have the responsibilities for alimony and/or child care.

PROBLEM 32.4 (p.395)

a. In all states, the property belongs to Veronica because she acquired it before her marriage.

b. In community property states (listed in the Student Edition), the vacation home belongs equally to Frances and Leon because it was acquired during the marriage and would be divided equally between the two upon divorce. In most other states, property acquired during the marriage is marital property, belonging to both spouses. Upon divorce in these states, however, if equitable distribution is the guiding principle, a court will consider a number of factors in distributing the marital property, which means that it may or may not be split between Frances and Leon, and that split may not be equal. This question presents students with an opportunity to discuss what factors should be considered in the equitable distribution of property. It also highlights the policy that unless specifically contracted otherwise, property acquired during marriage (except by gift or bequest) belongs to the marital unit rather than to either individual.

c. Arguments for the equitable distribution of property include the following:

- Spouses who bring more financial assets to the marriage are compensated accordingly.
- In longer marriages, it provides compensation for the in-kind (nonmoney) contributions of nonworking spouses.
- Both spouses' needs are considered in the distribution of property so as not to disadvantage a spouse who does not have the means to provide for himself or herself.
- Some people believe that consideration of the length of marriage is an advantage in deciding what is equitable.

    On the other hand, in community property states, the length of the marriage is irrelevant, so marital property is distributed equally no matter how long or short the marriage is.

- Some argue that this system unfairly rewards nonworking spouses and penalizes individuals with the means to acquire property and assets during a marriage.

Note: Some community property states give judges discretion to use some equitable principles in determining property division. If yours is a community property state, consult with a lawyer who practices in this area before explaining the law to students.

DISCUSSION—CHILD SUPPORT

Note: The state's general interest is in making sure that children receive adequate support, both for the children's sake and to diminish the need for government support. Ask students to consider the results if a separated or divorced parent does not make alimony and/or child support payments required in their separation or divorce agreements. Pose the following questions to students.

- What should courts do if a parent will not or cannot pay child support?
- Should the nonpaying parent be fined or sent to jail? Would this help the situation or make the problem worse?
- Should support payments be deducted directly from the delinquent parent's paycheck?
- Should the parent responsible for making support payments be forced to seek work?

Remind students that the *Family Support Act of 1988 (FSA)*[4] requires states to establish clear guidelines for child support and also to provide support to help locate parents who have failed to provide the required support. The *FSA* allows states to deduct child support payments from salaries and to track delinquent parents by their Social Security numbers. The *Uniform Child Custody Jurisdiction and Enforcement Act (UCCJEA)*[5] requires states to accept and enforce custody agreements established in other states unless very specific and unusual circumstances arise. Among other things, this helps provide families with the stability that might otherwise be threatened if one ex-spouse decides to "shop around" for states that have more favorable laws after a custody agreement has already been reached in the state where the family lived when the couple was still married.

The Medical School Degree

PROBLEM 32.5 (p.396)

This problem is based on a 1984 case in which the genders were reversed, but the situation was essentially the same. The plaintiff, Janet Sullivan, lost at the trial level and then again on appeal. The California Supreme Court reversed the decision and sent it back to the trial court.[6] The trial court could have decided to compensate Sullivan for half the cost of her husband's education. California law requires reimbursement of one spouse's contribution to education that enhanced the other's earning capacity. Other state courts have been split on this issue. A few consider the value of the degree, many award restitution for contributions, and a few give nothing.

In a 1982 New Jersey case, the state court ruled that the professional degree was *not* subject to equitable distribution, but that the spouse who supported the degree earner may be entitled to alimony because she contributed to her spouse's professional education with the expectation of deriving material benefits from the degree later. The Court stated:

> "Marriage cannot be a free ticket to professional education for anyone without subsequent obligations. . . . One spouse ought not to receive a divorce complaint and the other receive a diploma. Those spouses supported through professional school should recognize that they would be called upon to reimburse the supporting spouses with financial contributions they received in pursuit of professional training. And they cannot deny the fairness of this result."[7]

In New York, the state courts have found that professional degrees are marital property, and in one precedent-setting case for that state, the wife who supported her husband while he earned a professional degree was entitled to half of the value of that degree. The court determined the degree's value, which could be set by its cost, its earning potential over the doctor's lifetime, or over a set number of years.[8]

a. Roberto is asking for part of Marta's income as a doctor because he worked to support her while she completed medical school. When they divorced, they had very little property to divide, and Roberto felt he should receive some of the value of the medical degree that his earnings helped Marta to earn. He also felt that he should receive some of the degree's future earning potential.

b. Students' answers will vary. This is one of the most difficult issues in divorce cases. Some argue that college and professional degrees are property and that, for property settlement purposes, a value (that is, lifetime increased earning potential) can be placed on a degree. Others say that if one spouse agrees to stay home with the children or contribute earnings so that the other can pursue a degree, this constitutes a gift between the spouses and therefore should be left free of interference. Still others say that the person who actually earned the degree deserves its full value.

Opponents of this view argue that those who worked hard and sacrificed to support their spouse are often taken advantage of by the student-spouse. They state that the spouse who supported the student did so based on the belief that increased future earnings were implicitly promised.

Some call for a middle ground in which the working spouse is reimbursed the amount of tuition that he or she paid. Others advocate giving the spouse partial compensation for the value of the degree.

PROBLEM 32.6 (p. 397)

Note: A mediator trained in family conflicts or an attorney specializing in divorce law could add depth and expertise to this discussion.

a. Students' answers will vary. If Carmen obtains custody of the younger children, she is likely to be awarded substantial child support and possibly rehabilitative alimony. The alimony she receives is likely to be short-term, covering the time it takes for Carmen to receive any needed training and to get a job. The amount of child support awarded may be determined by state guidelines. Because the children are young, she will need child care and support for a longer period of time than Miguel. His larger income will probably require him to pay child support.

b. Students could argue that Angela should pay alimony until Leroy gets a regular job and can provide his own support. Angela could argue that her salary is not large enough to support them both. She might point out that Leroy chose to be a writer, and she should not have to pay for his lack of success. Leroy might also be required to provide a portion of his income for child support.

STEPPARENTS (P. 397)

Learning Outcomes

After completing this section, students should be able to:

1. explain how the changing makeup of families in the United States relates to the rights and responsibilities of stepparents;
2. describe the conditions under which a stepparent can adopt his or her stepchildren; and
3. define the term *in loco parentis*.

BACKGROUND—STEPPARENTS AND STEPCHILDREN

The number of stepchildren in the United States is not known. According to the National Stepfamily Resource Center (NSRC), this number is difficult to determine, in part because the Census has changed the ways it reports marriages, divorces, and remarriages. According to the "Step Family Fact Sheet" from the website of the NSRC (www.stepfamilies. info):

- 12.3% are part of a stepfamily,
- 69.8% live with two parents,
- 62.5% live with their biological mother and father,
- 4.5% live with their biological mother and stepfather, and
- 1.2% live with their biological father and stepmother.

According to the 2010 census, the number of stepchildren was approximately 4.1 million, accounting for roughly 5 percent of all American children.

To learn more about organizations and websites devoted to supporting positive relationships between stepparents and stepchildren, visit the National Stepfamily Resource Center online at www.stepfamilies.info.

CAPTION ANSWER (P. 397) Stepparents can become full parents by adopting their stepchildren.

NOTES

(1) *Palmore v. Sidoti*, 466 U.S. 429 (1984).

(2) *Federal Parental Kidnapping Prevention Act of 1980*, 28 U.S.C. § 1738A (1980).

(3) *Orr v. Orr*, 440 U.S. 268 (1979).

(4) *Family Support Act of 1988*, Pub. L. No. 100–485, 102 Stat. 2343 (codified as amended in scattered sections of 42 U.S.C.).

(5) *Uniform Child Custody Jurisdiction and Enforcement Act (UCCJEA)*, 9 (1A) U.L.A. 657 (1999).

(6) *In re Marriage of Sullivan*, 691 P.2d 1020 (1984).

(7) *Mahoney v. Mahoney*, 91 NJ 488 (1982).

(8) *O'Brien v. O'Brien*, (new citation) 66 N.Y.2d 576 (1985).

The case on page 392 of the Student Edition, in which the U.S. Supreme Court struck down a Washington state law that allowed visitation rights to anyone who could show that visitation would be in the best interests of the child, was *Troxel v. Granville*, 530 U.S. 57 (2000).

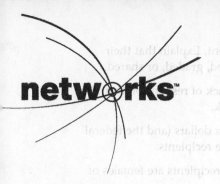
networks™

Congress has passed many laws creating social programs that provide economic, educational, housing, and health benefits to millions of Americans since the Great Depression of the 1930s. These programs have been met with open arms by some and with opposition by others.

In the twenty-first century, government social programs are a continuing source of controversy in the United States. This chapter discusses which groups of people benefit from government support programs, what the criteria are for inclusion in them, and how these programs operate.

INTRODUCTION (PP. 398–399)

Learning Outcomes

After completing this section, students should be able to:
1. explain how the government determines who is poor and how many children and adults are estimated to live in poverty;
2. name several government support programs designed to help poor people; and
3. name several government support programs designed to help all Americans, regardless of income.

DISCUSSION—WHOM SHOULD THE GOVERN-MENT HELP?

Core issues for this chapter include what role, if any, the government should play in helping people; who should qualify for assistance; and when it should be provided. Elicit students' views on this issue by using a continuum exercise. This activity will be most effective if used before students read Chapter 33.

Post signs reading "Yes" and "No" at opposite ends of the classroom, and ask students to place themselves along the continuum between the signs to indicate their answers to each of the following questions. Postpone requests for clarification. Tell students to focus on how they feel *in principle* about each group.

Should the government provide financial help and/or social programs for:

- elderly people?
- drug addicts?
- homeless people?
- poor children?
- farmers?
- home owners?
- poor families?
- people who have AIDS?
- people who lack health insurance?
- military veterans?
- people who have immigrated to the United States legally?
- undocumented immigrants?
- large corporations?
- small businesses?
- people with physical disabilities?
- alcoholics?
- people with developmental disabilities?
- people who suffer from mental illness?

- college students?
- people who have lost their jobs?
- millionaires?
- people who are hungry?
- all families with children regardless of income?

In a follow-up discussion, tell students that every group listed in the continuum exercise benefits to some extent from government programs or assistance. Explain that students will learn more about these programs in this chapter.

If time permits, have students examine assumptions people make. For example, some people argue that every society includes citizens who are disadvantaged and/or helpless to some degree. A society that regards itself as civilized must provide a "safety net" to minimize suffering. From this point of view, social programs are a necessary function and a responsibility of government.

Other people believe that our society prizes self-reliance, and they assume that when the government provides assistance, individuals lose the motivation to support themselves and their families, undermining self-reliance. From this point of view, government social programs do more harm than good to those they are intended to assist.

Another issue is what criteria are used in determining who should receive assistance from the government. Ask students what criteria they applied as they took positions along the continuum. Possible answers include: having an income below a certain level; having children or being a child; having a disability; being elderly; having a health problem; being a target of discrimination; living in a depressed area; and being unable to find employment. Governments may also assist certain groups as a way of investing in the future or as a means of reducing future spending. This may serve as a rationale for funding education or public health programs.

LEGAL RESOURCE PERSONS

Legal resource persons can provide valuable insights into the assumptions behind, rationale for, and inner workings of various government programs. Officials from government agencies, legislators, social workers, or lobbyists could visit your class to describe why social programs exist and how they are administered.

ACTIVITY—DEBUNKING WELFARE MYTHS

Give students a handout with the following statements about welfare. Ask students to indicate whether they think "most people" would agree or

disagree with each statement. Explain that their answers will not be collected, graded, or shared.

1. Poverty results from a lack of responsibility and an unwillingness to work.
2. A large proportion of tax dollars (and the federal budget) supports welfare recipients.
3. The majority of welfare recipients are females of color.
4. People on welfare often become permanently dependent on government support.
5. Welfare recipients use government benefits to fund extravagant, luxury purchases.

After students have completed their individual work, review each statement with the class and ask students to discuss whether they think most people would agree or disagree with the statement. Make sure students understand that they are not necessarily revealing their own answers—just what they think most people would say. After students guess about answers, reveal the facts for each statement. This is an opportunity to debunk common myths.

1. Poverty most often results from low wages. In fact, most people who are poor and who are old enough to work do work. However, they do not earn enough money from their jobs. These people are often known as the "working poor."
2. Welfare costs equal approximately 1 percent of the federal budget and 2 percent of state budgets.
3. Most welfare recipients are children. Most women on welfare are white.
4. Movement off welfare is frequent. The majority of welfare recipients use benefits only on a temporary basis.
5. Welfare families continue to live far below the poverty line despite receiving government assistance.

Conclude the activity by asking students to discuss the following questions:

- How does this information compare to your initial impressions?
- From where do most people get their impressions about welfare and welfare recipients?
- Why might the media's portrayal and the public perception of the welfare system differ from reality?
- How do myths about welfare affect people and policies?

As an extension activity, have students examine newspapers, magazines, and the Internet to find examples of articles about poverty, government assistance programs, and politicians' speeches about welfare. Ask students how these sources illustrate the welfare system and the people who use welfare benefits. Ask students why they think this is the case.

PROBLEM 33.1 (p.399)

a. Students' answers will vary. The causes of poverty and the appropriate responses to it cannot be addressed comprehensively in a law class. Economics and sociology courses typically focus on this issue in greater depth. Nevertheless, without a basic understanding of the causes of poverty, students will have difficulty comprehending why government programs have been created to assist people who face poverty.

The concept of a cycle of poverty may help students understand why it is difficult for people born into impoverished families to escape that poverty. Many forces operate against poor people, including poor nutrition and health, poor housing, dangerous neighborhoods, families in crisis, discrimination, limited job opportunities, etc.

Many people argue that upward economic mobility is tied to education. If a child's school is poorly funded and his or her home environment is not conducive to success in school, then it is very difficult to break out of poverty. The income gap between workers with a college education and those without a college education has grown dramatically in recent years. Most contemporary service-sector jobs available to people without higher education do not pay enough to keep a family above the poverty level.

Structural economic factors also contribute to poverty. The mixed-market economic system in the United States experiences market fluctuations and recessions, both of which create unemployment. Economists consider a 3–4 percent unemployment rate to be "full employment," meaning that at any given time many workers will be without jobs through no fault of their own—even when the economy is healthy. The loss of manufacturing jobs and the disappearance of farms and numerous factories and stores in cities have created substantial unemployment. Housing costs have increased dramatically as the supply of affordable housing has diminished.

Ask students to explain their answers regarding problems the government can solve. For those it cannot, are there other groups that could help? (religious groups, philanthropic groups, corporate or personal foundations)

b. Students' answers will vary. Those who favor standardizing the amount of aid people receive argue that unequal payments cause poor people to move to states with higher government assistance allotments, creating fiscal problems for some states while allowing other states to avoid their responsibility to the poor. Opponents argue that the cost of living in some states is higher than in others and that states with lower payments generally have less money for all purposes. An alternative to standardization is adjusting welfare payments according to the cost of living in each state.

In 1999, the U.S. Supreme Court examined the issue of whether a state may restrict the amount of benefits it pays to welfare recipients who have moved from a different state to only the amount that the recipient would have received had he or she not moved. The state of California wished to decrease benefits to new recipients moving to the state in an attempt to dissuade poor families from immigrating simply to receive welfare. The Supreme Court considered the constitutional guarantees of equal protection and the right to travel.[1] The Court held that our system of federalism and the privileges and immunities clause of the Fourteenth Amendment require states not to hinder the rights of citizens to travel and move among the states. The Court struck down the California policy because it was discriminatory toward citizens who were moving from states that offered lower welfare benefits. The Court recognized and rejected California's attempt to discourage lower-income citizens from taking up residence in the state.

ECONOMIC BENEFITS FOR INDIVIDUALS AND FAMILIES (PP. 399–403)

Learning Outcomes

After completing this section, students should be able to:

1. describe the Social Security system and name three benefits it provides;
2. identify beneficiaries of the federal Supplemental Security Income program;
3. summarize the criticism of the welfare system before it was changed in 1996;
4. describe the benefits of the *Personal Responsibility and Work Opportunity Reconciliation Act of 1996* and the requirements and limitations of those benefits; and
5. identify who benefits and the types of benefits derived from food stamps, and housing assistance and mortgage interest deductions.

ACTIVITY—REFLECTION ABOUT ASSISTANCE TO NEEDY FAMILIES AND WELFARE REFORM

Remind students that the reforms that came as a result of the *Personal Responsibility and Work Opportunity Reconciliation Act of 1996*[2] remain controversial. Give students a handout with the following questions and ask them to privately answer the questions about their own views of welfare reform.

- Should people who receive assistance in this program be required to work or to attend a vocational training program? Should the age of the recipient make a difference? Why or why not?

- Should there be a limit on how many years a family can receive assistance in this program? Should it affect their eligibility if a family makes a successful transition off welfare and then experiences difficulty again years later? Explain your answers.

- Should immigrants be denied welfare? Should it affect their eligibility whether they are documented or undocumented immigrants? Why or why not?

- Should unmarried minors who are parents be required to stay in school or return to school and to live in an "adult-supervised setting" in order to receive benefits? Explain your answer.

- Should the government have a duty to ensure that all parents who are trying to make the transition to work can get affordable child care and health insurance? Should it limit this duty that the costs of these benefits would be very high for communities and states—possibly leading to tax increases or to cuts in other programs? Why or why not?

- Should states be required to move a certain percentage of people from welfare to work in a specified period of time or risk losing federal funding? Should it affect states' qualifying for federal funds if states have difficulty paying for welfare reform programs, especially if the economy is poor? Explain your answers.

BACKGROUND AND RESEARCH— HUNGER IN AMERICA AND FOOD ASSISTANCE PROGRAMS

As mentioned in the Student Edition, the Census Bureau estimated nearly 15 million households were "food insecure" in 2018. According to the U.S. Department of Agriculture, more than 37.2 million people living in 14.3 million households (11.1 percent of U.S. households) were struggling with hunger in 2018. Of them, 6 million were children, representing 13.9% of all children. The Student Edition also noted that the average benefit under the Food Stamp Program (Supplemental Nutrition Assistance Program/SNAP) was about $1 per meal. In 2017, the average SNAP household received about $254 a month (about $126 per month per recipient) which is approximately $1.40 per meal.

Students who are curious about the extent of hunger in their own states and across the country, as well as government and private programs designed to end hunger, should consult the websites of the following agencies or groups:

- **The Food Research and Action Center (FRAC)** is a nonprofit organization that advocates for improved public policies and public-private partnerships that will end hunger and poverty. Their website offers extensive and easy-to-read information about demographics, poverty, food stamp participation, and state-by-state data and resource information. Find them at www.frac.org.

- **The United States Department of Agriculture (USDA)** administers the SNAP program and the Special Supplemental Nutrition Program for Women, Infants, and Children, commonly known as WIC. USDA also runs other child nutrition programs such as the National School Lunch Program (which serves 31 million children each day), School Breakfast Program, the Summer Food Service Program, and the Child and Adult Care Food Program. Find them at www.usda.gov using the search term "child nutrition."

ACTIVITY—CONDUCTING AN INTERVIEW

Ask students to work individually, in pairs, or in small groups to interview people who work in agencies that provide government benefits in your area. During the interview students should ask for samples of forms that applicants must complete. Then they should examine and discuss them during the interview. Students should create their own questions for the interview or use some of the following:

- Who is eligible for benefits?
- What steps must someone take to obtain benefits?
- What rules affect the amount of benefits a person can obtain?
- Is there a waiting period before benefits begin?
- How long are benefits available?
- Do people have a right to a hearing if they are denied eligibility or if their benefits are reduced or terminated?
- How essential are these benefits to those who receive them? Does this program benefit children? If so, how would their lives be different if they could not obtain these benefits?
- In your opinion, do most recipients of these benefits tend to lose motivation to take responsibility and be self-sufficient because they receive this assistance?
- Did welfare reform legislation alter your program? If so, how? Do you regard these reforms as a success or a failure? Why?
- Do people who really need and deserve assistance slip through the cracks in this system? If so, what are the consequences?
- Suppose recipients want to live without these benefits. What obstacles might they face as they seek independence?
- What problems exist with these programs? Can they be solved?

When their interviews are complete, students should synthesize what they have learned about government support for families and individuals and then present their findings in side presentation to the class.

ACTIVITY - WHAT BENEFITS SHOULD VETERANS ENJOY?

Ask students what benefits they believe someone who has received an honorable discharge from the armed services should enjoy. Have students work in small groups to generate a list. Make a master list by bringing the class back together and calling on groups to give one benefit until groups have given all the benefits on their lists. Tell students that the veteran saw active duty in a combat zone and received significant injuries resulting in being confined to a wheel chair. Ask students if they would add to the master list? Tell students some veterans experience difficulty finding employment when they return home. Ask them if they would like to add to the master list. Tell students that veterans often report dealing with PTSD (post traumatic stress disorder), depression, substance abuse, and suicidal thoughts after returning from tours in combat zones. Ask them if they would add to the master list. Tell students some veterans eventually succumb to their injuries and pass away. Ask them if they would all to the master list. Have students visit the U.S. Department of Veterans Affairs' website at https://www.va.gov/ and read the benefits and health care available to veterans. As a class cross check the list you made with the list of benefits. Did the class think of benefits that the government does not provide? Does the VA provide benefits the class did not put on the list? Conclude with a class wide discussion on whether Veterans are provided with adequate benefits.

PROBLEM 33.2 (p.402)

a. Students' answers will vary. Students who oppose safety net programs might argue that they are costly; that taxpayers should not have to forfeit hard-earned dollars to support people who should be supporting themselves; and that these programs make people dependent, creating more harm than good for those who receive benefits.

   Students who support safety net programs might argue that they are necessary to limit the suffering of children, the elderly, and others who are helpless to some degree or who face disadvantages; and that we pay taxes to promote the common good. They may also argue that all people in the United States are entitled to basic human rights, including social and economic rights such as the right to food, shelter, and health care.

b. Expanded safety net programs would require higher taxes, spending cuts for other government programs, or both.

c. If we fail to provide safety net programs, we will likely face other costs. If, for example, preventive health care is eliminated, then more people will likely get serious illnesses that will cost more money to treat. In addition, children who are malnourished will suffer educationally, which will make them less employable or less productive as workers. Crime rates will also rise in communities if people lack basic necessities and skills.

ACTIVITY—CONDUCTING RESEARCH

The federal government chartered two private corporations to help low- and moderate-income families become homeowners. Fannie Mae and Freddie Mac are regulated by the U.S. Department of Housing and Urban Development. Both organizations provide information and access to financing programs that make paying for a home possible. Direct students to the "resources" pages at www.fanniemae.com or www.freddiemac.com where they can find resources explaining how to get a mortgage, select a home, and achieve home ownership. Ask students to survey these sites and summarize how these programs help individuals and families.

BACKGROUND—HOUSING ASSISTANCE AND HOMELESSNESS

Remember that in Chapter 27 students can learn more about the rights of tenants and landlords as well as about the problems relating to homelessness. There are also materials about these topics in Chapter 27 of the Teacher Manual.

Before government agencies can provide housing assistance to people who need it, they must know the extent of the problems relating to housing so they can plan and budget accordingly. As indicated in the Student Edition, some people estimate that more than half of the families eligible for housing assistance do not receive it. Ask students to hypothesize why so many people who are eligible do not receive support.

One group of people who are particularly difficult to support is the homeless population. Government(s) and advocacy groups need to plan for the number of people who will need help. The size of the homeless population is difficult to estimate because it changes daily, and many homeless people do not remain in a single location long enough to be accounted for. There may be a number of explanations for differences in estimates between government agencies and homeless advocates.

Government officials who collect census data may have difficulty finding homeless people because they take their census counts from mail-in surveys, visits to people's homes, and online surveys. Homeless advocacy groups, who serve this population directly, may have a better sense of its dimensions and trends. Advocacy organizations that seek funding and favorable legislation also need to paint a dramatic picture of the problem to win more funding, while others might minimize the problem for political or economic reasons.

Just prior to the 2000 census, many homeless advocates and the executive branch of government wanted to use a new form of collecting census data that would allow for statistical sampling because, they said, the results would include more traditionally undercounted people and would be more reliable. Critics said this proposal would violate the law and would overestimate people who are typically difficult to count, such as people who are homeless or poor people who move frequently. The controversy went to the U.S. Supreme Court, which ruled that census law prohibits statistical sampling for this purpose.[3]

Investigating the Law Where You Live

(p. 402) If students have trouble finding the public housing options that exist in their community, suggest they visit the website for the U.S. Department of Housing and Urban Development and follow the links to their own state at http://portal.hud.gov/hudportal/HUD?src=/program_offices/public_indian_housing/pha/contacts. The site also offers fact sheets about public housing, as well as information about renting, buying, and other resources for people looking for housing support. Much of the information is available in Spanish as well as in English.

CAPTION ANSWER (P. 402) The government allows tax deductions on the interest paid on a mortgage in order to encourage home ownership and to make homes more affordable. The majority of homeowners who benefit from this deduction are in the middle and higher-income brackets.

HEALTH BENEFITS (PP. 403–405)

Learning Outcomes

After completing this section, students should be able to:

1. identify groups of Americans who are least likely to have health insurance benefits;
2. explain the requirements and benefits of *The Patient Protection and Affordable Care Act;*
3. describe Medicare and Medicaid programs in terms of benefits and eligibility;
4. explain the purpose of the State Children's Health Insurance Program (SCHIP); and
5. describe the benefits of the *Family and Medical Leave Act* and who is eligible for these benefits.

BACKGROUND—MEDICARE REFORM

There has been much debate over the system of Medicare and calls for reform since its inception in 1965. For almost 40 years, contentious policy debates resulted in no substantial alterations to the system. This changed in December 2003, when the *Medicare Prescription Drug Improvement and Modernization Act of 2003* was signed into law.[4] The reforms were achieved amid much controversy. Supporters of the new plan were pleased that it provides many seniors and people living with disabilities with a prescription drug benefit, a health savings account, and various other health care options. Critics argued that the plan did not provide enough benefits for senior citizens, that the reforms significantly overburden future taxpayers, and that the reform demonstrates a shift toward privatization of Medicare that benefits drug companies and insurance companies more than it serves citizens.[5]

To learn more about Medicare reform, visit the following websites:

- The Center on Budget and Policy Priorities, which opposes the reform, www.cbpp.org/11-18-03health2.htm.
- The National Center for Policy Analysis, which opposes the law, www.nationalcenter.org using the search term "Medicare reform."
- AARP, which supports parts of the reform, www.aarp.org using the search term "Medicare reform."
- The Department of Health and Human Services Centers for Medicare & Medicaid Services, which supports and administers the program, www.cms.hhs.gov/. This site also contains information about Medicaid and the SCHIP program.

Center for Medicare Advocacy which works for comprehensive Medicare and health coverage for all people at https://www.medicareadvocacy.org/medi-care-info/medicare-and-health-care-reform/.

BACKGROUND AND ACTIVITY— ADOLESCENTS AND HEALTH INSURANCE

Health care can be extremely expensive without insurance, even for routine checkups and procedures, not to mention prescriptions, emergency care, and hospitalization. As a result of the Affordable Care Act, the number of Americans with health insurance has increased, however some Americans still do not have health insurance. People without health insurance use fewer health services, receive care less frequently, return for fewer follow-up appointments, use fewer preventative and healing medicines, and are more likely to seek care in an emergency room. As a result, health problems tend to become more acute in people without health insurance, and the expenses tend to increase dramatically.

Some people even cite the lack of health insurance as a cause of poverty and homelessness. Clearly, health insurance plays a critical role in ensuring access to appropriate health services. During the past decade, federal and state governments have made a significant effort to expand health insurance coverage to children and adolescents in low- and moderate-income families through programs such as Medicare and the State Children's Health Insurance Program (SCHIP), as described in the Student Edition. Additionally, under the Affordable Care Act, children may now continue to be covered by a parent's or guardian's policy until age 26.

While most adolescents are healthy by traditional medical standards, a significant number of young people experience a serious physical or mental health problem. For example, approximately 1 in 5 adolescents suffers from at least one serious health problem such as asthma or depression; and about 1 in 4 is believed to be at risk for early unprotected sexual intercourse or substance abuse.[6] The rapid rise in the obesity rates for children indicate that a growing number of children face serious current and future health problems. Adolescents are known to take risks and to believe that they are immune from harm, even when they know there are negative consequences for certain behaviors. According to the Centers for Disease Control, risk-taking behaviors account for 70 percent of adolescent illness, injury, and death.[7]

Adolescents in low-income and minority families have higher rates of death, illness, and health-risk behaviors. Other adolescents who are eligible for SCHIP—such as those who live in foster or group homes, are homeless or have run away from home, are incarcerated or involved in the juvenile correction system, or who are pregnant and parenting—have even more complex and acute health care needs.[8]

As students learned in Chapter 2, "Lawmaking," writing and implementing effective laws and policies are quite complicated processes. Legislators must write laws that will truly address the problem they have identified. The people who set up and administer the programs must run them in ways that accomplish the legislative goals. Most analysts would say that, through the expansion of SCHIP, the federal and state governments have made significant strides toward accomplishing their goals of providing health insurance coverage.

However, millions of poor and low-income adolescents remain uninsured. Researchers note that adolescents (ages 12–17) are more likely to be uninsured than younger children, and older adolescents (ages 18–24) were the most likely of any age group to be uninsured. Many of these adolescents are eligible for one of the assistance programs but simply are not enrolled.[9] Many program administrators and policy leaders are searching for new ways to reach out and enroll more eligible adolescents.

Ask students to consider ways in which they would design a campaign to "get the word out" in order to inform eligible adolescents that they may be eligible for SCHIP. Encourage them to think about the following questions:

- What sorts of materials and media do adolescents read or view? *bus signs, leaflets, Internet pop-ups, public service announcements on television, etc.*
- If you were to develop a poster or flyer, where would you hang it to have the best chance of reaching adolescents? *the school nurse's office, movie theaters, recreation centers, shopping malls, family planning clinics, etc.*
- How might your campaign attract the attention and reach special groups of adolescents that could benefit from SCHIP, such as youths who are homeless or runaways, pregnant or parenting, or in immigrant families? *county health clinics, community centers, work sites, etc.*

- Besides print publications, what other strategies should SCHIP administrators use to reach and enroll eligible adolescents? *Post something on a social networking site, hire teen and young adult employees who might make potential enrollees more comfortable, make the process for enrolling easier, etc.*

Then tell students to create a public awareness campaign designed to enroll more eligible adolescents into the SCHIP program. Students may work alone, in pairs, or in groups. When finished, students should share a general description of their campaigns and at least one promotional piece with the class. They might also send their plans and work to the agency that runs the SCHIP program in their state. Better still, invite a person from the local office that runs SCHIP to coach students as they work on their educational campaigns.

CAPTION ANSWER (P. 404) Medicaid covers most common medical services, including hospital and outpatient care, nursing-home services, hearing aids, eyeglasses, prescription drugs, dental care, physicians' office fees, medical supplies, and transportation to and from hospitals or doctors' offices.

PROBLEM 33.3 (p. 404)

a. Students' opinions will vary. Students should develop persuasive arguments to support their positions. Students could argue that people with health insurance would be more likely to visit their doctor on a regular basis, focusing on preventative healthcare rather than expensive emergency care. Having health insurance can actually keep overall medical care costs down by treating health issues before they become more serious. Students could also argue that health insurance may not be necessary for everyone. Wealthier Americans might be able to afford healthcare without insurance. Others may oppose requiring health insurance for ideological reasons—they may fear it would be another step toward socialized medicine, a model they oppose. Students may point to the Universal Declaration of Human Rights (Article 25: "Everyone has the right to a standard of living adequate for the health and well-being of himself and of his family, including food, clothing, housing and medical care and necessary social services.") as a foundation for health care as a right. Others may point to the fact that health care is not guaranteed in any of the U.S. foundational documents.

b. Students' opinions will vary. Students should develop persuasive arguments to support their positions. The strongest argument supporting the mandate requiring Americans to purchase health insurance or face a tax penalty is that by increasing the overall insurance pool, costs for everyone will decrease. Health care costs related to treating uninsured patients, who often rely on expensive emergency room care, and limiting the overall health insurance pool to only those Americans who have access through their employment, actually drive premiums up. Requiring all Americans to have health insurance spreads the expense of being sick over a larger number of people, thus lowering premiums. Students who do not support the mandate requiring Americans to purchase health insurance or face a tax penalty might argue that the decision to have health insurance should be a personal one and that the government should not be involved in such decisions. Some see this step as an infringement upon personal liberty and an unwelcome step toward socialized medicine, a model they oppose.

Investigating the Law Where You Live

(p. 404) The federal Social Security Administration's website has links to local or "field" offices where people can apply for Social Security and/or Medicaid. Note that the same field office handles both applications. Simply go to www.ssa.gov, click on "Requesting a Social Security Card," enter a zip code, and find the results for the nearest field office.

BACKGROUND—THE *FAMILY AND MEDICAL LEAVE ACT*

Review who is eligible for benefits provided by the *Family and Medical Leave Act (FMLA)*.[10] In addition to the requirements listed in the Student Edition, covered employees are those who have worked for the employer a minimum of one year, for a minimum of 1,250 hours (an average of 25 hours per week) during the 12 months prior to the start of the *FMLA* leave, and are employed at a location with at least 50 employees at the location or within a 75-mile radius. The law requires that employees returning from leave be restored to the positions they would have been in if they had not taken the leave or to equivalent positions.

Family and medical leave can be taken one day at a time (e.g., for weekly chemotherapy treatments).

If an occurrence is foreseeable, 30 days oral or written notice is required. Otherwise, employees must notify their employers as soon as possible. Where state law grants longer leaves or shorter notification requirements (where state law is more generous than federal law), state law supersedes the *Family and Medical Leave Act.* Employees can take advantage of both by using each in separate years.

If rights to family and medical leave are violated, an employee can file a complaint with a local or regional office of the U.S. Department of Labor's Wage and Hour Division, Employment Standards Administration.[11]

EDUCATIONAL BENEFITS (PP. 405–407)

Learning Outcomes

After completing this section, students should be able to:

1. explain whether the federal government or state governments have more involvement in elementary and secondary education;
2. describe the goals of Head Start and Early Head Start; and
3. identify three federal government grant and loan programs that help students attend colleges and universities.

ACTIVITY—UNDERSTANDING EDUCATION REQUIREMENTS

Organize students into small groups and ask them to discuss and answer the following questions.

1. Develop a hypothesis to explain why state and local governments must provide a free public elementary and secondary education to each child. Tell students that not all countries provide this benefit.

2. States set the age at which someone can legally drop out of school. At what age do you think a student should be permitted to drop out of high school? Explain your answer.

3. Employers argue that workers in the future will need a far better education and more technological skills than many are getting today. In order to strengthen educational programs:

   - should states require students to attend school year-round?
   - should states lengthen the school day?

- should states further restrict the number of hours a student can be employed?
- should states add an additional year to high school?

4. States set graduation requirements. Do you think different states should have different requirements or would a national curriculum be an improvement for the country? Are there any requirements your state should add or drop?

Have the groups present, defend, and compare their answers. In discussing the activity, ask students to identify assumptions that they make about the role of government in education. Have students speculate about how others, such as employees or parents, might answer the same questions.

PROBLEM 33.4 (p.406)

Decide whether you want to share with students the background information about school funding provided above before or after they answer this problem.

a. Those in favor of equalizing funding might argue the following points:

- It is necessary to help people in the poorest districts, which are most in need of resources and are most disadvantaged by educational funding systems based on property taxes.
- Inequalities in basic education perpetuate inequalities in society, and, therefore, make it more difficult to break the cycle of poverty that may persist for generations in some communities.
- Despite the Supreme Court's decision in *Rodriguez*, unequal funding violates the equal protection clause of the Fourteenth Amendment because some children receive an inferior education.
- Students who receive a superior education at public expense have an unfair advantage over others.
- Housing discrimination remains a very real problem, which, in effect, excludes children whose parents are targets of discrimination from the best schools and thus from equal opportunities.

b. Those who oppose equalizing funding might argue the following points:

- Equal opportunity is not tantamount to equal spending or equal outcome.
- Citizens who live in districts with strong schools pay more for housing and higher

taxes, and their children should benefit from these investments.

- The children of more affluent citizens should not be penalized because of their parents' success, which would happen if "their" tax dollars were redistributed to schools in poorer communities.
- Equalizing school funding would violate traditional local control of education.
- There is not necessarily a correlation between funding and quality of education. States that have adopted equalizing plans have not always seen an improvement in the quality of education in the poorer districts. In fact, in some states, the poorest performing districts currently spend the most money per student.

c. Students' answers will vary. Ask students to explain their opinions.

Investigating the Law Where You Live

(p. 406) Answers will vary. Encourage students to research to find out about the various early childhood education programs available in your community. Have students share their findings with the class.

CAPTION ANSWER (P. 407) In addition to the Federal Work Study Program, college students in need of financial assistance may utilize grants and loans.

BACKGROUND—ECONOMIC INEQUALITY AND SCHOOL FUNDING

In 1973, the U.S. Supreme Court heard and decided a case—*San Antonio Independent School District* v. *Rodriguez*—that challenged disparities in education funding based on property value. San Antonio's public elementary and secondary schools were funded by a combination of state funding and local property taxes. The San Antonio Independent School District (SAISD), acting on behalf of students whose families resided in poor districts, challenged this funding scheme. SAISD claimed that the reliance on assessable property caused severe interdistrict disparities in per-pupil expenditures. The Court held that Texas's public education finance system, although failing to distribute funding equally among its school districts, did not violate the Fourteenth Amendment's equal protection clause.[12]

As students will learn in Chapter 41, when courts review discrimination cases, they tend to apply one of three tests: the rational basis test, the strict scrutiny test, or the substantial relationship test. In the *Rodriguez* case, the Supreme Court applied the rational basis test, which indicated that the Court believed that education is not a fundamental right guaranteed by the U.S. Constitution. It also indicated that poor people, as a class, do not receive heightened protection by courts or by the Fourteenth Amendment.

In an impassioned dissent, Justice Thurgood Marshall, who was famous for his role in opposing discrimination based on race in arguing *Brown* v. *The Board of Education of Topeka*,[13] wrote that education is a fundamental right. Although not explicitly mentioned in the U.S. Constitution, adequate education is a basic welfare right that is necessary to equip citizens with the knowledge and ability to take advantage of other rights. According to Justice Marshall:

> "[T]he fundamental importance of education is amply indicated by the prior decisions of this Court, by the unique status accorded public education by our society, and by the close relationship between education and some of our most basic constitutional values.

> . . . [Education] is required in the performance of our most basic public responsibilities, even service in the armed forces. It is the very foundation of good citizenship. Today it is a principal instrument in awakening the child to cultural values, in preparing him for later professional training, and in helping him to adjust normally to his environment. . . ."

Since the *Rodriguez* decision, efforts to equalize funding have been challenged at the state level because all states do grant their citizens the right to education. Some state constitutions even specify that every state resident is entitled to an "adequate" education, a guarantee that has been used to challenge inequities in education. For example, the New Jersey court ruled in *Abbott* v. *Burke*[14] that inadequate and unequal funding denies students in urban districts a thorough and efficient education. The New Jersey court required the state to equalize funding between suburban and urban districts for regular education and to provide extra or "supplemental" programs to "wipe out disadvantages as much as a school district can." Still, the New Jersey example underscores the reality that inequities in education go beyond spending and require long-term solutions. Some of the districts in New Jersey that continue to perform the poorest now have the highest per-student expenditures.

ACTIVITY—CONDUCTING AN OPINION POLL

Ask students to poll teens and adults in the community to weigh public opinion on government-funded educational programs.

Students should ask the following questions:

Would you be willing to pay increased taxes to fund government programs in order to:

- improve public schools?
- provide college education for all students?
- ensure that all Americans have decent housing?

As a follow-up, if respondents express willingness to pay more taxes, ask how much more money they would be willing to pay. Have students compile and interpret their data and present their results in a written report.

DISCUSSION AND DEBATE— GOVERNMENT SPENDING POWER/ GOVERNMENT AUTHORITY

As high school students know, they must follow rules and decisions of their parents or guardians because they rely on them for food, shelter, health care, and financial support. Students may have heard their parents say: "As long as you live under my roof, you will obey my rules," or "I'm not paying for you to___." Ask students how reasonable it is for parents to expect to have a say in how their money is spent. Are there limits?

Like parents, Congress has considerable discretion in how it chooses to exercise its spending power. For example, the drinking age is established by state, not federal, law. However, Congress made highway funding contingent on states adopting 21 as the minimum drinking age. Because states rely on this important source of funding, every state has adopted 21 as the minimum drinking age—in essence, establishing a national minimum drinking age. Ask students to hypothesize whether the following statements are true or false. Then students should debate whether the "true" scenarios are reasonable exercises of Congress's spending power:

- Any private university whose students receive federal student loans may not discriminate on the basis of race. *true*
- Students who are convicted of drug use lose eligibility for federal student loans. *unclear*
- Government-issued food stamps may not be used to purchase alcohol or tobacco. *true*

- Libraries that receive federal funding must install government-specified screening software on all public computers. *true*
- Any person receiving welfare entitlements must obtain government permission before purchasing a nonessential appliance, such as a television. *not true*
- Recipients of unemployment benefits must demonstrate reasonable attempts and willingness to find a job. *true*
- Medicaid recipients may not use government funds for an abortion, even where the life of the mother is at risk and even though abortion is legal. *true*
- A person receiving any form of government assistance may not criticize the government. *not true*

At the conclusion of the discussion and debate, ask students to consider the broader theme by asking the following questions.

- To what degree must a person sacrifice individual autonomy (personal freedom) to receive government assistance?
- What if the result of government assistance is that people who are poorer are able to exercise fewer rights than the general population?

ACTIVITY—CONDUCTING A DEBATE

As students complete their study of this chapter, have them debate the purpose of government and whether the government should do more or less to support families and individuals. Rather than taking the issue as one broad topic, assign groups of students to debate each of the three categories highlighted in this chapter: economic benefits, health benefits, and educational benefits. Within each category, one or two smaller groups should argue each side of the issue. Invite at least two legal resource persons—legislators, people from government agencies, advocacy groups, or political parties—with opposing views to help students prepare to debate.

NOTES

(1) *Saenz* v. *Roe*, 526 U.S. 489 (1999).

(2) *Personal Responsibility and Work Opportunity Reconciliation Act of 1996*, Pub. L. No. 104-193, also known as *PRWORA*.

(3) *Department of Commerce* v. *United States House*, 525 U.S. 326 (1999).

(4) *Medicare Prescription Drug Improvement and Modernization Act of 2003*, Pub. L. No. 108-173, 117 Stat. 2066 (2003).

(5) Park, Edwin, et al. "The Troubling Medicare Legislation," *Center On Budget and Policy Priorities*, December 8, 2003.

(6) Brindis, Claire D., Madlyn C. Morreale, and Abigail English. "The Unique Health Care Needs of Adolescents," *Health Insurance for Children*. Volume 13, Number 1. Spring, 2003. p. 117.

(7) Kann, L., Warren, C., Harris, W., et al. *Youth risk behavior survey–United States, 1997*. Atlanta: Surveillance and Evaluation Research Branch, Division of Adolescent and School Health, Centers for Disease Control and Prevention, 1998.

(8) Brindis, Morreale, English, p. 117.

(9) Brindis, Morreale, English, p. 126.

(10) *Family and Medical Leave Act*, Pub. L. No. 104-1, 109 Stat. 9, tit. 1, part A (1995).

(11) "News You Can Use: A Tour Through the Law: Your Basic Rights," *U.S. News and World Report* (August 2, 1993).

(12) *San Antonio Independent School District* v. *Rodriguez*, 411 U.S. 1 (1973).

(13) *Brown* v. *The Board of Education of Topeka*, 349 U.S. 294 (1955).

(14) *Abbott* v. *Burke*, 100 N.J. 269, 495 A.2d 376 (1985).

UNIT 6
Individual Rights and Liberties

Unit 6 introduces students to constitutional law and civil rights law. The topics are controversial; many reasonable people disagree about whether the government has done enough, too much, or too little to protect the rights of people. As legislatures pass laws, the executive branch carries out laws, and courts have interpreted laws, there is much disagreement about the proper balance between the rights of individuals and the needs of communities. Despite the controversies, or perhaps because of them, the Bill of Rights, the Fourteenth Amendment, and various civil rights laws are the hallmarks of the political and social freedoms Americans enjoy and many others admire.

CHAPTER 34
Introduction to Constitutional Law

Chapter 34 introduces the study of constitutional law. It describes how the Constitution establishes the basic framework of government and how the Bill of Rights protects basic individual rights.

CHAPTERS 35–37
Freedom of Speech, the Press, and Expression in Special Places

Chapters 35–37 focus on freedom of expression and its importance in maintaining a democracy. The chapters investigate the scope of the government's ability to regulate expression and, in certain instances, to prevent and punish it.

CHAPTER 38
Freedom of Religion

Chapter 38 explains how the establishment clause and the free exercise clause work together to ensure that the government protects religious freedoms. The chapter provides examples in which the right of individuals to practice their religion sometimes clashes with the government's obligation not to establish or favor any religion.

CHAPTER 39
Due Process

Chapter 39 explores the concept of due process, which concerns both fair procedures and protection from government interference with certain rights.

CHAPTER 40
The Right to Privacy

Chapter 40 focuses on the contested right to privacy.

CHAPTER 41
Discrimination

Chapter 41 deals with discrimination law and the controversial issue of affirmative action.

SERVICE LEARNING AND SPECIAL PROJECTS

1. **Debate:** There are several rich topics for debate in this unit, such as school censorship, school prayer, cameras in courtrooms, government access to private records, and affirmative action.

2. **Survey About Controversial Public Policy Issues:** Students could survey other students, parents, or community residents to determine their knowledge and opinions of individual rights. This could include, but is not limited to topics such as marriage equality, school censorship, school prayer, and cameras in courtrooms.

3. **Student Advocacy and Service Learning:** While community service is educational and meaningful on many levels, service learning takes it to "the next level" by connecting service with classroom learning and reflection. The following activities are suggested to help students enhance what they learn in Unit 6 by serving their communities.

   - Research the activities of hate groups in your community or state and devise strategies to counter these groups. Keep in mind the right to free speech.
   - Present a mock trial about the First Amendment to younger students.
   - Research and write a synopsis of a landmark case relating to the First Amendment, due process, privacy, or discrimination. Make the synopsis available for other students in civics and government classes.
   - After conducting the survey described in item **2.**, devise a strategy for educating peers, parents, and community members about their rights and responsibilities under the Bill of Rights.

UNIT RESOURCES

Using Legal Resource Persons

1. A representative from your state's legislature might be invited to discuss public policy issues related to discrimination and First Amendment issues.

2. Representatives from advocacy groups could discuss how citizens can work together to bring about changes in laws and policies that protect people from discrimination.

Other useful websites include:

- www.landmarkcases.org. This site, developed by Street Law, Inc. and the Supreme Court Historical Society, features lesson plans, links to Supreme Court cases and arguments, and resources that help students analyze the ways key Court decisions have influenced law and society.
- www.washingtonpost.com/politics/courts-law/. The *Washington Post*'s Supreme Court reporters provide information about the Court, the justices, this term's cases, and cases from the past few terms.
- www.law.cornell.edu. The site of the Legal Information Institute at Cornell Law School includes a list-serve that enables teachers or students to receive daily summaries of the Court's decisions as they are announced.
- www.oyez.org. Northwestern Law School's site provides a synopsis, analysis, and audio of oral arguments for cases from the past several decades.
- www.firstamendmentcenter.org. The First Amendment Center has an extensive site devoted to freedom of speech, the press, religion, assembly, and petition.
- www.publicagenda.org. Public Agenda provides a wealth of balanced information about controversial issues, including public polls on various issues.
- Two sites will help teachers embrace the teaching of controversial issues in appropriate ways that ultimately help students learn important citizenship skills such as researching policy questions, evaluating evidence, formulating opinions, expressing opinions, and advocating for effective policies. *The Civic Mission of Schools* report specifically encourages teachers and administrators to embrace controversial issues. It is available at https://www.carnegie.org/publications/guardian-of-democracy-the-civic-mission-of-schools/. The National Council for the Social Studies (www.ncss.org) offers suggestions for teaching controversial issues.

networks™

INTRODUCTION AND AMENDMENTS TO THE CONSTITUTION (PP. 410–412)

The U.S. Constitution is the framework of our government. It guarantees each American certain basic rights and certain protections from excessive power by the federal government. In this chapter, students will learn about the purposes of the most significant constitutional amendments, how amendments are made to the Constitution, and basic constitutional law principles, including the idea that "rights are not absolute," the use of "balancing tests," and the "constitutional floor" for rights.

Learning Outcomes

After completing these sections, students should be able to:

1. define the terms *amendment* and *due process*;
2. outline two methods of amending the U.S. Constitution;
3. summarize the rights guaranteed to individuals in each amendment in the Bill of Rights;
4. explain what the Bill of Rights was designed to protect citizens from;
5. explain how the courts have interpreted the Fourteenth Amendment to apply the Bill of Rights to protections from state and local governments;
6. list the prohibitions in the Thirteenth Amendment; and
7. explain how voting rights of American citizens were affected by the Fifteenth, Nineteenth, Twenty-third, Twenty-fourth, and Twenty-sixth Amendments to the U.S. Constitution.

BACKGROUND—CONSTITUTIONAL LAW

In contrast to other chapters of the text, the material in Chapter 34 is derived primarily from constitutional law. The main body of the U.S. Constitution grants only limited powers to the federal government. Therefore, the federal government cannot act unless permitted to do so by the Constitution. The Bill of Rights (the first ten amendments to the Constitution) was added to the Constitution to allay fears that the federal government would become too powerful. The Bill of Rights and subsequent amendments regulate government action in two ways. They prohibit the government from taking certain actions (e.g., "Congress shall make no law respecting an establishment of religion... or abridging the freedom of speech, or of the press...."), and they require certain actions (e.g., "In all criminal prosecutions, the accused shall enjoy the right to a speedy and public trial....").

Emphasize to students the difference between constitutional protections and statutory protections. In theory, laws passed in a democratic republic are representative of the collective wisdom of the majority. While unpopular laws can be amended or repealed, the fundamental protections provided by constitutional amendments cannot be amended nearly as easily as can state and federal statutes. For example, it would be unconstitutional to pass a law that abridged or denied the freedom of speech of unpopular groups such as the Communist or Nazi Parties. Even if an overwhelming percentage of citizens found these political doctrines to be abhorrent, the First Amendment grants every citizen freedom of speech. However, this freedom is not absolute. While the Bill of Rights bestows many rights upon American citizens, the government does have the power to regulate when, where, and how (time, manner, and place) those rights are exercised.

While the basic principles underlying the constitutional amendments remain the same, the interpretation of those underlying principles by the Supreme Court of the United States changes over time to reflect society's changing needs, values, and opinions. This view treats it as a "living constitution." Some jurists advocate this approach to constitutional interpretation. However, there is an alternative school of thought that says treating the Constitution as a living document injects unnecessary subjectivity and uncertainty by allowing too much judicial discretion. Proponents of this view argue for an interpretation of the Constitution that focuses on close reading of the constitutional text and adherence to the original intent of the Framers of the Constitution. One criticism of the "strict interpretation" or "textualist" approach is that it perpetuates the status quo and traditional biases in the legal system and society. In areas of law where the Supreme Court's justices are most deeply divided, one can see the interplay between the "living constitution" and "strict interpretation" approaches to applying constitutional law.

CAPTION ANSWER (P. 411) The passage of the Fourteenth Amendment meant that all people born in the United States were citizens and guaranteed equal protection under the law. It also provided that no state can deprive any citizen of "life, liberty, or property without due process of law." The Fifteenth Amendment guaranteed the right to vote for citizens (male only), regardless of race, color or previous servitude.

PROBLEM 34.1 (p. 412)

a. Once students have ranked these rights in order of importance, ask them to give the reasons behind their choices. An alternative way to approach this problem is to use the activity "Which Rights are More Important?"

b. Students' answers will vary. The rights in this problem come from four of the twelve amendments proposed during the 109th Congress. This is a typical number of proposed constitutional amendments for each congressional session. Students' answers will vary in terms of whether any of these amendments are needed.

To extend this discussion, you may want to mention and debate the following additional amendments that have been proposed in recent years:

- prohibit flag burning as protected speech
- grant rights to victims of crimes
- permit organized prayer in public schools
- institute a "flat tax" in which all Americans pay the same percentage in income tax
- regulate campaign finance
- permit the line-item veto by the president
- establish term limits for elected officials

Both the Equal Rights Amendment and the D.C. Voting Rights Amendment were passed by Congress but failed to win ratification by three-fourths of the states. The Twenty-seventh Amendment was proposed in 1789 and ratified in May 1992 when Michigan became the thirty-eighth state to ratify it. This amendment delays the implementation of a salary increase that Congress votes for itself until after the next Congress convenes.

ACTIVITY—WHICH RIGHTS ARE MOST IMPORTANT?

Note: The following activity can be used as an alternative way to approach question **a.** in Problem 34.1, or it may serve as a useful review activity upon completion of this unit.

Tell students that Senator Stingy is worried about the federal budget. Recognizing that the protection of individual rights can often be costly, she has proposed that some of the individual liberties in the Constitution be sacrificed. Assume that she will use the amendment process to achieve this goal. Organize the class into committees and give each an envelope containing the following rights printed on individual slips of paper:

- free speech
- freedom of assembly
- freedom of the press
- freedom of religion
- right to bear arms
- freedom from unreasonable search and seizure
- protection against self-incrimination (right to remain silent)
- right to an attorney
- right to an impartial jury of peers
- protection against cruel and unusual punishment

- right to vote
- due process of law
- equal protection of law

Give the committees about ten minutes to reach consensus on which three of the rights they will eliminate. Have the committees share, compare, and justify their choices. Record the committees' choices on the board so the class can identify patterns in the choices.

Repeat the activity by asking each committee to sacrifice three more of their rights. Continue this process until each group is left with only one remaining right. At the end of the activity, have students reflect on the difficulty in deciding which rights to give up and which one to retain.

Challenge students to identify rights enjoyed by people in the United States that are not included in the list. Then challenge students to name rights that people in the United States do not currently enjoy.

DISCUSSION—AMENDING THE CONSTITUTION

Ask students to develop hypotheses to explain:
- why the Framers made the Constitution difficult to amend;
- why relatively few amendments have been ratified in our history;
- which of the proposed amendments, if any, listed in question **b.** of Problem 34.1 are likely to be ratified (students should justify their selections); and
- how the Framers might regard any of the amendments added to the Constitution since the Bill of Rights.

BASIC CONSTITUTIONAL LAW PRINCIPLES (PP. 412–414)

Learning Outcomes

After completing this section, students should be able to:
1. explain why rights guaranteed in the U.S. Constitution are not, and cannot be, absolute;
2. describe how courts use "tests" as they decide cases;
3. define the term *compelling interest test* and describe how it is applied to free-speech rights;

4. explain why the U.S. Constitution does not generally protect citizens from the actions of private individuals, organizations, or businesses;
5. explain how the U.S. Constitution functions as a "floor" for basic rights that cannot be taken away by federal, state, or local governments; and
6. compare the kinds of rights included in the U.S. Constitution with those in the Universal Declaration of Human Rights.

BACKGROUND—CONSTITUTIONAL RIGHTS

As noted in the Student Edition, state constitutions are another important source of rights. Federal constitutional rights are a minimum that the states must guarantee, but they may choose to grant more expansive rights in their state constitutions. Some states interpret their own state constitutional rights in the same way as the U.S. Supreme Court has interpreted federal constitutional rights. Other states grant their residents greater rights than those granted by the U.S. Constitution. For example, some states grant greater free-speech rights and greater privacy protections than does the U.S. Constitution.

Another interesting feature of the U.S. Constitution is that many—but not all—of the rights that it provides are granted to all people within the United States, and not just citizens. For example, the equal protection and due process clauses of the Fourteenth Amendment apply to all persons within the territorial jurisdiction, regardless of citizenship status.

LEGAL RESOURCE PERSON

Consider inviting a constitutional law expert to describe for students how their state constitution is interpreted regarding various rights. A law professor might be willing to discuss their views of the ways in which the state constitution has evolved, if any, and describe the proposed amendments currently under consideration. Students might also investigate the process by which their state's constitution is amended to determine whether citizens can force consideration of proposed amendments through ballot measures.

PROBLEM 34.2 (p.414)

a. Although every citizen is afforded constitutional rights, the government may, at times, place reasonable restrictions on an individual's exercise of those rights. Courts often balance the government's interest against an individual's given right. Students may suggest a variety of examples to illustrate that "rights are not absolute." For example, freedom of speech is not absolute. Government can regulate speech using reasonable rules regarding time, place, and manner, such as when and where a person operating a sound truck (a vehicle with a loudspeaker attached) can broadcast messages throughout a community. The case mentioned in the Student Edition relating to falsely yelling "fire" in a crowded theater is similar to the case of *Schenck* v. *United States*.[1] In *Schenck* v. *United States* (1919), the Supreme Court ruled that distributing pamphlets advocating disobeying the draft during World War I presented a "clear and present danger" to national security and could be prohibited by the Espionage Act. In the opinion of the unanimous Court, Justice Oliver Wendell Holmes compared the pamphlets to falsely yelling "Fire!" in a crowded theater. Other examples include applying the Fourth Amendment's protection against unreasonable searches and seizures, where courts have created many exceptions to the requirement of a warrant based on probable cause.

b. Tests serve as objective standards that were created by the Court to provide a framework for the justices to analyze future cases raising similar issues. For example, in the *Miranda* v. *Arizona*[2] case, the Court created a test for the admissibility of confessions obtained by police from an accused person. According to this test, the police must inform a person in a situation of custodial interrogation of his or her right to remain silent and have an attorney present, in order for a confession to be admissible at trial against the accused person.

c. Students' examples of economic rights will vary. The Fifth Amendment requires that when the government is going to take property from people, it must use fair procedures and offer fair compensation. Students may identify a range of economic rights that are not provided for in the U.S. Constitution, such as the right to a home, to a job, quality health care, a good education, to earning a minimum or "living" wage, and an adequate standard of living. Have students debate the merits of including such rights within the Constitution.

ACTIVITY—COMPARING AND CONTRASTING

Ask students to create charts in which they compare and contrast rights included in the U.S. Constitution with those listed in the Universal Declaration of Human Rights (UDHR). Both documents are included in the Appendix of the Student Edition with plain language versions accompanying the original language. Have students, working individually or in pairs, decide which rights in the UDHR should be added to the Constitution. Have students provide justification for their choices.

NOTES

(1) *Schenck* v. *United States*, 249 U.S. 47 (1919).

(2) *Miranda* v. *Arizona*, 384 U.S. 436 (1966).

networks™

The First Amendment guarantees freedom of speech—the right to express and receive information and ideas. It protects all forms of communication: speeches, books, art, newspapers, television, radio, and other media. The First Amendment exists to protect ideas that may be unpopular or different from those of the majority or those in power. Persons *making* the communication, as well as persons *receiving* it, are protected. People have a right to hear, see, read, and in general be exposed to different points of view. Although courts are very protective of the right to freedom of speech, it is not absolute.

INTRODUCTION AND THE IMPORTANCE OF FREEDOM OF SPEECH (PP. 415–417)

Learning Outcomes

After completing these sections, students should be able to:
1. identify forms of communication protected by guarantees of freedom of speech;
2. explain three reasons why the First Amendment's protection of speech is central to democracy in our country; and
3. describe the relationship between the First Amendment and the concept of a "marketplace of ideas."

BACKGROUND—CATEGORIES OF SPEECH

The U.S. Supreme Court has created many categories of speech, which are examined with various levels of judicial scrutiny. (Judicial scrutiny is covered in greater depth in Chapter 41. Generally, the higher the level of judicial scrutiny a particular right or interest receives, the broader the protection of the right or interest.) Depending upon which category is being addressed, different tests are applied to determine the scope of restraints that are permissible on the type of speech.

Regulation, or restraint, of speech can fall into the category of either content-based or content-neutral speech. A regulation that is content-based prohibits speech on the basis of the ideas or information contained in the speech. To implement such a regulation, there must be a compelling government interest, and there must be no less restrictive way to achieve the government's interest. Examples of content-based restrictions include speech that is limited because it contains confidential government information or because it is likely to cause an immediate danger to public safety.

A restriction on speech that is content-neutral regulates speech to avoid an evil that is not connected to the content of the speech. Generally, these include time, place, and manner restrictions. This type of restriction must have a substantial governmental purpose and be narrowly tailored to meet that purpose. Also, other means of communicating the content must be available. For example, a community that allows rallies and marches only on weekends so as not to interfere with traffic during business days has made a content-neutral prohibition on speech. All speech, regardless of the message, is limited in that form on weekdays because of its likelihood to disrupt traffic, not in an effort to censor the particular message.

There is also a distinction between pure speech and symbolic speech. All pure speech receives some constitutional protection. Symbolic speech is nonverbal conduct by which one intends to convey a message. Regulation of symbolic speech must pass a four-part test to be constitutional:

1. It is within the government's interest.

2. It furthers an important or substantial government interest.

3. The government's interest is unrelated to the suppression of free expression.

4. The incidental restriction on free speech is not greater than necessary to further that interest.

CAPTION ANSWER (P. 416) Conflicts concerning free speech are difficult to resolve because they often involve a clash of fundamental values. The need for peace and public order must be balanced against the fundamental right to express one's point of view.

BACKGROUND—FREE SPEECH AND THE PLEDGE OF ALLEGIANCE

The case involving saluting the flag and reciting the Pledge of Allegiance mentioned in the Student Edition is *West Virginia Board of Education* v. *Barnette*.[1] In this case, the Court ruled that requiring students to salute the flag while reciting the Pledge of Allegiance is "compelled speech or compelled symbolic speech" and was in violation of free speech protected by the First Amendment. The students' freedom of religion was also an issue in this case (see pages 340–341 in this Teacher Manual for more information).

PROBLEM 35.1 (p.417)

a. This quotation is from an opinion written by Justice Oliver Wendell Holmes.[2] The phrase goes to the core of the First Amendment, which asserts that certain activities (beliefs or actions) are protected against government interference regardless of their popularity. Ask students whether they believe freedom of speech should apply to speakers from the Ku Klux Klan, Communist Party, or American Nazi Party. If their speech is *not* restricted, what might occur? If their speech is restricted, what short-term and long-term consequences might follow?

b. Ask students to explore how their emotional reactions to unpopular speech might conflict with the civil liberties perspective that speech should be protected regardless of its political context. (This question can also introduce the flag-burning case in the Student Edition.)

c. The revolutionary spirit of protest and the commitment to the right to freely criticize government policy were motivating factors behind the adoption of the First Amendment. Protest can also be seen as patriotic because it reflects active citizenship, passion, and concern for values and ideas, and a desire to influence decision making. In 1954, award winning journalist Edward R. Murrow famously said, "We must not confuse dissent with disloyalty" while criticizing Senator Joseph McCarthy and the House Un-American Activities Committee. However, some people argue that during a war domestic protest may damage our international image, undermine our solidarity, and lower the morale of the troops. Nonetheless, having a government that allows protest in tumultuous times demonstrates the depth of our commitment to the free expression of ideas and the democratic values for which the United States often engages in wars to protect and promote.

The tone of war protests has shifted somewhat since the Vietnam War, which generated substantial public opposition. During the Vietnam War, some protesters combined their condemnation of U.S. foreign policy with hostility toward U.S. soldiers. During subsequent demonstrations, protesters have largely distinguished their disapproval of government policy from their support of the troops.

ACTIVITY—INTERPRETING QUOTATIONS

Ask students to carefully read and interpret the quotations from Justice Brandeis and Thomas Jefferson about free speech shown below.

"Those who won our independence believed that the final end of the State was to make men free to develop their faculties; and that in its government the deliberative forces should prevail over the arbitrary. They valued liberty both as an end and as a means. They believed liberty to be the secret of happiness and courage to be the secret of liberty. They believed that freedom to think as you will and to speak as you think are means indispensable to the discovery and spread of political truth; that without free speech and assembly, discussion would be futile; that with them, discussion ordinarily affords adequate protection against the dissemination of noxious doctrine; that the greatest menace to freedom is an inert people; that public discussion is a political duty; and that this should be a fundamental principle of the American government."

—Justice Brandeis's concurring opinion, *Whitney* v. *People of the State of California* (1927)

"We have nothing to fear from the demoralizing reasoning of some, if others are left free to demonstrate their errors and especially when the law stands ready to punish the first criminal act produced by the false reasoning; these are safer corrections than the conscience of a judge."

—This quote from Thomas Jefferson was included in a footnote to the Brandeis opinion in *Whitney* et. al.[3]

After students have read the quotes and you have reviewed any questions they may have about vocabulary and meaning, ask students to decide whether they agree or disagree with the authors. Ask those who agree whether they think that speech should never be restricted. Have students brainstorm situations in which speech should be restricted.

BACKGROUND AND DISCUSSION— POLITICAL SPEECH

Ask students to develop a hypothesis to explain why political speech is the most highly protected of all forms of speech. Students should share their hypotheses with the class.

Explain that the U.S. Supreme Court ruled in *McIntyre* v. *Ohio Elections Commission*[4] that an Ohio statute banning the writing or distribution of anonymous political campaign literature violates free speech. It said that combating fraud and libel and providing the electorate with relevant information are not sufficiently compelling interests to justify a ban on unsigned flyers. It was significant in this case that the banned literature was political in nature, the most highly protected of all speech. However, the Supreme Court did uphold a Florida Bar Association rule that prohibited lawyers from sending targeted mail solicitations to accident and disaster victims within 30 days of the incident.[5] Ask students to develop a hypothesis to explain why the Court upheld this rule.

COMMERCIAL SPEECH (PP. 417–419)

Learning Outcomes

After completing this section, students should be able to:

1. define the term *commercial speech*;
2. describe and assess how protection of commercial speech has evolved over time;
3. describe the reasons behind the U.S. Supreme Court's decisions regarding advertising by pharmacists and lawyers; and
4. describe three kinds of commercial speech that government can ban.

BACKGROUND—COMMERCIAL SPEECH

The case referred to in the Student Edition involving beer companies that wanted to disclose the alcohol content of their products, Rubin v. Coors Brewing Co, was decided by the Supreme Court in 1995.[6]

In a 1980 case, *Central Hudson Gas and Electric Corp.* v. *Public Services Commission of New York*,[7] the Supreme Court announced a special set of rules for determining whether or not commercial speech such as advertising is protected by the First Amendment. First, to be protected the speech must involve lawful activity. Second, the speech must not be misleading. Unlike political speech, where a wide variety of opinions—true or not—are tolerated, commercial speech must be reasonably accurate to be protected. Laws against false advertising, therefore, do not generally violate the First Amendment. Nonetheless, the Court has held that legitimate commercial speech warrants protection, and laws that regulate it must serve substantial governmental interests and must be carefully tailored to achieve those ends. Note that this is a lesser standard than the "compelling interest" required to regulate other forms of speech.

CAPTION ANSWER (P. 418) In general, courts allow the government to ban commercial speech that is false or misleading or that provides information about illegal activities.

Learning Outcomes

After completing this section, students should be able to:

1. define the term *obscenity* in relation to free speech;
2. summarize guidelines for determining whether or not an expression is obscene as established in *Miller* v. *California;*
3. describe strategies state and local governments have developed for dealing with pornography;
4. weigh the merits of permitting the government to censor publications and media;
5. describe U.S. Supreme Court decisions regarding child pornography; and
6. explain why the U.S. Supreme Court has found some legislative attempts to protect children from pornography on the Internet unconstitutional.

BACKGROUND AND DISCUSSION— COMMUNITY STANDARDS FOR OBSCENITY

The difficulties confronting the U.S. Supreme Court in obscenity cases are perhaps best summarized by Justice Potter Stewart's now famous language, "… I know it [obscenity] when I see it, and the motion picture in this case is not that."[8] The Court standards on obscenity set out in the Student Edition were first established in *Roth* v. *U.S.*[9] These were modified in *Miller* v. *California,*[10] and then again in *Jenkins* v. *Georgia.*[11] The case *Smith* v. *United States* gave juries considerable discretion to rely on their own knowledge of community standards to determine whether an expression is obscene.[12]

Because the Court has relied on "community standards" to determine what is obscene, expression that some communities consider obscene might be protected in others. To determine community standards, lawyers in obscenity cases have traditionally introduced into evidence the range of sexually-explicit magazines and movies available locally as well as the number of adult entertainment establishments in a particular community. In one unique defense in 2008, a defense attorney in a federal obscenity case attempted to force Google

Trends to provide search trends in a given area (Pensacola, Florida) to show that searches for terms like "orgy" were more common than searches for "apple pie," which, he says, indicates that community standards are fairly tolerant of material that others call "obscene."[13]

As mentioned in the Student Edition, determining "community standards" for Internet users creates an additional challenge for courts and for those involved in this debate. Ask students to answer the following questions and to explain the reasons for their answers:

- Does it make sense for the First Amendment to be applied differently in different places?
- Would it be possible to set a national standard for obscenity? Would it be desirable?
- How has the development of the Internet as a major form of communication made regulation of obscenity more difficult?

In 1986, the Supreme Court upheld a zoning ordinance that prohibited adult motion picture theaters from being located within 1,000 feet of any residential zone, single-or multiple-family dwelling, church, park, or school. The Court upheld the ordinance for three reasons: (1) The ordinance did not ban the free expression of the theater owners; (2) the regulation served a substantial government interest in preserving the quality of life in the community; and (3) the ordinance was a reasonable method of regulating the time, place, and manner of the expression. About 5 percent of the city's land area was still available for use by adult theater operators.[14]

The Supreme Court case on child pornography referred to in the Student Edition is *New York* v. *Ferber.*[15] This case involved a challenge to a New York law that made it illegal to produce or distribute materials depicting children performing sexual acts. In *Ferber*, the Court recognized that not all of the outlawed materials would meet a strict definition of obscenity, but held unanimously that the state's compelling interest in safeguarding the physical and psychological well-being of minors outweighed the First Amendment interest of the pornographer.

Out of concern that children could be privy to sexually explicit telephone messages, Congress enacted a law in 1989 that would have essentially put the "dial-a-porn" industry out of business. The Supreme Court unanimously struck down the law, which prohibited the commercial transmission of indecent telephone messages, as a violation of the First Amendment. Justice White asserted that "the government may not reduce the adult population to … only what is fit for children."[16]

In its decision, the Court held that although indecent sexual expression is protected, it may be regulated only to promote a compelling state interest by the least restrictive means. The Court determined that alternatives such as increased oversight by the Federal Communications Commission, making the purchases available only by credit card transactions, granting access codes to adult service users, and scrambling rules were less restrictive than the government's total prohibition on the messages. The Court noted that there was no evidence that the alternatives would not be effective in achieving the government's interest.[17] As mentioned in the Student Edition, in May 2008 the Supreme Court upheld a federal law that punishes those who distribute child pornography.[18]

The case referred to in the Student Edition in which the Court found that video games are considered speech is *Brown* v. *Entertainment Merchants Association*.[19]

CAPTION ANSWER (P. 419) The Court has found some efforts to protect children from adult content on the Internet unconstitutional because the laws have not been sufficiently clear about exactly what expression is prohibited.

PROBLEM 35.2 (p.420)

a.–b. Students' answers will vary. This problem raises public policy as well as constitutional issues. The rationale *for* allowing government to regulate obscenity is: (1) the potential for corruption of youths and others; (2) the lowering of society's moral values; and (3) the possibility that sexual permissiveness or violence will be encouraged.

The rationale *against* allowing government restriction is that: (1) society benefits from all forms of artistic expression; (2) the reasons for censorship are groundless (i.e., it is not harmful); (3) defining what materials qualify as pornography is imprecise, and (4) pornography serves as a useful sexual release for some. The Supreme Court has stated that obscenity can be defined by community standards. Of course, as community standards change over time, so does the definition of *obscenity*.

c. Students' opinions will vary. Some students will likely argue that certain types of pornography encourage violence. Other students may point out that many people view pornography and do not engage in violent acts. This topic continues to be quite controversial.

In 1984, the city councils in both Minneapolis and Indianapolis passed ordinances that made trafficking in pornography a *per se* form of discrimination against women. The mayor of Minneapolis vetoed the law. The Indianapolis law, once passed, immediately became the subject of a lawsuit. In 1985, the Seventh Circuit Court of Appeals held that pornography, defined as "graphic sexually explicit subordination of women," did not pass constitutional muster under the three-part test for obscenity from *Miller* v. *California*. In *American Booksellers Association, Inc.* v. *Hudnut*, the U.S. Supreme Court denied certiorari, saying:

"The ordinance discriminates based on the content of the speech. Speech treating women in the approved way—in sexual encounters 'premised on equality'—is lawful no matter how sexually explicit. Speech treating women in the disapproved way—as submissive in matters sexual or as enjoying humiliation—is unlawful no matter how significant the literary, artistic, or political qualities of the work taken as a whole. The state may not ordain preferred viewpoints in this way."[20]

d. Students' answers will vary. Several special problems are involved with First Amendment challenges to Internet material. Current law defines *obscenity*, in part, as material that violates a community's standards. However, the question remains, what is the "community" in regard to the Internet? Also, what technologies are available to block the transmission of offensive content to minors without interfering with the rights of adults who should be able to lawfully access such content?

BACKGROUND—INTERNET FILTERING SOFTWARE ON COMPUTERS IN PUBLIC LIBRARIES

Many students (and teachers) have been surprised and occasionally frustrated to find that appropriate and educational content has been blocked by filtering software installed on their schools' computers. While the Supreme Court has not heard cases relating to public school computers, it would likely find that installing filtering software on a computer in a public school library would not be a violation of the First Amendment. The school has an interest in regulating the content of material accessible to students, particularly where pornography is involved. Any inconvenience caused by the tendency of filtering software to exclude some historical and religious sites could be resolved through a disabling device that is available to the librarians at their discretion.

The Supreme Court has, on three occasions, wrestled with a related issue involving congressional efforts to set conditions for library funding on the installation of filtering devices on public computers. After striking down two previous congressional acts for vagueness, the Court upheld the *Children's Internet Protection Act (CIPA)* in *United States, et.al.* v. *American Library Association, et al.*[21]

Congress passed *CIPA* in 2000. It requires public libraries to have anti-pornography filtering software on their computers in order to receive government funding for the library or discounts on computer technology. A clause in *CIPA* allows an administrator of the library to turn off the filtering software for an adult who is doing legitimate research or otherwise lawfully using the computer. Failure of a library to comply with *CIPA* means losing critical federal funding and assistance in purchasing computer technology.

The American Library Association challenged *CIPA*, arguing that the software grossly censors library patrons' use of the computer by "overblocking" legitimate sites, thus violating the First Amendment. In upholding the law, then Chief Justice Rehnquist's plurality opinion rejected the notion that such stipulations induce libraries to violate the First Amendment rights of their patrons. While recognizing the need for libraries to have broad discretion in deciding what materials to offer patrons to best facilitate learning and provide cultural enrichment, the Court was not concerned with the tendency of filters to "overblock" and prevent research efforts because the filter could be disabled in such instances. The Court viewed the government's interest in protecting young library users from inappropriate material as worth the small burden placed on adult users.

Justice Souter's dissent argued that content-based restrictions on communication in the library's control are unconstitutional. He did not think that any library should be able to install pornographic filters on machines that were meant to give adult patrons full Internet access.

DEFAMATION (PP. 421—422)

Learning Outcomes

After completing this section, students should be able to:

1. define the term *defamation* and explain its relationship to the First Amendment;
2. define the terms *slander* and *libel* and distinguish between them;
3. state how proof that a statement is true affects the outcome of a defamation suit; and
4. describe the U.S. Supreme Court's rules regarding whether and when public figures can collect damages in a defamation suit.

THE **CASE** OF...

The Public Official's Lawsuit for Libel

PROBLEM 35.3 (p.421)

Note: This problem is based on *New York Times* v. *Sullivan*.[22]

a. Students' opinions will vary. Arguments consistent with the Court's opinion include: debate on important public issues must be wide open; mistakes of fact that are not intentionally made or made without reckless disregard for their accuracy should not subject the speakers to defamation liability; if speakers about public issues could be sued, it would lead to repression of speech. Arguments opposed to the Court's opinion include: false statements that harm a person's reputation should subject the speaker to liability; it is incumbent on the speaker to verify the accuracy of the information, persons who happen to be in the public arena should have the same rights to protection of their good names as those who are not public figures.

b. Public officials do have reduced privacy rights because other persons can lawfully make inadvertently false statements about them that harm their reputations, provided the speakers do not know that the information is false or act with a reckless disregard for the truth. Private individuals do not have to prove recklessness or malice to recover damages in defamation suits for false statements made against them. The rationale most often given for the differing treatment of public and private figures is that public officials implicitly consent to greater public scrutiny as a result of their position. Also, a public figure's status and access to the media places such a person in a better position to correct any untrue information that may surface.

c. The Court balanced the value of communicating information about a public issue of great concern with the interest of public officials in avoiding being hurt by false statements.

FIGHTING WORDS, OFFENSIVE SPEAKERS, AND HOSTILE AUDIENCES (PP. 422–427)

Learning Outcomes

After completing this section, students should be able to:

1. define the terms *fighting words, clear and present danger test, incitement test,* and *hate speech;*
2. explain how the Court's tests relating to protected speech have evolved over time with the "clear and present danger" test, the "balancing" test, and the "incitement" test;
3. evaluate the arguments supporting and opposing the punishment of hate speech; and
4. distinguish between court decisions regarding hate speech and decisions on laws that increase criminal punishments for bias-motivated violence and intimidation.

LEGAL RESOURCE PERSONS

Police officers who handle protests or demonstrations are good resource persons to address freedom of assembly, offensive speakers, and hostile audiences. The local authority who receives applications for demonstrations and approves permits would also serve as a helpful resource person. Students should ask what permits are required to hold a demonstration where they live and how police decide when a protest or demonstration needs to be halted.

PROBLEM 35.4 (p.422)

a. Terminiello gave a speech in which he denounced Jews and African Americans. A large crowd formed outside to protest his views. The police felt that Terminiello's speech was stirring public anger, inviting dispute, and creating a disturbance. The police arrested Terminiello because his conduct and speech violated a Chicago ordinance.

b. Students' opinions will vary. Arresting the speaker in such situations permits a "heckler's veto" in that the crowd's response and the subsequent arrest of the speaker would, in effect, stifle the exchange of ideas. Not arresting the speaker could have led to a riot if there were not enough police to control the crowd.

Terminiello claimed that his arrest violated his First Amendment rights. He argued that people should be allowed to express their opinions in a public forum even if the views expressed are not popular with some people. The right to free speech would be meaningless if people thought they would be arrested for expressing their views.

c. The U.S. Supreme Court overturned the city's peace ordinance, saying that it was too vague and that it punished speech that should have been protected. Justice Douglas analyzed the purpose of free speech and found the city ordinance contradictory to the arrest. He stated: "A function of free speech... is to invite dispute. It may indeed best serve its high purpose when it induces a condition of unrest, creates dissatisfaction with conditions as they are, or even stirs people to anger."[23]

Speech is often provocative and challenging. It may strike at prejudices and preconceptions and have profound unsettling effects as it presses acceptance for an idea. If the Court had upheld Terminiello's arrest, they would have encouraged the standardization of ideas either by legislatures, courts, or dominant political or community groups.

d. Students should give reasons for their opinions. Recall that the rights protected by the First Amendment are not limitless. Courts often balance the individual's right to speak with the harm that may occur if that right is exercised or with some other substantial and compelling government interest.

DISCUSSION—FREE SPEECH AND HOSTILE AUDIENCES

The Court case mentioned in the Student Edition is *Dennis v. United States,* (1951).[24]

This activity will be more compelling if a police officer helps to lead the discussion. Such cases present police with difficult problems.

During a period of racial turmoil in the late 1960s, Dick Gregory and a group of civil rights advocates staged a peaceful and orderly march from city hall to the home of Chicago's mayor. The purpose of this march was to demand desegregation of Chicago's public schools. As the demonstrators marched through the mayor's neighborhood, several thousand bystanders cursed at and threatened the marchers. The police, fearful that they could no longer contain the large crowd, ordered the demonstrators to disperse. When the demonstrators refused, they were arrested for disorderly conduct. Use the following questions for a class discussion.

1. As a police officer, how would you have handled the situation? Would you have arrested the demonstrators or the hecklers? *Students' opinions will vary. The police obviously have a very difficult job in these situations. Consider this passage from Justice Black's concurring opinion in* Gregory v. Chicago:

"Both police and demonstrators made their best efforts faithfully to discharge their responsibilities, (but) they were nevertheless unable to restrain these hostile hecklers within decent and orderly bounds. These facts disclosed by the record point unerringly to one conclusion, namely, that when groups with diametrically opposed, deep-seated views are permitted to air their emotional grievances, side by side, on city streets, tranquility and order cannot be maintained even by the joint efforts of the finest and best officers and of those who desire to be the most law-abiding protesters of their grievances."[25]

Ask students what choice, other than arresting the demonstrators, police have when they cannot quell the mob surrounding a demonstration.

2. Assume that Gregory is convicted for disorderly conduct. As a judge, how would you rule on his appeal? *The Supreme Court called this "a simple case" and reversed the defendant's convictions. The Court found the convictions to be totally devoid of evidentiary support showing that the conduct was disorderly. According to the Court, the acts in question were clearly entitled to First Amendment protection.*

The Supreme Court used the incitement test in its decision in *Brandenberg v. Ohio.*[26] This case presents the balance that has been struck between the speech rights of protesters and the need for public order and safety.

CAPTION ANSWER (P. 424) Those who support punishment for hate speech argue that strong measures should be taken because of the emotional and psychological impact hate speech has on its victims and the victims' communities. Supporters also say that hate speech amounts to fighting words and therefore does not qualify for First Amendment protection. Opponents of punishment for hate speech argue that speech codes designed to promote tolerance for certain groups of people are vague and difficult to enforce. They claim that such codes make the government act as censor—favoring certain content or viewpoints and disfavoring others—in violation of the First Amendment.

PROBLEM 35.5 (p.425)

In addition to discussing the specific actions, students should analyze the policy to determine whether or not it is vague or overbroad. It appears to be both.

a. Under a broad reading of this policy, all the actions listed would be violations. However, student opinions are likely to vary greatly regarding the reasonableness of punishing certain actions.

b. Such a policy might reduce the incidence of insensitive, bigoted speech. Also, it puts the school on record as taking a stand against racism, homophobia, and bigotry. Psychological research suggests that attitudes follow behavior; that is, the most effective way to alter attitudes is to alter behavior.[27] Hence, if the norms in school change and students no longer feel free to express insensitive, bigoted, or hateful speech, research suggests that over time they may become less insensitive, hateful, or bigoted.

Opponents of the policy would argue that it is vague, overbroad, regulates content, and violates the First Amendment. Prejudice and hatred live within a person, and banning such speech may not eradicate the tension among the various groups. Moreover, racism can be communicated in more subtle ways which are difficult, if not impossible, to regulate. These types of policies do not easily hold up against legal challenge. In addition, such a policy might produce a backlash of resentment among students and result in increased tension.

Have students brainstorm other steps that the school, groups within the school, and individuals might take to achieve the same purposes. Students and teachers interested in this challenge could explore the website of the American Psychological Association, which has numerous resources devoted to understanding and reducing prejudice. Of particular note is the article "Understanding and Preventing Hate Crimes," available at www.apa.org/monitor/nov01/hatecrimes.aspx.

Although the Supreme Court has not ruled on school speech codes, other courts have unanimously concluded that they violate the First Amendment.[28]

Some states that have adopted "anti-hate" legislation use a breach-of-the-peace model. These statutes punish a speaker who utters abusive or insulting words with the intent to promote a breach of the peace. Even though this model places restrictions on speech, it is considered more acceptable because the restrictions are tied to the violence and not to the speech itself.

c. Students' opinions will vary. Discuss other ways in which regulators of media and businesses could promote similar objectives.

d. Both racial and ethnic slurs and fighting words may incite immediate physical retaliation. Racial and ethnic slurs can increase tensions among groups, not just the individuals involved, and promote negative stereotypes. Fighting words need not be related to race or ethnicity.

DELIBERATION

Should hate speech be banned in our democracy? (p. 426–427)

An overview of the deliberation method is discussed in the front of this Teacher's Manual. For free deliberation materials, student handouts, and an instructional video visit https://store.streetlaw.org/deliberations/.

If this is your first deliberation, consider devoting significant time to establishing norms for deliberations and civil discourse. Introduce the process of deliberations, including careful reading, clarification,

preparing and presenting initial positions, reversing positions, free small group discussion, search for common ground, and whole-class discussion.

Begin class by introducing the deliberation issue: the regulation of hate speech. Ask students to brainstorm what kinds of speech might be classified as hate speech. As a class, develop a working definition of hate speech. Explain that this deliberation will focus on whether hate speech should be banned by the government.

Take students through the deliberation steps as outlined in the front of this Teacher Manual.

Debrief by instructing students to:

- Raise your hands if you changed your position on the issue.
- Raise your hand if you considered a new opinion that you had not considered before today.
- Raise our hand if you felt listened to during the deliberation.
- Follow up by asking students, how they might translate this activity to conversations outside the classroom.

Consider having students perform a self-assessment on the process and their contribution to it.

For the more information on government regulation of hate speech, students may wish to visit:

- **"Hate Speech is Protected Free Speech, Even on College Campuses"** https://www.vox.com/the-big-idea/2017/10/25/16524832/campus-free-speech-first-amendment-protest
- **"The Case for Restricting Hate Speech"** http://www.latimes.com/opinion/op-ed/la-oe-nielsen-free-speech-hate-20170621-story.html
- **"The Hate Debate"** https://www.npr.org/podcasts/481105292/more-perfect
- **"Hate in America"** http://hateinamerica.news21.com/

TIME, PLACE, AND MANNER RESTRICTIONS (PP. 428–431)

Learning Outcomes

After completing this section, students should be able to:

1. distinguish between regulations of expression based on content and regulations based on when, where, and how the speech takes place;
2. identify examples of regulations that may govern the time, place, and manner in which expression takes place;
3. define the term *public forum;*

4. explain what the law says about regulating viewpoint-neutral speech in public and in nonpublic forums; and

5. evaluate a court's decision to allow an American Nazi Party demonstration in Skokie, Illinois.

BACKGROUND—RESTRICTIONS ON EXPRESSION

Ask students whether they feel it is fair to require that music be played at a lower volume under certain circumstances, such as late at night or in other circumstances when it may disturb others. A 1989 case demonstrates how time, place, and manner regulations can be used to control the communication of a particular message. In *Ward* v. *Rock Against Racism (RAR)*,[29] the U.S. Supreme Court held that New York City's regulation of music volume at outdoor rock concerts was a legitimate time, place, and manner restriction. It found that the government had a substantial interest in protecting the well-being of other persons in the park and those living near it. The regulation was content-neutral because it served purposes unrelated to the content of the expression. Furthermore, the regulation left open ample alternative avenues for communication since it only controlled the volume, not the expression.

Explain to students that the federal, state, and local governments often restrict the time, manner, and place of demonstrations on public lands. Ask students if it restricts free speech when individuals or groups must first get permits in order to be able to demonstrate. Interested students may want to visit the American Civil Liberties Union website's page "Know Your Rights: Protesters' Rights" at https://www.aclu.org/know-your-rights/protesters-rights/ for up to date information.

THE **CASE** OF...

The Nazis in Skokie

PROBLEM 35.6 (p.428)

a. More than six million Jews were killed in the Holocaust during World War II. Many members of the large Jewish population of Skokie were survivors of Nazi concentration camps or relatives of those who lost their lives. Many people in Skokie and all over the country despised the American Nazi Party. In addition, many Jewish groups maintained that European Jews and others had remained passive for too long during the Nazi rise to power. Their slogan "Never Again" refers to a heightened commitment to combat anti-Semitism wherever it is encountered.

b. Students' opinions will vary. Motive is generally not a factor in determining whether or not speech will be protected. The exception is when the speaker's motive is to produce imminent lawlessness and when the speech is, in fact, likely to have this result.

c. Under the First Amendment, content should not be a consideration in determining whether or not speech should be protected. This was the main argument of the Nazi Party and of the American Civil Liberties Union (ACLU). The ACLU lost many members after it accepted this case because, for some, protecting the civil liberties of Nazis was simply too personally offensive to support.

d. The town of Skokie passed a law that was not viewpoint-neutral; that is, it regulated certain viewpoints but not others. For example, it banned racial and religious viewpoints and military-style uniforms. The requirement for liability insurance appears to be content-neutral so long as every group had to purchase it. However, because the town could waive the requirement (though it appears that it would not waive it for the Nazi Party), it applied the law in a discriminatory way. In other words, it appeared that the town was actually trying to censor a particular group by invoking a type of time, place, and manner restriction.

e. Students' opinions will vary. The town could have required the demonstration to be held at a certain time or place so as not to obstruct traffic or unduly interfere with other city activities. In *Collin* v. *Smith*, the federal district court for the Northern District of Illinois found the ordinances to be unconstitutional.[30] The Seventh Circuit Court of Appeals affirmed.[31] The insurance ordinance also included a provision allowing it to be waived. Here, the court ruled that because no principled standard existed for determining exemption and such insurance coverage was unavailable to controversial groups such as the Nazi Party, this ordinance was an "abridgement in the guise of regulation" and therefore unconstitutional.

Although racial slurs might not be protected speech under the fighting words doctrine, that doctrine extends only to abusive and insulting speech that is used in an abusive manner and in a way that presents an actual danger. The U.S. Supreme Court found Skokie's ordinance to be overbroad and unduly vague because the "First Amendment does not permit the government to restrict discussion of such sensitive and emotion-charged public issues [as race and religion] to the sanitary prose of legal and social science technical jargon."[32]

With the Nazi demonstration scheduled for June 25, 1978, the city of Skokie sought a U.S. Supreme Court stay of the Seventh Circuit Court of Appeals ruling pending review. On June 12, 1978, however, the Supreme Court denied the request for a stay.[33] With all legal obstacles to the march removed, the American Nazi Party canceled the demonstration three days before it was to take place, explaining that the aim of the planned Skokie march had been "pure agitation to restore our right to free speech" and admitting that they had "used the threat of the Skokie march to win the right to rally in Chicago." A Nazi rally was subsequently held in Chicago's Marquette Park on July 9, 1978. No serious incidents took place.

CAPTION ANSWER (P. 429) Courts analyze time, place, and manner restrictions by determining whether the site is a public forum. If the site is a public forum, the regulation will be overturned unless it serves an important government interest. If the site is a nonpublic forum, the regulation will be upheld so long as it is reasonable.

PROBLEM 35.7 (p. 429)

a. This is a restriction of manner (it prohibits only the posting of signs) and place (the prohibition applies only to public property). The ordinance is content-neutral; it regulates all types of signs regardless of their content. The U.S. Supreme Court upheld this ordinance.[34]

b. This is a restriction on manner (it prohibits sleeping) and place (the prohibition applies only to certain national parks). This regulation also is content-neutral, although some argument can be made that the prohibition discriminates against certain speakers. The regulation was challenged by a group of homeless people who sought the right to sleep in Lafayette Park in Washington, D.C., across from the White House, as part of a demonstration of their plight. The National Park Service regulation was upheld by the Supreme Court in *Clark* v. *Community for Creative Non-Violence*.[35]

c. This is a content restriction because it regulates the type of idea (editorials) rather than the time, place, or manner of communication. Moreover, some view this as the worst type of content restriction, because it bans political opinions, the very heart of free speech protection. The Supreme Court struck down this regulation.[36]

d. This is based on an actual case. In *Metromedia, Inc.* v. *City of San Diego*,[37] the Supreme Court found this to be a place and manner restriction. The restriction on all billboards is an unreasonable regulation that could interfere with the flow of protected expression. However, the Court did say that a prohibition that applied only to commercial billboards would probably be upheld, perhaps reflecting the idea that commercial speech has less protection.

e. The Supreme Court held this content-based restriction to be unconstitutional.[38] Although the Court assumed for First Amendment purposes that the District of Columbia had a compelling interest in protecting the dignity of foreign diplomats and shielding them from criticism, it found that the regulation was not tailored narrowly enough. The government's interest could have been achieved through less restrictive options such as prohibiting the intimidation, coercion, or harassment of foreign officials.

f. This is loosely based on *Bray* v. *Alexandria Women's Health Clinic*.[39] The town ordinance is not content-neutral. The law prevents people from exercising their First Amendment rights by preventing them from voicing their antiabortion message. The sidewalks, in all likelihood, would be considered a public forum. Thus, the ordinance could not legitimately target a specific kind of speech. However, the town could place time, place, and manner restrictions on the protesters. For instance, a regulation could prohibit demonstrations within 100 feet of the clinic to ensure access for those wanting to enter the clinic. A blanket exclusion of all picketing, on any topic, may be constitutional.

g. In 1992, the Supreme Court held that a public airport is a nonpublic forum and that because it is a nonpublic forum, it is reasonable to ban repetitive solicitation of funds inside the terminal. The Court distinguished, however, between solicitation of donations and the distribution of leaflets. The Court felt that solicitation would interfere with the traditional and historical use of the terminal—that is, processing passengers and baggage, thereby facilitating air travel. However, a ban on the distribution of literature inside the terminal, which does not interfere with passenger flow as severely, would violate the free speech clause. The political or religious groups would therefore have the right to solicit funds on the sidewalks in front of the terminal.[40]

THE **CASE** OF...

The Flag Burning

PROBLEM 35.8 (pp.430–431)

Be sure students have read the section on symbolic speech in the Student Edition before they complete this activity. Students' answers will vary. When students have completed their letters, have them exchange them with each other to compare answers and reasons.

This case is based on the U.S. Supreme Court decision in *Texas v. Johnson*.[43] Opinion A is based on the majority's decision, and Opinion B is based on the dissent. This 5-to-4 decision was controversial when it was announced in 1989. Justices Kennedy and Scalia, both known for their conservative views, voted with the more liberal justices of the Supreme Court. Following the *Johnson* case, many members of Congress found its outcome so objectionable that they passed a federal statute making it a crime to deface the flag. This federal statute was challenged and struck down by the Supreme Court in 1990.[44] Congress has since explored passing a constitutional amendment to remove flag-burning from constitutional protection. Anti-flag desecration is one of the top ten subjects of amendments proposed in Congress.

The case of *Texas v. Johnson* is one of several cases featured at www.landmarkcases.org, a website of Street Law, Inc. and the Supreme Court Historical Society. The site includes numerous background articles, teaching materials designed for a variety of reading abilities, links to the majority and dissenting decisions, teaching suggestions, articles about the proposed constitutional amendment banning flag-burning, and other resources dedicated to this topic.

Note: This case provides an opportunity to use legal resource persons who represent opposing views on this topic. Students could also conduct a

simulated moot court or mini-moot courts on this case. For suggestions about how to prepare students to conduct a moot court, see the section called "Teaching Strategies" in the front of this Teacher Manual, or visit https://www.streetlaw.org/programs/scotus-in-the-classroom and click on the "Resources" tab.

SYMBOLIC SPEECH (PP. 432)

Learning Outcomes

After completing this section, students should be able to:

1. define the terms *symbolic speech*; and *expressive conduct*
2. list five examples of symbolic speech;
3. describe how courts decide whether nonverbal expression constitutes protected symbolic speech; and
4. weigh arguments for and against permitting demonstrators to burn the American flag.

BACKGROUND—SYMBOLIC SPEECH AND GOVERNMENT INTEREST

A famous symbolic speech case, *United States v. O'Brien*,[41] dealt with burning a military draft card. In that case, the defendant argued that he had burned his Selective Service draft card intentionally as an act of political protest against the Vietnam War. The U.S. Supreme Court held that his political views and his actions were separate. The Court stated that Congress had good reason for making it a crime to destroy a draft card. The Selective Service system requires that everyone have a card readily available; burning one's card makes it unavailable. The Court ruled that O'Brien had been punished for reducing the effectiveness of the draft law, not for expressing his opposition to the war. Although expression of opposition in itself was protected by the First Amendment, interfering with the draft was not. In its decision, the Court pointed out that "when 'speech' and 'nonspeech' elements are combined in the same course of conduct, a sufficiently important government interest in regulating the nonspeech element can justify incidental limitations on First Amendment freedoms."[42]

ACTIVITY—IDENTIFYING SYMBOLIC SPEECH

Share the cases below with students and ask them to identify the speakers' interests in expressing their positions and the government's interest in regulating their expression. Then have students decide whether the action in each case should be protected by the First Amendment as symbolic speech.

1. Bill Spence taped a peace symbol to an American flag. When he hung the flag upside down—a symbol of distress or danger—in the window of his apartment, he was arrested and convicted for violating a state law against improper use of the flag. *Spence's interest was in expressing his political belief that the nation was in trouble. The government's interest was in avoiding desecration of a national symbol. This case is based on* Spence v. Washington.[(45)] *The Supreme Court reversed Spence's conviction and pointed out four important factors:*

   • *The flag was privately owned.*
   • *The flag was on private property.*
   • *There was no risk of breach of the peace, incitement to riot, or disorderly conduct.*
   • *Spence's action was a form of communication (i.e., symbolic speech). The Court rejected the state's arguments concerning the importance of respect for our national emblem. However, the Court left open the possibility of prosecuting someone if the factors listed above did not apply.*

2. Raul Ortega believes that discrimination against Hispanic Americans is widespread. To protest this discrimination, he throws a rock through a school window. Taped to the rock is the message, "End Discrimination Now!" *Ortega's interest is in protesting discrimination against Hispanic Americans. The government's interest is in protecting property from destruction. Although a message was taped to the rock, the thrown rock would not be considered protected symbolic speech, and Ortega could be prosecuted for his action.*

VAGUENESS AND OVERINCLUSIVE LAWS (PP. 432–434)

BACKGROUND—VAGUENESS OF LAWS

Vagueness is a difficult but important concept. Courts are careful to ensure that laws regulating speech do not have a "chilling effect" on protected expression. For this reason, and because of the requirements of due process, laws regulating speech must be clear and specific and cannot prohibit any protected expression. For example, the issue of vagueness arose when a Massachusetts man was arrested for wearing a four-by-six-inch flag sewn to the seat of his blue jeans. He was arrested for violating a state statute which read, "Whoever publicly mutilates, tramples upon, defaces or treats contemptuously the flag of the U.S. ... whether such flag is public or private property ... shall be punished by a fine of ... not more than 100 dollars or by imprisonment for not more than one year, or both." The Supreme Court said that the "treats contemptuously" language was too vague, especially in light of clothing fashion standards at the time.[(46)]

CAPTION ANSWER (P. 432) Courts determine whether conduct is symbolic speech by asking whether the speaker intended to convey a particular message and whether it is likely that the message was understood by those who viewed it.

a. The suspect was prosecuted because the prosecutor believed that he or she had enough evidence to prove that he trespassed on private property, erected and burned a cross intending to arouse the fear, anger, and alarm of the African American family in violation of the city's ordinance. The prosecution also believed it could convince a jury that the suspect's actions were motivated by racial hostility.

b. The defendant's alleged conduct could have violated several other Minnesota statutes carrying significant penalties: terrorist threats, arson, criminal trespass, or criminal property damage. The prosecutor may have chosen to use the hate crime ordinance to demonstrate that St. Paul will not tolerate hate crimes. It is also possible that the prosecutor was looking for a test case to determine whether the ordinance was constitutional.

c. Students might identify the word symbol and the phrases "... or has reasonable grounds to know..." and "arouses anger, alarm, or resentment." They might say that one cannot predict how others might react to a particular symbol, so it is hard to know in advance what action would violate the law.

d. Upon appeal, the defendant could argue that the hate crime ordinance, as written, is vague because a reasonable person cannot understand what expression is prohibited. An ordinance should be drafted in a manner that is clear as to what activity will be considered illegal. The defendant could also argue that the ordinance interferes with his First Amendment right of free speech and expression. All citizens have the right (albeit not absolute) to express their opinions, even if those opinions might be offensive to the vast majority.

The state of Minnesota could argue that the rights guaranteed by the Constitution are not absolute, even the right of free speech. Thus, the government could argue that the ordinance is narrowly tailored toward accomplishing the government interest of protecting the community against bias-motivated threats to public safety

and order. Additionally, the state could argue that, although the ordinance regulates content-based expression, those hateful expressions have no value and are so evil that the restrictions outweigh the right to free expression. The Supreme Court has held in the past that certain limited categories of speech so lack the values the First Amendment was designed to protect that the Constitution affords no protection to that expression (e.g., child pornography, obscenity, and libel).

e. Students' answers will vary, particularly when they express their opinions about whether they agree or disagree with the defendant's lawyer. Students may say that the attorney is expressing a view that is supported by the Constitution. The mere fact that expressive activity or speech causes hurt feelings, offense, or resentment does not render that expressive conduct or speech unprotected. No matter how much one might disagree with their opinions, racists and Nazi groups, for example, have the right to spread their opinions by legal means without government interference. The attorney apparently felt that the ordinance as written interfered with his client's First Amendment rights. If the ordinance was held to be constitutional, it would have far-reaching effects on other opinions and messages.

f. Students' answers will vary. They should give reasons for how they believe the case should have been decided. This problem is based on the 1992 U.S. Supreme Court case, *R.A.V.* v. *City of St. Paul, Minnesota.*[47] In its decision, the Court determined that the ordinance was unconstitutional because it was content-based—that is, it discriminated on the basis of the content of the opinion expressed. The law did not apply to all fighting words, but instead selected only fighting words based on race, color, creed, religion, and gender. The law excluded fighting words based on political affiliation, union membership, sexual orientation, and other factors. The fact that such ideas may not be popular should not affect a speaker's right to communicate the message. A concurring opinion expressed the view that the ordinance was overly inclusive because it proscribed both unprotected speech and speech that causes only hurt feelings or resentment.

In a different case just one year later involving a Wisconsin statute, the U.S. Supreme Court ruled unanimously that the First Amendment allows enforcement of a criminal assault charge with a more severe penalty when the offender acts on the basis of racial hatred.[48] Note that in

2003, the Court held that a state could ban cross burning that was intended to intimidate, provided the burden was on the state to prove intimidation. Therefore, there are ways to write hate crime ordinances that are not vague or overly broad.

g. In 2007–2008, there were numerous reports of nooses being displayed on college campuses and in work sites. While these acts are vile and insensitive, it can be very difficult for cities or states to enforce laws that prohibit these acts because the ordinances or statutes must not be vague or overly broad. Ask students to investigate a news report of a noose being displayed near their community and then to report how the act was investigated and what authorities did to respond to it. Beyond criminal prosecution, college administrators and government officials at all levels can model open and productive communication among groups, promote and support prosecution for actions that constitute crime, and demonstrate intolerance to hate crimes.

DISCUSSION—CROSS BURNING REVISITED

In response to increasing racial tension, Virginia enacted a law in 1952 that banned all cross burning on other people's property. Over many years the Ku Klux Klan used burning crosses to intimidate African Americans. In 1968, the law was expanded to ban cross burning in all public places. Ask students to examine the statute and answer the questions that follow.

"It shall be unlawful for any person or persons, with the intent of intimidating any person or group of persons, to burn, or cause to be burned, a cross on the property of another, a highway or other public place. Any person who shall violate any provision of this section shall be guilty of a Class 6 felony... Any such burning of a cross shall be prima facie evidence of an intent to intimidate a person or group of persons."

1. How is the Virginia statute different from the Minnesota statute in *R.A.V.? The Virginia statute is much narrower than Minnesota's because it applies only to cross burning that causes intimidation. In contrast, the Minnesota statute applied to various symbols that "included but was not limited to" those listed in the statute. Also, the Virginia statute places part of the burden of proof on the defendant instead of on the state.*

2. The Virginia statute says that the "burning of a cross shall be *prima facie* evidence of an intent to intimidate a person or group of persons." In other words, a person who burns a cross in public will be assumed to have intended to intimidate unless the person can prove otherwise. How does this shift the burden of proof that generally exists in a criminal case? What arguments might justify such a shift? *By shifting the traditional burden of proof from the state (prosecution) to the defendant, the statute says that cross burners are guilty of intending to intimidate unless and until they can prove otherwise. Some people, including Justices Thomas and Scalia, argue that such a shift is appropriate in this unique context because a burning cross can rarely if ever be separated from the racial terrorism that was historically associated with it. Others argue that the burning cross is also a symbol of ideology (i.e., the Ku Klux Klan's) and ideological symbols, unlike acts of intimidation, must be protected.*

3. In light of *R.A.V.*, should this statute be upheld? *During the 2002–2003 term, the Supreme Court revisited the issue of cross burning in* Virginia v. Black.[49] *This time the Court said that a ban on cross burning that was intended to intimidate would be constitutional provided the state, not the defendant, bears the burden of proving intimidation.*

Defendants in two separate cases challenged the Virginia law as unconstitutional under the First Amendment. On the night of May 2, 1998, several drunken teenagers in Virginia Beach, Virginia, decided to retaliate against an African American neighbor who had complained about the firing range in one of the teen's yards. To get back at the African American neighbor, the teens built a cross and placed it on the neighbor's lawn. The teens tried to light the cross and failed, leaving the cross and burn holes on the lawn. The family found the cross the next morning and called the police. Initially angry, they became fearful of more violence and moved to a different town. The teenagers pled guilty to charges of attempting to burn a cross.

In a separate case four months later, Ku Klux Klan member Barry Elton Black held a large rally on private property. A 25-foot cross was burned at the rally, visible to nearby homes and motorists on the state highway. Black was arrested for intimidation. At trial, both white and African American witnesses testified that they were intimidated or frightened by the rally and the cross burning. A jury found Mr. Black guilty of violating the law against cross burning. The defendants in both cases challenged the Virginia law on First Amendment grounds, relying on the Court's decision in R.A.V.

The Court held that the state could ban cross burning in public, provided the state could prove the requirement of intent to intimidate. Justices Scalia and Thomas would have maintained the Virginia law in its entirety. They argued that the intent to intimidate could be assumed because public cross burning, unlike symbolic speech, could not be separated from its effect of intimidating. Justice Souter's dissent argued that upholding a ban on cross burning was a content-based restriction that was rooted in the government's opposition to the message conveyed. His position was based on the notion that the strength of the First Amendment is its protection of ideas that the majority finds distasteful and obnoxious.

DISCUSSION—SOCIAL MEDIA THREAT OR RAP LYRIC?

Social media has amplified personal speech and given average people the ability to broadcast their posts and tweets to potentially world wide audiences. With this development comes increased importance and new questions about which speech should be protected and which should be restricted.

Ask students if they think social media posts should be protected like other forms of speech? What if the speech in question were violent rap lyrics? Do lyrics of songs have special protections as artistic expressions as well as speech? What if those lyrics were perhaps meant as a threat toward an individual? At what point should the speech be restricted?

Explain to students that the Supreme Court has long held that a "true threat" is an exception to the First Amendment protection. However, it has never defined exactly what a "true threat" is. The federal government has made it illegal to transmit any communication threatening to injure another person.

This scenario is based on a U.S. Supreme Court case from 2015, *Elonis* v. *United States*[50]. After his wife left him and he was fired from his job, Anthony Elonis began posting violent rap lyrics (some of which he wrote himself) on Facebook. Elonis' ex-wife felt the graphically violent lyrics were meant for her, so she altered authorities and obtained a restraining order. When he began posting about local law enforcement and a kindergarten class, it attracted the FBI's attention. A female FBI agent interviewed Elonis about his posts, and soon after he posted new lyrics that communicated thoughts about killing an FBI agent and her family. He was arrested and convicted under the federal law that banned interstate threats because a "reasonable person" would regard the statements as

threats. Elonis appealed arguing that the lyrics were only a "true threat" if the speaker intended to threaten someone, which he did not.

The question before the Court was: "Does the First Amendment require proof of the defendant's intent to threaten in order to convict him of threatening another person? Or is it enough to show that a "reasonable person" would regard the statement as threatening?"

Ask students if they would find for Elonis or the U.S. government in this case. Discuss possible First Amendment arguments for each side.

Inform students that the Supreme Court found for Elonis. The Court held that the government had to prove more than just a reasonable person would have felt threatened. They wrote that "wrongdoing must be conscious to be criminal." The prosecution would have had to prove that Elonis intended to threaten his ex-wife or the FBI agent and known that this posts would be viewed as threats.

TAKING ACTION: LAW AND DEMOCRACY
Advising Your City Council

PROBLEM 35.10 (p.434)

The Supreme Court has a history of examining the constitutionality of legislation restricting charitable solicitation. The Court first extended First Amendment protection to the area of charitable solicitation in the case of *Cantwell* v. *Connecticut*.[51] Later, in *Village of Schaumburg* v. *Citizens for a Better Environment*,[52] the Court struck down an ordinance prohibiting the solicitation of contributions by charitable organizations that do not use at least 75 percent of their receipts for charitable purposes. Remind students of the Court's decision involving the religious groups soliciting for funds at the airport described in Problem 35.7 part **g.**

Note: This problem asks students to draft a paper advising the council member. An alternative approach could be to have a legislative hearing in which students advise the council member through their testimony. To take it a step further, students could be grouped into hypothetical groups who have a stake or opinion about the proposed legislation, and those groups could testify. For suggestions about how to conduct a legislative hearing, see the section called "Teaching Strategies" in the front of this Teacher Manual.

a. Students' opinions will vary. Criminal laws that could be used to address the problem are laws that prohibit harassment, obstructing the flow of pedestrian traffic on side walks, vagrancy, or public nuisance. In some cases public health laws, quality of life laws, and criminal trespass laws may also apply. The key to designing laws that target these problems and that withstand constitutional challenge is ensuring that the laws specifically criminalize conduct and not speech. Also, the criminal laws noted above would have to be enforced consistently against both "help the homeless" panhandlers and others.

b. The words "Help the homeless" would be protected speech. They might even be viewed as political speech. Explore with students whether panhandling might be viewed as symbolic speech.

c. Students may draft a law to regulate the blocking, threatening, and harassing behavior. Some cities have drafted ordinances that use the term aggressive panhandling to describe appeals for money that escalate into repeated demands, threatening body contact, shouting obscenities, and other intimidating behavior.[53] Alternatively, there might be certain non-public locations from which this speech could be banned. For instance, in New York City a statute prohibiting panhandling in transit facilities was upheld.

d. Students' laws should be examined for vagueness and over inclusiveness. If a student's law bans protected speech along with unprotected speech, it can be struck down as over inclusive. If it is not clear exactly what is banned under the student's law, it may be struck down as vague.

e. Students should recognize that citizens will vary in their views. Arguments in favor of this type of law include the concern for safety, maintaining the quality of life, the deterioration of urban quality of life that some citizens and tourists are offended or feel harassed by any panhandling, and loss to businesses as shoppers choose to avoid these areas.

Opposing arguments include that people who are homeless and needy have a right to ask for money, that society has no right to jail them as they are merely a manifestation of society's unfairness, that free speech protects solicitation for money, that the law is overly broad and vague, and that police use the threat of the law to move people along.

NOTES

(1) *West Virginia State Board of Education* v. *Barnette*, 319 U.S. 624 (1943).

(2) U.S. v. Schwimmer, 279 U.S. 644 (1929) (Holmes, J. dissenting).

(3) *Whitney* v. *People of the State of California*, 274 U.S. 357 (1927).

(4) *McIntyre* v. *Ohio Elections Commission*, 514 U.S. 334 (1995).

(5) *Florida Bar* v. *Went For It Inc.*, 515 U.S. 618 (1995).

(6) *Rubin* v. *Coors Brewing Co.*, 514 U.S. 476 (1995).

(7) *Central Hudson Gas and Electric Corp.* v. *Public Services Commission of New York*, 447 U.S. 557 (1980).

(8) *Jacobellis* v. *Ohio*, 378 U.S. 184 (1964).

(9) *Roth* v. *U.S.*, 354 U.S. 476 (1957).

(10) *Miller* v. *California*, 413 U.S. 15 (1973).

(11) *Jenkins* v. *Georgia*, 418 U.S. 153 (1974).

(12) *Smith* v. *United States*, 431 U.S. 291 (1977).

(13) Richtel, "What's Obscene? Google Could Have An Answer," *New York Times*, June 24, 2008.

(14) *City of Renton* v. *Playtime Theatres, Inc.*, 475 U.S. 41 (1986).

(15) *New York* v. *Ferber*, 458 U.S. 747 (1982).

(16) *Sable Communication of California, Inc.* v. *Federal Communication Commission et al.*, 492 U.S. 115 (1989).

(17) Id. at 126.

(18) *U.S.* v. *Williams*, 553 U.S. 285 (2008).

(19) *Brown* v. *Entertainment Merchants Association*, 564 U.S. 786 (2011).

(20) *American Booksellers Association* v. *Hudnut*, 771 F.2d (7th Cir. 1985), aff'd mem., 475 U.S. 1001 (1986).

(21) *The Children's Internet Protection Act*, 114 Sta. 2763A-6335 and *United States et al.* v. *American Library Association, Inc., et al.*, 539 U.S. 194 (2003).

(22) *New York Times* v. *Sullivan*, 376 U.S. 254 (1964).

(23) *Terminiello* v. *Chicago*, 337 U.S. 1 (1949).

(24) *Dennis* v. *United States*, 341 U.S. 494 (1951).

(25) *Gregory* v. *Chicago*, 394 U.S. 111 (1969).

(26) Brandenburg v. Ohio, 395 U.S. 444 (1969).

(27) Pettigrew, T.F. (1997). "Combatting Racism: Creating Norms for Intergroup Harmony." Paper presented at the annual meeting of the American Psychological Association, Chicago, August 18, 1997.

(28) *Booher* v. *Board of Regents, Northern Kentucky University*, 163 F.3d 395 (1998); *Dambrot* v. *Central Michigan University*, 55 F.3d 1177 (6th Cir. 1995); *UWM Post, Inc.* v. *Board of Regents of the University of Wisconsin System*, 774 F. Supp. 1163 (E.D. Wis. 1991); *Doe* v. *University of Michigan*, 721 F. Supp. 852 (E.D. Mich. 1989).

(29) *Ward* v. *Rock Against Racism (RAR)*, 491 U.S. 781 (1989).

(30) *Collin* v. *Smith*, 447 F.Supp. 676 (N.D. Ill. 1978).

(31) *Collin* v. *Smith*, 578 F.2d 1197 (7th Cir. 1978).

(32) Id. at 1201.

(33) *Smith* v. *Collin*, cert. denied, 439 U.S. 916 (1978).

(34) *Los Angeles City Council* v. *Taxpayers for Vincent*, 466 U.S. 789 (1984).

(35) *Clark* v. *Community for Creative Non-Violence*, 468 U.S. 288 (1984).

(36) F.C.C. v. *League of Women Voters*, 468 U.S. 364 (1984).

(37) *Metromedia, Inc.* v. *City of San Diego*, 453 U.S. 490 (1981).

(38) *Boos* v. *Barry*, 485 U.S. 312 (1988).

(39) *Bray* v. *Alexandria Women's Health Clinic*, 506 U.S. 263 (1993).

(40) *International Society for Krishna Consciousness, Inc.* v. *Lee*, 505 U.S. 672 (1992).

(41) *United States* v. *O'Brien*, 391 U.S. 367 (1968).

(42) Id. at 376.

(43) *Texas* v. *Johnson*, 491 U.S. 397 (1989).

(44) *U.S.* v. *Eichman*, 496 U.S. 310 (1990).

(45) *Spence* v. *Washington*, 418 U.S. 405 (1974).

(46) *Smith* v. *Goguen*, 415 U.S. 566 (1974).

(47) *R.A.V.* v. *City of St. Paul, Minnesota*, 505 U.S. 377 (1992).

(48) *Wisconsin* v. *Mitchell*, 508 U.S. 476 (1993).

(49) *Virginia* v. *Black*, 538 U.S. 343 (2003).

(50) *Elonis* v. *U.S.*, 135 S.Ct. 2001 (2015).

(51) *Cantwell* v. *Connecticut*, 310 U.S. 296 (1940).

(52) *Village of Schaumburg* v. *Citizens for a Better Environment*, 444 U.S. 620 (1980).

(53) Charles Mitchell, "Aggressive Panhandling Legislation and Free Speech Claims: Begging for Trouble," 39 N.Y.L. Sch. L. Rev. 697 (1994).

networks™

The First Amendment guarantees freedom of the press. It protects us from government censorship— the suppression of material the government considers offensive—of newspapers, magazines, books, radio, television, and film. Traditionally, the courts have protected the press from government censorship. However, freedom of the press sometimes clashes with other rights, such as a defendant's right to a fair trial or a citizen's right to privacy. In these instances, the courts must determine the best way to resolve the conflict.

INTRODUCTION (PP. 435–437)

Learning Outcomes

After completing this section, students should be able to:
1. define the term *censorship* and state how it occurs;
2. explain why an independent press is sometimes called "the fourth branch" of government;
3. state how democracy is threatened in the absence of a free press;
4. identify other rights with which freedom of the press sometimes collides; and
5. weigh obligations of government-owned television stations to give access to political candidates.

RESOURCE PERSONS

Newspaper editors and reporters may be particularly good resources in conjunction with discussions of censorship, prior restraint, and defamation.

ACTIVITY—INTERPRETING QUOTATIONS

Ask students to examine Thomas Jefferson's quotation below:
"If it were left to me to decide whether we should have a government without a free press or a free press without a government, I would prefer the latter."

Then ask students to work individually or in pairs to complete the following:

- Develop hypotheses to explain why Jefferson felt so strongly about the importance of a free press.
- Decide whether you agree with Jefferson.
- Defend your position.

ACTIVITY—ANALYZING POTENTIAL CONFLICTS BETWEEN THE PRESS AND A FAIR TRIAL

Have students examine the quotation, "justice cannot survive behind walls of silence." This quote is from the famous Sam Sheppard court case.[1] In that case, Dr. Sam Sheppard was accused of brutally murdering his wife. There was an enormous amount of pretrial publicity, and Sheppard was convicted. In 1966, the U.S. Supreme Court overturned his conviction, in part because of all the adverse publicity. He was acquitted in his second trial, in which F. Lee Bailey represented him. Many people believe Sheppard's story inspired the television series and feature film *The Fugitive*.

Ask students to interpret the quote and explain how having a free press is related to getting a fair trial. Ask students whether they can identify circumstances when having a free press might interfere with getting a fair trial.

To explore these issues, you may want to examine several current high-profile cases. Have students consider:

- the difficulty of obtaining an impartial jury in these cases;
- what steps have been taken or might have to be taken to reduce juror bias and the influence of the media and the general public (e.g., sequestering the jury, change of venue, or gag orders on the attorneys).

For additional information about juries and impartial juries, see Chapter 5.

ACTIVITY—THE FOURTH BRANCH OF GOVERNMENT

Ask students why they think some people refer to the press as "the fourth branch" of government. To what extent does the press provide a check on the three (other) branches of government? Does the press scrutinize each branch equally?

To test their hypotheses, ask students to examine print newspapers, news magazines, or online news sites with national circulation. Once they have selected their news sources, ask students to find articles related to the executive branch (including the president, cabinet departments, agencies, the military, etc.), the legislative branch (including senators, representatives, congressional committees, and the legislation they consider), and the judiciary branch (including various levels of courts and their decisions). Have students consider the following questions.

- What is the purpose and tone of each article?
- Which person or group appears to be the most closely scrutinized? Least closely scrutinized?
- Do the articles tend to focus more on the decisions themselves or on the decision makers?
- Should citizens know about the topics and issues presented in the article?
- Does the article support or refute the claim that the press serves an important function as the "fourth branch" of government?

BACKGROUND—THE MEDIA, THE FIRST AMENDMENT, AND THE FAIRNESS DOCTRINE

Although the courts have been protective of the First Amendment rights of the media, they have also recognized the media's responsibility to present both sides of important public issues. In the case of *Red Lion Broadcasting* v. *FCC,* the U.S. Supreme Court dealt with the problem of relatively few private corporations controlling the mass media and possibly giving a one-sided presentation of issues, thereby restricting the people's right to know.[2]

The question was whether or not the Federal Communications Commission's (FCC) "fairness doctrine," an agency policy that at one time required broadcasters who had presented one side of a controversial issue to give free time to a presentation of the other side, violated the broadcaster's First Amendment rights. The Supreme Court held that the fairness doctrine was not a violation of the broadcaster's First Amendment rights because it is "the right of viewers and listeners, not the right of the broadcasters, which is paramount."

Broadcasters operate under licenses granted by the federal government, and the number of licenses that can be granted is limited. Broadcasters can be required to share the scarce resource with which they have been entrusted in order to ensure that there will be the "uninhibited marketplace of ideas" that the First Amendment was intended to create.

Although the fairness doctrine has been abandoned, complex and controversial issues remain for the FCC involving the best policies for ensuring a balanced dissemination. The debate includes how much time is given to various sides of an issue as well as the number of media outlets that can be owned by a single person or entity. Some people argue that government regulation regarding media ownership is overly restrictive and that media ownership should be driven by pure market forces with minimal government interference. Others argue that media ownership differs from other commodities because it controls people's access to information. Therefore, they say, increased government regulation is appropriate to prevent monopolies selecting what information the public will receive. Ask students to consider the extremes of each position. What would happen if one person or organization (or a small group of them) controlled the entire flow of news and information? Does our community benefit from news coverage from more than one source (or ownership)? Is news coverage balanced? If not, what can we do to seek more balance?

a. The television station can argue that its decision is viewpoint-neutral, based on Forbes's lack of serious voter support. It can also argue that the debate is not a public forum.

b. Forbes can argue that the debate is a public forum and the television station's assessment of Forbes as not politically viable is not a compelling or narrowly tailored reason for excluding him from the debate. Forbes can also claim that a state-owned television network must have pre-established, objective criteria for determining who is included and excluded.

c. Students' answers will vary. In *Arkansas Educational Television Commission* v. *Forbes*,[3] the Supreme Court ruled that the debate was a non-public forum with selective access for individual speakers and that the TV station's decision to exclude Forbes from the debate was a reasonable, viewpoint-neutral exercise of professional journalistic discretion consistent with the First Amendment. There was no evidence to show that the station had excluded Forbes based on his views.

d. Students' answers will vary. Ask students whether they have ever watched debates and whether they believe that the presence or absence of particular candidates at debates influenced them or might influence other voters. The effort made by political candidates to participate in televised debates indicates that the candidates find debates to be one of the most effective avenues for communicating their positions to voters.

e. A third-party candidate can draw support away from one of the two major-party candidates, thus potentially affecting the outcome of the election. For example, some people believe that Independent Party candidate Ross Perot pulled conservative voters who might otherwise have voted for George Bush, leading to Bill Clinton's first election in 1992. Some analysts also believe that Green Party candidate Ralph Nader pulled liberal voters who would otherwise have voted for Al Gore, contributing to the historically close election that landed George W. Bush in the

White House in 2000. It is possible for a third-party candidate to defeat both major-party candidates. This occurred in Minnesota in 1998 when Jesse Ventura, a Reform Party candidate, defeated both the Democratic and Republican candidates in the gubernatorial race.

f. Students' opinions will vary. Many citizens feel that our electoral system should do more to encourage candidates who are not from the two major parties. Others believe that the two-party system works well in the United States and has provided more political stability than the multi-party systems in some other countries.

g. Students' opinions will vary. Those arguing for an automatic right of access for all may point to the role of money in elections.

Those without access to large sums of money have no chance of running a viable candidacy. Requiring government-owned stations to include all candidates would temper this problem. Those opposing an automatic right of access might argue that the "lunatic fringe" would then gain access and detract from serious candidates. Since fringe candidates have far less voter support, allowing them to participate would waste broadcast time and turn off viewers.

This problem may lead to a discussion of campaign finance reform, a controversial topic that touches upon many First Amendment issues. For more information about election reform, see Chapter 3 in the Student Edition.

PROHIBITING PUBLICATION (PP. 437–438)

Learning Outcomes

After completing this section, students should be able to:

1. define the terms *prior restraint* and *gag order*;
2. identify three circumstances when prior restraint is permitted;
3. weigh the relative importance of a free press against a defendant's right to a fair trial;
4. describe the reasoning behind the U.S. Supreme Court's decision in *New York Times* v. *United States*; and
5. identify one circumstance when government censorship of the press would be upheld.

BACKGROUND—THE FEDERAL COMMUNICATIONS COMMISSION AND PRIOR RESTRAINT

The Federal Communications Commission (FCC) is a five-person political body that determines whether the content of material is appropriate for radio, network television, and cable television. Those who violate FCC rules can be issued a fine. In an effort to avoid violations, even live events are broadcast on a slight audio delay so that potential violations can be censored before they hit the airwaves.

Students may be surprised to learn that the government cannot stop a network from using particular language before the fact, but may impose fines after the fact. The result is that the networks must censor themselves. The distinction between the government actively censoring television programming and the government imposing fines after a violation is key. It may seem like "splitting hairs," but the distinction is significant in First Amendment jurisprudence. Government censorship in the form of a prior restraint is examined with the strictest judicial scrutiny and almost never survives judicial review. Prior restraint was particularly offensive to the Framers as they crafted the First Amendment. The idea is that a network, or any private speaker, should not be prevented from circulating ideas (unless they cause imminent danger), although they may have to accept the consequences (such as fines or, in some cases, imprisonment) for the expression if it violates a government regulation or law.

THE **CASE** OF...

The Gag Order

PROBLEM 36.2 (p. 437)

Before students answer this problem, be sure they have read the entire section about prohibiting publication.

a. A brutal murder in a small town received widespread media coverage. In order to preserve the chances of having an unbiased jury at trial, the judge, with both parties' agreement, prohibited the press from publishing the confession and other information introduced at a pretrial hearing. The media sued.

b. Students' opinions will vary. The facts here raise the interesting question of whether or not the press and the public have a First Amendment "right to know" about criminal proceedings.

The judge and both sides agreed to keep the press from publishing the information. Also note that this is a gag-order case, not a closed-trial case. The Sixth Amendment guarantees the defendant a public trial which he will still have even if the gag-order stands. Ask students which is preferable: allowing the media in but ordering them not to publish, or closing the hearings to the media altogether.

c.–d. Obviously both rights are very important. In *Nebraska Press Association* v. *Stuart*,[4] the case on which this problem is based, the U.S. Supreme Court held that the trial judge must try to protect the rights of the defendant without barring media coverage or closing the trial to the media and public. These steps could include postponing the trial, changing the location (venue) of the trial, permitting extensive questioning of jurors regarding their knowledge of the case, and carefully instructing the jury at the end of the trial.

DISCUSSION—THE PENTAGON AND THE PRESS

The government's attempt to impose censorship was the issue in the case of *New York Times Co.* v. *United States*.[5]

Ask students to discuss whether the government is ever justified in censoring coverage of a war, and if so, when. The debate over the role of the press in times of war took on a new dimension during the war in Iraq in 2003, when the government allowed reporters to be "embedded" with the troops. Ask students how this arrangement might benefit the government, the press, and the public. How might the responsibilities of the military and the troops be compromised by this relationship? How might this approach be a disservice to the public? For a comprehensive look at the policy of embedding reporters and the history of military-media relations, visit www.rcfp.org/ and use the search term "embedded journalists."

a. Students' answers will vary. The government has an interest in protecting or prosecuting the publication of confidential information and communications, particularly those related to military operations and international relations. The government could argue that the release of top-secret documents would endanger military members and intelligence officers actively involved in missions abroad. Further, release of confidential communications could prove embarrassing or diplomatically compromising for the United States in terms of its internal and foreign relations.

b. Students' answers will vary. The website has an interest in uncovering the truth. The website could argue that Americans have the right to know what is being shielded from them by government and corporations. The website could argue that it is their duty to provide a check against the unfettered abuse of power by government generally and the military in particular.

c. Students' answers will vary. This case is based on the website WikiLeaks, established in 2006 by Julian Assange. The publication on the website of thousands of classified and confidential documents has led many governments, including the United States, to attempt to censor WikiLeaks. Supporters of WikiLeaks have argued that the First Amendment was designed to protect exactly this type of investigative journalism. On the other side, critics of Mr. Assange and WikiLeaks have argued that in order for governments to function, particularly in military and international situations, certain information must be held confidential in order to protect those individuals risking their lives in service of the country. In deciding *New York Times* v. *United States*[6], the U.S. Supreme Court addressed the issue being examined here. In that case, the Court refused to censor the publication of the Pentagon Papers because the court held that releasing the documents would not cause grave and irreparable danger. The U.S. government would have to prove the grave and irreparable danger standard in order to be successful in censoring WikiLeaks.

DENYING THE PRESS ACCESS TO INFORMATION (PP. 439–440)

Learning Outcomes

After completing this section, students should be able to:

1. explain why access to information from the government is essential to maintaining a democracy;
2. describe the relationship between a free press and access to information from the government;
3. identify requirements of the 1966 *Freedom of Information Act (FOIA)*; and
4. outline steps in making a *FOIA* request.

BACKGROUND AND DISCUSSION— ACCESS TO CRIMINAL TRIALS

Press and public access to criminal trials has been the cause of considerable U.S. Supreme Court litigation. In 1979, the Court permitted exclusion of the press and public from pretrial hearings under limited circumstances in *Gannett Co., Inc.* v. *DePasquale*.[7] Since then, the Court has emphasized the traditional preference in American law for open criminal proceedings. The year following *Gannett*, the Court ruled that the press and public have a First Amendment right of access to criminal trials that is independent of the defendant's Sixth Amendment right to a public trial. This means that the defendant cannot waive the press or the public's right of access.[8] In 1984, the Court extended this presumption of openness to the voir dire (jury selection) process[9] and to pretrial suppression hearings.[10] The Court set forth guidelines in those cases whereby trial judges could close proceedings to the press and public on a limited basis for extraordinary reasons. These cases seem to have repudiated much of the Court's reasoning in *Gannett*. The Court has also since permitted state courts to televise criminal trials.[11] Ask students to identify the advantages and disadvantages of televising criminal trials by asking the following questions:

- What are the benefits and costs of televising trials?
- Are local trials televised where you live?

- Should U.S. Supreme Court oral arguments be televised or otherwise broadcast? *Currently they are not, although this is a hotly debated topic. There have occasionally been bills proposed by members of Congress to require the sessions to be televised, however to date, none of those bills have become law. For some exceptional cases, the Court provides same-day audio recordings. For all cases, the Court posts same-day transcripts online and audio recordings by the Friday of the week the case is argued.*

DISCUSSION—THE *FREEDOM OF INFORMATION ACT*

The *Freedom of Information Act (FOIA)* was amended by the *Electronic Freedom of Information Act Amendments of 1996.*[12] Among the amendments are the requirements that records created on or after November 1, 1996, be made available electronically within one year and that a general index of records be made available electronically by December 31, 1999.

Ask students to think about the year 1966, when the *Freedom of Information Act* was passed. Ask students questions that might help them develop a hypothesis about why *FOIA* was enacted at that time. For example: What was happening (politically) in our country at that time? How were many peoples' attitudes about the government changing at that time? Have you heard about COINTELPRO? If so, do you know what it was and what it did?

If students are unfamiliar with COINTELPRO, give them a little background about it. It was an FBI counterintelligence program that operated under the leadership of J. Edgar Hoover between 1956 and 1971 that engaged in secret and often illegal activities that monitored, disrupted, and smeared the reputations and images of groups and individuals it considered politically subversive. All of those targeted were Americans. Some were members of the Communist or Socialist parties. Some were entertainers, and others were leaders of the civil rights movements. It even targeted Puerto Ricans who were part of that island's independence movement. Its activities were made public and became the focus of a congressional inquiry by the Church Committee, which exposed its unconstitutional activities and record keeping.

PROBLEM 36.4 (p.439)

This problem is based on *JB Pictures Inc.* v. *Department of Defense.*[13] The Defense Department policy was put into effect during the Persian Gulf War in 1991. Out of respect for families' privacy, defense officials do not allow media coverage at any site to which remains are transferred. All four military service branches participated in the formulation of this policy. The government defends the policy on the theory that media access would compromise the mission of the mortuary to prepare remains with dignity, care, and respect. Some media and other organizations challenged this policy, claiming the First Amendment allowed them access to Dover Air Force base, the location of the largest Defense Department mortuary for the remains of soldiers, sailors, pilots, and marines that is responsible for handling identification and funeral preparations.

a. Students' answers will vary. The veterans group and media who opposed the policy argued that war and its cost cannot be accurately depicted without showing those killed and wounded. Because enlisted men and women are dying in the service of the nation and because political decisions regarding military action are in part based on public sentiment, it is important that the public not be shielded from the effects of military action. Also, allowing the press and veterans groups access to the mortuary ensures that the government is accurately reporting the death toll and the manner in which soldiers are dying.

b. Students' answers will vary. The Washington, D.C., Circuit Court of Appeals determined that the government had sufficient interest to limit access to the base to reduce the hardship on grieving families and to protect their privacy. Where death and national service or public figures are involved, it is often difficult to balance the family's interest in privacy against the public's interest in monitoring government honesty.

CAPTION ANSWER (P. 440) Having reporters embedded with the troops during the initial invasion of Iraq provided the public with a great deal of information—virtually in real time—about the early stages of the war.

a. Students' answers will vary. This hypothetical situation is based on the U.S. Supreme Court case *Houchins* v. *KQED, Inc.*[14] In that case, the Supreme Court held that the press has no broader rights of access to the prison than the general public and that they could not enter the institution and interview whomever they wished. The Court found that such a special privilege of access was not essential to guarantee the freedom of the press to communicate or publish.

b. The actual case did not include an *FOIA* request. The newspaper could ask for information by sending an *FOIA* request letter. Hypothetically, the newspaper had the right to make the request and to receive a response in 20 days. It does not have the right to receive medical records, personnel records, or investigatory records. Without those, it would be particularly difficult, but not impossible, to investigate this story.[15]

c. The prison has a right and a duty to protect the inmates and to maintain security within its walls. The prison might argue that unregulated access by the media would infringe on inmates' privacy; that interviews tend to create "prison celebrities," who in turn generate internal problems and undermine security; and that unscheduled tours could disrupt institutional operations.

d. Students' answers will likely vary about how they would decide the *FOIA* request.

e. Students' answers will vary. For example, students (or reporters) can obtain information about which programs the federal government funds or expenses related to those programs.

REQUIRING THE PRESS TO DISCLOSE INFORMATION (P. 441)

Learning Outcomes

After completing this section, students should be able to:
1. explain why journalists may refuse to reveal their sources of information;
2. describe the relationship between maintaining a free press and protecting the confidentiality of reporters' sources; and
3. identify rights that conflict with shield laws.

a. Students' responses will vary. Some might argue that the drawings were an essential component of the story and therefore showing them was very important. In addition, the editorial director might argue that in reporting news, the outlet regularly presents views and shows pictures that offend different people. Alternatively, an editorial director could decide that the story could just as effectively be told without showing the drawings and unnecessarily offending some Muslim communities.

b. Students' answers will vary. If Congress passed such a law and it were challenged in the federal courts the strongest argument against such a law would be that it is an unconstitutional infringement on free speech. However, in *Brandenburg* v. *Ohio*, the Court said that speech can be prohibited if it is "directed at inciting or producing imminent lawless action" and it is "likely to incite or produce such action."[16] It could be argued that the speech could incite a terrorist act and, therefore, the limitation of free speech is justified.

DISCUSSION—SHOULD JOURNALISTS BE REQUIRED TO REVEAL THEIR SOURCES?

A reporter and/or a lawyer who specializes in First Amendment law could add depth and interest to this discussion. He or she can help students grapple with these questions. As of 2019, 39 states plus the District of Columbia had adopted shield laws with varying degrees of protections. (Go to www.rcfp.org and use the search term "shield laws" to connect to a state-by- state analysis.) There is no federal shield law, although there have many proposed and a few that have passed one house of Congress.

In 2004, *New York Times* reporter Judith Miller went to jail for "contempt of court" when she refused to testify to a federal grand jury investigating the leak of the name of a CIA agent. (Miller had not published a story revealing the name, but she apparently had information important to the investigation.) This was a highly politicized case because the CIA agent,

Valerie Plame, was married to Ambassador Joseph Wilson, who, just two days before the leak, had published an Op-Ed article criticizing the Bush Administration for "twisting" intelligence to justify the war in Iraq. It was widely speculated that top Bush administration officials had leaked Plame's name in retaliation for her husband's comments. Eventually, after serving for about 75 days, Miller was released from prison when, she says, her source(s) agreed to allow her to reveal their identities. She later testified against Lewis "Scooter" Libby, Vice President Cheney's Chief of Staff, who was convicted of perjury, obstruction of justice, and making false statements to federal investigators looking into the leak. Journalists remain divided about Miller's stance. Some questioned her First Amendment claims, saying that she was simply trying to cover for people she was close to in the White House.

In a class discussion, ask students to:

- Identify parties likely to oppose requirements that journalists reveal sources.
- Identify parties likely to support requirements that journalists reveal sources.
- State how justice might be served by requiring journalists to reveal sources.
- State how justice might be threatened by requiring journalists to reveal sources.
- Identify short- and long-term consequences of requiring journalists to reveal sources.
- State how far they might be willing to go as journalists if the government tried to force them to reveal their confidential sources of information about a story.
- Discuss whether the press can truly be free if journalists may be forced to reveal sources.

NOTES

(1) *Sheppard* v. *Maxwell*, 384 U.S. 333 (1966).

(2) *Red Lion Broadcasting* v. *FCC*, 395 U.S. 367 (1969).

(3) *Arkansas Educational Television Commission* v. *Forbes*, 523 U.S. 666 (1998).

(4) *Nebraska Press Association* v. *Stuart*, 427 U.S. 539 (1976).

(5) *New York Times Co.* v. *United States*, 403 U.S. 713 (1971).

(6) Ibid.

(7) *Gannett Co., Inc.* v. *DePasquale*, 443 U.S. 368 (1979).

(8) *Richmond Newspapers, Inc.* v. *Virginia*, 448 U.S. 555 (1980).

(9) *Press Enterprise* v. *Superior Court*, 464 U.S. 501 (1984).

(10) *Waller* v. *Georgia*, 467 U.S. 39 (1984).

(11) *Chandler* v. *Florida*, 449 U.S. 560 (1981).

(12) *The Freedom of Information Act*, 5 U.S.C. § 552, as amended by Public Law No. 104–231 (1996).

(13) *JB Pictures Inc.* v. *Department of Defense*, 86 F.3d 236 (D.C. Cir. 1996).

(14) *Houchins* v. *KQED, Inc.*, 438 U.S. 1 (1978).

(15) *The Freedom of Information Act*, 5 U.S.C. § 552(j) (1988).

(16) *Brandenburg* v. *Ohio*, 395 U.S. 444 (1969).

The First Amendment free-doms of speech and assembly present problems when schools, military bases, and prisons are involved. The rights of students, military personnel, and inmates may, at times, conflict with the rights of others or interfere with the need to preserve order. When this conflict occurs, courts must balance the competing interests in each case.

As a general rule, courts allow greater freedom of speech and assembly in public parks and on street corners than in schools, military bases, and prisons. The courts speak of places such as public parks and street corners—where First Amendment rights are traditionally exercised—as public forums. According to a well-established series of court decisions, however, schools, military bases, and prisons provide only a limited forum for the exercise of First Amendment freedoms. In these places, one can usually exercise his or her rights, but only as long as the expression does not interfere with the purpose of the facility.

INTRODUCTION (P. 442)

Learning Outcomes

After completing this section, students should be able to:
1. identify three types of facilities in which First Amendment rights may be limited; and
2. define the term *public forums*.

DISCUSSION—SPEECH IN SPECIAL PLACES

Discuss with students the reasons why greater restrictions on speech are (or are not) needed in places such as schools, prisons, or military bases. Ask the following questions to stimulate class discussion:

- What might result if no restrictions on speech existed in these institutions?
- What might result if political speech was not allowed in these institutions?
- What other institutions or places restrict speech? *courts, libraries, legislatures, post offices, places of worship, etc.*
- Do you think those restrictions infringe on a person's constitutional rights?

ACTIVITY—FREE SPEECH IN SCHOOLS

Use a continuum activity (See the Teaching Methods section in the front of this Teacher Manual) to explore students' initial views on various issues related to free speech in schools. Post signs at opposite ends of the room, one saying "Schools SHOULD Permit" and the other saying "Schools SHOULD NOT Permit." As you read the following statements, have students take positions along the continuum to express their opinions.

Should students be able to wear T-shirts or other clothing on campus during school hours at public schools:

- with logos or other advertisement for beer?
- that promote animal rights?
- that make fun of animal rights and depict the slaughter of animals?
- that state opposition to abortion?
- that say "Be Happy. Not Gay"? (A case involving this T-Shirt reached the U.S. Seventh Circuit Court of Appeals in 2008.)
- with religious messages?
- with swastikas?

- that glamorize guns or other weapons?
- with illustrations of marijuana leaves?
- that promote recycling?
- that make fun of environmentalists?
- that mock the school principal or a teacher?
- with racist messages?
- with the Confederate flag?
- with messages that criticize current U.S. foreign policy toward a particular country?
- with anti-immigrant messages?
- promoting a particular political candidate?
- with words that phonetically spell an expletive? (The brand FUCT was recently the subject of the Supreme Court case *Iancu v. Brunetti* regarding offensive brand names receiving patents.)

Follow up by asking students whether they have heard the statement "Where you stand is based on where you sit." If so, ask them to explain what it means. *It means that people tend to form their positions on various questions based on their jobs, their stations, their social status, and/or their vantage point.* Then ask students to think about how people in various positions (with varying perspectives) might answer these questions differently.

For example, would parents, teachers, principals, school security officers, superintendents of schools, guidance counselors, community police officers, and members of the ACLU all be likely to answer the clothing questions the same way?

Have students weigh the relative value of freedom of expression versus safety and accomplishment of the school's primary educational mission.

Note: This activity could be repeated after students complete the reading and activities in this chapter. Ask students whether they view any of the issues differently as a result of what they learned in this chapter. Students might also take positions along the continuum as if they were U.S. Supreme Court justices of different eras, including 1969, when the Court ruled on *Tinker* v. *Des Moines School District*,[1] and 1988, when the Court ruled on *Hazelwood* v. *Kuhlmeier*.[2]

THE FIRST AMENDMENT IN PUBLIC SCHOOLS (PP. 443–445)

Learning Outcomes

After completing this section, students should be able to:

1. describe the free expression issues raised by the case of *Tinker* v. *Des Moines School District*;

2. identify the circumstances under which student expression can be limited according to the *Tinker* decision;
3. describe the First Amendment issues raised by the *Hazelwood* v. *Kuhlmeier* case;
4. describe the reasoning of the U.S. Supreme Court in *Hazelwood*;
5. explain how school dress codes relate to the First Amendment; and
6. apply standards established in the *Tinker* and *Hazelwood* cases to various expression issues in public schools.

THE **CASE** OF...

The Student Armbands

PROBLEM 37.1 (p.443)

The historic *Tinker* decision was the first U.S. Supreme Court opinion to recognize that the U.S. Constitution protected student expression rights in public schools. Before reviewing the facts with students, be sure to provide the historical context of the late 1960s and the Vietnam War. There was no clear Supreme Court precedent that required the case to be decided in favor of the students.

a. The students could argue that they were exercising their First Amendment right to free expression by wearing the armbands. The armband itself was not disruptive to the educational process nor did it interfere with the rights of other students. Further the armbands were symbolic of the students' objection to the Vietnam War. The students were expressing a political belief, a form of speech that is most protected under the First Amendment. Finally, the students were in a public school, where principles of democratic government should be respected as well as taught.

b. The principal could argue that he must ensure a positive, disruption-free learning environment for all young people in his school. He could argue that the armbands are disruptive and would distract other students from their studies. While this form of protest might be appropriate outside of school, it is inappropriate in school.

c. Students' answers will vary. The armbands at school could be considered a form of free expression protected by the First Amendment. Wearing an armband is symbolic and minimally disruptive to the school environment. Alternatively, some students could argue that this form of protest will always be distracting to other students and is therefore inappropriate in the school environment.

d. Students' answers will vary. The U.S. Supreme Court ruled in favor of the students holding that the armbands were protected speech and that the expression was not materially and substantially disruptive of the educational process nor did it interfere with the rights of the other students.

ADDITIONAL TEACHING RESOURCES

The First Amendment Center devotes a section of its website to K–12 student expression cases, including lesson plans for teachers. Visit www. firstamendmentcenter.org for the latest information about student dress codes, student publications, cyberspace issues, hate speech, and speech codes.

The Landmark Supreme Court Cases website, presented by Street Law, Inc., and the Supreme Court Historical Society, features the *Tinker* case, the *Hazelwood* case, and other landmark decisions. Visit https://www.landmarkcases.org/ to find lesson plans, activities, links to oral arguments, excerpts of decisions, background materials for various reading levels, and resources about the aftermath of the cases.

The Student Press Law Center—online at www. splc.org—is a national organization that provides legal advice and assistance to student journalists and the educators who work with them. The Journalism Education Association also provides materials online at www.jea.org.

ACTIVITY—CONDUCTING RESEARCH AND INTERVIEWS

Ask students to conduct research on students' rights to freedom of speech, press, religion, assembly, privacy, due process, and freedom from discrimination. Does their school have written rules regarding these rights? Are they outlined in the school's student handbook? Do the rules vary for different age groups? Students might interview school administrators and teachers and examine back issues of the school newspaper to determine whether problems occurred involving these rights and, if so, how they were resolved.

DISCUSSION AND ACTIVITY— CENSORSHIP OF THE SCHOOL NEWSPAPER

Students may find the case of *Hazelwood School District* v. *Kuhlmeier*[3] very interesting. Invite a number of people to discuss censorship of school newspapers in your school and the *Hazelwood* case. You could invite a school administrator, journalism teacher, student editor, and/or attorney specializing in school law or constitutional law to add depth and interest to the discussion of this problem.

As a class, review the facts of the case as described in the Student Edition. (Or you may find additional teaching materials on the landmark cases website at www.landmarkcases.org) Confirm students understand the facts and the constitutional question involved.

Then, put students into small groups to discuss the best arguments in support of the student editor's position.

While students are working, ask the visitors to walk around the room to listen to the students discuss their ideas. Ask students to report their best arguments to the rest of the class. *Students may say the principal violated their First Amendment rights by deleting the pages on which articles appeared. His actions may violate the school's publication policy. The articles are neither obscene nor defamatory. They are merely accounts of the students' feelings and thoughts and are therefore entitled to protection.*

According to the U.S. Supreme Court's decision in Tinker, *students cannot be punished for personal expression unless the speech materially and substantially interferes with the educational process, can be reasonably predicted to have that effect, or invades the rights of others.*

There is no evidence in the record that the principal could reasonably forecast that the articles would have materially disrupted the educational process.

Moreover, the principal's actions were overinclusive in that he deleted articles that he did not find offensive. The principal deleted all the articles for the sake of "administrative convenience." The U.S. Supreme Court has recognized previously that constitutional rights outweigh the government's interest in administrative convenience.[4]

Finally, students can argue that school officials could censor the articles on an invasion of privacy theory only if they can show that publication of the articles could result in the school being sued for damages in a tort suit. Based on the tone of the articles, there is no threat of this happening.

Invite your guests to add additional arguments in favor of the student editor if they wish.

Then ask students to go back to their small groups to discuss the best arguments to support the principal's point of view. After they work in their small groups, ask students to report out their best arguments in favor of the principal. *The principal could argue that the school is not required to tolerate student speech that is inconsistent with its basic education mission. Hence, school officials retain the right to impose reasonable restrictions on school-sponsored publications without violating students' First Amendment rights.*

Accordingly, educators may exercise editorial control over the style and content of students' speech if their actions are reasonably related to legitimate educational concerns. The school could assert that its actions are reasonably related to these concerns. It found the articles to be inappropriate for younger students and to reveal private personal facts about members of the student body and their families. Additionally, the articles were slanted since only one side of the issues was presented. The school could argue that it finds this to be irresponsible journalism and thus exercised editorial control in deciding to ban the articles.

Invite your guests to add additional arguments in favor of the principal if they wish.

Ask students: How is this case similar to *Tinker*? How is it different? *Both Tinker and Hazelwood concern students' First Amendment rights in public schools. Tinker addresses "the educator's ability to punish a student's personal expression that happens to occur on the school's premises." Hazelwood, however, addresses "the educator's authority over school-sponsored publications, theatrical productions and other expressive activities that ... the public might perceive to bear the imprimatur of the school." In other words, Tinker holds that the First Amendment requires a school to tolerate certain nondisruptive speech, but it does not require that a school promote or endorse all speech just because the speech is nondisruptive.*

Ask students for their own opinions about what the Court should decide. They should support their opinions with reasons.

Before you reveal the Court's decision, ask the guests to discuss the policies for school newspapers at your school (if you have one).

Then, tell students that in the actual case, the U.S. Supreme Court reversed a lower court decision and ruled that school officials had properly exercised their editorial control over a school-sponsored newspaper produced in a journalism class.

YOU BE the JUDGE

High School Student Expression and the First Amendment (p. 445)

Note: Invite the principal or other officials from your school system (perhaps from the general counsel's office, if the school system is large) to help students with this activity or to analyze a state-specific case that deals with student expression issues.

a. Students' answers will vary and should be supported with reasons. Applying the thinking behind *Hazelwood*, this is a school-sponsored activity, so the principal can regulate the expression. It can be argued that the principal's actions are reasonably related to legitimate educational concerns. In this case, the student's speech is inappropriate and the school has an interest in protecting members of the audience from "lewd and indecent" language.

Tinker could be used in support of the student's right to free speech. It can be argued that he has a right to free speech and that right does not terminate merely because he has walked through the "schoolhouse gate." Although this right is not absolute, there is no real evidence that his speech "materially disrupted" the educational process. The speech may not have generated any more "student participation" than other rousing political speeches made during prior assemblies.

This problem is based on an actual case, *Bethel v. Fraser*.[5] The Court held that the First Amendment did not prevent a school district from disciplining a student for making an "offensively lewd and indecent speech" at an assembly.

b. Students' answers will vary. This question is based on a case heard by the U.S. District Court for Western Pennsylvania, *Layshock* v. *Hermitage School District*.[6] It required the judge to balance the freedom of expression of a student with the responsibility of a public school to maintain an environment conducive to learning. The judge found that because the student used an off-campus computer to create the profile, it cannot be considered school-related speech. There was also not enough evidence to prove that the profile created a substantial disruption in the school. According to the judge, the school district thus had no authority to regulate the student's speech. In 2010 the U.S. Court of Appeals for the Third Circuit found in favor of the students. The school district petitioned the Supreme Court of the United States to take the case, but the Supreme Court did not grant the petition. There will likely be many similar cases, raising the issue of school regulation of off-campus speech with an on-campus impact, in the future.

The case described above is similar to the case *Burch* v. *Barker*,[7] which was decided by the Supreme Court in 1998. The difference is that, in the *Burch* case, students had produced a newspaper off school property, distributed it off school property (at a senior barbeque) and without the knowledge and financial support of school authorities. In *Burch*, the Court determined that the school could not prohibit distribution of the paper without violating the First Amendment rights of the students because the policy was overbroad and no one could reasonably associate such communications with institutional endorsement.

c. Students' answers will vary. This case is purely hypothetical, not based on an actual case. A persuasive argument can be made for the school's right to regulate the expression. The majority in *Hazelwood* specifically held that theatrical productions may be regulated if the "public might reasonably perceive [it] to bear the imprimatur of the school."[8] The Court further stated that expressive activities, including theatrical productions, may be characterized as part of the school curriculum so long as faculty members supervise them and they are designed to impart knowledge or skills to the participants and the audience.

One may argue that, under *Tinker*, the school's action is impermissible without evidence that a substantial disruption will occur. Moreover, performances were scheduled for a Thursday and Friday night, not during school hours. Arguably, this is outside the scope of the principal's control since the educational process cannot be disrupted when school is not in session.

d. Students' answers will vary. This example is based on the 1982 case, *Island Trees Union Free School District* v. *Pico*.[9] In that case, the school board removed from school libraries books that it found to be "anti-American, anti-Christian, anti-Semitic, and just plain filthy."[10] Students challenged the removal of these books, claiming a denial of their First Amendment rights. In a limited holding, the Court found that the board's action in removing the books was motivated by the board members' personal, social, and political beliefs. The Court reversed the lower court judgment that had supported the board. "The right to receive ideas is a necessary predicate to the recipient's meaningful exercise of his own rights of speech, press and political freedom."[11] However, the

Court upheld prohibiting library books that were educationally unsuitable or pervasively vulgar. The decision did not address the board's authority to select books for the library or its authority to choose educational materials to be used in classrooms.

e. Students' answers will vary.

Note: This hypothetical case is based on the case of *Morse* v. *Frederick*, decided by the Court in 2006.[12] This case makes an excellent moot court subject. For teaching suggestions about conducting moot courts, see the Teaching Methods section in the front of this Teacher Manual, on Street Law's website page "SCOTUS in the Classroom" (www.streetlaw.org/programs/scotus-in-the-classroom), or *Street Law's Guide to Mock Trials and Moot Courts,* available at www.streetlaw.org.

In the actual case, the main argument from Deborah Morse, the principal, was that this is a case about student speech. Joseph Frederick was at a school-sponsored event, and so was subject to school rules. He was disciplined for displaying a message that advocated illegal drug use, which contradicts the school's policy of discouraging the use of illegal substances. In addition, Morse argued that, as in *Hazelwood*, the school should be able to limit Frederick's speech during a school-sponsored event, because otherwise it appears to the public as though the school is endorsing the message. Finally, Morse argued that this case is consistent with *Tinker* because Frederick disrupted a school activity by displaying the banner and could have interfered with the work of the school by bringing about an increase in drug use.

Frederick, the student, argued first that this case is not about student speech, because he was not on school property when he displayed the banner and because he had not gone to school at all that day. Thus he should have the same rights adults have, and the school should not be able to limit his speech. He then argued that even if it was considered student speech, his banner was like the armbands in *Tinker*. It was displayed peacefully and did not "substantially interfere" with school work. In addition, Frederick argued that this case is not like *Hazelwood*, because the pro-drug banner was not part of the curriculum or an official school activity. He argued that no reasonable person would think the pro-drug message was endorsed by the school.

The Court ruled 5-to-4 for Principal Morse, concluding that she did not violate the First Amendment by confiscating a pro-drug banner. The Court dismissed Frederick's argument that this case did not involve school. It emphasized that participation in the Torch Relay was approved by the school, monitored by teachers, occurred during school hours, and included performances by the school band and cheerleaders.

Relying on its earlier decision in *Hazelwood*, the Court explained that a public school student does not have the same rights that adults have, and that the *Tinker* disruption analysis is not the only way to evaluate whether student speech can be limited. It said it was reasonable for the principal "to conclude that the banner promoted illegal drug use—in violation of established school policy—and that failing to act would send a powerful message to students in her charge, including Frederick, about how serious the school was about the dangers of illegal drug use." In the end, it ruled that a principal may restrict student speech that is "reasonably" viewed as promoting illegal drug use.

BACKGROUND AND ACTIVITY—CENSORSHIP IN PUBLIC SCHOOL LIBRARIES

Question and answer **d.** in the *You Be the Judge* feature provide an interesting example of how expression in special places deals with the right of students, parents, administrators, and teachers to remove books from school libraries or classrooms. Obviously, choices must be made in acquiring school materials. The line between censorship and legitimate selection can be difficult to establish. On the one hand, there is a strong tradition of local control of curriculum in the United States. The Supreme Court has been reluctant to become involved in these controversies. Yet, as the *Tinker* case establishes, the First Amendment does apply to schools.

Direct students to the website of the American Library Association (ALA) at www.ala.org and ask them to read the information provided when they use the search term "Intellectual Freedom and Censorship." After reading that section, ask students to use the search terms "Challenged and Banned Books" to locate lists of books that have been subjects of censorship or attempted censorship in schools. Then assign students the following tasks:

- Identify the stance of the ALA on this issue.
- Infer the criteria that censors are applying as they seek to censor books.
- Identify the assumptions censors make regarding censorship.
- Identify the assumptions the ALA makes regarding censorship.
- Evaluate the wisdom of censoring specific books for specific groups of students (e.g., by age or grade level).

BACKGROUND AND DISCUSSION—SCHOOL DRESS CODES

Note: This activity is a natural continuation of the T-shirt activity at the beginning of this chapter. Now that students have learned more about the circumstances under which the Court has allowed or not allowed schools to regulate student expression, this activity can serve as a review.

To address the issue of school violence and the decline in academic achievement, a growing number of public schools are mandating dress codes and even requiring school uniforms.[13] Dress codes may prohibit students from wearing clothing that is identifiable as gang clothing, such as bandanas, particular colored handkerchiefs, college jackets, earrings, and other accessories.

Opponents of school dress codes claim that they violate an individual's right to free speech and expression. Additionally, they claim that there is no certainty that they reduce school violence or improve academic achievement. Sometimes a strict dress code is adopted in a school that has no gang problems, which undermines the justification for the code.

Supporters of dress codes claim that they reduce classroom violence and improve the educational environment. They prevent students from being mistakenly targeted as gang members because of their clothing, and they promote discipline.

Cases concerning regulating students' hair length and obscenity preceded today's challenges to school dress codes. In the hair length cases, the federal circuits were split in their rulings about whether school authorities had the authority to regulate hair length. Some of the circuits that struck down hair regulations determined that there is a constitutional right to govern one's appearance, although it is not based on the First Amendment.[14] Later, the courts began to hear cases involving students wearing T-shirts printed with slogans deemed to be obscene. In light of the *Bethel* v. *Fraser* ruling that public schools could (and should) regulate vulgar and offensive speech, courts have upheld school districts' decisions to discipline students for wearing T-shirts with sexual, offensive, or vulgar messages.[15]

The current focus of school dress regulation has been gang clothing and symbols. A rule was upheld in one school banning male students from wearing earrings after school officials determined that many males wore earrings to indicate gang membership.[16]

Ask students how the courts should analyze mandatory uniform rules. Pose the following questions:

- Should student clothing be considered a form of protected speech?
- Is clothing expressive conduct or symbolic speech?
- What standard or test should a court use to determine whether or not the rules are constitutional?

THE FIRST AMENDMENT IN PRISONS AND THE MILITARY (P. 446)

Learning Outcomes

After completing this section, students should be able to:

1. compare the ways that different purposes of schools, prisons, and military bases shape limits on expression;
2. summarize key rulings on limits of expression in prisons and military bases; and
3. define the term *penological*.

BACKGROUND—FREE SPEECH IN THE PRISON CONTEXT

Today, free speech cases in prisons and jails are decided by balancing the inmate's right to free speech against the institution's interest in security, safety, orderly running of the facility, rehabilitation (for convicted inmates), or in some cases, equal opportunity. Some recent free-speech issues in institutions include whether or not inmates have a right to various publications, visitors, and uncensored mail.

Four questions help spell out how the balancing test should be applied:

1. Is there a logical, rational connection between the restriction imposed by officials and the interests they claim justify the restriction?

2. Assuming the inmate cannot exercise a particular right in a particular way because of the restriction imposed by officials, are there alternative ways the inmate can exercise the right in question? For instance, if the inmate cannot receive a particular publication, can the inmate still exercise the right to free speech in other ways?

3. If the inmate's request is granted, what impact would that have on other inmates, staff, and institution resources? Where there is a "significant ripple effect on fellow inmates or on prison staff, courts should be particularly deferential to the informed discretion of prison officials."[17]

4. Are there ready alternatives available to officials that would allow the inmate's request to be met at a minimal cost or threat to a legitimate penological interest? The existence of such alternatives suggests that the official's response is exaggerated and not reasonably related to a legitimate concern.

In general, the federal courts, and certainly the U.S. Supreme Court, defer to the judgments of prison administrators when inmates attempt to exercise expression rights. For example, in a 2004 case, the Supreme Court denied that an inmate had a First Amendment right to provide legal counsel to another inmate.[18] In a different case, as mentioned in the Student Edition, the Court denied that a prison had violated an inmate's First Amendment right by refusing to provide him with a daily newspaper.[19] In both cases, the Court upheld regulations that interfered with an inmate's constitutional rights as long as those regulations were reasonably related to legitimate penological (corrections) objectives.

BACKGROUND—INDIVIDUAL RIGHTS, MILITARY DECISIONS, AND NATIONAL SECURITY

Where national security is asserted as the government's interest in a particular regulation, courts tend to tread cautiously and defer to the government's position. Judges prefer not to impose their judgments over those of top military and government officials given the unique conditions of military life and where national security may be threatened.

As a result, the military is afforded considerable discretion in limiting expression, as well as other constitutional rights, of its members. The military has often successfully argued that conformity and strict regulation are essential to its training program and ability to carry out its function.

National security is considered such a significant government interest that it is often offered in support of regulations affecting people outside the military context. For example, in the *Korematsu* case, during World War II the Supreme Court upheld the government's policy of confining American citizens of Japanese descent to internment camps, despite the fact that it was race-based discrimination arguably in violation of the equal protection clause of the Fourteenth Amendment.[20] Nonetheless, the government's assertion of national security interests does not afford it carte blanche for limiting rights. At times the Court does not tolerate actions that regulate expression in the name of national security, as it did in the case of *New York Times v. United States*,[21] discussed in Chapter 36.

People enlisted in the military are always subject to stricter regulation of speech, because it is their job to be prepared for national threats. Further, ordinary citizens may experience greater limitations on their rights anytime the country is perceived to be particularly vulnerable, such as in times of war or terrorist activity. See Chapter 44, "Law and Terrorism," for more information about this topic and www.landmarkcases.org, for Street Law's teaching resources about the *Korematsu* case.

CAPTION ANSWER (P. 446) Individual rights and freedom of expression are limited on military bases to protect the safety of soldiers, as well as national security.

ACTIVITY—SHOULD THIS EXPRESSION BE PERMITTED?

The following cases give students an opportunity to examine expression rights in a variety of special places. For each case, ask students to give arguments for and against permitting the expression. Then have students decide whether or not the First Amendment should protect the expression and explain their reasoning.

Summaries of the actual court decisions are given below each question.

1. Candidates for national political office sought permission to enter Fort Dix military base to distribute literature and discuss issues with military personnel. Permission was denied because Fort Dix had a regulation against "demonstrations, sit-ins, picketing, protest marches, political speeches," and similar activities. *The U.S. Supreme Court held that the basic function of Fort Dix was to train soldiers and not to provide a public forum.*[22] *In addition, the ban on speeches and demonstrations had been evenly applied to all partisan political campaigns. The dissenters (Justices Brennan and Marshall) argued that Fort Dix was an "open" post and for that reason the proposed leafleting had to be allowed in the street and parking lots that were open to civilians.*

2. A group of college students marched to the county jail to protest the arrests of other students who had taken part in a civil rights demonstration. The sheriff warned them that they were trespassing and told them to leave immediately. Some left, but others did not. Those who remained were arrested and charged with trespass. *In a 5-to-4 decision, the Supreme Court upheld the conviction of the students based on the trespass statute. The Court rejected the idea that the trespass statute was unconstitutional, vague, or that it was being used selectively to suppress the civil rights of minorities. "Nothing in the Constitution prevents Florida from even-handed enforcement of its general trespass statute against those refusing to obey the sheriff's order.... The state, no less a private owner of property, has power to preserve the property under its control for the use to which it is lawfully dedicated." In short, jails are not proper places for protest.*[23] *The dissenters believed that the jailhouse, like an executive mansion, courthouse, or legislative chamber, is one of the seats of government and therefore an obvious center for protest.*

3. Several hundred African American students marched to the grounds of the state capitol to protest against segregation. A large crowd of police and onlookers gathered to watch. The protesters carried signs that read "Down with Discrimination" and sang freedom songs. After being warned to disperse, the protesters were arrested and charged with breach of the peace. *With no violence or threat of violence and ample police protection, the Court reasoned (8 to 1) that the convictions infringed on the defendants' constitutionally protected rights of free speech, free assembly, and freedom to petition for redress of grievances. This case differs from the preceding case in that: (1) the conviction here was based on a vague breach-of-peace statute (historically subject to some abuse by law enforcement); and (2) the state capitol was viewed as a public forum and therefore, a proper place to protest.*[24]

4. An urban high school has a long-standing rule against wearing partisan buttons and badges. When students wear buttons, school officials require them to be removed. A student wears a "White Power" button to school. When the student refuses to remove the button, she is suspended. *The court acknowledged that the Tinker case (1969) would control, but here a long-standing rule had been enforced against all partisan buttons and badges (not just armbands, like in Tinker), and the trial judge had made a finding*

that the "White Power" button, if worn, would have "materially and substantially disrupted the educational process."[25]

5. High school students were suspended for refusing to remove buttons worn in support of a teachers' strike. The buttons read, "Do Scabs Bleed?" and "I'm Not Listening, Scab." *The court ruled that the buttons could only be banned if they substantially interfered with the educational process or the rights of others.*[26]

NOTES

(1) *Tinker* v. *Des Moines School District*, 393 U.S. 503 (1969).

(2) *Hazelwood* v. *Kuhlmeier*, 484 U.S. 260 (1988).

(3) *Hazelwood* v. *Kuhlmeier*, 484 U.S. 260 (1988).

(4) *Stanley* v. *Illinois*, 405 U.S. 645, 656 (1972); *Thomas* v. *Review Bd. of Ind. Employment Sec. Div.*, 450 U.S. 707, 719 (1981).

(5) *Bethel* v. *Fraser*, 478 U.S. 675 (1986).

(6) *Layshock* v. *Hermitage School Dist.*, No. 2:06-cv-116, 2007 U.S. Dist. LEXIS 49709 (W.D. Pa. July 10, 2007).

(7) *Burch* v. *Barker*, 861 F.2d 1149 (9th Cir. 1988).

(8) *Hazelwood* v. *Kuhlmeier*, 484 U.S. 260 (1988).

(9) *Island Trees Union Free School District* v. *Pico*, 457 U.S. 853 (1982).

(10) *Id.* at 856.

(11) *Id.* at 857.

(12) *Morse* v. *Frederick*, S.Ct. 2618 (2007).

(13) Amy Mitchell Wilson, "Public School Dress Codes: The Constitutional Debate," 1998, *BYU Educ. & L.J.*, 145 (Spring 1998).

(14) E.g., *Richards* v. *Thurston*, 424 F. 2d 1281 (1st Cir. 1970).

(15) *Broussard* v. *School Board of City of Norfolk*, 801 F. Supp. 1526 (E.D. Va. 1992); *Pyle* v. *South Hadley School Committee*, 824 F. Supp. 7 (D. Mass. 1993).

(16) *Olesen* v. *Board of Education of School District No. 228*, 676 F. Supp. 821 (N.D. Ill. 1987).

(17) *Turner* v. *Safley*, 482 U.S. 78 (1987).

(18) *Shaw* v. *Murphy*, 532 U.S. 223 (2001).

(19) *Beard* v. *Banks*, 548 U.S. 521 (2006).

(20) *Korematsu* v. *United States*, 323 U.S. 214 (1944).

(21) *New York Times Co.* v. *United States*, 403 U.S. 713 (1971).

(22) *Greer* v. *Spock*, 424 U.S. 828 (1976).

(23) *Adderley* v. *Florida*, 385 U.S. 39 (1966).

(24) *Edwards* v. *South Carolina*, 372 U.S. 229 (1963).

(25) *Guzick* v. *Drebus*, 431 F.2d 594 (6th Cir. 1970).

(26) *Chandler* v. *McMinnville School District*, 978 F. 2d 524 (9th Cir. 1992).

Religious freedom in the United States is protected from government interference by two clauses in the First Amendment to the U.S. Constitution. The establishment clause forbids the government from creating a state religion. It also forbids the government from endorsing or supporting religion and from preferring one religion over another. The free exercise clause protects the right of individuals to worship or believe as they choose; the government cannot prohibit or unduly burden the religious practices of individuals. Some people believe that, taken together, these two clauses require the government to be neutral toward religion. Others believe that the establishment and free exercise clauses require the government to accommodate religious belief and practice, as long as it does not establish or promote a state or national religion.

340

INTRODUCTION (PP. 447–448)

Learning Outcomes

After completing this section, students should be able to:
1. define the terms *establishment clause* and *free exercise clause*;
2. explain what the establishment clause of the First Amendment prohibits the government from doing; and
3. explain what the free exercise clause of the First Amendment prohibits the government from doing.

ACTIVITY—THE PLEDGE OF ALLEGIANCE AND FREEDOM OF RELIGION

Begin class by asking students to recite the Pledge of Allegiance. Then ask students to say it again, this time as the Pledge was recited during the 1920s and 1930s. *(The words "under God" were not yet included and individuals saying the pledge would begin with one hand on their heart and then, when they said the words "the flag", they would extend that arm to a straight, stiff position, pointing their palm upwards toward the flag.)* Ask students if anyone felt uncomfortable about saying the pledge in this fashion. Students may point out the similarity to the Nazi salute, which was nearly the same, just with the palm down.

Then tell students about the case of *Minersville School District* v. *Gobitis*[1] in which the Court upheld the right of a democratically elected school board to create a requirement that students recite the Pledge of Allegiance. The Court emphasized the nature of representative democracy, saying that people who did not like the school board's rules could elect a new board. In reaching that conclusion, the Court rejected the arguments of students who were Jehovah's Witnesses who claimed that reciting the Pledge and saluting the flag were sacrilegious in the view of their religion and that the requirement violated their First Amendment rights.

Three years later, the Court reversed itself in its ruling in *West Virginia State Board of Education* v. *Barnette* (this case was discussed in reference to freedom of speech in Chapter 35).[2] The Court said that requiring students to recite the Pledge is "compelled speech or compelled symbolic speech" and was in violation of Free Speech protected by the First Amendment. In one of the Court's most eloquent statements about its responsibility to protect liberties, it said, "If there is any fixed star in our constitutional constellation, it is that no official, high or petty, can prescribe what shall be orthodox in politics, nationalism, religion, or other matters of opinion or force citizens to confess by word or act their faith therein."

As an optional follow-up, students can research the case *Elk Grove Unified School District* v. *Newdow*.[3] In 2000, the parent of an elementary school student sued the school district claiming that the school district policy of leading students in the recitation of the pledge (containing the words "under God") violated the First Amendment protection from establishment of religion. In 2002, the federal Ninth Circuit Court agreed with Mr. Newdow and issued an opinion that ignited a dramatic national reaction and debate. In 2004, the Supreme Court heard the appeal and issued an opinion that was based on reasons that surprised many. The Court dismissed the suit because Mr. Newdow was not the custodial parent, so he had no standing to bring the suit.

BACKGROUND—RELIGIOUS HOLIDAYS IN THE PUBLIC SCHOOLS

The issue of how to deal with religious holidays in the public schools—sometimes called the December Dilemma—is a challenge for school administrators, teachers, parents, and students. However, it does provide an opportunity to enhance understanding of religious liberty in the United States. The general notion is that in our diverse society, it is permissible to teach about religious holidays, as long as the instruction is tied to secular educational goals, but that celebration of religious holidays is not appropriate. A wide range of educational and religious organizations have come together to create a guide on this topic. It is in a larger publication called *Finding Common Ground: A Guide to Religious Liberty In Public Schools*, available for free online at www.freedomforum.org. Have students study the suggested guidelines and compare them to their school's practices and policies.

For additional background information about a variety of U.S. Supreme Court decisions related to schools and religious freedom, visit the website of American Civil Liberties Union at www.aclu.org and then search under its section called "Supreme Court" for the term "religion."

THE ESTABLISHMENT CLAUSE (PP. 448–450)

Learning Outcomes

After completing this section, students should be able to:

1. identify five actions the government cannot take as a result of the establishment clause;
2. explain why the "wall of separation" between church and state is incomplete;
3. summarize the three parts of the Lemon test used to determine whether or not a government law or action meets the requirements of the establishment clause;
4. explain how the endorsement test is used in guiding establishment clause decisions;
5. describe decisions of the U.S. Supreme Court in cases involving prayer in schools and funding parochial schools; and
6. interpret a case involving religious expression in a public school ceremony.

BACKGROUND—THE ESTABLISHMENT CLAUSE

Ask students to review the Student Edition where it describes the actions the government is prohibited from doing. Then remind students that the establishment clause is not absolute and does not forbid every action by government that benefits religion or every contact between government and religion. Strongly worded opinions in some recent establishment clause cases suggest that several members of the Court see the clause as a prohibition against establishing or endorsing a state or national church, or coercing anyone to hold a religious belief or participate in a religious activity, but not as requiring absolute neutrality between government and religion. These justices believe that the First Amendment requires the government to accommodate religion.

Congress passed the *Equal Access Act*[4] in 1984 in an attempt to redraw the line between separation and accommodation of religion and state as it applies to public schools. This statute makes it illegal for any public secondary school that has a limited open forum (meaning it has one or more noncurriculum-related student groups meeting at the school during nonschool hours) to deny equal access to, or to discriminate against, any students who wish to conduct a meeting on the basis of religious, political, philosophical, or other content of the speech at such meetings. Under the *Equal Access Act,* the meeting must be voluntary and student-initiated with no sponsorship by the school or government. The employees of the school or government can be present only in a nonparticipatory capacity. The Supreme Court ruled that the statute does not violate the establishment clause.[5] After the passage of the act and the Court's upholding of it, political cartoonists had a field day portraying school administrators being required to allow meetings of fringe political and religious groups on their campuses—which was certainly not the original intent of Congress.

In *Agostini* v. *Felton,*[6] the Supreme Court ruled in a 5-to-4 decision that publicly paid teachers can go into parochial schools to provide *Title I* educational services without violating the establishment clause. (*Title I* is a federal program to improve academic achievement among students who are financially disadvantaged.)

In addition to the cases listed above, the Student Edition refers to important establishment clause cases without mentioning their names. While the names of all of these cases may not be important for a general study of freedom of religion, if students (or teachers) wish to know more details about a particular case, the case names may be helpful.

- The case that established the "endorsement test" is *Lynch* v. *Donnelly.*[7]
- The cases in which the Court has allowed states to provide bus transportation, computers, and loans of certain textbooks to parochial school students are: *Everson* v. *Board of Education*[8] for buses, *Board of Education* v. *Allen* for textbooks,[9] and *Mitchell* v. *Helms* for computers.[10]
- The Ohio case in which the Court approved the use of vouchers for helping to pay tuition at a variety of nonpublic schools, including religious schools, is *Zelman* v. *Simmons-Harris.*[11]
- The Court decisions that say public school-sponsored prayer violates the establishment clause are *Lee* v. *Weisman*[12] and *Santa Fe Independent School District* v. *Doe.*[13]
- The case in which the Court found a violation of the First Amendment when a government ordered schools or courthouses to display the Ten Commandments is *McCreary County* v. *ACLU.*[14]
- The case in which the Court did not find a First Amendment violation when a private organization donated a monument including the Ten Commandments for placement near the Texas state capitol is *Van Orden* v. *Perry.*[15]

BACKGROUND—TEACHING ABOUT EVOLUTION, CREATIONISM, AND INTELLIGENT DESIGN IN PUBLIC SCHOOLS

As problem **f.** in the *You Be The Judge* feature on page 453 in the Student Edition and its answer illustrate, teachers, students, and parents often struggle with questions about what should be taught and what should be learned in public school science classes. The debate has been going on for years among families, teachers, school boards, state boards of education, and even state legislators.

Creationism is defined as arguments put forward to support the belief that life was created consistent with the creation story in the Old Testament of the Bible. The most famous case involving the teaching of creationism is known as the Scopes Trial[16] of 1925, in which a teacher was convicted for violating a statute prohibiting the teaching of the scientific theory of evolution. The conviction was overturned on appeal to the Tennessee Supreme Court based on a legal technicality and an interest in ending the media circus the case had created. The appeals judge said that the jury, and not the judge, should have assessed the fine of $100. Because Scopes was no longer employed by the state, the court saw "nothing to be gained by prolonging the life of this bizarre case." The court held that the case should not be retried in the interest of "the peace and dignity of the state."

Teachers may also be interested in the "John T. Scopes" chapter in the book *Great Trials in American History.* For more information about this publication, visit www.mheducation.com/prek-12.

In more recent cases, the Supreme Court has been clear that laws requiring the teaching of creationism and laws that require a curriculum based on religious beliefs violate the First Amendment. For example, the Court ruled in 1987 that

Louisiana's *Creationism Act*, forbidding the teaching of the theory of evolution in public elementary and secondary schools unless "creation science" is also taught, violated the establishment clause because it lacked a clear secular purpose.[17]

Since that decision, supporters of creationism have focused on teaching "intelligent design" instead of "creationism." The Discovery Institute, a leading supporter of intelligent design (ID) theory and advocate for its teaching in public schools, defines ID as the assertion that "certain features of the universe and of living things are best explained by an intelligent cause, not an undirected process such as natural selection [suggested by the theory of evolution]." They also believe that ID is a scientific theory and that the "intelligent cause" is directed by the Christian view of God and His design.[18] Others say ID is just creationism that has been rebranded and repackaged. The U.S. National Academy of Sciences, the American Association for the Advancement of Science, and the U.S. National Science Teachers Association have called ID "pseudoscience," saying that "creationism, intelligent design, and any other claims of supernatural intervention in the origin of life or of species are not science because they are not testable by methods of science."[19]

A high-profile case involving intelligent design came to the U.S. District Court in 2005. In *Kitzmiller v. Dover Area School District*,[20] a group of parents claimed that the school district's requirement that science teachers present the theory of intelligent design as an alternative explanation of the origin of life violated the First Amendment. The federal judge agreed and issued a rather sharply worded ruling that the requirement violates the Establishment Clause of the First Amendment because intelligent design is not a science and that it "cannot uncouple itself from its creationist, and thus religious, antecedents..."

THE CASE OF...

The Rabbi's Invocation

PROBLEM 38.1 (p. 450)

Before students answer the questions presented in the Student Edition, ask:

- Does the school district's practice of inviting Christian ministers and Jewish rabbis

represent students of all faiths? Does it represent atheists?

- Is this a problem? If so, how should it be addressed?

Note: Be sure that students read the entire section on the establishment clause before they try to answer this problem, which is based on the 1992 U.S. Supreme Court case of *Lee v. Weisman*.[21]

a. Mr. Weisman objected to the local rabbi delivering an invocation at his daughter's middle school graduation. Mr. Weisman alleged that the invocation and benediction violated the First Amendment requirement to separate church and state. Students may be interested to read or to hear the rabbi's prayers.

INVOCATION

God of the Free, Hope of the Brave: For the legacy of America where diversity is celebrated and the rights of minorities are protected, we thank You. May these young men and women grow up to enrich it. For the liberty of America, we thank You. May these new graduates grow up to guard it. For the political process of America in which all its citizens may participate, for its court system where all may seek justice, we thank You. May those we honor this morning always turn to it in trust. For the destiny of America, we thank You. May the graduates of Nathan Bishop Middle School so live that they might help to share it. May our aspirations for our country and for these young people, who are our hope for the future, be richly fulfilled. Amen.

BENEDICTION

O God, we are grateful to You for having endowed us with the capacity for learning which we have celebrated on this joyous commencement. Happy families, give thanks for seeing their children achieve an important milestone. Send Your blessings upon the teachers and administrators who helped prepare them. The graduates now need strength and guidance for the future; help them to understand that we are not complete with academic knowledge alone. We must each strive to fulfill what You require of us all: to do justly, to love mercy, to walk humbly. We give thanks to You, Lord, for keeping us alive, sustaining us, and allowing us to reach this special, happy occasion. Amen.[22]

b. Students' answers will vary. The Weismans could argue that because the invocation and benediction referred to God in several places, the school was, in effect, advancing religion by creating an identification of the school with a deity. The Weismans could also argue that the principal's invitation to the rabbi to give the invocation and benediction could present a symbolic union of the state and its public schools with religion and religious practices. Furthermore, while attending graduation may be voluntary, it is an important rite of passage. To expect a student to skip graduation to avoid exposure to a prayer is a high price to pay.

c. Students' answers will vary. The school could argue that general civic acknowledgments of religion in public life do not violate the establishment clause, as long as they neither threaten the establishment of an official religion nor coerce participation in religious activities. Attendance at the graduation was voluntary, and no student was required to stand or participate while the prayers were said. The school could also argue that nondenominational prayer to God at public celebrations is a long-standing American tradition and should be allowed during such a significant occasion.

d. This question asks students to compare the *Weisman* case to the cases explained in the Student Edition. The Supreme Court has held that a public school cannot sponsor prayer. *Weisman* is similar to previous school prayer cases in that the school is holding an official school event and sponsoring prayer at that event.

This case differs from the other school prayer cases because the prayers in dispute were daily and this prayer occurred only once. Also, school attendance is mandatory, while graduation attendance is voluntary. Another difference between this case and other school prayer cases is that the prayer at the graduation ceremony was not drafted by school administrators.

e. Students' opinions will vary. The U.S. Supreme Court held that public school benedictions and invocations offered by clergy who had been invited by the school principal violate the First Amendment ban on government establishment of religion. The Court felt that officially sponsored prayer at graduation ceremonies could coerce students into participation in religious exercises in violation of the Constitution.[23]

f.–g. Students should examine each of the scenarios in light of the *Lee* v. *Weisman* decision, the *Equal Access Act*, the endorsement test, and the three-part establishment clause test (the *Lemon* test) described in the Student Edition.

ACTIVITY—CROSS SHAPED PUBLIC MONUMENTS

Begin this discussion by asking what crosses symbolize. Once students state the religious symbolism, ask them to think of how else they have seen the cross symbol used. Students might suggest grave markers, first aid stations or kits, the logo for the Red Cross displayed on armor or flags during in the Crusades, and other uses.

Give students this scenario: A town in Maryland has a 40 foot tall World War I memorial in the center of a very busy traffic circle. The names of soldiers are written on a brass plate and the words *valor, endurance, courage,* and *devotion* inscribed in the base. The state government did not build the monument which has stood for over 90 years, but nows pays for the maintenance and grounds-keeping around it with taxpayer money. A group of citizens claims that Maryland is violating the Establishment Clause by paying to maintain the monument.

In small groups, ask students to consider the question: Is Maryland violating the Establishment Clause by spending taxpayer money on the cross shaped monument? Ask them to write down their arguments for each on index cards or small pieces of paper. Have them sort the arguments into "yes" and "no" piles. Then have them lay the index cards on the desk with the arguments arranged from their most persuasive at top to their least persuasive at the bottom for each side. When all groups are done sorting, have students travel around the room to see other groups' arguments.

Have students return to their seats and lead a large group discussion. After the discussion, disclose that this was a real Supreme Court case, *American Legion* v. *American Humanist Association*[24]. The Supreme Court decided that the cross does not violate the Establishment Clause because the passage of time creates a presumption that a long-standing monument is constitutional.

For a case summary of the consolidated case, *Maryland-National Capital Park and Planning Commission* v. *American Humanist Association*, go to www.store.streetlaw.org. For instructions on how to conduct a moot court and mini-moot courts, visit Street Law's SCOTUS in the Classroom page at www.streetlaw.org/programsscotus-in-the-classroom.

THE FREE EXERCISE CLAUSE
(PP. 451–453)

Learning Outcomes

After completing this section, students should be able to:

1. distinguish between beliefs and actions in terms of protection of freedom of religion;
2. predict how the U.S. Supreme Court is likely to rule when a valid, neutral law interferes with religious practice;
3. summarize the U.S. Supreme Court decision in *Wisconsin* v. *Yoder*; and
4. describe the *Religious Freedom Restoration Act*.

BACKGROUND—THE FREE EXERCISE CLAUSE

The free exercise clause protects the right to freely exercise one's religion. However, the courts place some limits on the exercise of religion.

For example, no court would hold that the First Amendment protects human sacrifice even if a particular religion required it. The Supreme Court has interpreted this clause to mean that the freedom to *believe* is absolute, but the ability to *act* on those beliefs is not. Questions of free exercise usually arise when a person's civic obligation to comply with a law conflicts with his or her religious beliefs or practices. If a law singled out a specific religion or particular religious practice, under current Supreme Court rulings that law would violate the First Amendment. Controversy arises when a law is generally applicable and religiously neutral but has the accidental or unintentional effect of interfering with a particular religious practice or belief.

Students may find the case of *Church of the Lukumi Babalu Aye* v. *City of Hialeah*[25] interesting. After the opening of the Church of the Lukumi Babalu Aye which practices Santeria, the city of Hialeah in Florida passed an ordinance prohibiting animal sacrifices. The church sued claiming the city was violating their free exercise of religion. The case was appealed to the Supreme Court who decided unanimously for the church. The Court found that the ordinances did not pass strict scrutiny and singled out the Santeria practitioners based on their religion.

The Student Edition refers to several famous free exercise cases. The 1878 case, *Reynolds* v. *United States*, in which the Supreme Court upheld the conviction of a Mormon man who practiced polygamy focused on the constitutional difference between freedom to believe and freedom to act. Although a person might endorse the practice of polygamy based on religious beliefs, the government is allowed to ban such a practice given the government's strong interest in protecting the institution of marriage.[26] Similarly, in the peyote case mentioned in the text, *Employment Division* v. *Smith*, the Court ruled that because the government has a strong interest in regulating the use of drugs and alcohol, the government may impose regulations on such substances even where they are being used as part of religious ceremonies.[27] In both cases, the Court said the government had a legitimate interest in the regulation, and the effects on religious exercise were incidental to the regulation, not the purpose of it.

For additional free teaching materials about the 2014 *Hobby Lobby* case mentioned in the Student Edition, please go to www.streetlaw.org and search for the case name under the resources tab.

Ask students to consider the tension that exists between the establishment clause and the free exercise clause. The government has to be careful not to intentionally interfere with exercise of religion while at the same time stopping short of an endorsement of religion that might violate the establishment clause.

For more information about cases related to the free exercise clause, including links to major cases and explanations intended for high school students, see http://law2.umkc.edu/faculty/projects/ftrials/conlaw/freeexercise.htm.

THE **CASE** OF...

The Amish Children

PROBLEM 38.2 (p.451)

The U.S. Supreme Court's opinion in *Wisconsin* v. *Yoder*[28] is interesting and well written and one that most students could read. Justice Douglas's concurring opinion argues forcefully that the children's rights were ignored in this case. Some believe that the Yoders would lose before today's

Court because Wisconsin's student attendance law was neutral and did not target a specific religion.

a. Students' answers will vary but should show an understanding of the conflict between the state's view of education and the Amish view of education. Students should also note that the Court emphasized the unique characteristics and long history of the Amish community. Because Amish children were not expected to grow up and participate in mainstream society, a traditional high school education might be inconsistent with the skills and knowledge necessary to function as productive adults within their community.

b. Students' answers will vary. The dissenters may argue that the state has an interest in requiring secondary education because it provides people with the basic skills necessary to participate effectively in a democracy. They might also have expressed concern that the interests of an Amish child might be different from those of their parents. (See answer **c.** below.)

c. Students' answers will vary. Some students may argue that without a high school education, Amish children are deprived of the necessary instruction and exposure to eventually make independent judgments as adults as to whether or not they will stay in the Amish community or live in modern society. Without a high school education, an Amish person would be at a severe disadvantage if he or she chose to leave the Amish community, thereby limiting personal liberty and autonomy.

Investigating the Law Where You Live

(p. 452) Discussions about holiday traditions, decorations, and celebrations may be sensitive subjects. You may wish to consult with your school administration prior to this lesson to discuss your school's or district's policies. For additional information on this subject, visit the Baptist Joint Committee's website at bjconline.org or the National Education Association's website at www.nea.org/tools/15287.htm.

CAPTION ANSWER (P. 452) The Supreme Court's rule is that a valid, neutral law—that is, a law that does not specifically target a religious belief or practice—will be upheld even if it interferes with religious practice.

YOU BE the JUDGE

Religion and K-12 Public Education (p. 453)

Most of these questions contain fact patterns based on actual Supreme Court decisions pertaining to the establishment and free exercise clauses. Representatives from various religious organizations, civil liberties groups, or attorneys specializing in constitutional law can add depth and interest to this discussion by helping students think through the dilemmas posed in this problem. To present a balanced viewpoint, it may be best to bring in two people or a panel of people with different perspectives.

a. This case involves the establishment clause. Students' opinions about whether this government action violates the First Amendment will vary. In 1993, the Court held that the establishment clause does not prevent a public school district from furnishing a disabled child enrolled in a parochial school with a sign-language interpreter in order to facilitate the child's education. Government programs that neutrally provide benefits to a broad class of citizens defined without reference to religion are not subject to an establishment clause challenge just because the religious school may also receive an attenuated financial benefit.[29]

b. This case involves the establishment clause. Students' opinions about whether this government action violates the First Amendment will vary. In *Wallace* v. *Jaffree,* the Court found a violation of the establishment clause because the legislature's purpose was to restore prayer in public schools.[30] The law, which originally required a moment of silence for meditation, was later amended to specify that the time could be used for meditation or prayer. The amendment suggested religious motivations. This being the case, the purpose was not secular in nature. However, state statutes allowing local school districts to provide a moment of silence—not tied to the issue of prayer—have been upheld in the federal courts of appeals.[31]

c. This case involves both the free exercise clause and the establishment clause. Students' opinions about whether this government action violates the First Amendment will vary. This situation is based on *Board of Education of Westside Community Schools* v. *Mergens.*[32] In that case, the Supreme Court held that a public high school, whose existing student clubs included those unrelated to the curriculum, must afford equal access to a student Bible study group. In reaching this decision, the Court applied the federal *Equal Access Act of 1984*,[33] which they determined did not violate the establishment clause. A majority of justices also found that the principal's decision violated the First Amendment speech rights of the students because the principal's decision discriminated against a certain group of students based on the content of what they proposed to say.

d. Students' opinions about whether this government action violates the First Amendment will vary. The coach-led prayer would most likely be a violation of the establishment clause. As the Court recognized in *Lee* v. *Weisman*,[34] it is unfair to expect a student to remove himself or herself from an important activity in order to avoid being subjected to state-endorsed prayer. In *Santa Fe Independent School District* v. *Doe*[35], the Court held that the tradition of a broadcast student-led prayer at the beginning of a football game was a violation of the establishment clause because it was at a school-sponsored activity and required use of the school's public address system. However, if several of the football players decide they want to pray among themselves before a football game, the school could not interfere because doing so would be a violation of their free exercise rights. Note the tension that often arises between the efforts of the government to avoid anything that appears to establish religion and its efforts not to infringe on the free exercise rights of citizens.

e. This case involves the free exercise clause. Students' opinions about whether this government action violates the First Amendment will vary. This exact case has not come before the appellate courts. The general idea is that school systems should be sensitive to the religious needs of all students, including those from minority groups. If the public school system is unable to change the date of the testing, it must offer alternative dates for these students to take the exams. If the school system failed to provide an alternative for the Muslim students, the school might be violating their free exercise rights by having them choose between important testing and celebration of the religious holiday. Reasonable accommodations must be made, where feasible, to avoid an infringement on the right to free exercise.

f. This case involves the establishment clause. Students' opinions about whether this government action violates the First Amendment will vary. The Supreme Court has struck down laws requiring the teaching of creationism and those preventing the teaching of evolution, because requiring a curriculum based on religious beliefs is a violation of the establishment clause.

However, in the process of teaching evolutionary theory, a science teacher may state that some people reject this belief in favor of creationism or intelligent design theory. Educating students about divergent beliefs and theories would be a secular educational purpose, which is permitted under the First Amendment.

g. This case would most likely be analyzed as an establishment clause case, but it does seem to involve a student's free exercise rights. Students' opinions about whether this government action violates the First Amendment will vary. There is no doubt that many public schools have a Christmas tree or celebrate the Christian holiday in some way. However, in recent decisions, the Supreme Court has held that displays of religious symbols such as nativity scenes on public property contravene the establishment clause if they convey a message that is primarily religious rather than secular.[36] Ask students whether they think the national Christmas tree and Hanukkah menorah in Washington, D.C., violate the Constitution because they are on public land, or if there is something unique about school settings.

h. This hypothetical case involves the free exercise clause. Students' opinions about whether this government action violates the First Amendment will vary. The school should probably make an exception to its "no hats policy" to avoid infringing on the free exercise right of religious students. The purpose of the rule—to foster a safe school environment and awareness of traditional manners—should not be undermined by an exception for religious purposes. Further religious head coverings do not interfere with the educational process.

Note: The Supreme Court has held that the military context is somewhat distinct because of a greater need for conformity and specific rules that allow greater latitude in constitutional infringements. The Court upheld an Air Force rule prohibiting hats as applied to a soldier wearing a yarmulke.[37] Congress later passed a law lifting the ban on religious headwear in the military.[38]

DISCUSSION—FREEDOM OF RELIGION IN COMMUNITY SPACES AND IN PUBLIC LIFE

Note: The questions posed in the Student Edition focus on religion and public schools. Use these additional cases to help students understand the concept of separation of religion and government in other settings. Ask students to discuss and decide which of the following scenarios violate the First Amendment.

1. A state government pays a chaplain to open each legislative session with a prayer. *Students' answers will vary. In* Marsh v. Chambers, *a 6-to-3 majority found no violation of the establishment clause.*[39] *The Court said that "the practice of opening legislative sessions with prayer has become part of the fabric of our society."*

2. A state law prohibits members of the clergy from holding certain public offices. *Students' answers will vary. In 1978, the Supreme Court stated that if the purpose of the state law or other governmental action is to single out religion for adverse treatment, or to hinder or discriminate against a particular religion, that is a violation of the free exercise clause. The Court found such a violation in this case.*[40]

3. A state requires citizens receiving unemployment benefits to accept any appropriate job that becomes available. A citizen is denied continued unemployment compensation because she refused to accept a job that would require her to work on the day that she celebrates her Sabbath. *Students' answers will vary. The case of* Frazee v. Illinois Dept. of Employment Security *was used as a model for this problem. A unanimous Court held that the free exercise clause was violated when the state refused to provide Mr. Frazee with unemployment benefits. The Court found that Frazee was entitled to constitutional protection since his refusal to work on Sunday was based on a "personal professed religious belief."*

   The Frazee case has combined an interesting twist. Apparently, Mr. Frazee was not a member of an established religious sect or church. He did not claim that his refusal to work on Sunday was a requirement of a tenet, belief, or teaching of an established religious body. Justice White indicated that the sincerity of an individual's belief is the key issue. As long as the belief is sincerely held, then it is unconstitutional to deny benefits just because the person is not a member of a specific religious organization or denomination.[41]

4. A town begins its public board meetings with a prayer. The prayer is followed by the town's normal business, including a public forum and a portion of the meeting where business owners and residents apply for zoning changes or various permits. Since the tradition began, nearly all of the clergy invited to deliver the prayer have been Christian. Most clergy delivered prayers that were Christian in nature (referring to Jesus or Christ). Other clergy delivered more generally religious prayers. *In* Town of Greece v. Galloway *(2014) the Court upheld the town's prayer by a vote of 5 to 4.*[42]

Additional free teaching materials about this case are available at www.streetlaw.org.

NOTES

(1) *Minersville School District* v. *Gobitis*, 310 U.S. 586 (1940).

(2) *West Virginia State Board of Education* v. *Barnette*, 319 U.S. 624 (1943).

(3) *Elk Grove Unified School District* v. *Newdow*, 542 U.S. 1 (2004).

(4) *Equal Access Act*, 20 U.S.C. 4071 (1984).

(5) *Board of Education of the Westside Community Schools* v. *Mergens*, 496 U.S. 226 (1990).

(6) *Agostini* v. *Felton*, 521 U.S. 203 (1997).

(7) *Lynch* v. *Donnelly*, 465 U.S. 668 (1984).

(8) *Everson* v. *Board of Education*, 330 U.S. (1947).

(9) *Board of Education* v. *Allen*, 392 U.S. 236 (1968).

(10) *Mitchell* v. *Helms*, 530, U.S. 793 (2000).

(11) *Zelmon* v. *Simmons-Harris*, 536 U.S. 639 (2002).

(12) *Lee* v. *Weisman*, 505 U.S. 577 (1992).

(13) *Santa Fe Independent School District* v. *Doe*, 530 U.S. 290 (2000).

(14) *McCreary County* v. *ACLU*, 545 U.S. 844 (2005).

(15) *Van Orden* v. *Perry*, 545 U.S. 677 (2005).

(16) *State of Tennessee* v. *Scopes*, 278 S.W. 57 (Tenn. 1925).

(17) *Edwards* v. *Aguillard*, 482 U.S. 578 (1987).

(18) www.discovery.org/csc/topQuestions. php#questionsAboutIntelligentDesign and www.citizenlink.org/content/A000006139.cfm, accessed July 8, 2008.

(19) www.aaas.org/news/press_room/evolution/ qanda.shtml, accessed July 8, 2008.

(20) *Tracy Kitzmiller et al.* v. *Dover Area School District*, 400 F. Supp. 2d 707 (M.D. Pa. 2005).

(21) *Lee* v. *Weisman*, 505 U.S. 577 (1992).

(22) Ibid. at 581–82.

(23) Ibid.

(24) *American Legion* v. *Am. Humanist Ass'n*, 139 S.Ct. 2067 (2019).

(25) *Church of the Lukumi Babalu Aye* v. *City of Hialeah*, 508 U.S. 520 (1993).

(26) *Reynolds* v. *United States*, 98 U.S. 145 (1878).

(27) *Employment Division* v. *Smith*, 494 U.S. 872 (1990).

(28) *Wisconsin* v. *Yoder*, 406 U.S. 205 (1972).

(29) *Zobrest* v. *Catalina Foothills School District*, 509 U.S. 1 (1993).

(30) *Wallace* v. *Jaffree*, 472 U.S. 38 (1985).

(31) For example, in 2000 Virginia enacted a statute requiring public schools to begin each day with a moment of silence, during which a student, "in the exercise of his or her individual choice," could "meditate, pray, or engage in any other silent activity...." Va. Code Ann. § 22.1-203 (Michie 2000). In a 2-to-1 split, the Fourth Circuit Court of Appeals held that the Commonwealth's statute did not offend the establishment clause. *Brown* v. *Gilmore*, 258 F.3d 265 (4th Cir. 2001).

(32) *Board of Education of Westside Community Schools* v. *Mergens*, 496 U.S. 226 (1990).

(33) *Equal Access Act*, 20 U.S.C. 4071 (1984).

(34) *Lee* v. *Weisman*, 505 U.S. 577 (1992).

(35) *Santa Fe Independent School District* v. *Doe*, 530 U.S. 290 (2000).

(36) See *Allegheny* v. *ACLU*, 492 U.S. 573; *Lynch* v. *Donnelly*, 465 U.S. 668 (1984).

(37) *Goldman* v. *Weinberger*, 475 U.S. 503 (1986).

(38) *National Defense Authorization Act for Fiscal Years 1988 and 1989*, 10 U.S.C. § 776.

(39) *Marsh* v. *Chambers*, 463 U.S. 783 (1983).

(40) *McDaniel* v. *Paty*, 435 U.S. 618 (1978).

(41) *Frazee* v. *Illinois Dept. of Employment Security*, 489 U.S. 829 (1989).

(42) *Town of Greece* v. *Galloway*, 572 U.S. 565 (2014).

CHAPTER 39
Due Process

The concept of due process of law includes the idea that government should treat people fairly. But determining what is fair is seldom easy. The language of the due process clause—no person shall be deprived of life, liberty, or property without due process of law—has been interpreted to mean that a person cannot lose life, liberty (freedom), or property unless fair procedures are first followed by the government. This is part of what the due process clause means, and it is often called "procedural due process." However, courts have also interpreted the due process clause as a limit on the substantive powers of government, meaning that the laws themselves have to be fair. This is called "substantive due process." When courts consider substantive due process cases, they look at whether a government passed a law or action that unreasonably interferes with a fundamental or basic right. The Fifth Amendment's due process clause protects against action by the federal government. The Fourteenth Amendment has almost the same due process language and protects people from actions by state and local governments.

INTRODUCTION (P. 454)

Learning Outcomes

After completing this sections, students should be able to:
1. define the terms *procedural due process*, and *substantive due process; and*
2. explain how procedural due process differs from substantive due process.

PROCEDURAL DUE PROCESS (PP. 455–457)

Learning Outcomes

After completing this section, students should be able to:
1. identify what procedural due process helps to prevent and the reasons for procedural safeguards;
2. give examples of government actions that deprive a person of life, liberty, or property; and
3. name at least six procedures the government might have to follow before it deprives someone of life, liberty, or property.

BACKGROUND—PROCEDURAL DUE PROCESS

Note: If students have already studied the criminal justice system in Unit 2, they may be familiar with certain due process procedural protections that apply to criminal defendants.

Most due process issues concern what is called procedural due process. The focus is on what procedures must accompany the government's decision to take away a citizen's protected interest in life, liberty, or property. When a court is concerned about procedural due process, it is less concerned with the final decision the government may make than about the procedural steps the government goes through in making the decision. ("It's not what you do, it's how you do it.")

The goal of procedural due process is fairness. Requiring that certain procedures be followed before depriving someone of life, liberty, or property provides the public more protection from the government. For example, a typical procedural due process right is the right to be notified of the government's intention and the right to a hearing in which the person can present his or her side of the issue. The amount of "process due" varies from one type of situation to another. Just as with other constitutional rights, the court tries to balance the individual's interest in having more procedural rights and the severity of the potential loss the person is facing against the government's interest in being able to make decisions quickly and efficiently.

The procedural due process cases mentioned in the Student Edition are: *Conn. Dep't of Pub. Safety* v. *Doe*,[13] which relates to due process under Megan's Law, and *Goldberg* v. *Kelly*,[14] relating to the requirement of the government to provide due process before cutting public assistance to a person.

Remind students that if they believe the government has not followed fair procedures when taking some action that affected their life, liberty, or property interest, they may want to consult an attorney. With the attorney's advice and assistance, they may be able to file a complaint directly with the government agency. They may also be able to go to court and seek an order that the government follow due process when dealing with them.

THE **CASE** OF...

Goss v. Lopez

PROBLEM 39.1 (p.456)

The case of *Goss* v. *Lopez* is a leading student rights case.[4] The facts of this case make an interesting role-play when approached seriously by students. The first role-play could take place before the *Goss* decision, and a follow-up role-play could show how the due process requirements have changed under *Goss*.

a. The students were suspended for their presence at, or their participation in, a demonstration conducted at the school. The U.S. Supreme Court held that the students had a right to be informed of the charges brought against them, to be given an explanation of the charges if the students deny the wrongdoing, and to be given an opportunity to be heard.

b. Students' answers will vary. Students may want the right to call and cross-examine witnesses. They may also want to have an impartial person preside over the proceeding and to have an attorney present. These rights will give the students more protection, but they are time-consuming and expensive and were not required by the Court under *Goss*.

c. Students' opinions will vary. *Goss* provides an opportunity to emphasize the flexible nature of

due process, the importance of fair procedures in avoiding government errors, and the time and money due process may require. Discuss with students whether or not the procedures required by *Goss* are adequate.

After discussing *Goss*, students may be interested to learn that the Court held that dismissal of a medical student for academic (as opposed to disciplinary) reasons did not necessitate a due process hearing.[5]

THE **CASE** OF...

The Deportation of Permanent Residents

PROBLEM 39.2 (p.457)

Note: This problem may be sensitive or awkward for students who immigrated to this country with or without proper documentation. See Chapter 42 for additional background about the deportation—now commonly called "removal"—of noncitizens. Tell students that while this case was decided by the Court in 2003, there is still a vigorous public debate about reforming the way the U.S. detention system works and the rights people should have if they are facing the possibility of deportation.

This case is based on the 2003 case of *Demore* v. *Kim*.[6] The question before the Court was the constitutionality of the *Immigration and Nationality Act*,[7] which allows the Immigration and Naturalization Service (INS now called USCIS for United States Citizenship and Immigration Services), to detain without bail any noncitizen (legal or undocumented immigrants) who are deportable for various offenses. These people may be deported if found guilty of any of a list of specific crimes, including aggravated felonies. Petty theft, combined with prior convictions, like Kim's conviction, is considered an aggravated felony.

In Kim's case, neither party disputed Kim's burglary, petty theft, or prior convictions. Both parties also agreed that these offenses made Kim deportable under the act. The question was whether Kim could be detained by the INS without bail during the deportation hearings. Kim argued that the law violated his Fifth Amendment right to due process.

The Fifth Amendment guarantees that no person will be deprived of life, liberty, or property without due process of law. This means that the government cannot take your life, your freedom of movement, or your property without proceedings that typically give a person notice of the charges and an opportunity to be heard.

a. Students' answers will vary. Arguments *opposing* the Court's decision to allow Kim's deportation without a bail hearing include:

- Bail hearings are due process rights available to all defendants. As Justice Souter wrote, making these hearings unavailable to (legal) permanent residents violates the precedents that have been set in nearly 100 years of cases.
- Kim has been convicted of relatively minor crimes and does not pose a danger to the community.
- Kim should have the right to prove that he does not pose a flight risk or a danger to the community.
- Kim should not be discriminated against on the basis that he is not yet a U.S. citizen.

Arguments in support of the Court's decision and the constitutionality of the act include:

- As then Chief Justice Rehnquist wrote, the Court has repeatedly allowed Congress to make laws for noncitizens that would not be acceptable if applied to citizens.
- The length of detention is not a significant period of time to be held without bail.
- Congress has determined that (noncitizen) immigrants pose a significant flight risk during deportation proceedings. Congress designed the law to ensure that dangerous aliens are removed from the United States.
- There is no intention by Congress to treat permanent lawful residents any differently than any other class of noncitizens.
- Kim is not in a favored group and should not be allowed a bond hearing. The Court recognizes the right of the government to limit the rights of people who have broken the law.

b. Students' answers will vary. Note that this particular question may require sensitivity in handling the discussion among students.

Materials in Chapter 41, "Discrimination," and in Chapter 42, "Immigration Law," can be used to expand the discussion.

ACTIVITY—MOOT COURT OF *KELO* V. *CITY OF NEW LONDON*

Begin this activity by asking students to review the Fifth Amendment's "takings" provision and its connection to due process. Then, review how the Fourteenth Amendment applies constitutional

protections from actions of state and local governments.

With that background, ask students to conduct a moot court of the case of *Kelo* v. *City of New London*,[8] decided by the U.S. Supreme Court in 2005. The case summary for this case is available at streetlaw.org under the "Resources" tab. The issue in the case was: Does the term *public use* as articulated in the Fifth Amendment (and made applicable to the states and local government through the Fourteenth Amendment) permit a local government to take the private property of one party and lease it to another, even if the property is not run-down or causing a public nuisance? The relevant precedent cases are *Berman* v. *Parker*[9] and *Hawaii Housing Authority* v. *Midkiff*,[10] also available at www.oyez.com. Depending on the skill levels of your students, you may want to give them only the facts, issues, and precedents so they can develop their own arguments for both sides in the case. If more scaffolding is needed, you may also wish to provide them with bulleted arguments for each side. Reserve announcing the Court's decision until student justices have reached and explained their own conclusions.

For additional suggestions about teaching using the case study or moot court methods, see the Teaching Methods section in the front of this Teacher Manual and Street Law's website page SCOTUS in the Classroom at www.streetlaw.org/programs/scotus-in-the-classroom. *Street Law's Guide to Mock Trials and Moot Courts* may also be helpful. Information about it is available at www.mheducation.com/prek-12.

SUBSTANTIVE DUE PROCESS (PP. 158–159)

Learning Objectives

After completing this section, students should be able to:

1. define the term *unenumerated rights;*
2. name several fundamental rights listed in the Constitution and protected by due process rights; and
3. name several unenumerated fundamental rights protected by due process.

CAPTION ANSWER (P. 458) Substantive due process is used by courts to protect basic freedoms by making sure that government does not violate a fundamental right without good reason. Procedural due process is a citizen's right to fair treatment by the government.

BACKGROUND AND DISCUSSION—THE CONCEPT OF LIBERTY AND CONTROVERSIES OVER SUBSTANTIVE DUE PROCESS

The Fifth and Fourteenth Amendments guarantee that no person will be deprived of life, liberty, or property by a local, state or federal government without due process of law. *Life* and *property* have been interpreted fairly literally. For example, the government cannot execute a person or impose heavy fines without first following fair procedures, such as a trial or hearing. The government cannot build a highway through someone's private backyard without following procedures for notifying property owners and giving a fair price for the land.

However, *liberty* is a more nebulous concept. Ask students what liberty means to them. What does liberty allow them to do? Are they free to exercise their liberties without government interference? What should happen if the government thinks it has a compelling reason to interfere with their liberties?

People interpret the Constitution in different ways. As mentioned in the Student Edition, there is typically more agreement across philosophical lines when it comes to providing due process protections to rights specifically named (enumerated) in the Constitution. There is much more philosophical conflict over the application of due process protections to unenumerated rights, such as education, the right to die, workers' rights, and in various privacy issues such as intimate relations between consenting adults and in reproductive choices such as abortion.

For further background about the right to privacy and substantive due process, see Chapter 40, "The Right to Privacy," and Chapter 41, "Discrimination."

BACKGROUND AND ACTIVITY—DUE PROCESS IN HISTORY

Students (and teachers) with an interest in U.S. history may appreciate the historical context and foundation of due process rights. Assign students the following research questions and ask them to report their findings in creative ways (oral reports, posters, role-plays, written reports, etc.) to the class.

- Why do you think the framers of the Constitution (especially Anti-Federalists) included the Fifth Amendment due process rights? From which other historical document have you heard the phrase "right to life, liberty and...."
- When was the Fourteenth Amendment added to the Constitution? Why do you think it was added? Why did the Radical Republicans push hard for it to be added?
- What were the basic facts, main constitutional questions, and the U.S. Supreme Court decision in the following cases? What did the Court say in each case about the "liberty of contracts," the "liberty interests" of workers, and the application of the Fourteenth Amendment? In your opinion, how did the Court's decision reflect that period of history?

a. The 1905 case of *Lochner* v. *New York*?[1]

b. The 1937 case of *West Coast Hotel Co.* v. *Parrish*?[2]

- What were the facts, constitutional questions, and Court decision in the 1967 case of *Loving* v. *Virginia*?[3] How does this case show that some substantive due process cases also deal with discrimination and the application of the Fourteenth Amendment's equal protection clause? In your opinion, how does this case reflect that period of history? (For more information about the *Loving* case, see Chapter 29. Chapter 41 deals extensively with discrimination and the Fourteenth Amendment's equal protection clause.)

THE **CASE** OF...

The Right to Die

PROBLEM 39.3 (p. 459)

Note: This topic may be particularly sensitive for students with friends or relatives who are terminally ill or who have contemplated or committed suicide.

a. Students' answers will vary. These two cases are similar in that both involved adults who (apparently) did not want to prolong their lives. Both cases involved quality-of-life issues and the degree to which other people can be involved in the death of someone who is gravely ill. Both cases also involve liberty and medical ethics, as courts have to sort out who has the right to make decisions and to take actions that support death. The two cases are different in that the woman in *Cruzan* was not able to make this decision for herself because she was unconscious.[11] In the assisted suicide cases, competent adults made their own choices. Also, *Cruzan* involved passive euthanasia, not assisted suicide.

b. Students' answers will vary. Arguments in favor of allowing physician-assisted suicide include that competent adults should have the right to determine the time and manner of their death and to choose a humane and dignified death. Generally, people in the final stages of a terminal illness may lawfully order the removal of their life-support systems or may have signed "do not resuscitate" orders. However, terminally ill patients who are not on life support cannot have assistance to hasten their deaths.

c. Students' answers will vary. Arguments against allowing physician-assisted suicide are that the country has consistently rejected any right to commit suicide or to allow another to assist in committing suicide. Society has a legitimate interest in prohibiting intentional killing (murder) and preserving human life, preventing suicide, protecting the medical profession's integrity and ethics, and maintaining physicians' role as healers. Some also fear that legalizing assisted suicide may unduly pressure sick and elderly people to terminate their lives to avoid burdening their families financially and emotionally. Society has a legitimate interest in protecting vulnerable people and groups of people from being pressured to end their lives.

d. Students' opinions will vary. In two separate cases, the U.S. Supreme Court upheld statutes which make it a felony to knowingly assist in a suicide.[12]

e. Students' answers and reasons may vary. To extend this activity, ask students to debate the question(s) or to write persuasive speeches or essays on the topic.

BACKGROUND—THE RIGHT TO DIE

It may be helpful to clarify the differences between passive euthanasia (refusal of medical treatment), active euthanasia (assisted suicide for a terminally ill or suffering patient), and suicide. The right to refuse medical treatment is a constitutionally recognized right. The government cannot pass a law requiring a person to accept medical treatment against his or her will. However, the government can require that medical treatment be continued in the absence of evidence of the person's intentions, as the state of Missouri did in the case of Nancy Cruzan. The right to assisted suicide is constitutionally permissible but not constitutionally required, that is, a state may choose to make it a crime or may choose to allow it.

In many states, suicide is a crime. However, a person who attempts suicide and is unsuccessful is treated as a victim and generally directed to proper medical and mental health care. The law may confine a person who is believed to be a danger to himself or herself to prevent that person from committing suicide.

Public Agenda, a nonprofit opinion research organization, provides facts, cases, polling information, and the latest news about the right to die at www.publicagenda.org.

Suicide and the right to die are also examined in the criminal law material in Chapter 9.

NOTES

(1) *Lochner v. New York*, 198 U.S. 45 (1905).

(2) *West Coast Hotel Co. v. Parrish*, 300 U.S. 379 (1937).

(3) *Loving v. Virginia*, 388 U.S. 1 (1967).

(4) *Goss v. Lopez*, 419 U.S. 565 (1975).

(5) *Board of Curators of the University of Missouri v. Horowitz*, 435 U.S. 78 (1978).

(6) *Demore v. Kim*, 538 U.S. 510 (2003).

(7) *Immigration and Nationality Act*, 8 U.S.C. § 1226 (1996).

(8) *Kelo v. City of New London*, 545 U.S. 469 (2005).

(9) *Berman v. Parker*, 348 U.S. 26 (1954).

(10) *Hawaii Housing Authority v. Midkiff*, 467 U.S. 229 (1984).

(11) *Cruzan v. Director, Missouri Dept. of Health*, 497 U.S. 261 (1990).

(12) *Washington v. Glucksberg*, 521 U.S. 702 (1997), used a due process analysis for assisted suicide; *Vacco v. Quill*, 521 U.S. 793 (1997), used an equal protection analysis for assisted suicide.

(13) *Conn. Dep't of Pub. Safety v. Doe*, 538 U.S. 1 (2003).

(14) *Goldberg v. Kelly*, 397 U.S. 254 (1970).

Although the words *right to privacy* and *right to be let alone* do not appear anywhere in the U.S. Constitution, many people contend that privacy is a basic right that should be protected. Since the mid-1960s, the U.S. Supreme Court has recognized a constitutional right to privacy. Privacy is protected when people want to make certain kinds of important decisions, such as marriage and family planning, free from undue government interference. Because privacy has been found to be a fundamental right, the Court sometimes justifies privacy protection in terms of substantive due process.

The right to privacy generally protects citizens from unreasonable interference by the government. However, the right to privacy sometimes conflicts with important government interests. In such cases, the government can regulate certain acts or activities, even though a person's right to privacy is affected.

INTRODUCTION (PP. 460–462)

Learning Outcomes

After completing this section, students should be able to:

1. state when the U.S. Supreme Court began to recognize a constitutional right to privacy;
2. identify two general circumstances when the right to privacy is protected;
3. list five zones of privacy created by the U.S. Constitution and explain their significance;
4. give examples of U.S. Supreme Court decisions that have found that someone has a privacy right; and
5. give examples of U.S. Supreme Court decisions that have expressed a limit to someone's privacy right.

PREVIEW ACTIVITY—QUOTE ANALYSIS AND WRITING

Post the following quotation from Justice Brandeis's dissenting opinion in the 1928 case of *Olmstead* v. *United States*[1] for all students to see:

"The makers of our Constitution . . . conferred, against the Government, the right to be let alone—the most comprehensive of rights and the right most valued by civilized men."
—U.S. Supreme Court Justice Louis Brandeis

Ask students to write a short journal entry explaining whether they agree or disagree with Justice Brandeis. They should also write about their reasons. After students have completed their work, ask student volunteers to share their views with the class or with another student who sits nearby. Use these student viewpoints to introduce the chapter.

ACTIVITY—ANALYZING PRIVACY EXPECTATIONS AND PROTECTIONS

Organize students into small groups and have them consider the following questions. Each group may answer all the questions or each group can focus on one setting (home, school, work, etc.). In either case, tell students to discuss the questions and prepare to discuss their group's findings with the rest of the class.

1. What does privacy mean to you? At home? At school? At work? On the phone? In other places?
2. Why is it important to have your privacy respected and protected?

3. How would you feel if someone listened in on your phone calls, opened your mail, inspected your locker, gained access to your e-mail, or looked at your medical or tax records without your permission?

4. In what other ways can privacy be invaded?

5. To what extent do you expect privacy in each of these places or situations?

6. To what extent are your privacy rights protected in each of these places or situations?

7. How can the law protect the right to privacy?

As students prepare their group responses, ask them to formulate a list of reasons for privacy (e.g., to prevent embarrassment, to protect people from government interference in their lives, to prevent self-incrimination, etc.) and have them consider what legitimate reasons the government might have for taking actions that interfere with an individual's right to privacy (e.g., preventing crime).

With regard to the role of the law in protecting privacy, note that the law can protect the right to privacy because it allows people who believe their privacy has been violated to sue. This is known as taking a tort action. The law can also criminalize certain invasions of privacy. For example, in California it is a misdemeanor to intentionally disclose medical, psychiatric, or psychological information if the wrongful disclosure results in economic loss or personal injury for the individual to whom the information pertains.

DISCUSSION—HOW PRIVATE IS YOUR INFORMATION AND HOW MUCH DO YOU CARE?

Organize students into groups of three and ask them to discuss the following questions among themselves. Do you worry about your personal information being taken or your privacy being invaded when you:

- purchase something with a credit card?
- shop online using a credit card?
- download something from a computer?
- pass through a metal detector?
   Explain the new version of metal detectors called millimeter wave scanners, in which passengers step into a booth whose cameras can peer through their clothing to photograph the body underneath. According to the Electronic Privacy Information Center, "The image resolution is. . .

high so the picture of the body presented to screeners is detailed enough to show genitalia." The American Civil Liberties Union said "If Playboy published [those images], there would be politicians out there saying they're pornographic."[2]

- post or view something on YouTube?
   In July, 2008, a federal judge ordered YouTube to divulge to Viacom all of its log-in names and Internet Protocol addresses associated with those names. At the time, Viacom was trying to build the case that most of what is viewed on YouTube is unauthorized material that infringes on copyrights.[3]

- send an e-mail?
   E-mail can be easily intercepted by anyone with enough technical skill. Encryption programs can prevent that, but they are not used widely by individuals or by businesses, and some law enforcement officials are concerned that criminals and terrorists would use these programs to send unbreakable messages.

- search the Internet?
   "Cookies" store information that will identify the user the next time he or she visits that site. Other marketing software can track where Internet users "go" and send them advertisements or other information to entice them to buy their products.

- carry a cell phone?
   For years, consumers could buy Global Positioning System (GPS) devices that use satellites to help them pinpoint exactly where they are on a map or a trail. Smart phones take GPS further and allows users to track each other. The result is that parents can track children, spouses can track each other, employers can track employees, friends can find one another, and police can find someone who is missing quickly. The manufacturers believe that purchasers want to know how to find each other and to know where their friends and relatives "hang out." From a marketing standpoint, merchants can track potential customers and send them more targeted messages like "Angie, you are about one mile from a great restaurant, whose specials tonight include. . . " The unanswered privacy questions include: Can someone turn the technology off? Delete past information? Control who collects the information and who they share it with?[4]

Ask students whether they think different generations view issues of technology and privacy differently. Do they predict their parents, guardians, or grandparents would have the same level of concern as they have? Are their parents confounded by the level of personal information they post or read on social networking sites? Finally, ask students whether they think the government should pass more laws (or fewer) to protect privacy. If so, what should those laws say?

BACKGROUND

Two cases in which the U.S. Supreme Court had to weigh privacy interests with other compelling state interests are highlighted in the Student Edition. The case involving a government agency's requirement that contractors undergo a background check including questions about illegal drug use was *National Aeronautics and Space Administration* v. *Nelson*.[5] For more information about the Court's decision to uphold a state law requiring public notice that a convicted sex offender lives in the area (Megan's Law)[6], see Chapters 7 and 39 in this Teacher Manual.

As noted in the Student Edition, the U.S. Supreme Court began to recognize a constitutional right to privacy in the mid-1960s. The right to privacy is generally considered to derive from the 1965 U.S. Supreme Court opinion in *Griswold* v. *Connecticut*,[7] which is mentioned in detail in the section "Reproductive Rights and Privacy" in the Student Edition. The right to privacy, though not explicitly articulated in the U.S. Constitution, has generally been recognized as a substantive due process right. It is largely derived from the liberty guarantee of the due process clause of the Fifth and Fourteenth Amendments. It is based on the theory that personal liberty requires the government to respect the realm of privacy. The Court has also looked to the Third Amendment's prohibition of quartering troops in peacetime to show privacy within the home and the Fourth Amendment's guarantee against unreasonable searches as a source of privacy rights. For more on substantive due process and its relationship to the Constitution, see Chapter 39 in this Teacher Manual.

Those supporting privacy rights do not fall neatly along liberal and conservative lines. The right to privacy sometimes collides with other constitutionally protected values. Picking up on the idea that one's home is one's castle, there is strong popular antagonism against telemarketers calling people at home. In response, Congress created the National Do Not Call Registry, which is managed by the Federal Trade Commission (FTC) and the Federal Communications Commission (FCC). Among its

many provisions is one that prohibits most types of businesses from calling consumers who have registered with the FTC. However, the registry does not prohibit political organizations, charities, public opinion researchers, or companies with which registrants have an existing business relationship from calling to sell another product or service.

Violators are subject to significant fines and other penalties. While the registry was instantly hailed by many consumers and other privacy rights supporters, critics of the registry say it violates the free speech rights of businesses. These critics found support in some federal court decisions. To register a phone number on the National Do Not Call Registry or get the most, up-to-date information about the fate of the National Do Not Call Registry, visit www.donotcall.gov.

CAPTION ANSWER (P. 461)   Students' answers will vary.

PROBLEM 40.1 (p.462)

Note: If you want to give students another scenario to explore, you could ask them to consider what privacy interests are in conflict and what arguments could be made on either side about a public school policy that restricts the length of a boy's hair. Ask the students to predict the Court's answer on this question and then encourage them to research the case of *Breen* v. *Kahl*.[8] They should report on the Court's reasoning and how it compares and contrasts with their own views on the question. (This case was decided in a lower federal court, not the Supreme Court.)

Some of the situations in the student texts are based on actual cases. As you discuss the answers with students, stress that knowing the court's position is not as important as students identifying the rights and interests in conflict, providing arguments for each side, taking a stand, and supporting their positions with reasons.

Students' responses and reasons for agreeing or disagreeing with each law or policy will vary.

a. The conflict is between a taxpayer's right to be free from self-incrimination and the government's interest in collecting taxes. In 1961, the Supreme Court held that income from illegal activity is taxable and that the Internal Revenue Service (IRS) requirement that this income be reported does not violate the taxpayer's Fifth Amendment rights.[9]

b. The conflict here is between the sunbather's right to dress (or not to dress) as he or she desires, the right of others not to have to view people in the nude, and the interest of the community in establishing moral standards. Very few places in the United States allow nude sunbathing, although it is more common in some other countries.

c. The conflict here is between an inmate's right to be free from an invasion into his personal privacy (and free from cruel and unusual punishment under the Eighth Amendment) and the interests of the prison officers, administrators, and other inmates in the security of the prison. In 1979, the Supreme Court held that strip searches were not punishment and that, under certain circumstances, they were a reasonable method of assuring security in the institution.[10] However, the Court has stressed that these searches cannot be used to harass, embarrass, or degrade inmates.

d. The conflict is between the individual's freedom to ride a motorcycle unencumbered by a helmet and the state's interest in regulating use of the highways in ways reasonably designed to improve safety, reduce injury, and protect the public from higher overall insurance premiums. As of 2019, 19 states and Washington, D.C. require all riders to war helmets, 28 states have age requirements, and 3 states have no helmet laws.

e. The conflict here is between an individual's right to use the telephone free of government surveillance and the government's interest in gathering information related to criminal activity. In 1979, the Supreme Court held that telephone users do not have an expectation of privacy in the phone numbers they dial, since the telephone companies keep a record of all numbers dialed.[11]

f. The conflict here is between the emergency room doctors' need to know what medication a patient is taking in order to provide proper case and avoid adverse drug interactions and the patient's right to privacy in the medications they take. The information your doctors, nurses, and other health care providers put in your medical record is private and protected under HIPAA (*Health Insurance Portability and Accountability Act*). In addition, conversations your doctor has about your care or treatment with nurses and others is also confidential and protected under HIPAA. While you cannot be forced to share all medications, if an adverse reaction occurs as a result of

a patient's failure to disclose medications, that may negate liability on the part of the hospital or emergency room staff.

PRIVACY IN THE HOME AND IN EDUCATIONAL SETTINGS (PP. 462–464)

Learning Outcomes

After completing this section, students should be able to:

1. explain the phrase "A person's home is his or her castle.";
2. describe how the U.S. Supreme Court reversed its earlier decision involving two consenting adults who argued their privacy right to be "let alone" in their own home;
3. explain the purpose of the *Family Educational Rights and Privacy Act of 1974 (FERPA)*; and
4. describe the U.S. Supreme Court cases that have limited students' right to privacy.

BACKGROUND—PRIVACY AT HOME

While privacy in the home receives strong protection, the protection is not absolute, and society's changing attitudes toward "private" behavior may affect the Supreme Court's decisions. As noted in the Student Edition, in 1986 the Supreme Court upheld a Georgia law that made sodomy a crime punishable by up to 20 years in prison, even if that sexual activity occurred between two consenting adults in the privacy of their own home.[12] However, the Court was sharply divided in that case, known as *Bowers* v. *Hardwick*, and eventually reversed itself in 2003 in the case of *Lawrence* v. *Texas*. In the *Lawrence* case, the Court ruled that laws prohibiting private consensual sex between same-sex partners invaded the privacy and substantive due process rights of the petitioners.[13] For more information about the right to substantive due process, see Chapter 39 in this Teacher Manual. For more information about the *Lawrence* case, see Chapter 41.

CAPTION ANSWER (P. 462) Police usually need a valid search warrant in order to search a person's home.

PROBLEM 40.2 (p.463)

a. Students' answers will vary. This case is based on *Stanley* v. *Georgia*.[14] In that case, Justice Marshall said that the Georgia law was equivalent to a state asserting that it has the right to control the moral content of a person's thoughts, a philosophy wholly inconsistent with the First Amendment.

b. Students' answers will vary. Students should analyze these situations to determine how far the right to privacy should extend. The Supreme Court has limited *Stanley* to cases of private possession and use of obscene material.

c. Students' answers will vary, but charging people to view movies would most likely compromise the individual's freedom from government regulation that was recognized in this case. The Court recognizes a broader interest in the state's regulation of commercial activities (even when those activities take place in the home) than it does in an individual's private, noncommercial conduct in the home. The Court has permitted the government to prohibit the importation of obscene material for commercial distribution.[15] The Court has also upheld a state's court order to stop a commercial theater from showing obscene films, even though the patrons were restricted to adults who had notice of the nature of the films.[16]

d. In 1975, the Alaska Supreme Court reversed the conviction of an individual for possession of a small amount of marijuana at home, based on the right to privacy guaranteed in the state's constitution.[17] However, two years later the Arizona Supreme Court refused to make the same ruling, even though the right to privacy in their state's constitution is similar to Alaska's.[18] Several local jurisdictions, however, have decriminalized possession of small amounts of marijuana, making it subject only to a civil fine.

e–f. The hypothetical marijuana case is similar to the *Georgia* obscenity case in that the defendant acted in a private environment. The main difference is that reading obscene material is at least arguably a protected activity under the First Amendment, while possession of marijuana is not protected in any way by the Constitution. The U.S. Supreme Court has not yet considered a privacy defense in a marijuana possession case, but it seems unlikely that it would extend the right to privacy to such an action. The Court has refused to accept medical use of marijuana (even where it was authorized under state law) as a defense to violation of federal drug laws.[19] In 2012, Colorado legalized the use of marijuana for personal use and since then several states have followed.

BACKGROUND AND DISCUSSION— PRIVACY AT SCHOOL

Remind students of the student search case, *New Jersey* v. *TLO*.[20] In this case the school principal found evidence of marijuana use in a student's purse. The Supreme Court recognized that the student did have a reasonable expectation of privacy while at school, but upheld the search of the student's purse. This case is discussed in Chapter 12 in both the Student Edition and this Teacher Manual.

One area of school privacy law that has received significant attention in recent years is the issue of drug testing. To learn more about how the Court has interpreted the privacy rights of students, refer to the Student Edition and to the corresponding notes and activities in Chapter 12 of this Teacher Manual.

Ask students whether they agree with the purpose of the *Family Educational Rights and Privacy Act (FERPA)*[21] described in the Student Edition. Some districts routinely allow students under the age of 18 to inspect their files. Have students weigh the merits of such a policy.

In 1994, Congress passed the *Improving America's Schools Act*,[22] giving states the right to enact legislation that would allow schools to disclose education records to juvenile justice agencies in an effort to involve educators in addressing juvenile delinquency. The rules for disclosure must meet the following four criteria:

1. State law must specifically authorize the disclosure.

2. The disclosure must be to a state or local juvenile justice system agency.

3. The disclosure must relate to the juvenile justice system's ability to provide preadjudication services to students.

4. State or local officials must certify in writing that the institution or individual receiving the information has agreed not to disclose it to a third party other than another juvenile justice system

agency. With parental consent, educators can disclose information from a juvenile's education record at any time.

Ask students whether they agree or disagree with the purpose of this law.

THE CASE OF...

Peer Grading

PROBLEM 40.3 (p.464)

This problem is based on *Owasso Independent School District* v. *Falvo*[23] and relates to the *Family Education Rights and Privacy Act (FERPA)*.[24] *FERPA* is a series of laws meant to protect schoolchildren's privacy. The act protects the release of education records or personally identifiable information in the records. Records also usually include grade books and administrative papers. To gain certain information under the act, written consent must be provided by the parents. To change information on records, parents may ask for a hearing, or a formal meeting where the school and the parents, together with their lawyers and a neutral person, will decide what the records should say.

In this case, Mrs. Falvo was particularly concerned about her son Phillip, who received special education support for speech and language problems in addition to his regular classroom instruction. Mrs. Falvo was concerned that Phillip would be embarrassed by peer grading, and she believed that *FERPA* protects the grades on assignments.

Encourage students to debate the issues highlighted in this case. Should students have a right to privacy regarding their grades? Even on individual assignments? Do the benefits of peer grading (such as immediate feedback and the opportunity to review answers again) outweigh the loss of privacy?

Ask students whether they think *FERPA* applies to a situation like the one in this case.

a. Students' answers will vary. *FERPA* applies only to school records and protects the release of these records (i.e., protects the privacy interest in school records). Grades on in-class assignments would not be protected by *FERPA* unless that particular assignment is part of a school record. (This was the issue before the Supreme Court in this case.)

b. Students' opinions will vary. Justice Kennedy wrote the unanimous opinion that held that

student assignments are not considered education records under *FERPA*. A student's privacy rights are not violated under *FERPA* by peer grading or by calling out the grades in class. A student is not acting for the school when he or she is grading another student's paper. Under the language of *FERPA*, this means that assignments are not "education records" because they are not "maintained" by the school administration; they are maintained by the teacher. Education records are limited to those documents that are held in a central place at the school.

INFORMATION GATHERING AND PRIVACY (PP. 464–466)

Learning Outcomes

After completing this section, students should be able to:

1. describe how the right to privacy is being challenged by technology, especially newer technologies; and
2. explain the privacy protections and requirements of the *Privacy Act of 1974*, including remedies if the government violates a person's rights under this law.

BACKGROUND—THE *RIGHT TO FINANCIAL PRIVACY ACT*

The *Privacy Act of 1974*[25] and other statutes and case laws protect a person's general right to privacy by prohibiting the government from releasing certain personal information without that person's consent.

A concern among a growing number of people is the privacy of their financial transactions with banks, credit unions, savings and loans, and credit card companies. As far back as 1976, in *United States* v. *Miller* the Court held that a bank depositor had no reasonable expectation of privacy for checks and deposit slips in large part because the bank, not the depositor, holds that documentation. In response, Congress passed the *Right to Financial Privacy Act (1978)*,[26] giving federal government officials access to consumer financial records in certain situations, such as when the customer gives permission, or when the government obtains an administrative or judicial subpoena or search warrant.

The *USA PATRIOT Act* amended the RFPA. See Chapter 44 of the Student Edition and in this Teacher Manual.

BACKGROUND—THE *FREEDOM OF INFORMATION ACT (FOIA)*

The *Freedom of Information Act (FOIA)* establishes procedures that the federal government must follow when the public seeks information.[27] The basic purpose of the act is to provide the public with certain information gathered and held by the federal government. However, the act, originally passed in 1967 and amended several times since then, excludes nine types of information, including personnel and medical files, "the disclosure of which would constitute a clearly unwarranted invasion of personal privacy."[28] For more information about *FOIA*, see Chapter 36 of this Teacher Manual.

An attorney who handles *FOIA* cases would be a good resource person for a discussion of why this law was passed and how it has been used by citizens to learn more about the information the U.S. government collects.

BACKGROUND—ELECTRONIC COMMUNICATIONS AND PRIVACY

The *Electronic Communications Privacy Act*[29] prohibits the government from accessing or reading e-mail unless it is in conjunction with routine maintenance or by court order. In addition, third parties are prohibited from reading e-mail unless it is on an internal network, such as in an office. This means that employers may read and monitor their employees' e-mail, and school personnel can access information created on school computers.

Students may be familiar with some of the privacy issues related to the Internet, especially those who spend a lot of time online at home or at school. The rising number of electronic databases and the increasing frequency of Internet usage have added to concerns about privacy. In Oregon, for example, someone posted state license plate numbers on the Internet, enabling anyone to identify a vehicle's registered owner. In another case, an officer was discharged from the Navy when an employee of America Online disclosed the officer's identity and sexual orientation to a Navy investigator. After suing the Navy and America Online for violating his right to privacy, the officer received money damages and military retirement with full benefits.[30]

The *USA PATRIOT Act* was passed in an effort to improve national security after the terrorist attacks of September 11, 2001. The act made numerous changes to the amount of privacy citizens can expect when they are using computers in their homes, at work, and at public libraries.[31] See Chapter 44 of the Student Edition and this Teacher Manual for more information.

THE **CASE** OF...

The Police Officers' Texts

PROBLEM 40.4 (p.466)

This case is based on the 2010 case *City of Ontario* v. *Quon*.[32] After the Chief of the Ontario Police Department discovered that a number of officers had exceeded the limits on their department issued pagers, further investigation occurred. It was discovered that a number of the pages sent were not work-related, and some were sexually explicit. Quon, one of the officers, was disciplined. Quon then sued the department and city for violation of his Fourth Amendment right against unreasonable searches and seizures. However, the U.S. Supreme Court ruled that because the pager was issued by the department, and the search of the pager messages was work-related, the search was reasonable. The Court ruled that no violation of the Fourth Amendment occurred in this case.

a. The police department conducted a search of pager messages made by officers who had exceeded the monthly texting limit of their pagers.

b. Students' answers will vary. According to the Court in *Quon*, the officers did not have a reasonable expectation of privacy because the pager was issued by the department for work-related use. Therefore, the officers should have known that use of the pagers would be monitored and messages reviewed.

c. Students' answers will vary. The police department had good reason to review the texts in order to determine if they needed to increase the texting limits for the officers. Because the intent of the search was work-related and the warrantless search itself was reasonable, all information uncovered in the process of that search is deemed reasonably obtained as well.

REPRODUCTIVE RIGHTS AND PRIVACY (PP. 466–468)

Learning Outcomes

After completing this section, students should be able to:

1. describe key decisions about contraception made by the U.S. Supreme Court in 1965 and in 1972;

2. explain how the issue of privacy pertains to constitutional questions involving contraception and abortion;

3. describe how the trimesters of pregnancy determine the right to abortion as defined by the *Roe* v. *Wade* decision;

4. summarize U.S. Supreme Court decisions on abortion since *Roe* v. *Wade* with regard to laws that might require the consent of the father of the fetus or of the parents of pregnant minors;

5. describe the U.S. Supreme Court decision in *Planned Parenthood of Southeastern Pennsylvania* v. *Casey*; and

6. describe how the issue of abortion has affected appointments to federal courts and how it has affected elections.

Note: Abortion, possibly the most divisive health law issue, continues to be controversial in state and federal courts and legislatures.

Consult with the principal or school district officials to determine whether there are any policies that restrict or guide classroom discussion of the abortion issue. Great care and sensitivity are needed in teaching these issues. The goal should be to bring out both sides of the issue, identify reasoning that supports each position, and explain the current state of the law. You will need to explore current state law on the issue.

BACKGROUND—PRIVACY RIGHTS, BIRTH CONTROL, AND CONTRACEPTION

The 1965 case mentioned in the Student Edition is *Griswold* v. *Connecticut*. In that case, the executive director and medical director of Connecticut's Planned Parenthood League had been convicted for giving information on contraception to married persons under a state law prohibiting any persons from using a "drug, medicinal article or instrument for the purposes of preventing conception." In reversing the conviction, Justice Douglas spelled out the

origins of the right to privacy and noted that the state law impinged on the "intimate relation of husband and wife and their physician's role in one aspect of that relation."[33]

The 1972 case mentioned on the same page is *Eisenstadt* v. *Baird*,[34] which declared unconstitutional a law prohibiting the sale of birth control to unmarried people. The U.S. Supreme Court has affirmed that there is a constitutional right to procreate.[35] It has also upheld the right of a doctor to provide contraceptive information.[36] In 1977, the U.S. Supreme Court ruled that a New York law prohibiting the sale of contraceptives to minors was unconstitutional.[37]

BACKGROUND AND ACTIVITY—*ROE* V. *WADE*

Street Law, Inc., recognizes that teaching about controversial public policy questions can be challenging. However, properly done, such lessons help students learn vital skills to help them consider public policy deeply and to engage in public policy discussions in a civil way. Teachers who are interested in balanced materials, resources, lesson plans, and background materials about key Supreme Court decisions about controversial issues (including the *Roe* v. *Wade* decision) should go to www.landmarkcases.org. The content on the site is written by Street Law, Inc., with funding from the Supreme Court Historical Society.

The material is available free of charge and contains links to oral arguments and decisions, as well as information about the impact of *Roe* since the decision.

BACKGROUND—ABORTION LAW

After students have read about the Court's decision in *Roe* v. *Wade*,[38] ask them to hypothesize about why the Court concluded a woman has a constitutional right to an abortion, but that the government may regulate that right more as the pregnancy progresses. The issue is one of viability. In 1973, the Court weighed the privacy right to an abortion with the right of an unborn baby by using then-current scientific evidence regarding the point at which a baby could survive outside the womb. At that time fetal viability became possible in the third trimester.

Nearly 20 years—and many technological advances—later when the Court ruled in the *Casey* case, it rejected the trimester framework and the essentially absolute right to an abortion in the first and second trimesters that had been recognized in

Roe. Instead the Court adopted a viability test, holding that the government's interest in life outweighed the mother's right to an abortion at the point at which a fetus is viable outside the womb. This ruling concerns proponents of the right to abortion because advances in technology constantly redefine the point of viability.

The most recent developments have focused on efforts in many states to regulate late-term abortions. A Nebraska statute was the first law to reach the U.S. Supreme Court, in the case of *Stenberg* v. *Carhart.*[39] This law banned late-term abortions except when necessary to preserve the life of the mother. The law was challenged based on the argument that the statute failed to include an exception for protecting the health of the mother and because the definition of the procedure was ambiguous and could also apply to other commonly used early-term abortion techniques. The Court struck down the law on the basis that it did not allow an exception for late-term abortion where necessary to protect the health of the mother.

To some, Justice O'Connor's concurrence seemed to be a road map for how the government might constitutionally limit late-term abortions, namely by providing an exception for the life and health of the mother. As mentioned in the Student Edition, in 2007 the Supreme Court found that a federal law that criminalized late-term abortions was not a violation of the Constitution.[40]

Perhaps because society is so divided over the scientific, legal, moral, and political issues entwined with the right to privacy and its relationship to the right to an abortion, there will always be attempts to limit and to extend legal protections for abortion procedures.

CAPTION ANSWER (P. 466) Abortion is such a controversial issue because it goes to the core of people's values. Opponents of abortion believe that life begins at conception. They feel that the life of a defenseless, unborn child should be protected. Those who support abortion argue that it is a constitutional right and a private matter to be decided by the woman.

DISCUSSION—GOVERNMENT FUNDING OF ABORTION

The U.S. Supreme Court has held that neither a state nor the federal government is obligated, under the Constitution, to pay for abortions.[41] The Court upheld the *Hyde Amendment,* which said that no federal money that would otherwise pay for medical services for the indigent could be used to fund abortions. However, the funds could be used for most other medical services, including prenatal care and childbirth. Some critics argued that the *Hyde Amendment* indirectly allowed the federal government and the states to violate a woman's constitutional right to abortion established in *Roe* v. *Wade.* [42] The Supreme Court rejected this argument. It ruled that the decision is up to legislatures, and there is no constitutional right to a free abortion. The Supreme Court has held that the government may express its preference for life in choosing not to subsidize abortions.

Ask students what freedom of choice means for a woman who cannot afford an abortion. Some people argue that if the government will not fund abortions for poor women, then it must offer more services for poor mothers and their children. On the other hand, many people are morally opposed to abortion. Ask students whether the public should have to pay for a procedure that many people oppose on moral grounds.

PROBLEM 40.5 (p.467)

a. Students' answers will vary. Abortion is a controversial issue because it involves people's deeply held values and often religious beliefs. Those who oppose abortion uphold the sanctity of the life of the fetus. Those who support abortion value a woman's right to choose, to control her reproduction, and to bring children into the world when and if she is ready to be a parent. It is difficult to identify compromise positions in this area.

b. Students' answers will vary.

c. The advantages of parental consent laws are that when parents are included in such a significant and difficult decision and medical procedure, they can help guide their daughter in making the right decision, ensure proper follow-up care and support, and provide financial assistance.

   The disadvantages of parental consent laws include that a young woman who has a difficult relationship with her parent(s) may experience further strain on the relationship. Some people think a young woman should be able to make this private decision without parental interference. Others worry about the physical and emotional consequences to young women (and their babies) if parents attempt to prevent an abortion that the daughter wishes to have.

PROBLEM 40.6 (p.468)

a. Those who support such a law would argue that the father has rights as well as the mother. In 1976 the Court held that states cannot give a husband veto power over his wife's decision to have an abortion. This type of veto power places an undue burden on a person who wishes to obtain an abortion. It restricts the woman who is carrying a fetus from making decisions concerning her body. The Court also feared that women who suffered from spouse abuse would be hindered from getting an abortion.[43]

b. As noted in the discussion notes about government funding of abortion, the courts have said that the right to have an abortion is not the same as the right to obtain a free abortion if one is poor. The inability of poor women to obtain an abortion has not been seen by the courts as the government imposing an undue burden on obtaining an abortion.[44]

c. This question is based on the case of *Planned Parenthood of Southeastern Pennsylvania* v. *Casey*. In that case, the petitioners challenged Pennsylvania's abortion statute requiring women undergoing an abortion procedure to give certain information prior to the procedure, to give an informed consent, and to wait 24 hours except in the case of medical emergency. The Supreme Court held that the law did not violate the Constitution by creating an undue burden on women seeking an abortion. Three of the seven justices said that these requirements do not constitute an undue burden. The other four justices expressed the view that the waiting period reasonably furthered the state's interest in assuring that a woman's consent was fully informed.[45]

d. Remind students that parental consent is typically required before doctors provide any medical care to minor children. One exception is in the case of an emergency. In 1979, the Supreme Court ruled that the type of law described in this question places an undue burden on unwed minors to get consent from one or both parents. The state must provide alternate procedures for obtaining authorization.[46] In two 1990 cases, the Court further considered the issue of parental

consent for minors. While generally continuing to allow states greater discretion to legislate in this area, the Court found that some parental consent laws may place an undue burden on a woman's right to obtain an abortion, unless the state establishes a "judicial bypass" provision, allowing consent to be obtained from a judge who would hear the case and make a decision in place of a minor's parents.[47]

e. This requirement was upheld in the 1983 case of *Planned Parenthood* v. *Ashcroft*[48] in which the Court held parental consent requirements constitutional so long as they meet certain conditions. The Court said that a law can only require parental permission if: (1) there is a mechanism to allow the unmarried minor to establish that she is mature enough to make the decision on her own; (2) there is some judicial review involved; and (3) it is in her best interests. This view was also upheld in the 1992 *Casey* decision.[49]

f. This requirement was struck down in a 5–3 decision in *Whole Woman's Health* v. *Hellerstedt*[50]. The Court stated that the medical benefits gained by requiring the admitting privileges did not outweigh the "substantial burden" imposed on women seeking to exercise their constitutional right to choose an abortion. They based this on the fact that only 7 or 8 clinics in the entire state would be able to function if these restrictions went into place. At the time of publication, the Supreme Court is considering a similar case, *June Medical Services LLC v. Gee*[51]. This case challenges a Louisiana statute requiring physicians who perform abortions to have admitting privileges at a local hospital.

NOTES

(1) *Olmstead* v. *United States*, 277 U.S. 438 (1928).

(2) Akers, Becky. "Get Ready To Strip at Reagan National." *Washington Post*, June 22, 2008.

(3) Menn, Joseph and Jessica Guynn. "Ruling Against YouTube Worries Privacy Advocates." *Los Angeles Times*, July 4, 2008.

(4) Nakashima, Ellen. "When the Phone Goes With You, Everything Else Can Tag Along." *Washington Post*, July 12, 2008, p. A1.

(5) *National Aeronautics and Space Administration* v. *Nelson*, 562 U.S. ___ (2011).

(6) *Connecticut Dept. of Public Safety* v. *Doe*, 538 U.S. 1 (2003).

(7) *Griswold* v. *Connecticut*, 381 U.S. 479 (1965).

(8) *Breen* v. *Kahl*, 296 F.Supp. 702 (W.D. Wisc. 1969), aff'd 419 F.2d 1034 (7th Cir.) (1969).

(9) *James* v. *United States*, 366 U.S. 213 (1961).

(10) *Bell* v. *Wolfish*, 441 U.S. 520 (1979).

(11) *Smith* v. *Maryland*, 442 U.S. 735 (1979).

(12) *Bowers* v. *Hardwick*, 478 U.S. 186 (1986).

(13) *Lawrence* v. *Texas*, 539 U.S. 558 (2003).

(14) *Stanley* v. *Georgia*, 394 U.S. 557 (1969).

(15) *U.S.* v. *Thirty-Seven Photographs*, 402 U.S. 363 (1971).

(16) *Paris Adult Theatre* v. *Slaton*, 413 U.S. 49 (1973).

(17) *Ravin* v. *State*, 537 P.2d 494 (Alaska 1975).

(18) *State* v. *Murphy*, 570 P.2d 1070 (Arizona 1977).

(19) *United States* v. *Oakland Cannabis Buyers' Coop.*, 532 U.S. 483 (2001).

(20) *New Jersey* v. *T.L.O.*, 469 U.S. 325 (1985).

(21) *Family Educational Rights and Privacy Act*, Pub. L., No. 93-380, 88 Stat. 571 (1974).

(22) *Improving America's Schools Act*, Pub. L., No. 103–382, 108 Stat. 3518 (1994).

(23) *Owasso Independent School District* v. *Falvo*, 534 U.S. 426 (2002).

(24) *Family Education Rights and Privacy Act (FERPA)*, 20 U.S.C. § 1232 g.

(25) *Privacy Act of 1974*, 5 U.S.C. § 552(a) (2000)

(26) *United States* v. *Miller*, 425 U.S. 435 (1976), and the *Right to Financial Privacy Act*, 12 U.S.C. § 3402.

(27) *Freedom of Information Act (FOIA)*, 5 U.S.C. § 552 (1988).

(28) Id.; see also *U.S. Department of State* v. *Washington Post Company*, 456 U.S. 595 (1982).

(29) *Electronic Communications Privacy Act*, 18 U.S.C. § 2701 (1986).

(30) *McVeigh* v. *Cohen*, 983 F.Supp. 215 (D.D.C. 1998).

(31) United States, 107th Congress, *Uniting and Strengthening America by Providing Appropriate Tools Required to Intercept and Obstruct Terrorism Act (USA PATRIOT Act)* (2001). Online posting, U.S. Department of Justice www.justice.gov.

(32) *City of Ontario* v. *Quon*, 560 U.S. 746 (2010).

(33) *Griswold* v. *Connecticut*, 381 U.S. 479 (1965).

(34) *Eisenstadt* v. *Baird*, 405 U.S. 438 (1972).

(35) *Skinner* v. *Oklahoma ex rel. Williamson*, 316 U.S. 535 (1942).

(36) *Griswold* v. *Connecticut*, 381 U.S. 479 (1965).

(37) *Carey* v. *Population Services Int'l.*, 431 U.S. 678 (1977).

(38) *Roe* v. *Wade*, 410 U.S. 113 (1973).

(39) *Stenberg* v. *Carhart*, 530 U.S. 914 (2000).

(40) *Gonzales* v. *Carhart*, 550 U.S. (2007).

(41) *Harris* v. *McRae*, 448 U.S. 297 (1980).

(42) *Roe* v. *Wade*, 410 U.S. 113 (1973).

(43) *Planned Parenthood of Central Missouri* v. *Danforth*, 428 U.S. 52 (1976).

(44) *Harris* v. *McRae*, 448 U.S. 297 (1980).

(45) *Planned Parenthood of Southeastern Pennsylvania* v. *Casey*, 505 U.S. 833 (1992).

(46) *Bellotti* v. *Baird*, 443 U.S. 622 (1979).

(47) *Ohio* v. *Akron Center for Reproductive Health*, 497 U.S. 502 (1990); and *Hodgson* v. *Minnesota*, 497 U.S. 417 (1990).

(48) *Planned Parenthood* v. *Ashcroft*, 462 U.S. 476 (1983).

(49) *Planned Parenthood of Southeastern Pennsylvania* v. *Casey*, 505 U.S. 833 (1992).

(50) *Whole Woman's Health* v. *Hellerstedt*, 136 S.Ct. 2292 (2016).

(51) *June Medical Services LLC* v. *Gee*, 586 U. S. ____ (2019).

INTRODUCTION (PP. 469–471)

Learning Outcomes

After completing this section, students should be able to:
1. describe different ways of defining *equality*;
2. compare and contrast the U.S. Supreme Court decisions in *Plessy* v. *Ferguson* and *Brown* v. *Board of Education* and their power to prohibit and to promote equality;
3. give examples of how the government may respond to discrimination;
4. identify examples of civil rights laws and programs that collide with each other;
5. explain how discrimination can harm all Americans—not just its targets; and
6. define the terms *Jim Crow laws* and *national origin*.

DISCUSSION—EQUAL PROTECTION

Post the following quote from U.S. Supreme Court Justice John Marshall Harlan on the board: "In respect to civil rights, all citizens are equal before the law. The humblest is the peer of the most powerful." Ask students whether they agree with the view Justice Harlan expressed in his dissent in the case of *Plessy* v. *Ferguson*.[1] Have students write about this issue, both before and after they study Chapter 41.

Discuss with students what some have described as the relationship between people's hearts and society's laws. Instruct students to examine the Fourteenth Amendment and try to identify the equal protection clause ("No State shall . . . deny to any person within its jurisdiction the equal protection of the laws."). Then, have students consider the quote from the Declaration of Independence that appears in the Chapter 41 opener in the Student Edition. Ask students which must come first, fair laws or a commonly felt commitment to equal opportunity. How might this question be seen as analogous to the conundrum "Which came first, the chicken or the egg?"

Discuss with students the importance of enforcing just laws. Remind students that the Thirteenth, Fourteenth, and Fifteenth Amendments, as well as numerous laws, were intended to guarantee equal opportunity and equal protection, but they were not enforced for decades. This discussion offers an opportunity to reinforce the relationship among the three branches of government. If laws are not enforced, they mean very little. Ask students to think about where discrimination takes place now and where it has taken place in our country's history. (*They may say discrimination has*

Although the promise of equality set forth in the Declaration of Independence is one of the most ambitious ideals of the United States, the question of just what equality means is not answered simply. Does it mean that everyone receives the same treatment? Or does it mean that everyone has equal opportunities? To the extent that neither treatment nor opportunities are equal, individuals and institutions in society must decide how to respond to the challenges of discrimination in a way that is effective and fair to all. The government may respond to discrimination through laws, regulations, amendments, and court decisions. The Thirteenth, Fourteenth, and Fifteenth Amendments to the Constitution were ratified in attempts to make greater equality a reality. U.S. Supreme Court decisions have brought dramatic changes that helped to stop discrimination.

played out in voting booths, on athletic fields, in public spaces, in workplaces, in neighborhoods, etc.)

Then ask students to brainstorm how American society might be different today if we had never had discrimination based on race, national origin, citizenship status, gender, religion, sexual orientation, age, or disability. How has our history of discrimination and the struggles to correct it shaped the character of modern society?

BACKGROUND—STATE ACTION AND EQUAL PROTECTION

This chapter presents material on the Fourteenth Amendment's equal protection clause. For background material on the historical context of the clause and its framers, refer to Chapter 39 of this Teacher Manual. Remember that "state action" must be present for the Fourteenth Amendment to apply.

Receiving federal money may cause a private institute to be treated as a state actor and therefore subject to the Fourteenth Amendment and other laws guaranteeing equal protection by the government. For example, most private universities must ensure that their affirmative action policies conform to constitutionally permissible guidelines because they receive federal financial aid and education funding programs.

Some of the most pernicious forms of discrimination have come from private actors. Congress and state and local legislatures have had to be particularly creative in crafting anti-discrimination legislation that is constitutional. For example, segregation in restaurants and hotels throughout the country was once a major problem. However, these policies were generally perpetuated by the private owners of these businesses, placing them outside the reach of the Fourteenth Amendment. In outlawing segregation in these establishments, Congress relied on its powers under the commerce clause. The U.S. Supreme Court upheld such laws, accepting the rationale that segregation had an adverse effect on interstate commerce because it discouraged minorities from traveling.[2] Major federal civil rights laws are summarized in the Appendix of the Student Edition. There is also extensive legislation at the state and sometimes the local level.

ACTIVITY—RESEARCH: WHEN THE SUPREME COURT CHANGES COURSE

To illustrate that the Supreme Court sometimes directly overrules precedent, have students read about the decision in *Plessy* v. *Ferguson*,[3] the case which upheld the "separate but equal" doctrine

which was subsequently overturned by *Brown* v. *Board of Education*.[4] After *Brown*, the Court also found segregation to be unconstitutional in public facilities such as beaches, buses, golf courses, courtrooms, and prisons.[5]

Information and support for teaching about the *Brown* and *Plessy* cases is available online at www.landmarkcases.org. This site was developed by the Supreme Court Historical Society and by Street Law, Inc. It includes case summaries, primary source materials, political cartoons, links to the Court's decisions and to audio recordings, as well as lesson plans and reading materials geared to students of various reading abilities.

There is continuing controversy over the nature of acceptable affirmative action programs. These plans, either voluntary or mandatory, are designed to undo the continuing effects of past discrimination and to promote diversity in the future. The Supreme Court's 2003 affirmative action decisions concerning programs at the University of Michigan undergraduate programs and law school are described in the Student Edition and treated in further detail later in this chapter of the Teacher Manual.[6]

CAPTION ANSWER (P. 470) Thurgood Marshall argued against separating schoolchildren by race, asserting that segregation is inherently unequal. He stated that equal facilities did not characterize the practice of Jim Crow laws anywhere in the United States.

ACTIVITY—CONNECTING *KOREMATSU* AND *BROWN* IN HISTORY

In addition to the connections between the *Brown* case and the history of slavery, racial discrimination, and the civil rights movement, *Brown* is also an excellent opportunity for students to research and study both the internal and external politics at work on the U.S. Supreme Court. Have students research Earl Warren's appointment to the Court shortly before the *Brown* case was heard and his campaign to secure a unanimous decision. Students may be interested to learn that Warren was nominated to the Court as part of a political deal with President Eisenhower, who did not expect that Warren would fight for desegregation. Guide students in researching Warren's role in the Japanese internment during World War II and how it contrasts with his position on the desegregation of schools.

Students might also research topics comparing and contrasting the Court's decision in *Korematsu* v. *United States*[7] (upholding the policy of Japanese internment) and the Court's decision in *Brown*. (To learn more about both cases, including lesson plans for teaching about them, consult www.landmarkcases.org.) Students may debate whether national

41.1 TM Figure

Test	When is this test used?	Who must prove what under this test?
Rational Basis Test		
Substantial Relationship Test (also known as the Intermediate Scrutiny Test)		
Strict Scrutiny Test		

security is a compelling state interest that justifies treating racial minorities, people of particular ethnicities, or people who immigrate from certain countries differently. These issues have received considerable attention since the terrorist attacks of September 11, 2001.

WHAT IS DISCRIMINATION? (PP. 471–474)

Learning Outcomes

After completing this section, students should be able to:

1. define the term *discrimination*;
2. give examples of laws that discriminate but are reasonable and constitutional;
3. describe the rational basis test and how it is applied to determine if a law or practice is constitutional;
4. explain the strict scrutiny test and the types of discrimination cases judges apply it to;
5. identify two requirements of the substantial relationship test and name the type of discrimination cases to which it is typically applied; and
6. explain the equal protection clause of the Fourteenth Amendment.

ACTIVITY—IDENTIFYING LEGAL VERSUS ILLEGAL DISCRIMINATION

Post this excerpt of the Fourteenth Amendment and questions a.–b. on the board:

"No State shall . . . deny to any person within its jurisdiction the equal protection of the laws."

Does treating people equally mean treating them the same? What is discrimination? Have students write responses to the questions and then discuss

them as a class. In the large group discussion, ask students:

- Do you think that treating people equally means sometimes treating them differently? For example, to make sure disabled students have access to a public education, we provide special accommodations such as ramps or additional staff.
- Can you think of examples of discrimination that are not necessarily negative or unfair?

Tell students that *discrimination* means choosing or distinguishing between two or more things based on some criteria. Individuals, groups, institutions, and governments discriminate all the time. The problem arises when discrimination is unfair and illegal. The focus of this section is how the government and the courts determine what types of government discrimination are fair and legal.

After students have read about the rational basis, strict scrutiny, and substantial relationship tests in the Student Edition, ask them which test is "easier" on the government. In other words, if the government takes an action or passes a law that is challenged in court because someone thinks it violates the equal protection clause, which test would the government rather have the courts apply? *The rational basis test provides the lowest amount of protection against discrimination.*

Which test is "hardest," or offers the most protection against discrimination? *The strict scrutiny test is hardest to win.*

To review these equal protection tests, ask students to create a chart like the one shown in **41.1 TM Figure** above. Then ask students to fill it in, applying what they have learned in this section of the chapter.

CAPTION ANSWER (P. 472) Judges will uphold a law or practice that treats some people differently than others if there is a rational basis for the differential treatment or classification.

A rational basis exists when there is a logical relationship between the treatment or classification and the purpose of the law.

BACKGROUND—REASONABLE VERSUS UNREASONABLE DISCRIMINATION

After reading the material on equal protection tests in the Student Edition, students should begin to see that courts will not allow discrimination against certain categories of people unless the circumstances are exceptional. These protected classes of people (categorized by race, national origin, immigration status, or gender) have traditionally been viewed by the courts as politically powerless. In addition, these personal characteristics have been considered by the courts as unlikely to reflect on one's individual abilities. The courts do not treat age as a protected classification, although a federal law protects against age discrimination in employment. While no federal law forbids discrimination based on sexual orientation, state and local governments are beginning to provide legal protections.

The "beer sales to males" case referred to in the discussion of the substantial relationship test in the Student Edition is *Craig* v. *Boren*.[8] The Supreme Court case mentioned in the Student Edition that declared unconstitutional the Virginia law that prohibited interracial marriage is *Loving* v. *Virginia*.[9]

CAPTION ANSWER (P. 473) Equal protection cases are controversial because there are different beliefs about which groups of people the Fourteenth Amendment was meant to protect. Some people argue that when the Fourteenth Amendment was ratified in 1868, Congress intended it to protect only against racial discrimination. Others argue that it was intended to protect only African Americans against discrimination, and that other racial minorities, women, or whites are not protected. Still others claim that the Fourteenth Amendment embodies the national commitment to the fundamental value of equality, and that all unfair forms of government discrimination should be prohibited by the equal protection clause.

PROBLEM 41.1 (p.474)

This problem requires students to make a judgment about the reasonableness of particular forms of discrimination and to support their decisions with reasons. In discussing the problem, make some generalizations about reasonable and unreasonable discrimination (e.g., discrimination based on gender is often rooted in stereotypes that deny an individual equal opportunity and therefore is unreasonable). Some of these situations are based on actual cases, but students should focus on what is reasonable rather than on what a court may have decided.

a. Courts would probably uphold this discrimination based on the notion that people lose certain reflexes as they get older and may endanger the safety of themselves or others. This case is similar to "The Case of the Forced Retirement" in the Student Edition. However, the legal analysis in this case is troubling. Some individuals are perfectly capable of piloting a plane after age 60 and some are incapable of doing so before age 60.

b. This seems to be unreasonable discrimination based on gender stereotyping.

c. This discrimination based on disability appears unreasonable. The health concerns associated with HIV and its transmission do not apply to working as a prison guard.

d. Discrimination based on age for admission to certain films has been upheld as a reasonable form of discrimination.

e. This is clearly unreasonable discrimination. The *Rehabilitation Act of 1973* and the *Americans with Disabilities Act*[10] prohibit discrimination based on a disability.

f. In *Personnel Administrator* v. *Feeney*, the Supreme Court ruled 7 to 2 that state laws giving veterans absolute and permanent preference in hiring are not gender-based discrimination.[11] The Court reasoned that such laws merely draw a distinction between veterans and nonveterans. Since veterans are both male and female, the Court found no gender-based discrimination. Veterans' preference rules are specifically exempt from *Title VII* of the *Civil Rights Act of 1964*.

g. *Title IX* allows the federal government to cut off aid to schools that discriminate on the basis of gender. Therefore, the school would have to start a girls' team or let girls try out for the boys' team.

h. This discrimination is legal even though some young, unmarried persons are safer drivers than some older, married persons. Instead, rates are based on statistics drawn from the accident rates of large numbers of drivers of various ages. Also, insurance companies are private businesses, so the Fourteenth Amendment would not apply.

i. This is unreasonable discrimination. Employers may hire on the basis of gender only when it is reasonably necessary to the normal operation of the employer's business. Projecting a classy image by having only male servers wear tuxedos (and therefore hiring only males) is not reasonably necessary to the normal operation of the business and constitutes illegal gender discrimination.

DISCRIMINATION BASED ON RACE (PP. 474–484)

Learning Outcomes

After completing this section, students should be able to:

1. identify at least four complex questions raised as government seeks to help Americans who are subject to, or affected by, racial discrimination;
2. summarize the arguments for and against busing as a remedy for discrimination in public schools;
3. evaluate the merits of affirmative action as a remedy for discrimination and as a method for promoting diversity in schools and in the workplace;
4. identify trends in U.S. Supreme Court decisions related to affirmative action in education;
5. identify and explain the provisions of constitutional amendments and significant federal legislation that expanded voting rights;
6. explain the arguments for and against gerrymandering in order to create majority-minority legislative districts; and
7. define the terms *remedy, affirmative action, certiorari,* and *gerrymandering.*

BACKGROUND—RACIAL DISCRIMINATION CASES

The case referred to in the Student Edition in which the Court upheld the town's refusal to rezone land was *Arlington Heights (Ill.) v. Metropolitan Housing Development Corporation.*[12] The first busing case to reach the U.S. Supreme Court was *Swann v. Charlotte Mecklenburg Board of Education,* in which the Court acknowledged that busing was one possible method that lower courts could use to end school desegregation.[13]

DISCUSSION—TENSION AMONG THE THREE BRANCHES AND BETWEEN STATES AND THE FEDERAL GOVERNMENT

The three branches of government established by the U.S. Constitution have distinct roles—making the laws (legislative); interpreting the laws (judicial); and enforcing the laws as made and interpreted

(executive). However, this relationship can break down in the face of a court opinion that is politically unpopular (as the *Brown* decision was in many communities that resisted the notion of desegregation).

Perhaps the most notorious example of this breakdown occurred when President Andrew Jackson ousted Native Americans from their land and forced them to endure the Trail of Tears in outright defiance of a U.S. Supreme Court decision favoring the Native Americans' position.[14] In the 1950s and 1960s—aware that there would be fierce resistance to integration and that communities would need time to develop workable plans—the Court instructed state government and local officials to implement desegregation with "all deliberate speed."[15]

Some people believed this approach was the only way to make compliance with the Court decision feasible; others argued that the ambiguous language gave many school districts license to drag their heels and abandon any genuine attempt at desegregation. Eventually desegregation was achieved when Congress threatened to withhold federal funding from segregated schools under the *Civil Rights Act of 1964. Title IV* of the act empowered the attorney general to file a civil suit on behalf of parents whose children were being denied equal protection of the laws.

Additionally, with *Title VI*'s prohibition on segregation in any program or activity receiving federal money, states could not afford exclusion from unprecedented, lavish funding.

Some people, even some who believe in desegregation, have asserted that the Supreme Court did not have the authority to desegregate schools and other public facilities. They say that the Court was not really interpreting the Constitution but instead was substituting its policy preference for that of the legislature, which had chosen not to outlaw segregation. Ask students which is the proper government body for making such decisions.

Have students list arguments for and against each branch's authority and each level of government's authority in the area of desegregation.

Arguments for the Court include the fact that the legislative process was too slow; the majority should not be allowed to dictate the rights of the minority; and courts must step in to correct flaws in the process that prevent disfavored political groups from combating abuse. Arguments for the legislature include the idea that the Court is given too much power when it invalidates laws without a sound constitutional rationale for doing so; policy decisions should be made by democratic means in a democracy; and Court-imposed solutions to social ills fail to get to the heart of the issue and threaten to exacerbate tensions.

BACKGROUND AND DISCUSSION— SEGREGATION AND SCHOOLS

Discuss methods used to desegregate schools when residential patterns produce schools that are not well integrated. To give historical context, review the *Plessy* and *Brown* cases and the responses in many states to the desegregation orders that followed. Prince Edward County, Virginia, for example, closed its schools altogether for five years rather than integrate.[16] In many areas, white parents sent their children to private schools, which seriously compromised the nationwide desegregation of public schools. Ongoing housing discrimination continues to exacerbate the problem.

The Brown Foundation has prepared and posted extensive materials about the case at www.brownvboard.org. You will also find information and support for teaching about the *Brown* and *Plessy* cases at www.landmarkcases.org.

PROBLEM 41.2 (p.476)

a. Students' answers will vary. Students who think the government should do more to integrate schools should propose government programs to encourage greater integration. Students who do not think the government should take more steps to integrate public schools should give their reasons why it should not.

b. Students may argue that a school that has at its core one minority group may best address cultural issues and build knowledge and skills for that group's students. Alternatively, students may argue that separating people of different races can never be good because students need to learn to live and work together in an integrated society.

THE CASE OF...

Affirmative Action in Higher Education

PROBLEM 41.3 (p.478–479)

This problem is based on two cases that were decided by the U.S. Supreme Court in 2003 involving separate challenges to the University of Michigan's undergraduate admissions policy (*Gratz* v. *Bollinger*) and law school admissions policy (*Grutter* v. *Bollinger*).[17] These cases represented the first time the Court had revisited the issue of affirmative action in higher education since *University of California Regents* v. *Bakke* in 1978.[18] Although the Court rejected the quota system in *Bakke*, in which a fixed number of seats were set aside at a state medical school, Justice Powell's concurring opinion in that case seemed to provide guidelines for schools that wanted a constitutional approach to promoting diversity. Justice Powell expressed the view that race may be used as a factor in admissions—so long as the program does not mandate racial quotas, and so long as factors other than race are similarly being considered in an individualistic assessment of how an applicant may contribute to the diversity of the student body.

Note: Information and support for teaching about the *Bakke* case is available at www.landmarkcases.org.

a. Both cases involved the affirmative action policies at the University of Michigan, at the undergraduate level and in the law school. Both policies were adopted to address the problem of the underrepresentation of certain minority groups in the undergraduate and law school student populations. The undergraduate admissions policy automatically awarded 20 points, of the 100 needed to gain admission, to any member of an underrepresented minority group. The law school admissions program looked at each application individually but gave consideration to the contributions that a person from an underrepresented minority could make to achieve the goal of a more diverse student body. Both policies were race-conscious, not race-neutral. However, the law school's policy allowed for a case-by-case consideration of each candidate. One reason for the differences in these two policies is administrative realities. The undergraduate program receives significantly more applications than the law school program, making case-by-case examination difficult.

b. Students' answers will vary. Arguments *for* the use of affirmative action include:

- The university has a legitimate interest in having students from every type of religious, ethnic, geographic, and racial background. Selective admissions processes help to create that.
- Students in a more diverse setting will be better able to understand and discuss "minority viewpoints."
- There is no alternative available that would allow the university to create and maintain a diverse student body.

- Based on the national test scores of African Americans, the loss of subjective admissions would result in a severe decrease in the number of African Americans admitted to the university. A race-blind system would cause a dramatic drop in the percentage of minority students, with an equivalent increase in the percentage of white students.
- The university is following the *Bakke* decision in making race one factor among many in determining admissions. While there are no quotas based on race, diversity is considered a plus in the admissions process.
- The special admissions program allows the university to remedy past effects of discrimination against minorities, in addition to creating a diverse student body.

Arguments *against* the use of affirmative action include:
- The university's goal of creating a more diverse student body by admitting a critical mass of minority students is equivalent to a quota.
- Accepting students with lower scores, based on their race or ethnicity, is reverse discrimination.
- The university should look for race-neutral ways to enhance diversity and improve admissions.
- Applicants should be admitted without any regard to race, ensuring that no race is discriminated against.
- The state's interest in a diverse student body is not compelling enough to justify a special admissions policy that excludes qualified students.
- Race-conscious policies perpetuate race as a divisive issue in this country and have the potential to create backlash. Where affirmative action policies are used, the legitimacy of a minority's acceptance to a particular school will also be questioned, diminishing the individual's accomplishments.
- A race-neutral alternative to a policy of affirmative action is for the school to sacrifice its exclusivity and adopt admissions criteria that produce a more diverse student body without consideration given to the race of each applicant. The idea that racial diversity creates intellectual diversity is based on the incorrect notion that members of a group all have the same ideas.

c. The Court issued separate opinions for each case. Taken together, they reaffirmed the importance of diversity and the role of affirmative action in

achieving it so long as candidates are viewed as individuals and rigid quota-like systems that mechanically award advantages to all minorities are not used. Therefore, the law school admissions policy was upheld, while the undergraduate process was found to be unconstitutional based on the equal protection clause of the Fourteenth Amendment.

Justice O'Connor, the swing vote in the 5-to-4 decision in the law school admission case, delivered the majority opinion, which endorsed the central holding in *Bakke* that diversity is an important state interest that permits some race-conscious approaches to assessing applicant pools in order to achieve a "critical mass" (but not a quota) of underrepresented minorities. She did not focus on affirmative action as reparation for past injustice against minorities. Instead her reasoning was more future-oriented, recognizing the role of universities in educating tomorrow's leaders and providing a diverse workforce.

In his dissent in the law school case, Justice Thomas criticized the majority opinion as suggesting that "classroom aesthetics yield educational benefits" and the law school's failure to find a race-neutral policy that could achieve similar diversity. The dissenters also suggested that schools should have to choose between selectivity and diversity, rather than using a race-conscious process to achieve the twin goals.

The Court ruled 6 to 3 that the automatic point system used in the undergraduate admissions process was unconstitutional. Then Chief Justice Rehnquist wrote the majority opinion that objected to the undergraduate program's failure to consider applicants on an individual basis as required by *Bakke*. The undergraduate program may still use affirmative action but in a form that is less mechanical and mathematical.

In her dissent in the undergraduate case, Justice Ginsburg argued that a system of automatic points in achieving diversity might be preferable to other methods because it was an honest, open approach to the role that race plays in the process and is necessary to correct for disparities among the races created by a legally endorsed racial caste system that persisted in the country for many years. She feared that less mathematical approaches simply camouflage the use of race as a factor.

d. Students' answers will vary. The Supreme Court found that promoting diversity is a compelling state interest that justifies limited discrimination based on race. Such measures are necessary to achieve diversity because this country's history of discrimination and exclusion puts members of certain minority groups at a disadvantage in the college application process and, by extension, in the employment market. By suggesting a time frame of 25 years, the Court seemed to reinforce the message that affirmative action is a means to an end. If affirmative action programs are successful, the theory goes, affirmative action will no longer be necessary in the next generation because there will be a diverse group of leaders whose presence and influence will erase the stain of past discrimination.

Although both opponents and proponents envision a day when affirmative action will no longer be necessary to achieve proportionate representation, many people disagree over the exact time frame that is needed. The issue of a time frame for affirmative action was central in the *Bakke* case.

According to a biographer, during the Supreme Court's private conference on the 1978 *Bakke* case, Justice Stevens said that preferences "might be acceptable as a temporary measure but not a permanent solution. . . . Justice Powell agreed. The problem was one of transition to a colorblind society. Perhaps, Stevens added, African Americans would not need these programs much longer, but at this point Justice [Thurgood] Marshall broke in to say that it would be another hundred years. This remark left Powell speechless. . . . He recoiled from the prospect of generation upon generation of racial quotas."[19]

Justice Stevens, one of two justices who were on the Court for both *Bakke* and the Michigan cases, voted to uphold both the undergraduate and law school admissions policies at the University of Michigan.

Some people also argue that affirmative action is merely a Band-Aid, and the problems that undermine minority achievement go much deeper. Such problems, including poverty and substandard elementary and secondary schools, require long-term solutions that may take more than a generation to achieve. Interestingly, *Bakke* was decided about 25 years after *Brown*, and the Michigan cases were decided about 25 years after *Bakke*.

e. Students who believe the university should adopt a policy of affirmative action based on race should advise the university president to design a system similar to that of Michigan's law school and avoid the use of any formula that appears too mechanical or that too closely resembles a quota system in order for the proposed program to be constitutional. Students may want to explore more creative solutions to the problem that address potential causes for the underrepresentation of these minority groups.

PROBLEM 41.4 (p.482)

Surprisingly, Justice O'Connor, who wrote the majority opinion upholding affirmative action in the University of Michigan Law School case, had warned about the "stigmatic harm" of racial classifications, and Justice Thomas reiterated this theme in *Grutter*.[20] Justice Thomas, the only African American on the Supreme Court at the time of the Michigan cases, wrote a powerful dissent in *Grutter*, even citing studies that suggest that heterogeneity in education hurts minority students.

Justice Thomas feared negative consequences if "overmatched students" are admitted to elite institutions where they cannot remain competitive. He also argued that affirmative action insulted minorities by undermining their accomplishments; even minorities who would have been accepted to a school regardless of their race are assumed to have benefited from affirmative action policies.

Justice Thomas's position has stirred controversy, particularly because many people viewed his nomination by President George H.W. Bush to the Court as race-motivated in part. Some argue that it is hypocritical for Justice Thomas to criticize a program from which he may have benefited. However, others argue that Thomas, who has discussed how uncomfortable he felt as a minority student attending Yale Law School, is in the best position to understand the harmful effects of affirmative action.

BACKGROUND—EMPLOYMENT DISCRIMINATION

In 1997, the U.S. Supreme Court ruled that *Title VII*'s ban on retaliation for making discrimination charges applies to former employees as well. In the case, the employer gave a negative reference to a prospective employer in retaliation for the former employee's charge of race discrimination. This violated *Title VII* of the *Civil Rights Act of 1964*. The case was *Robinson* v. *Shell Oil Co.*[21]

The federal government agency established to deal with employment discrimination is the Equal Opportunity Employment Commission (EEOC). Their website (www.eeoc.gov) includes an explanation of each of the types of discrimination discussed in Chapter 41. The site also explains how to contact EEOC field offices to file a charge of discrimination.

The case discussed in the Student Edition is *United Steelworkers of America* v. *Weber*.[22] The case involving the government policy to set aside a certain number of contracts for minorities to work on publicly funded projects is the case of *Adarand Constructors* v. *Pena*.[23]

BACKGROUND—GERRYMANDERING

While the U.S. Constitution guarantees at least one seat in the House of Representatives to each state, it does not explain how these representatives are to be elected. Congress and the courts have struggled to determine what is a fair selection process. After trying a variety of methods, all states began using single-member districts to select their congressional representatives. There are two difficulties with using such districts: malapportionment (having districts that are not equally sized) and gerrymandering (designing districts exclusively to reduce or enhance a particular faction's voting power).[24]

There has been a steady flow of cases to the U.S. Supreme Court that deal with challenges, based on the *Voting Rights Act*,[25] to changes in legislative districts within states. This is an important topic, but it is complex and generally beyond the scope of the *Street Law* text.

The Center for Voting and Democracy collects materials on this topic, including a fact sheet on gerrymandering, at www.fairvote.org/research-and-analysis/redistricting/.

CAPTION ANSWER (P. 482) Until the passage of the *Voting Rights Act of 1965*, obstacles to full voting rights included poll taxes, literacy tests, and the intimidation of African Americans who wanted to exercise their voting rights.

THE **CASE** OF...

The Redistricting Commission and the State Legislature

PROBLEM 41.5 (p.483)

a. Article 1, Section 4 reads: "The Times, Places and Manner of Holding Elections for Senators and Representatives shall be prescribed in each state by the Legislature thereof. . ." Interpreted literally, only the legislature of a state has the power to create laws and make decisions related to elections. Therefore, it is unconstitutional for the people of the state (the commission was established through ballot measure) to take that power away from the legislature. Also, because the legislature is a "representative body," it is in the best interest of the citizens of the state of Arizona that the legislature make decisions regarding elections, rather than an unelected state commission.

b. The phrase "by the Legislature thereof..." found in Article 1, Section 4 of the Constitution could be interpreted as the legislative process. Because the redistricting commission was created through the ballot process and the members of the commission were chosen by the legislature, then it could be argued the commission is a "legislative" or law-making process. Further, if the people of Arizona want an unelected commission to make decisions regarding redistricting, then that form of "direct democracy" should not be ignored by the state legislature. What better way to avoid gerrymandering, or manipulation of political boundaries in favor of a party or candidate, than taking the power of redistricting away from those who would seek to use redistricting power for political gain. Finally, traditionally the Supreme Court has granted wide authority when it comes to the ways states govern themselves. A decision to strike down the commission would run counter to that tradition.

c. Students' responses will vary. If the Court strictly interprets Article 1, Section 4, then the Court will likely find the Arizona redistricting commission, and other similar commissions, unconstitutional. However, some justices may see the redistricting commissions as an acceptable solution to the gerrymandering problem. In the case of Arizona, the commission was created "by the people" of the state. The Court would need to have a strong justification to overturn the "will of the people." The case being discussed here is *Arizona State Legislature* v. *Arizona Independent Redistricting Commission*,[26] which was heard by the U.S. Supreme Court in 2015. In a 5-4 decision, the Supreme Court held that the Elections Clause did not preclude an initiative-created independent commission from drawing district boundaries.

DISCRIMINATION BASED ON NATIONAL ORIGIN AND CITIZENSHIP STATUS (PP. 484–486)

Learning Outcomes

After completing this section, students should be able to:

1. describe how courts have generally treated government laws and policies that discriminate based on national origin and citizenship status; and
2. evaluate opposing arguments about whether state laws may deny a free public school education to children of parents who are undocumented immigrants.

BACKGROUND—IMMIGRANTS AND DISCRIMINATION

A study conducted by Robert L. Bach of the State University of New York at Binghamton concluded that immigrants as a whole are more likely to have legal problems than other low-income people. Nearly every aspect of the legal system presents challenges to immigrants. Newcomers are often victimized by discrimination in the workplace, housing market, and schools. Unscrupulous employers capitalize on their vulnerabilities. Immigrant women who are victimized by domestic violence and depend on a husband who is a U.S. citizen for legal status may be afraid to seek help. The primary legal resource for poor people, the federally funded Legal Services Corporation, has been restricted by Congress from helping people seeking U.S. legal status.[27]

With respect to the national origin cases referred to in the Student Edition, the Supreme Court case on noncitizens and professional licenses is *Examining Board of Engineers* v. *Floresde Otero*.[28] The case dealing with noncitizens and government employment is *Sugarman* v. *Dougall*.[29] In 1982, the Court held that a citizenship requirement for peace officers did not violate the equal protection clause.[30] For much more information about immigration law and immigrants, see Chapter 42.

BACKGROUND AND RESEARCH—IMMIGRATION AFTER SEPTEMBER 11, 2001

As part of the war on terrorism that began after the September 11, 2001, tragedy in the United States, the federal government took numerous actions that have targeted noncitizens and even citizens who are from, or appear to be from, certain countries in the Middle East. The federal government used immigration law violations, rather than the traditional criminal justice process, to arrest thousands of Muslims, very few of whom were ever charged in connection with terrorist actions.

As mentioned in Chapter 39, in the 2003 case of *Demore* v. *Kim*, the Supreme Court upheld a federal law that required detention of noncitizens without bail or a hearing after their release from prison for commission of certain crimes while they were being processed for deportation.[31] In this case, the Court essentially said that legal permanent residents were not entitled to the same due process rights as citizens, who would be entitled to a hearing prior to detention of any sort.

For a variety of viewpoints about the *USA PATRIOT Act*, including its impact on documented and undocumented immigrants to the United States see:

- www.immigrationforum.org (from the Immigration Forum)
- www.americanimmigrationcouncil.org (from the American Immigration Council)
- www.adc.org (from the Arab-American Anti-Discrimination Committee)
- www.aclu.org/action (from the American Civil Liberties Union).

Immigration law is rapidly evolving. For the latest on immigration policy visit FindLaw's website at https://immigration.findlaw.com/ and the U.S. government's website at https://www.usa.gov/immigration-and-citizenship.

THE CASE OF...

Educating the Children of Undocumented People

PROBLEM 41.6 (p.485)

This problem asks students to evaluate which opinion should be the Court's decision. Ask students which opinion they most closely agree with and why.

This case is based on the 1982 case of *Plyler* v. *Doe*.[32] In this case, the Court handed down an important but controversial decision concerning the rights of schoolchildren of undocumented immigrants. In a 5-to-4 decision, the Court held for the first time that undocumented immigrants were "persons" and therefore entitled to equal protection under the Fourteenth Amendment. For this reason, similar to the reasons given in Opinion A, Texas was precluded from denying to undocumented school-age children the free public education it provides to other children. Opinion A represents the majority opinion in the case, and Opinion B represents the views of the dissenters.

To extend this conversation, teachers may ask students to participate in a deliberation about whether the U.S. government should make it easier for unauthorized immigrants who came to this country as children to pay for college. Deliberation teaching materials about this topic available are at https://store.streetlaw.org/deliberation-immigration/.

CAPTION ANSWER (P. 486) *Title VII* of the *Civil Rights Act of 1964* protects against employment discrimination based on national origin.

Investigating the Law Where You Live

(p. 486) Student answers will vary based on location. Encourage students to visit the U.S. Equal Employment Opportunity Commission at https://www.eeoc.gov to learn more employment discrimination.

DISCRIMINATION BASED ON SEX (PP. 486–494)

Learning Outcomes

After completing this section, students should be able to:

1. identify steps people should take if they believe they have been targets of gender discrimination;
2. explain the requirements and protections of the *Equal Pay Act* and *Title VII of the Civil Rights Act of 1964*;
3. differentiate between quid pro quo sexual harassment and hostile environment sexual harassment;
4. explain the standard set out by the U.S. Supreme Court for deciding when a hostile or abusive work environment constitutes sexual harassment;
5. summarize the U.S. Supreme Court decisions involving sexual harassment cases in schools;

6. describe the requirements and the impact of *Title IX* of the *Education Act of 1972*;
7. analyze hypothetical cases to determine whether *Title IX* has been violated; and
8. define the terms *sexual harassment, quid pro quo,* and *hostile environment.*

BACKGROUND—THE EQUAL RIGHTS AMENDMENT

Students can learn about some of the varying perspectives on the efforts to pass the Equal Rights Amendment at the Eagle Forum (www.eagleforum.org/era), a conservative organization that opposed the amendment since it was first introduced. The Alice Paul Foundation and the National Council of Women's Organizations also provide information about the Equal Rights Amendment online at www.equalrightsamendment.org.

CAPTION ANSWER (P. 487) The ERA would have prohibited federal, state, and local governments from passing discriminatory laws or enforcing laws unequally based on gender.

BACKGROUND—GENDER DISCRIMINATION AND THE EQUAL PROTECTION CLAUSE

The 1971 case in which the U.S. Supreme Court first recognized that gender discrimination could violate the equal protection clause was *Reed* v. *Reed*.[33] In *Reed*, the Court overturned a state law establishing an absolute preference for men as executors of wills where no executor was named. The Court found no rational relationship between the law's classification and purpose.

Among other decisions of the Supreme Court, a California statutory rape law under which males but not females could be prosecuted was found not to violate the equal protection clause.[34] The federal draft registration's exclusion of females was also found not to violate equal protection.[35] In the draft case, the Court reasoned that the equal protection clause requires that Congress treat similarly situated persons equally. However, because of the military's combat restrictions on women, men and women are not considered similarly situated for purposes of the draft.

The Supreme Court's 1990 decision in *Johnson Controls* unanimously struck down as unconstitutional a policy designed to protect women[36] but which in fact denied jobs to women.

The company had instituted rules that prohibited women from working in a particular job that exposed workers to levels of lead that were considered unsafe by OSHA, the federal Occupational Safety and Health Administration. To work in those jobs, women had to prove they were infertile because there is a widely recognized risk to fetuses exposed to high levels of lead. However, men did not have to prove they were infertile to work the same job, despite the fact that exposure to lead is also hazardous to male reproductive systems.

THE CASE OF...

The Single-Sex School

PROBLEM 41.7 (p.488)

a. Virginia argued that Virginia Military Institute (VMI), with its history dating to 1839, has a distinctive mission of producing citizen soldiers who are prepared for leadership in civilian life and military service; therefore, since women are not allowed to serve in combat, the school should be permitted to have an all-male training program. Also, VMI uses an "adversative" educational method, featuring physical rigor, mental stress, absolute equality of treatment, absence of privacy, minute regulation of behavior, and indoctrination in desirable values. If forced to admit females, VMI would have to change its adversative education methods, to the detriment of the school's mission.

b. The United States argued that excluding women from this state school violated the equal protection clause. Virginia offered unique educational benefits only to males. Admitting women to VMI would not affect the goal of producing citizen soldiers. VMI's program was not inherently unsuitable for women. In addition, VMI graduates constitute a valuable network for leadership positions in careers in the military as well as business, industry, and government.

c. Students' opinions will vary. Ultimately, the Supreme Court required that VMI admit women to the school.[41] Initially, the Supreme Court appeared to agree with the court of appeals that the state of Virginia had the option of: (1) admitting women to VMI and adjusting the program to implement that choice; (2) establishing parallel institutions or parallel programs; (3) abandoning state support of VMI, giving VMI the option to pursue its own policies as a private institution; or (4) coming up with some creative strategy.[42]

Virginia attempted to create a parallel institution, which the Supreme Court later ruled did not equal VMI, stating that the new school's student body, faculty, course offerings, and facilities hardly matched VMI's. Further, the graduates of the new school could not anticipate the benefits associated with VMI's long history, prestige, and its influential alumni network.

d. Students' answers will vary. The Supreme Court ruled that certain aspects of the state's program would have to be changed (for example, privacy concerns would require separate bathrooms for men and women).

e. Students' answers will vary. In order for a state to justify a single-sex school, it must show that parallel opportunities are available. In recent years, single-gender public education has gained popularity, particularly in some inner cities. Unlike racial segregation, it appears that it is possible to create "separate but equal" schools based on gender, and research suggests benefits for each gender. The education law officially known as the No Child Left Behind Act clarified the previously ambiguous status of same-sex public education in the United States. The law makes it clear that single-sex public education in the United States is legal, provided that comparable courses, services, and facilities are made available to both sexes.[43] The U.S. Department of Education's Office for Civil Rights has a list of requirements single-sex schools must meet to be in compliance with civil rights laws at https://www.ed.gov/news/press-releases/education-department-clarifies-requirements-offering-single-sex-classes.

PROBLEM 41.8 (p.489)

a. This is based on *Mississippi University for Women* v. *Hogan*,[37] where the Court found that the school's policy of not accepting men violated the equal protection clause. The Court rejected the school's argument that its single-gender policy was a form of affirmative action designed to compensate for past gender discrimination. The state could not prove that women lacked opportunity to get nursing training when the school was established or that women were deprived of such opportunity.

b. The owner of a used-car lot probably does have a legitimate interest in hiring sales staff who are presentable. However, a legitimate interest cannot legally be expressed by rejecting male applicants who lack "sex appeal."

c. *Title VII* specifically states that women "affected by pregnancy" or related medical conditions shall be treated the same for all employment-related purposes as other disabled employees. Employment-related purposes include the receipt of fringe benefits (maternity/parental leave, disability). Therefore, employees on maternity leave and employees on parental leave or disability should be allotted benefits for the same length of time.

Treatment of pregnancy-related issues is a matter of considerable disparity among states. The Supreme Court has examined a few state statutes dealing with employment and pregnancy.[38] The Court has indicated in its opinions the importance of providing equal treatment to employees with pregnancy-related disabilities and employees who have disabilities not related to pregnancy.

In related issues, the Equal Employment Opportunity Commission (EEOC) guidelines state that an employer is under no obligation to provide health care coverage for an employee's dependents. But if an employer covers the medical expenses of spouses of female employees, then it must equally cover the medical expenses of spouses of male employees, including expenses arising from pregnancy-related conditions.

A father won the first sex-discrimination case under the federal *Family and Medical Leave Act*[39] in February 1999, when a federal jury in Baltimore awarded $375,000 in damages to a Maryland state trooper who had been denied paternity leave to care for his newborn daughter solely because of his gender.[40]

d. **The equal protection clause of the Fourteenth** Amendment requires that laws and regulations generally treat similarly situated persons equally. However, because of the military's combat restrictions on women, men and women are not similarly situated for purposes of front-line fighting.

BACKGROUND—WOMEN AND THE LAW

Many online resources deal with equal rights for women. Equal Rights Advocates (www.equalrights.org) works to secure equal rights and economic opportunities for women through litigation and advocacy. The American Civil Liberties Union (www.aclu.org) has a women-and-the-law project.

DISCUSSION—SEXUAL HARASSMENT

Sexual harassment is common in the workplace and in schools throughout the United States. Ask students how they would define *sexual harassment*. Have students share definitions and discuss why it is difficult to agree on a definition. Discuss to what extent sexual harassment is a problem in their school and in the middle schools that students attended. Ask students to discuss how targets of sexual harassment are harmed and whether they think sexual harassment creates a poor school environment—even for people who are not direct targets of such harassment. Finally, ask students to recommend what school administrators, teachers, other staff, and fellow students can do to reduce the instances and impact of sexual harassment in schools.

ACTIVITY—CONDUCTING RESEARCH

Have students conduct research and interview administrators to identify school policies that address the issue of sexual harassment and to determine how such cases are typically handled. Have students produce an article on the topic for the school newspaper. The article should include advice from administrators and guidance counselors on how a student should respond to sexual harassment.

As an alternative, have students interview parents and other adults who work outside their homes, and ask them if they think sexual harassment is an issue in their workplace, what policies their employers have to address sexual harassment, and whether they think those policies work.

THE **CASE** OF...

The Obnoxious Remarks

PROBLEM 41.9 (p.490)

Students should read the entire section about sexual harassment before they attempt to answer this question.

a. *Title VII* of the *Civil Rights Act of 1964* makes it "an unlawful employment practice for an employer . . . to discriminate against any individual with respect to his [or her] compensation, terms, conditions, or privileges of employment, because of such individual's race, color, religion, sex, or national origin." The Supreme Court has stated that this language is not limited to economic or tangible discrimination. The phrase "terms, conditions, or privileges of employment" strikes at the entire spectrum of disparate treatment of men and women in employment. This would include a hostile and abusive work environment. Sexual harassment can create a hostile work environment, and its effects can be discriminatory in that some women (or men) would be treated differently than other employees because of that unwanted sexual attention. Harassment could also provide an obstacle to being hired or promoted and, in that sense, is directly related to *Title VII*'s goal of equal opportunity in the workplace.

b. This case is based on *Harris* v. *Forklift Systems, Inc.*[44] In *Harris*, the Supreme Court held that an employee must show only that he or she was offended by the conduct in question and that a reasonable person would also find the conduct offensive. An employee no longer has to establish that the abusive conduct seriously affected his or her psychological well-being, which was the standard the trial judge used.

c. Students' answers will vary. Harris's attorney could argue that: (1) Hardy's conduct created a hostile and abusive work environment because of his consistent sexual references and innuendoes; (2) any reasonable woman in Harris's position would have found the conduct abusive and hostile; and (3) Hardy's conduct was pervasive enough to alter the conditions of the work environment so that Harris was unable to properly perform her duties.

Hardy's attorney would argue that:

(1) Hardy's conduct may have been offensive, but it did not rise to a level where it made the environment hostile or abusive; (2) Hardy's comments were made only as jokes and, therefore, they were not abusive; (3) Harris quit her job because she had developed a problem with alcohol; and (4) a reasonable person would not have found Hardy's conduct and comments hostile and abusive. As evidence of this, other female employees testified at the trial that they had considered Hardy's comments to be jokes and were not offended. Students' answers about how they would judge the case will vary.

d. As the Supreme Court set out in 1998, employers must establish policies making it clear that harassment will not be tolerated in the workplace, communicate these policies to employees, and provide a meaningful process for handling complaints.[45] If a company does not have a policy, it should draft one with the help of a labor attorney, train its employees, and implement a meaningful complaint process. The company should also ensure confidentiality and protect victims and witnesses against retaliation.

CAPTION ANSWER (P. 491) In general, the law will protect women from unwanted sexual advances in any work context, whether or not it has been traditionally dominated by men. Additional sensitivity training may be necessary for jobs that have not traditionally included women to ensure a smoother transition to a gender-integrated workforce.

An employee who believes that he or she has been a victim of sexual harassment should try to document the harassing behavior, tell a trusted friend what happened or is happening to establish a "witness" to the problem and the timeline of the problem, and be sure to tell the offender that his or her behavior is offensive.

Further, a harassed employee should follow the procedures delineated in the employer's policy on sexual harassment. In fact, the Supreme Court has ruled that an employer will not be held vicariously liable for hostile-environment sexual harassment when it can prove that it took reasonable steps to prevent sexual harassment and that the alleged victim failed to take advantage of the available preventive measures.[46] If the employee is not satisfied with the outcome from following this procedure (or the company does not have a policy), the employee can file a complaint with the Equal Employment Opportunity Commission and/or retain a lawyer. The employee should exhaust all available administrative remedies before filing a court case.

Whether mediation is an appropriate strategy remains controversial. One view holds that because of the power imbalance between the alleged victim and the employer, mediation should not be used. The other view holds that mediation is the most appropriate dispute resolution strategy, and that litigators do not necessarily have a positive effect on any power imbalance.

BACKGROUND—STUDENT-TO-STUDENT SEXUAL HARASSMENT

It is important that students understand the serious consequences of sexual harassment and that legal remedies exist if a school fails to protect students from sexual harassment.

In *Davis* v. *Monroe*, the U.S. Supreme Court held that a school board may be held liable under *Title IX* in cases of student-to-student harassment if: (1) the funding recipient (school) has actual knowledge of the sexual harassment; (2) the funding recipient is deliberately indifferent to the harassment; and (3) the harassment is so severe, pervasive, and objectively offensive that it can be said to deprive the victim of access to the educational opportunities and benefits provided by the school.[47] More information about the facts and legal issues involved in this case is available at www.oyez.org.

PROBLEM 41.10 (p.492)

In analyzing questions a.–h., students should apply the definitions of sexual harassment found in the Student Edition.

a. With the facts given, this example does not constitute sexual harassment. There may be a quid pro quo harassment claim if Fernando made Sylvia's career advancement conditional on her submission to sexual demands. Moreover, there could be a hostile environment claim if Fernando's behavior in the future creates an intimidating and offensive workplace.

b. Under the *Harris* case (discussed in Problem 41.10), the welder is a victim of hostile-work environment sexual harassment. The continuous and pervasive display of pornography and use of demeaning comments "may be found to create an atmosphere in which women are viewed as men's sexual playthings rather than as their equal coworkers."[48] This type of atmosphere violates *Title VII* of the *Civil Rights Act of 1964*.

c. The Equal Employment Opportunity Commission guidelines state that the harassed employee's occasional use of sexually explicit language will not necessarily negate a claim that the defendant's conduct was unwelcome. But a harassment claim will not be allowed if Ella used "extreme and abusive or persistent sexual comments." In *Ferguson* v. *E.I. Dupont de Nemours and Co.*,[49] the court held that "sexually aggressive conduct and explicit conversation on the part of the plaintiff may bar a hostile environment claim."

d. The facts do not support a sexual harassment claim. If Stephanie was offering Victor a promotion in exchange for (unwelcome) sexual favors, there may be a quid pro quo claim. If Stephanie's conduct is found to unreasonably interfere with Victor's work performance or if it creates an intimidating or offensive workplace, there may be grounds for a hostile environment claim.

e. While the supervisor's comments were inappropriate, they are not sufficient grounds for a sexual harassment claim. The Court tends to treat an isolated comment differently than repeated comments. If the supervisor makes repeated comments or interferes with the new staff member's work, there could be grounds for a harassment claim. In 1998, in a unanimous decision, the Supreme Court made it clear that a male has a legal claim under *Title VII* of the *Civil Rights Act* when male coworkers subject him to sexual harassment.[50]

f. These facts do not suggest sexual harassment. The teacher's comment regarding his student's physique may have been inappropriate, but it probably does not give rise to an actionable claim. Reports from school systems show a rising number of sexual harassment complaints involving teachers, staff, and students. It seems likely that the increase is due to increased awareness of the problem, as opposed to changes in behavior. Larger school systems may have administrative staff with training/monitoring/investigation expertise in sexual harassment who would be excellent classroom resources for discussing these issues.

The Supreme Court ruled in 1998 that a student who was sexually harassed by a teacher may not be able to collect damages from the school district under *Title IX* unless a school district official with the appropriate authority has actual notice of, and is deliberately indifferent to, the teacher's misconduct.[51] The idea is that a school district cannot be held responsible for everything that a teacher may say, but it can be held liable where it has notice of a problem and chooses to ignore the situation. Legal action could, however, be taken against the individual teacher.

g. There are not enough facts to make a determination. This fact pattern is based loosely on the confirmation hearing of Supreme Court justice Clarence Thomas. Professor Anita Hill testified at the confirmation hearing that, in the past, Justice Thomas had sexually harassed her while they worked together. Under the later *Harris* opinion—which Justice Thomas joined—if Professor Hill brought a legal claim, she would have had to show only that the conduct was unwelcome and that any reasonable woman in her position would have found Mr. Thomas's conduct abusive or hostile. The Thomas hearing helped bring the issue of sexual harassment in the workplace to the nation's attention.

h. While his behavior was inappropriate and may have caused the girl to be very upset and embarrassed, the facts presented in this problem do not suggest that his actions are part of a larger pattern of hostile actions toward the girl. Nor do the facts suggest that school personnel ignored the claims or concerns of the girl. This situation is an example of where school staff and parents can work together to support the girl and to help teach these young children—and others—about what is acceptable behavior before negative patterns develop.

ACTIVITY—ANALYZING THE EFFECTS OF *TITLE IX*

Have students interview school personnel, including administrators, athletic directors, and coaches, to evaluate the impact of *Title IX* at their school. Students should determine whether elementary, secondary, and postsecondary schools in their area that receive federal funding have changed their athletic programs to accommodate the needs and interests of female students. To what extent do females compete in interscholastic athletics? Are opportunities equal for members of both sexes? Should they be? Students might also interview female classmates who are athletes, as well as women who attended high school prior to *Title IX*, to identify how attitudes about sports may have changed among young women. Students should present their findings in a written report.

The American Association of University Women has developed an extensive fact sheet and tool kit about *Title IX*, available from their website https://www.aauw.org/title-ix/.

CAPTION ANSWER (P. 493) The impact of *Title IX* is controversial for several reasons. Some people are simply reluctant to let go of old stereotypes that might suggest that competitive sports are not appropriate for women. Others object to the increased funding of women's sports, which has reduced funding for some men's sports teams.

Investigating the Law Where You Live

(p. 493) The National Women's Law Center has a site that can guide readers through a series of easy-to-answer questions that can help answer the larger question of whether the athletic programs at their schools treat both male and female students fairly. Ask students to visit https://nwlc.org/issue/education-title-ix/ for more information.

PROBLEM 41.11 (p.494)

a. This is not a violation of *Title IX*; a separate but equal program is permissible. The law does not require that educational institutions have glee clubs or athletic teams. It does require, however, that these programs be open to all on equal terms.[52]

b. This may or may not be a violation. *Title IX* does not require purchases of new equipment for each team. It is reasonable for the school to provide used equipment, replacing items with new equipment as needed. However, the school could not have a policy of passing used equipment to women's teams and buying new equipment only for men's teams.

c. This is not a violation. *Title IX* does not affect school textbooks. Although gender stereotyping is considered an important issue in analyzing contemporary curriculum materials, the federal government has not regulated textbooks because of the conflict with the First Amendment.

d. This hypothetical case is based on *Clark* v. *Arizona Interscholastic Association*.[53] The Court held that the policy was a permissible means of attempting to ensure equal opportunity for girls in interscholastic sports and of redressing past discrimination. But in *Gomes* v. *Rhode Island Interscholastic League*,[54] the court held that exclusion of boys from the girls' volleyball team was prohibited when no boys' team was offered. This appears to be the correct *Title IX* analysis. Similarly, the Massachusetts supreme court found that the exclusion of boys from a girls' team was prohibited under a strict scrutiny analysis mandated by the state's equal rights amendment.[55]

e. Teams separated based on gender are permissible, but the university's athletic scholarship program is a violation. *Title IX* requires that the total amount of assistance awarded to men and women must be substantially proportionate to their participation rates in athletic programs.[56]

f. This question has not yet reached the Supreme Court of the United States, however the U.S. Department of Education has issued guidance on the matter. Once the school accepts funds raised by the parent booster clubs, it becomes subject to *Title IX,* therefore this scenario would likely be a violation.

DISCRIMINATION BASED ON SEXUAL ORIENTATION AND GENDER IDENTITY (PP. 495–498)

Learning Outcomes

After completing this section, students should be able to:

1. give examples of laws in cities and counties that protect against discrimination based on sexual orientation;
2. identify how federal law treats discrimination based on sexual orientation;
3. describe the compromise policy known as "don't ask, don't tell" as it applied to people serving in the military;
4. summarize the U.S. Supreme Court's opinion invalidating the *Defense of Marriage Act*; and
5. explain the U.S. Supreme Court's decision in *Lawrence* v. *Texas* and how it overturned the *Bowers* v. *Hardwick* precedent.

Note: Teaching this topic requires care. Increasing numbers of schools have student clubs for gay, lesbian, bisexual, transgender, and questioning (LGBTQ) students, but in other schools mention of (much less teaching about) these issues could be risky. Still, the topic is similar to other controversial issues in law and public policy. You can provide an important service by teaching students the skills to research topics, evaluate evidence, and formulate and express opinions in a thoughtful way. After all, these are skills citizens need in a democracy.

Organizations representing several different viewpoints and nonpartisan perspectives offer research to support the teaching of controversial issues and recommend the most effective approaches. *The Civic Mission of Schools,* a report recommending how to revitalize the teaching of civics and civic participation, is available at https://civicyouth.org/special-report-the-civic-mission-of-schools/. The National Council for the Social Studies (www.socialstudies.org) also provides viewpoints and recommendations about teaching issues that arouse controversy.

BACKGROUND—SEXUAL ORIENTATION, DISCRIMINATION, AND RIGHTS

The Human Rights Campaign (www.hrc.org) works for LGBTQ equal rights and helps to keep people informed about legislative and judicial developments at the state and federal levels. Human Rights Watch (www.hrw.org) places these issues in a larger, global context. The Lambda Legal Defense and Education Fund (www.lambdalegal.org) attempts to advocate for civil rights through impact litigation, education, and public policy work.

Discrimination in schools against LGBTQ students continues to be a difficult and, at times, devastating problem. The Gay, Lesbian and Straight Education Network (GLSEN) conducts a biannual study about school climate. In the 2017 report, they reported that 59.5% of students in their survey felt unsafe at school because of their sexual orientation and 44.6% because of their gender expression; 70.1% report having been verbally harassed and 28.9% report being physically harassed at school within the last year. The report also showed a direct relationship between in-school victimization, grade-point average, and the college aspirations of LGBTQ students. For more information about this report, or to learn about this group's recommendations for improving school climate and reducing bullying, visit their website at www.glsen.org.

CAPTION ANSWER (P. 495) State and Local laws have been passed regarding issues such as: anti-conversion therapy, employment discrimination, gender updates on identification documents, hate crimes, marriage equality, adoption, school anti-bullying, transgender healthcare, and more.

BACKGROUND—SUPREME COURT DECISIONS

While the 2003 case of *Lawrence* v. *Texas* is the featured case in the Student Edition, the Court has considered cases related to discrimination based on sexual orientation several times, beginning in the late 1990s. The 1996 case from Colorado discussed in the Student Edition is *Romer* v. *Evans*.[57]

In 2015, marriage equality was achieved through *Obergefell* v. *Hodges*[58] which challenged state bans on same-sex marriage and the refusal of some states to recognize marriages performed in other states. In a 5-4 decision, the Supreme Court ruled for the same-sex couples and stated that marriage is a fundamental liberty protected by the Due Process Clause of the Fourteenth Amendment. The decision also said that the bans on same-sex marriage violate the central aspects of the Equal Protection Clause. The majority recognized that people may object to same-sex marriage based on their religious beliefs, but said those objections cannot overcome the rights protected by the Constitution. The justices did reaffirm the rights of those people to speak out about their beliefs, however. A case summary can be found at https://store.streetlaw.org/.

Three LGBTQ employment discrimination cases were argued in October 2019. In *R.G. & G.R. Harris Funeral Homes Inc.* v. *EEOC*[59], Aimee Stephens, a transgender woman, was terminated when she announced to her employer that she intended to begin presenting herself as a woman. In *Bostock* v. *Clayton County, Georgia*[60] and *Altitude Express* v. *Zarda*[61], two gay employees allege that they were fired because of their sexual orientation. All three cases focus on *Title VII* of the *Civil Rights Act of 1964*, which makes it unlawful for an employer to fire or refuse to hire an individual or to base their wages or benefits on the basis of their "race, color, religion, sex, or national origin." The question in these cases is: Does discrimination against an employee because of their sexual orientation or transgender status amount to discrimination "because of...sex"? The decisions in these cases may have a large impact on LGBTQ rights in the workplace. Case summaries for these cases are available at https://store.streetlaw.org/.

THE **CASE** OF...

Lawrence v. Texas

PROBLEM 41.12 (p.497)

a. Students' answers will vary. Lawrence could argue that the Texas statute denied them equal protection of the law because it prohibited sexual acts among gay and lesbian people that were permitted among heterosexual couples. They could also argue that the due process clause of the Fourteenth Amendment protects the liberty and privacy interests of same-sex and opposite-sex couples, thereby prohibiting a state from criminalizing private, consensual sex acts among adults. (See Chapter 39 for more information about due process rights.)

Texas could argue that the Court should not create new, unwritten rights. The right to intimate relationships does not protect every type of sexual activity. Also, fundamental liberty interests are found in "deeply rooted" tradition. In this case, there is no deeply rooted tradition that provides for a right to practice homosexual sodomy. There is instead a centuries-old tradition of criminalizing sodomy. Under a rational basis review, the Texas legislature's belief that sodomy is immoral provides the rational basis needed for this law.

b. Students' answers will vary but should be supported with reasons.

c. Students' answers will vary. Some people have said that *Lawrence* v. *Texas*[62] is the *Brown* v. *Board of Education* for the LGBTQ community. This case opened the door to greater legal protections for these groups and led the way to decisions such as *Obergefell* v. *Hodges*.

d. Justice O'Connor believes that the state has the right to pass a law that relates to intimate relations but must do so in a way that applies to all couples equally.

e. Students' answers will vary. Some students will agree with Justice Kennedy's opinion that the liberty guaranteed by the Constitution protects all citizens from government intrusion into personal moral decisions. Others will argue that to some degree all laws are based on a community's sense of morality. Therefore, elected officials—who are accountable to the people—and not judges, are the most qualified to make these types of decisions in a democracy. So, if locally elected people make laws criminalizing certain behavior, this is simply an example of democracy at work.

PROBLEM 41.13 (p.498)

---

a–c. Students' answers will vary. This problem asks students to consider three fairly common perspectives on this issue. It might be helpful to have students visit www.publicagenda.org to gain greater understanding about the issue and to identify the public's concerns about the issue before deciding which perspective they support. Homophobia is not uncommon among high school students, and this is likely to be a challenging discussion. Whether "out" or not, there is a good chance that there are LGBTQ students in your class.

DISCRIMINATION BASED ON AGE (PP. 498–500)

Learning Outcomes

After completing this section, students should be able to:

1. describe the purpose of the *Age Discrimination in Employment Act* and the types of discrimination it outlaws;
2. explain the types of workers and employers subject to the *Age Discrimination in Employment Act*;
3. note the types of exceptions included in the act; and
4. summarize at least three laws or practices that involve the government's legal and constitutional discrimination of young people.

CAPTION ANSWER (P. 499) Students' answers will vary, but age should be a bona fide job qualification for the jobs they identify.

BACKGROUND—COMBATING AGE DISCRIMINATION

The Equal Employment Opportunity Commission (EEOC) is the federal agency responsible for enforcing the *Age Discrimination in Employment Act*.[63] In 2014, the EEOC received nearly 20,500 complaints related to age discrimination in employment. For more information on age discrimination, go to www.eeoc.gov/eeoc/publications/age.cfm.

THE **CASE** OF...

The Forced Retirement

PROBLEM 41.14 (p. 499)

This case is based on the 1976 case *Massachusetts Board of Retirement* v. *Murgia*.[64] Students should explore the arguments on both sides and identify those with which they most closely agree. Arguments in favor of Murgia include that an age maximum is arbitrary and an alternative exists to achieve the state's goals. The state would argue that age, unlike race and gender, is not a "suspect" class. A mandatory retirement age provides administrative convenience and creates positions for new officers.

Students can also analyze the other side of this issue, in which they have a personal stake, and consider whether it is arbitrary that the law says a person must be 18 before engaging in certain activities (e.g., voting, serving on juries, bringing and defending lawsuits, entering binding contracts). Clearly, some teenagers younger than 18 are mature enough to participate in these activities responsibly, but the law has to draw the line at some age. In this context, students are likely to raise the issue of the drinking age as well. It might interest students that prior to ratification of the Twenty-sixth Amendment, in many places a person could drink beer and wine at age 18 but could not vote. The situation is generally reversed today.

Age discrimination laws are more often interpreted by courts to protect older people than young people.

DISCRIMINATION BASED ON DISABILITY (PP. 500–504)

Learning Outcomes

After completing this section, students should be able to:

1. explain what it means to have a disability according to the *Americans with Disabilities Act (ADA)*;
2. summarize major legislation that prohibits discrimination against people with disabilities and what those laws require;
3. describe and evaluate U.S. Supreme Court decisions in cases involving people with disabilities; and
4. interpret hypothetical cases to determine whether laws against discrimination based on disability should apply.

BACKGROUND—DISABILITY LAW

Many people believe that the *Americans with Disabilities Act of 1990 (ADA)* was the most important civil rights act of the last quarter of the twentieth century. However, interpreting the act has kept the federal courts very busy.

Questions presented to the U.S. Supreme Court have ranged from what constitutes a disability to whether courtrooms must be made accessible to disabled litigants and whether state employees can sue their employers (i.e., their governments) in federal court for violations of this law. The first prong of the *ADA* definition of disability provides that a condition constitutes a disability if it "substantially limits one or more of the major life activities of such individual."[61] This requirement serves to weed out from *ADA* protection physical or mental impairments that are too minor or insignificant to be considered disabilities. The Supreme Court has interpreted the *ADA* to say that, a condition must substantially limit one or more major life activities to qualify as a disability under the act. According to disability advocates, while a few of the Court's statements regarding that requirement may prove beneficial to certain plaintiffs, the overall effect of the Court's decisions has been to make it more difficult to establish a substantial limitation on a major life activity. Chapter 45 of this Teacher Manual discusses how the *ADA* has been interpreted in the employment context.

The U.S. Department of Justice provides information for businesses and governments to help them comply with the *ADA*. It also provides links to other federal agencies with *ADA* enforcement responsibility. Visit www.ada.gov for more information. The Bazelon Center for Mental Health (www.bazelon.org) frequently files an amicus brief in support of those seeking disability rights appearing before the U.S. Supreme Court. The Bazelon Center raised concern that over the previous ten years, the Supreme Court had narrowed the interpretation of *ADA* so dramatically that many people with mental illnesses and other disabilities were no longer covered by the law.

THE **CASE** OF...

The Student with a Disability

PROBLEM 41.15 (p. 501)

Students' answers will vary but should be supported with reasons. Tell students the U.S. Supreme Court's thinking appears to have shifted since the 1982 *Rowley* decision.

The *Rowley* case arose before the passage of the *Americans with Disabilities Act* in 1990. In the 1980s, the rights of physically and intellectually disabled persons were the subject of frequent litigation. Much of the litigation raised questions about the scope of the *Education for All Handicapped Children Act*.[66] For example, in the *Rowley* case, the U.S. Supreme Court held that the act did not require a public school to provide an interpreter for a deaf child.[67] Two years later, a unanimous Court ruled that a public school was required to provide a disabled student with catheterization, during school hours.[68]

In 1999, the Supreme Court interpreted the *Individuals with Disabilities Education Act* (IDEA, the successor to *EAHC*) to say that public schools must provide a wide range of medical care for disabled children attending public school classes.[69] In that case the Court required the school district to provide all-day nursing care to a quadriplegic high school sophomore who had been paralyzed from the neck down since age four. Those opposed to this decision argued that it would seriously strain the financial resources of many school districts. They also argued that this decision went beyond providing educational supports for children with disabilities and was instead providing medical care.

For more information and background about IDEA and its protection for school-aged children with disabilities, see Chapter 30.

THE **CASE** OF...

The Dentist and His HIV-Positive Patient

PROBLEM 41.16 (p.502)

a. Student answers may vary. As noted in the Student Edition, individuals who are HIV positive have been held to be disabled under the *ADA*. A disability is a physical impairment that substantially limits one or more of an individual's major life activities, including his or her ability to reproduce and have children. From the moment of infection and throughout every stage of the disease, HIV infection satisfies the statutory and regulatory definition of a "physical impairment."

b. The Court of Appeals had ruled that treating a patient in a dentist's office would not have posed a direct threat to the health and safety of others. In making the ruling, the court relied on the 1993 Dentistry Guidelines of the Centers for Disease Control and Prevention (CDC) and on the 1991 American Dental Association Policy on HIV.

On appeal, the Supreme Court, in its first case addressing HIV,[70] examined the following questions: (1) whether asymptomatic HIV is a disability under the *ADA*, so that people without visible symptoms can claim the protection of the law; (2) whether reproduction is a major life activity under the *ADA*; and (3) whether courts should defer to a health care professional's judgment that providing treatment to a particular patient poses a direct threat of harm to the professional. Although the Supreme Court stopped short of concluding that HIV is always a disability for purposes of coverage under the *ADA*, it did note that the concept of "asymptomatic HIV" is something of a misnomer because of the virus's activity in the body from the moment of infection. The Court decided that HIV is always an impairment under the *ADA*.

By a vote of 5 to 4, the majority of the Court then concluded that HIV is an impairment that substantially limits reproduction, and that reproduction is a major life activity. The majority also held that medical professionals are not entitled to any special treatment or deference to their views when they are defendants in a discrimination case. However, the Court determined that the First Circuit Court of Appeals needed to clarify the basis of its conclusion that treating this patient did not pose a direct threat to the doctor. The

Court sent the case back to the appeals court for further proceedings on this issue. On remand, the First Circuit Court of Appeals again affirmed the district court's judgment in favor of the patient.[71]

c. Students' opinions will vary but should be supported by reasons.

THE **CASE** OF...

The Golfer and His Golf Cart

PROBLEM 41.17 (p.503)

a. Martin can claim that by failing to allow him to use a cart, the Professional Golfers' Association (PGA) failed to make its tournaments accessible to individuals with disabilities, in violation of the *ADA*.

b. The PGA can claim that it is a private organization, and therefore the *ADA* does not apply. It can also claim that walking is a substantive rule of its competition and that a waiver of the rule would fundamentally alter its competitions, which the *ADA* does not require. One aspect of walking as a substantive rule is that all the other golfers walk the course and endurance is one of the qualities required to win tournaments.

c. Students' opinions will vary. The U.S. Supreme Court ruled that the *ADA* requires the PGA to allow a disabled professional golfer to ride in a golf cart between shots at tour events. Allowing Martin to use a golf cart "is not a modification that would fundamentally alter the nature" of the PGA Tour, said Justice Stevens, who delivered the majority opinion.[72]

YOU BE the JUDGE

Discrimination and Disabilities (p. 504)

The *ADA* defines *disability* as a physical or mental impairment that substantially limits one or more major life activities; for example: walking, seeing, speaking, or hearing. Students should keep this definition in mind when analyzing the fact patterns.

a. The student clearly has a disability as defined by the act. The school would be required to build a ramp for the graduation ceremony unless doing so would impose an undue hardship. Building a ramp for just one occasion may prove to be excessively expensive and therefore an undue hardship. Awarding the diploma in front of the stage may be a reasonable alternative.

b. Employers may reject applicants or fire employees who pose a "direct threat" to the health and safety of other individuals in the workplace. The firefighter with HIV probably does not pose such a direct threat. An argument can, therefore, be made for labeling the city's conduct as illegally discriminatory. The case is based on *Doe* v. *District of Columbia*.[73] The Court determined, after hearing expert testimony on HIV transmission, that there was no measurable risk that the firefighter might infect another person on the job.

Transmission of the disease is rare. The three known transmission methods include sexual contact, contaminated needles, and blood-to-blood contact. The first two methods were inapplicable, and an expert testified that transmission from blood-to-blood contact would be extremely rare. In addition, each firefighter wears substantial protective gear. The Court held that the firefighter had been discriminated against based on his disability and ordered that he be reinstated with back pay.

c. The Little League coach has a disability. Although the coach is being treated differently than other coaches, the rule was implemented for the safety of the players as well as the coach. However, the Little League would have to demonstrate that the coach's presence on the field posed a real safety risk.

Under the *ADA*, a determination of a health or safety risk cannot be based on speculation. It must be based on specific objective data. Depending on the construction of the dugouts, it may be that the coach is no safer there. On the other hand, the coach must be able to maneuver quickly out of the way of either a batted or thrown ball or the players while in his wheelchair. If he could not move quickly enough, it is possible that he would pose a danger to a player running toward him. It is possible that no accommodation is needed and that the rule is reasonable.

d. The regulations implementing the *ADA* state specifically that cancer is a disease covered by the act. The executive director has been the subject of discrimination. Her superiors cannot fire her simply because she has cancer. The company should make reasonable accommodations so that the woman can function at work as well as she can for as long as she can be productive.

e. The issue here is whether or not being overweight is a disability that requires accommodation under the *ADA*. The Equal Employment Opportunity Commission (EEOC) states in its *ADA* implementing regulations that weight

that is within a normal range and not the result of a physiological disorder does not constitute impairment. Based on this guidance, the EEOC has argued the inverse—that a person's weight could be an impairment if it is either outside the normal range or the result of a physiological disorder.[74] The fact that she was denied the position even though she was otherwise qualified to perform her job demonstrates that she was a victim of discrimination. Only if her weight was outside the normal range or the result of a physiological disorder will the employer be required to accommodate her weight.

HOUSING DISCRIMINATION (PP. 504–507)

Learning Outcomes

After completing this section, students should be able to:

1. describe who is protected from housing discrimination by the *Fair Housing Act of 1968* and its 1988 amendments;
2. define the term *steering*;
3. describe forms of housing discrimination and methods used to determine when it is happening, including steering and redlining;
4. describe at least two forms of housing discrimination that are legal;
5. interpret situations to determine whether illegal housing discrimination has taken place;
6. describe the purpose of the *Community Reinvestment Act of 1977* and its results; and
7. identify steps individuals should take if they have been targets of housing discrimination.

BACKGROUND—ENFORCEMENT OF HOUSING DISCRIMINATION LAWS

The federal department of Housing and Urban Development (HUD) has the primary responsibility for enforcing federal fair housing laws. Visit the HUD website at https://www.hud.gov/program_offices/fair_housing_equal_opp/fair_housing_and_related_law for explanatory materials and https://www.hud.gov/program_offices/fair_housing_equal_opp/online-complaint for complaint forms in English and Spanish. HUD's research on housing discrimination is available at www.huduser.org/portal/home.html. For additional background on housing law, see Chapter 27 of the Student Edition and this Teacher Manual.

THE CASE OF...

The Unwanted Tenant

PROBLEM 41.18 (p.505)

a. Mrs. Weaver operates a five-unit apartment building. She refuses to rent to Mr. Tran because she believes other tenants will leave if she rents to someone from a minority group.

b. *The Fair Housing Act*[75] forbids discrimination on the basis of race and national origin in the rental of apartments of four or more units. Therefore, Mrs. Weaver's actions have violated federal law.

c.–d. Students should discuss the conflict between an individual's control of personal property and actions that discriminate against others. Students should also explain which right they believe to be more important.

e. If Mr. Tran discovers that the unit was not rented at the time he looked at it, he can complain to the local antidiscrimination agency or the U.S. Housing and Urban Development's Fair Housing Office. He could call the media's attention to this illegal act. He has many options, including looking elsewhere for a place to live. Discuss with students the benefits and costs of pursuing such cases of illegal discrimination.

CAPTION ANSWER (P. 506) Some older people choose to live in retirement residences because specific facilities and services for the elderly are provided.

Investigating the Law Where You Live

(p. 506) If students need assistance locating information regarding laws prohibiting housing discrimination in their state and which agencies handle complaints and enforce those laws, direct them to www.fairhousing.com.

Students should look for "housing laws," select the option for "state laws," and then enter in their state name.

YOU BE the JUDGE

The Federal Fair Housing Act (p. 507)

a. This advertising appears to violate the *Fair Housing Act (FHA)*. Part of the act (Section 804) outlaws notices, statements, or advertisements, with respect to the sale or rental of a dwelling, which indicate any preference, limitation, or discrimination based on race, color, religion, sex, handicap, familial status, or national origin, or an intention to make any such preference, limitation, or discrimination.[76] In one case, the court found a violation where, over a period of more than two years, a leasing agency ran 34 newspaper advertisements for its properties using only white models.[77] The court reasoned that an ordinary reader, viewing the advertisements as many times over the same time period, as did the African American plaintiffs, would naturally interpret them to indicate a racial preference.

b. This may be a violation of the *Fair Housing Act*. Landlords are not allowed to discriminate against families, although the landlords may limit renting to a family when the living space is not adequate to house them. There is insufficient information to determine whether this two-bedroom apartment is inadequate for four people.

c. The *FHA* now protects people from discrimination based on sexual orientation, so this is not legal under the FHA. For more information regarding housing discrimination and persons identifying as LGBTQ visit the Department of Housing and Urban Development's website at https://www.hud.gov/program_offices/fair_housing_equal_opp/housing_discrimination_and_persons_identifying_lgbtq.

d. This is a violation of the *FHA* as illegal discrimination on the basis of race and/or national origin.

e. The mere fact that a woman is divorced does not make her a poor credit risk. However, if her income is significantly reduced as a result of the divorce, then it could legitimately affect her creditworthiness. If the bank has a legitimate reason to believe that the woman's divorce makes her a financial risk, then it could legally deny her credit under the *FHA* because banks can lawfully refuse to lend to poor credit risks. Still, state or local law may prohibit discriminating on the basis of marital status.

f. This question prompts students to review the activities covered in the *FHA*, which are selling, leasing, and financing. This is not a violation of the *FHA*, since blocking a zoning change is not a covered action under the federal statute.

g. This is a violation of the *FHA*, which prohibits discrimination on the basis of disability. In addition, the *ADA* includes drug users in treatment as having a disability.

h. This type of discrimination is legal under the *FHA* since the musician does not fall within one of the protected groups.

i. The *FHA* does not forbid discrimination on the basis of age in the financing of homes; however, laws such as the *Equal Credit Opportunity Act* might offer protection here.

j. When the owner removed the ramp and encouraged the tenant to move elsewhere, he violated the *FHA* ban on discrimination on the basis of disability.

STATE AND LOCAL LAWS AGAINST DISCRIMINATION (PP. 508–509)

Learning Outcomes

After completing this section, students should be able to:

1. describe why state and local governments may provide more protections against discrimination than the federal government; and
2. list specific steps a person can take when his or her rights have been violated.

ACTIVITY—CASE STUDY: THE LGBTQ STUDENT CLUB AND THE RELIGIOUS UNIVERSITY

This case study is based on *Gay Rights Coalition of Georgetown University Law Center* v. *Georgetown University*.[78] Share with students the background information provided here and have them consider the questions that follow.

A large university affiliated with the Roman Catholic Church set aside some funds from tuition to support registered student clubs. A group of LGBTQ students applied to become a club at the university and was turned down. The reason given was that the religious teachings of the institution did not approve of homosexuality. A human rights law in the city where the university was located protected individuals against discrimination based on sexual orientation. The students sued the university. Ask students the following questions:

1. What arguments can the students make? *The students may argue that the university's action is in direct contradiction to the local law that prohibits an educational institution from discriminating against*

any individual on the basis of sexual orientation. While students may say that the university's action placed content-based restrictions on the gay students' speech and violated the equal protection clause by denying benefits that heterosexual students received, remind them that these First and Fourteenth Amendment rights do not apply to a private university.

2. What arguments can the university make? *The university could argue that the free exercise clause of the First Amendment protects it from having the government compel it to endorse an organization which challenges its religious tenets.*

3. How should this case be resolved? Would your answer be different if a state university were involved? *Students' answers will vary. The District of Columbia's Court of Appeals found that the government had a compelling interest in eliminating discrimination based on sexual orientation. This interest outweighed the burden it placed on the university's religious freedom. The court held that the local Human Rights Act does not compel uniformity of philosophical attitudes, but it does require equal treatment in educational institutions. Thus, the university could not be compelled to grant official "recognition" to LGBTQ student groups. Nevertheless, the university must provide the students with the facilities and services other student groups enjoy.*

The Court of Appeals noted that a public university would not be able to impose these content-based restrictions on speech. Furthermore, it would not be able to use its student body "recognition" process to comment on the "rightness and wrongness of homosexual conduct." A private university has no such restrictions.

4. Should there be a national law that protects individuals against discrimination based on sexual orientation, or should the development of policy in this area be left to state and local governments? Give your reasons. *Students' answers will vary. Students should consider whether they would also leave it up to states and localities to set their own protections of other groups (women, people with disabilities, and people of various races, ethnicities, and national origins).*

NOTES

(1) *Plessy* v. *Ferguson*, 163 U.S. 537 (1896) (Harlan, J. dissenting).

(2) See *Heart of Atlanta Motel* v. *United States*, 379 U.S. 241 (1964).

(3) *Plessy v. Ferguson*, 163 U.S. 537 (1896).

(4) *Brown v. Board of Education*, 347 U.S. 483 (1954).

(5) See generally, *Dawson v. Mayor of Baltimore*, 220 F.2d 386 (4th Cir. 1955); *Browder v. Gayle*, 142 F. Supp. 707 (M.D. Ala. 1956); *Holmes v. City of Atlanta*, 223 F.2d 93 (5th Cir. 1955); *New Orleans City Park Improvement Association v. Detiege*, 252 F.2d 122 (5th Cir. 1958); *Johnson v. Virginia*, 373 U.S. 61 (1963).

(6) *Gratz v. Bollinger*, 539 U.S. 244 (2003); *Grutter v. Bollinger*, 539 U.S. 306 (2003).

(7) *Korematsu v. United States*, 323 U.S. 214 (1944).

(8) *Craig v. Boren*, 429 U.S. 190 (1976).

(9) *Loving v. Virginia*, 388 U.S. 1 (1967).

(10) *Rehabilitation Act of 1973*, 29 U.S.C. §§ 701–796. and *The Americans with Disabilities Act of 1990*, 42 U.S.C. §§ 12101 et seq.

(11) *Personnel Administrator v. Feeney*, 442 U.S. 256 (1979).

(12) *Arlington Heights (Ill.) v. Metropolitan Housing Development Corporation*, 429 U.S. 252 (1977).

(13) *Swann v. Charlotte Mecklenburg Board of Education*, 402 U.S. 1 (1971).

(14) *Worcester v. Georgia*, 31 U.S. 515 (1832).

(15) *Brown v. Board of Education II*, 349 U.S. 294, 301 (1955). *Note: There were two* Brown v. Board of Education *cases. The first (Brown I) ruled on the constitutionality of segregation, holding that separate but equal was inherently unequal; the second (Brown II) ruled on the implementation of integration, adopting the loosely interpreted "all deliberate speed" time frame.*

(16) *Griffin v. County School Board*, 377 U.S. 218 (1964). However, a municipality under court order to desegregate its publicly owned swimming pools was held to be entitled to close the pools instead, so long as it ceased operation of them entirely. *Palmer v. Thompson*, 403 U.S. 217 (1971).

(17) *Gratz v. Bollinger*, 539 U.S. 244 (2003); *Grutter v. Bollinger*, 539 U.S. 306 (2003).

(18) *University of California Regents v. Bakke*, 438 U.S. 265 (1978).

(19) John C. Jeffries, Jr. *Justice Lewis F. Powell, Jr.: A Biography*. Riverside, NJ: Scribner's, 1994.

(20) *Richmond v. J.A. Croson Company*, 488 U.S. 469, 509 (1989); *Grutter v. Bollinger*, 539 U.S. 306 (2003) (Thomas, J., dissenting).

(21) *Robinson v. Shell Oil Co.*, 519 U.S. 337 (1997).

(22) *United Steelworkers of America v. Weber*, 443 U.S. 193 (1979).

(23) *Adarand Constructors v. Pena*, 515 U.S. 200 (1995).

(24) Jan Witold Baran and Jason P. Cronic, "Congressional Districting: A Historical Overview," *Update on Law-Related Education*, Vol. 20, No. 3 (1996): 28.

(25) *Voting Rights Act of 1965*, 42 U.S.C. § 1973 et seq. (2000), *Voting Rights Act Amendments of 1970*, Pub. L. No. 91–285, 84 Stat. 314, *Voting Rights Act Amendments of 1982*, Pub. L. No. 97–205, 96 Stat. 131, *Voting Rights Act Reauthorization and Amendments Act of 2006*, Pub. L. No. 109–246, 120 Stat. 577.

(26) *Arizona State Legislature v. Arizona Independent Redistricting Commission*, 135 S.Ct. 2652 (2015).

(27) Christina DeConcini, Jeanine S. Piller, Margaret Fisher, "The Changing Face of Immigration Law," *Social Education*, Vol. 62, No. 7 (November/December 1998).

(28) *Board of Engineers v. Floresde Otero*, 426 U.S. 572 (1976).

(29) *Sugarman v. Dougall*, 413 U.S. 634 (1973).

(30) *Cabell v. Chavez-Salido*, 454 U.S. 432 (1982).

(31) *Demore v. Kim*, 538 U.S. 510 (2003).

(33) *Plyler v. Doc*, 457 U.S. 202 (1982).

(33) *Reed v. Reed*, 404 U.S. 71 (1971).

(34) *Michael M. v. Superior Court of Sonoma County*, 450 U.S. 464 (1981).

(35) *Rostker v. Goldberg*, 448 U.S. 1306 (1980).

(36) *UAW v. Johnson Controls, Inc.*, 499 U.S. 187 (1991).

(37) *Mississippi University for Women v. Hogan*, 458 U.S. 718 (1982).

(38) *Newport News Shipbuilding and Dry Dock Co. v. EEOC*, 462 U.S. 669 (1983); *California Federal Sav. and Loan Ass'n. v. Guerra*, 479 U.S. 272 (1987).

(39) *Family and Medical Leave Act (FMLA)*, 29 U.S.C. § 2601 (1993).

(40) *Knussman v. Maryland*, 935 F. Supp. 659 (D. Md. 1996).

(41) *United States v. Virginia*, 518 U.S. 515 (1996).

(42) *United States v. Virginia*, 976 F. 2d 890 (4th Cir. 1992), cert. denied 508 U.S. 946 (1993).

(43) *No Child Left Behind Act*, Pub. L. No. 107– 110, 115 Stat. 1425 (2002) (codified at 20 U.S.C.A. §§ 6301–6578 (West Supp. 2002)).

(44) *Harris v. Forklift Systems, Inc.*, 510 U.S. 17 (1993).

(45) *Burlington Indus., Inc. v. Ellerth*, 524 U.S. 742 (1998); *Farragher v. City of Boca Raton*, 524 U.S. 775 (1998).

(46) Id.

(47) *Davis v. Monroe County Board of Education*, U.S. 629 (1999).

(48) *Barbetta v. Chemlawn Services Corp.*, 669 F. Supp. 569, 573 (W.D.N.Y. 1987).

(49) *Ferguson v. E.I. Dupont de Nemours and Co.*, 560 F.Supp. 1172 (D. Del. 1983).

(50) *Oncale v. Sundowner Offshore Services, Inc.*, U.S. 75 (1998).

(51) *Gebser v. Lago Vista Independent School District*, 524 U.S. 274 (1998).

(52) *Hoover v. Meiklejohn*, 430 F. Supp 164 (Colo. 1977).

(53) *Clark v. Arizona Interscholastic Association*, F.2d 1126 (9th Cir. 1982).

(54) *Gomes v. Rhode Island Interscholastic League*, F.2d 733 (1st Cir. 1979).

(55) *Attorney General et al. v. Massachusetts Interscholastic Athletic Assoc.*, 393 N.E.2d 284 (1979).

(56) *Requirements Under Title IX of the Education Amendments of 1972*, U.S. Department of Education, Office for Civil Rights.

(57) *Romer v. Evans*, 517 U.S. 620 (1996).

(58) *Obergefell v. Hodges*, 135 S.Ct. 2584 (2015).

(59) *R.G. & G.R. Harris Funeral Homes Inc. v. EEOC*, ____ U.S. ____ (argued Oct. 8, 2019).

(60) *Bostock v. Clayton Cty., Ga.*, ____ U.S. ____ (argued Oct. 8, 2019).

(61) *Altitude Express Inc. v. Zarda*, ____ U.S. ____ (argued Oct. 8, 2019).

(62) *Lawrence v. Texas*, 539 U.S. 558 (2003).

(63) *Age Discrimination in Employment Act*, 29 U.S.C. §§ 621–634 (2000).

(64) *Massachusetts Board of Retirement v. Murgia*, 427 U.S. 307 (1976).

(65) *Americans with Disabilities Act (ADA)*, 42 U.S.C. § 12102(2)(A).

(66) In 1975, Congress passed Public Law 94-142 *(Education for All Handicapped Children Act)*, now codified as *IDEA (Individuals with Disabilities Education Act)*.

(67) *Hendrick Hudson Board of Education v. Rowley*, 458 U.S. 176 (1982).

(68) *Irving Independent School District v. Tatro*, 468 U.S. 883 (1984).

(69) *Cedar Rapids Community School District v. Garrett F.*, 526 U.S. 66 (1999).

(70) *Bragdon v. Abbott*, 524 U.S. 624 (1998).

(71) *Abbott v. Bragdon*, 163 F.3d 87 (1st Cir. 1998).

(72) *PGA Tour, Inc. v. Martin*, 532 U.S. 661 (2001).

(73) *Doe v. District of Columbia*, 796 F. Supp. 559 (D.D.C. 1992).

(74) Major Amy M. Frisk, "Obesity As a Disability: An Actual or Perceived Problem?" 1996 *Army Law*: 3 (1996).

(75) *Fair Housing Act*, 42 U.S.C. § 3604.

(76) Id.

(77) *Ragin v. Harry Macklowe Real Estate Co.*, 6 F.3d 898 (2d Cir. 1993).

(78) *Gay Rights Coalition of Georgetown University Law Center v. Georgetown University*, 536 A.2d 1 (D.C. App. 1987).

UNIT 7
Contemporary Issues in Law

network™

The chapters in *Street Law* have traditionally been organized around unit topics that correspond with courses taken in the first or second year of law school. Naturally the presentation of the content has been adapted for high school students with a much greater focus on practicality, skill development, and civic engagement. However, some topics that are now very practical for high school students do not fall neatly within the traditional *Street Law* units. These five topics—immigration law, intellectual property, law and terrorism, rights and responsibilities in the workplace, and environmental law—are presented in this final unit.

CHAPTERS IN BRIEF

CHAPTER 42
Immigration Law

Chapter 42 introduces students to the complex and contested issue of immigration law. The chapter explains naturalization, visas, and asylum and challenges students to come up with public policy for dealing with the millions of immigrants in the country without legal status.

CHAPTER 43
Intellectual Property

Chapter 43 provides an overview of intellectual property with sections on patents, copyright, and trademark law. Students also learn about the challenge of dealing with counterfeit goods.

CHAPTER 44
Law and Terrorism

Chapter 44 explains the unique legal and practical issues our country faces as part of the war on terror. Students learn about the laws of war and have to think about whether those laws also apply when fighting non-state actors (who may not adhere to the laws of war). Throughout this chapter there is a need to strike a sensible balance between security interests and individual freedoms.

CHAPTER 45
Rights and Responsibilities in the Workplace

Chapter 45 explores rights and responsibilities in the workplace, providing an overview of the law that young people encounter getting, keeping and also losing a job. Related material dealing with statutory and constitutional protections against employment discrimination can be found in Chapter 41.

CHAPTER 46
Environmental Law

Chapter 46 provides an overview of major environmental law legislation, explores whether these problems are best dealt with at the state, federal, or global level, and introduces the challenge of climate change.

SERVICE LEARNING AND SPECIAL PROJECTS

1. **Debate and deliberations:** Several controversial issues in this unit lend themselves to debates and deliberations. Topics could include: (a) immigration reform; (b) the *USA PATRIOT Act*; (c) use of drones in military action; (d) Internet file-sharing and copyright infringement; and (e) the advantages and disadvantages of unions.

2. **Survey on Controversial Issues:** Students could survey other students, parents, or community residents for their opinions on the issues described above and other questions raised throughout the unit.

3. **Student Advocacy and Service Learning:** While community service is educational and meaningful on many levels, service learning takes it to "the next level" by connecting service with classroom learning and reflection. The following activities are suggested to help students enhance what they learn in Unit 7 by serving their communities.

   - Students can volunteer at a community center that serves immigrants. Students can talk with clients for whom English is not their native language and help them practice their English.
   - Students can also volunteer with local non-profit organizations to help immigrants prepare for the citizenship test.
   - Together with teachers, students can host an intellectual property information session advising students about how to protect their rights, and how to register works with the Copyright Office.
   - Students can work with local online media companies to develop a list of rights and responsibilities for students regarding the use of and illegal use of online media. Students can then construct a web page for others about copyright violations.
   - Students can work with a local military office and organize a food/supplies drive at school and prepare care packages for American troops abroad.
   - Students can work with a school counselor to set up a job fair to inform students about their rights at a job. Set up opportunities for students to teach others about their rights during an interview, during employment, and when they leave a job.
   - Students can organize a highway, stream, or park clean up.
   - Students can lead a recycling effort in their community or school.

UNIT RESOURCES

Using Legal Resource Persons

One of the "best practices" in law-related education is to invite outside resource people to co-teach lessons in your classroom. These guests should not be asked or expected to lecture on a topic, but to engage students in interactive activities that showcase student work with the guidance of an expert. It is ideal to ask a particular resource person to work with the same group of students repeatedly. This significantly amplifies students' retention of the content and has also been shown to increase the likelihood that those students will pursue careers in the legal field. You might consider inviting the following people to co-teach one of the topics in this unit.

1. Representatives from the private sector could discuss how immigrants contribute to the economy.

2. Federal and state representatives could discuss public policy issues related to immigration, law and terrorism, and the environment.

3. A dean or member of the faculty of a local university could discuss the issue of plagiarism, how to avoid infringing on the property rights of others and the impact for students who fail to adhere to those rules.

4. Attorneys who specialize in labor relations could discuss how laws affect the rights and responsibilities of individuals in the workplace.

5. In addition, attorneys who specialize in intellectual property could provide insights they have gained through their work in cases involving copyright, trademark and patent infringement.

6. Attorneys who specialize in environmental law or policy could co-facilitate a deliberation or debate on a current environmental policy such as fracking.

networks™

America has been a land of immigrants for many more than 500 years—more if you count the earlier migrations of Native Americans across the Bering Strait. Our nation's laws and policies regarding immigrants continue to change with each historical era, reflecting a persistent tension between the view that immigrants should be welcomed and celebrated and the view that immigration should be restricted.

In this chapter, students will learn how people gain legal entry to the United States as visitors, guest workers, and as lawful permanent residents. Students will also learn about the requirements and qualifications for citizenship. How the country accommodates people seeking asylum from persecution and how the government removes people who are here illegally are also explored. Finally, students will learn about the government agencies that have jurisdiction over immigration and the intense policy debates over the best ways to address undocumented immigration and the extent of government support for immigrants.

ADDITIONAL RESOURCES

The following organizations offer lesson plans and materials to assist educators in teaching about immigration:

- Teaching Tolerance http://www.tolerance.org/lesson/immigration-myths.
- Center for Educational Telecommunications http://www.cetel.org
- New York Times Learning Network (www.nytimes.com/learning/), Justice Learning (www.justicelearning.org), and Annenberg Classroom (www.annenbergclassroom.org) offer resources for teaching this chapter. Of special note is a lesson plan from Annenberg Classroom called "Modern Immigration Debates," written by Judith Painter and edited by Street Law, Inc.

INTRODUCTION (PP. 512–513)

Learning Outcomes

After completing this section, students should be able to:

1. describe the role immigration has played in the creation of the U.S. as a nation;
2. explain how immigration laws are created;
3. identify the government agencies responsible for overseeing immigration; and
4. define *quotas*.

ACTIVITY—REFLECTIONS ON LIBERTY

Note: This activity can be completed before students begin studying this chapter or as a summary activity at the conclusion of this chapter, or both, to track how their attitudes may have changed.

Write the following phrase on the board: . . . *with liberty and justice for all.*

Ask students to spend about ten minutes reflecting on its meaning and creating a short essay, drawing, poem, or list of ideas that reflects their response to the phrase. Then ask students to switch papers with a neighbor and to review their classmate's reflections and to ask questions about it.

Have students discuss what the idea of liberty means to them. Liberty to do what? *(To earn a decent wage and to have a decent standard of living? To get an education? To express their ideas? To practice their religion freely? To give their children better opportunities than they had?)* Liberty from what? *(From poverty? From famine? From persecution? From war? From government intervention?)*

Where do those liberties come from? Does every person have them as part of their human rights? Do those liberties derive from rights gained by citizenship to a particular country? By living in a country that protects those liberties?

Then ask students to view the photograph of the Statue of Liberty in the Student Edition. As the text indicates, millions of people saw "Lady Liberty" on their way to Ellis Island when they arrived as immigrants in New York. It is estimated that more than 100 million people living in America today can trace their ancestry to people who passed through Ellis Island.

Ask students: What do you think immigrants thought of when they saw her? What did she represent to them?

Explain to students that much has been written about the symbolism integrated into the statue's design. (*She is based on the Roman goddess of freedom from slavery, oppression, and tyranny. One of her feet is trampling on shackles. The seven spikes on her crown represent the seven continents and seven seas. Her torch symbolizes enlightenment, and her tablet signifies knowledge and shows the date of the Declaration of Independence.*) If students want to learn more about the statue's history and symbolism, direct them to www.libertyellisfoundation.org.

Finally, ask students whether they think their relatives were drawn to the United States by liberty and whether they think they have found it. Is liberty still a draw for today's immigrants? Which liberties?

BACKGROUND—TEACHING ABOUT IMMIGRATION LAW

Immigration law is very complex, in part because it changes often and because there are so many factors that determine how the law treats immigrants in the United States.

Street Law, Inc., encourages teachers to work with legal professionals who have expertise in immigration. Many major cities and other communities with a large number of immigrants are home to law firms specializing in this area of the law. Invite lawyers, advocates, and judges to co-teach these topics and to help lead the interactive student activities throughout this chapter.

Immigration law information is also available online. The National Immigration Law Center's (www.nilc.org) mission is to protect and promote the rights of low-income immigrants and their families. Cornell Law School's Legal Information Institute (www.law.cornell.edu/topics) provides an overview of immigration law.

With the increase in the immigrant population throughout the United States, their legal rights have become a national political issue. These issues, with facts, policy options, and political perspectives, are presented online at www.publicagenda.org and www.procon.org.

ACTIVITY—TRACING IMMIGRATION LEGISLATION THROUGH HISTORY

TM Figure 42.1 lists many key court decisions, federal laws, and executive actions relating to

TM Figure 42.1

Date(s)	Name of Legislation, case, or executive action	What did it say? What did it do?	How did its passage reflect that period of history?	What was its impact?
1790	*Naturalization Act of 1790*			
1798	*The Alien and Sedition Acts of 1798*			
1807	*The Act Prohibiting Importation of Slaves*			
1819	*Immigration Act of 1819*			
1841	*United States v. The Amistad*			

TM Figure 42.1

Date(s)	Name of Legislation, case, or executive action	What did it say? What did it do?	How did its passage reflect that period of history?	What was its impact?
1848	Treaty of Guadalupe Hidalgo			
1868	The Fourteenth Amendment			
1882–1943	Chinese Exclusion Act of 1882			
1891	Immigration Act of 1891			
1901	The Anarchist Exclusion Act			
1907	Immigration Act of 1907 and "The Gentleman's Agreement" with Japan			
1921 and 1924 until about 1950	Quota Act of 1921 and National Origin Quota Act of 1924			
1924	Immigration Act of 1924			
1952	The Immigration and Nationality Act of 1952 (also known as the McCarran-Walter Act)			
1953	Refugee Relief Act			
1964 and 1965	Immigration and Nationality Act (as amended)			
1980	The Refugee Act			
1982	Plyler v. Doe			
1986	Immigration Reform and Control Act of 1986 and the Immigration Marriage Fraud Amendments of 1986			
1996	Illegal Immigration Reform and Immigrant Responsibility Act and the Anti-Terrorism and Effective Death Penalty Act of 1996			
2001	USA PATRIOT Act			
2002	Homeland Security Act of 2002			
2005	REAL ID Act of 2005			

TM Figure 42.1

Date(s)	Name of Legislation, case, or executive action	What did it say? What did it do?	How did its passage reflect that period of history?	What was its impact?
2006	*The Secure Fence Act of 2006*			
2012	*Deferred Action for Childhood Arrivals (DACA)*			
2012	*Arizona v. United States*			

immigration in the United States. Assign small groups of students to learn about these cases and legislation and then report on one or two of the laws and cases in the table. Or, ask students to create an annotated timeline for the class to create together.

To conduct research, students may simply search for the name of the case or law in news media or may consult a website such as www.law.cornell.edu. The important element in this activity is for students to make a hypothesis about how each action reflected the attitudes of courts and lawmakers at the time it was announced.

After students have reported on the laws they studied and completed their charts or timeline by listening to the presentations of their fellow students, ask students:

1. Which of these actions shows the United States opening its doors to immigrants and which shows the United States closing its doors to immigrants?

2. During which years was preference given to immigrants from certain countries or regions? (Or, when were immigrants from certain [other] regions or countries excluded through quotas?)

3. During which years was preference given to immigrants related to U.S. citizens and to highly skilled workers?

ACTIVITY—MAPPING THE MELTING POT

Ask students where their families lived before they came to the United States. They should be as specific as possible, naming at least the continent their ancestors came from and, if possible, the specific country or region.

Since many people have ancestors or relatives from numerous places, encourage students to name as many places as possible. Students may need to talk to their parents or guardians to get this information. Students who are adopted should be invited to list the home countries of their adoptive families and, if known, of their birth parents.

Once students have collected their lists, ask them to create a class map or circle graph that shows how many cultures are represented in the class and which countries are most represented. For example, how many push pins are placed on Canada or India or Italy on the map?

If possible have students conduct research online to learn about the broader migration patterns of others from the same region or country of origin. Direct students to the website of the Migration Policy Institute (MPI). From the homepage at www.migrationinformation.org, students should search for the MPI Data Hub, where they can find maps indicating where other people from their home countries have settled and a state-by-state demographic analysis of foreign-born people, including their countries of origin, citizenship status, education, and income levels. Finally, ask students to compare their class maps with the "pictures" of immigration they found online.

CITIZENSHIP (PP. 513–514)

BACKGROUND—MEETING CITIZENSHIP REQUIREMENTS

The U.S. Citizenship and Immigration Services (USCIS) offers a multitude of online resources for immigrants at www.uscis.gov. The site includes forms, frequently asked questions guides, and general information about immigration and immigration processes.

ACTIVITY—CITIZENSHIP TEST PANEL

Explain to students that after years of criticism and testing backlogs, the government began the process of revising the citizenship test for people who want to become naturalized citizens.[1] Ask students who they think would (and should) be involved in giving input to the government for the new test. (*Answers might include people representing immigrant advocacy groups, educators with expertise in history and civics, English literacy groups, Members of Congress from both political parties, immigrations officials, etc.*)

Organize students into small groups and tell them that each group will serve as a panel of advisers to USCIS that is responsible for preparing the new test. Ask each panel to make recommendations by discussing and reaching a consensus about the following questions. (Depending on class size and time, each group could answer all the questions, or each group could answer one question and report back to the class.)

- Should applicants for naturalization be required to demonstrate knowledge of U.S. history? If so, what should they know? Be specific.
- Should applicants be required to demonstrate knowledge of U.S. government? If so, what should they know?
- Should applicants be required to show what they know about the U.S. Constitution, other documents, laws, or Supreme Court decisions? If so, which documents? What should they know about those documents? Be specific.
- Should applicants be required to show what they know about U.S. culture? If so, what should they know?
- Should applicants be required to demonstrate proficiency in English? If so, how should they be expected to prove it? How proficient should they be? (Note: The test is currently administered orally. Is that the best way to continue?)

Ask the groups to present their findings to the class and then discuss these questions with the larger group:

- If your recommendations are accepted, how would you imagine applicants would learn the information they need to know?
- How long do you think the test should be? (How many questions?)
- Should there be a shorter test for senior citizens who have lived in this country legally for more than 20 years? (Note: The current test does allow legal permanent residents who are 65 or older to take a shorter test.)
- Do you think you could pass the test this class has recommended? Explain.
- Do you think most U.S. citizens could pass the test you have recommended?
- Think about your relatives who came to America before you. Do you think they could answer these questions? If not, should they have been turned away?
- In what ways, if any, does an applicant's knowledge of the topics your class has suggested improve his or her ability to be a good citizen?

Conclude by telling students that the revised test went into effect in October 2008. They can find information about the test, sample questions, vocabulary lists, and other study guides at www.uscis.gov.

DISCUSSION—IMMIGRANTS SWEARING ALLEGIANCE TO THE UNITED STATES

Remind students that before immigrants can become naturalized citizens, they must swear their allegiance to the United States. Use the questions for a class discussion:

- Do you think this requirement is reasonable prior to naturalization? Explain your reasons.
- Do you think all citizens, not just naturalized citizens, should be required to swear their allegiance to the United States? Why or why not?

According to USCIS, the oath of allegiance is:

"I hereby declare, on oath, that I absolutely and entirely renounce and abjure all allegiance and fidelity to any foreign prince, potentate, state, or sovereignty of whom or which I have heretofore been a subject or citizen; that I will support and defend the Constitution and laws of the United States of America against all enemies, foreign and domestic; that I will bear true faith and allegiance to the same; that I will bear arms on behalf of the United States when required by the law; that I will perform non combatant service in the Armed Forces of the United States when required by the law; that I will perform work of national importance under civilian direction when required by the law; and that I take this obligation freely without any mental reservation or purpose of evasion; so help me God."

In some cases, USCIS allows the oath to be taken without the clauses: "...that I will bear arms on behalf of the United States when required by law; that I will perform noncombatant service in the Armed Forces of the United States when required by law..." In addition, USCIS will permit the oath to be taken without reciting the words, "so help me God."[2]

Review the case of *West Virginia Board of Education* v. *Barnette*[3] with students. In 1941, the state of West Virginia passed a law that required all public and private school teachers and students to participate in activities for the purposes of "teaching, fostering, and perpetuating the ideals, principles and spirit of Americanism... [and] the government of the United States and of the state of West Virginia." Part of that requirement was "honoring the Nation represented by the Flag." Those who refused were considered "insubordinate" and could be punished by expulsion. Students who were expelled could not be re-admitted to school until they agreed to pledge. Parents of students who were

absent for five or more days of school could be charged with delinquency, and if convicted, subject to fines of $50 and up to 30 days in jail.

Walter Barnette and other Jehovah's Witnesses sued the school board, challenging the compulsory nature of the flag salute and Pledge. In one of the U.S. Supreme Court's most famous statements about protecting civil liberties, the Court said: "If there is any fixed star in our constitutional constellation, it is that no official, high or petty, can prescribe what shall be orthodox in politics, nationalism, religion, or other matters of opinion or force citizens to confess by word or act their faith therein."

Ask students whether the decision in this case changes their opinions about whether the requirement for naturalized citizens to swear their allegiance is reasonable and appropriate. Is there a difference between people coming into this country for the first time and people who have been here before?

Note: Extension teaching materials about this case are available in Chapter 38 of this Teacher Manual.

CAPTION ANSWER (P. 513) Citizenship by birth occurs when persons are born in the United States regardless of the citizenship status of their parents. The only exception is children born to diplomats.

PROBLEM 42.1 (p.514)

Students' responses will vary. Study guides and sample test questions for the civics test administered by the U.S. Citizenship and Immigration Service can be found at www.uscis.gov/citizenship/learners/study-test/study-materials-civics-test.

PROBLEM 42.2 (p.514)

a. Wilfred is a U.S. citizen because both his parents are U.S. citizens. It does not matter where he was born or that his mother is in the military.

b. Because Jose was born in the United States, he is a citizen. However, as a minor he may have to leave the country with his parents if there is no one left to care for him. He will be able to enter the United States for visits and to return as an adult.

c. Yes. Margot meets all the requirements for naturalization. Her application for naturalization is likely to be approved.

d. Ying's son may automatically be a citizen because his father became a citizen while his son was still a minor.

VISITORS AND LAWFUL PERMANENT RESIDENTS (PP. 514–516)

Learning Outcomes

After completing this section, students should be able to:

1. differentiate between different types of non-immigrant visas, including visas for tourists, students, and temporary workers;
2. describe the requirements of employer-sponsored immigrant visas;
3. explain how family-sponsored visas are determined and prioritized;
4. summarize the limits on who can receive green cards and lawful permanent resident (LPR) status; and
5. describe the purpose and requirements of the *Immigration Reform and Control Act of 1986;* and define the terms *visa, non-immigrant visa, immigrant visa, lawful permanent resident (LPR),* and *green cards.*

CAPTION ANSWER (P. 515) Tourists, temporary workers, athletes, musicians, government employees, ship or airline crew members, foreign media representatives, and participants in cultural or student exchanges may need a non-immigrant visa to enter the United States for a specified period.

DELIBERATION—SHOULD THE U.S. GOVERNMENT MAKE IT EASIER FOR UNAUTHORIZED IMMIGRANTS WHO CAME TO THIS COUNTRY AS CHILDREN PAY FOR COLLEGE?

Facilitate a deliberation on the following question: Should the U.S. government make it easier for unauthorized immigrants who came to this country as children to pay for college?

An overview of the deliberation method is available at the beginning of this Teacher Manual. A detailed lesson plan, instructional video, readings, and student handouts for this deliberation are available at https://store.streetlaw. org/deliberations/.

FIGURE 42.1 CAPTION ANSWER (P. 516) Family-sponsored green cards are issued the most (66.4%). Student answers will vary. Students may feel family-sponsored green cards are important to reunite families. Other students may feel that refugees from dangerous situations need green cards more urgently.

PEOPLE SEEKING HUMANITARIAN PROTECTION (PP. 516–518)

Learning Outcomes

After completing this section, students should be able to:

1. list what a person has to prove if he or she is seeking asylum in the United States;
2. explain the process an asylum seeker must go through; and
3. define the terms *asylum* and *refugee.*

Investigating the Law Where You Live

(p. 516) The primary legal resource for low-income people, the federally funded Legal Services Corporation, has been restricted by Congress from helping people seeking legal status in the United States. Still, many nonprofit organizations provide legal aid to immigrants who are facing deportation or other legal issues. Most of the organizations that offer legal aid operate locally, while several national organizations focus on training pro bono lawyers and advocating for immigrant rights. The National Immigration Law Center (www.nilc.org) and the Immigrant Legal Resource Center (www. ilrc.org) are two such organizations. The Immigrant Advocates Network (IAN) has a national network at www. lawhelp.org that includes professionals from public interest organizations, bar associations, and lay people. The U.S. Department of Justice (www.justice.gov/eoir/probono/states. htm) also provides listings of free legal aid sorted by state.

To find contact information for immigration courts throughout the United States, students can check the Department of Justice website at www.justice.gov/eoir/ sibpages/ICadr.htm.

BACKGROUND—REFUGEES AND ASYLEES IN THE U.S.

According to the Department of Homeland Security,[4] in 2017, 53,691 refugees were admitted to the United States—a 37 percent decrease from 2016. The decrease was due in large part to additional security vetting procedures. Admissions reached a low point in 2002, due in part to changes in security procedures and admission requirements after September 11, 2001. The number of refugee arrivals subsequently increased and reached a post-2001 peak in 2009. After decreasing from 2009 to 2011, refugee admissions increased sharply from 2012 to 2016. In 2017, the leading countries of nationality for individuals admitted as refugees were the Democratic Republic of the Congo (17 percent), Iraq (13 percent), Syria (12 percent), Somalia (11 percent), and Burma (9.5 percent). The leading states of residence of refugees admitted to the United States in 2017 were the most populous states—California, Texas, and New York, which resettled the most refugees (10, 9.0, and 6.0 percent of admitted refugees, respectively), Nebraska, North Dakota, and Washington resettled the most refugees per capita.

The total number of persons granted asylum in the United States increased 31 percent from 20,340 in 2016 to 26,568 in 2017. The leading countries of nationality of persons granted asylum were China (21 percent), El Salvador (13 percent), and Guatemala (11 percent). Nationals of these countries accounted for 45 percent of all persons granted asylum. In 2017, 58 percent of persons granted asylum were between the ages of 18 and 44. Like refugees, asylum seekers are, on average, younger than the native-born U.S. population: the median age of persons granted asylum in 2017 was 24 years (as to compared to 37 for native born population). Fifty-two percent were male, and 48 percent were married. In 2017, the leading states of residence for individuals granted asylum were California (46 percent) and New York (9.4 percent).

CAPTION ANSWER (P. 517) Persons seeking asylum in the United States must claim to have been persecuted (or have a justifiable fear of persecution) in their home country because of their race, religion, nationality, political opinion, or membership in a particular social or ethnic group.

PROBLEM 42.3 (p.518)

a. This practice, known as female genital mutilation (FGM), is outlawed in the United States and is condemned by the international human rights community. It may be grounds for granting asylum, but Grace will have to prove that she has a well-founded fear of being subjected to the practice and that the government of her country is unable or unwilling to stop the practice. She might enlist testimony from others about conditions in her country. If she can prove these requirements, her asylum is likely to be approved.

b. It is well known that the Chinese government has targeted some religions and arrested their members. Wong will have to prove that he belongs to a group that is targeted and that his fear is well founded. If he can prove this, his asylum is very likely to be granted.

c. Mohammed must prove that he has a reasonable fear of future persecution. His testimony establishes only that he has been threatened once, but it does not show that other such arrests or prohibitions on such political organization have taken place. Most likely, he will have to provide other evidence supporting his claim that he will be arrested. Without that, his request will likely be denied.

d. Domestic violence is sometimes allowed as grounds for asylum, but Eva must show that she could not find protection from domestic violence in her home country. She may be able to show that her husband is connected to the government in their home country or that domestic violence is not against the law there. Many people, however, argue that protection from domestic violence is not available in many countries and that women should be protected. Failing that evidence, Eva's request will likely be denied.

e. Rashid will not likely be able to receive asylum because he once fought against the United States. Access will almost certainly be denied.

UNDOCUMENTED IMMIGRANTS (P. 518)

Learning Outcomes

After completing this section, students should be able to:

1. explain the circumstances that would exist for an immigrant to be undocumented;
2. describe the difficulties that undocumented immigrants experience in the U.S.; and
3. define *human trafficking*.

BACKGROUND—IMMIGRANTS AND HUMAN TRAFFICKING

Coming to the United States can be an expensive and risky decision. While some immigrants attempt to enter the country illegally on their own, many others may pay thousands of dollars to a "coyote"—someone to help smuggle them in. The slang term developed because of the coyote's reputation for being furtive and untrustworthy. There have been many news stories about "coyotes" abandoning undocumented immigrants to die in some remote location, and some have been known to sell female immigrants into slavery.

In one particularly gruesome case, 19 Mexican and Central American immigrants died after being sealed in the back of an airless tractor-trailer truck that was left abandoned in a truck stop.[8] Two members of the smuggling ring were later convicted of "alien smuggling resulting in death."

If you ask most people, they will say that slavery ended in this country when the Civil War ended, or more accurately, with the passage of the Thirteenth Amendment in 1865. Perhaps that is why it is shocking to learn that human trafficking, slavery, and its related forms of involuntary servitude still exist here.

Human trafficking is defined as "the recruitment, harboring, transportation, provision, or obtaining of a person for labor or services, through the use of force, fraud, or coercion for the purposes of subjection to involuntary servitude, peonage, debt bondage or slavery."[9] The basic idea is that someone who is seeking a better life and better employment—often outside their home country—may fall prey to unscrupulous and criminal people and arrive in a life of slavery or bondage. According to a report from the U.S. State Department, some of the most common victims are women who are exploited while working as domestic help in private homes or as sex slaves, children who are sold as sex slaves, men who are imprisoned on the ships where they work, and people who are forced into labor with no compensation.

The International Labor Organization of the United Nations estimates that there are 12.3 million people in forced labor, bonded labor, forced child labor, and sexual servitude at any given time.

While the problem exists around the world, the estimated numbers in the United States are also alarming. According to government-sponsored research completed in 2018, between 600,000 and 800,000 people are trafficked across national borders. About 80 percent of these victims are women and girls, with approximately half being minors.[10] Some highly publicized cases in the United States include:

- In 2008, a suburban Washington, D.C.-area man pled guilty to holding a teenage girl as a slave for five years. When she was 14, the girl's father in Nigeria had been promised that she would be paid and could attend school in the United States if she cared for a doctor's five children. This doctor brought her to the United States using his oldest daughter's passport. She was never paid, became a domestic servant, and was not allowed to attend school. She was routinely raped by her employer, and his wife regularly beat her.[11]

- Thirty men came to the United States legally with guest worker visas. When several of them sustained life-threatening injuries and one was electrocuted, they organized to ask for safer working conditions. Their lives were threatened, and they fled the Texas work site. After another recruitment agency offered them jobs, they were left in Alabama for six days with no food or water. They escaped again and were in Mississippi when the captain of a local police department told them that the Alabama recruiter was their "owner" and that they had to go with him or face prison. When they resisted, the officer forced them into vans at gunpoint to return to the recruiter.[12]

- Twenty-two Thai men entered the United States legally with the help of a labor contracting company. Upon arrival, the contractor confiscated their passports, temporary agricultural worker visas, and return plane tickets. They were under constant guard, housed in a small storage building, and threatened with arrest and deportation if they left. Shortly after Hurricane Katrina, they were transported from North Carolina to New Orleans, where they lived in the same condemned building that they were working to tear down. They were not paid for their work, and some resorted to trapping and eating pigeons.[13]

As a sign of its complexity, and perhaps as part of the problem, more than 26 federal agencies in eight federal departments are involved in preventing trafficking, rescuing victims, and investigating and prosecuting claims. The United Nations has six offices and sub-organizations involved.

DETENTION AND REMOVAL OF NONCITIZENS (P. 519)

Learning Outcomes

After completing this section, students should be able to:

1. name the federal department and agency responsible for prosecuting immigration violations and for detaining and removing people who are in the country illegally;
2. describe the current situation as it relates to the detention of people suspected of being undocumented immigrants;
3. describe the rights of people accused of immigration violations;
4. explain where some people facing immigration charges may find legal help; and
5. describe the appeals process in cases where a person loses his or her removal case with the initial immigration judge.

ACTIVITY—SHOULD IT BE A DEPORTABLE OFFENSE?

Organize students into groups of three or four and have students assign each group member to be a reporter, recorder, or facilitator. Ask students to discuss each of the situations below and to decide whether the action should be a removable offense. Then students should rank the offenses from least serious to most serious. Remind students that at this stage, the point is not what the law says, but what students think it should say.

a. a person convicted of aggravated assault

b. a person convicted of carrying a handgun without a license

c. a person who was addicted to illegal drugs while living in the United States but who is now clean

d. an undocumented worker who is also the mother of a toddler born (with citizenship) in the United States

e. a person who filed for a visa extension in a timely manner but had not been notified by the time his visa expired

f. a person who has been convicted of sexually abusing a child

g. a person convicted of two cases of food stamp fraud on two separate days

h. a person convicted of the misdemeanor crime of soliciting sexual contact with a non-spouse

i. a person charged with (but not yet convicted of) a crime that could result in two or more years in prison, who fails to appear in court when ordered

j. a person who attempted to vote in a local election, but who was not a registered voter

After the groups have concluded their discussions and rankings, ask representatives to indicate and explain their group's rankings. In conclusion, tell students that each of these actions is, in fact, a removable offense.[14] These laws apply to immigrants who are in the country illegally as well as those with lawful permanent resident status, regardless of how long ago the crime was committed or whether time was served.[15]

CAPTION ANSWER (P. 519) In addition to evidence that removal would create a hardship for family members, an order of removal may be canceled if an immigrant has at least ten years of residence in the United States, no criminal convictions, and good moral character.

BACKGROUND—PATTERNS IN IMMIGRATION, REMOVAL, AND DETENTION

The U.S. Immigration and Customs Enforcement Agency (ICE) enforces federal laws governing border control, customs, trade and immigration. Each year ICE publishes a report on immigration removals. Here is a summary of 2018 immigration removal and detention patterns from the report.[16]

ICE conducted 256,085 removals in 2018. Of the interior removals ("an individual removed by ICE who is identified or apprehended in the U.S. by an ICE officer or agent)"[17], 145,262 involved individuals previously convicted of a crime. For updated immigration data visit the Department of Immigration and Customs Enforcement's website at https://www.ice.gov/statistics.

IMMIGRATION LAW AND POLICY (PP. 520–523)

After completing this section, students should be able to:

1. describe a range of views regarding the value that undocumented immigrants have in U.S. society;
2. explain which level of government has traditionally had responsibility to set and enforce immigration laws and policies;
3. formulate and express an opinion about various immigration reform proposals; and
4. summarize recent executive action on immigration.

BACKGROUND—GOVERNMENT SERVICES FOR IMMIGRANTS

California Proposition 187 was introduced in 1994 to deny undocumented immigrants (or those suspected of being so) social services, health care, and public education.[18] The proposition came before voters in the general election, where it received 59 percent of the vote and became law the next day. Its constitutionality was immediately challenged in several cases. A few days later, a federal judge issued a temporary restraining order against it, relying on the ruling in the 1982 case of *Plyler* v. *Doe*.[19] (Students may recall from their study of Chapter 41, that in the *Plyler* case, the U.S. Supreme Court handed down an important but controversial decision concerning the rights of schoolchildren of undocumented immigrants. In a 5-to-4 decision, the Court held for the first time that undocumented immigrants were "persons" and therefore entitled to equal protection under the Fourteenth Amendment.[20] In 1998, newly elected California Governor Gray Davis—who had opposed the proposition—had the case brought before mediation. He then dropped the appeals process before the courts, effectively killing the law.

In another challenge, the state of Texas unsuccessfully filed suit to require the federal government to pay the educational, medical, and criminal justice expenses allegedly incurred as a result of the presence of undocumented immigrants in Texas. Concluding that the complaint raised questions of policy rather than constitutional or statutory violations, the Supreme Court dismissed the lawsuit.[21]

ACTIVITY—TAKE A STAND FOR IMMIGRATION REFORM

This activity may be particularly sensitive for some students. You may wish to offer an alternative assignment for students who do not wish to particulate.

Post signs along the longest wall in your classroom. On one end, the sign should say "strongly agree," on the other end it should say "strongly disagree," and in the middle it should say "convince me, I'm not sure." Then, as you read each of the following policy proposals, ask students to stand along the wall to indicate their "stance" on the proposal.

For each example, after students have moved, ask a few volunteers to give their reasons why they chose that position, and then ask students whether they wish to move, based on the views expressed by their classmates.

- Undocumented immigrants may not use local services such as schools, libraries, or parks.
- Give immigration judges more leeway to consider each individual's circumstances when making decisions about asylum and removal.
- The government should create more ways for immigrants to enter the country legally, including addressing bureaucratic barriers to legality.
- Only English should be used in government notices about laws and regulation, and only English can be spoken by local government workers.
- Grant all people living in the United States the same due process rights in every legal proceeding.
- Employers may not hire undocumented workers. The criminal fines for employers who hire undocumented workers should be raised to $5,000 for the first offense and $75,000 and jail time for repeat offenses.
- The border with Mexico is still too "porous" and too many people are getting through illegally. We should build a (longer) fence between our two countries, hire more border patrol agents, and allow concerned U.S. citizens to help the Immigration and Customs Enforcement Office (ICE) monitor the border.
- ICE is not doing enough to remove undocumented immigrants. Even accounting for a wide range of estimates, the number of undocumented people living in the United States is too high. Local and state police departments should play a more active role in identifying undocumented immigrants and turning them over to ICE agents.

Note: To extend this activity or help students prepare to debate other immigration policy controversies, check out the website www.procon.org, which provides balanced pro and con arguments on many immigration reform topics.

CASE STUDY—IMMIGRATION LAW AND POLICY IN THE SUPREME COURT

The Supreme Court case about the constitutionality of the travel ban referenced in the Student Edition on page 521 is *Trump* v. *Hawaii*[22]. On September 24, 2017, President Trump issued a proclamation that limited travel to the United States to people from certain countries. According to the U.S. government, these countries either did not share enough information with the United States about terrorism risks and the identity of visitors, or they posed some other national security risk. These countries were given 50 days to bring their practices into compliance. Several of those countries did not change their practices, so the president issued a proclamation suspending some or all travel by their citizens to the United States. The eight affected countries were Chad, Iran, Libya, North Korea, Somalia, Syria, Venezuela (where the ban only applies to certain government officials), and Yemen. Chad was later removed from the ban. The government could grant waivers to individual travelers. The ban had no expiration date, but the U.S. government would review it every six months.

President Trump said that this measure was necessary to keep Americans safe. Opponents of the action, however, argued that the proclamation unlawfully targeted Muslims. The president issued two earlier orders banning citizens from several Muslim-majority countries from entering the United States. These two previous orders were struck down by federal courts.

The state of Hawaii, the Muslim Association of Hawaii, and several individuals sued the federal government over the president's September 2017 proclamation, arguing that it violated federal immigration law and unlawfully targeted Muslims. The Supreme Court considered several issues: Did the September 2017 executive action banning travel to the United States by nationals of several named countries violate federal immigration laws set forth in the *Immigration and Nationality Act*? Did the September 2017 executive action violate the Establishment Clause of the First Amendment?

In a 5-4 decision, the Supreme Court found for President Trump. The Court found that the travel ban did not exceed President Trump's authority under the *Immigration and Nationality Act*. Chief Justice John Roberts wrote that for national security reasons, the president may suspend travel of non-citizens from counties that do not share adequate information about the people migrating to the United States. The Court believed that President Trump's action regarding the ban passed the "rational basis test" because he provided legitimate national security interests that admitting non-citizens from other countries might pose a national security risk. Although five of the seven countries are Muslim-majority, the Court did not find evidence that the countries were chosen based on their majority religion. Because religion could not be proven to be the primary reason for their selection, there was no violation of the First Amendment Establishment Clause.

For a full case summary of *Trump* v. *Hawaii* (2018), visit Street Law's website at https://store.streetlaw.org/.

The *Deferred Action for Childhood Arrivals (DACA)* policy is still being ligated in the Supreme Court of the United States (as mentioned on page 521 of the Student Edition). The case, *Department of Homeland Security* v. *Regents of the University of California*[23], will decide if the Trump Administration can legally wind down the *DACA* policy. Updated information can be found at https://www.scotusblog.com/case-files/cases/department-of-homeland-security-v-regents-of-the-university-of-california/.

PROBLEM 42.4 (p.521)

a. Student answers will vary. Some students might feel that all undocumented immigrants should be deported regardless of age. Some may feel that since the United States is the only home these young people know, they should be permitted to remain in the country.

b. Student answers will vary. Students who feel they should be legal residents might again site the lack of proper immigration and naturalization processes. Students who advocate citizenship may cite that young children are not culpable for violating immigration law because they are minors.

c. Student answers will vary. Students may state that an executive order is permissible because immigration policy is carried out by the executive branch which the president has the right to command. Others may feel that the Framers meant for such an important issue to be decided by Congress since Article I give only the

Congress the power to "establish a uniform rule of naturalization." Article I establishes that powers over citizenship require the federal government to act, not the individual states.

THE CASE OF...

State or Federal Authority Over Immigrant Enforcement

PROBLEM 42.5 (p.522)

a. Arizona

b. U.S.

c. U.S.

d. Arizona

e. U.S.

f. U.S.

g. Arizona

The case referenced in this problem is *Arizona* v. *United States* (2010)[24]. This case can be explored further using Street Law's case study strategies. For further explanation of the strategies, download the "Using Case Studies in the Classroom" guide at https://store.streetlaw.org/using-case-studies-in-the-classroom/. These strategies are also outlined in the front of this Teacher Manual. The case summary for *Arizona* v. *United States* can be found at https://store.streetlaw.org/ by typing the case name in the search box.

TAKING ACTION:
LAW AND DEMOCRACY

PROBLEM 42.6 (p.523)

As students discuss which reforms they might support as a representative of their district, check in with each role group to make sure they are clear on their role and perspective. When student groups come together to search for consensus on an immigration reform bill, make sure each group is allowed

equal time to voice their perspectives. The intended outcome of the activity is for students to create a bill that not only incorporates multiple perspectives but also create a bill that could "pass" a vote from the majority of representatives.

NOTES

(1) Sachs, Susan. "Pressed by Backlog, U.S. Rethinks Citizenship Test," *The New York Times*. July 5, 1999.

(2) Policy Manual, Chapter 3, Part J, Volume 12, U.S. Citizenship and Immigration Services, http://www.uscis.gov/policymanual/HTML/PolicyManual-Volume12-PartJ-Chapter3.html.

(3) *West Virginia State Board of Education* v. *Barnette*, 319 U.S. 624 (1943).

(4) Mossaad, Nadwa, *Annual Flow Report: Refugees and Asylees 2017*, Office of Immigration Statistics, Department of Homeland Security, 2019.

(5) *Antiterrorism and Effective Death Penalty Act*, Pub. L.No. 104–132, 110 Stat. 1214 (1996) and the *Illegal Immigration Reform and Immigrant Responsibility Act*, Pub. L.No. 104–208, 110 Stat. 3009 (1996).

(6) "U.S.: Mandatory Deportation Laws Harm American Families: Legal Residents Often Deported for Minor Crimes," *Human Rights Watch*, Press Release. July 18, 2007.

(7) Schrag, Philip G. and David Ngaruri Kenney, *Asylum Denied: A Refugee's Struggle for Safety in America*. University of California Press. 2008.

(8) Barnes, Steve. "Conviction in Immigrant Deaths Case," *The New York Times*. December 24, 2004.

(9) Trafficking in Persons Report, June, 2018. U.S. Department of State accessed at https://www.state.gov/wp-content/uploads/2019/01/282798.pdf.

(10) Ibid.

(11) "Md. Man Pleads Guilty to Holding Teen Slave," *The Associated Press*. July 16, 2008.

(12) Sturgis, Sue. "Modern-day slavery on the Gulf Coast: Pascagoula Police Captain Kidnaps Guest workers," *The Institute for Southern Studies*. August 22, 2007.

(13) Collins, Kristin. "Workers: Promise Became A Prison: Thai Men Sue N.C. Contractor," *The News & Observer*. March 10, 2007.

(14) For cases **a.**, **b.**, **f.**, **i.**, and **j.**, see: *Immigration and Nationality Act* 8 U.S.C. § 1227 (2000). For case **d.**, see: Preston, Julia "As Deportation Pace Rises, Illegal Immigrants Dig In," *The New York Times.* May 2, 2007. For cases **c.**, **e.**, **g.**, and **h.**, see: Kurzban, Ira J. *Immigration Law Sourcebook, Tenth Edition* American Immigration Law Foundation 2006. pp. 52, 128, 133, and 135.

(15) www.pbs.org/independentlens/ sentencedhome/immigration.html, accessed July 2008.

(16) Fiscal Year 2018 ICE Enforcement and Removal Operations Report, U.S. Immigration and Custom Enforcement, https://www.ice. gov/doclib/about/offices/ero/pdf/ eroFY2018Report.pdf.

(17) See 16.

(18) *Plyler* v. *Doe,* 457 U.S. 202 (1982).

(19) *Reed* v. *Reed,* 404 U.S. 71 (1971).

(20) *Plyler* v. *Doe,* 457 U.S. 202 (1982).

(21) *Michael M.* v. *Superior Court of Sonoma County,* 450 U.S. 464 (1981).

(22) *Trump* v. *Hawaii,* 138 S.Ct. 2392 (2018).

(23) *Department of Homeland Sec.* v. *Regents of the Univ. of Cal.,* ____ U.S. ____ (argued Nov. 12, 2019).

(24) *Arizona* v. *U.S.,* 567 U.S. 387 (2012).

networks™

Intellectual property is a product of the human mind—music, art, literature, inventions, scientific discoveries, and technological innovations. Intellectual property is protected by the law just as tangible property is protected. However, because creations of the mind are not physical objects, intellectual property law is very different.

Today intellectual property is more accessible than ever because of the widespread and growing use of computers, digital music players and handheld devices. As well, each year intellectual property becomes a bigger part of the U.S. economy. Therefore, it is important for students to understand how intellectual property law protects not only those who create intellectual property, but also those who lawfully consume an assortment of intellectual property every day. In this chapter students will explore how intellectual property is classified and protected by the law.

INTRODUCTION (PP. 524–525)

Learning Outcomes

After completing this section, students should be able to:
1. define the terms *intellectual property, patent, copyright, trademark,* and *infringement;* and
2. list at least three examples of intellectual property.

ACTIVITY—IDENTIFYING INTELLECTUAL PROPERTY

One way to introduce students to the difference between a copyright and a patent is to tell half of the class that they are inventors, and instruct them to invent something. Tell the other half of the class that they are authors, and instruct them to write something. Provide no further instructions. After a couple of minutes, ask the class to raise their hands if they have anything written down. Chances are that the authors will all have something written, because authors express themselves and expression must be recorded or fixed in some manner. By contrast, inventors deal in the realm of ideas. Ask the inventors what makes their idea an invention. The answer is that it is novel: nobody has thought of it before. Ask the authors what makes them authors: they have expressed themselves. The activity could be used to elicit many of the differences between copyright and patent. Copyrights protect fixed, creative expression; patents protect novel inventions and discoveries.

PATENTS (PP. 525–526)

Learning Outcomes

After completing this section, students should be able to:
1. describe the characteristics of what should be patented;
2. explain the patent process; and
3. distinguish between monopoly and public domain as they apply to patents.

a. Light that was not produced by candle or gas-light so is safer and easier to maintain.

b. A more convenient, safer way to shave.

c. A more convenient way to apply liquids such as deodorant and hair spray.

d. A more convenient, safer way to heat foods and liquids.

e. A more intuitive way to navigate on a computer screen.

ACTIVITY—MINI-MOOT COURT: SHOULD GENES BE PATENTABLE?

Recently there has been a great deal of debate surrounding the issue of whether human genes should be patentable. There are strongly held views on both sides of the debate and the U.S. Supreme Court ruled on the issue in 2013.[1] For this activity, divide the class into three even groups. Make one group "pro," one group "con," and one group "judges." Distribute the "Overview" paragraph below to the whole class and then distribute the pro and con bullets only to the appropriate side. (The judges should not receive copies of the arguments.)

Have each group meet to go over their material and brainstorm additional arguments they can make. Have the judges review the background information and discuss the format for their mini-moot.

When the groups are ready, pair one pro student with one con student and one judge. Have each group simultaneously conduct mini-moot courts. Finally have the judges from each group decide the "winner" and state the strongest argument from each side. Discuss the results.

When the classroom discussion is complete, tell students that in the case of *Association for Molecular Pathology* v. *Myriad Genetics,* the U.S. Supreme Court ruled that the genes in this case were not patentable because Myriad did not create anything. Simply isolating the genes from the bloodstream did not change the genes from their natural form. However, the Court left open the possibility that if a company did alter the form of the genes, a patent might be appropriate.

Overview

Patents may be obtained on useful inventions and discoveries that are novel or new. Recently there has been a great deal of debate as to whether individual human genes should be patentable. A company called "The Gene Company" identified two genes that are indicators of increased risk of breast and ovarian cancer. The company applied for and obtained a patent on the two genes. Because of these patents, if anyone wants to be tested to determine if they have these genes, they must go to The Gene Company for such testing. In addition, if anyone wants to examine, research or study these genes in any way, they must get the permission of The Gene Company. Because of the obvious value of these genes, investors have invested large sums of money in The Gene Company, relying on the strength of the gene patents.

Suggested Pro Arguments

1. The Gene Company invested a great deal of time, expertise, and money in identifying the links between these genes and specific cancers. This discovery has been crucial in identifying women at increased risk for cancer and allowing those women to take steps to minimize or eliminate that risk. If companies like The Gene Company cannot recoup the cost of that investment, these types of scientific advancements will not occur.

2. Financial investment from outsiders in scientific research is critical to its continuation. If the genes are not patentable, then there will be no incentive for individuals and corporations to invest money in this area of science.

3. Although The Gene Company did not create the genes, it was the first to identify them.

4. Just because The Gene Company has a patent on these genes does not mean that other researchers cannot use them. It simply means that others must obtain permission from The Gene Company first.

5. Patents are granted for a specific period of time, not forever. After that time period has expired, the genes will be available for any researcher to use without permission.

Suggested Con Arguments

1. Obtaining a patent on a part of the human body—something that every human possesses—is absurd. What if the first scientist who discovered the human heart had patented it? Would every doctor thereafter who wanted to listen to a patient's heartbeat have to get permission first?

2. The Gene Company simply took the genes out of the human body. They did not create those genes and they did not make anything out of those genes, so their actions do not meet the requirements for a patent.

3. If The Gene Company is permitted to maintain its patent on these genes, it will prevent future inventors from using those genes to make additional important discoveries.

4. Products of nature should not be eligible for a patent. A tree cannot be patented, but a baseball bat made from a tree is patentable. The Gene Company is looking to patent the tree, not the bat.

5. Changes in science occur very quickly. Asking inventors and other scientists to wait 20 years before they may conduct research would severely hinder further scientific advances in this area.

Additional information for this activity was obtained from the ACLU[2] and SCOTUSBlog.[3] For additional information about teaching moot courts, see the Front of this Teacher Manual or download the "Mini-Moot Courts Bundle" which includes an instructional video, detailed instructions, and student handouts at https://store.streetlaw.org/videos/. In addition, you may be interested in *Street Law's Guide to Mock Trials and Moot Courts* (2006). You can find out more about that at www.streetlaw.org.

COPYRIGHTS (PP. 527–528)

Learning Outcomes

After completing this section, students should be able to:
1. describe how copyright works when applied to original works;
2. distinguish between patents and copyrights;
3. explain why someone would want to register a copyright;
4. explain situations when "fair use" of copyrighted material would apply; and
5. define *first sale* and *fair use*.

DISCUSSION—IDENTIFYING COPYRIGHTS

Ask students to raise their hands if they think they own a copyright. The class will be surprised to learn that each of them owns many legally enforce-

able copyrights and that once they fix any type of creative expression, they own the copyright to that work. Copyright notice (which is optional) can be illustrated by a scavenger hunt through the classroom for copyright notices.

Once students are aware that they own copyrights, ask them what they think their copyrights protect against. The five exclusive rights are reproduction, production of derivative works, distribution, performance, and display.

Clarify the doctrine of first sale with students. Buying a painting, for example, does not give the new owner the right to copy it, although the owner may display or resell the painting. The practice of software licensing, on the other hand, allows software companies to avoid the harsh effects of first sale, which allows the owner of an individual work to resell or dispose of that particular copy of the work. For example, if computer programs were sold to consumers outright, the first buyer could install the program on his or her computer and then give it to a friend, who could install it on his or her computer and give it to another friend, and so on.

Computer programs are not subject to the first-sale doctrine, however, because they are typically licensed to consumers through shrink-wrap licenses rather than sold. Shrink-wrap licenses are distributed via notices that inform the consumer that opening the outside wrapping of the software constitutes agreement to the licensing terms contained inside.

DISCUSSION AND ACTIVITY— PLAGIARISM

Use the topic of intellectual property to discuss plagiarism. Discuss and clarify the meanings of plagiarism and paraphrasing, reasons why teachers prohibit plagiarism, and how they are related to intellectual property concepts.

Describe consequences students may face if they are found guilty of plagiarism, such as expulsion or loss of course credit.

Discuss the implications of this issue in the digital age. How might a student get into trouble when downloading text or photos from a website and incorporating them into a homework assignment? How can students use copyrighted material appropriately?

Educating About Intellectual Property (www.educateip.org) has a series of lessons designed around specific intellectual property issues. You can find links to the lessons under the Curriculum Tab. Lesson 4 deals specifically with plagiarism.

BACKGROUND AND ACTIVITY—THE FAIR USE DOCTRINE

Copyright provides legal protection for written/tangible works including art, books, and music. When a work is copyrighted the owner has exclusive control over what can be done with the work. This means that it cannot be copied or used by another person without permission.

As with many legal protections there are some exceptions to the rule. One major exception to copyright law is called the "Fair Use Doctrine." According to www.copyright.gov, the doctrine of "fair use" has developed through a substantial number of court decisions over the years and has been codified in section 107 of the copyright law.[4]

"Fair use" occurs when a person using copyrighted material maintains that it is a reasonable and limited use of a copyrighted work or a portion of that work. Examples include news reporting, teaching, scholarship or research. The distinction between what is "fair use" and what is infringement in a particular case will not always be clear or easily defined. There is no specific number of words, lines, or notes that may safely be taken without permission. If you are not sure if your use of the copyrighted material falls under "fair use," the safest option is to get permission from the copyright owner before using copyrighted material.

Educating About Intellectual Property (www.educateip.org) has a series of lessons designed around specific intellectual property issues. You can find links to the lessons under the Curriculum Tab. Lesson 3 deals specifically with "fair use."

PROBLEM 43.2 (p.528)

a. This is an example of "fair use." It is legal for Gloria to sell the DVD under what is referred to as the "first sale doctrine." The "first sale doctrine" provides that an individual who purchases a copy of a copyrighted work from the copyright holder receives the right to sell, display or otherwise dispose of that particular copy.

b. Buying CDs and then copying them and selling the copies are obvious violations of copyright law. Gloria should not do this.

c. This is another example of "fair use." Gloria is not selling the photograph; rather, she is using it as part of a school project. In this situation, the rights of the television network are not being violated.

ACTIVITY: FAIR USE

Shepard Fairey, an artist, created the artwork that was one of the best-known images during the 2008 presidential campaign. He created a shaded image of Barack Obama looking upwards. Others took his image and sold it on hundreds of thousands of buttons, posters, websites, and t-shirts. The image is based on an Associated Press (AP) photograph, taken in April 2006 by Mannie Garcia on assignment for the AP. The AP said it owns the copyright and wanted credit and payment. Fairey disagreed.

Find and display side-by-side pictures of the original photo and the Shepard Fairey poster (for example, http://www.npr.org/blogs/thetwo-way/2011/01/12/132860606/shepard-fairey-and-ap-settle-copyright-dispute-over-hope-poster).

Organize students into small groups, and assign half of the groups to generate arguments that Shepard Fairey could make that his poster was "fair use." Assign the other half to generate arguments that the AP could make that his poster was copyright infringement. After allowing time for students to work, call on the groups in an alternating fashion (a Fairey group, then an AP group, etc.) to list one of the arguments they came up with.

In the actual case, Shepard Fairey argued that his use of the image fell under "fair use" because his artwork significantly changed the photo upon which it was based. He also argued that his art was intended for political use, not commercial. He said that he did not receive any money from the sale of the posters and other items. He pointed out that the use of the photo had not diminished its value—if anything, the photo's value had increased since he created his art.

The AP argued that the image is very recognizable, had not really been modified or altered, and was not part of a collage or other art form. They said that since he took the entire photo, which is itself an artistic work, and used it for commercial purposes, it is not "fair use."

Ultimately, the two parties reached a settlement before the case went to trial. In their unusual settlement, both sides agreed to share the rights to make posters and other merchandise using the Hope image. They also agreed to collaborate on a new series of images that Fairey would create using photographs by AP. Moving forward, Fairey agreed to get a license from AP before he uses another AP photo in his work.

DISCUSSION—PARODY

In small groups, ask students to generate a list of parodies of popular culture. Encourage groups to share their ideas with the class, and write student answers on the board. Ask the groups to consider this list and develop a working definition of the word *parody*. Discuss what parodies have in common with the original work and how they differ. Ask students when, if ever, a parody should be considered a copyright infringement of the original work. Encourage groups to write a rule courts could use to decide infringement cases.

Tell students that the Supreme Court of the United States decided a case, *Campbell* v. *Acuff-Rose Music, Inc.*[5] that considered this question. The band 2 Live Crew produced a song "Pretty Woman," which was a parody of the song "Oh, Pretty Woman," by Roy Orbison. They asked Acuff-Rose Music, the record company with the copyright, for a license to use the song but the company denied the request. 2 Live Crew produced the parody without permission. Acuff-Rose Music sued Luther Campbell and the other members of the band 2 Live Crew for copyright infringement. They argued that the song was a commercial for-profit venture, so should not be protected by "fair use." 2 Live Crew argued that it was an artistic parody so should be protected by "fair-use."

To help decide the case, the Court considered all four of these factors: (1) the purpose and character of the use, including whether such use is of a commercial nature or is for nonprofit educational purposes; (2) the nature of the copyrighted work; (3) the amount and substantiality of the portion used in relation to the copyrighted work as a whole; and (4) the effect of the use upon the potential market for or value of the copyrighted work.

In a unanimous decision, the Court found for the band. They ruled that even if a parody makes a profit, it can still be protected by "fair use" and not amount to a copyright infringement because it did not copy extensively from the original.

Details of the case can be found at https://www.oyez.org/cases/1993/92-1292. A C-Span video taped days before *Campbell* v. *Acuff-Rose Music, Inc.* was argued at the Supreme Court would be interesting background for teachers and is available at https://www.c-span.org/video/?52141-1/campbell-v-acuff-rose-music-inc.

After discussing the case, have groups revisit their original list of parodies. Ask students to consider each parody and discuss how they would rule if they were a court deciding whether or not it was a copyright infringement.

BACKGROUND—ONLINE PIRACY AND FILE SHARING

According to the Recording Industry Association of America (RIAA), the U.S. economy loses $12.5 billion in total output annually as a result of music theft. Digital music theft has been a major factor behind the decline in music sales over the past 20 years. From 2004 through 2009 alone, approximately 30 billion songs were illegally downloaded on file-sharing networks.[6]

Peer to peer file sharing was the subject of several federal appellate court cases in the last 15 years. In *MGM Studios* v. *Grokster*[7], the Supreme Court decided companies that encourage and profit from peer to peer file sharing (which violates copyrights) could be held liable for damages.

TRADEMARKS (PP. 529–531)

Learning Outcomes

After completing this section, students should be able to:

1. describe situations when a trademark would be used;
2. distinguish between the four categories of trademark: fanciful, arbitrary, suggestive, and merely descriptive;
3. explain the trademark registration process; and
4. define *counterfeit goods* and explain the problems that occur when the public has access to *counterfeit goods*.

PROBLEM 43.3 (p.530)

Students' responses and opinions may vary. However, students might consider:

a. The strength of T. Markey's mark is the unique spelling of the name and the detailed logo.

b. The relatedness of the goods is strong because both products are apparel.

c. The marks are very similar, the names sound the same when said aloud, and the graphics are identical but an inverse of each other. They do, however, differ in the spelling of the name, the names are written in a noticeably different font, and the graphics are facing opposite directions.

d. Evidence of actual consumer confusion is lacking, but the original company alleges it.

e. The sophistication of the purchasers is unclear in this case.

f. Tee Marque states that his intent was parody.

The problem is loosely based on an actual case between The North Face and a Missouri teenager, Jimmy Winkelmann, the creator of a company called The South Butt. According to Winkelmann, who created the company to make money for college, The South Butt was created as a parody of The North Face. Beyond the oppositional name, The South Butt's tag line was "Never Stop Relaxing,"while The North Face's tagline was "Never Stop Exploring." The North Face sued Winkelmann for infringement and eventually the two parties settled the case out of court.[8]

Discuss with your students whether they think The South Butt was parody or piracy. What is the difference? Should it matter in terms of the outcome?

ACTIVITY—REVIEW

To review the three categories of IP, create Mystery Intellectual Property Bags. Prepare one brown paper bag for every four students in the class. Include in each bag 4-5 common household items that have components that are trademarked, copyrighted, or patented. Ideas for objects: small package of facial tissues, tube of toothpaste, gum a shoe, a magazine, a pen, packaged food item, etc. Place students in groups of four.

Give each group a Mystery Intellectual Property Bag and instruct them to identify anything in the bag that is subject to copyright, patent, or trademark protection. Ask each group to choose a recorder to keep track of their conclusions. Allow about ten minutes for the students to work through their bags and discuss, and then have the groups report out on their findings. Discuss their ideas and the items in each bag. Point out any copyrights, patents, or trademarks they may have missed.

TAKING ACTION:
LAW AND DEMOCRACY

Counterfeit Goods

PROBLEM 43.4 (p.531)

a. Students' responses will vary. First, purchase your prescription medications from a trusted pharmacy, preferably one that you have worked with before. Second, when you receive your medication, examine it to ensure it looks exactly as it has in the past. Counterfeit medications often have subtle differences such as changes in pack-

aging or lettering on the medication. Finally, if you need to use an Internet pharmacy, make sure it is a credible one. How can you tell? The FDA has a website called the Counterfeit Alert Network (https://www.fda.gov/drugs/drug-safety-and-availability/counterfeit-alert-network) to bring attention to online pharmacies that have distributed counterfeit medications.

b. Yes. The creation and distribution of counterfeit products is a form of infringement. When a pharmaceutical company creates and sells a drug, the company generally takes out a patent for that particular medication. When counterfeit medications are created and marketed as patented medications, that is a form of patent infringement.

c. Students' responses will vary. If you suspect you have taken a counterfeit medication, contact your doctor immediately. If you suspect you have received a counterfeit medication, bring it to your local pharmacy for further inspection. If you come across a website that you suspect might be associated with counterfeit prescription drugs, contact the Food and Drug Administration at www.fda.gov.

NOTES

(1) *Association for Molecular Pathology* v. *Myriad Genetics, Inc.*, 133 S. Ct. 2107 (2013).

(2) The Fight to Take Back our Genes, *American Civil Liberties Union*, https://www.aclu.org/fight-take-back-our-genes.

(3) Denniston, Lyle, Argument recap: Analogies to the rescue, *SCOTUSBlog*, April 15, 2013, http://www.scotusblog.com/2013/06/opinion-recap-no-patent-on-natural-gene-work/.

(4) *Limitations on exclusive rights: Fair use*, 17 U.S. Code section 107 (1990).

(5) *Campbell* v. *Acuff-Rose Music, Inc.*, 510 U.S. 569 (1994).

(6) 2019 Piracy Impact: The True Cost of Sound Recording Piracy to the U.S. Economy, Recording Industry Association of America, https://www.riaa.com/reports/the-true-cost-of-sound-recording-piracy-to-the-u-s-economy/.

(7) *Metro-Goldwyn-Mayer Studios Inc.* v. *Grokster, Ltd.*, 545 U.S. 913 (2005).

(8) Hines, Alice, "The Butt Face, The North Face Spoof, Agrees to Halt Clothing Sales," *The Huffington Post*, October 25, 2012.

CHAPTER 44
Law and Terrorism

The terrorist attacks against the United States on September 11, 2001, fundamentally changed U.S. foreign policy. The war on terror that started with these attacks and a focus on one terrorist organization, Al-Qaeda, has developed into a "war" with several terrorist organizations in many different countries. The war on terror is a source of continuing debate and controversy. Civil liberties groups and others claim that many provisions of the laws that have been created as part of the war on terror are not justified in terms of security and therefore go too far in restricting individual rights when the United States is not officially at war. This chapter will explore the legal frontier associated with the threat of contemporary terrorism. The terrorist attacks on September 11, 2001, and concerns about future attacks led President George W. Bush, Congress, state legislators, and mayors of U.S. cities to institute new laws and policies to protect Americans.

INTRODUCTION (PP. 532–533)

Learning Outcomes

After completing this section, students should be able to:
1. explain how laws governing war have changed;
2. describe the debate over laws and policies put into place as part of the war on terror; and
3. define the term *habeas corpus*.

BACKGROUND—WHAT IS TERRORISM?

Although an act of terrorism can be easy to recognize, the term itself is difficult to define. The trouble in formulating a precise definition stems from the charged nature of the word itself. Terrorism has as many different definitions as there are political perspectives. Acts that are labeled as "terrorist" by some are perceived as dutiful, heroic, and courageous by others. For these people, displays of loyalty to a cause through violent acts serve a greater good. For others, an act of terrorism is an intentional, vicious, and unjustifiable act carried out against a group of typically nonmilitary innocent people for purposes of intimidation or coercion.

Most definitions agree that terrorism is a premeditated criminal act intended not only to harm its direct victims but also to have an intense and lasting psychological impact on others. There are other elements of terrorism worth noting:

- Most people believe terrorism targets civilians.
- Most experts agree that terrorism is highly strategic.
- Most people see terrorism as politically or socially motivated.
- According to the United States Department of State, terrorism is defined this way by U.S. law:

  (1) the term "international terrorism" means terrorism involving citizens or the territory of more than one country;

  (2) the term "terrorism" means premeditated, politically motivated violence perpetrated against non-combatant targets by subnational groups or clandestine agents; and

  (3) the term "terrorist group" means any group practicing, or which has significant subgroups which practice, international terrorism.[1]

- Both the U.S. Department of State and the Central Intelligence Agency (CIA) define terrorism as "premeditated, politically motivated violence perpetrated against non-combatant targets by subnational groups or clandestine agents, usually intended to influence an audience."

Although people have yet to reach a consensus definition of terrorism, experts have identified elements that are typical of most terrorists and their motivations. According to the Constitutional Rights Foundation article "What Is Terrorism?" terrorist acts are typically carried out by individuals or groups who:

- lack the political power to peacefully change policy that they find unjust or wrong;
- seek to intimidate, create or increase anxiety and fear, coerce a population or government to succumb to their ideals and demands, and create a situation in which a government will change its policies to avoid further disruptions;
- seek to attract as much media attention as possible to disseminate fear and anxiety to a larger group and create social awareness of their cause; and
- often justify their acts on ideological or religious grounds."[2]

In addition to Street Law's materials and lesson plans, teachers may want to consider resources offered by the Constitutional Rights Foundation (http://www.crf-usa.org/america-responds-to-terrorism/what-is-terrorism.html). In addition, the United States Institute of Peace offers a three-lesson teaching guide targeted for grades 11–12 entitled "Teaching Guide on International Terrorism: Definitions, Causes and Responses." This guide is available online at https://www.usip.org/publications/2001/11/international-terrorism-definitions-causes-and-responses.

BACKGROUND—RIGHTS DURING WARTIME

After President Lincoln suspended habeas corpus during the Civil War in 1862, the U.S. Supreme Court ruled in 1866 that Lincoln had gone too far when he ordered civilians to be tried in military courts. In *Ex Parte Milligan*,[3] the Court held, "The Constitution of the United States is a law for rulers and people, equally in war and peace, and covers with the shield of its protection all classes of men, at all times and under all circumstances."

During World War I, Congress and many state and local governments passed laws that restricted oral and written speech criticizing government involvement in the war. In a landmark case involving free speech from that era, *Schenck* v. *United States*,[4] the Supreme Court ruled, "When a nation is at war many things that might be said in a time of peace are such a hindrance to its effort that their

utterance will not be endured so long as men fight and that no Court could regard them as protected by any constitutional rights." The Court also established in this case the requirement that the government must show that there is a "clear and present danger" before suppressing speech.

Note: The *Schenck* decision and the tests it provided for free speech remained the law of the land for many years. In 1969, the case of *Brandenburg* v. *Ohio* created a new standard, updating the "clear and present danger" test from *Schenck*.

In *Brandenburg*, the court said that speech can be prohibited only if it is "directed at inciting or producing imminent lawless action" and if it is "likely to incite or produce such action."[5] Even speech advocating violent action is protected by the First Amendment unless it is "likely to incite imminent lawless action."

The U.S. Supreme Court upheld many of the restrictions on Japanese Americans during World War II. When the Court upheld curfews for Japanese Americans, Justice William O. Douglas, one of the most liberal judges ever to sit on the Supreme Court, wrote: "Where the perils are great and time is short, temporary treatment on a group basis may be the only practical expedient."[6] In the case of *Korematsu* v. *United States*, Justice Hugo Black ruled that the internment of Japanese Americans was constitutional, saying, "Hardships are part of war, and in greater or lesser measure, citizenship has its responsibilities as well as its privileges."[7] While many students may know that the United States government interned 112,000 Japanese Americans during World War II, they may not know that about 250 Italian Americans were also interned and that many Italian immigrants waiting for citizenship were classified as enemy aliens and subject to curfews and other restrictions[8] Though *Korematsu* was never explicitly overturned, the United States now considers the internment to have been wrong and has provided reparations.

PROBLEM 44.1 (p.533)

a. Students' answers will vary. The restriction of individual rights and privacy since September 11, 2001, is justified by its advocates in the name of national security, just as were the restrictions employed during the Civil War, World War I, and World War II.

The war on terror is different from other wars because it is not fought against nation-states, but rather against nonstate actors such as al-Qaeda and ISIS, which operate out of a number of different countries. Because terrorists are not readily identifiable like most military personnel, it is harder to determine who might be a terrorist. Unlike World War I and World War II, there has been no formal congressional declaration of war in the war on terror. A formal declaration of war extends the powers of Congress and the president.

During World War II, the U.S. government justified its internment of Japanese Americans because it feared that they would be loyal to Japan. Today, law enforcement agencies focus on people from the Middle East and South Asia for similar reasons. It is important to note that during World War II, no Japanese American was ever convicted of espionage; in fact, many fought and died in the war against Japan.

None of the people from the Middle East and South Asia who were interrogated by the FBI shortly after the attacks of September 11, 2001, was charged with a terrorist offense.

Since the September 11, 2001, attacks, Muslims and Arab Americans say they have experienced discrimination from some in the government and hate crimes like those experienced by German Americans, Italian Americans, and Japanese Americans during World War I and World War II. The U.S. government has vigorously denied that it uses racial or religious profiling and says that it aggressively prosecutes hate crimes against Muslims and Arab Americans.

b. Students' answers will vary. Students may respond that they would want to be able to deploy troops without congressional approval, set curfews at home, investigate individuals or groups without a cumbersome warrant process, or use advanced interrogation techniques.

c. Students' answers will vary. Encourage students to check the website of the American Civil Liberties Union at www.aclu.org.

d. Students' answers will vary. This quote comes from a book Rehnquist wrote in 1998, before the terrorist attacks of September 11, 2001, and before the beginning of the war on terror.[9] In his book, Rehnquist writes about the history of courts during wartime and concludes that it is necessary to restrict rights during such times. Rehnquist's writings are cited by those who favor restricting some rights during the war against terror.

SURVEILLANCE AND SEARCHES (PP. 533–535)

BACKGROUND AND DISCUSSION— PATRIOTISM AND THE *USA PATRIOT ACT*

Just weeks after the terrorist attacks of September 11, 2001, Congress passed the *USA PATRIOT Act*[10] giving new powers to law enforcement entities. The name is an acronym, which stands for "Uniting and Strengthening America by Providing Appropriate Tools Required to Intercept and Obstruct Terrorism."

Those who defend the *USA PATRIOT Act* often call themselves "patriots" because they feel it is patriotic to stand behind the government's efforts to protect Americans from terrorists, even if it must restrict constitutional rights to do so. Critics say its supporters wrongly imply that opponents of the act are unpatriotic because they oppose the government's actions to strip civil liberties and rights. They say that by protecting our constitutional rights, they are the real patriots. They argue that we can be free and safe without many of the provisions of the *USA PATRIOT Act.*

Help students analyze how patriotism relates to the arguments about antiterrorism measures. Ask them to define the word patriot and then, working on their own or in small groups, brainstorm a list of characteristics of a patriot. Have students share their definitions and characteristics with the class and try to come up with a generally accepted definition of the word patriot.

One of the philosophical differences that comes up is defining the word patriot in times of war. Some students may say that patriots should unite behind the government in times of war. Others may say that patriots in a democratic country are responsible for exercising their First Amendment rights of free speech and free press to ensure that the country they love is doing the right thing.

ACTIVITY—DEFINING PATRIOT

Share with students the following ideas on the characteristics of a patriot, adapted from Colin Greer's book *A Call to Character*,[11] and from a speech by President Ronald Reagan, available at https://www.reaganlibrary.gov/sspeeches/major-speeches-1964-1989. Have students individually or in small groups review each of the "definitions" of a patriot and choose the one that resonates most to them. Students should then share their answers and support their choice.

1. A patriot is a citizen. President Harry Truman said upon leaving office that he was now "going to ascend to the highest office in the land, the office of citizen."

2. A patriot stays informed on current events, learns from history, gets involved in his or her community, votes for or works for candidates or issues, and accepts the results of free and fair elections.

3. A patriot has courage. Like the firefighters and police officers who rescued others after the September 11, 2001, terrorist attacks—many at the cost of their own lives—and like the passen-

gers who fought back on hijacked Flight 93, a patriot places a high value on the well-being of others, even in the face of danger. Eleanor Roosevelt described courage as "the strength to face pain, act under pressure and maintain one's values in the face of opposition."

4. A patriot shows compassion and caring, exhibiting kindness, showing empathy, and helping others through service. As the Greek philosopher Plato said, "Please, my friends, be kind; everyone you meet is fighting a hard battle."

5. A patriot exhibits conscience by standing up for what he or she believes is right, even in the face of opposition from the majority. A patriot supports the law of the land but may in good conscience oppose existing law, even in some cases committing civil disobedience in support of an important moral principle.

6. A patriot acquires knowledge of the history, traditions, and fundamental principles upon which our country and Constitution are based.

7. A patriot possesses a positive attitude, believing that even the most difficult task is not impossible. A patriot is optimistic that society can improve and works hard to solve problems and rebuild after loss. The United States' emergence from the Great Depression and its efforts to help rebuild Germany and Japan after World War II demonstrate the magnitude of accomplishments that can occur with determination.

8. A patriot is idealistic and believes one person can make a difference. A patriot believes in the words of poet Shirley Kaufman: "It's not what I wake up to but what I dream."

9. A patriot understands how democracy works and knows that citizens in a democratic society can contribute to bringing about constructive change. A patriot works to protect democracy and the rule of law. In the words of Ronald Reagan, "This democracy of ours which sometimes we've treated so lightly, is more than ever a comfortable cloak, so let us not tear it asunder, for no man knows once it is destroyed where or when he will find its protective warmth again."

10. A patriot fights for his or her country and for freedom, yet acts responsibly. Point out to students that responsibility and freedom are closely connected. Freedom is what allows a patriot to possess all of the previously mentioned characteristics. Yet freedom requires that

people take responsibility for their actions and even their unforeseen consequences. Freedom is not a license to act in any way one desires. Real individual freedom requires self-discipline, imposed by responsibility and morality.

11. A patriot understands that he or she is a member of a community. The success of a community is based upon each individual's recognition of his or her impact on others. Gandhi said that social evil can run rampant when there is:

- politics without principle
- wealth without work
- commerce without morality
- pleasure without conscience
- education without character
- science without humanity
- worship without sacrifice

As this discussion demonstrates, a patriot does not embody one specific defining quality. Many traditional notions of a patriot, including those of Greer and Reagan, portray a patriot as highly positive, moral, and courageous. However, uninformed or blind patriotism can lead to jingoism, intolerance, hatred, and bigotry. Discuss with students these ideas and how they relate to patriotism, especially during a time of war.

BACKGROUND—THE DEPARTMENT OF HOMELAND SECURITY

The creation of the Department of Homeland Security is one of the most substantial bureaucratic changes in the post–September 11, 2001, era. The Department of Homeland Security unites many government agencies under one department in the name of domestic security. The hope is that autonomous agencies such as the Federal Emergency Management Agency, the Immigration and Naturalization Service (INS), the Coast Guard, and the Customs Service, which were once part of larger departments (Justice, Transportation, Treasury, etc.), will collaborate more closely and more efficiently in an effort to improve domestic intelligence and security under the umbrella of the Department of Homeland Security to improve national security.

Have students visit the Department of Homeland Security's website located at www.dhs.gov for more information on the organizational structure of the department; recent news and press; and information about how to protect themselves in the event of biological, chemical, nuclear, explosive, or radiation threats.

CAPTION ANSWER (P. 534) The *USA PATRIOT Act* was passed by Congress in response to the September 11, 2001, terrorist attacks on the World Trade Center and the Pentagon. The Act broadened the powers of the government and was intended to combat terrorism by tracing and monitoring sources of money that fund terrorist activities, finding and detaining terrorists who have entered the United States, and intercepting communications among terrorist groups.

PROBLEM 44.2 (p.535)

Both parts of this problem lend themselves to a continuum activity. Create a classroom continuum along one wall of the room.

As you read each statement, have students move to a position under the sign that most closely resembles their opinion. After several students have explained their reasons, ask students if anyone has reconsidered and wants to move to a new spot on the continuum.

a. Students' answers will vary depending on their personal views about the importance of protecting civil liberties and the sacrifices they are willing to make to protect themselves from acts of terrorism.

b. Students' answers will vary.

- Under current law, if the employer consents to the search, it is permissible. Note that employers generally have the right to look at their employees' files and e-mail on work computers because the employers, not the employees, own the computers. If the employer does not consent to the search, the government would have to obtain a court order to conduct the search.
- Home computers have generally been free of such surveillance unless a search warrant has been issued.
- Many local and state governments have installed surveillance cameras to catch speeding drivers and red-light runners. In addition, some have placed closed-circuit televisions (CCTV) on streets and in parks for general surveillance in the hopes of catching drug dealers and others who may commit crimes in public. The use of cameras for these anti-crime purposes has generally been upheld by the courts. Those who oppose this practice say that it violates the privacy of every individual that the cameras photograph and makes the United States a police state like Big Brother in George Orwell's *1984*, where the

state is constantly monitoring its citizens. Those in favor of anti-crime surveillance cameras say it helps to reduce crime and catch criminals. This practice, however, has generally been used more as an anti-crime measure than an antiterrorism measure.

- If law enforcement has evidence that someone is a terrorist, they can probably install such cameras with a court order. Depending on whether law enforcement goes through a regular court or the Foreign Intelligence Surveillance Court, they may have to show probable cause that the person has committed a crime. To obtain a warrant from the Foreign Intelligence Surveillance Court, law enforcement may have to show minimal evidence or perhaps no specific evidence. Those opposed to installing these cameras would argue that installing cameras without showing probable cause violates the suspect's civil liberties and privacy.

- Before the *USA PATRIOT Act* was revised in 2006, the government could obtain library records without a court order, and librarians were subjected to gag orders preventing them from disclosing to library patrons that a law enforcement agency had seen their library records. After much public criticism and debate, this provision was dropped when the *USA PATRIOT Act* was reauthorized.

- The *USA PATRIOT Act* and U.S. Customs and Immigration Services (USCIS) laws allow the government to check travel records. This is true whether or not the country is at war or in a time of heightened security. Even the targeting of specific groups of people for these security checks, such as people traveling to and from certain countries that are thought to be associated with terrorism, would likely be upheld.

BACKGROUND—*PROTECT AMERICA ACT*

In December 2005, New York Times reporters James Risen and Eric Lichtblau published an article that sparked a major national debate over national security, privacy, and the Fourth Amendment. The article described a secret surveillance program that had been going on for at least three years, which included warrantless domestic wiretapping ordered by the Bush administration and carried out by the National Security Agency with the cooperation of several major telecommunications companies.[12]

More investigative reporting and public exposure of the warrantless search program continued, as did

the debate over privacy rights and the need for new and better investigation and monitoring tools. Some said the warrant rules under the *Foreign Intelligence Surveillance Act (FISA)* were insufficient for collecting vital data, particularly because new technologies, such as disposable cell phones and Internet-based communications, provided new intelligence challenges needing new procedures. Others said the *FISA* rules did not provide enough protection for people's rights. In August 2007, Congress passed and the president signed into law the *Protect America Act of 2007*.[13]

To get a sense of how polarizing the bill and law were at the time, one need only note the differences in how the Act was described on the websites of the White House and of the American Civil Liberties Union. President Bush and the White House described it as "Legislation Modernizing Foreign Intelligence Law to Better Protect America." In explaining his decision to sign the bill into law, President Bush said "...the Director of National Intelligence has assured me that this bill gives him the most immediate tools he needs to defeat the intentions of our enemies."

The ACLU called it "The Police America Act" instead of its actual legislative name, saying that it allows for "massive, untargeted collection of international communications without court order or meaningful oversight by either Congress or the courts. It contains virtually no protections for the U.S. end of the phone call or e-mail, leaving decisions about the collection, mining, and use of Americans' private communication up to this administration."

a. Under the *Protect America Act of 2007*, the government does not need a warrant to listen to the phone calls and read e-mails and faxes, because one of the parties is located outside the United States. The government can also search the premises of the place where Ed makes the calls. They probably would be able to go to a bank or other financial institution and obtain Ed's financial statements using a National Security Letter subpoena. This law is designed to enable the government to uncover terrorist plots and catch terrorists without taking the time needed to obtain a warrant. An argument against the law is that it violates the Fourth Amendment to the U.S. Constitution, which forbids unreasonable searches and usually requires a warrant before a search takes place.

b. Considering the facts given in the problem, the government does not have enough evidence to arrest Ed. However, if the government had evidence that Ed and his friend talked about giving the money to his brother or supporting terrorism, then it would have enough evidence to arrest him. The transfer of money to support terrorist groups is known as "providing material support for terrorism" and is a crime. (Syria is also a country listed by the U.S. State Department as one that supports terrorist groups.) Others might counter that there is no evidence that Ed said or did anything wrong and that he has the freedom of speech to talk to someone whom he does not know is a terrorist.

c. Students' answers will vary. If Abdul was attending terrorist group meetings in Syria, this would increase the government's case that Abdul was a terrorist and that the money transferred may have gone to support a terrorist group. Ed could still argue that he was transferring the money to help Abdul's family and that he knew nothing about terrorist groups in Syria. This defense might not be successful.

LAW AND INTERNATIONAL TERRORISM (PP. 536–537)

Learning Outcomes

After completing this section, students should be able to:

1. explain how the war on terror started;
2. differentiate between the war on terror and other wars;
3. describe the role of law during times of war or armed combat;
4. explain how the U.S. has changed its approach to military action;
5. identify and explain the advantages and disadvantages of using drones in military situations; and
6. define *drones*.

CAPTION ANSWER (P. 536) The U.S. government stated that the Geneva Conventions of War did not apply to prisoners or detainees taken in for interrogation in Afghanistan and Iraq because this was "not a war against a country" but a war against the Taliban and al-Qaeda, groups that were not working for the cause of one country.

LAW, TORTURE AND DETAINEES (PP. 538–540)

Learning Outcomes

After completing this section, students should be able to:

1. explain opposing views about whether the Geneva Conventions apply to the detainees held at Guantánamo Bay;
2. explain the intent of and controversy associated with the *Military Commissions Act (MCA)*;
3. describe how the Geneva Conventions as well as other laws and international treaties define torture and penalize people who torture others;
4. take and defend a position about how the U.S. government treats people it detains in connection with the war on terrorism; and
5. define the terms *combatant*, *unlawful combatant*, and *civilian*.

ACTIVITY—DETENTION

Use the following case study to examine the issue of detention further. Tell students these "facts": Achmed, 26, is a university student from a country in the Middle East. He is in the United States on a student visa. He goes to his state's motor vehicle administration office to renew his driver's license. Since the September 11, 2001, attacks, federal law enforcement officials have been stationed around this facility to help gather information on possible terrorists. Achmed is pulled out of line and questioned about when and why he entered the United States. His answers sound suspicious to the officers, and they decide to detain him while they investigate his background further. He is not allowed to talk to anyone outside the detention facility, including his family or a lawyer. He is held for four months and then is released without having been charged with a crime.

a. If you were a government official charged with locating possible terrorists, what reasons would you give for detaining Achmed?

Students' answers will vary. The background provided does not specify what sounded suspicious in Achmed's answers or why the government officials detained him. Under present law, if Achmed was in violation of his visa, he could be held indefinitely without access to a lawyer. In fact, the 1996 *Illegal Immigration Reform and Immigrant Responsibility Act*[14] requires such detentions to ensure that people who have entered the United States illegally not only will be detained but deported.

Officials also may have based their decision to detain Achmed on factors such as whether he is from a country where some terrorists have originated, whether he entered the United States around the time of a terrorist attack, or whether his answers about his course of study or place of residence sounded plausible.

Achmed may have been held so long in detention because officials were either unable to find much information on him or because they had some information but not enough to clear him of suspicion of terrorist activity.

b. Should the government be allowed to detain people for these reasons? Students' opinions will vary, but they should support their answers with reasons.

c. Were Achmed's rights violated? If so, how?

Defenders of Achmed's detention might argue that immigrants in the United States do not have the same expectation of civil rights as citizens, and since immigration law allows these kinds of detentions the action was legal. Opponents of his detention might argue that all people have certain human rights, as detailed in the Universal Declaration of Human Rights, Article 9 ("No one shall be subjected to arbitrary arrest, detention or exile") and Article 11 ("Everyone charged with a penal offence has the right to be presumed innocent until proved guilty according to law in a public trial at which he has had all the guarantees necessary for his defence"). The United States is a signer of the Universal Declaration of Human Rights.

BACKGROUND—TORTURE

Much of the attention on the torture question has revolved around the military's use of torture in interrogation. However, in recent years, it has been alleged that the CIA did not follow international treaties or U.S. laws when it took people into custody who were suspected members of terrorist organizations.

The CIA was also accused of a practice known as "extreme rendition" where alleged terrorists were sent to camps called "black sites" in other countries to be detained and tortured. These were countries,

such as Egypt, Pakistan, and some European countries, that condoned torture. Many European governments were very critical of this practice, as were many people in the United States.

Victims of torture have usually found it extremely difficult to bring a civil lawsuit against the U.S. government. This is because the government raises the so-called state secrets privilege, meaning that "there is a reasonable danger" that such a disclosure of information in the court case "will expose military matters which in the interest of national security should not be divulged."[15] When the courts allow the government to invoke this privilege, it usually results in the termination of the lawsuit, leaving prisoners without recourse. The use of this privilege has been widely criticized.

CASE STUDY—THE GENEVA CONVENTIONS AND THE CASE OF *HAMDAN* v. *RUMSFELD*

Before teaching the section about detention, interrogations, and torture, teachers may want to use the case study teaching strategy to explore the issues presented in the section.

Street Law, Inc., has developed background materials about the Geneva Conventions and the case of *Hamdan* v. *Rumsfeld*.[16] To access these materials, visit Street Law's website at www.store.streetlaw.org/ and type *Hamdan* v. *Rumsfeld* in the search box. To learn more about how to use the case study method, download the "Using Case Studies in the Classroom" guide at https://store.streetlaw.org/using-case-studies-in-the-classroom/, or see the "Teaching Methods" section in the front of this Teacher Manual.

PROBLEM 44.4 (p.540)

This problem is designed to illustrate the difficulty of defining and applying such definitions to actual practices in order to determine what is and what is not torture. The first definition is from the UN Convention Against Torture. Students may be surprised to learn that the second definition listed is one put forth by the Justice Department during the Bush administration.

a. Students' responses may vary.

- Loud music: this would probably not be torture under either definition.
- Hooding: under the first definition, it could be argued that being hooded and being in

total darkness for an extensive period would cause mental suffering and be considered torture. Under the second definition, it would not.

- Water boarding: this has been declared to be a form of torture under the first definition, and it arguably could be considered torture under the second if the action impeded breathing, a bodily function. It appears that water boarding has been used by the military and by the CIA during the Bush Administration, as some internal Justice Department memoranda did not find it to be torture. After a great deal of adverse publicity and criticism by members of Congress, human rights advocates, and the press, the government announced it would not continue to allow the practice.
- Yelling: this would not be torture under either definition.
- Hanging the person upside down: this would seem to be torture (mental suffering) under the first definition and not under the second.
- Keeping the person in total darkness: this also would seem to be torture (mental suffering) under the first definition and not torture under the second definition.
- Keeping a person naked in a cage: this would seem to be torture (mental suffering, degrading treatment) under the first definition, but not necessarily under the second.

b. The main difference between the two definitions is that the first definition makes pain or suffering the principal criterion for something to be considered torture, while the second definition centers on the requirement of a serious physical condition or injury, such as death, organ failure, or serious impairment of bodily function.

Consequently, one would probably consider many acts that are classified as torture under the first definition unlikely to be torture using the second definition.

c. Under present law, torture is not permitted in any circumstances. Those who argue that torture should not be available even in this situation would say that if you allow torture in one instance, it will be used in others. They also state that torture is an inhuman act that dehumanizes the torturer. It also may lead to our military or civilian personnel being tortured when they are captured. Those who would allow torture in this situation might say that it would save lives, and that goal is more important than other values.

They also might argue that the president has an inherent authority as commander-in-chief that gives him or her power to override the torture treaty and anti-torture laws. These arguments were used after September 11, 2001, in the period 2001–2003 by some in the U.S. Justice Department to justify "aggressive interrogation techniques" such as water-boarding by the military and the CIA. Those criticizing this approach say that the president does not have the power to overrule laws and treaties, which are the highest law of the land. They argue that the president is not above the law. They point out that these positions by the Justice Department led to well-publicized abuses which took place in the early 2000s at the Abu Ghraib prison in Iraq and in Guantanamo Bay, Cuba. All this is part of the debate about the extent of presidential power during a war against terror.

d. Students' responses will vary. The late Senator John McCain made this statement as part of a speech in support of legislation he was sponsoring to outlaw the use of torture. Senator McCain's argument was that although terrorists are evil people, how we, as a nation, choose to treat prisoners defines us not them. He is arguing that we can choose to uphold our national principles against these types of abuses or we can choose to abandon those principles and lose the just society we are fighting to protect.

ACTIVITY—MOOT COURT: ACCESS TO THE COURTS FOR DETAINEES

The case addressing the legality of the *Military Commissions Act of 2006*[17] in the Student Edition is *Boumediene* v. *Bush*.[18]

Before they read about the Court's decision, give students the opportunity to learn about the case by using the moot court teaching method.

To learn more about this teaching method, including steps to take to make it successful, see the "Teaching Methods" section in the front of this Teacher Manual.

For the background content needed for the moot court, go to https://store.streetlaw.org/ and type *Boumediene* v. *Bush* in the search box. You may also wish to consider using a mini-moot court for this activity. Full instructions, an instructional video, and student handouts are available at https://store.streetlaw.org/mini-moot-courts-resource-bundle-and-video/.

NOTES

(1) "Country Reports on Terrorism, 2013" Bureau of Counterterrorism, U.S. Department of State, http://www.state.gov/j/ct/rls/crt/2013/224830.htm, accessed 4/1/15

(2) "What is Terrorism?" Constitutional Rights Foundation, http://www.crf-usa.org/america-responds-to-terrorism/what-is-terrorism.html, accessed 4/1/15

(3) *Ex Parte Milligan*, 71 U.S. 295 (1866).

(4) *Schenck v. United States*, 249 U.S. 47, 52 (1919).

(5) *Brandenburg v. Ohio*, 395 U.S. 444 (1969).

(6) *Hirabayashi v. United States*, 320 U.S. 214 (1944).

(7) *Korematsu v. United States*, 323 U.S. 214 (1944).

(8) O'Brien, Edward L. "In War, Is Law Silent?" *Social Education*, National Council for the Social Studies, November/ December, vol. 65, (7) pp. 419–425, paraphrased with permission.

(9) William Rehnquist, *All The Laws But One: Civil Liberties In Wartime*, 1st edition, Knopf Publishers, 1998.

(10) United States, 107th Congress, *Uniting and Strengthening America by Providing Appropriate Tools Required to Intercept and Obstruct Terrorism (USA PATRIOT Act) Act* 2001. 26 Oct. 2001. 7 Nov. 2003. Online posting, U.S. Department of Justice. Washington: GPO, 2001.

(11) Greer, Collin and Herbert Kohl, eds. *A Call To Character*, HarperCollins Publishers, 1995.

(12) Risen, James and Eric Lichtblau "Bush Lets US Spy on Callers Without Courts," *New York Times*, December 16, 2005.

(13) *Protect America Act*, Pub.L. 110–55, § 1, Aug. 5, 2007.

(14) *Illegal Immigration Reform and Immigrant Responsibility Act of 1996*, 8 U.S. C. Section 1372.

(15) *U.S. v. Reynolds*, 345 U.S. 1 (1953).

(16) *Hamdan v. Rumsfeld*, 548 U.S. 557 (2006).

(17) *The Military Commissions Act of 2006*, P.L. 109–366, § 6(c) (3), Oct. 17, 2006.

(18) *Boumediene v. Bush*, 553 U.S. 723 (2008).

networks™

Both federal and state laws govern the workplace by outlining the rights and responsibilities of job applicants, employers, and employees during a job search, on the job, and in the event of job loss. When looking for a job, a person should keep in mind that there are legal and practical issues to consider. For example, employers may ask questions about an applicant's race, gender, or age. In some instances, such questions are legitimate and necessary. In other Instances, such questions may be illegal and constitute discrimination. Once on the job, an employee finds that there are laws that deal with wages and hours, taxes and benefits, Social Security, unions, health and safety, and privacy issues. Although job loss can occur through firings or layoffs, the law provides some protections and assistance for workers who have lost their jobs.

INTRODUCTION AND LOOKING FOR A JOB (PP. 541–545)

Learning Outcomes

After completing these sections, students should be able to:

1. distinguish between appropriate and inappropriate questions that an employer may ask in a job interview;
2. distinguish between appropriate and inappropriate tests employers may administer to applicants for specific jobs, including polygraph tests, drug tests, and aptitude tests;
3. explain how the *Americans with Disabilities Act (ADA)* applies in employment contexts; and
4. define the terms *bona fide occupational qualification (BFOQ)* and *polygraph test.*

ACTIVITY—LOOKING FOR A JOB

This section gives you the opportunity to teach students some basic job application and interviewing skills. Have students access listings from an online job search site. Also provide sample job application forms from local businesses and have students fill them out. You may also consider having students craft a resume and cover letter, as well as a personal essay or statement of goals, which may be useful for students in applying for jobs and to colleges. Set up mock job interviews to give students practice with this important skill and also to demonstrate appropriate and inappropriate interview questions. The interview activity described here is similar to question **b.** in Problem 45.1.

CAPTION ANSWER (P. 542)   Under the *Americans with Disabilities Act (ADA)*, employers are not required to hire a person with a disability who is not qualified for the position. The *ADA* does state, however, that it is illegal to discriminate against a "qualified individual with a disability."

CAPTION ANSWER (P. 543)   Employers can also ask for general contact information and past work experience. For young workers, employers can ask for evidence that they are old enough to work (which might include a work permit, depending on state law). For some jobs, employers can ask about prior criminal convictions.

> **PROBLEM** 45.1 (p.543)

a. Assuming the questions are somehow related to the job for which Jill is interviewing, Mr. Marconi's inquiries into her particular interest in the job, citizenship status (because it pertains to work eligibility), willingness to move for the job, and ability to speak another language would all be permissible. The other questions raise more complex issues:

Age: Age less than 40 years is not a specifically protected category under federal and most state laws, however this question is inappropriate unless it is suspected that Jill may be too young for employment.

Family planning: This question is illegal. Interviewers are not permitted to ask prospective employees questions about family planning. It is a violation of *Title VII* the *Civil Rights Act of 1964* which prohibits employment discrimination based on sex and the *Pregnancy Discrimination Act of 1978.*

Prior arrests: Since this question asks about arrests and not convictions, it may be more difficult to justify. Some states have determined that it is an unfair practice to ask about arrests because an arrest alone is no indication of guilt, and historically minorities have suffered from unequal law enforcement practices. Questions about convictions may relate to legal policies of employers not to hire ex-felons, depending upon the particular job. Some states may make it illegal to discriminate on the basis of prior conviction, unless the conviction reveals the presence or absence of qualifications for the job.

Height and weight: A hiring decision based on the answer to this question may be illegal. This is because height and weight requirements often have a disparate impact on women, and they appear to have no relevance to the position for which Jill is applying.

The U.S. Supreme Court addressed this issue in *Dothard* v. *Rawlinson*.[1] In *Dothard*, the Alabama Board of Corrections established a 120-pound minimum weight requirement and a 5'2" minimum height requirement for prison guards. The plaintiff, a female applicant, proved that the requirement would exclude 41.13 percent of the female applicants while excluding less than 1 percent of the male applicants. The Supreme Court found that the plaintiff had a valid gender discrimination claim but ruled in favor of the defendant (the Board of Corrections) because in a prison setting physical size is a valid consideration. For more information about discrimination based on gender, see Chapter 41, "Discrimination."

Credit Rating: Generally, employers have a right to conduct a credit check. The investigation must comply with the federal *Fair Credit Reporting Act.*[2] The employer must notify the employee in writing that an investigative report is being compiled. Upon request, the employer must also provide the employee with a copy of the report. Refusing to hire an applicant on the basis of a bad rating may constitute evidence of discrimination because the percentage of nonwhites with low credit ratings is disproportionately higher than the percentage for whites, assuming the question is asked only to rule out minority applicants and has no relevance to the job.[3] For more information about issues related to credit, see Chapter 24, "Credit and Other Financial Services."

Dinner Plans: This is an improper question because it may concern Jill that her hiring is dependent on her answer. It also puts the interviewer in a difficult position even if he chooses not to hire her for relevant reasons. It is best to avoid such a question during a job interview.

Mental Health/Medical History/Disability Issues: The *Americans with Disabilities Act (ADA)* in all likelihood makes the question and accompanying checklist an illegal, discriminatory practice. The employer cannot refuse to hire an applicant because of a disability if he or she can perform the essential functions of the job with an accommodation. An employer cannot ask a job applicant whether he or she is disabled or ask about the nature or severity of a disability. An employer can ask whether the applicant can perform the duties of the job with or without reasonable accommodation.

b. Students should critique the role-play and provide possible alternative responses. You may wish to conduct the role-play a second time, or in small groups, followed by a large class discussion, providing the opportunity for sharing the different responses.

c. Have students indicate how successfully Jill asserted her rights and maintained a proper demeanor in the context of a job interview.

d. Discrimination claims can be made to either the Equal Employment Opportunity Commission (EEOC) or a state agency, or resolved through a lawsuit.

BACKGROUND—THE *ADA* IN THE EMPLOYMENT CONTEXT

The *Americans with Disabilities Act (ADA)* makes it unlawful to discriminate in employment against a qualified individual with a disability. This part of the law is enforced by the U.S. Equal Employment

Opportunity Commission (EEOC), as well as state and local civil rights enforcement agencies that work with the commission. Job discrimination against people with disabilities is illegal if practiced by private employers, state and local governments, employment agencies, labor organizations, and labor-management committees. If a person has a disability and is qualified to do a job, the *ADA* protects the individual from discrimination based on the disability. Under the *ADA*, a person has a disability if he or she has a physical or mental impairment that substantially limits a major life activity. A substantial impairment is one that significantly limits or restricts a major life activity such as hearing, seeing, speaking, walking, breathing, performing manual tasks, caring for oneself, learning, or working. In 1999, the U.S. Supreme Court declined to expand the *ADA* from persons whose impairments "substantially limit" a major life activity to employees whose conditions are improved by medication or corrective devices such as eyeglasses.[4]

A person with a disability must be qualified to perform the essential functions or duties of a job, with or without reasonable accommodation, in order to be protected from job discrimination by the *ADA*. An employer cannot refuse to hire a person if his or her disability does not interfere with functions essential to the job. The *ADA* permits an employer to refuse to hire an individual if he or she poses a direct threat of substantial harm to the health or safety of himself or herself or others in the workplace. The employer must also consider whether a risk can be eliminated or reduced to an acceptable level with a reasonable accommodation.

The EEOC offers information about the *ADA* in the employment context online at https://www. eeoc.gov/eeoc/history/ada25th/ including a timeline of historic milestones. Additional information about the consideration of disabilities of job applicants is included in answer **a.** to Problem 45.1. Major provisions of the *ADA* are listed in the Student Edition, and the subject of discrimination based on disability outside the employment context is covered in Chapter 41, "Discrimination."

CAPTION ANSWER (P. 545) Students' answers will vary and will likely depend on the type of job the applicant is seeking.

PROBLEM 45.2 (p.545)

Students' answers will vary. Employees who will work with the public must have reasonable language skills and accurate math skills (to calculate bills, make change, etc.). Cashiers also have to be trustworthy. Drug testing may be permitted. Polygraph testing is not likely to be permitted. The manager might check references with past employers (if any) and may check social networking sites to help determine character. If the job involves driving (such as delivering food) a careful employer will certainly check an applicant's driver's license records.

CONDITIONS ON THE JOB (PP. 546–558)

Learning Outcomes

After completing this section, students should be able to:

1. summarize the work hours, minimum wage, and overtime wage requirements of the *Fair Labor Standards Act (FLSA)* and which jobs are not covered by the act;
2. list fringe benefits employers may offer to workers;
3. describe the requirements of the *Family Medical Leave Act (FMLA)* and which employers are exempt;
4. debate the benefits and criticism of unions and of collective bargaining for workers;
5. differentiate between right-to-work states and non-right-to-work states;
6. summarize what union members have the right to do and what actions by unions and employers would constitute unfair labor practices;
7. describe how the Occupational Safety and Health Administration (OSHA) acts to protect workers on the job;
8. summarize how much privacy a worker might expect regarding his or her appearance, personnel records, medical records, drug use, use of the telephone, Internet, e-mail, and other computer-related tasks; and
9. define the terms *fringe benefits, union, collective bargaining agreement, right-to-work laws, strikes, picketing,* and *unfair labor practice.*

BACKGROUND—EMPLOYMENT LAW

The online information available from the Department of Labor (www.dol.gov/) can answer any further questions regarding workers' rights, regulations, and laws.

More information about the *Employment Polygraph Protection Act*[5] is available from the American Polygraph Association online at www.polygraph.org/.

426 Contemporary Issues in Law

Investigating the Law Where You Live

(p. 546) The Department of Labor's website (www.dol.gov/dol/topic/youthlabor/) provides state-by-state comparisons and information about hours, wages, and other work rules. It also links visitors to state laws regarding youth employment. The National Conference of State Legislature's website has information on state minimum wages at http://www.ncsl.org/research/labor-and-employment/state-minimum-wage-chart.aspx.

Investigating the Law Where You Live

(p. 547) If students need help finding answers to this problem, they should ask a labor lawyer in their community. They can also visit the Job Accommodation Network at http://askjan.org.

DELIBERATION—SHOULD OUR STATE OR COMMUNITY RAISE THE MINIMUM WAGE?

Facilitate a deliberation about raising the minimum wage in your community. An overview of the deliberation method is available at the beginning of this Teacher Manual. A detailed lesson plan, instructional video, readings, and student handouts for this deliberation are available at https://store.streetlaw.org/deliberations/.

PROBLEM 45.3 (p.547)

a. Students should debate whether or not all persons should be covered by a minimum wage. Having a lower minimum wage for young people would encourage employers to hire younger people who may not yet have well-developed job skills. This would give youth an opportunity to get a job and to learn responsibility. Additionally, paying youth less money would decrease the economic strain placed on small businesses, giving them a greater opportunity to prosper. Finally, many younger people do not have the expenses that adults have. An employer who spends less on salaries can lower prices and become more competitive. In turn, all citizens would benefit from the lower prices. On the other hand, adults who do not have well-developed job skills may lose employment opportunities to youths. Many adults need the income to support their families.

The Fair Labor Standards Act (FLSA)[6] establishes minimum wage, overtime pay, record keeping, and child labor standards affecting full-time and part-time workers in the private sector and in federal, state, and local governments. In addition to setting the federal minimum wage, the *FLSA* requires employers to provide any eligible employee written notice of the training wage's requirements and remedies before the employee begins employment. The act prohibits displacing employees, or reducing their hours, wages, or benefits for the purposes of hiring employees who satisfy the training wage requirements. Employers who violate the act will be disqualified from employing any individual at the lower wage.

This issue is one of ongoing concern for Congress. Some argue that the existing minimum wage results in an increasing number of jobs that do not pay a living wage, while others contend that the market is a better regulator of wages than the government. Note that if a state establishes a minimum wage that is higher than the federal minimum wage (it cannot adopt one that is lower), an employer in that state must then meet the state minimum.

b. The employee should ask to speak to the manager directly. The employer could have made an honest error in computing the employee's salary. Additionally, the other cook may be paid more because he has more seniority or more experience. If the employee's conversations with the employer are unsuccessful, the employee has several options.

Refer students to the *Steps to Take* feature in the Student Edition. Discuss with students the options listed on the transparency. The employee could contact the Wage and Hour Division of the U.S. Department of Labor, the state or local employment government agency, or the company's union, if one exists. While the right to sue exists, it appears to be inappropriate here to sue for the small amount that is owed. You may want to role-play the employee's meeting with the employer and then critique it.

Remind students that as they read in the Student Edition, the *Fair Labor Standards Act* does not require overtime for all employees.

c. The employer's policy or the employment contract, if there is one, will dictate whether or not Vana is required to reimburse the owner for the amount she is short. The employee should have been given notice of the policy before being required to pay money to the restaurant owner. The main argument for her paying is that her job is to collect the right amount of money for sales and make change. An argument against this is that everyone makes mistakes on a job and usually such a person is not required to pay the company back. You may wish to discuss with students whether this is fair, and ask what other method the restaurant owner might use to account for receipts.

BACKGROUND—FAMILY AND MEDICAL LEAVE

Review with students the benefits of the *Family and Medical Leave Act (FMLA)*[7] described in the Student Edition. In addition, students may want to know that the federal legislation does not apply to all employees. It covers employees who have worked for the employer a minimum of one year; a minimum of 1,250 hours (an average of 25 hours per week) during the 12 months prior to the start of the *FMLA* leave; and are employed at a location where at least 50 employees are employed at the location or within a 75-mile radius. It also does not cover "highly compensated" employees. The law requires that employees returning from leave be restored to the positions they would have had, or to similar positions, if they had not taken the leave.

CAPTION ANSWER (P. 548) Taxes withheld from workers' paychecks are used to provide government services, such as education, law enforcement, national defense, trash collection, and road building and maintenance.

PROBLEM 45.4 (p.549)

a. Students' answers will vary. If Bethany returns to school while she is working, she may want tuition reimbursement. She may also be interested in training, meals, retirement benefits, health insurance, vacations, sick leave, holidays, and breaks. If she thinks she might have children, she might want to know about parental leave policies, as well as child care on or near the premises.

b. Chandler may argue that the denial of paternity leave is gender discrimination and therefore violates *Title VII* and/or the *Family and Medical Leave Act (FMLA)*. Providing women with 10 days of paid maternity leave treats female employees more favorably than male employees. Note that a father won the first gender-discrimination case

under the federal *FMLA* in 1999, when a federal jury in Baltimore awarded Kevin Knussman $375,000 in damages. The Maryland state trooper had been denied paternity leave to care for his newborn daughter.[8]

Korey may argue that pregnant female employees and male employees are not similarly situated. As students learned in Chapter 41, paid leave for pregnant employees is a form of disability compensation. Since male employees are entitled to other forms of disability payments, there is no discrimination. Korey may argue that the *FMLA* does not apply to companies with fewer than 50 employees, as in this case.

c. Students' answers will vary. Since Russell is interested in working for several years before attending college, he would probably be interested in obtaining free uniforms, health insurance, sick leave, vacations, use of an automobile, reimbursement for gas expenses or use of a company gas card, and insurance coverage.

CAPTION ANSWER (P. 551) Students' answers will vary

PROBLEM 45.5 (p.552)

Note: The Student Edition refers to the *National Labor Relations Act (NLRA)*[9].

a. Reasons workers may want a union include a desire for higher wages, better working conditions, other benefits, and protection from losing their jobs. They may also feel protected by the bargaining strength of large numbers of workers. National and international unions, such as the AFL-CIO, protect the workers' interests and regulate the entire industry in a uniform manner. National and international unions have political power and support legislation that would be beneficial to their members. Automobile manufacturing is a large industry with several manufacturers and thousands of employees. Theoretically, employees as individuals often lack the power to negotiate effectively with their employer on a one-to-one basis.

Those opposed may see union dues as too expensive and union demands driving the company either out of business or out of the country. Some workers may oppose unions because they further group interests at the expense of individual employees.

An employee who is considering supporting the formation of a union can acquire information prior to a union election. Employers and the prospective union have the right to give speeches, send letters, hold meetings, and send pamphlets in order to disseminate information in support of or against the union.

b. In right-to-work states, employees can work for companies and not be forced to pay dues or fees to the union. Those opposed to right-to-work policies say they undermine the financial security of unions and promote discontent among workers. They argue that they also allow some workers to get a free ride because the union works to get better wages and benefits for all employees, not just for union members. They might also argue that if 50 percent of workers have voted for a union to be their sole bargaining agent, then all should at least support the union financially. Those who favor right-to-work laws argue that workers should have a right not to be required to financially support unions that they oppose. They see this as their personal freedom.

c. Students' answers will vary. Arguments against a strike by the sanitation workers include the impact that not collecting garbage will have on the community. Some states and localities have laws against strikes by public employees or those performing essential services such as garbage collection and transportation. Arguments in favor include the fact that striking is the strongest employee tactic toward gaining fair treatment (particularly if it results in public pressure on the city to improve wages) and that it has been more than five years since the sanitation workers have had a pay raise. If the workers have a collective bargaining agreement, the grievance can be taken to arbitration. The arbitrator can be anyone on whom the parties mutually agree to decide the dispute. The arbitrator's decision is generally binding on all parties involved.

d. Students' answers will vary but should be supported with reasons. Generally, public employees do not have a right to strike because they are performing government services that are considered essential (e.g., police, fire, sanitation). However, teachers have been allowed to strike in certain places, and "work to the rule" efforts and other methods have been used by government employees to gain attention for their demands. Where public employees do have the right to strike, it is highly regulated by state law. Many of their rights are covered by their collective bargaining agreement and civil service regulations. In some cases, public employees have bargained for greater rights including, for example, the right to a hearing before they lose their jobs.

PROBLEM 45.6 (p.553)

Students' answers will vary. In the facts given, it appears that the Occupational Safety and Health Administration (OSHA) was slow to act following the inspection. If it had issued orders requiring changes sooner, the accident might not have occurred. The construction companies should have corrected the violations cited by OSHA as they were legally bound to do. Additionally, if workers continued to make complaints about safety conditions and practices, it might have kept up pressure on OSHA to act.

CAPTION ANSWER (P. 554) OSHA requires employers to keep records of all job-related illnesses and injuries among their workers. OSHA also conducts on-site inspections, orders changes, and sometimes fines employers if inspections show that health or safety hazards exist.

PROBLEM 45.7 (p.555)

a. The Occupational Safety and Health Administration (OSHA) was created by the *Occupational Safety and Health Act* to assure safe and healthful working conditions and to preserve our human resources.[10] OSHA sets safety standards and regulations and conducts investigations to determine whether or not the standards are upheld. If a workplace does not comply, OSHA can order a correction of the hazard. It has the authority to impose monetary fines as well.

Though OSHA enforcement has been criticized and some feel it overregulates, most students will probably see the need for health and safety regulation. It might be a useful exercise to explore one local industry to determine what OSHA regulations apply and have an industry representative describe how industry regards OSHA. Additional information about OSHA is available at www.osha.gov.

b. Students' answers will vary. Employees like Jack can exercise their safety and health rights without fear of repercussions, such as being fired for complaining. Generally, a worker cannot be retaliated against for filing a claim or complaining about unsafe working conditions. Even if it turns out that the workplace is safe after an inspection, the employer cannot fire the worker if the complaint was made in good faith. If Jack believes he was fired for his complaint, he has the right to report the company's action to OSHA within 30 days of the layoff. OSHA will conduct an investigation of the circumstances surrounding the layoff. OSHA may find that other coworkers were also laid off and Jack's dismissal was not a product of his complaint. Without other discriminatory actions by the company, Jack's layoff would be justified.

c. Students' answers will vary.

CAPTION ANSWER (P. 555) The federal government has instituted right-to-know laws that require employers using certain hazardous materials to inform their employees about the accident and health hazards of chemicals in the workplace. Employers must also train their employees to properly handle such materials to minimize problems. In addition, many employers now offer training programs to inform employees of possible health hazards.

CAPTION ANSWER (P. 556) Students' answers will vary. Those who work for the federal and some state governments generally have greater privacy rights than those who work for private employers.

ACTIVITY—CASE STUDY: PRIVACY, EMPLOYMENT RECORDS, AND RECOMMENDATIONS FOR EMPLOYEES

Give students a hypothetical case based on the background information below. Then ask students the questions that follow.

A man working in a school district was accused of sexual misconduct by several students. The man later applied for a job in a different school district. His former employer (school district) wrote letters recommending him for employment without disclosing the facts regarding his prior charges of sexual misconduct. These letters stated that the man had "genuine concern for students" and "outstanding rapport with everyone," and concluded that he "wouldn't hesitate to recommend the man for any position." A new school district hired the man, and he later sexually assaulted a 13-year-old girl. The first employing school district was found liable in tort for the sexual assault occurring at the second school district.[11] If an employer recommends an employee to a prospective employer, covering up known serious problems, the prior employer may be liable in tort for the harm caused by the employee at the new place of employment.

Does this court decision surprise you? Do you agree or disagree with it? Think back to the elements

of negligence that were studied in Unit 3, "Torts" (duty, breach, causation, damages). Did the first employer commit a tort?

Were the employee's privacy rights violated? What if the charges were never proved in a court of law?

BACKGROUND—SUBSTANCE ABUSE ON THE JOB

The law relating to employers' rights and obligation to address substance abuse by employees is complex. Public employees are protected by the Fourth Amendment ban on unreasonable searches and seizures. A blood or urine test used to detect drugs or alcohol is a search and seizure subject to constitutional requirements of reasonableness. To determine whether or not a particular test is unreasonable under the Fourth Amendment, a court will first determine the degree of privacy the employee is reasonably entitled to expect and then balance that expectation of privacy against the public employer's interest in the safe and efficient performance of job duties.

Pursuant to the enactment of the *Drug Free Workplace Act* of 1988,[12] recipients of federal contracts or grants are required to take specified actions designed to assure drug-free workplaces. The act is the result of congressional concern over potentially defective military equipment, satellites, rockets, and space shuttles made by an impaired workforce.

One of the requirements of the act includes a written drug-awareness program to inform the employees of the hazards of drug use. The program must include information regarding drug counseling, rehabilitation, and employee assistance programs. The employer's failure to adhere to the act's regulations may result in the withholding or suspension of payments under the contract, suspension or termination of the contract, or a maximum five-year suspension or debarment of the employer from the receipt of federal contracts.

As a general rule, an employee's expectation of privacy will prevail over an employer's interest, unless the employer has objective, individualized suspicion that the employee is impaired. An employer may be exempt from the requirement to use individualized suspicion if: (1) the employer is a government and it can show that it has a compelling government interest, usually public safety or protecting highly sensitive information;[13] or (2) employers may test if they are in industries subject to pervasive federal regulations, such as the nuclear power industry.[14]

THE CASE OF...

Testing Customs Agents for Drugs

PROBLEM 45.8 (p.557)

a. Students' answers will vary. Drug-testing advocates contend that the tests will reduce drug use and will deter the drug users from applying for jobs in workplaces with testing programs. Additionally, reductions in drug and alcohol abuse have been linked to improvements in safety, work quality, attendance rates, and employee morale.[15] Also, employers arguably have the right to insist that their employees report to work without drugs in their system.[16]

Remind students that the Supreme Court upheld a railroad's drug testing program after an accident. In that case, the Court said that the industry has important safety concerns and that the importance of finding out whether drugs were involved in railroad accidents was held to warrant this action.[17]

In the case presented in this problem, the testing program involved only employees in "sensitive positions." Employees in these positions came in contact with drugs, carried firearms, and handled classified information about drugs. The dangers are, therefore, so great that drug testing is warranted.

b. Students' answers will vary. Opponents of this particular policy may object to the fact that it appears not to allow for an employee to contest the drug-test results or for a second test to confirm the results. Opponents of drug testing in general argue that drug tests can produce erroneous results, create difficulties in employee/union relations, invade employee privacy, and fail to indicate whether or not an employee is actually impaired by the drug.[18] Another argument against testing is that it tends to regulate the employees' off-duty behavior.

In the facts of this case, only 5 of 3,600 people tested positive. Opponents may argue that the small number may make the drug-testing effort seem unwarranted. It also may indicate to the employees a lack of trust by the employer, and this might lead employees to return that lack of trust toward their employer. Finally, the testing requirement here applies only to persons applying for promotion to sensitive positions. The policy seems to indicate that people already in such positions will not be tested. If the nature of the work is, at least in part, the reason for the testing, then it would seem to justify testing all people in those sensitive positions.

c. Students' answers will vary. This case is based on the case of *National Treasury Employees Union* v. *Von Raab*,[19] which held in a 5-to-4 decision that it was proper for the government to do this because of the risk involved in these sensitive jobs.

YOU BE the JUDGE

Employees' Right to Privacy (p. 558)

Emphasize to students that the questions ask whether the law *should* protect these employees, not whether the law *does* protect them. Therefore, for questions **a.–f.**, students' answers will vary.

a. Generally, private employers are entitled to discuss former employees with prospective employers. State laws regulate the type of information the employer is permitted to disclose. Union contracts may also limit the employer's power to disclose information. Significantly, employers may be liable for defamation if they convey information about the employee that they know to be false. Government employers have greater restrictions on releasing information to others.

b. Generally, an employer may dictate how you, as an employee, should dress, how you wear your hair, and whether or not you may wear a beard or mustache if the employer's requirement is reasonable under the circumstances and the employer implemented and enforced the regulation in good faith.

In *Kelley* v. *Johnson*, the U.S. Supreme Court upheld the police department's hair length and shaving requirements.[20] The Court found a rational relationship between the requirement and the public employer's needs. The Court stated that hair length is not an "immutable characteristic," thus it is afforded less protection. Since Lionel's employer is specifically prohibiting dreadlocks—a hairstyle worn by some members of the African American community—the employer's action would be looked at more closely by the court because of its impact on protected persons and its potential violation of antidiscrimination laws. In another case, two Rastafarian correctional officers sued the prison, challenging the grooming regulation under which they were ordered to cut their dreadlocks. The officers claimed that forcing them to change their hairstyle violated their religious rights protected under the *Religious Freedom Restoration Act (RFRA)*.[21] This was later struck down by the Supreme Court in 1997.[22] The federal court ruled for the officers, stating that the employment regulations constituted a substantial burden to the plaintiffs' right to free exercise of religion under *RFRA*.[23] In this case, Lionel did not claim that his hairstyle was connected to his religion.

c. Generally, private employers are permitted to search employees or their purses, desks, and lockers to obtain evidence of theft. If a *private employer* conducts the search, then the evidence seized could be used against the employee. The search would not violate the Fourth Amendment since a private employer, and not the government, gathered the evidence.

 In this example, Jasper asked the police to search the handbags. In order to stay within the bounds of the Fourth Amendment, the police must have probable cause and a search warrant. The fact that something is missing will not, by itself, result in probable cause to justify getting a warrant to search a specific place. Any evidence the police obtain illegally will be suppressed and not be available for use against the employee/defendant at trial.

d. Barnes has a right to know what his employees are doing while they are on company time. Employers have the right to observe their employees themselves or appoint someone else to observe them. Though the law may not require it, Barnes should investigate any allegations Sally makes before taking action against Jenny, and Jenny should be afforded an opportunity to be heard. Having a nonsupervisory employee spy on another may be considered by many a poor management practice, but it is not illegal.

e. Jay is permitted to install the mirrors. Generally, employers may use electronic surveillance reasonably to protect their property or monitor employee performance. Often, state statutes do not provide much employee protection in this situation. Ask students whether they believe the law should be changed to protect employee privacy in this type of situation.

f. For the most part, employers are allowed to monitor electronic mail sent between company employees. Assuming that Hugo's comments are untrue and/or unjustified, Tami could terminate his employment.

LOSING A JOB (PP. 558–565)

Learning Outcomes

After completing this section, students should be able to:
1. contrast how employees in government or union jobs may be fired or laid off with those who have employment-at-will contracts;
2. assess the fairness and merits of at-will employment;
3. explain why whistle-blowers may be protected from being fired;
4. interpret situations to decide whether firings are legal or illegal;
5. describe how different employers may legally follow differently the procedures regarding notification, severance pay, and extending health care benefits when they fire or lay off a worker;
6. describe unemployment compensation and the kinds and limits of benefits one can expect;
7. list the steps a person must take to apply for unemployment benefits;
8. interpret situations to determine which employees are eligible for unemployment compensation; and
9. define the terms *employment-at-will contract, whistle-blowing,* and *severance pay.*

BACKGROUND—PROTECTION FOR WHISTLEBLOWERS

 As mentioned in the Student Edition, the federal laws protecting whistleblowers include the *Fair Labor Standards Act, Title VII* of the *Civil Rights Act of 1964,*[24] and the *Occupational Safety and Health Act.* In addition, in 2008 the Supreme Court issued two decisions protecting workers from retaliation when they reported discrimination on the job. In *Gomez-Perez* v. *Potter,* the Court ruled that federal employees (like private-sector employees) are protected against retaliation for reporting age discrimination violations. In *CBOCS West, Inc.* v. *Humphries,* the Court said that it is not permissible to retaliate against an employee who reports discrimination against another employee in the workplace.[25] For more information about whistle-blowers and laws related to protection for whistle-blowers, visit the

Government Accountability Project (GAP) online at www.whistleblower.org. GAP is a nonprofit public interest and law firm that publicizes whistle-blower concerns and defends whistle-blowers in government and business settings. GAP also advocates occupational free speech and ethical conduct, government and corporate responsibility, and empowering citizen activists.

CAPTION ANSWER (P. 559) Students will have their own opinions about this issue. Explain that under the doctrine of employment-at-will, employees can quit anytime they wish, and employers can discharge them at any time for any reason or for no reason at all. However, an employee's firing cannot violate some other law, such as an antidiscrimination law.

PROBLEM 45.9 (p.560)

Note: Be sure that students have read all of the material in the Student Edition before they try to answer the questions in this problem.

The company's policy does not establish an at-will employment contract because, according to the handbook, the employer can discharge an employee for just cause. Therefore, in order to respond to questions **a.–g.**, students must determine what constitutes just cause. This term is used in the Student Edition, but you may want to clarify it further before assigning this question. Courts have found just cause to include: chronic absenteeism or lateness, insubordination or failure to follow orders, inefficient or incompetent work performance, disloyalty, disclosure of trade secrets, intoxication, gross negligence, fighting, and participating in an illegal strike.

a. Warren could be charged with chronic lateness or insubordination because his tardiness continued even after he was warned against it three times. If the facts permit, it could also be argued that Warren has breached the employment contract since he is not abiding by its terms. A breach of contract, under these circumstances, could terminate the employee/employer relationship. It would be very important for the company to have accurate attendance and time records for its employees and copies of the warnings that Warren received about his tardiness.

b. Leona would have a wrongful discharge claim against the employer, since the reason for her termination (refusing to engage in illegal activity) violates public policy.

c. Pierre could lawfully be discharged for intoxication, but it could be argued that this is a health problem and should be treated as such. The *ADA* protects alcoholics who are in treatment.

d. The employer may successfully argue that Naomi's work performance is inefficient and incompetent, and therefore the discharge was justified.

e. John could be fired for starting the fight. Company policy will dictate whether or not both parties participating in the fight will be reprimanded. Employers have the right to decide who was at fault.

f. The company can argue that Chloe was disloyal and disclosed trade secrets to the competition and could fire her for her actions.

g. D'Angelo would be protected under applicable whistle-blowing laws. These laws protect D'Angelo from a retaliatory firing once he informs the appropriate authorities of his employer's dishonest and possibly illegal conduct.

h. Although it may appear harsh and unfair, Marnie's firing is likely to be legal. Had Marnie been on the job for a longer period of time, it is possible that the *Family Medical Leave Act (FMLA)* may have protected her.

THE CASE OF...

The Shoe Store Firing

PROBLEM 45.10 (p.562)

a. Since there is not an employment contract, employee handbook, nor a collective bargaining agreement, Mr. Brady has an employment-at-will contract. This type of contract allows the employer to fire the employee without notice for any reason or no reason at all (but not for an illegal reason). Similarly, the employee may quit a job without notice and for any reason.

b. Students' answers will vary. Supporters of at-will contracts say that by giving both parties the ability to terminate the employment relationship freely, the employer and the employee can escape an unfavorable work situation or they can benefit from an unexpected opportunity. Furthermore, employers should be able to hire and retain the best personnel possible. The at-will doctrine ensures this kind of flexibility.

Opponents of at-will contracts argue that the doctrine can be used as a pretext for discriminatory actions. Moreover, unfair treatment and loss of valuable employees and serious injury to employee morale are cited as consequences of the doctrine. Some argue that the law should at least require a period of notice before job termination.

c. Conduct and critique the role-play. Students should examine the manner in which the employees stated their views and the employer responded. Were these the best ways to communicate? What may have been some alternatives?

d. Organize the class into small groups. Each group should come up with a list, which may include items such as incompetent job performance, continual late arrival and/or early departures from work, insubordination, use of abusive or obscene language, sexual harassment, etc. The fairness of the rules may be determined by looking at how clear and understandable they are and whether they lend themselves to arbitrary enforcement. Are the words in the rules defined so that both employer and employee understand and agree on their meaning?

e. A third party could also be hired to write a handbook or to act as a mediator between Mrs. Hinoshita and the employees. However, a mediator should be neutral, and this may not be possible if Mrs. Hinoshita were to hire the person and pay for the work. Perhaps the shoe store employer is not concerned with the opinions of her employees in this matter.

BACKGROUND—PROCEDURES BEFORE JOB LOSS

When there is a "just cause" requirement for firing, management must adequately and fairly investigate the charges before any disciplinary action is taken. Additionally, the punishment administered must be consistent with prior practices and must not be discriminatorily or arbitrarily applied.

In the absence of a contract or an agreement entered into by the employee and the employer, an employee is not required to give notice prior to severing the employment relationship. However, employers may sue employees for breach of contract and recover monetary damages if the employee leaves the job without providing the notice required by the contract.

The law requiring certain employers to warn their employees that the plant may be closing is the *Worker Adjustment and Retraining Notification Act of*

1988.[26] The law that requires certain employers to give their terminated employees health coverage for a certain length of time (at the employee's expense) is the *Consolidated Omnibus Budget Reconciliation Act (COBRA)*.[27]

PROBLEM 45.11 (p.564)

Though the law may not require extensive procedures before the firing in these cases, students should be able to list basic due process procedures they might want, such as notice, an opportunity to rebut the charges, a hearing with rights to testify, confrontation and cross-examination of witnesses against them, the right to an attorney, an impartial decision maker, and the right to appeal if they lose.

a. Students' answers will vary. Assuming the computer software company is private, employees are entitled only to the procedures delineated in the employment contract, collective bargaining agreement, or the employee handbook, if any of the above exist. If the employer refuses to honor the procedures in the employment contract, the employee may sue the employer in court to enforce the document. Some courts have even enforced the employer's policies found in the employee handbook. The steps this employee might take could depend on whether he or she is a member of a union. If the employer does not abide by the procedures set out in the collective bargaining agreement, the employee must lodge a complaint with the immediate supervisor. If the matter is still not resolved, the employee may file a grievance with the union. Another alternative is to hire a lawyer who specializes in labor law.

b. Students' answers will vary. Arguments in favor of notifying employees are that they need to know the status of their employment in order to provide adequately for themselves and/or their families. Notice will enable employees to search for a job while they are still employed without worrying about finances. Severance pay would lessen the financial burden placed on the employees while they seek alternative employment and await the issuance of unemployment compensation.

Sometimes employers feel they cannot inform their employees of the business's impending failure because the employees will leave and seek other employment opportunities. In the absence of a clause in individual contracts or collective bargaining agreements entitling an employee to severance pay, employers are not required to give notice or make such payments. Some state laws, however, require notice and payment under certain circumstances.

c. Students' answers will vary. Some jobs might lend themselves to a requirement of notification, such as jobs where the employer's business would be severely harmed or a danger created by an employee leaving without notice. For example, a life-guard or security guard giving no notice may put people or property in danger. If a job requires a special technical skill and a replacement cannot be readily hired, the employer might suffer major financial loss because of this, therefore advance notice may be justified.

CAPTION ANSWER (P. 564) Students' answers will vary, but should be supported by reasons.

CASE STUDY—TERMINATION BASED ON SEXUAL ORIENTATION AND TRANSGENDER STATUS

One key provision of the *Civil Rights Act of 1964* is *Title VII*, which makes it unlawful for employers to make employment decisions including termination based on a person's race, color, religion, sex, or national origin. Since 1964, Congress has amended *Title VII* and passed additional laws making it unlawful for employers to discriminate based on other factors, such as pregnancy, age, and disability. While a bill called the *Equality Act* passed in the U.S. House of Representatives on May 17, 2019, as of the publication of this manual it has not been taken up by the Senate, so there is no federal law that explicitly provides protections for LGBTQ workers against discrimination. Some federal courts have concluded that the protections against "sex" discrimination already contained in *Title VII* also restricts employers from discriminating based on sexual orientation or gender identity. Other federal courts have reached the opposite conclusion.

In October 2019, the U.S. Supreme Court heard cases concerning alleged workplace discrimination against two gay men because of their sexual orientation, *Bostock* v. *Clayton County, Georgia*[28] and *Altitude Express* v. *Zarda*[29]. On the same day, it heard oral arguments about a transgender woman who was terminated from her job as the director of a funeral home, *R.G. & G.R. Harris Funeral Homes* v. *EEOC*[30]. As of the publication of this manual, the cases have not been decided but may set precedents for the legality of terminations on the basis of sexual orientation and transgender status.

These cases and the issues they present can be explored further using Street Law's case study strategies. For further explanation of the strategies, download the "Using Case Studies in the Classroom" guide at https://store.streetlaw.org/using-case-studies-in-the-classroom/. These strategies are also outlined in the front of this Teacher Manual. Case summaries for these cases can be found at https://store.streetlaw.org/ by typing the case names in the search box.

BACKGROUND—UNEMPLOYMENT COMPENSATION

Generally, a person is ineligible for unemployment compensation if discharged for misconduct. Many courts have found "misconduct" to mean the employee's willful or wanton disregard of an employer's interests, the employee's deliberate violation of the employer's standard of behavior, or consistent carelessness or negligence. In contrast, an employee's mere inefficiency, good-faith errors in judgment, or failure to provide a good performance as a result of some inability or incapacity are not considered acts of misconduct. Unemployment compensation eligibility requirements and restrictions vary from state to state.

Investigating the Law Where You Live

(p. 565) A simple internet search will help students find out where people in their community can apply for unemployment compensation. If students need additional direction, send them to www.careeronestop.org/ReEmployment/UnemploymentBenefits/what-is-unemployment-insurance.aspx where they can search their state's unemployment insurance program.

PROBLEM 45.12 (p.565)

a. Based on the facts, it appears that Maggie is willfully disregarding her employer's interests. Arguably, her inaction constitutes misconduct. Maggie would therefore be ineligible to receive unemployment compensation. However, the facts do not say why Maggie disliked him, and she may have a claim if he has done something illegal to her.

b. Smoking an illegal substance at work clearly violates the standard of behavior an employer would expect from his or her employees. Phillip's actions constitute misconduct, so he is ineligible for unemployment compensation.

c. Based on the facts, Sybil has an argument for why she missed work but may still not be eligible for unemployment compensation. Employers have an interest in having their employees show up for work and perform their duties. It can be argued that Sybil is willfully disregarding her employer's interests. She is unable to satisfy the employer's interests because of her family obligations. If given adequate notice, many employers might be understanding of Sybil's family problems and help her figure out a way to do her job well and take care of her family at the same time. It is also possible that Sybil may be eligible for protection/leave under the *Family and Medical Leave Act*. There are not enough specific facts in the scenario to be sure.

d. Alonzo is eligible for unemployment compensation. He is unemployed due to no fault of his own. Alonzo may be disqualified, however, if the company's new offer is deemed "suitable employment." Employment may be unsuitable if it is too distant from the employee's home, and 1.5 hours could be considered a long commute.

NOTES

(1) *Dothard* v. *Rawlinson*, 433 U.S. 321 (1977).

(2) *Federal Fair Credit Reporting Act*, 15 U.S.C. § 1681 (1988).

(3) Fischer, Mark A. "Minorities score lower in 'colorblind' credit ratings," *Columbus Dispatch*, April 14, 1999.

(4) *Sutton* v. *United Air Lines, Inc.*, 527 U.S. 471 (1999); *Albertsons, Inc.* v. *Kirkingburg*, 527 U.S. 555 (1999); *Murphy* v. *United Parcel Service, Inc.*, 527 U.S. 516 (1999).

(5) *Employment Polygraph Protection Act (EPPA)*, 29 U.S.C. §§ 2001 et seq. (1988).

(6) *Fair Labor Standards Act (FLSA)*, 29 U.S.C. §§ 201 et seq. (1999).

(7) *Family Medical Leave Act (FMLA)*, 29 U.S.C. §§ 2601 et seq.

(8) *Knussman* v. *Maryland*, 935 F. Supp. 659, (D. Md. 1996).

(9) *National Labor Relations Act (NLRA)*, 29 U.S.C. §§ 151 et seq. (1935).

(10) *Occupational Safety and Health Act (OSHA)*, 29 U.S.C § 651 (1988).

(11) *Randi W.* v. *Muroc School District*, 929 P.2d 582 (Cal. 1997).

(12) *Drug Free Workplace Act*, 41 U.S.C. § 705 (1988).

(13) *Skinner* v. *Railway Labor Executives Ass'n*, 489 U.S. 602 (1989).

(14) *Alverado* v. *WPPSS*, 759 P.2d 427 (Wash. 1988), cert. denied, 490 U.S. 1004 (1989).

(15) Hartstein, "Drug Testing in the Workplace: A Primer for Employers." 12 *Employee Relations Law Journal* 577 (1987).

(16) Id.

(17) *Skinner* v. *Railway Labor Executive Association*, 489 U.S. 602 (1989).

(18) Hartstein, "Drug Testing in the Workplace: A Primer for Employers." *Employee Relations Law Journal* 577 (1987).

(19) *National Treasury Employees Union* v. *Von Raab*, 489 U.S. 656 (1989).

(20) *Kelley* v. *Johnson*, 425 U.S. 238 (1976).

(21) *Religious Freedom Restoration Act (RFRA)*, 42 U.S.C. §§ 2000bb et seq. (1993).

(22) *City of Boerne* v. *Flores*, 521 U.S. 507 (1997).

(23) *Francis* v. *Keane*, 888 F. Supp. 568 (S.D.N.Y. 1995).

(24) *Civil Rights Act of 1964*, 42 U.S.C. § 2000(e) (2000).

(25) *CBOCS West, Inc.* v. *Humphries*, 128 S. Ct. 1951 (2008) and *Gomez-Perez* v. *Potter*, 128 S. Ct. 1931 (2008).

(26) *Worker Adjustment and Retraining Notification Act of 1988*, 29 U.S.C. §§ 2101–2109 (2000).

(27) *Consolidated Omnibus Budget Reconciliation Act of 1985*, 29 U.S.C. §§ 1161–1168 (2000).

(28) *Bostock* v. *Clayton Cty., Ga.*, ___ U.S. ___ (argued Oct. 8, 2019).

(29) *Altitude Express Inc.* v. *Zarda*, ___ U.S. ___ (argued Oct. 8, 2019).

(30) *R.G. & G.R. Harris Funeral Homes Inc.* v. *EEOC*, ___ U.S. ___ (argued Oct. 8, 2019).

Environmental law is a relatively new and still evolving branch of law in the United States. Until the 1960s there was almost no regulation of natural resources. The Environmental Protection Agency and several wide-reaching pieces of federal legislation were born out of the environmental crisis in the 1970s. Now, with increasing global interdependence, nations across the world are joining together to combat the causes of climate change.

INTRODUCTION (PP. 566–567)

Learning Outcomes

After completing this section, students should be able to:
1. identify early land conservation efforts in the United States;
2. describe the conditions that led to the establishment of environmental protection laws in the 1970s; and
3. define the term *environment*.

ACTIVITY—IDENTIFYING PAST AND PRESENT THREATS TO THE ENVIRONMENT

Before students read the chapter, project images from the Documerica Project, photographs funded by the Environmental Protection Agency (EPA) from 1971-1977 to document environmental problems and everyday life in America. These photographs are now digitized and available at the U.S. National Archives website (https://www.flickr.com/photos/usnationalarchives/collections/72157620729903309/).

In small groups instruct students to list all of the environmental problems they saw in the photographs from the mid-seventies. Explain to students that the EPA was created to address many of these problems and has made remarkable progress in the past 50 years. Ask students if all of the problems on the list have been solved. Then ask students to consider the list again and rank the most imminent threats to the environment today from 1-3 (with 1 being the most imminent threat to the environment today). Once groups have ranked their ideas and identified their top 3 current threats to the environment, instruct students to visit https://www.epa.gov/environmental-topics to investigate each further. Students may reevaluate their rankings. Have groups make a poster with a symbol and a fact about the greatest threat to the environment today. Alternatively, students could explore the site on their own.

DISCUSSION—*SILENT SPRING*

Ask students if they are familiar with the book *Silent Spring* by Rachel Carson. If students are, ask them to brief the class about its significance. If not, explain that *Silent Spring* was published in 1962 (almost a decade before the earliest major environmental legislation and the establishment of the EPA). Rachel Carson was a birdwatcher who discovered that the overuse of pesticides was killing birds and making the forests "silent." The book documented the harmful effects of pesticides such as DDT and was critical of both the chemical industry and the U.S. government for their roles in the crisis. Many consider this book a wake-up call and a rallying point for the environmental grass-roots movements.

Display the following quote from Rachel Carson's *Silent Spring* large enough for the class to read or hand out copies to students:

"We stand now where two roads diverge. But unlike the roads in Robert Frost's familiar poem, they are not equally fair. The road we have long been traveling is deceptively easy, a smooth super-highway on which we progress with great speed, but at its end lies disaster. The other fork of the road—the one less traveled by—offers our last, our only chance to reach a destination that assures the preservation of the earth."[1]

Ask students to discuss what this quote says about the urgency of environmental problems in the 1960s and why that message was so powerful. Ask students to consider this quote from today's per-spective. In hindsight, which road did the United States take, or did it forge a third road? Conclude by having students consider if this quote is still rele-vant to today's environmental issues.

PROBLEM 46.1 (p.567)

Student answers will vary. Students may inter-pret this quote as meaning that nature gives people who avail themselves of it an added perspective that cannot be gained elsewhere. They may see it as a justification for preserving nature.

THE NATIONAL ENVIRONMENTAL PROTECTION ACT (PP. 567–569)

Learning Outcomes

After completing this section, students should be able to:

1. describe the provisions of the *National Environmental Policy Act* (*NEPA*);
2. apply *NEPA* to various government activities;
3. define the term *environmental impact state-ment* (*EIS*) and explain the EIS process; and
4. explain the function of the *Council on Environmental Quality* (*CEQ*).

BACKGROUND—ORIGINS OF THE EPA

In the 1960s many factors worked together to create public awareness, concern, and demand for action regarding the environment. During this time, Ohio's Cuyahoga River was ablaze, Rachel Carson's

Silent Spring was published, Americans were seeing the first photographs of Earth from space, and smog was choking cities across the country. In response, President Richard Nixon issued a plan to address these issues. The plan contained 37 points including seeking legislation to end dumping in the Great Lakes, approving a contingency plan for oil spills, and creating national air quality standards and emissions guidelines for vehicles. President Nixon also sent the U.S. Congress a plan to consolidate many of these responsibilities in one federal agency. In 1970 President Nixon signed the *National Environmental Protection Act (NEPA)* which formed the Council on Environmental Quality and required federal agencies to file environmental impact statements.

The new EPA was officially established on December 2, 1970. It was created to conduct research on important pollutants, monitor the bio-logical and physical environment, establish environ-mental baselines to measure pollution control efforts, set and enforce air and water quality stan-dards, support states in their environmental efforts, and more. Within a month of the creation of the EPA, the *Clean Air Act* was passed.[2]

Further information on the origins of the EPA is available at https://www.epa.gov/history/ori-gins-epa. A timeline of important events in the EPA's history is available at https://www.epa.gov/history#timeline.

PROBLEM 46.2 (p.568)

a. The school board should address whether the new school would "significantly affect" the envi-ronment. It should address both the effects on the natural environment (such as digging up land, disturbing wetlands, etc.) and the human environment (such as an increase in traffic, noise, vehicle emissions). An EIS would be required because federal funds will be used and the construction will significantly affect the environment.

b. The benefits of seeking public input before mak-ing environmental decisions is that the public has a chance to provide input before the con-struction and implementation begins. Often resi-dents have knowledge of the immediate environment that the EPA may find helpful in assessing the impact of a project. The costs are the time and effort needed to accumulate and analyze the feedback. A by-product of public input is that often groups take a "Not In My Backyard" (NIMBY) approach, fighting a facility they see as harmful if it is built close to their home, but not elsewhere. This sometimes means that more affluent neighborhoods—which are better equipped to mobilize and advocate for themselves—are able to stave off projects that then move to underserved areas where there are fewer resources to oppose them.

ACTIVITY—*NEPA* WHERE YOU LIVE

Begin this activity by asking students if they are aware of any government projects in their state that might require an Environmental Impact Statement (EIS) such as major highway construction or new government buildings (including schools). Have students explore the EPA website at https://www.epa.gov/nepa. Students should choose "Find EPA NEPA contacts and EISs by state" under the heading "NEPA Where You Live." Students should click on their region and then their state. Ask students to look at the titles of the projects and try to categorize them into types of projects. Then ask students to notice the list of the agencies seeking the EIS. Are there agencies that appear more often than others? Can they make any conclusions about that? Ask students to choose one project and predict what types of impact on the environment it might have. As an extension, you may wish to have students download the EIS for that project and skim it to test their hypothesis, however the vocabulary and scientific knowledge needed may make this difficult for most students.

THE CLEAN AIR ACT (P. 569)

Learning Outcomes

After completing this section, students should be able to:
1. describe the hazards presented by air pollution;
2. explain factors that contribute to air pollution;
3. describe the provisions of the *Clean Air Act* (*CAA*); and
4. evaluate the impact of the *CAA*.

BACKGROUND

The *Clean Air* Act requires the EPA to set "National Ambient Air Quality Standards" for pollutants considered harmful to public health and the environment. *Primary standards* provide public health protection, including protecting the health of "sensitive" populations such as asthmatics, children, and the elderly. *Secondary standards* provide public welfare protection, including protection against decreased visibility and damage to animals, crops, vegetation, and buildings.[3]

PROBLEM 46.3 (p.569)

a. Students can find the air quality of their area by visiting www.airnow.gov and either entering their zip code or state. Air quality will be rated as good, moderate, unhealthy for sensitive groups, unhealthy, very unhealthy, or hazardous. There will also be a numeric "air quality index" score.

b. Students can find the forecast for tomorrow's air quality by clicking on the "forecast" tab.

c. Answers will vary. Students can find this information in the "AQI Pollutant Details" section to the right of the map.

d. Answers will vary. In many cases the air quality in a nearby zip code will remain the same. This is because often the factors that affect air quality are similar in areas in close proximity. In some cases, they may differ due to a change in rural, suburban, and urban areas.

CAPTION ANSWER (P. 570) Answers will vary. Students who live in rural areas are more likely to experience harmful agricultural runoff. For more details, the EPA offers a fact sheet on agricultural runoff at https://www.epa.gov/sites/production/files/2015-09/documents/ag_runoff_fact_sheet.pdf.

DISCUSSION—WORLD'S AIR POLLUTION

Ask students to make a hypothesis about which regions of the world have the best air quality and which have the most dangerous. Ask which factors might influence a region's air quality. Have students explore the interactive map *World's Air Pollution: Real-time Air Quality Index* available at https://waqi.info/. Instruct students to scroll down to see more information about the air quality ratings and the health implications and cautionary statements. Have students zoom on their state and city on the map. Then have students revisit their hypothesis based on the data and revise as necessary. As a whole class, discuss the disparity in global air quality, the factors that impact it, and some possible solutions to help the regions that are the most negatively impacted.

THE CLEAN WATER ACT (P. 570)

Learning Outcomes

After completing this section, students should be able to:

1. describe the historic practices that led to water pollution and their effects;
2. describe the provisions of the *Clean Water Act* (*CWA*) and *Safe Drinking Water Act* (*SDWA*);
3. evaluate the limitations of the *CWA* and the *SDWA*; and
4. define the terms *point source pollution* and *nonpoint source pollution*.

BACKGROUND

The Clean Water Act (*CWA*) established a permit system that regulated the discharge of pollutants from point sources. It also monitors water quality of surface waters and classifies them for their uses (e.g., fishable, swimmable). The history of the *CWA* can be found on the EPA's website at https://www.epa.gov/laws-regulations/history-clean-water-act. A summary of the *CWA* is available at https://www.epa.gov/laws-regulations/summary-clean-water-act.

PROBLEM 46.4 (p.573)

a. Student answers will vary. The EPA's website has information on recent news, resources, and environmental information regarding air, water, clean ups, and more for each state.

b. Student answers will vary. Initiatives can be found under the "clean ups" and "news" tabs.

ACTIVITY—MOCK TRIAL: *RICKI JONES V. METRO CITY*

The D.C. Street Law Clinic at Georgetown University Law Center developed a mock trial about water quality and negligence. The mock trial simulates a civil suit brought by the parents of an AIDS patient who sue Metro City for negligence when their son dies after drinking tap water from the city's contaminated pipes. The trial can be downloaded from Street Law's website at https://store.streetlaw.org/ricki-jones-v-metro-city/.

Instructions for conducting a mock trial can be found at the front of this of this Teacher Manual, on Street Law's website at https://www.streetlaw.org/teaching-strategies/mock-trial, and in Street Law's Classroom Guide to Mock Trials and Moot Courts available at https://store.streetlaw.org/classroom-guide-to-mock-trials-and-moot-courts/.

THE ENDANGERED SPECIES ACT (P. 571)

Learning Outcomes

After completing this section, students should be able to:

1. describe the provisions of the *Endangered Species Act* (*ESA*); and
2. explain the role of the U.S. Fish and Wildlife Service (FWS) and the National Marine Fisheries Service (NMFS) in implementing the *ESA*.

ACTIVITY—ENDANGERED SPECIES WHERE YOU LIVE

Students can learn about endangered species in their state by accessing the U.S. Fish & Wildlife Service's website at https://www.fws.gov/endangered/species/. Students can select their state by clicking on the map of the United States. They can then view a profile for each species on the results page and use the status code to identify the current status for each species. Each results page also contains documents about conservation efforts and a recovery plan.

Arrange students in small groups and allow them to choose a species. Have students use the results page to make a list of efforts by the U.S. Fish & Wildlife Service to help preserve the species. Ask groups to present their species and recovery plan to the class.

ACTIVITY—ENDANGERED SPECIES AROUND THE WORLD

Using the World Wildlife Fund's website at https://www.worldwildlife.org/species students can explore endangered animals from around the globe such as marine animals, primates, big cats, and more. After they have become familiar with the animals, have students view at least one "Conversation in the Classroom," to hear WWF experts share stories of their experience working to protect species and habitats around the world available at https://www.worldwildlife.org/teaching-resources/.

EXTENSION—MINECRAFT: *EXTINCTION! A BIODIVERSITY CRISIS*

As an extension, have students explore WWF's Minecraft curriculum: *Extinction! A Biodiversity Crisis*. Students can play the popular interactive game to learn about species extinction, ecological niches, and conservation solutions at https://education.minecraft.net/blog/we-teamed-up-with-world-wildlife-fund-for-an-interactive-science-curriculum-on-biodiversity/.

LAND POLLUTION (PP. 571–572)

Learning Outcomes

After completing this section, students should be able to:
1. provide examples of land pollution;
2. describe the provisions of the *Resource Conservation and Recovery Act* (*RCRA*) and *Comprehensive Environmental Response, Compensation, and Liability Act of 1980* (*CERCLA*);
3. explain the requirements of Superfund site current and post owners to clean up and rehabilite the sites; and
4. investigate and discuss the disparate impact of environmental hazards on low income communities.

BACKGROUND

The *Resource Conservation and Recovery Act* (*RCRA*) is an example of a "cradle to grave" law, meaning it monitors hazardous waste from generation to disposal. The term *RCRA* is often used interchangeably to refer to the law, regulations to support the law, and the EPA policy to regulate compliance with the law. Detailed information about *RCRA* is available at the EPA's website at https://www.epa.gov/rcra. It includes an interactive timeline of milestones in the *RCRA's* history at https://www.epa.gov/rcra/resource-conservation-and-recovery-act-timeline.

The *Comprehensive Environmental Response, Compensation, and Liability Act of 1980* (CERCLA) is more commonly known as Superfund. It was established as a response to toxic waste dumping sites such as Love Canal. It gives EPA authority to clean up contaminated sites. Detailed information on CERCLA is available at https://www.epa.gov/superfund/learn-about-superfund. It includes an interactive timeline of the Superfund Program at https://www.epa.gov/superfund/superfund-history.

PROBLEM 46.5 (p.572)

a. Information on Superfund sites can be found at www.epa.gov under the heading "Key Topics." Students should select "Superfund," then under "Learn About Superfund," they should select "Sites where you live."

b. Students may be able to observe a pattern where less affluent areas, often rural communities, are more likely to be the location of a Superfund site. For more information, students may want to visit the EPA's environmental justice page at https://www.epa.gov/environmentaljustice.

OTHER FEDERAL ENVIRONMENTAL PROTECTION LAWS (PP. 572–573)

Learning Outcomes

After completing this section, students should be able to:
1. describe the provisions of the *National Historic Preservation Act* (*NHPA*) and explain its connection to the environment; and
2. explain the harm caused by noise pollution and the efforts of the *Federal Noise Control Act of 1972* to reduce it.

CAPTION ANSWER (P. 572) To find the location of sites on the National Register of Historic Places, students may visit the National Park Service's website at https://www.nps.gov/maps/full.html?mapId=7ad17cc9-b808-4ff8-a2f9-a99909164466. Students can enter the name of their town/city and state. The map will display the location and basic information on the historic sites in their area.

PROBLEM 46.6 (p.573)

a. Student answers will vary. Some noise control regulations set "quiet hours" or "quiet zones." Others regulate aircraft, highway traffic, and commercial and industrial noise to certain decibel levels. Most assign fines for individuals or companies who violate them.

b. Answers will vary based on location. Students might suggest writing elected officials, starting a petition, or volunteering with groups that advocate for noise control regulations.

ENVIRONMENTAL REGULATION AT VARIOUS LEVELS OF GOVERNMENT (PP. 573–575)

Learning Outcomes

After completing this section, students should be able to:

1. provide examples of how EPA works with other agencies, industry and environmental groups, and with state, tribal and local governments;
2. describe the critical role played by state and tribal agenies in enforcing environmental regulations;
3. compare the advantages and disadvantages of federal and state governments making envrionmental legislation and regulations;
4. define the term *cooperative federalism*;
5. compare the advantages and disadvantages of cooperative federalism in making environmental legislation and regulations; and
6. deliberate the question: "Should the federal government ban hydraulic fracturing (or fracking)?"

Investigating the Law Where You Live

(p. 573) To find the agencies in their state responsible for environmental protection, students should visit www.epa.gov, go to "Your Community," and enter the student's state. Contacts for state agencies are available under "Federal & State Contacts."

PROBLEM 46.7 (p.573)

a. The advantages of the federal government making environmental legislation or regulations are that environmental issues don't stop at state borders; they are nationwide so a national policy to combat them is needed. The federal government can more easily see the big picture of problems and solutions and has greater resources with which to address them. The disadvantages are that the federal government may not recognize state-specific problems, understand state economies, and represent the needs of groups within a state.

b. The advantages of the state government making environmental legislation or regulations are that states are more likely to have a better understanding the specific problems, state industry and agriculture sectors, and the impact of possible solutions on the state and local economies. The disadvantages of the state government making environmental legislation or regulations are that environmental issues don't stop at state borders; they are nationwide so there should be a national policy to combat them. The state government has fewer resources than the federal government.

c. The advantage of cooperative federalism in making environmental legislation and regulations is that by sharing the responsibility and costs, the federal and state governments work together to find stronger solutions to environmental issues. Together the federal government and states have many resources. The disadvantages of cooperative federalism in making environmental legislation and regulations are that it can make the process time consuming and allow issues to worsen before they are addressed. When the federal and state governments are unable to compromise, gridlock can occur.

DELIBERATION

Should the federal government ban hydraulic fracturing (or fracking)? (pp. 574–575)

An overview of the deliberation method is discussed in the front of this Teacher Manual. For free deliberation materials, student handouts and an instructional video visit https://store.streetlaw.org/deliberations/.

If this is your first deliberation, consider devoting significant time to establishing norms for deliberations and civil discourse. Introduce the process of deliberations including careful reading, clarification, preparing and presenting initial positions, reversing positions, free small group discussion, search for common ground, and whole-class discussion.

Begin class by introducing the deliberation issue: fracking. Explain that this deliberation will focus on whether fracking should be banned by the federal government. It is likely that students may not be familiar with the mechanics of fracking. It may be helpful to provide them with the graphic available at https://insideclimatenews.org/content/infographic-hydraulic-fracturing-explained-health-risks.

Students will strive to reach consensus on some aspect of the issue, but are not required to agree on an answer to the deliberation question. Take students through the deliberation steps.

Debrief by instructing students to:

- Raise your hands if you changed your position on the issue.
- Raise your hand if you considered a new opinion that you had not considered before today.
- Raise your hand if you felt listened to during the deliberation.
- Follow up by asking students how they might translate this activity to conversations outside the classroom.

Consider having students perform a self-assessment on the process and their contribution to it.

For the more information on government regulation of fracking, students may wish to visit:

- *"How Does Fracking Work?"* (https://www.youtube.com/watch?v=Tudal_4x4F0): A six-minute animated video from TED-Ed explaining how the fracking process works and some impacts of fracking.
- *FracFocus* (https://fracfocus.org/): FracFocus allows the public to search fracking records, including where wells are located, publicly available lists of chemicals used at wells, and more.
- *"How Hydraulic Fracturing Works"* (https://www.nationalgeographic.org/media/how-hydraulic-fracturing-works/): A National Geographic Education resource that uses video and text to explain fracking and allow students to explore facts, vocabulary, and other resources.

CLIMATE CHANGE (P. 576)

Learning Outcomes

After completing this section, students should be able to:

1. discuss the current and possible future effects of climate change;
2. explain the scientific consensus on causes of climate change;
3. propose possible steps to mitigate climate change in the global context; and
4. describe the provisions of the Montreal Protocol.

DISCUSSION—COUNT DOWN YOUR CARBON

Begin the discussion by asking students what they can do to help reduce their carbon footprint. Make a list of suggestions on the board.

Have students explore ways to reduce their carbon footprint by using the interactive carbon calculator, *Count Down Your Carbon* at http://www.countdownyourcarbon.org/calculator.php. Students will see how their choices about which light bulbs to use, planting trees, adjusting their thermostat, carpooling, food choices, and recycling impact carbon dioxide emissions. After students have completed the activity, ask them if there is one thing that they can commit to in their daily life to help reduce emissions. Make a classroom poster and have students write their contribution to display in the classroom.

PROBLEM 46.8 (p.576)

The biggest contributors of greenhouse gases, including carbon dioxide, include transportation (gas and diesel), electricity generation (coal and natural gas), industry, and agriculture. Steps to reduce emissions include reducing consumption by using alternative forms of transportation (fewer trips, public transit, biking, etc.), using more fuel efficient vehicles (fuel standards, hybrid or electric vehicles), using more fuel efficient appliances and fixtures (for heat and electricity), and using alternative sustainable fuels (solar energy, biofuels, and wind power).

Emissions on a global basis are analyzed based on the United Nations Framework on Climate Change (UNFCCC), a treaty to prevent "dangerous" human interference with the climate system. The UNFCCC analyzes information gathered under the Kyoto Protocol and Paris Agreement. The Kyoto Protocol legally binds countries who sign to emission reduction targets. The Paris Agreement is a commitment by signatories to reduce emissions and invest in solutions in order to keep global temperature rise below 2 degrees Celsius this century.[4]

Global regulations cannot be enforced. While the Kyoto Accord is technically binding, there is no international entity to enforce compliance.

ACTIVITY—COMPARING CLIMATE CHANGE LAWS AROUND THE WORLD

Climate change is a global phenomenon, but legislation varies widely from country to country. Students can compare laws by exploring the interactive map available at https://www.carbonbrief.org/mapped-climate-change-laws-around-world. In small groups, have students compare one industrialized nation (other than the United States), one developing nation, and the United States. Have students create a Venn diagram showing the types of laws the countries share and those that are unique. Students could make a power point slide or a poster to share with the class. In whole group discussion, the class should create a hypothesis about what factors influence a country's climate change legislation.

NOTES

(1) Carson, Rachel, Lois Darling, and Louis Darling. *Silent Spring*. Boston : Cambridge, Mass.: Houghton Mifflin, 1962.

(2) The Origins of EPA, https://www.epa.gov/history/origins-epa accessed November 2019.

(3) Criteria Air Pollutants, https://www.epa.gov/criteria-air-pollutants/naaqs-table accessed November 2019.

(4) United Nations: Climate Change, https://www.un.org/en/sections/issues-depth/climate-change/ accessed November 2019.